AREA SECTIONS—C

MW00850385

Endorsements

Diana has done it again! Like all of her books, this one also raises the bar on the subject. San Diegans and anyone visiting the region's wilder side will greatly benefit from her latest work. The book shares her wide-ranging knowledge about hundreds of our most notable trails in a style that is both interesting and easy to reference. I plan to own several copies: one to hold, one to go, and at least one to give.
—John D. Mead, President, Adventure 16

Diana Lindsay and her team of authors/Canyoneers have compiled the finest collection of San Diego County hikes, along with the regional habitats, plants and animals ever put together in one guidebook. What an accomplishment!
—Mark Jorgensen, Retired Superintendent, Anza-Borrego Desert State Park

Whether you are a San Diego resident or visitor, Coast to Cactus *should be your hiking bible. This is the most complete guidebook yet to trails in the San Diego region, but it is also much more than that. There are exquisite pearls of natural and cultural history information waiting to be discovered in every hike description. The trip summaries feel both intimate, like the information is coming from your favorite hiking buddy, and authoritative, thanks to the book's partnership with the San Diego Natural History Museum. Sun hats off to the Canyoneers and Sunbelt Publications for this masterful work.*
— Annette McGivney, Southwest Editor, *Backpacker Magazine*

An exciting new guide to help California native plant lovers, gardeners, botanists, San Diego County residents, and visitors enjoy and learn about the county's wide range of native plants and natural resources. All of our members will want a copy!
— Bobbie Stephenson, President, California Native Plant Society,
San Diego Chapter

This trail guide is a wonderful resource to help people explore our local wilderness and discover its unique treasures. It's replete with trail information and different habitat descriptions—definitely a key to finding the right hike and the right place to enjoy and learn from San Diego's remarkable natural diversity.
—Duncan McFetridge, Director, Cleveland National Forest Foundation

This book is directed not only to hikers but to all southern Californians who should read the Introduction to promote appreciation for and stimulate efforts to protect the unique beauty that surrounds us. In our time, when the challenges of population, energy, and water requirements impose stresses on our environment, it is important to make all aware of the value and beauty of the land.
—Janet Anderson, President, Desert Protective Council

The Coast to Cactus *trail guide is the ultimate resource for anyone who is interested in exploring and learning about everything San Diego County has to offer. Whether you have just moved to San Diego, or have lived here your entire life, everyone should take advantage of the wealth of information the book provides.*
—Roy Coffman, Store Manager, Patagonia Cardiff-by-the-Sea

This is a book that should be owned by all who enjoy getting out into nature in San Diego County. The descriptions of the plants, birds, and other features encountered on each walk should deepen ones awareness of the beauty and diversity of our county's environmentally rich areas.
    —David Kimball, President, San Diego Audubon Society

This guide fills a gap in outdoor books available in San Diego. Its detailed and comprehensive coverage makes it possible for people to find nature right in the neighborhood.
    —Carrie Schneider, President, San Diego Canyonlands

The San Diego Reader *is delighted to have provided the means for developing this new trail guide through its weekly publication of Canyoneer articles for the* Reader's *"Roam-O-Rama" column. This book combines the best in county hiking trails with the right amount of interpretive detail to provide a learning experience every time someone takes a hike.*
    —Jim Holman, Editor and Publisher, *San Diego Reader*

This book is truly indispensable to anyone hoping to gain the most out of their backcountry adventures! Diana Lindsay's guide is sure to become the essential "pocket naturalist" for all San Diego trail explorers striving to get more out of their outdoor experiences!
    —Davin Widgerow, Chair, Steering Committee, Sierra Club San Diego

This book needs to be part of every adventurer's library. In addition to being a comprehensive hiking guide, it brings people closer to nature and inspires people to get out and explore, which is precisely why Subaru is a proud supporter of the book and the Canyoneers program.
    —Eric Park, Zone Retail Marketing Manager, Subaru of America

This book is a fine addition and update to the aging library of San Diego hiking books. The inclusion of plants and animals likely to be encountered on each hike is a useful feature. The book can encourage people to follow Walkabout International's motto, "Walk for the health of it."
    —Robert Buehler, President, Walkabout International

This is a very well written, user friendly trail guide of San Diego County. A great addition to any hiker's library, —be they beginner or seasoned—one that will be recommended as a resource to our leaders as they prepare their own hikes for our Club.
    — Karen Eagleton, President/Chairman of the Board,
    The Wilderness Association of San Diego and San Diego Hiking Club

Published in Cooperation with:

California State Parks

Mission Trails Regional Park
(City of San Diego)

San Diego County Department
of Parks & Recreation

San Diego Natural
History Museum

San Dieguito River Park
Joint Powers Authority

The San Diego River Park
Foundation

COAST TO CACTUS

The Canyoneer Trail Guide to San Diego Outdoors

Edited by
Diana Lindsay, Managing Editor
Paula Knoll
Terri Varnell

Contributors Listed
in the Acknowledgments

Sunbelt Publications, Inc.
San Diego, California

Coast to Cactus: The Canyoneer Trail Guide to San Diego Outdoors

Sunbelt Publications, Inc.
Copyright © 2016 by Diana Lindsay
All rights reserved. First edition 2016. Fourth printing 2021.
Printed in Korea

Managing Editor Diana Lindsay
Edited by Paula Knoll and Terri Varnell
Trail maps by Patric Knoll
Cover, area maps, and book design by Barry Age
Typography by Simone Matern
Project management by Deborah Young

Sunbelt Publications, Inc.
P.O. Box 191126
San Diego, CA 92159-1126
(619) 258-4911, fax: (619) 258-4916
www.sunbeltpublications.com

24 23 22 21   7 6 5 4

Library of Congress Cataloging-in-Publication Data

Names: Lindsay, Diana, 1944- editor. | Knoll, Paula, editor. | Varnell, Terri, editor.
Title: Coast to cactus : the canyoneer trail guide to San Diego outdoors /
edited by: Diana Lindsay, managing editor, Paula Knoll, Terri Varnell
Other titles: Canyoneer trail guide to San Diego outdoors
Description: First edition. | San Diego, CA : Sunbelt Publications, Inc., 2016.
Identifiers: LCCN 2016005617 (print) | LCCN 2016007246 (ebook) | ISBN
9781941384206 (pbk. : alk. paper) | ISBN 9781941384237 (ebook)
Subjects: LCSH: Hiking--California--San Diego--Guidebooks. |
Trails--California--San Diego--Guidebooks. | Natural
history--California--San Diego--Guidebooks.
Classification: LCC GV199.42.C22 S2635 2016 (print) | LCC GV199.42.C22
(ebook) | DDC 796.5109794/98--dc23
LC record available at http://lccn.loc.gov/2016005617

Cover photo by Ellen Esch taken at Scripps Reserve
Back cover photo by Alan King
Flap photo by Don Endicott taken in Anza-Borrego Desert State Park
Inside back cover photos by Jon Lindsay

We strive for accuracy. If you see something that needs to be corrected in the next printing,
please let us know: info@sunbeltpub.com

DEDICATION

Helen Vallejo Chamlee

Her passion for and appreciation of San Diego's natural resources
inspired the development of the Florida Canyoneers in 1973.

Alan Marshall

A Canyoneer extraordinaire whose passion led to expanding walks
outside of Florida Canyon and throughout the county.

Paula Knoll

A 30-year veteran Canyoneer who was instrumental in introducing
new hiking areas to county residents and was a tireless editor
and contributor to *Coast to Cactus*.

Subaru loves the earth.

Coast. Wetlands. Chaparral. Mountains. Desert. If there is anything that says "San Diego" it is the incredible biodiversity of this county. There are so many different environments to discover it can be challenging to know just where to start. Fortunately, the San Diego Natural History Museum and the Canyoneers have you covered. This hiking guide will open new worlds to both the novice and expert outdoor enthusiast. **Join Subaru—love the earth and explore.**

Subaru is a proud partner of the San Diego Natural History Museum and the Canyoneers program.

SUBARU

EDITOR'S NOTE
How to learn more about species featured in this book

When information about a species is featured in the trip description, its scientific name appears in **bold** with the common name. For descriptive information about other species mentioned by common name only, look in the index either under the common or scientific name; the **bolded** page number is where additional information about that species can be found. Go to the appendix to learn about habitats in which species can be found.

Inland North Hikes

Inland South Hikes

Mountain Hikes

Desert Hikes

Foreword

Dear Reader,

You are about to embark on a remarkable journey through our fascinating and diverse region, guided by this book which was created by a dedicated group of San Diego Natural History Museum volunteers, the Canyoneers.

The hikes presented in *Coast to Cactus: The Canyoneer Trail Guide to San Diego Outdoors* offer an in-depth exploration of San Diego County and its unique habitats, which together makes our county one of only 35 global biodiversity hotspots.

These habitats—and the geologic past which has influenced the evolution of this remarkable variety—are highlighted at the San Diego Natural History Museum (theNAT) in two of our core exhibitions: *Fossil Mysteries* and *Coast to Cactus in Southern California*. TheNAT provides an introduction to the underlying natural history of the area's geology, paleontology, and resulting biodiversity, serving as an informal visitor center with the goal of introducing our residents and visitors alike to this amazing place we call home.

A great exhibition is one that inspires the visitor to learn more, and through the hikes presented in this guide you will have the opportunity to experience our region firsthand.

The Canyoneers, our volunteer naturalists trained to teach appreciation of plants and animals in southern California, have made that possible for more than 40 years through free, guided hikes. These hikes are now available to everyone in this comprehensive guide, which was made possible through the passion of many devoted volunteers—including Diana Lindsay, who has served as a tireless advocate as well as the book's project manager and lead editor—collaboration with numerous regional agencies, and also through generous support from Subaru of America, official corporate sponsor of the book and this year's Canyoneer hiking season. As you explore our region, we hope you will be inspired to promote stewardship of our environment and to help protect and preserve our quality of life.

Thank you for your support of the San Diego Natural History Museum, and special thanks to the Canyoneers for their dedicated service to the Museum and our community.

Michael W. Hager, Ph.D.
Past President & CEO
San Diego Natural History Museum

Dear Outdoor Enthusiast,

We are delighted to offer the combined wisdom and experience of over 40 years of San Diego Natural History Museum Canyoneer nature walks in this beautifully illustrated and easy-to-use guide. The Canyoneers lead free guided hikes throughout San Diego County, and this is the first time we've compiled our experiences into a book. Whether you are a short-term visitor or an experienced southern California naturalist, you'll find surprising and delightful routes, tips, and commentary about the ecological richness of our area.

Of course you'll want to begin your hike by visiting the Museum in Balboa Park and seeing our award-winning exhibition, *Coast to Cactus in Southern California*. There you can find an overview of the entire region and view some of the key habitats, plants, and animals. It is an excellent starting point for your journey through one of the most ecologically remarkable regions on the planet.

TheNAT is dedicated to understanding and inspiring appreciation of our natural world in southern California and Baja. With this exceptional guide we hope you'll be inspired to join us in studying and conserving our incredible region.

Judith Gradwohl
President & CEO
San Diego Natural History Museum

Preface
From the Managing Editor of *Coast to Cactus*

In 2001 I presented the idea of publishing a trail guide from the perspective of the San Diego Natural History Museum Canyoneers to Paula Knoll and Alan Marshall. They immediately became proponents of the idea, and it was presented to the Canyoneers at a meeting held on January 5, 2002. The vision was to create a book that would be a "Virtual Canyoneer" that accompanies the outdoor adventurer interested in learning more about this area that is a world-class biological hotspot. The idea seemed daunting at that time.

The idea tossed around for years until 2011 when *San Diego Reader* publisher Jim Holman called for someone to take over Jerry Schad's "Roam-O-Rama" column (as Jerry had passed away that fall). Paula, Alan, and I discussed the possibility of the Canyoneers answering the call and using the weekly "Roam-O-Rama" columns as a framework for creating the Canyoneer trail guide. Once again the concept was presented to the Canyoneers, and this time it met with enthusiasm. A memorandum of understanding was signed by Alan Marshall, then president of the Canyoneers, Michael W. Hager, President and CEO of the Museum, and me as President of Sunbelt Publications, Inc. The first Canyoneer "Roam-O-Rama" article was published in the *San Diego Reader* on January 5, 2012. The vision is now a reality thanks to a great number of dedicated and talented people and supporting agencies who are mentioned in the Acknowledgments.

Paula, Diana, and Alan introducing the book concept at a 2002 meeting of the Canyoneers

This unparalleled hiking guide is from the perspective of the Canyoneers who are San Diego Natural History Museum volunteers and citizen scientists trained to lead guided nature walks that teach appreciation for the great outdoors. When you hike with a Canyoneer, you are encouraged to stop, look, listen, touch, smell, and examine—to understand the interactions in nature.

With this book, hikers have their own "Virtual Canyoneer" to the best of San Diego County outdoors and even to some of the lesser-known places in the region. There are some 250 hiking options presented in this book and over 500 different species of plants, birds, mammals, reptiles, and invertebrates featured in the trip descriptions.

Readers are encouraged to use this guide in conjunction with the permanent exhibition *Coast to Cactus in Southern California* at the San Diego Natural History Museum in Balboa Park. After gaining a sense of how incredibly special this region is, use this guide to go out into the field and experience it firsthand.

The Canyoneers have donated their time and talent to create this guide. Purchase of this book will help support the San Diego Natural History Museum's mission to interpret the natural world through research, education, and exhibits; to promote understanding of the evolution and diversity of southern California and the peninsula of Baja California; and to inspire in all a respect for nature and the environment.

Take a hike with your "Virtual Canyoneer" and enjoy the great outdoors!

Diana Lindsay, Canyoneer and Board Member, San Diego Natural History Museum
Managing Editor, *Coast to Cactus: The Canyoneer Trail Guide to San Diego Outdoors*

Preface
From the President of the Canyoneers

Over 40 years ago, in 1973, San Diego Natural History Museum's associate botanist, Helen Vallejo Chamlee, proposed the idea of having a cadre of citizen-scientists offer nature walks in Balboa Park's Florida Canyon. The volunteers would be trained by the Museum, with a mission of introducing and enlightening the people of San Diego County about the amazing diversity of plants and animals in the region. Originally named the Florida Canyoneers, this group of naturalist guides eventually moved beyond Florida Canyon and into every corner of San Diego County.

Over the intervening years, hundreds of volunteers from all walks of life have been trained to lead their fellow San Diegans into the wonders of our natural environment. While not all of those Canyoneers remain with us in body, I have to believe they are still with us in spirit within the pages of this book. It is to all Canyoneers, past, present, and future, that I want to give my heartfelt thanks for all that you do. And, I want to give a special thanks to all of the public who have joined us on our hikes, because without you there would be no need for Canyoneers.

I am sure that some of you who are picking up this book have been on at least one Canyoneer nature hike. I also imagine there are those who are not familiar with the Canyoneers and their schedule of more than 70 hikes per season, from September through late June. I hope this book will give you some insight into what it's like to be out on the trail with the Canyoneers, while also providing an introduction to this amazingly rich and diverse part of the planet in which we live.

Canyoneer hikes are free with no reservation needed. What could be a better way to spend part of your day? Better yet, bring your entire family. A Canyoneer hike isn't meant as an aerobic event, even if some of them do get your heart pounding and blood flowing. Rather, you are encouraged to stop, look, listen, smell, touch, and think about all that surrounds you. There is nothing sweeter to the ears of a Canyoneer than the sound of someone asking a question about some aspect of nature. It is through this process of discovery that we hope you will learn something new and interesting along the way. For a list of Canyoneer hikes or to sign up to receive email notices of upcoming hikes, go to www.sdnat.org/canyoneers.

Between the covers of this book you will find a wealth of exciting trails to explore, including many of my favorite hikes in San Diego County. Yet everyone has individual preferences and needs when it comes to hiking. That's why you'll find hikes of varying lengths, difficulties, and locations from the coast to the desert, and from the middle of the city up to the mountains. Let your imagination soar as you thumb through these pages. The most important thing is to just get out there and begin to discover for yourself the joy, beauty, and wonder of nature that many of us take for granted in our busy lives. In doing so, I hope you will find that you want to become a steward of our public lands. By deciding that our environment is something of immense value and worth the time and effort to help protect and preserve, you will have taken an important step in passing it on to future generations.

I look forward to seeing you on the trails.

Jim Varnell
Canyoneer President 2014-2016

Introduction:
San Diego County's Ecosystems and Habitats

San Diego County's 4500 square miles offer an abundance of hiking trails of various distances and difficulties through diverse habitats within several ecosystems. This guide is a useful companion for your explorations of these natural areas, whether your goal is to add to your previous hiking experiences or to discover new trails. It will serve as your personal naturalist guide to these areas, providing information to enrich your enjoyment of the home of numerous plants and animals.

San Diego County's natural areas are truly exceptional places thought to be the most biodiverse land in the United States. Year-round opportunities await your exploration in any season—coastal areas are pleasant in any month, mountain landscapes warm up during the summer, and the desert regions cool and appeal to all visitors in the winter and spring. San Diego County's subtle seasons bring new discoveries in every ecosystem throughout the year. Bird migrations, the onset of winter rains, and the flowering and fruiting of plants are some of nature's phenological cues signaling changing seasons.

These life-cycle events, in addition to entire ecosystem adaptation, can vary substantially in their timing across years, depending on factors that are not part of living organisms. This is particularly well illustrated by increased productivity of ecosystems during the high rainfall of El Niño years or community progression through successional stages after fire. There are many nuances waiting to be uncovered in our natural areas that influence biodiversity. This book is your personal trail guide—your portable Canyoneer—that can provide you with a perspective and an interpretation of those nuances that make San Diego County such a special place.

You are likely to encounter a unique find each time you're on the trail because the diversity of life is exceptionally high. Much of San Diego County lies within the California Floristic Province, a region encompassing most of the State of California and extending into southwest Oregon and northern Baja California, Mexico. The California Floristic Province is globally recognized as one of 35 hotspots identified for high biodiversity in combination with high rates of habitat loss. These biodiversity hotspots contain about 35% of the Earth's vertebrate animals and 44% of its vascular plants, despite covering only 1.4% of Earth's land surface. In San Diego County alone, 2672 plant species have been documented. A high degree of endemism exists in the county, with many species occurring only within, or nearly within, the borders of San Diego County.

Cascading effects of plant biodiversity can be observed in other phyla as well. For example, the large numbers of native insect pollinator species may be attributed, in part, to the diversity of plants. The diversity of ecosystems found in the county also provide habitat to many mammal and reptile species. Further, San Diego County straddles the Pacific Flyway, bringing many bird species to our region during their yearly migrations, resulting in more than 500 species of either year-round residents or migrants recorded in the county. Hikes around dawn and dusk hours generally lend themselves to better chances of sighting mammals and bird foraging and signing behaviors, as many of these species are crepuscular, or active near twilight hours. Warm, bright, and sunny days often enliven snake and lizard activity as these reptiles are commonly diurnal, or active during the day.

The varied topography and Mediterranean climate, with cool, wet winters and dry summers throughout most of the county, are largely to thank for this diversity of flora. Starting at the Pacific Ocean, the Peninsular Ranges, predominately the Laguna Mountains in San Diego County, divide the county into three main regions. West of the mountains, on the cismontane side, the coastal plain region is largely dominated by chaparral and coastal sage scrub, with other ecosystems sprinkled in. The Salton Trough region on the transmontane side is dominated by the Colorado Desert, but variation within this ecosystem also awaits your discovery. The mountains themselves, the montane regions, are home to majestic oak woodlands, meadows, and conifer forests.

These geographic regions also provide rough geological divisions for the county. Throughout the western coastal plain region, rounded cobbles, which are river-worn pieces of rhyolite rock, pepper the landscape. These distinctive cobbles were eroded over millions of years from mountains found in present-day Sonora, Mexico. Washed down by rivers to coastal areas, and then through the action of plate tectonics, these cobbles were moved about 300 miles northwards with the Baja California peninsula as the entire Pacific Plate shifted northward relative to the North American Plate along the San Andres fault, beginning some 6 million years ago. Today these cobbles are found in modern-day San Diego County.

Many different sandstone formations can be found in the coastal plain region. Over portions of geological history, this region was underwater, and deposits of marine sediment formed the sandstone. The mesa regions in western San Diego County are also testaments to the watery past, as they are former marine terraces. Sedimentary rocks characterize the Salton Trough area as well. Erosion from local mountains and deposition from the ancestral and modern-day Colorado River have filled this region over the past 24 million years with sediments up to 5 miles deep.

Marine fossils can also be found in the Salton Trough, thanks to the ancestral Gulf of California covering the area. More recent megafauna fossils from the Pleistocene epoch, which was over 11 thousand years ago, speak to the region's more temperate history and post-recession of the ancestral gulf. Moving into the Peninsular Range region, the Southern California Batholith was formed as magma cooled slowly within the Earth's crust, and as a result, granitic rocks are prominent on the landscape.

This geologic diversity has contributed to our biological diversity. The close proximity of the peninsular ranges to our coast combined with the cold California current has produced a Mediterranean climate while those same ranges have created a rain shadow desert only a 100 miles from the coast. This geographic setting has resulted in the creation of our diverse ecosystems.

This guide includes hikes that will introduce you to the nine main habitats in the county. Within any given hike, you may encounter several habitat types, as the borders between them overlap and small-scale local patterns and microclimates can influence vegetation type and community composition. As a result of the variation present in our region, many different methods for classifying habitats exist. Depending on the methodology used, some systems have over 20 habitat types for the county or agency websites may have localized habitats listed that are not included in the following habitat categories. In this guide we have chosen broad, easily understandable habitat categories, as identified by San Diego State University (SDSU) (http://interwork.sdsu.edu/fire/resources/san-diego-habitats.htm).

Descriptions of the nine main habitats found in the county follow this brief introduction, giving both the percentage of land mass and acreage that each habitat occupies. Total acreage for the nine habitats is 2,156,959 acres, or about 74.5 percent of the county's land mass (2,896,640 acres or 4526 square miles). The remaining 25.5 percent of the county's acreage falls under anthropogenic land use. An anthropogenic biome is an area where humans have fundamentally altered ecosystem properties to the point where human activities currently comprise the majority of land use, areas such as urban developments and roads.

Each hike in this book has one or more symbols in the "At a Glance" information found at the top of each trip description that represents the habitats that will be encountered.

Lists are provided in the appendix of the most common or distinctive plants, birds, mammals, reptiles, and invertebrates that can be found in each of the nine habitat types that are presented in this book. Each species has detailed descriptions embedded within trip write-ups that may be found by referring to the index. Look for page numbers in bold that will refer you to the location for more in-depth species-level information. Common plant names used in this book are those listed with the scientific names in the 5th edition of the *Checklist of the Vascular Plants of San Diego County* by Jon P. Rebman and Michael G. Simpson.

The natural spaces preserved within the county are excellent places to look for, observe, and appreciate our rich biological diversity. While absorbing the beauty and peace you find in San Diego County's natural landscapes, take a moment to reflect on what might not be immediately obvious. Some spaces have been compromised and fragmented and may be detached from a much larger and wilder ecosystem. There may be the background noise of a freeway or suburban development bordering open space or powerlines running through an area. Species that should be found in the habitat are often missing.

Our incredible biodiversity is threatened by pressure from many sources including habitat fragmentation and land conversion from increasing urbanization, invasion from non-native species, nitrogen pollution, increased fire frequency, and altered precipitation regimes, to name a few. These changes can fundamentally impact interactions both between and within species. Within a population, for example, roads restrict species movement, effectively decreasing gene flow as animals breed. Reduced genetic diversity lowers the potential of a population to adapt to future environmental changes or disease. Unprecedented drought severity can limit the germination, growth, and seed production of plants upon which many rodents feed. As a prey item, smaller rodent populations can result in further cascading effects throughout the ecosystem. On your explorations, challenge yourself to see the interconnectedness between plants and animals and imagine how they may change once the system is disturbed.

We encourage you to make this guide a resource for achieving greater understanding of our region. Take a friend or family member with you, share your knowledge and appreciation of this wonderfully complex region, and begin the dialogue of how we as humans fit into the fabric of our ecosystems and our responsibilities to the land. Visit the San Diego Natural History Museum and learn about the research by regional scientists to better understand the threats to our ecosystems and how principles from this research are being applied to mitigate these effects. We hope the information in this guide helps you to develop a deeper connection with the region—grounding, relaxing, and invigorating you. In turn, we hope that you will use your newfound knowledge to become an advocate for San Diego County's natural spaces, cultivating a wide-spread stewardship ethic, and ultimately helping protect these areas for future generations.

Ellen Esch, Canyoneer
Division of Biological Sciences
University of California, San Diego

San Diego County Land Mass: 2,896,640 Acres or 4526 Square Miles

The 9 habitats comprise 74.5% of the land mass or 2,156,959 acres
Anthropogenic land use is 25.5% or 739,681 acres

HABITAT	% COUNTY LAND MASS	ACREAGE
Beach/Salt Marsh/Lagoon	0.2%	6360 acres
Coastal Sage Scrub	7.9%	228,915 acres
Grassland	5.1%	146,833 acres
Chaparral	31.6%	915,857 acres
Oak Woodland	4.2%	120,859 acres
Riparian	1.8%	50,671 acres
Freshwater Marsh/Montane Meadow/Vernal Pool	0.9%	26,449 acres
Mixed Conifer Forest	2.6%	75,878 acres
Desert	20.2%	585,137 acres
TOTAL	74.5%	2,156,959 acres

The Nine Habitats Used in This Book

Beach/Salt Marsh/Lagoon

This habitat is the interface between the ocean and land and is highly influenced by the ocean tides. These areas contain a mix of aquatic and terrestrial organisms. During high tide, much of these ecosystems are underwater, while becoming exposed at low tides. There is also a mix of salt water with fresh water in coastal lagoons. Within these ecosystems, zonation patterns exist in which certain elevations are conducive to different dominant plant species.

In salt marshes, California cord grass (*Spartina foliosa*) generally dominates at the lowest elevations, providing habitat for the endangered light-footed Ridgway's rail—formerly the clapper rail (*Rallus obsoletus levipes*)—and is replaced by low-growing succulents such as pickleweeds (*Salicornia* **spp.**) and fleshy jaumea (*Jaumea carnosa*). These patterns are driven by interactions among plants and their tolerance of salinity and inundation.

Generally, higher elevations have more organic matter and clay-type soils, and less frequent inundation. As a more hospitable environment for vascular plants, the structure of plant communities of higher elevations is driven primarily by competition, while environmental constraints limit plant ranges at the lower elevations.

When the tide recedes twice each day, mudflats and saltpans are often exposed, and feeding shorebirds will provide hours of bird-watching entertainment. Gulls and shorebirds along with endangered and threatened species such as the western snowy plover (*Charadrius nivosus*) and least tern (*Sterna antillarum*) also frequent sandy beach areas and intertidal flats, feeding on invertebrates such as sand crabs and a variety of worms. In the spring, mating runs of California grunion (*Leuresthes tenuis*), a small fish, are one of the most distinctive events on sandy beach areas. Only 0.2% of the county's land surface (about 6360 acres) falls within this habitat.

Ellen Esch

Beach/Salt Marsh/Lagoon

Coastal Sage Scrub

Often described as soft chaparral, coastal sage scrub is characterized by low-growing, aromatic shrubs that are found from the coast to the foothills, generally not above 1500 feet in elevation. Aromatic compounds in these species may have evolved to attract pollinators, discourage animal browsing, or resist water loss with associated resinous leaf coatings. Many coastal sage scrub plants are drought deciduous, effectively reducing water loss by going into various stages of dormancy as they shed their leaves in the dry summer months.

Plants vary in their tendency to drop leaves under limited moisture scenarios, so while you might struggle to find nitrogen-fixing deerweeds (*Acmispon glaber*) and California encelia (*Encelia californica*) during the summer months, coastal sagebrush (*Artemisia californica*) and black sage (*Salvia mellifera*) will be more conspicuous as they generally retain more of their leaves. Other plants such as California buckwheat (*Eriogonum fasciculatum*), lemonadeberry (*Rhus integrifolia*), scrub oak (*Quercus* **spp.**), and coyote brush (*Baccharis pilularis*) rely on thicker, waxier leaves to avoid desiccation and are often in full foliage throughout the year.

North-facing slopes are good places to find these evergreen species of coastal sage communities. Less sun exposure compared to southern-facing slopes allows larger, moisture-intensive plants to flourish. Small rodents including woodrats and several mouse species are common dwellers in coastal sage scrub as are their predators, which include snakes, raptors, and coyotes. As the name implies, coastal sage scrub can be found near the coast but also exists in inland valleys. This habitat comprises 7.9% (228,915 acres) of the county's land surface.

Grassland

Grasslands are generally located in the lower elevations of San Diego County's interior valleys but can extend up to 4000 feet in elevation. This habitat generally falls into native- or exotic-dominated ecosystems. Native grasslands contain high densities of the California State Grass, purple needle grass (*Stipa pulchra*), in addition to other perennial bunchgrasses. Native herbs, which are plants without a woody base, splash color on grassland habitats in the spring. Geophytes, or plants that form underground energy stores, are among the most distinctive native herbs coloring grassland habitats in the spring.

Coastal Sage Scrub

Blue dicks or school bells (**Dichelostemma capitatum** subsp. **capitatum**) produce a small pom-pom like purple flower atop a single, long and leafless stalk originating from a corm, which is a swollen underground stem. The large and showy flowers of mariposa lilies (**Calochortus spp.**) originate at their bulb, which is a modified leaf with fleshy scales with a growing tip and a root, like an onion. Their distinctive three petals can be found in white, pink, or yellow. Blue-eyed-grass (**Sisyrinchium bellum**) is another common geophyte, arising from underground rhizomes, which are underground stems that grow sideways and develop roots and shoots of their own. The blue-eyed-grass presents a small iris-like flower. These species are important food sources for large and small vertebrates that seek out their underground energy storage organs.

Other characteristic spring flowers include the blue to purple Nuttall's snapdragon (**Antirrhinum nuttallianum**) and lupines (**Lupinus spp.**), orange California poppies (**Eschscholzia californica**), and yellow flowers of tarplants (**Deinandra spp.**). These characteristic herbs may be hard to find however, as most grasslands in southern California have been developed or converted into exotic-dominated areas. Disturbances, such as overgrazing by cattle or high fire frequencies, have facilitated conversion into non-native annual grasslands. Annual exotic grasses in this area notably do not include any bunch grasses, and instead, species like ripgut grass (**Bromus diandrus**), compact brome (**Bromus madritensis**), and slender wild oat (**Avena barbata**) are common. These species of annual grasses originate from the Mediterranean Basin in Europe and arrived in southern California in around 1850. The summer months turn these grasses a golden color, in contrast to perennial bunchgrasses, which often remain party green and are photosynthetically active during the dry months.

Exotic herbs such as filarees (**Erodium spp.**), black and short-pod mustards (**Brassica nigra** and **Hirschfeldia incana**), along with various exotic Centaurea thistle species, can also be found in high abundances in exotic grasslands. Birds of prey, rabbits, and rodent species are common in both native and exotic-dominated grasslands. This habitat comprises comprises 5.1% (146,833 acres) of the county's land surface.

Chaparral

Chaparral, also called an elfin forest, is characterized by dense woody shrubs with sclerophyllous or hard leaves and is widespread across the county in the higher ele-

Don Fosket

Grassland

vation foothills, generally found between coastal sage scrub and coniferous forests. It is the most widespread habitat in the county ranging in elevation from 500 to 4500 feet. In contrast to coastal sage scrub, most chaparral species are evergreen, retaining their leaves through the dry summer months and protecting themselves from water loss with their leathery, resinous leaves. They can also form impenetrable shrublands.

Presence of chamise (*Adenostoma fasciculatum*) often indicates chaparral habitat, though at higher elevations you may frequently see the charismatic and distinctive red-barked manzanita species (*Arctostaphylos* **spp.**), the aptly-named ribbonwood or red shank (*Adenostoma sparsifolium*), and mountain-mahogany (*Cercocarpus* **spp.**) that produces fuzzy, curly seeds. Following winter rains, spring in the chaparral brings brightly colored purple and white blossoms of Ceanothus species and large flower stalks with white blossoms of chaparral candle (*Hesperoyucca whipplei*) scattered across the landscape.

Chaparral species possess adaptations to dealing with fire such as the ability to resprout from underground root burls or successful seedling recruitment post-fire. However, fires occurring more frequently than once every 30 years limit the ability of chaparral communities to recover from repeated disturbance and may result in conversion to areas dominated by invasive grasses. Large fires in chaparral areas often occur as a result of the high temperature at which these woody and resinous species burn. However, most fires start with exotic annual grasses which have lower ignition points and then spread to the chaparral, at which point extinguishing the blaze is made more challenging due to hotter burn temperatures of the woody species.

Similar animals are found in chaparral habitats as are found in coastal sage scrub, though mountain lions are occasionally found in chaparral as it often occurs in larger, less fragmented regions. This large habitat comprises 31.6% (915,857 acres) of the county's land surface.

Oak Woodland

Areas populated by shade-casting oaks are classified as oak woodlands and are generally found in interior canyons and inland foothills between 1500 and 4500 feet in elevation. Commonly occurring oak species are California black (*Quercus kelloggii*), canyon live (*Quercus chrysolepis*), coast live (*Quercus agrifolia* **vars.** *agrifolia* and *oxyadenia*), Engelmann (*Quercus engelmannii*), and interior live (*Quercus wislizeni*) oaks. Distinguishing between spe-

Don Fosket

Chaparral

cies of oak can be challenging as some of these species hybridize, though leaf color and shape along with bark and acorn characteristics remain helpful traits. Extensive root systems with deep taproots give oaks access to water throughout the year, and as a result they retain their leaves year-round, with the exception of the deciduous California black oak and some Engelmann oak that are drought deciduous.

This year-round canopy offers protection from predation and sun exposure for wildlife, boosting the diversity of animals you are likely to encounter in this habitat. Over 300 species of terrestrial vertebrates use California oak woodlands for food, cover, and nesting, including at least 120 species of mammals, 147 species of birds, and 60 species of amphibians and reptiles.

Significant leaf loss and subsequent death may be indicative of damage caused by the goldspotted oak borer (*Agrilus auroguttatus*). This introduced, invasive pest, native to Arizona and Northern Mexico, poses a major threat to the integrity of oak woodlands in introduced ranges. Coupled with increased drought, the insect can more easily and quickly damage stressed oak trees. Infection rates are estimated at 90% of trees (as opposed to 4% in the native range) with mortality occurring 45% of the time (versus 2% in its native range).

Oak woodland understories often have high abundances of western poison-oak (*Toxicodendron diversilobum*), exotic grasses, and other herbs. Commonly found adjacent to chaparral communities, many similar species of animals can be found in both ecosystems, though acorn woodpeckers (*Melanerpes formicivorus*) and western scrub-jays (*Aphelocoma californica*) are especially fond of oak woodlands, as are southern mule deer (*Odocoileus hemionus*) and California ground squirrels (*Otospermophilus beecheyi*). About 4.2% (120,859 acres) of the county's land surface is oak woodland.

Riparian

Riparian areas are found along streams and lake edges in canyon bottoms and valleys at any elevation throughout the county. They are easily recognized by their dense year-round vegetation. Trees and shrubs such as willows (*Salix* **spp.**), western cottonwood (*Populus fremontii*), mule-fat (*Baccharis salicifolia*), and western sycamore (*Platanus racemosa*) are common plant species of this habitat type.

With abundant water resources, this is an especially productive ecosystem capable of producing dense understories. As a result, riparian areas support many animals that often arrive in search of water, food, and

Oak Woodland

shelter. A host of amphibians, reptiles, birds, and mammals can be found in these areas. Riparian areas can also provide important habitat connectivity and shelter for animals, creating a corridor to link landscapes fragmented by development and roadways.

While these communities have access to year-round water, surface water is not a requirement and underground water sources can support riparian communities. Riparian areas are highly influenced by the nature of the stream running through them and may range from only a few meters across where a stream runs through a steep canyon or may

Riparian

Freshwater Marsh/Montane Meadow/Vernal Pool

be wider as it reaches the coast. Hydrology, such as sediment transport during flooding events, can also influence the nature of riparian systems. Riparian habitats also provide riverbank stabilization, erosion control, and improved water quality. San Diego County has 1.8% (50,671 acres) of its land surface within this habitat.

Freshwater Marsh/Montane Meadow/Vernal Pool

These habitats are formed when areas are saturated with freshwater for most of the year regardless of elevation. Common plant species found in freshwater marshes and montane meadows are cattails (*Typha* **spp.**), rushes (*Juncus* **spp.**), bulrushes (*Schoenoplectus* **spp.**) and flatsedges (*Cyperus* **spp.**). Red-winged blackbirds (*Agelaius phoeniceus)* can be found perched on reeds in these habitats.

Whereas marshes are formed streamside, meadows occupy landscape areas too moist to support mixed conifer forest habitats, and vernal pools form in depressions in flat areas with an impermeable clay or rock substratum. Both marshes and meadows often have water year-round, while ephemeral vernal pools are seasonally filled by winter rains. Vernal pools support communities uniquely specialized to this environment and then dry up in the spring or early summer. Much of the suitable vernal pool habitat that was historically found on inland mesas, such as Kearny Mesa or Otay Mesa, has been urbanized. As a result, species, such as the San Diego fairy shrimp (*Branchinecta sandiegonensis*) are listed as federally endangered.

Only 0.9% (26,449 acres) of the county's land surface is within this habitat.

Mixed Conifer Forest

Mixed conifer forests contain a mix of needle-leaved conifers and broad-leaved trees and shrubs that occur at higher elevations (above 4500 feet) in the county's mountainous areas. Approximately 20 inches of precipitation are needed annually to support this community. As air rises along the western side of mountains, it cools with water vapor condensing to rain or snow leading higher elevation areas to receive more moisture. The effect creates a rain shadow, where dry air descends the eastern slopes of our mountain ranges.

In mixed conifer forests, Coulter (*Pinus coulteri*), Jeffrey (*Pinus jeffreyi*), or single leaf pinyon (*Pinus monophylla*) pines often form the canopy layer. California black oak (*Quercus kelloggii*) and canyon live oak (*Quercus chrysolepis*) may also comprise the canopy.

Don Fosket

Mixed Conifer Forest

California incense cedar (*Calocedrus decurrens*) and sugar pine (*Pinus lambertiana*) are important species found in the Lagunas, Cuyamacas, and on Palomar Mountain.

Under the top-most canopy layer, smaller trees and shrubs may be found in addition to grasses and herbs. Birds are abundant in mixed conifer forest and often include woodpeckers, owls, hawks, and jays. About 2.6% (75, 878 acres) of the county's land surface fall within this habitat.

Desert

Desert vegetation in eastern San Diego County arises as a result of the rain shadow created by the Peninsular Mountains (including the Laguna Mountains and Palomar Mountain). Within the desert portion of the county, a great range of vegetation types can be found, with elevation and direction of exposure often responsible for the division into vegetative subcategories. The desert habitat is second only to rainforests for the number and variety of plant and animal species found. It has the most diverse population of reptiles in North America and has thousands of invertebrate species. There are over 600 species of desert plants and more than 240 species of birds. Among the 60 species of mammals are some of the county's most charismatic megafauna, such as desert bighorn sheep (*Ovis canadensis nelsoni*) and mountain lion (*Puma concolor*).

Desert scrub is the most common of desert subcategories and can be identified by the dominance of creosote bush (*Larrea tridentata*). Spring paints common desert scrub species in bright colors that splash the landscape—indigo bush (*Psorothamnus schottii*) with purple flowers, creosote and desert agave (*Agave deserti*) with yellow flowers, and ocotillo (*Fouquieria splendens*) and chuparosa (*Justicia californica*) with red tubular flowers. The multiple colors of the cactus family including chollas and prickly-pear complement these species. Fields of annual flowers blooming in years of sufficient winter rains are also found in desert scrub.

Pinyon-juniper woodlands occur at higher elevations in the desert. As the name implies, pinyon pines (*Pinus monophylla* and *Pinus quadrifolia*) and California juniper (*Juniperus californica*) are common within this vegetative subcategory. Between low desert scrub and higher pinyon-juniper communities, the desert chaparral can be found. Across these subcategories, wherever water is found there will be riparian areas, often creating palm oases. Next to chaparral, the desert is the most common habitat in the county, occupying 20.2% (585,137 acres) of the county's land surface.

Desert

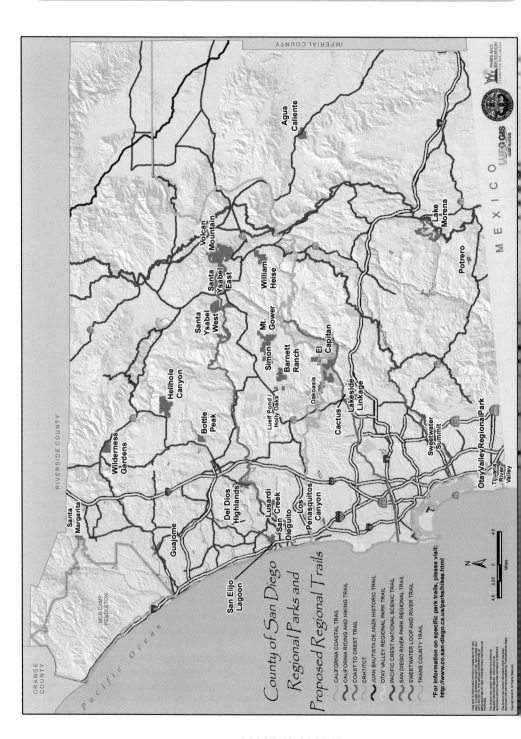

County of San Diego
Regional Parks and
Proposed Regional Trails

CALIFORNIA COASTAL TRAIL
CALIFORNIA RIDING AND HIKING TRAIL
COAST TO CREST TRAIL
CRHT/TCT
JUAN BAUTISTA DE ANZA HISTORIC TRAIL
OTAY VALLEY REGIONAL PARK TRAIL
PACIFIC CREST NATIONAL SCENIC TRAIL
SAN DIEGO RIVER PARK REGIONAL TRAIL
SWEETWATER LOOP AND RIVER TRAIL
TRANS COUNTY TRAIL

*For information on specific park trails, please visit:
http://www.co.san-diego.ca.us/parks/hikes.html

In 2000 the San Diego County Board of Supervisors affirmed that "Riding and hiking trails outside of County parkland and County road rights-of-way are a legitimate and necessary form of public recreation that the County should provide." A Trails Program Management Team was established using resources from the Departments of Parks and Recreation, Planning and Land Use, and Public Works. They were charged with developing a County Trails Program that encompasses both regional and community trails. An assessment was done and recommendations were made.

In 2005 the Board of Supervisors adopted the County Trails Program and the Community Trails Master Plan. The objective was to develop a system of interconnected regional and community trails and pathways that address the need for recreation and "provide health and quality of life benefits associated with hiking, mountain biking, and horseback riding throughout the County's biologically diverse environments."

The County Trails Program also includes a Regional Trails Plan that is part of the County's General Plan. The Regional Trails Plan has identified nine trails in the county that serve a regional function by covering long linear distances and transcending community and/or municipal borders; having state or national significance; or providing connectivity to existing parks and open space preserves. Some of the trails are established while others are in various planning stages. These nine trails provide significant north-south or east-west trail corridors that cross San Diego County.

Portions of these nine trails are included in the hikes described in this book. Because of the interconnectivity of these regional trails, some of the hikes are actually within two or more crossing corridors for the recognized trails within the Regional Trails Plan. The nine trails are the following, in alphabetical order.

California Coastal Trail (CCT). This 1000-mile-long trail is a work in progress that will extend from the Oregon border to the Mexican border when complete. The plan was developed in 1975, and in 2000 it was recognized as a statewide and national resource, now designated as California's Millennium Legacy Trail. The vision is a continuous trail connecting to parks, beaches and other trail networks that closely parallel the shoreline.

About 70% of this trail is complete in San Diego County.

California Riding and Hiking Trail (CRHT). In 1945 Governor Earl Warren signed the California Riding and Hiking Trail Act that would create a 3000-mile trail from the Mexican border north through the Tehachapi Mountains and the Sierra Nevada to the Oregon border. The route was to be established wherever possible over existing forest service trails and dirt roads on public lands. The vision for this trail has never been fulfilled, but San Diego County has the most continuous miles of trail in the state. A spur of the CRHT drops down to Anza-Borrego Desert State Park via the Mason Valley Truck Trail and winds its way north, up Grapevine Canyon and the Jasper Trail, and then down to Culp Valley and the Hellhole Canyon staging area in Borrego Springs. The Trans-County Trail utilizes a portion of the CRHT and the CRHT spur to the Hellhole Canyon staging area.

Coast to Crest Trail. In 1989 the San Dieguito River Valley Regional Open Space Park Joint Powers Authority was formed to conserve the natural habitat and to establish a trail in the San Dieguito River Valley that would extend 71 miles from Del Mar to Volcan Mountain. It was the first time that a regional trail was established within the county. The goal is to create a multi-use trail for hikers, bicyclists, and horseback riders. About 48 miles of the Coast to Crest Trail has been completed as of 2015. San Dieguito River Park also has auxiliary trails that are not part of the Coast to Crest Trail system. This guide lists 20 hikes that are part of the San Dieguito River Park, and 13 of those include segments along the Coast to Crest Trail.

Juan Bautista de Anza National Historic Trail. Congress authorized the creation of the Juan Bautista de Anza National Historic Trail in 1990—the first trail of its kind in the western US. The trail extends from Nogales, Arizona, to San Francisco, California, following as close as possible the route taken by Anza in the winter of 1775-76 when he brought 240 immigrants to California. Plans are currently underway to extend the trail into Mexico to Culiacan, Sinaloa, where the expedition began. When complete, it will be the first International Historic Trail in the world. Some of the trips described in this book in Coyote Canyon are along this historic trail.

Otay Valley Regional Park Trail. In 1990 the City of Chula Vista, the City of San Diego, and the County of San Diego utilized a Joint Exercise of Powers Agreement to plan and acquire land for a regional park that would provide open space and recreational opportunities for citizens of the region. When completed, a linear multi-use trail of 13 miles will be within 8000 acres of protected land. This trail will connect to the CRHT that will, in turn, connect to the Pacific Crest Trail. This book describes a hike within Otay Valley Regional Park.

Pacific Crest Trail (PCT). Teams of young men from the YMCA explored possible routes in the 1930s for a 2650-mile trail from Mexico to Canada that would cross three states. The Pacific Crest Trail became one of the first scenic trails in the National Trails System when it was authorized by Congress in 1968. It was dedicated in 1993. It is open to hikers and horses only. Vehicles and bicycles are not permitted. Dogs are permitted only in areas approved by managing agencies. Many of the east-west trails within the county will eventually connect with the PCT. The PCT utilizes small sections of the CRHT and TCT trails. There are 14 trips in the book that include sections of the PCT.

San Diego River Park Regional Trail. The vision of a 52-mile open space greenbelt along the San Diego River has long been the dream of The San Diego River Park Foundation (SDRPF). The Foundation engaged community members to create a San Diego River Park Conceptual Plan and then presented it to elected officials of the City of Santee, the City of San Diego, and San Diego County. In 2002 Governor Gray Davis signed a bill creating the San Diego River Conservancy, the eighth state-chartered conservancy in the state and the first dedicated to San Diego County. The act recognized the statewide significance of the San Diego River for both its natural and cultural resources. The Conservancy and SDRPF are working to create a system of parks, open spaces, and community places along the river. SDRPF owns three preserves and actively solicits funds to preserve other areas along the San Diego River.

This book has 23 trips that are part of the San Diego River Park. This includes 13 that are within Mission Trails Regional Park.

Sweetwater River and Loop Trail. In 1980, a licensed agreement was signed between San Diego County and the Sweetwater Authority allowing a segment of a loop trail on the south shore of Sweetwater Reservoir to be opened to the public. In 2002 the San Diego County Board of Supervisors authorized the County Department of Public Works to implement a plan to develop another loop trail along the north shore of Sweetwater Reservoir. The County continues to work with the communities of Spring Valley, Bonita, Valle De Oro, Crest-Dehesa, Rancho San Diego, and Jamul to expand the recreational opportunities in those areas. When completed, this trail will also connect to the CRHT in the Sloane Canyon area of the Dehesa Community. The Sweetwater River Trail is included in this guide with the 4.8 mile Sweetwater Riding and Hiking Trail extending the described hike by approximately 5 miles one-way.

Trans-County Trail (TCT). One of the most ambitious plans is a 110-mile trail that will extend from the staging area at Hellhole Canyon in Anza-Borrego Desert State Park (ABDSP) to Torrey Pines State Natural Reserve. About 70% of the route uses existing trails that are already open for public use, some of which are already part of the Regional Trails Plan. The creation of this trail is a cooperative effort of federal, state, county, and local governments all working together to connect existing public trails with public right-of-way. The TCT uses the CRHT where it passes through Cuyamaca Rancho State Park as it heads north to the Riverside County line. Then it follows the CRHT spur to the Hellhole Canyon staging area in ABDSP, at the edge of Borrego Valley. Although there has even been talk of the possibility of extending the desert portion of this trail to the Salton Sea to create a Sea to Sea Trail, that is not part of the County's RTP plan. The current plan is to get the trail completed to ABDSP. An extension to the Salton Sea could possibly be a future project.

Introduction:
Maximizing Your Outdoor Experience

This section offers tips and information that allow you to maximize your enjoyment and learning experience. You will find details that include the organization of the book, how to use its special features, and where to go for more information about equipment needed, safety issues, and trail etiquette.

How This Book Is Organized

All hikes in this book are arranged geographically into five sections—coast, inland north, inland south, mountains and desert. We use major freeways and corridors of travel as boundaries where possible for each of the areas, making it easier to spatially visualize the location of the hike, its trailhead, and its probable habitat. Refer to the map on the inside front cover to view the five sections.

All of the five sections are divided, in turn, into sub-sections based on major corridors of travel where applicable. Maps showing details of each of the geographical divisions are found in the front of each hike section of this book. Each section is also color-coded for quick reference. Hikes within the divisions have been listed generally north to south in the book, unless they have been clustered together within a specific group as a chapter, such as Mission Trails Regional Park and Cuyamaca Rancho State Park.

Understanding the Book's Special Features

Basic information for pre-hike planning is found in the "At a Glance" section that precedes the hike description. This includes distance, difficulty, elevation gain/loss, estimated hiking time, trail use, special notes regarding the hike, directions to the trailhead, trailhead GPS coordinates, available maps, and the name of the agency that manages the area.

Special features in the "At a Glance" section include symbols that indicate what habitats might be encountered on the hike and an atlas square number that can be used on the SDNHM's website for more information about the chosen hike area for further study. These features allow for more in-depth understanding of the ecology found in the hike area. Every hike also includes a map and photos of either the area or of species that might be encountered on the hike.

NOTE: Pay particular attention to the discussion below on the GPS coordinates so that you will end up at the right location for the trailhead.

Distance: Distance is indicated from the trailhead, followed by the type of hike described, which can be: out-and-back (following the same trail in both directions); a loop (either a complete circle/loop or a loop after a short out-and-back); or one-way (a point-to-point hike requiring a shuttle or pick-up at the other end). The distance is rounded to the 0.1 mile. Optional distances are indicated for extending a hike.

Difficulty Rating: All trips are classified according to a 1-5 rating system (using hiker symbols) that takes into account distance, hiking time, elevation gain/loss, and trail quality. Trails vs. cross-country travel along with steepness of grades will influence the rating.

🚶—a short trail, generally level, that can be completed in 1 hour or less with possible elevation gain/loss of up to 200 feet.

🚶🚶—a route of 1-3 miles with some up and down that can be completed in 1-2 hours with elevation gain/loss of up to 500 feet.

🚶🚶🚶—a long route, up to 5 miles, with uphill and/or downhill sections with elevation gain/loss of up to 1000 feet.

🚶🚶🚶🚶—a long or steep route, perhaps more than 5 miles or climbs of up to 1500 vertical feet.

🚶🚶🚶🚶🚶—the most challenging, both long and steep, more than 5 miles long with climbs of more than 1500 vertical feet.

Elevation Estimates: Rather than using a precise figure that can vary from one GPS to another, this book is using a general range that indicates the maximum of elevation gain/loss in increments of 100 feet. For example, an elevation gain/loss over 100 feet and up to 200 feet is shown as up to 200 feet. For essentially flat trails, elevation gain/loss is listed as minimal.

Hiking Time Estimates: Time is based on an average standard hiking speed of 2 mph for flats and then adding 30 minutes for each 1000 feet of climbing. Then, the time is rounded up to the nearest hour. These estimates are based on years of experience running public hikes for the Museum. An experienced, strong hiker will complete the hike before the estimated time. These estimates are hiking times only and do not take into account extra time that individuals may want to spend observing or studying the habitat they are exploring.

Trail Use: All trails listed in this book are open to hikers. If no listing appears, it means the trail is open to hikers only. It is assumed that they are NOT open to bicycles, horses, or dogs unless specifically listed in the trail use area. *When dogs are listed, it is ALWAYS with a leash.* Some wilderness trails may be open to horses but not dogs. Horses are herbivores and do not upset the balance within hunting territories, although their feces may introduce invasive plant seeds through their feed. Keeping horses on designated horse trails minimizes the impact to an area.

Dogs resemble predators like coyotes and foxes. They may frighten deer and small animals, even flushing out ground-dwelling animals or frightening birds from their nests while on a leash. Dog feces may also introduce parasites or diseases for which wild animals may have no immunity. This is why most state parks and wilderness areas do not allow dogs with the exception of designated vehicle roads and always on a leash. Wild areas and wildlife can be particularly hazardous to unleashed dogs—think cactus and rattlesnakes.

Bicycles are usually restricted to vehicle routes if allowed. Rules regarding dogs, horses, and bicycles vary from one agency to the next. It is best to call the agency if you are not sure. The "At a Glance" information includes the name of the managing agency. The appendix lists all of the agencies, their websites, and telephone numbers.

Contact the agencies directly for information regarding accommodation for hikers with special needs. Some agencies have ADA-approved facilities or trails. This book lists hikes that have specific ADA approval.

This book does not list hikes as good for children. What might be good for one child might not be appropriate for another child. Generally, the easier hikes are more appropriate for children.

Facilities and Water: This book is not indicating the presence of toilet facilities or water as their availability at many trailheads is constantly changing due to ongoing drought conditions. Rather, we are encouraging hikers to assume there will be no facilities or water at the trailheads and to plan accordingly.

Driving Directions: Driving directions are included for every hike in this book. The directions always start with an exit from a major highway and then describe the roads, turns and distances needed to reach the parking for the trailhead. Some hikes will have multiple directions if travel from various parts of the county requires the use of a different major highway.

While every attempt has been made to provide accurate directions, unforeseen factors could cause directions to change. These could include road closures, new roads, or starting from a location not accounted for in the directions. For this reason you are encouraged to use these driving directions as suggestions and to either use a printed map or digital mapping software to determine the best route from your personal starting point.

Setting Your GPS Device to Read Coordinates Correctly: GPS coordinates are provided for every hike in this book to help you find the recommended trailhead location to start your hike. GPS stands for Global Positioning System and is a satellite based navigation system that allows for the determination of an exact location anywhere in the world. There are a myriad of ways to express a geographic location when using GPS. Some of these are simply a matter of preference, while others depend on a specific task or need you are trying to accomplish.

We wanted to provide the simplest and least ambiguous format as possible for this purpose. To that end we have selected a format known as decimal degrees which consists of a pair of numbers that represent latitude and longitude. Each number begins with a hemisphere designator (N for the northern hemisphere of latitude and W for the western hemisphere of longitude) followed by either 2 or 3 digits before the decimal point and then 5 digits after the decimal point. For example, the degree decimal GPS coordinates for the San Diego Natural History Museum in Balboa Park is N32.73238, W117.14738.

Most GPS devices can be configured to accept and represent coordinates in decimal degrees (which also may be listed as dd.ddddd). If, after your GPS unit has been configured for decimal degrees, it does not accept the N or W, don't worry. You may simply drop the N and use a "-" (minus sign) in place of the W. Ensure your device is set to WGS84 if there are multiple map datum choices.

We have chosen to use 5 decimal places in order to get a resolution of approximately 1 meter. This is roughly the same accuracy as most handheld consumer GPS units on the market today. This level of resolution should easily get you to a position where you will be able to find the location of the trailhead for the start of a hike.

A full discussion of configuring and using your particular GPS device and the formats for representing geographic locations is beyond the scope of this book. There are many references, both printed and on the web, that will help you become familiar with this topic.

If you find that the decimal degree format isn't appropriate for your needs, there are many websites that have simple-to-use interfaces that allow you to enter our decimal degree format and convert it to a format better suited to your requirements.

Here are some examples of various representations expressing the geographic coordinates for the San Diego Natural History Museum:

N32.73238, W117.14738 (decimal degrees using N,W) (hdd.ddddd)
32.73238, -117.14738 (decimal degrees using +,-) (+/-dd.ddddd)
N32 43.943, W117 08.843 (degrees / decimal minutes) (dd mm.mmm)
N32 43 56.5680, W117 08 50.5680 (degrees / minutes / seconds) (dd mm ss.ssss)
11N 466191 3621628.8 (Standard UTM)

Agencies: Various agencies manage the hike areas, including federal, state, and local entities that include county and city governments, non-profit organizations, and private groups. Federal government agencies include the US Department of Agriculture Forest Service (Cleveland National Forest) and the US Department of the Interior (National Park Service, Bureau of Land Management, and the US Fish and Wildlife Service). State agencies include the California Department of Parks and Recreation (California State Parks) and the California Department of Fish and Wildlife. San Diego County manages several open space parks. Various cities such as San Diego, Poway, and Chula Vista also have parks that they manage. Other managing agencies include water districts and non-profit organizations.

Each agency has separate rules regarding trail use and hours of operation. Managing agencies are listed using abbreviated names. Check the appendix for the agency full name, website, and telephone number if more information is needed. Note: Gated trailheads can be closed due to weather conditions or restoration after a fire.

Notes and Optional Maps: Additional pertinent information needed for planning purposes is included in Notes, such as parking fees or required parking passes (e.g. National Forest Adventure Pass). Every hike has the name of one or more USGS 7.5 minute map(s) for the hike.

Habitat Designators: Each hike has one or more habitat symbols indicating the type of habitat(s) found on the hike. There are nine designators being used in this book. For detailed information, go to the top of this Introduction section to review information about the various habitats. These are the symbols for the nine habitats.

 Beach/Salt Marsh/Lagoon

 Coastal Sage Scrub

 Grassland

 Chaparral

 Oak Woodland

 Riparian

 Freshwater Marsh/ Montane Meadow/Vernal Pool

 Mixed Conifer Forest

 Desert

Atlas Square: The San Diego Natural History Museum has divided San Diego County into a grid system of squares 3 miles or 5 kilometers on a side based on the public land survey of townships, ranges, and sections, often following section boundaries represented on US Geological Survey topographic maps, the Cleveland National Forest map, and the Thomas Brothers road atlas. Most of the atlas squares represent one-quarter of a township or nine sections. Atlas squares are identified by letters from north to south and by numbers from west to east. An atlas square number appears in the "At a Glance" information section for each hike. The atlas square designator is keyed to the trailhead location of your hike. Use this designator to learn more about plants and animals that are in the trail area either before or after your hike. Go to www.sdnat.org/atlasprojects for a full list of resources and atlas projects (plants, birds, and reptiles) made available by the San Diego Natural History Museum.

Use of Scientific and Common Names with Featured Species: This book includes both common and some significantly important plants and animals that are found in specific hike areas or habitats. Over 500 plant and animal species are featured. If a particular species has some detailed information in a trip write-up, the common name will appear followed in parentheses with the scientific name, family, or phylum. The species will be listed in the index by both its scientific and common name with the page number for detailed information in **bold**. When a species is listed with no additional information, only the common name will be used. To find information about a species that is listed with no detail, refer to the index for the page number where it is featured.

All species featured in this book appear on lists found in the appendix and are sorted alphabetically by both scientific and common name. The scientific name is the best reference as it allows accurate identification of a species. A particular plant can have many common names that vary by region. This book uses the Checklist of the Vascular Plants of San Diego County, 5th Edition, by Jon P. Rebman and Michael G. Simpson (San Diego: San Diego Natural History Museum, 2014) for use of common names, including all punctuation and dashes that are used in this reference. As an example, *Toxicodendron diversilobum* is referenced as western poison-oak instead of poison oak. The lists also indicate in what habitats you may find a certain species. Note: Scientific names may differ over time as increased knowledge drives taxonomic and nomenclatural changes.

Finding More Information:

The best resource for finding more information about the county's natural resources and biodiversity is to visit the San Diego Natural History Museum. It has a wealth of information and resources available for the public, including the new permanent exhibition Coast to Cactus in Southern California. The exhibition makes use of specimens from the Museum's scientific collections alongside immersive environments with hands-on exhibits, live animals, and innovative media. It is the perfect place to visit in order to better understand what one will see and discover on hikes throughout the county.

Exhibition highlights include an oversized replica of a segment of mud from a local tidal flat. Young visitors can crawl inside where they will discover animals that survive in the mudflats in spite of tough intertidal conditions. There is also a re-creation of a residential patio overlooking an urban San Diego canyon that explores how humans share space with nature. It brings to light the impact of introduced species on native plants and animals. An immersive virtual storybook tells the tale of the dynamic chaparral ecosystem and how periodic fires are a natural part of life in this signature California habitat. There is also a multi-media exhibit with an Airstream trailer that explores the desert world at night. Exhibit elements are presented in both English and Spanish. The Museum website will give more information about the Coast to Cactus exhibition at www.sdnat.org/explore. This website includes information about habitats and photographs of many of the species that can be found in the various habitats.

Another interactive exhibition to visit while at the Museum is Fossil Mysteries. It explores big themes in science such as evolution, extinction, ecology, and Earth processes, including the geology of our region. One exhibit shows, through a time sequence covering millions of years, how the Baja California peninsula was ripped away from mainland Mexico as it moved and continues to move northwest on one of the Earth's moving plates—an event that is very important to the geologic history of San Diego. Other exhibits show how rocks and fossils reflect our geologic past. Rocks and their contained biological record document the evolution of this part of western North America. They tell about periods of high rainfall or drought and changing climate. Deciphering the geological and biological record is an ongoing process. Each year the Museum scientists add to our knowledge through new discoveries and new insights, showing that geology is not just about the past but it also gives us clues about our future. Exhibit elements are also presented in both English and Spanish.

While you are at the Museum, ask about special events, classes, and lectures, or visit www.sdnat.org to find the information you need. Pick up a Canyoneer brochure when you visit the Museum for a listing of FREE guided public hikes offered throughout the county, or get the hike schedule online at www.sdnat.org/canyoneers. If you can't attend a Canyoneer public hike, then take this book with you—it is your "Virtual Canyoneer."

Additional information about species or hike areas can be found online, including articles written by the Canyoneers that have appeared in the San Diego Reader: www.sandiegoreader.com/staff/canyoneers/. Search the websites for the various agencies listed in the appendix, give them a call, or send them an email if you have specific questions.

Recommended Equipment:

Much of maximizing your outdoor experience can be summarized in one word and done before leaving home—preparation. This guide describes more than 250 hikes that include several options sometimes offered in a single write-up. The hikes described range from easy paths, that are smooth and wide with minimal elevation change, to strenuous excursions, with higher elevation changes and/or narrow, rocky, or slippery surfaces. The preparation and equipment should be optimized for each experience with the following samples of just a few pre-hike questions to ask yourself; what are possible hazards and weather; what are the area characteristics and trail conditions; what and how is assistance available; what are the fees, regulations and operating hours; and what are items of interest? Many individuals pay little attention to these questions and, typically, it is not a significant problem. However, in some cases this lack of research can have serious consequences.

Virtually all books on wilderness travel devote a chapter to safety and include a Ten Essentials list. An online search will result in hundreds of returns from which you can derive your own list appropriate for different levels of hike distance, elevation change, possible time for medical response, and other factors. The majority of the walks in this book describe dayhikes, but the more difficult walks may necessitate preparations to survive overnight if injured, lost, or if there is a rapid change in weather or other unplanned occurrences during the trip.

Plan your water needs based on the distance, atmospheric aridity (are you hiking near the coast or in the desert), expected exertion level (pace, elevation change, terrain), and personal comfort. Since hydration needs or desires vary significantly between people (even those of the same age, weight, and physical conditioning), personal experience is the most useful guideline. If you have not been hiking on a regular basis, try some easy hikes in varied environments prior to tackling outings with difficult ratings in order to learn what your body requires in terms of hydration. Many of the hikes described in this book do not have water available, so it is critical to carry what you need to be safe. Consider all free-flowing water sources as contaminated. A basic rule is to drink water before starting the hike and to drink from 6-12 fluid ounces every 20 minutes during the hike.

Wear appropriate footwear and clothing geared to the location and expected weather conditions, even on relatively short trips. This can make a considerable difference on both comfort and safety levels. Flip-flops are generally ill advised for nearly all the trips described in this book. Many trails have various objects capable of abrading or puncturing skin and, while a snake bite is highly unlikely, the added protection of a decent trail shoe can also provide traction on steep trails.

Carry a snack on the hike. Longer hikes necessitate some form of body fuel that will equal about 200 calories an hour on the trail. Monitor water and fuel intake every 20 minutes on a long hike. A daypack at minimum should include sunscreen for body and lips (lip balm with sunscreen protection), a hat, and sunglasses to minimize sun exposure. As a minimum, carry water, a snack, a light jacket, a communication device, and first aid supplies for every trip.

Safety Issues:

These are the factors that lead to hazards and injuries, in order of importance:

1. Lack of preparation prior to leaving home.

2. Inattention while hiking and not being fully conscious of your surroundings, which could lead to you becoming lost. It is important to glance back for landmarks for your return hike as things will look different going the opposite direction!

3. Hubris/impulse control —thinking the unexpected won't happen and that it is okay just to do it. Know your personal comfort zone and restraints.

4. Rocks—by far the most common hazardous object in the environment: falling on a rock; falling off a rock; a rock falls on you; rock moves when stepped on.

The remaining dangers and hazards most people obsess on have a relatively miniscule probability of occurrence, such as the very common terror associated with snakes. Note that three of the four major hazards listed above are mental. The fourth is mostly a hazard because of the other three. As for the most touted advice on hazards, a few words:

Snakes: In San Diego the most common concern for many people is a rattlesnake bite. The consequences can be serious. But, like shark attacks, such events are very uncommon and, unlike sharks, rattlesnakes typically only strike when threatened. If you are bitten, remove yourself from the area where the snake is located. Sit down and assess the situation. If you have cell phone connectivity, call 911 and seek advice. If you are unable to contact 911, move at a moderate pace to an area where you can make cell connectivity, or have another person do that. What is important is to get yourself with focused speed and efficiency to a medical facility that has anti-venom serum.

Mountain Lions: An encounter with a mountain lion is an extremely rare possibility. Basic rules include: make yourself as large as possible and never bend or crouch; don't run; maintain eye contact and aggressively wave your arms; slowly, without turning around, create distance between you and the lion, and give the lion space and time to move away from you. If attacked, protect your neck and throat and fight back with whatever you have—trekking poles, rocks, tree branches, jacket, or backpack. Safety is always in numbers—
DON'T HIKE ALONE.

Other Attackers: The two most dangerous creatures that can be encountered in the county from a probability perspective are bees and ticks. People who are allergic to bee venom should carry an epinephrine pen to avoid possible anaphylactic shock. Tick bites are not an immediate threat but some transmit pathogens that can have serious long term medical consequences. Check for ticks after a hike.

Toxic Plants: Western poison-oak is very common in moist inland areas such as canyon bottoms, watersheds, and stream areas. For those who have a physical reaction, the result can be anything from a minor itching rash to significant blistering requiring hospitalization. Identification of the plant is problematic since it may look like a tree, a shrub, or a vine. It has leaves that can vary considerably in size and be of different colors, and it can extend itself out through the foliage of other plants. The plant's offending toxin is a relatively non-water soluble oil that is readily transmitted by contact with any part of the plant, except for the tiny flower. It can be retransmitted by contact with other parts of the body, clothing, furniture, or even by petting a dog who has rubbed against the plant. The warning adage of "leaves of three, let it be" provides some assistance, but this deciduous plant is still capable of transmitting its irritating substance even when leafless. For more information about recognizing, avoiding, and treating the results of an allergic reaction, refer to the Internet, which will provide copious instructions—often accompanied by photos of contact woes.

Flash Floods: Take care hiking in desert wash areas when it is raining or has recently rained in the mountains. Some of the most dangerous flash floods occur in our desert areas. Literally within minutes a seemingly dry desert wash can become a raging torrent. Pay attention to the weather and where it is raining or has recently rained. Flash floods happen when rain collects on distant mountains and ridgetops. It doesn't matter if the desert is dry and the sun is out. As runoff flows down to the desert, it picks up speed and debris. The desert soil is dry and becomes nearly impermeable to fast moving water. It only takes 6 inches of running water to knock a person down and carry him away. It is best to avoid narrow canyons and desert washes when rain is possible, even in distant mountains. If you are caught hiking in a desert wash or low area when it starts to flood, get to higher ground as quickly as you can. You may have only a few seconds of warning as you will hear it before you will see it coming. Think freight train! Keep off the tracks, or in this case, keep out of the washes when there is the potential of flash floods.

Wildfires: Be aware of current fire conditions when planning a hike. A good resource is the California Department of Forestry and Fire Protection or CAL Fire at www.fire.ca.gov. Obey any restrictions if camping overnight. San Diego County has burned in three of the top ten largest fires in California since 1932 with the 2003 Cedar Fire being number one, having burned more than 270,000 acres.

Other Considerations: Make a realistic assessment of your physical prowess and experience in similar environments. If you are not ready, you can prepare yourself by training through increased exercise. The best preparation is engaging in hikes that are similar to the ones you wish to do. Start at less difficult levels and gradually increase the effort until they resemble the hike(s) desired. It is best to maintain a steady pace that does not require you to stop to catch your breath. On steep sections, try to maintain the cadence with a shorter stride, or if very steep, alternate with a rest stop to conserve energy.

Equally, or more important, is thoughtful risk assessment. This involves determining the probability of encountering various challenges and how significant each would be should they occur. After this assessment is made, consider possible ways to avoid any detrimental challenges, and if such challenges do occur, how they should be addressed.

Make a realistic plan and stick to it. Always tell someone of your travel plans. Check the weather forecast for your destination. Plan clothing, equipment, and supplies accordingly. Dress in layers and always carry a jacket. Weather conditions can change unexpectedly. Carry identification and medical cards in case of an emergency and also a smartphone; you might need to make an emergency call. If the hike involves steep grades or loose rocks, consider taking trekking/hiking poles for support.

Carry both a flashlight in case you are caught out after dark and a first aid kit to take care of scratches, puncture wounds, or blisters. Other things you might want to consider are toilet paper, a trash bag, and a camera.

Trail Etiquette:

Leave only footprints; take only memories and photographs. Otherwise leave an area unaltered or improved by removing undesirable signs of human presence, such as trash. Follow good trail ethics:

- Stay on the trail—walking anywhere else, cutting switchbacks, and taking other shortcuts damages the environment, causing erosion and visual scarring.

- If hiking with a group and there are no trails or if the trail temporarily disappears, carefully spread out to disperse the impact of single file footsteps and to avoid creating a new trail.

- Comply with all information signs and respect barriers. Typical trail etiquette is bicycles yield to hikers and horses. Hikers yield to horses. Downhill hikers yield to uphill hikers.

- Try not to create trail markers with a cairn or otherwise flag your route. If there are times when you determine this is essential for your safety, do so sparingly and always remove these directional signs as you leave. Better yet, use a GPS device (dedicated GPS or a smartphone GPS application) or a map and compass.

- Avoid sensitive areas such as meadows, lakeshores, wetlands, streams, soils with a biological crust (cryptobiotic soils), and seasonal nesting or breeding areas. Trails typically avoid these areas, and you should also.

- Never alter, change, remove, or disturb any archeological or paleontological site and artifacts.

- Restrict electronically created sound so that it is detected only by the user.

- Carry a trash bag and pick up litter left by others.

- Pack out what you pack in.

- Before and after a hike, wash your gear and support vehicle to reduce the spread of invasive species.

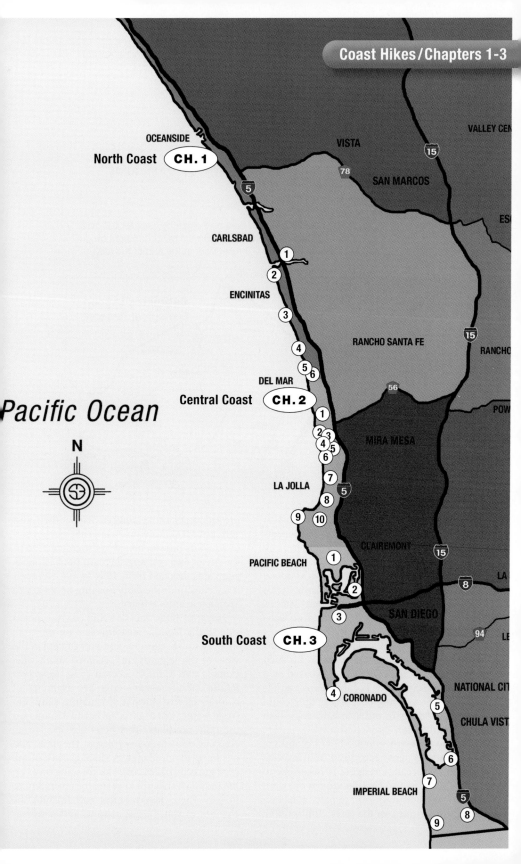

Pacific Ocean

N

North Coast CH. 1

Central Coast CH. 2

South Coast CH. 3

OCEANSIDE

VISTA

VALLEY CEN

SAN MARCOS

78

15

CARLSBAD

ENCINITAS

RANCHO SANTA FE

15

RANCHO

ESC

DEL MAR

56

POW

MIRA MESA

LA JOLLA

5

CLAIREMONT

15

PACIFIC BEACH

SAN DIEGO

8

LA

94

LE

CORONADO

NATIONAL CIT

CHULA VIST

IMPERIAL BEACH

5

Distance:	3 miles, out-and-back
Difficulty:	🚶🚶
Elevation gain/loss:	Minimal
Hiking time:	2 hours
Agency:	CDFW
Trail use:	Dogs
Notes:	Good birding area; visitor center open 9 a.m.- 3 p.m.
Trailhead GPS:	N33.09375, W117.30135
Optional map:	USGS 7.5-min *Encinitas*
Atlas square:	J6
Directions:	(Carlsbad) From I-5 go east on Poinsettia Lane for 0.3 mile. Turn right on Batiquitos Drive. Go 0.5 mile. Turn right on Gabbiano Lane. Go 0.3 mile. Park at the end of the road.

Habitat(s):

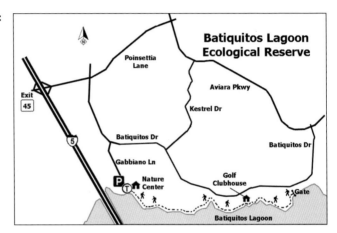

Batiquitos Lagoon is a 600-acre ecological reserve managed by the California Department of Fish and Wildlife and supported by the Batiquitos Lagoon Foundation. It has a drainage basin of 55,000 acres with inflow from San Marcos and Encinitas creeks with I-15 the eastern border of the San Marcos Creek watershed. It was designated an ecological reserve in 1983 to protect coastal wetland habitat and species. Although Batiquitos appears as a Spanish name, there is no such word in that language. Perhaps it is based on a Native American word. Local Indians considered it a little watering hole where they could follow tidal surges in order to gather shellfish and plants that they later consumed.

Looking west, you can see how I-5 and the railroad tracks have narrowed the lagoon's outlet to the ocean. Dredging is necessary to clear sand and silt so that Batiquitos does not become stagnant and can remain a lagoon flushed by the tides. In the early 20th century,

the lagoon became plugged from urban and agricultural activity upstream that carried soil down to its mouth, blocking the connection to the ocean and creating stagnant pools. The lagoon was dredged from 1994 to 1997 to open it once again to the daily flushing necessary to keep it a healthy estuary.

The trail hugs the shoreline on the north side of the lagoon. Heading east on the trail, freeway noise subsides, and you can enjoy the view of the lagoon's undeveloped south side. Cattails and California cord grass (*Spartina foliosa*) at the water's edge are examples of halophytes that survive fluctuating salty and fresh water. Cord grass grows in clumps on the tidal mudflats. This perennial has strong creeping rootstocks, is thick at the base, and has long, tough blades. A thick growth of tall cord grass provides cover for foraging birds on the mudflats that are in search of invertebrates to eat. These invertebrates can tolerate the changes in water level, salinity, and tempera-

California desert thorn

with imported species of eucalyptus and hot-tentot-fig, commonly referred to as iceplant. Volunteers regularly remove invasive species like castor bean, giant cane or Arundo, selloa pampas grass, tree tobacco, sweet fennel, and hemlock.

About halfway along the trail, a small freshwater creek, possibly created by runoff, is home to arroyo willow, mule-fat, and non-native palms. In the sandstone and clay banks, from time to time, layers of shell fragments are visible. These are middens, the trash heaps left by the native people who inhabited the area around the lagoon centuries ago. The middens show the extent of their harvesting activity. Archaeologists determined that Native Americans have harvested shellfish here for 9000 years!

Batiquitos hosts over 180 species of birds. Redwing blackbirds sing from the cattails, and egrets and great blue herons dot the shore. In winter, migratory shorebirds can be spotted on the mudflats along with ducks, coots, pelicans, gulls, and terns. Ospreys, or fish hawks, cruise over the water, and fall and winter songbirds like yellow-rumped warblers flit through the trees.

At a point where a steep slope heads up to a small parking lot, about 1.5 miles out, is a good place to turn and retrace your steps, although the trail continues almost to El Camino Real. More detailed information about plants, wildlife, history, and geology of the area can be found at www.batiquitosfoundation.org. Docents lead nature walks when the visitor center is open. A native plant garden is at the visitor center along with brochures for self-guided walks.

ture. They include various species of worms, clams, snails, and shrimp. Bulrushes, spiny rush, and sedges are found between the trail and the water. Pickleweed and salt grass are abundant in salty soil. In spring, alkali-heath, salty susan, seaside heliotrope, and salt marsh fleabane provide some color.

On the slope to your left, look for Mojave yucca and prickly-pear. Succulent chalk dudleya (**Dudleya pulverulenta**) grows sideways on the sandstone with its wide rosette covered in a chalky wax, which helps the plant avoid desiccation by reflecting the sunlight. Sharp-spined California desert thorn (**Lycium californicum**) spills over a rock just past the first turn in the trail. It is an entangled shrub with rigid pointed stems, fleshy leaves, and small white to purplish bell-shaped flowers that can be found on ocean bluffs and on borders of estuaries. California desert thorn is on a watch list by the California Native Plant Society because of its limited distribution along the coast and Channel Islands.

Familiar coastal sage scrub plants like coastal sagebrush, lemonadeberry, coastal deerweed, coastal goldenbush, and coyote brush mingle

Chalk dudleya

Distance:	5 miles, one-way or 10 miles, out-and-back
Difficulty:	🚶🚶 or 🚶🚶🚶, depending on length
Elevation gain/loss:	Minimal
Hiking time:	3 or 5 hours
Agency:	CSP-SDCD
Notes:	Check tide schedule; tidepools; good for birding; also see Trip 1-3 for a shorter hike
Trailhead GPS:	N33.08405, W117.31191
Optional map:	USGS 7.5-min *Encinitas*
Atlas square:	J6
Directions:	(Carlsbad) From I-5 go west on Poinsettia Lane for 0.4 mile. Turn left on Carlsbad Boulevard. Go 1.3 miles. Park along the side of the highway. If leaving a second car at the end of the 5-mile stretch, park near San Elijo State Beach.

Habitat(s):

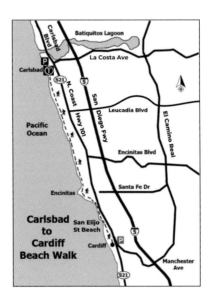

San Diego County's long coastline offers an abundance of beach hiking opportunities. This hike combines a relaxing beach walk with tidepools and can be done either as a 10-mile round trip or as a 5-mile one-way by having a car at each end of the route. The route starts in Carlsbad near the mouth of the Batiquitos Lagoon and ends at the San Elijo State Beach in Cardiff. Check the tide schedule, and time the hike for low tide to best view the tidepools.

Walking down the coast on the beach, note the difficult battle that local homeowners have with cliff erosion. The non-native hottentot-fig, often referred to as iceplant (*Carpobrotus edulis*), appears to provide a good, fast growing ground cover holding the cliff in place. However its roots are relatively shallow. In heavy rains, the succulent plants absorb water, increasing the weight of the mat, sometimes exceeding the weight the roots can hold, and thus the mat slides down the hill, making erosion worse. This plant also presents a unique fire hazard. The new plant growth showing on top looks green, but there may be a foot-and-a-half of flammable dead material underneath. This under-layer can burn quickly beneath the live layer on top, creating a chimney effect. Unfortunately, the more stable, native dune forming plants take much longer to establish themselves, so the battle against the forces of erosion and invasion continues.

Look for piles of kelp that wash ashore. Kelp is a brown alga that grows rooted to rocks in the offshore waters where it forms vast forests.

Sea anemone

Giant kelp (*Macrocystis pyrifera*) has the fastest growth rate of any plant—up to 2 feet each day under ideal conditions with some individuals reaching heights of almost 200 feet. The masses you see on the beach were torn from the rocks by storms and drifted onto the beach at high tide. The piles of kelp attract kelp flies (*Coelopa* spp.), which lay their eggs exclusively on piles of decomposing kelp. While they may be annoying, kelp flies fortunately do not bite people. The flies provide an important source of protein for shore and migratory birds. Creatures such as bean clams and moon snails that frequent the kelp beds are often washed ashore with the kelp and can often be seen by brave souls who dissect the piles of kelp. Common eel-grass (*Zostera marina*) is also frequently washed ashore and can be identified by its dark green, ribbon-like leaves. Interestingly, eel-grass is not seaweed, but a flowering plant (an angiosperm), meaning it produces pollen and seeds just like terrestrial grasses. The eel-grass acts as a nursery for young fish and invertebrates.

Also look for beach-rounded cobbles originating from the Lindavista Formation, similar to layers found in Tecolote Park. You will pass Moonlight Beach, which won the Best Restored Beach Award in 2011 from the American Shore and Beach Preservation Association. This route is a prime opportunity for birdwatching. In addition to gulls and pelicans, keep an eye out for grebes, long billed curlews, marbled godwits, royal terns, and many others.

If hiking at low tide, view tidepools and the associated marine creatures as you near Cardiff. The sea anemones (*Anthopleura* spp.) are quite delicate, so avoid stepping on them. They can be surprisingly hard to recognize at low tide. Anemones tend to collect bits of broken shells on their outer surface. When they curl up as the water level draws down, the shells protect the anemones from the sun's drying rays. At first glance, you may think you are looking at an area strewn with broken shells. Closer inspection will reveal dozens of curled up anemones. Anemones found in San Diego County are either solitary or aggregating, with the aggregating anemones being much more cryptic—camouflaged by the mass of broken shells.

Other sea creatures commonly found clinging to the rocks include gooseneck barnacles, mussels, small crabs, and sand tubeworms. These creatures are filter feeders, straining food from water by running it through specialized filtering structures. Sand tubeworms *(phylum Annelida)* build their tubes out of sand grains that they cement together with calcium secretions. The calcium is absorbed from the ocean by the worms. The tubes are very delicate despite their rock-like look and can easily be crushed with fingers. Treat these creatures gently to avoid hurting them.

Chitons and limpets *(phylum Mollusca)* tend to look like they are part of the rock they cling to with their muscular foot. If they are stuck tight to the rock that means they are alive. Chitons and limpets feed off of algae, using their tongue-like radula to scrape algae off rocks, which can also create burrows in the rock over time. Chitons have eight separate shell segments and look like a modern-day trilobite, while limpets have a single circular shells. Both will vary in color and size. Take a close look at the rocks where the various creatures live and notice that there are fossilized invertebrates under the live creatures. You are witnessing the ongoing process of reef transformation.

Intertidal life

Distance:	2.8 miles, out-and-back
Difficulty:	🏃🏃
Elevation gain/loss:	Up to 100 feet
Hiking time:	2 hours
Agency:	City of Encinitas
Notes:	Best at low tide; also see Trip 1-2 for a longer hike
Trailhead GPS:	N33.03450, W117.29231
Optional map:	USGS 7.5-min *Encinitas*
Atlas square:	K6
Directions:	(Encinitas) From I-5 go west on Encinitas Boulevard for 0.5 mile. Turn left on South Coast Highway 101. Go 1 mile to the turn off for Swami's parking lot on right, just south of Self-Realization Fellowship. If the lot is full, there may be additional parking available along the highway or on K Street.

Habitat(s):

The hike begins at the top of a cliff adjacent to a small park with a few artistic statues. A long stairway leads down to the beach. Here the ocean is the highpoint as it blends into the far horizon, creating a beautiful image. The area is popular among surfers, as well as shorebirds. Gulls (**family Laridae, subfamily Larinae**) and terns (**family Laridae, subfamily Sterninae**) seem accustomed to visitors and allow walkers to pass by at close range. The gulls tend to rummage through the kelp that has washed ashore. These scavengers attempt to find morsels of food clinging to the kelp. The wild-haired terns, on the other hand, hover and dive into the water for their food. Their time on the beach is meant for resting. Sanderlings (*Calidris alba*) are seen scurrying back and forth as each wave approaches and retreats, feasting on a host of creatures in the sand. Sanderlings are long-distant migrants

that breed in the Arctic and winter on sandy beaches as far as South America. These sandpipers pipe noisy "peeps" as they obsessively chase waves. They are light gray above and white below with black legs and black bills.

Keep on the lookout for squadrons of California brown pelicans (*Pelecanus occidentalis californicus*) gliding ever so close to the waterline. Their flying skills are amazing to watch and occasionally one will leave formation to plunge into the water from up to 60 feet for prey, mostly fish, and an occasional invertebrate. Once prey is caught, a pelican ejects the water by constricting its gular or distensible pouch against its body before tilting its head back to swallow. The gular pouch is yellowish, changing to red during courtship on the Pacific Coast. Local pelicans mostly nest on the ground or on low shrubs on islands off the coast. From March to May pelican numbers along San Diego's coast are gen-

California brown pelicans

erally smaller, as adult birds travel back to their nesting colonies, some in the Gulf of California. No pelicans nest in San Diego County, though non-breeders remain at popular roosting spots. Look for pelicans at jetties and piers and along fishing areas.

Walk south along the shoreline. The sandstone cliffs here are partially covered with vegetation. Non-natives, including several invasive species, dominate the native plants. There are the occasional natives—salt grass, native rushes, and salt heliotrope—amongst the plentiful non-native saltcedar, selloa pampas grass, hottentot-fig, and giant cane or *Arundo*, which can form dense stands on sand dunes. Watch for some sandstone blocks at the base of the cliffs near a tree tobacco plant (*Nicotiana glauca*). The exotic tree tobacco has long yellow tubular flowers that provide nectar for hummingbirds. Originally from Bolivia and Argentina, tree tobacco has become naturalized throughout the southwest within the last 100 years. Its establishment is somewhat dependent on ecological disturbance. The leaves are considered very toxic. Once you locate the blocks of sandstone, notice numerous fossilized clams embedded in the rock. Be on the lookout for ground squirrels or stray lizards that are occasionally found along these cliffs.

On the return to the shoreline, look for some dimples in the sand each time the water recedes. These are made by sand crabs (*Emerita analoga*), which tickle if you dig your toes into the sand. Upon close inspection, notice the feathery antennae that they use for filter feeding. Sand crabs and other beach-dwelling invertebrates are adversely affected by beach nourishment—the process of adding sand to beaches to combat erosion and increase beach width. A reduction in numbers of these small creatures often forces shorebirds to relocate, as they rely on these invertebrates as a food source.

Staircases lead down from the parking area and campground to San Elijo State Beach, and further down shore, the cliffs eventually lose elevation. Here, there is an interesting lifeguard tower on scaffolding, which is reminiscent of an erector set. This offsets the lower cliff line and allows the lifeguards greater visibility. Just beyond this tower, there is an inlet for the San Elijo Lagoon. This is the 1.4-mile turnaround point. If you choose to go further, you can (at low tide) wade across the river mouth or walk over the bridge to continue. If wading across, be cautious of the rounded cobblestones midstream. Beyond, there are a few restaurants along the beach and then a narrower stretch of sand, all part of Cardiff-by-the-Sea. It is about 1 mile from the inlet to the cliffs at the south end of this beach.

There is a lot to observe as you amble back along the coast. Be sure to sweep your focus from shore to sea. The reward may be a glimpse of a seal or porpoise visiting the area. If looking for solitude, the north end of the beach (nearest Swami's) tends to be less crowded. If invigorated with energy, venture a short distance to the north to explore the flat rocks covered with shallow tidepool depressions, black mussels, and gooseneck barnacles. After climbing the stairs back up to the park, walk north to the Self-Realization Fellowship (SRF) Meditation Gardens, which are free and open to the public. Enjoy the sweeping ocean views. Swami's Beach is named for Paramahansa Yogananda, the founder of SRF.

Tree tobacco

Distance:	1.5 miles, loop
Difficulty:	🚶
Elevation gain/loss:	Minimal
Hiking time:	1 hour
Agency:	San Diego County
Trail use:	Dogs
Notes:	Good birding area. Slot canyon and views. Visitor center open daily 9 a.m. to 5 p.m.
Trailhead GPS:	N33.00367, W117.27247
Optional map:	USGS 7.5-min *Encinitas*
Atlas square:	L7
Directions:	(Cardiff-by-the-Sea) From I-5 go west on Lomas Santa Fe Drive for 0.9 mile. Turn right onto North Rios Avenue. Go 0.8 mile. Park at the end of the road.

Habitat(s):

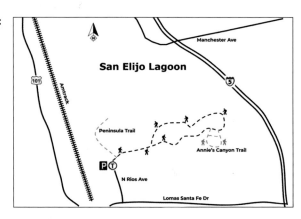

The San Elijo Ecological Reserve hosts more than 250 species of shore and water birds because they are attracted to the multiple plant communities found here that include coastal sage scrub, salt marsh, and riparian. A visit here is a good way to learn about the differences found in each of these communities and to see how one community transitions into another.

From the trailhead overlooking the large flat expanse of the lagoon, head down the slope to the right into a shady area of tall willows and western cottonwoods. Cottonwoods and willows are fast-growing trees that have a relatively short life span of about 100 years compared to slower growing tree species like oaks. Ecological strategies of plants can range from fast-growing species that uptake resources readily—water, light, and nutrients, for example—yet are poorly defended against browsing animals, disease, or have low tissue density making them susceptible to limb loss. Slow-growing species are often better defended, are able to persist in lower resource environments, and generally have longer life spans.

Other species encountered here are typical coastal sage scrub plants including lemonade-berry, California buckwheat, toyon, coastal sagebrush, black sage, laurel sumac, and arroyo willow. Behind a bench on the right, a large brown lump on the hillside is the exposed root of wild-cucumber. Poisonous western jimson weed, with its large white to pale violet trumpet-shaped flowers, is found on the trail.

In recent years, Lagoon Conservancy volunteers have removed non-native castor bean, and consequently blue elderberry (*Sambucus nigra*) is now more abundant. Native Americans used the blossom and fresh or dried leaves of the elderberry to make a tea that was given to babies with fever. Branches and twigs were used to make a variety of things such as musical instruments, tobacco pipes, whistles, and fire drills. The wood was used to make bows. Berry juice was used as a dye for basket making. Blue elderberry fruit is also a favorite food source for many bird species. The fruits ripen in the fall, and turn a deep bluish-purple to black color, which is often

Snowy egrets

masked by whitish powder. The fruit is used to make jams, jellies, syrup, and wine. This plant is a widespread species and can be found from San Diego's coast up into the mountains and all across the western United States.

After about 0.25 mile, the trail turns left, and sage scrub gives way to an open flat area closer to small channels. Notice how the plant communities change dramatically with minimal changes in elevation. Toward the water, salt marsh plants like spiny rush, pickleweed, salt grass, and alkali-heath dominate. Endangered bird species like Belding's savannah sparrow (*Passerculus sandwichensis beldingi*) and the light-footed Ridgway's rail (*Rallus obsoletus levipes*)—known as the light-footed clapper rail for many years—inhabit the marsh. With the elimination of 75% of southern California salt marsh areas, the breeding area for Belding's savannah sparrow is limited. This bird returns each year to the area where it was hatched. It is distinguished from other sparrows by a yellow patch in front of each eye. The light-footed Ridgway's rail has had more than 90% of its needed coastal wetland areas eliminated because of habitat degradation. There is concern about the rail's low genetic diversity and interchange with isolated populations.

Watch for mullet jumping out of the water. During the fall and winter migration, shorebirds and ducks explore the mud or shallow water for tiny crustaceans. Terns dart overhead, white-tailed kites hover over the water, ospreys make their rounds, and great blue herons stalk their prey.

Great blue herons are large blue-gray birds, yet only weigh about 4.5 to 5.5 pounds, thanks in part to their hollow bones. As stalkers, great blue herons often stand motionless in the water, waiting for their next meal to swim by before quickly stabbing it with their sharp beak. These birds are able to hunt both day and night with night vision enabled by the high percentage of rod-type photoreceptors in their eyes. The snowy egret (*Egretta thula*) is another prey-stalking bird you may see. Slender birds, their brilliant white plumage makes them stand out. The especially long and wispy plumage on their backs, necks, and heads is produced during the breeding season. These feathers were once prized in the fashion industry, particularly for hat plumes, causing their population to decline. However, the snowy egret populations started recovering in the 1930s with the passing of laws protecting the birds. Other birds with brilliant white plumage that you may see include the great egret and the juvenile little blue heron.

The trail loops back inland to high, drier ground where you will see typical coastal sage scrub plants. If you want a longer hike, add the loop for Annie's Canyon to climb a narrow slot and enjoy the view at the top. Turn right at the main trail to return to your car, or for a longer hike, go left toward I-5. Near the freeway in dense vegetation you might hear the California gnatcatcher, listed as threatened by the US Fish and Wildlife Service, or the least Bell's vireo, listed as endangered. As you return, enjoy the view of the steep, north-facing slope of the lagoon, covered in spots with dense chaparral as well as tenacious non-native orange nasturtium.

Finally, look for the San Elijo Nature Center across the lagoon on Manchester Avenue. Another trail beyond a metal gate leads down past saltbush plants to an observation area level with the lagoon, a favorite spot for birders. For information on additional trails and the San Elijo Lagoon Conservancy, visit their website: www.sanelijo.org.

Blue elderberry

Distance:	6 miles, out-and-back
Difficulty:	𝕏 𝕏
Elevation gain/loss:	Minimal
Hiking time:	3 hours
Agency:	SDRP
Trail use:	Bicycles, dogs, horses on some trails
Trailhead GPS:	N32.96775, W117.26012
Optional map:	USGS 7.5 min *Del Mar*
Atlas square:	M7
Directions:	(Del Mar) From I-5 go west on Via de la Valle for 0.3 mile. Turn left onto Jimmy Durante Boulevard. Go 0.9 mile. Just after crossing the bridge over the San Dieguito River, turn left onto San Dieguito Drive. Go 0.3 mile and park in the Lagoon Viewpoint at Old Grand Avenue Bridge lot on the left. For a shorter hike, park at the San Andres Drive trailhead. From I-5 go east on Via de la Valle. Turn right on San Andres Drive and park. Access trail at kiosk.

Habitat(s):

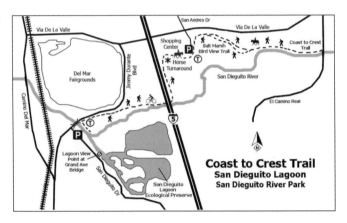

The San Dieguito Lagoon is the current start of the Coast to Crest Trail that follows the San Dieguito River watershed for 71 miles to its source on Volcan Mountain. There are 45 miles of the trail completed with 12 maps covering 14 trails listed at www.sdrp.org. There is a QR scan code that can be read using a mobile app to download information at 20 locations along the first 2 miles of the Coast to Crest Trail. The official San Dieguito Lagoon Staging Area is off San Andres Drive, which is an alternate starting point for a shorter hike. This hike, however, begins further west.

From the parking area, go to Jimmy Durante Boulevard and turn right, walking east until directly on the bridge, where 500 feet southeast is the Grand Avenue Bridge Overlook. In the 1920s there was a Navy emergency airfield here named San Dieguito Field, later noted in the Del Mar Racetrack song "Where the Turf Meets the Surf...take a plane." During WWII there were two blimps at the airfield in support of the anti-submarine patrols. The airfield was assigned to the Navy until returned to civilian control in 1947 when it was named Del Mar Airport. PSA flights were $16 from Burbank to Del Mar and back. The airport was closed in 1959 for the I-5 right-of-way, with a remnant of a blimp mooring dock circle on the west side until 2006.

Once past the bridge, make another right turn to the large San Dieguito River Park sign. From this point one can access the boardwalk trail along a portion of the river or the start of the Coast to Crest Trail (at the time of this writing a new trail section is planned along Jimmy Durante with views of the nearby restored wetlands). In 2016 the Boardwalk Trail will no longer provide direct access to the Coast to Crest Trail. It is 1.10 miles ahead to the San Dieguito Lagoon Staging Area off San Andres Drive. Walk along the Boardwalk where you can see current and remnant urn-

Willet, winter plumage

shaped nests attached on a vertical section under the Jimmy Durante Boulevard bridge. They are built of mud pellets and fibers and are used by birds that fly with open mouths, scooping up both insects and water. Look for birds with broad-based pointed wings, small heads, and deeply notched to square tails, which identify them as swallows. The nests belong to cliff swallows (*Petrochelidon pyrrhonota*), which have square-tipped tails, brick-red faces, dark backs, whitish foreheads and bellies, and pumpkin-colored rumps. The Boardwalk Trail continues for a few hundred yards where a turnaround and viewing platform will be established.

Continue east along a new section of the Coast to Crest Trail, along the edge of the Del Mar Fairgrounds towards the I-5 freeway. Once near the I-5 underpass, look for a mix of California horn snail shells, shore crabs with symmetric claws, and fiddler crabs (*Uca pugilator*) named for the males that have one large claw. The fiddler crab appears to be playing a fiddle when it waves its claw to attract females or when it picks up a small chunk of sediment and moves it to its mouth. The different appearance of males and females of this species is a clue into sexual dimorphism and mate selection. The large claw of a male signals a robust and healthy individual, which females prefer over smaller-clawed individuals. Fiddler crabs are detritivores—animals that feed on dead organic material. Their decomposed materials are important additions to the nutrient cycle. Other detritivores include dung flies, worms, sea stars, and sea cucumbers.

Continue on the Coast to Crest Trail under I-5, then past San Andres Drive where there is a slight incline onto the Salt Marsh Bird View

Trail (pedestrians only). Bikers and equestrians can continue on the adjacent Coast to Crest Trail. Both trails pass near the San Dieguito Lagoon open air classroom (Birdwing) with views of the wetlands. Birds that you might see here include the western sandpiper (*Calidris mauri*) and the willet (*Triga semipalmata*).

The western sandpiper is one of the most abundant shorebirds in North America. It is a migrant that breeds on the tundra in western Alaska and winters on the shores of much of North America, preferring mudflats, beaches, and ponds where it can forage for small worms, insects, crustaceans, and mollusks. Look for a small bird, plain gray on top and mostly white on the bottom with dark legs and a dark slightly curved bill. Before it departs in the spring, it grows many chestnut-red feathers on the upperparts.

The willet is also part of the sandpiper family. It is much larger than the western sandpiper with gray legs and a long, dark straight bill. The willet is dark gray above and lighter beneath with a stocky build. In flight it shows a bold black and white stripe on its wings. The tail is white with a dark band at the end. Also a migrant, it winters in the same locations as the western sandpiper and forages for similar but larger food. It is seen alone or in flocks, and when startled it makes a piercing call.

Follow the trail to El Camino Real, viewing the river whenever it is not hidden by the taller riparian plants. There is a riding school and horses in paddocks on the north side. At El Camino Real, turn around and head back to your vehicle. If parked at the end of San Andres Drive, modify the walk appropriately.

Shore crab and California horn snail

Distance:	1.6 miles, loop
Difficulty:	𝍌𝍌
Elevation gain/loss:	Up to 300 feet
Hiking time:	1 hour
Agency:	City of San Diego; SDRP
Trail use:	Dogs
Notes:	Brochures and trail maps available at the kiosk
Trailhead GPS:	N32.96288, W117.25528
Optional map:	USGS 7.5 min *Del Mar*
Atlas square:	M7
Directions:	(Del Mar) From I-5 go west on Via de la Valle for 0.3 mile. Turn left onto Jimmy Durante Boulevard. Go 0.9 mile. Just after crossing the bridge over the San Dieguito River, turn left onto San Dieguito Drive. Go 0.6 mile. This becomes Race Track View Drive. Continue through the stop sign and park on the road shoulder at the Crest Canyon kiosk.

Habitat(s):

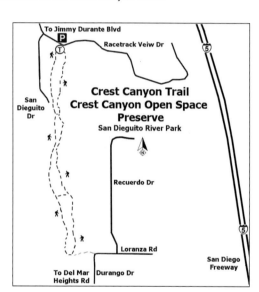

Crest Canyon Open Space Park was originally intended to be part of the Torrey Pines State Preserve Extension but was eliminated because of the cost of acquisition. Many young Torrey pines have taken hold in the shelter of this bowl-shaped canyon and have grown as large as those found in the Torrey Pines Extension. It is now managed by the City of San Diego and is part of the San Dieguito River Park. This open space has both a southern and northern entrance. The recommended route is the trailhead beginning at the lower or northern end of Crest Canyon.

Follow the wide gently sloping path up from the San Dieguito Lagoon through familiar coastal sage scrub vegetation including tele-graph weed, California buckwheat, and coastal goldenbush (*Isocoma menziesii* var. *vernonioides*). These plants are important for pollinators, as these species often flower later in the growing season and continue to flower over the summer and fall. The flowers provide an important nectar source during the dry months when few other plants are flowering. Coastal goldenbush is also a favorite host of the spittlebug (*Aphorphora* spp.), which is in the same insect order as aphids and leafhoppers. Those in the order Hemiptera have sucking mouthparts. Nymphs, who are the immature insects, attach to the plant and feed off the sugars. They are able to produce a frothy spit-like covering from their waste that serves as protection from

Spittle bug froth

predators and also from the sun's drying rays. The spittle covering also insulates against heat and cold.

Summer is a good time to look for the abundant number of small mustard-yellow flowers of big saltbush (*Atriplex lentiformis*) that grow in large gray-green clumps. Saltbush, a halophyte or salt-tolerant plant, makes itself saltier than the surrounding alkaline soil. This allows the plant to draw in water. Excess salt is then extruded as crystals on the underside of the leaves. These crystals are visible to the naked eye or with a magnifying lens.

In the middle of the canyon about halfway up, a large clump of arroyo willow indicates available fresh water. Further along on the right, amid dense stands of lemonadeberry, look for conical piles of sticks. These are either Bryant's (*Neotoma bryanti*) or big-eared (*Neotoma macrotis*) woodrat nests. These native woodrats have hair on their tails and look more like giant mice than rats. The non-native roof rat (*Rattus rattus*) has a bare tail. At a wide open space by a park sign, steep wooden stairs to the left ascend to another entrance to the preserve off Durango Drive.

A little further on, the coast sage scrub transitions to chaparral. Shrubs become denser and the sandy trail is narrow and slippery. San Diego mountain-mahogany, easily identified in summer by its fruit with a feathery tail, occurs here. Note that the species of mountain-mahogany you will see in the mountainous region of the county is another species (birch-leaf mountain-mahogany).

One animal that lives in this area, but likely not to be seen on a hike, is the nocturnal Virginia opossum (*Didelphis virginiana*). It is a marsupial that was introduced to California in the 1890s from the east coast. Opossums were deliberately brought to Los Angeles and have since spread throughout the state. They are opportunists and generalists that eat whatever is available. Sometimes it is roadkill, which can lead them to the same fate. The Virginia opossum is the only marsupial found in the United States. Its gestation is less than two weeks, with birthed young crawling into the mother's fur-lined pouch and attaching themselves to a teat where they continue to grow and develop for the next two and a half months before leaving the pouch. Opossums have long, hairless, prehensile tails that can be used to grab branches and carry small objects.

On the downhill return to the trailhead, take the parallel trail to the east side. It's higher up on the east side of the canyon and slightly steeper with a fine view of San Dieguito Lagoon and the Del Mar Fairgrounds. Rust-colored Lindavista Formation sandstone caps the canyon walls. Look for bushmallow with its pink flowers, fuzzy-leafed yerba santa, a huge Torrey pine with a broken limb, and Del Mar manzanita—a local rare and endemic species. About two-thirds of the way back, abundant pickleweed (*Salicornia* spp.) lines the trail. Another halophyte, this common salt-tolerant plant makes up most of the salt marsh. Pickleweed is both a salt excluder and a salt accumulator. Salt is either excluded at the roots or accumulated at the tips of the pickle-like branches. When the tips have accumulated more salt than can be tolerated, the segment cells break down, turn red, and then fall off.

As you leave Crest Canyon Open Space and head back toward Jimmy Durante Drive, visit the small observation area that overlooks the lagoon. This is a great spot in winter to see egrets, ducks, and other shore birds.

Woodrat nest

Distance:	2 miles, loop
Difficulty:	🚶
Elevation gain/loss:	Up to 200 feet
Hiking time:	1 hour
Agency:	CSP-SDCD
Notes:	Open 7:15 a.m. to sunset; bring only water, no food allowed
Trailhead GPS:	N32.93826, W117.25275
Optional map:	USGS 7.5 min *Del Mar*
Atlas square:	N7
Directions:	(La Jolla) From I-5 go west on Carmel Valley Road for 1.2 miles. Turn right onto Del Mar Scenic Parkway, passing condo developments. Park at the end of the road. The extension trails can also be accessed via Mar Scenic Drive and Mira Montana Drive.

Habitat(s):

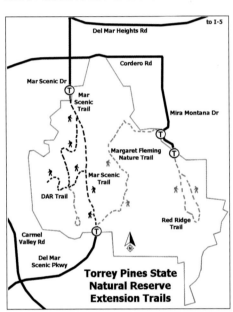

San Diego is a unique and exciting city for many reasons, and the remarkably rare Torrey pine is near the top of that list. Indeed, most San Diego residents can probably tell you where to find one, whether or not they realize the tree's uniqueness. That's because the well-known Torrey Pines State Natural Reserve between La Jolla and Del Mar offers beautiful ocean vistas, secluded hiking, and, of course, plenty of opportunities to see Torrey pines in their natural habitat. Slightly less famous, but equally worthwhile, is the Torrey Pines State Reserve Extension, located just across Los Peñasquitos Lagoon from the main reserve. These less-traveled extension trails offer spectacular pine specimens as well as a rich collection of other coastal sage scrub and chaparral plant life.

The dry, sandy soils favored by the Torrey pine are also preferred by a variety of other San Diego natives. This coastal sage scrub habitat is rich with wildflowers, various shrubs, and, as the name suggests, sage. Both white (*Salvia apiana*) and black sage (*Salvia mellifera*) can be found here, as well as the unrelated (except in smell) coastal sagebrush (*Artemisia californica*). Both black and white sage are members of the mint or Lamiaceae family while sagebrush belongs to the sunflower or Asteraceae family. Most species in the mint family can be identified by square-shaped stems and opposite leaves. While these three species are drought deciduous, coastal sagebrush is perhaps the most sensitive to moisture change, readily shedding its wispy leaves

White sage

and re-growing new foliage in response to the rainfall or fog regimes. Coastal sagebrush is a gray-green plant about 3 to 4 feet tall. Black sage falls in the middle of sagebrush and white sage in terms of its susceptibility to shed leaves. White sage is fairly tolerant to changing moisture along the coast, retaining most of its leaves even in the summer sun. This species can also be found in San Diego County's desert transition areas between chaparral shrublands and desert vegetation, while sagebrush and black sage remain more coastal. The whitish, lightly gray-green leaves of white sage are an adaptation to dealing with the sun, reflecting the sun's rays via the albedo effect—the lighter the surface and the more white it has, the greater the ability to reflect the sun's energy back into space, and, as a result, lighter-colored leaves remain cooler than would dark green leaves.

White sage was traditionally used by local Native Americans for respiratory problems and as a topical disinfectant, anti-inflammatory, and as an antioxidant. It was used for spiritual cleansing and to mask human odors before hunting. The young stalks were eaten raw and the seeds were roasted and eaten. Crushed leaves and water were used as a hair shampoo, a dye for graying hair, and as a hair straightener. It also cured dandruff.

Begin the extension trail at the end of Del Mar Scenic Parkway. The trail forks early and turning right will follow the Margaret Fleming Nature Trail to explore the east side of the wide basin. The 0.5 mile trail climbs the sandy red bluffs of the Lindavista Formation overlooking the entire basin and continues on to Mira Montana Drive. A trail to the left leads

to the top of Red Ridge. The north and west side of the reserve is explored by turning left at the fork and following the Mar Scenic Trail, which climbs to the other side of the basin and terminates at Mar Scenic Drive. The excellent Daughters of the American Revolution (DAR) trail can be accessed from this trail as well. Follow it along a ridge dotted with gnarled Torrey pines to reach spectacular views of Los Peñasquitos Lagoon and the open ocean. A short offshoot trail also descends from here into a pleasant, shaded pine grove.

Note that you can make a second loop from the trailhead by using the residential street Mira Montana Drive at the east end of the Margaret Fleming Nature Trail. Head north to Cordero Road and go left (west) five blocks to Mar Scenic Drive, where you turn left or south again to the Mar Scenic Trail that can be followed back to the trailhead at Del Mar Scenic Parkway.

If hiking in late winter to early spring, look for California poppy found here and note that the flowers are more yellow in coloration in this area than elsewhere in the county.

Coastal sagebrush

Distance:	1 mile, loop
Difficulty:	🏃🏃
Elevation gain/loss:	Up to 100 feet
Hiking time:	1 hour
Agency:	CSP-SDCD
Notes:	Open 7:15 a.m. to sunset; bring only water, no food allowed
Trailhead GPS:	N32.92296, W117.25542
Optional map:	USGS 7.5 min *Del Mar*
Atlas square:	N7
Directions:	(La Jolla) From I-5 go west on Carmel Valley Road for 1.6 miles. Turn left on South Camino Del Mar, which becomes North Torrey Pines Road as you cross into La Jolla. Go 0.9 mile to the park entrance to pay a day-use fee. The visitor center parking area is about 0.8 mile up the Torrey Pines Park Road. Free parking, if available, is by the beach on North Torrey Pines Road.

Habitat(s):

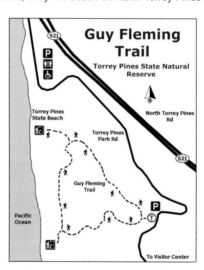

Torrey Pines State Natural Reserve is one of the most beautiful places to walk in San Diego. The reserve has ocean views from most trails, striking red and white sandstone outcrops, and interesting plants and flowers, including the rare Torrey pine.

The most popular walk in the reserve is the Guy Fleming Trail, named for the first caretaker of the park in 1921. He was hired by both Ellen Browning Scripps and the City to take care of their respective properties. Guy Fleming was also a Fellow at the San Diego Natural History Museum and was instrumental in recommending and including the Anza-Borrego Desert in the original State Park Survey authorized by the newly formed State Park Commission in 1928. Fleming was appointed the District Superintendent for all southern California State Parks in 1932.

First time visitors should go to the Torrey Pines Lodge Visitor Center. This small museum has interesting displays of human and natural history of the reserve and the Torrey pine. Ellen Browning Scripps constructed the Torrey Pines Lodge in a southwest pueblo style that was popular in 1922. She wanted to help draw attention to the pines and their need for protection. She had previously purchased land with several groves of pines, including the lodge land that was later incorporated into the park.

From the visitor center, walk back downhill on the paved road to the signed North Grove Guy Fleming trailhead on the left. It is a loop so either way is good with this description turning right at the start. Abundant examples of chaparral plants include chamise, lemonadeberry, laurel sumac, toyon, and coast prickly-pear. The visible cliffs are Torrey Sandstone outcrops

View toward the lagoon and beach

Alan King

which appear stark white unless capped by the iron oxide-rich Lindavista Formation, which then stains the white a light brown. Torrey Sandstone is a sedimentary formation that was deposited as a sandbar in the Eocene age, some 48 million years ago, where calcite bonded the composition of mostly quartz with some feldspar. The Lindavista Formation was deposited over the Torrey Sandstone a mere million years ago while the ocean retreated from the area.

The trail winds through old groves of Torrey pines and opens up to wonderful ocean views with cactus and low sage scrub vegetation. The north overlook has views of the ocean where sometimes (especially in winter) whales can be seen as well as the Torrey Pines State Beach and the brackish water in Los Peñasquitos Lagoon. Look at how the wind has shaped the trees and stunted the height of plants along the trail.

The south overlook can be closed when a wedding is performed, but when open and on a clear day, you can view the San Clemente and Santa Catalina Islands. The trail now turns east where there is coastal sage scrub, a habitat that occurs mostly in dry areas but also along the foggy coast and inland areas where the marine layer reaches. Plants tend to be soft-leafed, drought-deciduous, and shorter than plants in the chaparral ecosystems. Towards the end of the loop is chaparral, which is the dominant habitat of southern California consisting of woody plants that have sclerophyllous or stiff leaves that can be waxy or small as in lemonadeberry or the most common plant, chamise. This transition is a perfect example of loose habitat boundaries in the county, and the small-scale site characteristics influencing vegetation patterns vary locally. There is a bench at the end of the trail to take a rest before returning to your starting location.

Torrey Pines started out as a city park in 1899 when it was noted that these rare pines needed protection. Due to the special nature of the pines and surrounding acreage, this area has been designated a natural reserve, a more protected designation than a state park. Today over 2000 acres are preserved. Because this reserve was saved at an early date, it is a wonderful example of what the San Diego area was like before all of the development along the coastline. There are certain places on the trails where you can feel like you are in a wild place that has not seen the hand of man. Review the trail map and information handout so you know how to protect the reserve for future generations.

A hike any time of the year is great for enjoying ocean views and the picturesque wind-twisted pines, but late winter to early spring is best to view spring flowers. There are many common and uncommon flowers and plants in the coastal sage scrub, chaparral, riparian, and salt marsh plant communities at the reserve.

Don Fosket

Torrey Pines Lodge Visitor Center

Distance:	0.5 mile, loop
Difficulty:	犬犬
Elevation gain/loss:	Up to 100 feet
Hiking time:	1 hour
Agency:	CSP-SDCD
Notes:	Open 7:15 a.m. to sunset; bring only water, no food allowed; ADA compliant to viewpoint; 118 steep stone steps, no railing
Trailhead GPS:	N32.92146, W117.25517
Optional map:	USGS 7.5 min *Del Mar*
Atlas square:	N7
Directions:	(La Jolla) From I-5 go west on Carmel Valley Road for 1.6 miles. Turn left on South Camino Del Mar, which becomes North Torrey Pines Road as you cross into La Jolla. Go 0.9 mile to the park entrance to pay a day-use fee. The visitor center parking area is about 0.8 mile up the Torrey Pines Park Road. Free parking, if available, is by the beach on North Torrey Pines Road.

Habitat(s):

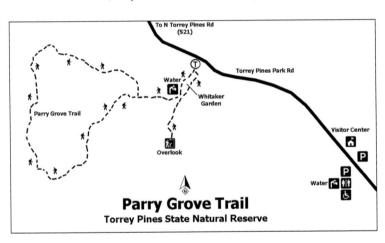

Parry Grove Trail
Torrey Pines State Natural Reserve

The Parry Grove Trail is one of the original hiking paths at this state reserve. The trail begins just north of the Torrey Pines Lodge Visitor Center at the top of the hill, with a walk through Whitaker Native Plant Garden, named for Thomas W. Whitaker, a plant scientist and longtime president of Torrey Pines Association. Follow the level trail out to the viewpoint that looks out over the original portion of the park, where steep canyons are eroded by water and wind. Backtrack a bit and descend the steep stone stairs to a sheltered bowl that once was home to the reserve's largest stand of the Torrey pine (*Pinus torreyana*). This tree is the rarest pine in North America. About 7000 individuals occur at the reserve and in Del Mar while another 2000 (a sub-species) are on Santa Rosa Island off of Santa Barbara. The California Native Plant Society considers it fairly endangered. It is a perfect example of

why San Diego is globally known as a biodiversity hotspot, a region with very high numbers of plant and animal species, particularly endemics, or species that occur nowhere else.

On seaside bluffs, the trees are low and twisted. In sheltered areas they can grow up to 60 feet tall, but are usually about 40 feet. Torrey pines have multiple major branches and 9- to 11-inch needles in bundles of five. To capture every drop of moisture, the serrated needles allow the trees to collect fog drip. The extensive root system helps prevent erosion. The taproot extends down 25 feet and lateral roots stretch 225 feet away from the trunk. Torrey pines start producing seeds around 12-18 years of age and exhibit delayed seed dispersal—seed fall beginning once cones mature about 2.5 years after pollination and continuing for the next 13 years. Most seeds fall from the cones by year 4 of

Canyon and ocean view

maturity, at which point only about 22% of seeds are retained.

The trail is a level loop meandering through dense chaparral and abundant wildflowers that include blue dicks, Nuttall's snapdragon, and southern pink during spring.

The native Kumeyaay lived in Torrey Pines and throughout coastal and interior San Diego County and northern Baja California. Spanish explorers used the Punta de los Arboles (Point of Trees) as a navigation landmark. In 1850, botanist Charles C. Parry described the pine and named it for his mentor, John Torrey. In 1883, Parry returned to San Diego and raised public concern about damage to the trees by picnickers, campers, and grazing cattle. In 1899, the City of San Diego set aside over 300 acres for a park, and Ellen Browning Scripps, a newspaperwoman and philanthropist, donated land comprising the North and Parry Groves. Over the next two decades, she purchased adjoining parcels, and in 1959, the adjoining parcels became part of the California State Park system to better protect the trees.

During a drought period in the 1980s hundred of pines in Parry Grove died because of severe bark beetle infestation. Their skeletons can still be seen. With adequate rain, the trees can produce enough pitch to withstand the insects, but in times of warmer temperatures and drought, beetles proliferate. The local culprits are called the five-spined engraver beetle (*Ips*

paraconfusus) and the red turpentine beetle (*Dendroctonus valens*). They burrow into the cambium or living part of the tree beneath the bark and eventually kill it. The females secrete chemicals called pheromones that attract mates. The long hanging black tubes seen throughout the reserve are pheromone traps for bark beetles. Young trees planted to restore the grove will face the same challenges as the original grove during times of drought.

The habitat is fragile and the reserve is in danger of being fragmented. Avoid the temptation to blaze your own way through the underbrush. Stay on the trails and help preserve this lovely place for future generations.

Torrey pine

Distance:	1.3 miles, out-and-back
Difficulty:	🏃
Elevation gain/loss:	Up to 300 feet
Hiking time:	1 hour
Agency:	CSP-SDCD
Notes:	Open 7:15 a.m. to sunset; bring only water, no food allowed
Trailhead GPS:	N32.91989, W117.25292
Optional map:	USGS 7.5 min *Del Mar*
Atlas square:	N7
Directions:	(La Jolla) From I-5 go west on Carmel Valley Road for 1.6 miles. Turn left on South Camino Del Mar, which becomes North Torrey Pines Road as you cross into La Jolla. Go 0.9 mile to the park entrance to pay a day-use fee. The visitor center parking area is about 0.8 mile up the Torrey Pines Park Road. Free parking, if available, is by the beach on North Torrey Pines Road.

Habitat(s):

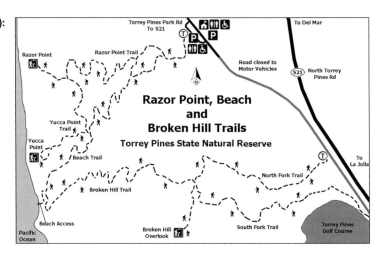

The Razor Point Trail in Torrey Pines State Natural Reserve offers stunning glimpses of the Pacific Ocean as it meanders through high quality southern maritime chaparral habitat before ending at an awe-worthy outlook. There are many well-placed benches to rest and enjoy the views, or for those interested in extending the hike, options to connect with other trails in the reserve.

This route begins following signs for the Beach Trail before the first junction directs you to the Razor Point Trail. Continue taking the right hand forks at the next junctions to keep you on the path to Razor Point. Chamise, California buckwheat, and felt-leaf yerba santa (*Eriodictyon crassifolium* var. *crassifolium*) are abundant at the start of the hike. You may see European honeybees on the flowers of California buckwheat and on the pale lavender flowers of yerba santa.

Yerba santa is highly valued by California Indians as a medicinal plant. The Spanish were so impressed with its healing qualities that they named it the holy plant. Look for a shrub with thick, velvet-like, gray-green woolly leaves that may have saw-toothed edges. Smell the fragrant leaves. Local Kumeyaay Indians would eat the leaves in addition to making a tea from the leaves to use for colds and coughs. This plant is found in coastal sage scrub and chaparral areas.

Ascending the steps up to Red Butte, take a moment to look at the hard, red rock under foot, part of the Lindavista Formation found in flat areas that has formed a hard cap that resists erosion and protects softer rock, like the Torrey Sandstone, found beneath it. The Lindavista Formation was deposited as the ocean retreated during the Middle Pleistocene, about a million years ago. It contains both marine and

Ellen Esch

Red Butte

land fossils and iron oxide, which colors the formation red. The oldest rock visible in Torrey Pines, found at the base of sea cliffs, is the Delmar Formation, which consists of lagoonal deposits of yellowish-green sandy claystone embedded with coarse-grained sandstone that was formed during the Eocene Epoch, more than 40 million years ago. While at Red Butte, notice the badlands to the south, made as the poorly cemented sandstone of the Bay Point Formation slowly erodes.

Descending along the trail down from Red Butte, observe mission manzanita and look for the two species of scrub oak that are common along the trail. Check the leaf undersides for trichomes or hairs to tell the difference between the two species. Nuttall's scrub oak (*Quercus dumosa*) trichomes are easily visible while those on Torrey's scrub oak (*Quercus Xacutidens*) are minute.

At Razor Point outlook, enjoy the view of the point jutting out beyond the end of the trail, the expanse of the Pacific Ocean, and more views of the badlands. The reserve's namesake species, the Torrey pine, are also easily visible from the outlook. On the way back from the lookout, take time to listen for the familiar sound of the wrentit (*Chamaea fasciata*), whose call is several whistled "chips," followed by an accelerating trill on an even pitch. Other "chips" heard may be coming from Anna's hummingbirds.

Walking back from the lookout, turn left to return the way you came or turn right to take an alternate trail past Big Basin with stunning views of the badland formations on the way to Yucca Point and the Beach Trail (which will take you back to the upper parking lot by turning left, or to Flat Rock and the beach by turning right).

Don Fosket

Felt-leaf yerba santa

Distance:	1.5 miles, out-and-back
Difficulty:	🚶🚶
Elevation gain/loss:	Up to 350 feet
Hiking time:	1 hour
Agency:	CSP-SDCD
Notes:	Open 7:15 a.m. to sunset; bring only water, no food allowed
Trailhead GPS:	N32.91981 W117.252956
Optional map:	USGS 7.5 min *Del Mar*
Atlas square:	N7
Directions:	(La Jolla) From I-5 go west on Carmel Valley Road for 1.6 miles. Turn left on South Camino Del Mar, which becomes North Torrey Pines Road as you cross into La Jolla. Go 0.9 mile to the park entrance to pay a day-use fee. The visitor center parking area is about 0.8 mile up the Torrey Pines Park Road. Free parking, if available, is by the beach on North Torrey Pines Road.

Habitat(s):

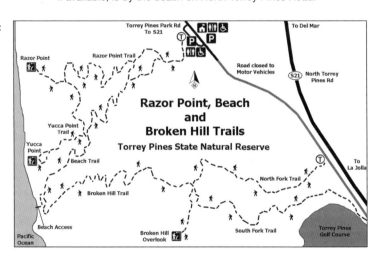

The Beach Trail is a very popular trail at Torrey Pines State Natural Reserve. Hikers and naturalists enjoy it for its spectacular ocean views and the opportunity to explore the rich natural history of this unique reserve. In addition to the Torrey pine, the reserve is home to a few rare species, including Nevin's barberry (***Berberis nevinii***) and the Del Mar manzanita (***Arctostaphylos glandulosa*** subsp. ***crassifolia***). Both species are components of the coastal sage scrub vegetation found here. Most other species of barberry and manzanita grow at higher elevations, in the foothills or mountains. Nevin's barberry was originally planted here by Guy Fleming, who also planted it on Palomar Mountain. It is native to the area on the north side of Agua Tibia Mountain in Riverside County. As of this writing, no natural occurrence of this plant has been recorded in San Diego County.

It is possible that both the Del Mar manzanita and the Torrey pine are relics of the ice age when southern California was cooler and had more rainfall. While the habitat here is generally considered to be coastal sage scrub, it is different from that found elsewhere in southern California. It has the usual coastal sage scrub species, such as coastal sagebrush, spineshrub, California buckwheat, black sage, and coast prickly-pear, but it also has many chaparral species. In addition to Del Mar manzanita and Nevin's barberry, it also has mountain-mahogany, yerba santa, and bush poppy, as well as an abundance of chamise, all typical chaparral species, and here referred to as maritime chaparral. The prevalence of fog probably makes this possible. Fog supplements the meager rainfall for this area's vegetation. Fog not only results in milder temperatures, but moisture from the fog condenses on the plant's leaves and drips into

View of Peñasquitos Marsh

the soil surrounding them. It has been demonstrated that the Torrey pines make significant use of water from fog.

The Beach Trail starts across the street from the Torrey Pines Lodge Visitor Center on the north side of the restrooms. It is 0.75 mile down to the beach from here, with a 340-foot elevation loss. There are 186 steps along the trail, most of which occur in the final 0.25 mile down to the beach as it descends through an eroded gulch. The trail is well maintained and signed, and careful attention to the signs will keep you from diverting onto one of the other trails that intersect with it. The trail passes a few Torrey pines. Keep a sharp eye out for the other interesting plants that grow here, particularly in the spring when many small annual plants are flowering.

Once you reach the beach, there may be dolphins playing in the surf, brown pelicans diving for fish, and gray whales offshore on their migration to and from Baja California lagoons. Sandstone cliffs tower above the beach. These cliffs are unstable as shown by the boulders at their foot. High tides and storm waves break at the foot of the cliff, undermining the soft sandstone. As a result, portions of the cliff break off periodically and come crashing down to the beach. While this is a danger that the beach goer faces, it also reveals the sedimentary layers that tell the geological history of the past 150 million years. Notice that the cliffs have the appearance of a gigantic layer cake, where each layer has a characteristic color and composition.

Millions of years ago coastal San Diego looked somewhat like the current eastern shore of the US. It was mostly flat with barrier islands a few miles offshore, which were composed of sand piled up on the shallow seabed by wave action. Lagoons formed between the barrier islands and the low continental shore.

Mud, silt, and sand accumulated at the bottom of the lagoon, and oysters and clams thrived. The movement of tectonic plates led to the formation of the San Andreas Fault and the uplift of coastal California. Compression of the lagoon sediments resulted in the formation of a fossil rich layer of yellow-greenish mudstone rock, known as the Delmar Formation. Flat Rock is a resistant fragment of Delmar Formation rock. Fossil clam and oyster shells embedded in Flat Rock are easily seen at low tide.

The sandstone layers above the Delmar Formation are known as Torrey Sandstone. Embedded within some of the component layers of Torrey Sandstone are round, river polished rocks known as San Diego cobble. These are derived from the beds of rivers that once flowed to the ocean from volcanic areas in Mexico. They are here now because coastal California and Baja California, Mexico, are on the Pacific Plate while the rest of the US is on the North American Plate. Currently, the Pacific Plate is moving toward Alaska at a rate of about 2 inches per year, relative to the North American Plate. It is expected to arrive there in 80 million years.

After exploring the beach, retrace your steps or take an alternate trail back, such as Razor Point Trail (see the previous trip).

Sandstone cliffs

Distance:	1 mile, out-and-back or 3 miles, loop
Difficulty:	🚶 or 🚶🚶
Elevation gain/loss:	Up to 800 feet
Hiking time:	1 or 2 hours
Agency:	CSP-SDCD
Notes:	Open 7:15 a.m. to sunset; bring only water, no food allowed; North Fork is ADA compliant to the first overlook; check at visitor center for possible trail closures due to restoration
Trailhead GPS:	N32.91625, W117.24778
Optional map:	USGS 7.5 min *Del Mar*
Atlas square:	N7
Directions:	(La Jolla) From I-5 go west on Carmel Valley Road for 1.6 miles. Turn left on South Camino Del Mar, which becomes North Torrey Pines Road as you cross into La Jolla. Go 0.9 mile to the park entrance to pay a day-use fee. The visitor center parking area is about 0.8 mile up the Torrey Pines Park Road. Free parking, if available, is by the beach on North Torrey Pines Road. Walk a short distance south from the visitor center to the trailhead.

Habitat(s):

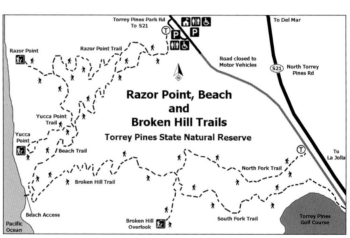

The Broken Hill Trail is the longest and one of the most scenic trails at Torrey Pines State Natural Reserve, winding through a thicket of chaparral until the trail opens up to reveal spectacular ocean views and then dropping down a steep canyon to Flat Rock and the beach below. The south fork route is heavily used by power walkers and joggers, alone or in groups.

Before beginning the hike, stop at the Torrey Pines Lodge Visitor Center to see exhibits on the natural and cultural history of the area and to pick up a brochure about the reserve and common plants found here. To reach the trailhead, walk south for 10-15 minutes on a paved segment of the original coast highway now restricted to hikers and bicyclists. The route is a national historic landmark first paved in 1915.

Its successor is the North Torrey Pines Road, a section of US-101 built in 1933. Further to the east roars I-5, constructed in the mid-1960s to speed the world to San Diego.

Look for the Broken Hill North Fork Trail sign. Initially flat, the light-colored, sandy path is easy to follow as it winds through densely packed manzanita, scrub oak, coastal sagebrush, coast spice bush, and yerba santa. Sunlit openings in the chaparral make room for spring wildflowers. Those areas are also strewn with marble-sized concretions, remnants of the rust-colored Lindavista Formation that caps the light-colored Torrey Sandstone at Broken Hill. When the trail forks, go right if Flat Rock is the objective, and head down to the beach. If a shorter loop is desired, then go left to the Broken Hill Overlook.

Sami Collins

Fragrant sage

The descent to the beach passes along a ridge with Fern Canyon to the north. Signs on the south side of the trail warn of unstable cliffs, which are easily damaged, so stay on the posted route. The trail gradually becomes less sandy and increasingly rutted where, over time, hikers have worn down the trail bed, exposing cobbles and roots. There are stairs in some spots so take care and stop at times to enjoy the area.

The shorter trail to the Broken Hill Overlook highlights the erosion-shaped geology of the reserve and its rare Torrey pines. While the softer Torrey Sandstone has eroded around Broken Hill, a segment still capped by the harder Lindavista Formation stands tall. From the overlook, gaze south across La Jolla Bay or look east to take in the emerald fairways of Torrey Pines Municipal Golf Course juxtaposed with the muted greens of the reserve's native chaparral.

In some areas along the North and South fork trails, footbridges and boardwalks have been built across areas where water drains in the rainy season. Smell an odor while walking here

in spring? It could be a small California native in the phlox family with a pretty purple flower called hooked pincushion plant or hooked skunkweed (*Navarretia hamata*), which has a skunky scent. Elsewhere in the reserve, hikers may catch a whiff of fragrance that could be bottled as perfume—another native known as fragrant sage or Cleveland sage (*Salvia clevelandii*), which is a bluish-purple-flowered perennial. This aromatic, compact shrub is an evergreen and is drought tolerant, which makes it popular as a cultivar in native gardens.

Along the trail, there may be a medium-sized, shiny, black stink beetle (*Eleodes* sp.). When disturbed or upon sighting a potential threat, the beetle will raise its rear end, but contrary to popular belief, local species of this genus do not expel a cloud of noxious vapor. There are those that do produce quinones or organic compounds that ooze out stinkiness—not really vapors—when threatened, but the cost of doing so is energetically draining. Then there are others that do not produce any quinones but mimic the threat behavior of those that do. In mimicry, some organisms will resemble another species or imitate a similar behavior to give them an evolutionary advantage, such as in the viceroy butterfly mimicking a poisonous monarch butterfly to have a survival advantage.

Walking east back along the Broken Hill Trail from the beach, turn right at the junction with South Fork Trail and immediately right again to take the spur trail to Broken Hill Overlook for some spectacular views of Torrey pines clinging to the eroded landscape. Return back to the junction with South Fork Trail and follow it back to the old coast highway and the visitor center.

Cyndy Cordle

Cliffside view

Bill Howell

Stink beetle

Distance:	0.5 mile, loop
Difficulty:	🚶
Elevation gain/loss:	Minimal
Hiking time:	1 hour
Agency:	NRS-UCSD
Notes:	Hours posted 8 a.m. to sunset
Trailhead GPS:	N32.87585, W117.24605
Optional map:	USGS 7.5 min *Del Mar, La Jolla*
Atlas square:	O7
Directions:	(La Jolla) From I-5 go west on La Jolla Village Drive for 0.9 miles. Continue onto North Torrey Pines Road. Go 0.4 mile. Turn left on La Jolla Shores Drive, and nearly immediately, turn right on La Jolla Farms Road. Go 0.1 mile. The gate for the Scripps Coastal Reserve will be on the left. Limited street parking is available on La Jolla Farms Road, and additional parking may be found on La Jolla Shores Drive or on the University of California, San Diego campus.

Habitat(s):

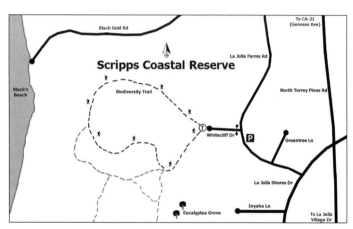

The Scripps Coastal Reserve or The Knoll offers spectacular views of the Pacific Ocean from coastal bluffs and an easy walk through coastal sage scrub habitat. It is part of the Natural Reserve System owned and managed by the University of California. The Scripps Coastal Reserve aims to provide a dedicated space for scientific research, education, and public service, contributing to stewardship and understanding of California's diverse ecosystems. The Biodiversity Trail offers an easy walk, with many signs posted along the trail informing visitors of the area's natural history, including plant and animal life and geology.

This route begins by walking through areas dominated by large stands of California encelia or bush sunflower and coastal sagebrush, which bloom in abundance from January to May. Both are in the sunflower family Asteraceae. This family is characterized by each

flower not being one flower but rather a composite cluster of several smaller flowers, which is an advantage in attracting pollinators to the flowerhead.

Follow the trail to the edge of the cliff where you will be rewarded with a commanding view of the Pacific Ocean, including the surf break at Black's Beach north of the overlook. A paved road offering pedestrian access to Black's Beach can be found further north of the reserve, past Black's Canyon, but there is no beach access from the Biodiversity Trail. The view to the ocean will be overlooking the Scripps and La Jolla submarine canyons, which plunge to over 2400 feet below the surface. Large marine life, such as gray whales, often take advantage of the deep waters off the coast during their yearly migrations. Keep a lookout from December to April as these mammals migrate from breeding to foraging grounds.

Coast bladderpod growing at cliff edge

Kelp beds in the La Jolla Cove to the south provide habitat to many species of marine life and appear slick on the water's surface. Over 265 fish species have been documented in the cove, representing half of all marine fish species found in California. Looking down between the overlook and the Scripps Research Pier, an exposed rocky intertidal zone at Dike Rock can be seen when water is left behind in pools at low tide.

Along the trail, look inland to see an area under various stages of restoration. Over 80% of original coastal sage scrub was lost by 1980 to agriculture and urbanization, with remain-

Crystalline iceplant

ing fragments facing pressure from invasion by non-native plant species. Invasive plant species of particular concern include crystalline ice plant (**Mesembryanthemum crystallinum**), which originates from South Africa and is recognized by water bubbles covering this prostrate succulent with red-tipped leaves. Others of concern originated from the Mediterranean basin and Eurasia, such as black mustard (**Brassica nigra**), which produces allelopathic chemicals that prevent native plants from germinating. Red-stem filaree or storksbill (**Erodium cicutarium**) is very aggressive and widespread and out-competes native plants. Various grasses, including compact brome (**Bromus madritensis**) and ripgut grass (**Bromus diandrus**) spread rapidly into various habitats where they increase fire frequency and convert native habitats into grasslands. These invaders can change habitat suitability for vertebrate and invertebrate species, displace native plants, and also affect other ecosystem services such as carbon storage and erosion control. Look for baby shrub seedlings that have been planted in areas where exotic plants have been removed, but please stay on the main path so as not to hinder their establishment.

Past restoration and conservation efforts at The Knoll have resulted in several nesting pairs of the federally threatened California gnatcatcher, whose habitat is limited to coastal

Wendy Esterly

Harlequin bug

sage scrub. Along this western edge of the reserve, look for an earthen bunker with two cuts into the bluff. During World War II, gun emplacements were constructed here to protect the coast.

As you return inland, look for a large coast bladderpod (***Peritoma arborea* var. *arborea***) that has a yellow bloom all months of the year on which often found is a red-throated, year-round resident of San Diego County—Anna's hummingbird (***Calypte anna***). It is often the largest and stockiest hummingbird in its range with a weight varying between that of a penny and a nickel. It drinks the nectar within the coast bladderpod bloom. Upon closer inspection of the coast bladderpod, there are likely harlequin

bugs (***Murgantia histrionica***), members of the stinkbug family with bright orange markings on their black back. Note the wings on bugs are crossed, forming an X or triangle versus the stink beetle with its fused parallel wing cases. The harlequin bug can spend his whole life on one plant. They feed on the plant with their sucking mouth-parts. When threatened, they will drop to the ground and feign death.

Closing the loop to the trailhead, notice the coast barrel cacti (***Ferocactus viridescens***) tucked beyond pockets of coastal sagebrush, many of which were saved and transplanted from area developments. Coast barrel cacti are often visited by native ant species for both protection and pollination. One species, the California harvester ant (***Pogonomyrmex californicus***), in turn, is an important food source for the conspicuous, yet shy, Blainville's horned lizards (***Phrynosoma blainvillii***). Unfortunately, both the California harvester ants and the horned lizards are disappearing, in part, because of the invasion of the very aggressive Argentine ant (***Linepithema humile***) that will destroy other ant colonies and, unfortunately, are not a food that horned lizards like. In fact, the Argentine ants will attack the horned lizards in large swarms. They may also decrease the number of pollinators that visit flowering plants by predating on larvae of pollinators.

Along this portion of the trail, Sumner Canyon drops off to the south. Other plants likely to be encountered on the trail include California buckwheat, lemonadeberry, and coyote brush. Careful observers may also be rewarded with desert cottontail, rattlesnake, western fence lizard, or wrentit sightings.

Wendy Esterly

Male Anna's hummingbird

Distance:	1 or 5 miles south or north, out-and-back
Difficulty:	🚶 or 🚶🚶🚶
Elevation gain/loss:	Minimal
Hiking time:	1 or 3 hours
Agency:	City of San Diego
Trail use:	Dogs, except between 9 a.m. and 4 or 6 p.m., depending on the month
Notes:	Check low tide schedule; the 5-mile hike requires scrambling over slippery rocks
Trailhead GPS:	N32.85718, W117.25725
Optional map:	USGS 7.5 min *La Jolla*
Atlas square:	P7
Directions:	(La Jolla) From I-5 N or CA-52 go west on La Jolla Parkway for 2 miles. Turn right at La Jolla Shores Drive, just past where West La Jolla Pkwy becomes Torrey Pines Road. Go 0.5 miles. Turn left on Calle Frescota, go 0.2 mile. Park in the lot just past Camino Del Oro. There is also limited parking on the surrounding streets. From 1-5 S go west on La Jolla Village Drive for 0.7 mile. Continue onto North Torrey Pines Road. Go 0.4 mile. Turn left on La Jolla Shores Drive. Go 1.8 mile. Turn right on Calle Frescota. Go 0.2 mile. Park in the lot just past Camino Del Oro. There is also limited parking on the surrounding streets. Best to park before 10 a.m.

Habitat(s):

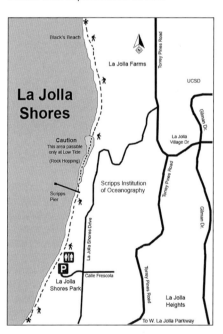

If you have been avoiding the beach thinking it is overcrowded with tourists, it pays to remember that timing is everything. Keep an eye on the tide schedules, get up early on the weekend, and head down to La Jolla Shores for a surprisingly relaxing and fascinating hike to the tidepools. The best time to arrive is at or a little before low tide. High tide will cover the tidepools and cut the accessible beach route by more than half. There are tidepools both to the north and to the south of the park on the beach, so choose either direction or start at one end and work your way to the other. The tidepools here are part of designated marine protected areas, similar to state parks. Collecting of any living marine resources is prohib-

Janine Kardokus

Sea anemones with and without shell cover

ited by the public in these areas, which in part is what helps them retain integrity and makes them such good places to go tidepooling.

Walking about 0.5 mile to the south, you will come to the end of a row of red roofed buildings. If the tide is low enough, walk around the corner toward smooth, flat-topped black rock formations that host many small tidepools. Sea anemones, small crabs, and fish frequent these hiding places. If lucky, you might spot the occasional nudibranch or sea slug (**class Gastropoda**), a small but often spectacularly-colored soft bodied, gastropod mollusk. The bright colors on nudibranchs serve to warn potential predators of their poisonous nature. The name nudibranch refers to the fact that they do not have a hard body shell but are nude instead, relying on chemical rather than physical defenses. A particularly spectacular and common nudibranch is the Spanish shawl (*Flabellina iodinea*), easily identified by its purple main body and bright orange cerata, or horn-like protrusions. You may also encounter a California aglaja (*Navanax inermis*), which is not a nudibranch despite also being brilliantly colored. In fact, the aglaja is a sea slug that is a predator of nudibranchs! Look for accents of bright blue, orange, and white that accentuate the aglaja's black body. Watch your footing, since the rocks can be slippery and the waves can surprise you when they shoot up between rock crevices.

If choosing to walk along the beach in the other direction, about 0.5 mile to the north, just past Scripps Pier, there is another set of tidepools in a rocky area with some very interesting rock formations in the Scripps Coastal Reserve area. Note the swirl patterns in sedimentary rock caused by earth movement, wind, and erosion. The cliff side provides a cross-sectional view back into geologic time, and it may be possible to spot a fossil or two embedded into the side of the cliff. As you explore the tidepools on this side, be aware that what looks like pieces of shells scattered among the rocks may actually be covering dozens of sea anemones. Take care to avoid stepping on the fragile bodies of the anemones.

Janine Kardokus

Tidepools are to the south of this rocky area.

Killdeer

In addition to the sea creatures, many shore birds enjoy these beaches. It is common to find yourself within a few feet of long-billed curlews, marbled godwits, plovers, and killdeer (*Charadrius vociferus*), as well as the ever-present western gulls. Brown pelicans can often be spotted soaring overhead or skimming the waters for a quick fish catch.

The killdeer, unlike many other shorebirds, can live in dry areas also. It is San Diego County's most widespread shorebird. In addition to mudflats and sandbars, it can be found in disturbed areas such as pasture lands, golf courses, athletic fields, urban lawns, and even along parking lots or airport runways. It has been recorded in oases in the Anza-Borrego Desert as well as in irrigated fields in Borrego Springs. Killdeers have a large rounded head, large eyes, and the short bill characteristic of plovers. They are tan on top and white below with two dark bars across their chest and white and black patches on their face. They have a pattern of walking, then running a few steps, and then stopping to look around. When disturbed they take flight and let out a shrill loud cry that almost sounds like "kill-deer," which is how the common name came to be. The species has also been called the chattering plover and noisy plover. When looking at an intruder, a killdeer bobs up and down. To distract a predator from a nest, the killdeer calls loudly, bobs up and down, and runs away, feigning a broken wing. To protect its ground nest from pasture animals that might step on the eggs, the killdeer may charge the animal to make it turn away. The killdeer is an omnivore eating crayfish, earthworms, beetles, insect larvae, seeds left in an agricultural field, and even frogs.

Continue past the tidepools all the way up to Black's Beach, for a longer distance, about 5 miles from the south to the north during low tide. There is a private residence at the base of the cliffs known as the mushroom guesthouse on Black's Beach. The Pavilion, with its round top atop a narrow column was designed and built in 1968 by Dale Naegle for Sam Bell of Bell's Potato Chips.

Rock formations north of Scripps Pier

Distance:	2 miles, out-and-back
Difficulty:	🚶
Elevation gain/loss:	Up to 100 feet
Hiking time:	1 hour
Agency:	City of San Diego
Trail use:	Dogs, except on beach
Trailhead GPS:	N32.84696, W117.27846
Optional map:	USGS 7.5 min *La Jolla*
Atlas square:	P7
Directions:	(La Jolla) From I-5 N or CA-52 go west on La Jolla Parkway for 1.8 miles. Continue west on Torrey Pines Road and go 1 mile. Turn right on Prospect Place. Go 0.6 mile. Turn right on Jenner Street, then left on Coast Boulevard. Begin looking for parking here to reach the starting point at Seal Rock or Children's Pool. Plan to be there early to park close by, especially on weekends. From 1-5 S go west on La Jolla Village Drive for 0.7 mile. Continue onto North Torrey Pines Road. Go 0.4 mile. Turn left on La Jolla Shores Drive. In 2.2 miles stay right on Torrey Pines Road and go 0.8 mile. Turn right on Prospect Place. Go 0.6 mile. Turn right on Jenner Street, then left on Coast Boulevard. Begin looking for parking here to reach the starting point at Seal Rock or Children's Pool. Plan to be there early to park close by, especially on weekends.

Habitat(s):

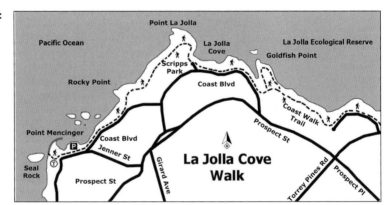

Enjoy a casual walk along one of the most picturesque parts of the San Diego coastline. This area is often featured in artwork and photography exhibits, the site for outdoor weddings, and a favorite destination of tourists visiting La Jolla. It can best be enjoyed in the early morning hours before crowds arrive, especially in the summer.

Begin the walk at Seal Rock, next to the historic wall commissioned by one of La Jolla's most influential women, Ellen Browning Scripps. Scripps built the wall over 100 years ago to create an artificial cove that was safe for children to swim in. The beach in front of the wall is a favorite location for harbor seals (***Phoca vitulina***) to lounge in the sun and, from December to March, to give birth to their pups. Just

over the fence, next to the sidewalk, is a colony of California ground squirrels, usually begging for handouts and chewing on either the Chilean sea-fig (***Carpobrotus chilensis***) or the South African hottentot-fig (***Carpobrotus edulis***) for moisture. These two non-native succulents are commonly known as iceplant. The sea-fig has small, magenta flowers, while the hottentot-fig has larger (2- to 6-inch diameter) flowers that are either light pink or yellow. The hottentot-fig is also more highly invasive, forming dense vegetative mats that can crowd out native plant species. The fruit of the hottentot-fig is edible and can be made into a jam.

Continuing on the sidewalk going north, there are high-rise condos inland and sand-

California sea lions

stone cliffs along the coast with some small, secluded beaches. An amazing sight to see near the water is California brown pelicans gliding directly overhead in formation, riding the updrafts from the cliffs or from the condos.

Eventually, the sidewalk winds past Ellen Scripps Park, which has a variety of tree life from around the world, including several mature Mexican fan palms, large Monterey pines, Australian tea trees, New Zealand Christmas trees, and a very large dragon tree from the Canary Islands. In addition to building a wall for the Children's Pool and bequeathing a park to the city, Ellen Scripps' philanthropy is also recognized by the many institutions she supported in La Jolla and San Diego, including the Scripps Institution of Oceanography and Scripps Hospital.

Just north of the park is the beach at La Jolla Cove, which has been a popular recreational spot since the late 1800s and offers some of the best snorkeling in San Diego. Below the water is the San Diego-La Jolla Underwater Park that encompasses 6000 acres, four habitats, and includes the Ecological Reserve and Marine Life Refuge.

Continuing along the sidewalk past the cove beach, head upward and notice the very mature Joshua tree (*Yucca brevifolia*) at the base of the hill. The Latin name of the Joshua tree refers to the short leaves. This desert species was planted here years ago. Above the cove are sandstone ledges frequented by several California sea lions (*Zalophus californianus*) with their accompanying pungent odor. Look for a gate along the fence to go down for a closer look, but use caution; the sandstone is slippery when wet and sea lions will bite if you get too close. There are distinct differences between sea lions and seals. Sea lions have ear flaps, can walk on land, are noisy and bark, and propel themselves in water with their front flippers. Seals are earless, move on

land on their bellies, make soft grunting noises, have small front flippers, and use their rear flippers to propel themselves in water.

Further up the hill, there is a spectacular view of one of La Jolla's seven caves. There are also sea lions in this area along with pelicans and Brandt's cormorants (*Phalacrocorax penicillatus*) resting on the sides of the cliff. The cormorants fish for their food—chasing prey underwater. The warmer ocean temperatures associated with El Niño can decrease the abundance of fish and reduce the cormorant's success in breeding. These birds have nested sporadically in La Jolla since about 1930, although the majority of the local population nests in much larger colonies on the Coronado and Channel Islands. Keep walking up and veer to the left into the grove of Torrey pine trees near the Cave Store.

For a small fee, you can enter the Sunny Jim Cave from inside the Cave Store. This is where the sidewalk ends and the dirt trail along the bluff begins. There is also a short side trail at the beginning with wooden steps going down to an observation deck. It is worth the stop for the beautiful views of the La Jolla cliffs. Usually a colony of Brandt's cormorants is perched on the vertical cliffs looking like a scene from a wildlife documentary of some remote distant land. Looking down when the ocean is calm, you will see the occasional bright orange flash of color from the California state fish called the garibaldi (*Hypsypops rubicundus*).

The bluff trail winds along the top of the cliffs above the caves through mostly native vegetation of coastal sage scrub variety. There are benches along the trail to rest and enjoy the wonderful views and solitude. The trail ends shortly at a small obscure public parking lot for two cars. Retrace your steps back to your vehicle.

Cormorants and brown pelicans

Distance:	1 mile, out-and-back
Difficulty:	👫👫
Elevation gain/loss:	Up to 400 feet
Hiking time:	1 hour
Agency:	City of San Diego
Trail use:	Dogs
Trailhead GPS:	N32.84315, W117.25988
Optional map:	USGS 7.5 min *La Jolla*
Atlas square:	P7
Directions:	(La Jolla) From I-5 N or CA-52 go west on La Jolla Parkway for 1.8 miles. Continue west on Torrey Pines Road and go 1.1 miles. Turn left on Exchange Place, then turn right onto Country Club Drive. Go 0.4 mile. Turn left on Romero Drive. Go 0.2 mile. Then turn left on Brodiaea Way. If available, park on the corner of Brodiaea Way and Encelia Drive (Parking is very limited). Walk up Encelia Drive for the trailhead. From 1-5 S go west on La Jolla Village Drive for 0.7 mile. Turn left on Torrey Pines Road. In 1.7 miles stay right on Torrey Pines Road and go 1.1 miles. Turn left on Exchange Place, then turn right onto Country Club Drive. Go 0.4 mile. Turn left on Romero Drive. Go 0.2 mile. Then turn left on Brodiaea Way. If available, park on the corner of Brodiaea Way and Encelia Drive. (Parking is very limited.) Walk up Encelia Drive for the trailhead.

Habitat(s):

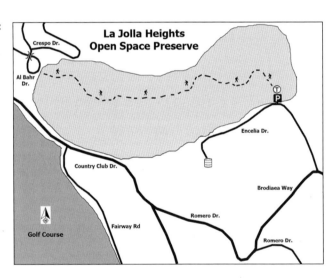

One of La Jolla's best-kept secrets is a small 42-acre open space preserve called La Jolla Heights that was set aside to preserve highly sensitive biological resources of the coastal mixed chaparral habitat. Begin the hike where Encelia Drive terminates at the summit of La Jolla Heights Open Space Preserve. A small succulent garden is found here. Agaves dominate the scene with their large lance-like leaves. At the downhill side of the garden is a sitting bench that provides a 180-degree view of the La Jolla area and the turquoise waters of the

Pacific Ocean beyond. La Jolla Shores and Torrey Pines State Natural Reserve are especially beautiful, so select a clear day for this hike to take advantage of the views. Spend time taking in the spectacular vista before beginning your descent along the narrow trail as it winds its way downhill through chamise and scrub oak. The low-lying vegetation provides opportunities for more views along the way.

On the way down the trail, note the many rounded cobblestones. The rocky trail surface can be challenging for hikers in some places.

View toward La Jolla Shores and cliffs

These stones are part of our geological history. They were worn smooth in rivers and traveled north from Mexico through movement of tectonic plates, millions of years ago. Our coastal land is still moving to the north about 2 inches a year. As you continue down the trail, there will be several trails that meander through the chaparral. In warmer weather lizards may be sighted darting in and out of the brush along the way. One of the lizards that might be seen is the southern alligator lizard (*Elgaria multicarinata*) with its slender, snake-like body. This lizard is common throughout southern California and can be found in several habitats throughout the county including coastal sage scrub, chaparral, oak woodlands, grasslands, and mixed conifer forests. It moves much like a snake with an undulating motion. The southern alligator lizard's tail is twice the length of its body. This lizard can quickly shed its tail when grabbed by a predator, leaving it as a wriggling distraction while the lizard makes a getaway. While the alligator lizard will re-grow the tail, doing so is energetically depleting.

A small side canyon will appear on the left as the trail heads down. From here a line of taller bushes will be visible along the left-hand side. Listen for numerous bird calls from this location. Continue downhill, keeping the treeline

to the left. There is a small riparian area and a bridge at the bottom of the trail, which borders a La Jolla neighborhood near Cowrie Avenue.

On the way back, there is the option of taking the wide access road to the left near the top. The wide road leads straight uphill to merge with Encelia Drive, where the trek first began. There are a variety of tall shrubs along the roadside that include chaparral broom, sweet fennel, and toyon. Note that this trek can also begin at the bottom of the hill leading to the summit and returning downhill. However, parking is very limited at the bottom of the hill and may require walking a distance to begin the hike.

Southern alligator lizard

Distance:	1 mile, loop
Difficulty:	🚶
Elevation gain/loss:	Up to 100 feet
Hiking time:	1 hour
Agency:	City of San Diego
Trail use:	Dogs
Trailhead GPS:	N32.81166, W117.23943
Optional map:	USGS 7.5 min *La Jolla*
Atlas square:	Q7
Directions:	(Pacific Beach) From I-5 go west on Garnet Avenue for 1 mile. Turn right on Lamont Street. Go 0.6 mile. Shortly after Lamont becomes Soledad Road, turn right on Park Drive into the parking lot. The trailhead is at the playground.

Habitat(s):

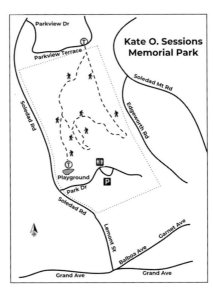

This 139-acre park, located on a hilltop between the communities of La Jolla and Pacific Beach, is named after a renowned San Diego horticulturist and nurserywoman. The high perch leads to some spectacular views. On a clear day one can see all the way to the hills of Mexico, along with views of Mission Bay and Fiesta Island. The 79-acre, manicured portion of the park contains a playground, a large grassy area for picnicking, and BBQ pits for cookouts. A 60-acre portion of Kate O. Sessions Memorial Park is preserved in a more natural state.

Starting on the slope behind the playground, look for an opening in the dense chaparral. This is your entrance to the trail into the wild side of Kate Sessions. This area contains a mile-long loop through the coastal sage scrub, with many offshoots created by both hikers and wildlife. Be wary of taking any of the offshoot trails, as many of them peter out, causing you to turn back to the main trail. The trail can be quite narrow and steep at times, as it is not officially maintained, yet it affords close-up looks at the native plants and animals. This space is an example of a well-planned urban park that has all the amenities for a great picnic spot as well as a preserved natural space to explore. The natural area is important for wildlife in an otherwise urban/suburban area. Ground squirrels, rabbits, rattlesnakes, and a wide variety of birds, spiders, and insects make good use of this "island" of preserved habitat. Keep an eye out for the striking orb-weaver spiders that like to make their homes in prickly pear cactus patches.

In many ways, this park is a perfect reflection of its namesake, Kate Sessions. Sessions was

Kate Sessions sculpture in Balboa Park

our loveliest natives into the horticulture trade, and now they can be found in gardens all over America.

The distinction between exotic, invasive, naturalized, and native species can, at times, be challenging. At Kate O. Sessions Memorial Park, you will be able to see plants belonging to all of these groups. Native plants are perhaps the easiest to define—a plant whose evolutionary history over hundreds or thousands of years is within that particular region or ecosystem. Exotic or non-native plants are anything other than this. These are plants brought either intentionally or unintentionally to a place where they were not previously found. Their fate can take a variety of routes. They may become naturalized, being able to reproduce and maintain populations over time without human help. A small subset of naturalized plants can get the further distinction of invasive if they are widespread and fast growing, causing disruption of native communities, often associated with economic or environmental harm. Look for invasive grasses, such as compact brome (***Bromus madritensis***) that fit this category.

Compact brome is recognized by its brush-like inflorescence that becomes purplish at maturity. Alternatively, exotic plants may not be able to reproduce without human intervention, like some of the ornamental pines. Some plants involved in the horticulture business can escape cultivation, however, and become either naturalized or invasive.

an avid horticulturist, known as the Mother of Balboa Park for importing and planting many of the exotic trees found there. She often started these trees in her gardens from seeds she collected all around the world. Many of the ornamental trees in the landscaped half of Kate O. Sessions Memorial Park are the very same species she imported, among which are Peruvian pepper trees, ornamental pines, and eucalyptus. However, Sessions was also one of the first proponents of using California native plants. She collected, grew, and introduced some of

The trail

Distance:	2 miles, loop
Difficulty:	🏃
Elevation gain/loss:	Minimal
Hiking time:	1 hour
Agency:	City of San Diego
Trail use:	Bicycles, dogs—unleashed permitted
Trailhead GPS:	N32.76897, W117.20947
Optional map:	USGS 7.5 min *La Jolla*
Atlas square:	R8
Directions:	(Mission Bay) From I-5 go west on Sea World Drive/Tecolote Road for 0.3 mile. Turn right onto East Mission Bay Drive, then turn left onto Fiesta Island Road. Use the parking lot at the corner of Mission Bay and Fiesta Island before crossing the water onto the island itself. If the lot is full, there is additional parking to the right once you drive onto the island. The trailhead is the island entrance.

Habitat(s):

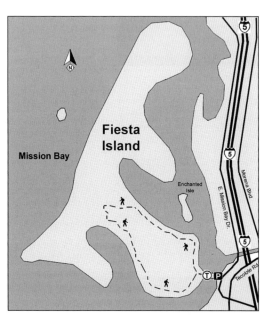

Fiesta Island on the east side of Mission Bay is a demonstration of the effects of man on the natural environment of San Diego. Mission Bay was originally a tidal marsh known as False Bay. The San Diego River emptied sometimes into False Bay and sometimes into San Diego Bay. In 1852 the US Army Corps of Engineers built a dike on the south side of the river to prevent it from flowing into San Diego Bay. This turned False Bay into an estuary outlet for the San Diego River. In later years the river was further constrained through levees, so that it no longer flowed into False Bay, which allowed for recreational development. In the 1940s the marsh was dredged to create today's Mission

Bay. The accumulated sand became the man-made Fiesta Island.

The relatively flat, easy trail that loops around the southern end of Fiesta Island is hidden from the road, but once you get past the dunes, you can see the variety of invasive plants that have colonized this disturbed area along with the native wildlife that still manages to call it home. Many of the invasive or non-native plants are those used in landscaping in the surrounding neighborhoods that have escaped from yards and businesses onto the island. Invasive plants exploit and colonize disturbed areas. They reproduce rapidly and are spread by wildlife, water, wind, and seeds. Found here are

Beach sun cup

species of ice plant and filaree, Sahara mustard, tree tobacco, tumbleweed, and castor bean.

Despite the abundance of invasive plants, there are native species that are thriving on Fiesta Island as well. Many of these plants, such as beach sun cup (*Camissoniopsis cheiranthifolia*), are specifically adapted to growing on the bare sand of natural dune areas. A member of the evening-primrose family, the sun cup grows in mats on the sandy surface. Others are generalists that can grow basically anywhere and tolerate a high degree of disturbance. The most common of these is coastal goldenbush. There are even five plant species that the state considers to be sensitive, including prostrate or Nuttall's lotus (*Acmispon prostratus*). Most of these are sand and dune specialists that are hard to find on the increasingly developed San Diego coast. The prostrate lotus is an annual herb with prostrate or trailing stems that can also form mats. The inflorescence is an umbel (umbrella-like) and the petals can vary in color from red, to orange, yellow, or purple and can be bi-color, streaked, or with spots.

In part because of the grassy habitat created by the many invasive plants, Fiesta Island is home to many interesting bird species, so remember to bring your binoculars! Grassland birds such as the western meadowlark and horned lark (*Eremophila alpestris*) are found commonly all year while the American pipit (*Anthus rubescens*) is here in winter. The sandy to rusty-brown horned lark has a black chest band and has whitish underparts. The male has a curved mask over its eyes and a head stripe with two feather tufts that look like horns. They are social birds that search the ground for seeds and insects. The American

pipit is a medium-sized songbird that resembles a sparrow. It has a thin bill and is often seen bobbing its tail. It breeds in the arctic and alpine tundra and winters along coastal beaches, marshes, and mudflats

The shoreline provides the mudflats and sandy beaches preferred by a variety of shorebirds. The island is also a nesting area for the western snowy plover. The northern tip of the island is fenced off as a least tern nesting area. Both species are designated threatened or endangered because of diminishing habitat needed for nesting. Raptors such as red-tailed hawks and barn owls take advantage of the many California ground squirrels and rabbits. The red-tailed hawk is the most common hawk in North America. The barn owl is a silent night predator.

This is a great hike for any would-be trackers. Because it is an island made of sand, every bird, lizard, insect, and mammal makes tracks for all to see. You may also see dog tracks as this is a favorite place for pet owners to legally run their dogs off leash.

Male horned lark

Distance:	2 miles, out-and-back
Difficulty:	🚶
Elevation gain/loss:	Up to 100 feet
Hiking time:	1 hour
Agency:	City of San Diego
Trailhead GPS:	N32.74812, W117.22936
Optional map:	USGS 7.5 min *Point Loma*
Atlas square:	R8
Directions:	(Ocean Beach) From I-8 W turn left on Sunset Cliffs Boulevard. Keep left onto Nimitz Boulevard and go 0.6 mile. Exit right on Famosa Boulevard/Catalina Boulevard. Turn left on Famosa Boulevard and go 0.4 mile to end of street and park in the lot. There are also entrances on the north side of West Point Loma Boulevard and along Famosa Boulevard. Any parking spot necessitates walking across West Point Loma Boulevard to experience both sides of the slough.

Habitat(s):

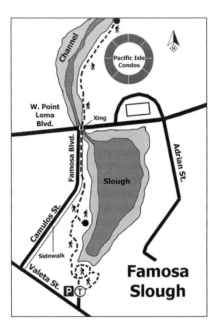

The Famosa Slough State Marine Conservation Area is a 37-acre wetland that connects to the San Diego River Estuary via a 12-acre natural channel. The slough includes fresh water, brackish, and salt march habitats. It is a go-to spot for birders, neighbors, and those interested in what is the remnant of the San Diego River delta at the south end of False Bay or Mission Bay wetlands.

Puerto Falso or False Bay was the name given by early Spanish explorers in 1542 to Mission Bay by some of Juan Cabrillo's men who went ashore to search for fresh water. When they came to Mission Bay and did not see the ship,

they thought at first that Cabrillo had sailed away without them. They named it False Bay to distinguish it from the larger San Diego Bay to the south. It continued to be called False Bay until officially changed to Mission Bay in 1915 by the US Board on Geographic Names.

To start the Famosa Slough portion of the walk, park in the dirt, then walk north through the yellow posts. To the right there is a short distance along a fence where the trail circles around one of the three sediment depressions. These have plants growing near and between concrete jacks and interlocking blocks to slow down runoff from the surrounding area. Water

Trestle ruins

will collect and enter into black catchment basins with rocks at the base to help defuse the water so that it soaks into the soil, or if there is a high volume of water, it will divert the surface water to the slough.

Circle the sediment depressions and then turn south for a short distance until crossing the concrete walkway to the end of Montalvo Street. Just beyond the fence, turn north and cross the end of Mentone Street. Follow the trail along the west side of the slough. Make a short detour to the right that is closer to the water to look for birds, such as ducks, coots, herons, and egrets. The elegant, long-legged, white great egret (***Ardea alba***) is a dazzling sight in flight with its impressive wingspan and its long black legs trailing along. It stands immobile or wades through water looking for fish, frogs, or other aquatic animals to stab with its long dagger-like yellow bill. It nests in colonies in high trees. The great egret is the symbol of the National Audubon Society.

Return to the main trail where it then rises up along Famosa Boulevard, turning again to the right when the path leads close to the water. Return to the main trail and continue to the corner of Famosa Boulevard and West Point Loma Boulevard. Turn right going east on West Point Loma Boulevard for a short distance and turn south on a wide gravel/dirt path where there is an excellent place to use binoculars to see how many different species of birds you can recognize. Follow the wide path, where there are a number of native plants along the way, until it turns up to West

Point Loma Boulevard. Turn right, and after a short distance, there is a crosswalk to carefully reach the other side. Turn west until there is a sign stating Famosa Slough. Turn right just past Orleans West where the remnants of a trestle are visible. Follow the trail until there is a wide area before retracing your steps back to the parking lot. More information can be found on the Friends of Famosa Slough website at www.famosaslough.org.

Great egret

Distance: 1.9 miles, out-and-back
Difficulty: 🥾🥾
Elevation gain/loss: Up to 400 feet
Hiking time: 1 hour
Agency: NPS
Notes: Fee required; hours posted 8 a.m. to 4 p.m.
Trailhead GPS: N32.67252, W117.24070
Optional map: USGS 7.5 min *Point Loma*
Atlas square: S7
Directions: (Point Loma) From I-8 W turn left on Sunset Cliffs Boulevard. Keep left onto Nimitz Boulevard and go 0.6 mile. Exit right on Famosa Boulevard/Catalina Boulevard. Turn right on Famosa Boulevard and continue onto Catalina Boulevard. After 2.7 miles continue onto Cabrillo Memorial Drive and follow it 2.5 miles to the monument.

Habitat(s):

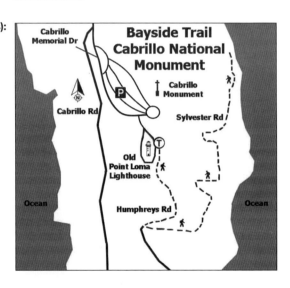

The view from the Bayside Trail at Cabrillo National Monument is stunningly beautiful. Visible from this trail are downtown San Diego, Coronado, San Diego Bay, and the Pacific Ocean. Whether you are visiting San Diego for the first time or are a life-long San Diegan who has never made it all the way down Point Loma, this trail is a wonderful way to learn a little bit about the nature and history of the area and to see it all from a lovely vantage point. It is also one of four National Recreation Trails in San Diego County. Although the trail is a scant 1.86 miles round trip, don't be fooled by the length. It is still a good workout as the hike back up the trail is all uphill with a 340-foot elevation gain. There are interpretive signs along the trail identifying many of the common plants that may be seen on the

hike. The signs also highlight the natural history and military importance of Point Loma and San Diego Bay.

The Bayside Trail is a perfect way to get acquainted with the coastal sage scrub ecosystem. This special habitat is becoming increasingly rare due to development in southern California. On this trail, however, one can experience the plants and animals that call the sage scrub habitat home. Black sage, California encelia, coastal sagebrush, laurel sumac, and lemonadeberry are some of the common plants that are encountered. The best time to view wildflowers in this coastal sage scrub community is February through May.

Point Loma is an important avian stopover on the Pacific Flyway. This means that during the spring and fall migration there are lots

Ocean view from trail

of bird species that may be viewed, many of which do not make their home in San Diego during the rest of the year. Be sure to bring your binoculars. Binoculars are also helpful when viewing the marine birds just offshore and the occasional sea lion that swims up to the fishing boats below.

The kelp forests visible just off of Point Loma are home to abalone, though their populations are much lower than historic numbers. Abalones face the plight of many marine species either currently or once prized for commercial fishing—slow growing with a high mortality of young. Reproductive success is contingent on having high population densities. This is especially important to a relatively sessile creature like the abalone that spawns by releasing gametes into the open water. Recent genetic studies of the adult pink abalone (*Haliotis corrugata*) in the Point Loma kelp forest shows that the population is below the threshold size needed for long-term viability and density must increase in order for this population to persist.

For history buffs, the Bayside Trail winds past several military bunkers that were part of the defense system used to protect the San Diego Bay during World Wars I and II. Point Loma is still important to the military and the entrance to the monument is on land belonging to the Department of the Navy. Pay

attention to the time while on the trail. The national monument closes at 4 p.m. and the exit gate through the military base closes at 5 p.m. Leave time to explore the visitor center to learn about Juan Rodríguez Cabrillo who discovered San Diego Bay in 1542. For years it was believed that Cabrillo was Portuguese, but recent evidence proves that he was born in Spain. A replica of his ship the *San Salvador* was built by volunteers of the Maritime Museum of San Diego and is now one of their exhibits.

Cormorants are commonly seen

Distance:	1.5 miles, out-and-back
Difficulty:	🚶
Elevation gain/loss:	Minimal
Hiking time:	1 hour
Agency:	USFW
Notes:	Hours posted 10 a.m. to 5 p.m.
Trailhead GPS:	N32.63993, W117.11098
Optional map:	USGS 7.5 min National City
Atlas square:	U10
Directions:	(Chula Vista) From I-5 take the E Street exit. Turn right on Gunpowder Point Drive and park. The free shuttle to the Discovery Center leaves from this location every 15 minutes between 10 a.m. and 3 p.m.

Habitat(s):

This short stroll within the San Diego Bay National Wildlife Refuge can be done at different times of the day to see the difference that both a high tide and low tide can have on marsh lands. The Living Coast Discovery Center, formerly known as the Chula Vista Nature Center, is located in the middle of this 326-acre refuge, which is also the headquarters for the San Diego Bay National Wildlife Refuge. Interpretive information in the center explains the relationship between the bay, the marsh, and upland habitats. The marsh is the transition between bay and upland areas that are not affected by tidal changes.

The center was opened in 1987, and two years later the US Fish and Wildlife Service established a refuge here to conserve and restore habitats and species in the salt marsh at Gunpowder Point. The name of the point derives from the fact that during World War I, the Hercules Powder Company processed giant kelp (*Macrocystis pyrifera*) that grows offshore

to produce potash, an ingredient of black gunpowder, and acetone, a component of cordite, a smokeless powder. In 1916 the Chula Vista plant was the largest kelp-processing plant along the southern California coast with 1500 employees. The plant was abandoned after World War I. The concrete foundation of the plant is still visible.

The refuge is a great place for birders and for an introduction to both shore birds and birds of prey for novices. The center has interpretive information about birds that explains the function of the various types of bills, toes, and leg length that determine how a bird feeds and rests. Birds in the sandpiper family (western sandpiper, long-billed curlew, and marbled godwit) have thin bills, straight or curved, that are often longer than their heads. Their long legs allow them to wade in water and walk along mudflats looking for food. Plovers have bills shorter than their heads and can be identified by their characteristic sprints and abrupt

Tidal marsh and coast bladderpod

stops. Diving birds that are clumsy on land include the lesser scaup, surf scoter, bufflehead, brown pelican, cormorants, ruddy duck, and the western grebe.

The idea of niche space is well illustrated by our shorebirds. For instance there are many birds that dig into the sand for their food items. Yet, having slightly different beak shapes and lengths along with preferences to forage at certain water depths, they are able to specialize on a certain size or species of prey. This segregation allows these bird species to use the shore habitat differently and to co-exist. There are many other resources other than food at play in determining niche space. Time is one such example—certain birds use the marsh's resources year-round, while others are only seasonal visitors.

The center has both a light-footed Ridgway's rail aviary and a raptor aviary. Permanence of the display is dependent on budgetary issues. Species that may be on display in the raptor aviary include golden eagle, bald eagle, American kestrel, long-eared owl, turkey vulture, and various falcons.

The trail begins across from the visitor center and heads west toward the bay. The trail spur to the right leads to a viewpoint where the remnants of the old gunpowder works may be seen. The spur trails to the left lead to other bay overviews, a pond, and mudflats. Plants seen on this walk include mule-fat, coast bladderpod, non-native tree tobacco, California buckwheat, lemonadeberry, black sage, white sage, coastal sagebrush, alkali heath, coast monkey flower, pickleweed, California cord grass, eucalyptus, coast cholla, and toyon.

Giant kelp

Distance:	1.4 miles, loop
Difficulty:	🚶
Elevation gain/loss:	Minimal
Hiking time:	1 hour
Agency:	USFW
Trail use:	Bicycles, dogs
Trailhead GPS:	N32.59444, W117.09083
Optional map:	USGS 7.5 min *Imperial Beach*
Atlas square:	V10
Directions:	(Chula Vista) From I-5 go west on Main Street and park at the Swiss Park staging area.

Habitat(s):

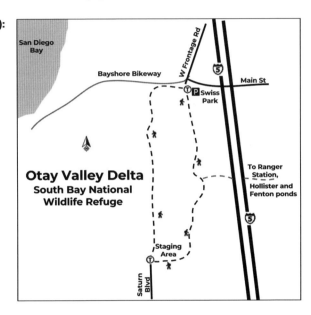

The Otay Delta Habitat Restoration Project is part of a much larger management plan to restore ecosystems and provide necessary habitat corridors for wildlife between San Diego Bay and Otay Mountain along the Otay River watershed. This former delta was fallow for over 30 years until non-native plants were removed and over 18,000 native trees, shrubs, and grasses were planted in 2012 on over 55 acres. The land is now part of the US Fish and Wildlife Service's San Diego National Wildlife Refuge. The Otay River watershed covers 160 square miles in San Diego County.

A watershed is an area of land whose rainfall all drains into a common body of water such as a river, bay, ocean, or underground aquifer. Watersheds range in size, population densities and area urbanized, percentages of land privately or publicly owned, and in how the area is used. Dif-ferent divisions of the area may be used for agriculture, residential, or open space. The unique characteristics of each watershed influence what minerals, soil, and pollutants travel through the watershed before it ultimately flows into the ocean. As such, stewardship to keep our watersheds clean is important. With such close proximity to the ocean in San Diego County, there is little chance for surface water to filter down through the soil and vegetation to be cleaned, accentuating the stewardship importance for our county. Limited water resources originating within the county also underscore the importance of protecting water quality. San Diego County has 11 watersheds that feed into the Pacific Ocean. East of the ridge in the Laguna Mountains there are five watersheds where water flows east to the Salton Sea and then into the Gulf of California. Watersheds ignore political

California buckwheat and mule-fat

borders, however, and there is overlap between our county's watersheds and those in neighboring counties of Orange, Riverside, and Imperial, along with Mexico, which contains over two-thirds of the Tijuana watershed.

Hikers, cyclists, dog walkers, and exercisers use the patchwork of trails throughout the refuge. A short stroll here is a good way to see restored riparian habitat along the lower Otay River. It also includes hiking a portion of the Otay Valley Regional Park on the south side of the river. From the staging area, walk south down a well-maintained trail of decomposed granite. Native plants such as California buckwheat, mule-fat, San Diego sunflowers and California roses abound adjacent to the fenced trail. Wild-cucumber vine intertwine through the shrubs and trees.

Trail view

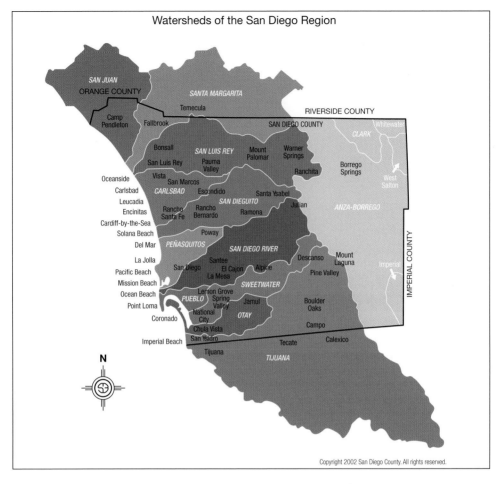

Watersheds of the San Diego Region

Look to the right and see a wide swathe of blue elderberry trees that have been planted in this area. Listen for bees that are busy collecting nectar and pollinating the abundant flowers of the numerous buckwheat and other plants.

There are more than 650 species of native bees (**superfamily Apoidea**) in San Diego County. Native bees are important pollinators for many native plants and some crops too, like squash and tomatoes. Most are solitary and do not live in hives, and many are specialists that can only get their food from certain host plants. Pollen is gathered to mix with nectar for baby food loaves. Only the adults feed on pure nectar. When the males wander too far in their work, they sometimes have to sleep out at night (or inside a flower, such as western jimson weed). Only female bees can sting.

After about half a mile, a junction is reached. If you make a left turn, you'll head towards Hollister and Fenton ponds and come to the Beyer Boulevard Ranger Station for the Otay Valley Regional Park. However, make a right turn and head towards the Saturn Boulevard staging area, and then north on a single lane paved road. The restored habitat of native plants continues along this path, although there is evidence of non-natives with mustard, hottentot-fig, and plumbago on the west side of the trail. Also seen in this area are salt heliotrope, spreading along the ground, and the prominent western jimson weed with its large white flowers. Swallows and western bluebirds are seen amongst the numerous local and migratory birds in this area. The trail turns back east near the Bayshore Bikeway back to the starting point.

Distance:	Variable, 4.5 miles total, out-and-back
Difficulty:	🏃 or 🏃🏃, depending on length
Elevation gain/loss:	Minimal
Hiking time:	1 to 3 hours
Agency:	CSP-SDCD
Trailhead GPS:	N32.57485, W117.12593
Optional map:	USGS 7.5 min *Imperial Beach*
Atlas square:	V10
Directions:	(Imperial Beach) From I-5 go west on Coronado Avenue (not the Coronado Bridge) and continue onto Imperial Avenue. After 2.4 miles, turn left on 4th Street. Follow 4th Street to Caspian Way and turn into the visitor center parking lot on left.

Habitat(s):

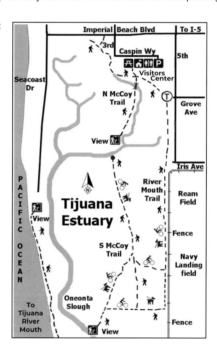

The Tijuana Estuary is one of the few estuaries in southern California that has natural, daily tidal flushing that enables this wetland to be among the most biologically productive systems. The trails described are in the north section of the Tijuana River National Estuarine Research Reserve, one of 35 designated Wetlands of International Importance. The trails are well marked and easy to follow. Trails are laid out to protect the multiple habitats that include salt marsh, coastal sage scrub, and riparian. These differ in amount of water, salt content, and soil types. Inches of elevation can also add to the habitat differences where indicator species differ from one section to another. Margins of habitats are active as different food sources

attract multiple birds and insects. Knowing bird feeding preferences, nesting sites, and behavior improves enjoyment of this wetland. Look for the reddish egret (*Egretta rufescens*), which is a medium-sized heron that is dark gray with a reddish neck and slate-gray long legs. It has a pink bill with black at the tip. It is uncommon but entertaining, dancing and darting erratically as it feeds along shallow coastal water.

The visitor center has a stand with free maps and pamphlets plus current information on any scheduled walks or updates in the area. Just south of the center is a native plant garden that includes salt heliotrope, California buckwheat, coastal sagebrush, and lemonadeberry. The path southwest of the center has a view of

Pacific pickleweed

a wooden trestle; this is all that remains of the structure built after WWII to support a sewer outfall pipe to the mouth of the river when the military used the area for coastal defense.

Walk south on the North McCoy Trail named after Dr. Mike McCoy, who along with biologists Joy Zedler and Paul Jorgensen, worked to build support to preserve the estuary in 1971. Pass over the bridge and notice two plants—Pacific pickleweed (*Salicornia pacifica*) and alkali-heath (*Frankenia salina*)—that tolerate the high salt content of the marsh, referred to as halophytes. The pickleweed has segmented fleshy stems that store the salt until concentrated and then break off when full. The flowers are very small and yellow with the leaves reduced to scales. The salty stem is known as a sea bean or sea asparagus and is valued for its culinary flavor. It is really not a bean but a succulent and is served in some restau-

rants. The alkali-heath shrub has a woody base with leaves that tend to roll under and tiny pink flowers. It grows on alkali flats or in salt marshes and excretes salt. Watch for egrets, curlews, and herons feeding along the inlets. Backtrack over the bridge, turning east then south along houses and an active naval aviation training facility. Continue on the River Mouth Trail to the end, then west at the water to view shorebirds.

Return to your car then drive to Imperial Beach Boulevard, turning right to Seacoast Drive until the end and park. Along the east side of the street, there are small patches of salt marsh bird's beak (*Chloropyron maritimum*), an endangered annual hemiparasite that is found in very few locations in California and

Salt marsh bird's beak

northern Baja California, Mexico. As a hemiparasite, this member of the broomrape family can photosynthesize but takes water and dissolved nutrients from a host, such as pickleweed or fleshy jaumea, through special root attachments called haustoria. Flowers are white to cream and pollinated by various bees. Look for plants with gray-green leaves often tinged purple that are salt encrusted.

Continue down the road to the viewing deck, then cross to the Pacific Ocean shore, and turn south to the Tijuana River mouth to watch the birds. It was here that from 1930 through the 1950s Alan Dempsey Holder pioneered California big-wave surfing over 1 mile from the shore. A 9- to10-foot surfboard was used at that time. Surfing was discontinued when pollution and flooding affected the area. Backtrack to return to your vehicle.

Alkali-heath

Distance:	22.5 miles of multi-use non-motorized trails available
Difficulty:	🚶 or 🚶🚶, depending on length
Elevation gain/loss:	Minimal
Hiking time:	1 to 3 hours, depending on length
Agency:	San Diego County
Trail use:	Bicycles, horses
Notes:	Hours posted dawn to dusk
Trailhead GPS:	N32.55427, W117.06300
Optional map:	USGS 7.5 min *Imperial Beach*
Atlas square:	W11
Directions:	(Imperial Beach) From I-5 go south on Dairy Mart Road. Drive 0.2 mile to parking lot on right with a Parks and Recreation, County of San Diego, Tijuana River Valley Regional Park sign.

Habitat(s):

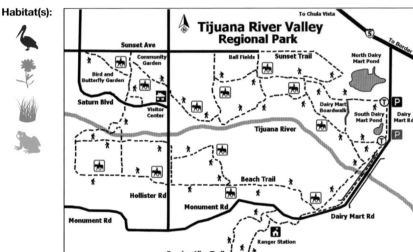

The Tijuana River Valley Regional Park provides a wide variety of year-round recreational opportunities within its 1800 acres that include a bird and butterfly garden. When visiting the garden, note that butterflies have knobbed antennae and close their wings above their backs to rest. Moths have antennae that are never knobbed and hold their wings outstretched at rest. Other recreational opportunities here include community gardens, multi-use open space turf area, and five ball fields.

This is also a good birding area. The park is part of the Pacific Flyway and is bisected by the west-flowing Tijuana River. The broad, flat flood plain provides an ideal environment to study the diverse vegetation communities that attract transient bird populations as well as amphibians and reptiles—lizards, skinks, snakes, whiptails, frogs, and toads. More than 340 bird species have been recorded in this area—that is two-thirds of all bird species recorded in the entire county!

One of the birds that may be seen is the black-crowned night heron (***Nycticorax nycticorax***). It is a light gray bird with a clearly defined black back and head with a white head plume. It is the most widespread heron in the world. Compared to other local herons, it is stocky with a thick neck and short legs, and it hunts at dusk and night. It is very social, both breeding and nesting in colonies.

The meandering trail system in this regional park provides a lush environment ideal for exploring. A good place to start is the Nature Observation Area around Dairy Mart Pond. Park at the north trailhead off Dairy Mart Road where there is an informational kiosk and trails to explore. You will see mixed

Donna Zoll

The pond

Wendy Esterly

use trail markers indicating the developed trails that can be explored. There are benches along the trails as well as bird blinds perfect for watching the birds around North Dairy Mart Pond. A wooden boardwalk borders a non-native grassland and an area of coastal sage scrub. Be on the lookout for snakes and other reptiles.

The flat river floor of this park consists of fill, alluvium, recent and old alluvial fan deposits, and terrace deposits. The area is prone to seasonal flooding. The ponds and surrounding riparian wetlands provide habitat for songbirds, rails, waterfowl, and shorebirds. The Mexican black-throated magpie-jay (*Calocitta colliei*), identified by its sharp contrasting colors of blue on top and white on the bottom, a long tail, and a black topknot, may be seen near the Bird and Butterfly Garden. This is an exotic bird in San Diego County, having escaped from captivity but nesting in the Tijuana River valley since at least 1997. This species is endemic to western mainland Mexico from Sonora to Jalisco and does not occur naturally in Baja California.

Native Americans first occupied this area some 9000 years ago. The Kumeyaay territory straddled both sides of today's international border. Spain and later Mexico claimed the area. When the Mexican-American War (1846-1848) ended, lines were drawn for the border between the two countries. Today the ancestral lands of the Kumeyaay are split along a political border with half of the Indian nation in the US and the other half in Mexico. In Baja California, the Kumeyaay are known as Kumiai.

Black-crowned night heron

Distance:	1.5 miles, out-and-back
Difficulty:	🚶
Elevation gain/loss:	Up to 200 feet
Hiking time:	1 hour
Agency:	CSP-SDCD
Trail use:	Bicycles, dogs only at Monument Mesa picnic area, horses
Notes:	Fee required at gate
Trailhead GPS:	N32.54358, W117.11501
Optional map:	USGS 7.5 min *Imperial Beach*
Atlas square:	W10
Directions:	(Imperial Beach) From I-5 go south on Dairy Mart Road for 1.2 miles. Continue onto Monument Road for 2.8 miles to the Border Field State Park entrance gate. After entering the park, drive past the entrance kiosk and follow the paved road as it turns south for 0.5 mile and then west 0.4 mile. The road leads to the top of Monument Mesa, where parking is available at Friendship Park. Note that the entrance gate is frequently closed due to flooding, but the park remains open. There is an alternate lot near the south side of the entrance gate. Proceed to the trailhead on foot or take the Beach Trail that intersects with the entrance road.

Habitat(s):

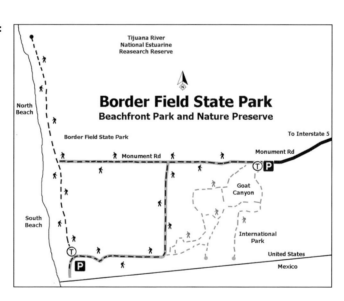

Border Field State Park is where delegations from the US and Mexico began the survey of the border in 1850 after the Treaty of Guadalupe Hidalgo was concluded on February 2, 1848, officially ending the Mexican-American War. From 1929 until the early 1960s, the park was home to a military base that included a radar installation, shore battery, auxiliary landing field, and fire control station. The flat area to the south was the site of an aerial gunnery target range, and a metal track was constructed to provide aircraft pilots with moving targets.

The Tijuana River watershed originates in the Laguna Mountains at the confluence of Cottonwood Creek and Tecate Creek. It then flows into Mexico where it is joined by the third major tributary, Rio Las Palmas. At this juncture the Tijuana River turns north and re-enters the US near San Ysidro. Over time, the river created a 3-mile wide valley. An ancient bay existed in the valley over 7000 years ago. The sea level then was much lower and the shoreline was located 0.75 mile offshore. Sea levels slowly rose, and sediments were carried

Donna Zoll

Road closed when flooded

downstream by the river and deposited near its mouth. These sediments gradually blocked the river mouth and restricted tidal flushing and, over time, created the estuary that is present today.

The hike along the beach and nearby dunes will surprise visitors with its beautiful views and diversity of animal and plant life. From the southwest corner of the continental United States, the trail system consists of the South Beach, North Beach, and Beach trails. The South Beach and North Beach trails follow the tide line along the coast and lead to the mouth

Alan King

Juvenile western snowy plover

of the Tijuana River, while the Beach Trail connects the beach to the park entrance road near the kiosk.

The South Beach trailhead is located on the beach at the west end of the road and turn-around below the north face of Monument Mesa, 200 yards north of the international border. It leads northward along the shoreline. The surface consists of soft beach sands. During spring and summer, hikers and others are restricted to walking along the wet portion of the sands to prevent disturbance of the least terns (**Sterna antillarum**) and western snowy plovers (**Charadrius nivosus**) nesting in the adjacent dunes. The terns hunt small fish in the estuary and ocean, while the plovers forage for small invertebrates on the sand. Many other waterbirds are visible as the trail passes along the beach, including the brown pelican, willet, and western gull. Seals, sea lions, dolphins, and whales can occasionally be spotted offshore.

The western gull (**Larus occidentalis**), like all gulls commonly called a seagull, is the only species of gull nesting in San Diego. There is a large colony on the Coronado Islands off the coast of Tijuana. The gulls commute regularly between the offshore colony and mainland. Brown pelicans also have a large colony on

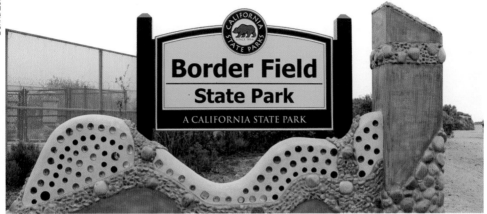

Entrance sign

the same islands. As a result of poisoning by DDT, the populations of some large birds at the top of the food chain, such as the brown pelican, osprey, and peregrine falcon, declined from the 1940s until the 1970s, when DDT was banned.

At the intersection of South and North Beach trails, approximately 0.6 mile north of the border, is the Beach Trail that serves as an access road for research sites in the area and leads to the gate entrance. It is near an abandoned concrete outfall remnant on the beach with the intersection marked with a wood and metal signpost. The Beach Trail is on a packed earth surface that leads east through the dune area, and crosses a series of salt flats. Here the vegetation includes blue elderberry, coast bladderpod, crystalline ice plant, Pacific pickleweed, grasses, and Shaw's agave. Look for Perez's marsh-rosemary (*Limonium perezii*) growing in salt marshes, coastal sage scrub upland habitats, and along sandy beach areas. It is one of the most widespread *Limoniums* in San Diego County and is native to the Canary Islands. This naturalized perennial is sometimes called a sea-lavender and is commonly used as a seaside garden plant.

The North Beach Trail continues along the shoreline for another 0.6 mile until it reaches the mouth of the Tijuana River. Bring binoculars to enjoy the abundance of bird life that includes migratory species that the estuary supports in coastal wetland and riparian habitats on this Pacific Flyway that extends from Alaska to the southern end of South America.

Western gull

Perez's marsh-rosemary or sea-lavender

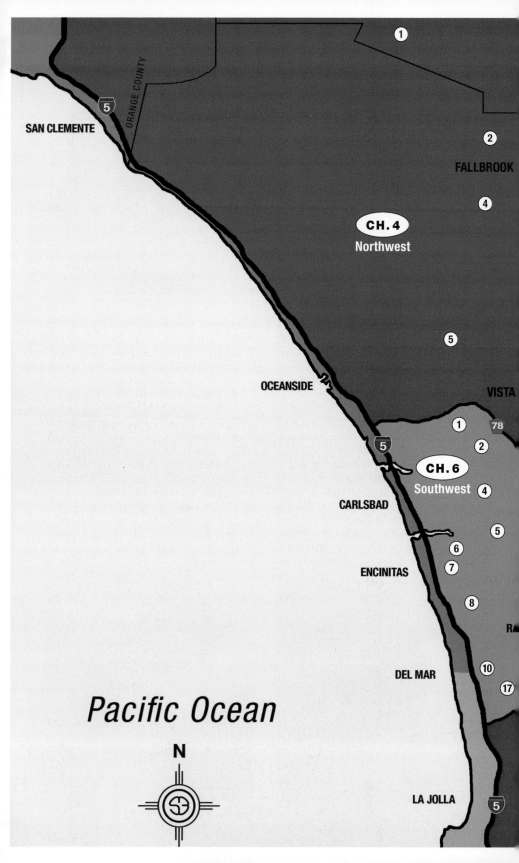

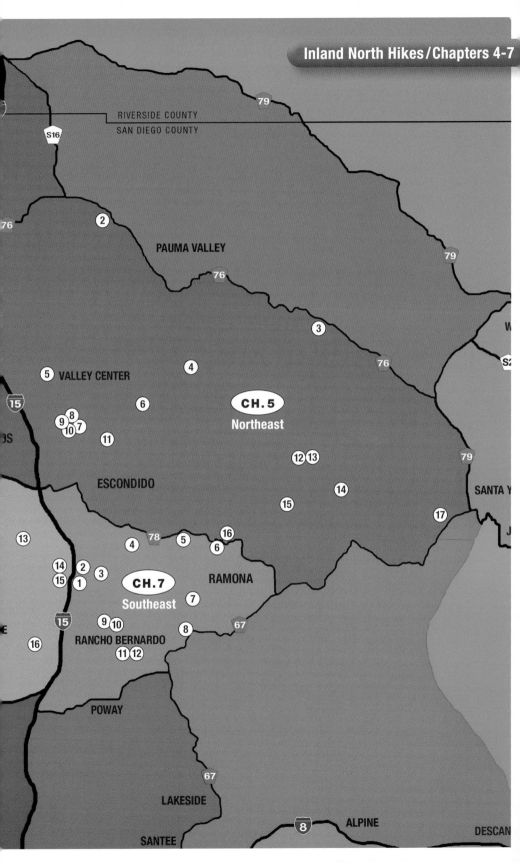

RIVERSIDE COUNTY
SAN DIEGO COUNTY

PAUMA VALLEY

VALLEY CENTER

CH. 5
Northeast

ESCONDIDO

SANTA Y

CH. 7
Southeast

RAMONA

RANCHO BERNARDO

POWAY

LAKESIDE

ALPINE

DESCAN

SANTE

SANTEE

Distance:	4.5 miles, loop
Difficulty:	🚶🚶🚶
Elevation gain/loss:	Up to 300 feet
Hiking time:	3 hours
Agency:	CDFW, Metropolitan Water District, Nature Conservancy, RCP, USFW
Notes:	Hours posted sunrise to sunset; day-use fee
Trailhead GPS:	N33.50881, W117.29393
Optional map:	USGS 7.5-min *Wildomar*
Atlas square:	N/A (Riverside County)
Directions:	(Murrieta) From I-15 go west on Clinton Keith Road for 5.2 miles. You will pass the visitor center at 4 miles. Continue onto Tenaja Road for 1.7 miles, then continue onto Via Volcano for 0.9 mile. Parking lot on left.

Habitat(s):

This hike explores an area just north of San Diego County in Riverside County that looks like California before subdivisions and freeways were built during and after World War II. The Santa Rosa Plateau Ecological Reserve is a rare gem waiting to be discovered. Inhabited for up to 8000 years by the earliest Indian bands followed by the ancestors of the Luiseño Indians, the reserve traces its recent history to Rancho Santa Rosa, which was granted to Juan Moreno in 1846. The preserve has long been recognized for its significant resources, which include two historic adobes, rare Engelmann oak woodlands, volcanic soils with vernal pools, running creeks, over 200 bird species, dozens of mammal species, and more than 50 rare, threatened, or endangered plant species.

A recommended hike is the Vernal Pool Trail to the adobes. Vernal pools form in shallow depressions after rains. They retain water for only a few months and dry out completely in the summer. A number of rare plants and animals have evolved mechanisms enabling them to survive and even depend on these special environmental conditions. Early spring, especially early to late March, is the best time to visit. The trail includes a boardwalk over a huge vernal pool where, if there has been a good rainfall season, and with some luck, you can search for fairy shrimp and tadpoles typically seen in early spring. Fairy shrimp (*Branchinecta* spp.) are small crustaceans up to 1.5 inches in size that rapidly complete their life cycle when water fills vernal pools. They swim upside down or ventral side up. After breeding, eggs settle to the bottom of the pool, to hatch out the next time the pool is filled. Tadpoles will eat fairy shrimp. Look for the two-striped garter-snake (*Thamnophis hammondii*) that may be sunning itself on the boardwalk, or it might be hunting, in turn, for the tadpoles who just consumed the fairy shrimp.

These aquatic striped snakes can reach up to 3 feet in length and are not dangerous to

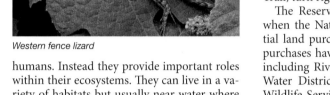

Pauline Jimenez

Western fence lizard

humans. Instead they provide important roles within their ecosystems. They can live in a variety of habitats but usually near water where they can find amphibians that are a large part of their diet, as well as earthworms, tadpoles, lizards, small fish, and fish eggs. They, in turn, are hunted by hawks, raccoons, crows, foxes, and squirrels. Females bear their young fully-formed after a two-three month gestation period. The young are on their own immediately after birth. A female may birth anywhere from 3-20 young snakes in a litter. Frogs and crayfish will eat the young. Although garter-snakes are among the most common snakes in North America, the two-striped gartersnake is limited in its territory and is a species of concern. There are two theories as to the origin of the common name for gartersnakes. One is that garter is a corruption of garden and may answer the question why they are also called garden snakes. The other theory is that the long stripes down their body resemble garters that men once wore to hold up their socks.

From the trailhead, follow the trail to the vernal pool boardwalk, then continue on the Vernal Pool Trail 1.7 miles to Ranch Road, and turn right, approximately 0.5 mile to the adobes. The trail to the adobes is surrounded by green meadows that transform to a buttery tan when they dry out in early summer. It passes beneath occasional massive blue-gray Engelmann oaks. The chocolate lily (*Fritillaria biflora*), which really is chocolate-colored and resembles a mission bell, is one of the attractions on this hike. Fat western fence lizards (*Sceloporus occidentalis*), or blue bellies as they are sometimes called because of the blue coloration on the ventral sides of their abdomens, often skitter along the trail or across the volcanic boulders protruding from the

meadow. The male western fence lizard is often seen sitting on a rock sunning itself and, as needed, performing territorial pushups.

From the adobes, follow Ranch House Road west to the Trans Preserve Trail and turn left or south. The trail climbs moderately to an oak forest, offering nice views of the valley and distant ridges. When you reach the Vernal Pool Trail, turn right to return to your vehicle.

The Reserve began to take shape in 1984 when the Nature Conservancy made the initial land purchase. Over the years, additional purchases have been made by various entities including Riverside County, the Metropolitan Water District, and the California Fish and Wildlife Service. It acts as a mitigation bank, with developers purchasing credits in the land bank to offset housing or other development of the land. Santa Rosa Plateaus Ecological Reserve's primary purpose is to protect the rare habitat, with a secondary purpose of recreation.

One of the rare and endangered plants found here is the Santa Rosa Basalt brodiaea (*Brodiaea santarosae*). Its discovery in 2007 was published in *Madroño*, the quarterly scientific journal of the California Botanical Society. It is endemic to this location in areas that were covered by the Santa Rosa Basalt, 8-11 million years ago before the mountains of southern California were uplifted. Only four known populations have been recorded. The small herb has what appears to be six large purplish petals, but they are actually tepals, which are the sepals and petals of the perianth that can't be easily divided into two kinds. Its large flowers and distinctive variable staminodes— sterile stamens that can't produce pollen— distinguish this from some other species found in southern California.

Walter Konopka

Two-striped garter snake

Distance:	3.2 or 5.4 miles, out-and-back
Difficulty:	🚶🚶 or 🚶🚶🚶
Elevation gain/loss:	Up to 500 feet
Hiking time:	2 or 3 hours
Agency:	FTC
Trail use:	Portions open to horses
Notes:	Hours posted 8 a.m. to sunset
Trailhead GPS:	N33.41326, W117.24128
Optional map:	USGS 7.5-min *Temecula; Fallbrook*
Atlas square:	C8
Directions:	(Fallbrook) From I-15 go west on Mission Road and continue onto East Mission Road for 4.9 miles. Turn right on North Pico Avenue, which becomes De Luz Road. Go 1.2 miles. Turn right on Sandia Creek Drive. Go 1.1 miles. Parking lot is on the right.

Habitat(s):

Santa Margarita River Trails (SMRT) is managed by the newly merged Live Oak Park Coalition and the Fallbrook Trails Council through an agreement with the Fallbrook Public Utility District. The utility district owns the property; the Fallbrook Trails Council maintains and repairs the trails and keeps them open for hikers, mountain bikers, and equestrians. The Santa Margarita River is one of the last free-flowing rivers in San Diego County. The river peacefully flows under a canopy of tall trees between banks lined with dense riparian growth. The river passes through three distinct managing agencies.

The 1400-acre SMRT property straddles the Santa Margarita River between San Diego County's Santa Margarita Preserve, north of Fallbrook, and San Diego State University's Santa Margarita Ecological Reserve at the Riverside County line. Both the preserve and SMRT are open to the public, while the univer-

sity's field station is closed to the public. SMRT has 14 miles of trails that loop and cross the river within the property. Wildlife, including deer and other large mammals, depend on this river corridor. The area is noted for raptors. The 2002 Gavilan Fire burned part of the area. The Fallbrook Trails Council worked to restore public access to the area after the fire and continues to make improvements on the property for trail users.

Begin hiking east from the parking area. The trail surface initially is soft sand, making the going easy for hikers but difficult for mountain bikers. Horses aren't permitted on this part of the trail, but you will encounter them later, further up the trail. Remember, horses have the right of way. Make way for any horse on the trail. The trail heads toward and under an array of tall trees, including coast live oaks, Goodding's black willows, western sycamores, white alders, western cottonwoods, and even a few

Alan King

Skunkbrush

dogwoods. The understory includes wild rose, western poison-oak, and skunkbrush, among many other plants.

Western poison-oak (***Toxicodendron diversilobum***) is abundant and highly variable. In some cases it is vine-like, climbing up the oaks and other trees. In other cases it is bush-like. Skunkbrush (***Rhus aromatica***), which is also called basket bush or three-leaf sumac, is also found here and is similar in appearance to western poison-oak with leaves of three. The difference is that poison-oak's middle leaf is free with a stem extending out. Steer your leashed dog away from poison-oak. If the contact dermatitis-causing chemical gets on its fur, petting your pet will be the same as touching poison-oak.

At about 0.25 mile, the trail crosses a steep hillside that is about 20 feet above the river. For the next 100 yards, it is necessary to climb over or around large rocks, the only somewhat difficult part of the trail. Afterwards, the trail is an easy stroll through the forest, though it remains about 20 feet above the river to avoid the dense growth of willows, sedges, and cat-tails lining the riverbank.

A number of short non-official use-trails go down to sandy river beaches and pools of clear water. Some other trails join the main trail from roads that end at streets, homes, or ranches on the hills above. Stay on the main trail, which has frequent numbered signs.

At about 1.6 miles, there will be a signed fork in the road directing hikers to go right, up the hill, and equestrians to continue to a river crossing via the trail on the left. This is a good place for hikers to turn around and go back the way they came, completing a 3.2-mile out-and-back hike. If you cross the river with the horses, be prepared to get wet, possibly up to your waist.

The trail to the right goes up hill out of the canyon, to the named 500-Foot Trail. Turn left here. It is part of the SMRT system, but here the hiking is through coastal sage scrub. The trail works its way back to the river in about 0.5 mile. Continue up the river to Rainbow Creek, about 2.7 miles from the trailhead. Here there is a delightful, open oak forest, a good place to rest a while in the shade before turning around and going back to the trailhead ending a 5.4-mile out-and-back hike.

Note that the swimming hole accessed from the parking area and across Sandia Creek Drive is not open to the public. The only trail from the parking area that is permitted is the one closest to Sandia Creek Drive, which connects the trail system to the county preserve staging area to the south. This staging area has a larger parking area that may be used if no parking is found at the SMRT trailhead. However, starting here will add an additional 2.4 miles to the trip and will call for crossing the river four times, twice going to, and twice returning from the trailhead.

Diana Lindsay

Western poison oak

Distance:	1 mile, loop
Difficulty:	🏃
Elevation gain/loss:	Up to 200 feet
Hiking time:	1 hour
Agency:	San Diego County
Trail use:	Dogs
Notes:	Hours posted 9:30 a.m. to 30 minutes before sunset
Trailhead GPS:	N33.36314, W117.20354
Optional map:	USGS 7.5-min *Bonsall*
Atlas square:	D8
Directions:	(Fallbrook) From I-15 go west on Mission Road. Turn left on Old Highway 395. Go 1 mile. Turn right on Reche Road. Go 2.2 miles. Turn right on Gird Road and go to the parking lot.

Habitat(s):

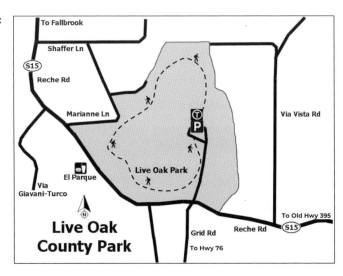

Live Oak County Park is one of the area's oldest parks and is where Fallbrook is said to have begun. It is a sprawling 27-acre tract in the middle of an old growth grove of coast live oaks (*Quercus agrifolia* var. *agrifolia*), some of which are over 100 years old. One oak has a much-branched trunk and reaches a height of over 30 feet. The leaves are dark green, oval, and spiny-toothed.

The park's paths, picnic tables, and jungle gyms nestle under the canopy of the oak grove. The north end of the park boasts well-groomed soccer fields and volleyball courts. The park also has a native garden with examples of plants found throughout the county and a small hiking trail. The real gem here is the multiple morteros or grinding rocks. This area was home to the Luiseño people who have inhabited the northwest corner of the county for several thousand years. It is easy to imag-

ine young children gathering acorns for the women to process into acorn meal as they worked while sitting under the oak canopy.

Acorns were ground in morteros and then the acorn meal was leached with water to remove tannins before it could be consumed. Acorns were a major staple because they could be stored all year in large granary baskets and used as needed. Ground acorn meal was mixed with water in cooking baskets to make a mush. The mush was cooked in the baskets by adding heated stones that were mixed in the mush. As stones cooled, they were removed and new hot stones were added until the contents were cooked. Sometimes berries or seeds were added or even fresh meat. Indians learned to cook in baskets because basketry was invented before pottery. When Indians learned to make pottery, they used the pots for storage and to hold water. Pottery was not used for cooking.

Picnic area under coast live oaks

The serenity of this area is occasionally broken by either the tapping sound or the raucous "wacka-wacka" call of a family of resident acorn woodpeckers (*Melanerpes formicivorus*) that are gathering acorns and storing them in their granary tree, in this case, oak silos. They custom-fit each acorn into a hole they make for storage, making sure the acorn fits tightly so that squirrels and chipmunks have difficulty stealing it. Acorn woodpeckers are unique in communally defending their centralized food store that has been added to over generations with the result of hundreds or even thousands of holes drilled and stuffed with acorns. Usually one individual in the group will stand watch, guarding against potential thieves who might steal from the stashed hoard. Acorn woodpeckers are also unusual in their breeding habits in that there is a communal effort among several males and females to raise their young in a single nest. Besides eating acorns or pine nuts, the acorn woodpecker also eats insects that it will catch on the fly, fruit, oak catkins, flower nectar, and occasionally grass seeds or lizards. Characteristic of this species is a red cap, a clownish black and white face, a black back, and black surrounding the bill. Females have a black forehead in front of the red cap. They have white wing patches and fly in an undulating pattern.

You may also see ground squirrels skittering amongst the leaves as they search for acorns that the woodpeckers have overlooked. Among other frequent visitors to the grove are the western scrub-jay, California towhee, and the white-crowned sparrow.

Male acorn woodpecker

Distance:	2 miles, loop
Difficulty:	
Elevation gain/loss:	Minimal
Hiking time:	1 hour
Agency:	FLC
Trail use:	Dogs
Trailhead GPS:	N33.35377, W117.24548
Optional map:	USGS 7.5-min *Bonsall*
Atlas square:	D7
Directions:	(Fallbrook) From CA-76 go north on South Mission Road for 4.4 miles. Turn right at the preserve entrance, just past Sterling Bridge, and go to the parking lot.

Habitat(s):

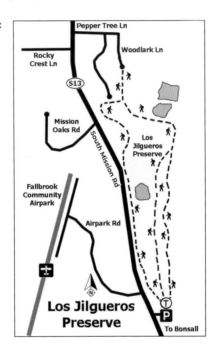

This 46-acre nature preserve was a farm before it was acquired by the Fallbrook Land Conservancy as its first acquisition. For its small size, it has a lot of diversity—from marsh wetlands to open fields, mature forest groves, and ponds. The conservancy has been planting native San Diego County plants and fixing up trails and birdhouses, giving this small retreat a pleasant garden-like quality. The primary trails are accessible and popular with local joggers and birdwatchers.

The preserve is home to a number of mammal and reptile species as well as over 122 bird species. *Los jilgueros* is Spanish for goldfinches. There are several species of this songbird found here. The most likely candidates honor-ed by the Spanish name are the lesser goldfinch (*Spinus psaltria*) and perhaps the American goldfinch (*Spinus tristis*).

More commonly seen is the lesser goldfinch, which happens to be one of the most wide-spread bird species in the county. However, the American goldfinch male is the more brilliant yellow of the two. The American goldfinch is all yellow with a black cap and black wings with some white markings. The lesser goldfinch is bright yellow beneath and also has a black cap and black wings with some white markings, but the back is all black or an olive green. The lesser goldfinch is the smaller of the two.

The American goldfinch is unusual in that it is the only finch that molts its body feathers

Wood bridge

twice each year, in late summer and again in late winter. After the winter molt, the golden feathers appear, indicating warmer months to come. Goldfinches are strict vegetarians feeding on various seeds. Brown-headed cowbirds (***Molothrus ater***) that parasitize a goldfinch nest are in for a rude awakening as the hatched cowbirds rarely survive more than a few days on a vegetarian diet.

Common reptiles found here include the western fence lizard, the southern alligator lizard, and the gophersnake. Common mammals include the bobcat, northern raccoon, Virginia opossum, coyote, California ground squirrel, and the long-tailed weasel.

From the south parking area, the trail heads west following a boardwalk into a wetland area where there are cattails and yerba mansa. The nature trail parallels the highway through a wooded glen before crossing back over the creek, where there is an old weir, an obstruction constructed to alter the flow of water.

Look for mule-fat or seep-willow (***Baccharis salicifolia***) near the water. It is a common indicator of riparian habitat because it forms thickets at seeps, drainages, and wet places. In the past when people were out on a journey and saw mule-fat in the distance, they knew they were nearing a reliable water source. It is a widespread shrub in San Diego County and is highly valued as wildlife habitat. The name mule-fat possibly came from the days when gold miners tied their mules to the trees and let them browse on the leaves all day. Another possibility for the name may be from its greasy smell that is reminiscent of the odor of rendered fat from mules, which the miners ate when nothing else was available. Native Americans used it at the first sign of hair loss, making a solution from the leaves to prevent further loss and baldness. The leaves are willow-like (the species name *salicifolia* means willow-leaved) and sticky when crushed, but it is not a willow and is often mistaken for a small willow. It is in the sunflower family, which has flowers in a tight cluster or head that usually resemble a single flower. Mule-fat flowers are nearly always in bloom or have persistent dried flowers at a terminal cluster. It is a dioecious species, meaning that there are separate male and female plants, so each produces only male flowers or female flowers. The flowers attract butterflies, especially queen butterflies that closely resemble their monarch cousins, especially in the caterpillar stage.

Look for arroyo willow (***Salix lasiolepis***), also near the water, to compare it to mule-fat. Arroyo willow is a true willow that is either a

Lesser goldfinch

Jon Lindsay

The weir

large shrub or small tree. The flowers are in yellow catkins (a cylindrical unisexual flower cluster). Hummingbirds use lint from the willow's catkins to line their nests. Willows have a single vein running down the length of the leaf while mule-fat will have two additional veins. The underside of mule-fat leaves are always

Don Fosket

Mule-fat

green. Some willow species have a silver underside. If the underside is silver, it is a willow. The family name for the willow genus is Salicaceae. Before salicylic acid was synthesized in chemical form to make aspirin, Native Americans and settlers would chew on willow bark or willow leaves as a pain reliever—especially for toothaches. They would also use the leaves to make baskets, especially grainery baskets

because the chemicals found in willow tend to ward off insects. Willows frequently grow where cottonwoods and sycamores are found and, like mule-fat, are indicators of riparian areas. Look for galls on willow leaves caused by the willow gall sawfly wasp (*Pontania* sp.). The galls are globular or oval in shape and can be green, yellow, or red in color. They form when the female oviposits (lays eggs) in the leaf tissue.

The north end of the preserve features a native plant garden that will have a splash of color in spring. The trail continues to a small pond before looping back along a dirt road abutting a housing development on one side and an open field on the other.

Alan King

Arroyo willow

Distance:	Variable, 4 miles, loops
Difficulty:	🚶 or 🚶🚶, depending on length
Elevation gain/loss:	Up to 100 feet
Hiking time:	1 or 2 hours
Agency:	San Diego County
Trail use:	Bicycles, dogs, horses
Notes:	Hours posted 9:30 a.m. to sunset; optional routes available; day-use fee
Trailhead GPS:	N33.24714, W117.27304
Optional map:	USGS 7.5-min *San Luis Rey*
Atlas square:	G7
Directions:	(Oceanside) From CA-76 go south on Guajome Lake Road. Turn right on Patiences Place and into the park entrance.

Habitat(s):

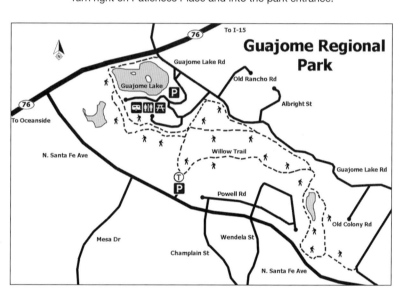

Guajome Regional Park is located less than 9 miles from Oceanside and the Pacific Ocean. This park offers a taste of some of San Diego County's most favorite habitats: woodlands, chaparral, grasslands, and riparian wetlands, including two small ponds that attract migratory birds. In the summer when most inland areas are arid and dry, cooling ocean breezes whisper through the trees. On weekday mornings, it has a secluded feel because most use is concentrated at the playground, picnic area, and adjacent campground.

The name Guajome is taken from the Luiseño word *wakhavumi*, which means frog pond. The Luiseño were the original inhabitants of the area who gathered wild seeds and nuts and hunted small game, reptiles, fish, and amphibians, which they found in local ponds. The Spaniards named this group of Indians after the mission they established in what later became the San Luis Rey Valley. The Franciscan padres used the surrounding lands where the Indians lived for grazing cattle and growing crops. Part of this land became Rancho Guajome. In 1845, 24 years after Mexico gained independence from Spain, California Governor Pio Pico gave the 2219-acre rancho to two Luiseño brothers, Andrés and José Manuel, who had been neophytes at Mission San Luis Rey. Soon after receiving the grant, the brothers sold the rancho for $550 to a wealthy rancher and merchant named Abel Sterns. Guajome Regional Park was part of the rancho lands. The Rancho Guajome ranch house is southeast of the park on Santa Fe Avenue. It is a National Historic Landmark and is worth a visit.

Pauline Jimenez

Upper pond

Start the hike at the main entrance, or else walk briefly along the sidewalk to another entrance at the night exit gate. The main hiking/biking trail circles 25-acre Guajome Lake and a shady gazebo, and the westernmost trail edges a willow-lined freshwater marsh with beckoning cottonwoods and entrancing cattails. Signs point toward a steeper trail to the upper pond, which offers a small fishing hole.

The park is a fascinating place for birdwatching. Over 150 species visit, and many stay year-round. Cassin's kingbirds often winter here, and there is the possibility of seeing San Diego's top bird predator, the golden eagle. Observed species include grebe, great blue heron, white-faced ibis, turkey vulture, goldfinch, duck, hawk, American kestrel, California quail, owl, gull, hummingbird, flycatcher, vireo, bluebird, wren, sparrow, warbler, northern mockingbird, and western meadowlark.

The park boasts at least 50 native plant species, as well as invasive and/or non-native species. A showy, highly invasive plant is the artichoke thistle (*Cynara cardunculus*), also called cardoon. It is easy to identify because the 5-foot-high plants dominate some park areas with purple flowerheads as big as your hand with spine-tipped leaves. Another highly invasive plant is the saltcedar or tamarisk (*Tamarix ramosissima*), which chokes out native vegetation. It was originally planted for shade and wind-breaks. The branches are airy with delicate pink flowers and small, scale-like leaves, which often have salt crystals on them. Individuals can produce 500,000 tiny seeds per year and cause drastic environmental impacts. Saltcedars lower the water table, which limits native plant and wildlife diversity. It has deep taproots that can intercept water required for other species. It traps alluvial sed-

Pauline Jimenez

Coyote melon

Pauline Jimenez

Yerba mansa

high, largely cone-shaped spike. The white petals at the base of the flower are actually bracts or modified leaves. This plant grows in very wet soils or shallow water and has a distinct musty, spicy scent. This plant had medicinal value to Native Americans, who boiled the leaves in a tea to aid in the cure for sore throat, stomach aches, asthma, and respiratory problems.

At the ponds, watercress, cattail, and bulrush are noticeable and usually mark the edges of important hunting and fishing areas for animals and humans alike. Look and listen for croaking frogs, warily basking lizards, muddy salamanders, and dragonfly acrobats that dart in the sun as they hold their wings flat, away from their bodies.

Staying on designated trails will help you avoid several dangerous plants in the park such as western poison-oak, stinging nettle, castor bean, poison hemlock, and jimson weed. This will also help prevent habitat destruction. Never touch, pick, or eat these plants or any plant that you cannot positively identify.

Duane Trombly

Saltcedar

iments that cause stream channels to narrow and flood more frequently and also increases fire frequency.

In early June when summer is ready to begin, you still can discover sacapellote (*Acourtia microcephala*), still clothed in bristly purple flowers with its large heart-shaped leaves, sticky with resin. There is salt heliotrope and white sage. Look for Pacific pickleweed and yellow coyote melon (*Cucurbita foetidissima*) in full bloom. Native American and Mexican tribes ate the coyote melon seeds, used the gourds for ceremonial rattles, and used other parts in cosmetics, detergents, and insecticides.

At the marsh, look for the curious-looking yerba mansa (*Anemopsis californica*), which is the only species in this genus and the only representative of the lizard's tail family in San Diego County. It has large waxy, gray-green leaves. The botanical name is from two Greek words that mean like an anemone and refers to its anemone-looking inflorescence on a 1-foot

Distance:	3.5 miles, out-and-back
Difficulty:	🚶🚶🚶
Elevation gain/loss:	Up to 1200 feet
Hiking time:	3 hours
Agency:	FLC
Trail use:	Bicycles, dogs
Notes:	Hours posted dawn to dusk
Trailhead GPS:	N33.36593, W117.15908
Optional map:	USGS 7.5-min *Bonsall*
Atlas square:	D9
Directions:	(Fallbrook) From I-15 go east on CA-76 for 0.7 mile. Turn left on Horse Ranch Creek Road. Go 2.2 miles. Parking is on the left just before Stewart Canyon Road. The trailhead is across the road.

Habitat(s):

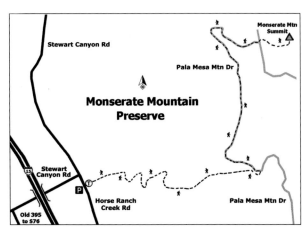

Monserate Mountain Preserve, located in San Diego's North County, is the second largest of 11 preserves within the 2700-acre Fallbrook Land Conservancy. The preserve began with an acquisition of 225 acres in 2000 with more acreage added a few years later to bring the current total to 340. The mountain is within what was once the 3323-acre Monserrate Land Grant claimed by Isidro Alvarado in 1846, which was located on both sides of I-15. Rancho Monserrate (Spanish for jagged mountain) was named for a famous mountain and monastery located in Catalonia, Spain. The name of the mountain today is a variant of the original spelling.

One of the rewards for climbing the steep trail to the 1567-foot mountain summit is the spectacular views of the Pacific Ocean to the west and the Agua Tibia Mountains to the east. Along the way is the additional visual treat of displays of native wildflowers such as Parry's phacelia, chaparral mallow, and blue dicks or school bells (*Dichelostemma capitatum*). When flowering, blue dicks send up a lovely purple-blue flower atop a fleshy stem originating from an underground corm or bulb. These corms were harvested with digging sticks and served as an important starch source for Native Americans. Many vertebrate animals also consume the corms.

The area has grown back nicely since the 2007 Rice Fire, which burned over 9000 acres. Spring is the best time for catching the most native color. There are additional rewards for the other senses as one climbs the mountain. The aroma of white sage and coastal sagebrush will fill the air on a warm afternoon while the songs of birds such as a California thrasher (*Toxostoma redivivum*) can be heard from the chaparral-covered hillsides. This brown bird is found only in California and Baja California, Mexico. It has a characteristically long tail and a long down-curved beak. Look for it under brush or on the ground under trees where it uses its long bill to dig for insects and worms, its main source of food. Males often advertise their territories by singing from the tops of tall shrubs. The song

Blue dicks or school bells

resembles that of the mockingbird, including mimicry, but is less strident, with fewer repetitions of each phrase.

Do not venture off the trail since the western rattlesnake (*Crotalus oreganus*) is known to inhabit the area. This is one of three rattlesnakes in cismontane (this side or western side of the mountains) San Diego County. The western rattlesnake is a heavy-bodied pit viper that is olive to black in color with distinct darker brown blotches on its back completely outlined by a lighter color. The blotches become bars near its tail. It is most likely to be active in the late afternoon and early evening in spring and summer. It becomes inactive when it begins to get colder in the fall. Rattlesnakes are solitary when active in spring and summer, but sometimes hibernate together in dens that can contain up to 100 individuals, especially in colder areas. In San Diego County, denning is not a typical behavior and snakes usually seek retreats individually. They mate shortly after emerging from hibernation, and about three months after mating, 8 to 10 live young emerge from eggs that hatch within the mother's body—they are ovoviviparous. They live on a diet of small mammals, birds, frogs, insects, and lizards, but hunt and eat only about once every two weeks. They kill their prey by their bite. The two fangs in their mouth are like hypodermics, injecting venom into the animal, which is quickly lethal to small animals, with the exception of some California ground squirrels that become immune to their bite. Rattlesnake venom is dangerous to humans and a bitten person should seek immediate medical attention. Humans are not rattlesnake prey, and most bites are done defensively. Many victims of rattlesnake bites were trying to catch the snake or handling it in some way.

The most direct way to conquer Monserate is a 3.5-mile out-and-back hike from the trailhead off of Pankey Road on the west side of the mountain. There is a well-marked trail leading to the summit with 1180 feet of elevation to be gained. The climb starts immediately and leads quickly to a gate that is the entrance into the preserve. At 0.5 mile beyond the gate, there is an intersection with a paved road; go left and the pavement soon gives way to a dirt trail. The sounds of the freeway begin to fade as one continues to ascend over the next mile. Both Red Diamond and the Canonita trails will intersect the main trail. Leave exploring them for another day and continue straight ahead and uphill. Eventually, there will be another intersection with the trail diverging in three directions. On the left is a false summit while the right leads to a water tower. A short climb up the middle path leads to the summit, where there is a large pile of rocks, a USGS marker, and an old metal registry box. After taking a well-earned rest and enjoying the expansive views, retrace your path down the mountain to your vehicle.

In 2010, the Fallbrook Firefighters Association began an annual 9/11 Memorial Hill Climb to honor the memory of the 343 firefighters who were killed when the Twin Towers collapsed. The event, held in September of each year, is a 5K hike up Monserate Mountain, which has an elevation gain similar to the height of the Twin Towers. For information, go to www.fallbrookfirefighters.org.

California thrasher

Distance:	Variable, 4 miles, loops
Difficulty:	🚶
Elevation gain/loss:	Up to 200 feet
Hiking time:	1 to 2 hours, depending on trails taken
Agency:	San Diego County
Notes:	Hours posted Friday through Monday 8 a.m. to 4 p.m.; the gate is locked at 4 p.m.; closed in August due to high temperatures
Trailhead GPS:	N33.34626, W117.02412
Optional map:	USGS 7.5-min *Pala*
Atlas square:	D12
Directions:	(Pala) From CA-76 go west on the Wilderness Gardens Preserve entrance/Bodie Boulevard, 9.7 miles east of I-15 and 25 miles west of CA-79. Parking is at the end of the paved road.

Habitat(s):

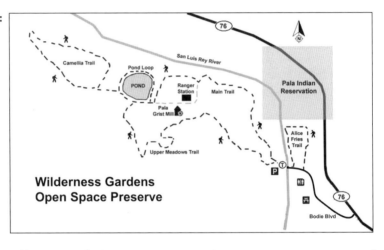

The 737-acre Wilderness Gardens Preserve is the oldest open space preserve managed by the San Diego County Department of Parks and Recreation. It sits astride the San Luis Rey River and includes a wide river valley with variously lush riparian and oak woodland vegetation and chaparral cloaked hills rising to the top of Pala Mountain. It has over 4 miles of hiking trails, most of which follow along the river and wrap around a pond, providing easy hiking from October through June. Picnic tables are available under shady oaks. The preserve is a birdwatcher's paradise.

The preserve has an interesting history. For thousands of years this site was a Native American encampment during the fall acorn collection season. Scattered about are deep-holed mortero grinding sites where the acorns were processed. The ruins of the historic Sickler's Grist Mill, which flourished here in the 1880s, remain and can be toured by appointment.

The last private owner was Manchester Boddy, the developer of Descanso Gardens in La Cañada as well as a Los Angeles politician, publisher, and horticulturist. He purchased the property in 1954 with the intent of creating a public garden along the lines of Descanso, which he had donated to Los Angeles County as a public park. He gave the property the name Wilderness Gardens, and intended to make it a garden to rival Descanso. He dug five ponds, built greenhouses, developed an extensive irrigation system, and planted an estimated 100,000 ornamental plants. However, he died in 1967 before this project was completed, and the property languished for several years thereafter.

Persuaded by Valley Center birder Alice Fries, San Diego County purchased it in the early 1970s and created its first natural lands preserve. It was, of course, far from a natural wilderness. Even though most of the horticultural plants died as Boddy's irrigation system

Cattails

evergreen shrub that is toxic in all of its parts and especially toxic to some animals, such as desert bighorn sheep.

Only one pond has survived, but its banks are choked with a dense growth of cattails (*Typha* **spp.**), making it difficult to see the water from all but a few vantage points. Notice the cattail flower stalk. The female part of the inflorescence is the brown, sausage-like head that becomes fluffy seeds. Above this female part of the plant, and on a continuation of the woody stalk above the fruit, is the male pollen producing flowers. Having both male and female flowers on the plant classifies it botanically as monoecious, as opposed to dioecious or having male and female flowers on separate plants. Most angiosperms have perfect flowers with both sexes. Cattails were highly useful plants for Native Americans. They used the edible starchy roots, ate the young flower shoots, and used the down from the seeds for padding and wound dressing.

Natural eutrophication, an aging process, will turn this small pond into a meadow in the not too distant future as the preserve becomes less a garden and more of a wilderness. Call the preserve office at (760) 742-1631 if there has been either continuous or significant rainfall, as the park may be closed.

decayed, plants like eucalyptus and oleanders (*Nerium oleander*), that are drought hardy, continue to thrive, particularly along the trails by the river. Oleander is an ornamental

Oleander—a hardy toxic exotic detrimental to some animals

Distance:	1 mile, out-and-back
Difficulty:	🏃
Elevation gain/loss:	Up to 200 feet
Hiking time:	1 hour
Agency:	USFS/CNF-PRD
Trail use:	Bicycles
Notes:	Short distance bounded by private property
Trailhead GPS:	N33.25414, W116.79404
Optional map:	USGS 7.5-min *Palomar Observatory*; *Mesa Grande*
Atlas square:	F15
Directions:	(Lake Henshaw) From CA-76 turn west into the US Forest Service San Luis Rey Picnic Area, 28 miles east of I-15 and 6.3 miles west of CA-79. The entrance is about 50 yards beyond the picnic area sign.

Habitat(s):

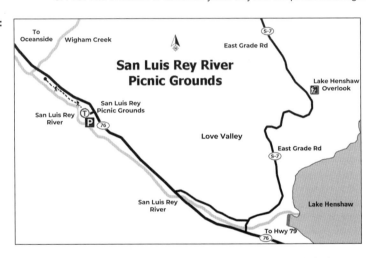

There are relatively few places where the public has access to the San Luis Rey River in its somewhat native wild state. For most of its 55-mile length it has been extensively modified by flood control projects, housing or shopping center developments, and intensive recreational use. Here, along CA-76 near Lake Henshaw, the flow of water is entirely dependent on when the Vista Irrigation District turns on the tap, using the river as a flume to transfer water from Lake Henshaw to its customers downstream. Luckily, the flow at the US Forest picnic area is somewhat steady, allowing visitors to experience this river in something approaching its original wild state. Here dense riparian vegetation and huge moss-covered boulders line the steady flowing river, providing a habitat for an amazing variety of birds and other wildlife. Not only is it a great place for birds, but also it is an excellent place for a family picnic and a hike along the river's banks. If the conditions permit, you could even take a dip in the river's cool waters.

The trail for the upstream hike begins on the left side of the information kiosk and continues for about 0.2 mile, passing through a dense forest of coast live oaks, western sycamores, black willows, western cottonwoods, and white alders (*Alnus rhombifolia*). It is the steady presence of water that makes this lush forest possible, but alders also contribute an important nutrient to this richness because their roots have nodules containing a strain of the bacterium frankia that is able to fix gaseous nitrogen and convert it to a form that plants can utilize.

Since there are also western cottonwoods (*Populus fremontii*) here, this is a good opportunity to compare a cottonwood and an alder. They can be similar in size and leaf shape with both having flowers that bloom in catkin form. Both can be found in riparian areas and sometimes, like here, in the same area. The bark of the cottonwood tends to be lighter in color and has deep furrows at maturity. The alder is usually darker and smoother. In spring, alders have

White alder

small female cones while cottonwoods have sticky buds. Seeds of a cottonwood are in a fluffy white matrix, giving the tree its name, while the alder seeds are in tiny cones that look like pine cones. The leaves of the alder are more egg-shaped and the veins are straight while those of the cottonwood are more triangular and the veins have an upward curve. Cottonwoods will also shimmer in the wind.

In addition to the dense canopy of trees, there is an equally dense understory of arroyo willows, California blackberry, wild rose, snowberry, and western poison-oak. Common snowberry (*Symphoricarpos albus*) is a plant that has small berries like poison-oak, though they are very white in contrast to poison-oak's cream berries. The white color, which lends the plant its common name, is an important food plant for numerous animals but is poisonous to humans.

This understory as well as the forest canopy above supports an amazing variety of birds. These include such common species as Steller's jay, black phoebe, the acorn woodpecker, plus several species of warblers and sparrows. Some birds are found here only in the summer. These are the neotropical migrants that are here in summer and then fly to South or Central America to escape our "brutal" winters. These migrants include the yellow warbler, lazuli bunting, and the black-chinned hummingbird, as well as the southwestern willow flycatcher (*Empidonax traillii extimus*), listed as endangered by the US Fish and Wildlife Service in 1995. The 40 to 50 pairs along this section of the San Luis River are the largest population remaining in California. Parasitism by the brown-headed cowbird and

clearing of riparian woodland led to the decline of this once common bird. The southwestern willow flycatcher often nests in stinging nettle or wild rose bushes along the river, or in the outer branches of oaks or willows hanging over the river. It is a small drab bird with light-colored underparts, olive-green upperparts, and two pale wing bars. It typically catches insects mid-air. It is easily recognized by its song, a burry "witcha-pew," or its call, "brrrritt!"

Toward the end of the upstream trail, there is a swimming hole that could be enjoyed on hot summer days in years that have normal rainfall, but during drought years, it is only a place to get your ankles wet. The advantage of low water is that it is more apt to be quiet here, with fewer people frolicking in the stream. Sitting here in solitude will increase the number of birds seen and make it easier to listen to their songs. However, be aware that poison-oak is prevalent here, and make sure you can identify it before sitting down or laying your clothes on low lying shrubs.

From the swimming hole, retrace your steps to return to the picnic area. However, the hike is not necessarily over. Walk to the opposite end of the road and find the last picnic table on a small rise that is between you and the river. Climb over the rise and down to the river where there is another swimming hole. Cross the river here and find another trail that will take you about 0.2 mile downstream, but don't attempt to cross the stream if the water is high. The forest canopy is more open here and the understory is less dense, but the mossy boulders are a rewarding sight. Note that hiking further downstream enters private property.

Southwestern willow flycatcher

Distance:	4 miles, loop
Difficulty:	𝍏𝍏
Elevation gain/loss:	Up to 500 feet
Hiking time:	2 hours
Agency:	San Diego County
Trail use:	Dogs, horses
Notes:	Hours posted Friday through Monday 8 a.m. to sunset; closed August due to high temperatures
Trailhead GPS:	N33.21678, W116.93395
Optional map:	USGS 7.5-min *Rodriguez Mtn*
Atlas square:	G13
Directions:	(Valley Center) From I-15 go east on El Norte Parkway for 4.6 miles. Turn left on Valley Parkway. Go 0.8 mile. Turn right on Lake Wohlford Road. Go 5.9 miles. Turn right on Paradise Mountain Road. Go 3.3 miles. Turn right on Los Hermanos Ranch Road and then immediately turn left on Kiavo Drive. Go 0.5 mile. Turn left on Santee Lane and drive to the parking lot.

Habitat(s):

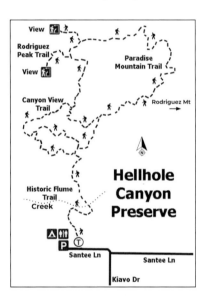

The 1907-acre Hellhole Canyon Preserve east of Valley Center is a valuable resource for wildlife, hikers, and equestrians because of running water, a scenic canyon, and spring wildflowers. It is a place to learn about the early history of water transport while observing ecological changes during fire recovery.

Hell Creek, which ironically flows into Paradise Creek, runs for about 3 miles through the preserve. Despite its name, Hell Creek is a delightful bubbling stream lined with sycamores, coast live oaks, and willows. It is a welcome refuge for thirsty animals, horses, and hikers on hot days. The preserve's terrain is fairly rugged, with a major part of the preserve on the southwest-facing slope of Rodriguez Mountain (3886'). The majority of the preserve is clothed with chaparral and coastal sage scrub, although there are patches of oak woodland in several of the smaller canyons and a continuous oak woodland ribbon and riparian community along Hell Creek.

One of the birds that frequents chaparral and coastal sage scrub is Bewick's wren (*Thryomanes bewickii*), a small gray-brown songbird with a fairly long tail crossed by fine black bars, tipped with white spots, and flicked energetically. It has a long white eyebrow and gray-white underparts. This wren searches through branches and leaves looking for insects. Once

Hell Creek flowing over boulders

restricted to natural habitats, Bewick's wren has become an urban adapter and is now seen in city gardens. Young males develop a repertoire of songs learned in their first year and retain them throughout their lives.

The Escondido Canal or Gamble Flume was built beginning in 1895 to bring water from the San Luis Rey River to Escondido through Hellhole Canyon. It consisted of long sections of a hand-dug ditch connected with a wooded flume. The canal still exists today, but it has been replaced by steel and concrete and now bypasses most of Hellhole Canyon after crossing it via a steel siphon constructed in the early 20th century. Hell Creek Trail follows the route of the old canal to the east for over 1 mile.

From the staging area, the first 0.25 mile of the trail is a gentle self-guided nature trail with signs identifying some of the major chaparral plants. The next half-mile leading down to Hell Creek has some steep places where trekking poles would be useful. The trail along the creek is nearly flat as it follows the contours of the hills for the next 1.3 miles angling progressively further from the creek. The trail ends 2 miles from the staging area. Older maps show the trail continuing for an additional 0.5 mile. It has since washed out. The trail going down to the creek and to the siphon is currently closed for habitat restoration. Those wanting a much longer and more strenuous hike can take the Canyon View Trail leading steeply up the hill.

Hellhole Canyon Preserve was completely burned by the Paradise Fire in 2003 and parts of the preserve were burned again in 2007 in the Poomacha Fire. A visit to the preserve shows how the coastal sage scrub, oak woodland, and chaparral plant communities can recover from fire. While the charred, twisted branches of the burnt shrubs are still visible, the preserve is alive with vigorously growing sage, manzanita, toyon, scrub oak, *Ceanothus*, and many other species that have sprouted from stumps not killed by the fire. The areas that burned again in 2007 are having difficulty recovering because four years is not enough time for the shrubs to build up a seed bank in the soil or root food storage.

Bewick's wren

Distance:	5 miles, loop
Difficulty:	🏃🏃🏃
Elevation gain/loss:	Up to 800 feet
Hiking time:	3 hours
Agency:	City of Escondido
Trail use:	Bicycles, dogs, horses
Notes:	Hours posted dawn to dusk
Trailhead GPS:	N33.20983, W117.08567
Optional map:	USGS 7.5-min *Valley Center*
Atlas square:	H11
Directions:	(Escondido) From I-15 go east on Mountain Meadow Road for 1.3 miles. Continue straight onto Hidden Meadows Road. Go 0.8 mile. Turn left on Granite Ridge Road. Go 0.2 mile. Turn right on Meadow Glen Way East. Go 0.3 mile. Turn right on Cougar Pass Road. Go 0.8 mile. Parking lot is on right. The last 0.5 mile is on dirt road; most passenger cars are able to pass.

Habitat(s):

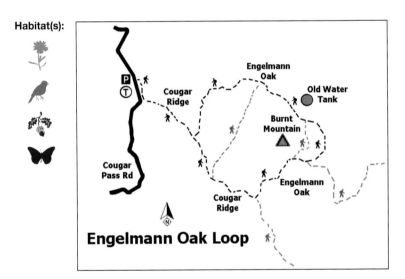

The 3058-acre Daley Ranch was acquired by the City of Escondido in 1996 as a conservation area to preserve biologically unique habitats that have regional importance. It is also a major recreational area with over 20 miles of trails available for hiking, mountain biking, running, and equestrian use. The property has rolling hills, mountainous areas, valleys, ponds, and seasonal streams. Originally it was home to bands of Kumeyaay and Luiseño Indians. In 1869 English immigrant Robert Daley moved into the valley and built a cabin. By 1875 he had acquired over 3000 acres. Over the years, the Daley family retained ownership and used the property for farming, raising horses, and a dairy before it was purchased by the City of Escondido.

Most visitors enter the ranch via La Honda Drive, off El Norte Parkway. The Engelmann Oak Trail is in a more secluded part of the ranch that can be reached via Cougar Pass Road. It offers a degree of solitude not found on the trails near the La Honda entrance.

Engelmann or mesa blue oaks (*Quercus engelmannii*) are found here. This stately oak is a somewhat rare live oak tree, usually with an upright trunk, twisted and symmetrically spreading limbs sparsely covered with flat, gray-green leaves. The main trunk can rise up to 80 feet. It is a majestic tree that grows only in a narrow band at least 20 miles inland from the ocean in the foothills of southern California down to Baja California, Mexico. They are found at elevations ranging from 500-4000

Don Fosket

A view toward Palomar

feet. It is considered a threatened species. The main threat it faces is development. It has been practically eliminated from the San Gabriel Valley and other areas where once it thrived. Most of the remaining Engelmann oaks are in San Diego's foothills and mountains. Engelmann oak woodlands often are savanna-like, with scattered trees set among grasslands or coastal sage scrub.

There are several different ways to hike the Engelmann Oak Loop, but the route described here is recommended for those who seek something different. After passing through the gate, follow the Cougar Ridge Trail as it passes near and then through a shady Engelmann and coast live oak woodland. As is the case with most Daley Ranch trails, this trail is an old dirt road originally used to move cattle or for fire protection. Although motorized vehicles will not be encountered, all ranch trails are popular with mountain bikers and equestrians.

After hiking 0.75 mile, the Engelmann Oak Trail branches off to the left. Take it and begin climbing this rather steep trail that is initially difficult. In less than 0.5 mile the hiking becomes easier approaching a grassy, gently

rolling ridge studded with well-spaced Engelmann oaks and patches of chaparral.

From February through early May, the hills are cloaked with a carpet of green grasses. Although the annual grasses turn brown by late May, blooming annuals and perennials continue to add color to the trail well into July. Depending on the month, a wide array of blooming shrubs and wildflowers such as a mariposa lily can be found along the trail.

A number of species of mariposa lily (*Calochortus* spp.) occur in the county, and all have fine hairs located within the flower. The lily is a monocot, which is the botanical term for a species that has only one (mono) cotyledon (cot) or seed leaf in the embryonic plant. Dicot, or plants that have two cotyledons, is the other classification option. Although cotyledons are often called seed leaves, they don't necessarily become green after seed germination. Common dicots include legumes (peas, beans, and peanuts), tomatoes, oaks, and daisies. Grasses and species that germinate from bulbs are common monocots, but this group also includes palm trees, agaves, yuccas, and orchids. There are several other

Engelmann oak

ways to distinguish between a monocot and a dicot. Monocots have flower parts in multiples of three—three petals or six petals usually. Dicots have flower parts in multiples of four or five. The major leaf veins of monocots are parallel, which are the plants traditionally used by Native Americans for fiber—yucca, agave, and palm, for example. Dicots have leaf veins that are reticulated, that is, in interconnecting lines, like a net.

After 1.7 miles, the Bobcat Trail goes off to the right, down through a shady canyon of coast live oaks. It eventually joins the Cougar Ridge Trail and would be a way to shorten your hike. However, to complete the Engelmann Oak Loop, stay to the left on the Engelmann Oak Trail. There will be another possible detour 2.2 miles into the hike when the Burnt Mountain Trail takes off to the right. Note that this trail does not lead up to the top of Burnt Mountain; it just bypasses part of the Engelmann Oak Trail.

The Hidden Springs Trail joins the Engelmann Oak Trail from the left at 2.75 miles. It leads down to Jack Creek and is a connection to the rest of the network of Daley Ranch trails. Continue following the Engelmann Oak Trail and pass through an oak woodland

containing numerous beautiful, huge coast live oaks, as well as a meadow that can become a small pond in a rainy winter. A little further on, the Engelmann Oak Trail ends as it joins the Cougar Ridge Trail at 3.35 miles. Go to the right, down the initially rather steep slope, and the Cougar Ridge Trail will follow along a stream and through an oak woodland, back to the trailhead and your vehicle.

Engelmann oak

Distance:	2 or 2.5 miles, out-and-back
Difficulty:	🚶 or 🚶🚶
Elevation gain/loss:	Up to 100 feet
Hiking time:	1 or 2 hours
Agency:	City of Escondido
Notes:	Open from 6 a.m. to sunset mid-December to early September, thereafter only on weekends
Trailhead GPS:	N33.17444, W116.99945
Optional map:	USGS 7.5-min *Valley Center*; *Rodriguez Mtn*
Atlas square:	H12
Directions:	(Escondido) From I-15 go east on El Norte Parkway for 4.6 miles. Turn left on Valley Parkway. Go 0.8 mile. Turn right on Lake Wohlford Road. Go 2.6 miles. Parking lot is on the right.

Habitat(s):

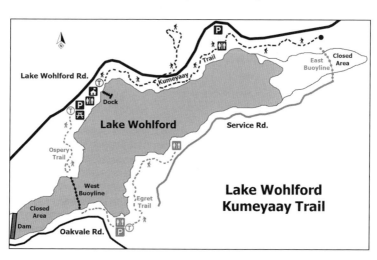

The Kumeyaay Trail is a testament to the use of the area by Native Americans who processed acorns from the coast live oaks and Engelmann oaks long before Escondido completed the construction of a dam in 1895. The dam was built to store water diverted via the Escondido Canal from the San Luis Rey River. The resulting reservoir, originally called the Bear Valley Reservoir, supplied water to area farmers, the City of Escondido, and Valley Center. The name was later changed to Lake Wohlford in 1924 to honor Escondido pioneer Alvin W. Wolford who was elected to the water district board in 1895 and served continuously until his death in 1924.

The Kumeyaay Trail follows a narrow path between Lake Wohlford and Lake Wohlford Road. The path is partially shaded by oaks. There are regular views of the lake as well as pleasantly situated benches for relaxation. Coast live and Engelmann oaks and rock formations are plentiful. Interesting boulders and rock slabs are coated with lichen and pigmented with yellow and red minerals.

The trail provides many opportunities for viewing waterfowl such as ducks, cormorants, egrets, herons, terns, and grebes. The pied-billed grebe (***Podilymbus podiceps***) is common in freshwater ponds across North America. This small, chunky brown bird with a thick chicken-like beak surface dives to forage for food or to quickly get out of danger. Depending on the circumstances, it can sink silently and inconspicuously or make a splash as it descends to avoid predators. It eats a variety of aquatic animals including fish, amphibians, crustaceans, mussels, insects, and snails. It builds a floating nest from surrounding vegetation.

There are occasional bald eagle sightings, as well as a resident osprey that may be seen on a nesting platform on the Osprey Trail, located at the west end of the parking lot. During the winter, white pelicans congregate along the

View looking south

buoy line at the east end of the lake. California quail and other woodland birds frequent the area with red-winged blackbirds seen among the cattails and sedges, near the docks.

The trailhead is to the left of the entrance, just beyond the Lake Wohlford office trailer. As you hike this trail, look for circular depressions in the rock called morteros. Hand stones, called pestles, were used in the morteros by the Kumeyaay to pound the acorns to break their shells and remove the nutmeat. Look for smooth grinding areas on boulders called slicks. Slicks and also portable milling stones, called metates, were used to grind the nuts down into a fine meal with a hand stone called a mano in an action much like using a rolling pin.

Cross a yellow bridge. Venture straight ahead and remain on the trail that parallels the road, as there are many side paths leading to the lake. The trail also becomes vague in places, so take care following this path. Look for a large-sloped boulder on the trail that provides the option for a side trip to the left leading to a lookout point. Cross the highway to take this steep trail. Be sure to watch for traffic, as there is a blind curve, and traffic can be heavy. After crossing the road, look to the right of the large oak tree for the trail. This side trip is well worth the effort. The lookout is built upon the remains of a homesite and is surrounded by a rock wall. The City of Escondido has improved the site by adding sitting niches among the rock and a bridge to span a gap at the top. The point provides a fabulous 330 degree view of the lake and surrounding area. When finished exploring, return to the large-sloped boulder to continue down the main trail. The steepness of the rock provides a challenge, but there are protrusions to assist your footing.

Now follow the main trail past rocky sections and some inviting sitting benches. When the trail opens up onto a dirt road, take the right fork past the porta-potty. Ignore the trail on the right and continue straight ahead where the trail becomes an indistinct narrow pathway, heavily shaded with tall boulders on the left. At the bottom, cross a green bridge and see the remains of an old well, which was once used to provide water to the homes at Lake Wohlford. Continuing down the trail are some patches of prickly-pear cactus with more morteros soon visible in front and to the right of the trail.

Soon there will be a collapsed culvert that is the recommended turnaround point. Here you can hop across at your own discretion or return. The trail continues a bit further from here and crosses another culvert via a wooden bridge with stone steps. The narrow trail eventually joins an old service road, which will soon be the required turnaround point. A no trespassing sign on a road gate marks the end of the trail. A shooting range is beyond this location. Return following the same trail.

Pied-billed grebe

Distance:	2.75 miles, loop
Difficulty:	🚶🚶
Elevation gain/loss:	Up to 750 feet
Hiking time:	2 hours
Agency:	City of Escondido
Notes:	Hours posted 6 a.m. to dusk; day-use fee weekends and holidays; bicycles restricted on some trails
Trailhead GPS:	N33.16624, W117.04989
Optional map:	USGS 7.5-min *Valley Center*
Atlas square:	I11
Directions:	(Escondido) From I-15 go east on El Norte Parkway for 3.1 miles. Turn left on La Honda Drive. Go 1.3 miles. Parking lot on the left, opposite the entrance to Dixon Lake.

Habitat(s):

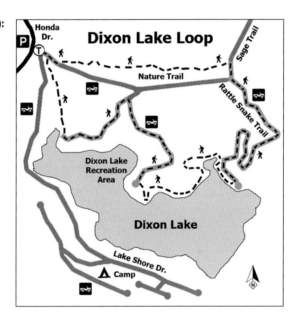

Dixon Lake is a multi-purpose recreation area adjacent to the Daley Ranch Open Space Preserve. Both are managed by the City of Escondido, but separately. The lake was named for James B. Dixon who was the superintendent for the Escondido Mutual Water Company. He had originally envisioned the construction of a reservoir near where his father had built a small dam to water his citrus trees in the late 1800s. Dixon Lake provides drinking water for Escondido. Activities here include boating, fishing, picnicking, camping, and hiking—swimming is not allowed. The hike described here goes through a variety of habitats with some surprising vistas, not only of the lake, but also of the growing city of Escondido down below.

Begin hiking east down the paved Dixon Lake entrance road, also signed as the Jack Creek Trail and named for the abundance of rabbits that were once seen here. About 500 feet ahead, take the hikers-only Dixon Lake Nature Trail on the left. The trail goes through a mix of lush chaparral and oak woodland. There are stately Engelmann oaks, spreading coast live oaks, and some quite large scrub oaks shading the trail as it passes by flowering California buckwheat, black and white sage, chamise, and bush monkey flower. Herbaceous corm and bulb producing perennials that may be seen are San Diego golden star and mariposa lilies (*Calochortus* spp.).

There are 81 species of mariposa lilies in Western North America, with 28 of them en-

Cyndy Cordle

Weed's mariposa lily

demic, found only, in California. Their flowers are somewhat unusual for lilies in having 3 petals and 3 sepals, where the petals and sepals differ in shape, size or color. Other lilies have tepals—sepals and petals that have the same appearance—so the flower, or perianth, appears to have 6 identical members. There are 9 different species of mariposa lilies in San Diego County, but in coastal areas you are most likely to find two: the splendid mariposa lily (*Calochortus splendens*), a striking pink- to violet-colored, bell-shaped flower, or Weed's mariposa lily (*Calochortus weedii* var. *weedii*) which has yellow flowers, often fringed with brown. Both are common in chaparral and coastal sage scrub but easily overlooked as their single flower is usually hidden under some shrubs or found among taller grasses. Native Americans used the mariposa bulbs for food. They were either eaten raw or cooked. Their bulbs were believed to have medicinal properties as well.

The trail continues for about 0.5 mile, ending as it emerges on the Sage Trail, one of the main Daley Ranch hiking and biking trails. Go right on the Sage Trail for about 0.10 mile where it ends in a T-junction with a lake access road. Go left on the road named the Rattlesnake Trail. It is not open to bicycles but can be used by motorized vehicles. Rattlesnake Trail goes up to a pass where there is the first glimpse of the lake, as well as the trail winding down to it. The trail ends at the lake, 1.35 miles from the entrance. A hikers-only trail begins just before the blue porta-potty at the end of the road. This shoreline trail continues for about 0.5 mile around Whisker Cove to Catfish Cove, where it ends at the Catfish Cove parking lot.

The lake, actually a reservoir, is stocked with rainbow trout yearly. Largemouth bass have been introduced and now reproduce here. Some grow to great size and can live for up to 16 years. In fact, an unofficial world's record largemouth bass was caught here that weighed over 25 pounds. Largemouth bass feed on smaller fish and a host of additional animals, including small birds, snakes, bats, and frogs.

A bird that you might see fishing or patrolling the lakeshore is the belted kingfisher (*Megaceryle alcyon*). It is a moderate sized (up to 14 inches) stocky bird with a large bluish-gray head with a shaggy crest. Its wings and back are also bluish-gray, but its underparts are white as well as its neck. It has a bluish-gray belt across the breast, and females have an additional rusty belt. The bill is long, straight, and thick. A belted kingfisher spends most of its time perched above the water looking for fish and aquatic animals in streams, ponds, lakes, or estuaries. When it spots some prey, the kingfisher takes flight and dives into the water, grabbing the prey with its pincer-like bill and returning to its perch, where it beats the prey against the perch and then swallows it whole, head first. Belted kingfishers build nests by burrowing into steep banks.

Follow the road leading up the hill from Catfish Cove, which is open to motor vehicles but receives little traffic. In 0.5 mile, take the road leading off to the left, which ends at Jack Creek Cove, about 0.25 mile ahead. The last leg of the journey is on the hikers-only trail that leads from the Jack Creek Cove parking area back to the landscaped picnic area near the Dixon Lake entrance. Along the trail, there are some interpretive signs explaining how Native Americans used some of the plants in the area.

Belted kingfisher

Distance:	4 miles, loop
Difficulty:	🏃🏃
Elevation gain/loss:	Up to 750 feet
Hiking time:	2 hours
Agency:	City of Escondido
Trail use:	Bicycles, dogs, horses
Notes:	Hours posted dawn to dusk
Trailhead GPS:	N33.16683, W117.05195
Optional map:	USGS 7.5-min *Valley Center*
Atlas square:	I11
Directions:	(Escondido) From I-15 go east on El Norte Parkway for 3.1 miles. Turn left on La Honda Drive. Go 1.3 miles. Parking lot is on the left.

Habitat(s):

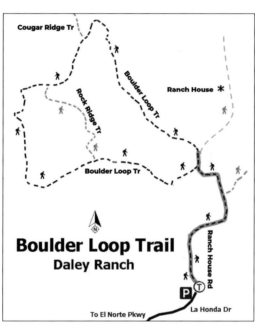

Development of the 3058-acre Daley Ranch in northeast Escondido was halted when the City of Escondido voted to acquire the property in 1996 to preserve it as a natural habitat and a place for outdoor recreation. As a result, it remains a treasure for anyone who likes to hike, run trails, mountain bike, ride horses, or just experience nature. The hills are clothed with coastal sage scrub and chaparral while in the valleys you will find ponds, oak woodlands, and grassy meadows. The trees include the increasingly rare Engelmann oaks as well as the more common coast live oak.

An intricate network of over 20 miles of trails winds through Daley Ranch making many hikes possible and hundreds of ways to plan a day's adventure. A few of the trails are single track but most are dirt roads maintained by a bulldozer for passage of emergency vehicles. However, other than bicycles, hikers won't encounter vehicles on any of these roads. The one exception is the Ranch House Road, but here vehicle traffic is confined to a shuttle bus that travels from the parking lot to the Ranch House and operates only on Sundays. Be alert for mountain bikers and horses on the trail.

One of the non-venomous reptiles that might be encountered is the gophersnake (*Pituophis catenifer*). It is one of the most commonly seen snakes in California. It is diurnal or active during the day. Its coloration and pattern can resemble that of a rattlesnake, and sometimes this beneficial snake is killed

Walter Konopka

Gophersnake constricting a chipmunk

Walter Konopka

Swallowing it

Walter Konopka

Only the tail is left

inadvertently when it is seen around residences. Gophersnakes help control rodents. They do not have the triangular shaped head of the rattlesnake and are much more slender, although they can reach a length of well over 4 feet. The head is small and almost indistinguishable from the neck. When threatened, it will rear up, puff up its body, flatten its head, and hiss, resembling a pit viper. It may also shake its tail to confuse potential predators. The tail does not have rattles and tapers to a point. The eyes have round pupils while those of the rattlesnake have vertical, cat-like pupils. Gophersnakes are constrictors that hunt mainly for small mammals but will also eat birds and eggs.

Rattlesnakes (*Crotalus* **spp.**) are important components of healthy ecosystems. They also help control rodents and, in turn, are prey items for other species. Pit vipers have a heat-sensing pit located between the nostrils and eyes on their diamond-shaped head that informs them of a nearby living creature. When striking, rattlesnakes have dry bites about 20% of the time in which no venom is injected. If you are lucky enough to see a rattlesnake eating prey, you will notice that their jaws allow for an extraordinary amount of movement, enabling them to fit entire rodents into their mouths. Snakes are able to breathe even when they are eating very large prey filling their entire mouths, thanks to an extendable glottis, which is a small opening behind the tongue that leads to the windpipe or trachea. This glottis also allows some snakes to hiss. They breathe out through their lungs, and in doing so vibrate a small piece of cartilage inside the glottis.

Boulder Loop is one of the many routes on the Daley Ranch. The best time to visit is January through July when wildflowers are out. Starting from the dirt parking lot off La Honda Drive, hike through the Daley Ranch gate and up the road toward the recently restored Ranch House, a structure built in 1928. Follow the Ranch House Road up over a small hill and down through an oak grove with views of some of the ponds that were once used for livestock grazing. The southern end of the Boulder Loop Trail is on the left about 0.7 mile from the parking lot. Proceed up the steep, eroded Boulder Loop Trail to the top of the ridge. Pause to catch your breath and

Don Fosket

Entrance gate

enjoy the vistas: south to Dixon Lake and beyond to Escondido; east to the Daley Ranch ponds with Stanley Peak rising above them; and west and southwest to suburbia sprawling over the neighboring valleys and crawling up the hills.

In spring, especially after a rain, you can hear Pacific treefrogs (***Pseudacris regilla***). These small amphibians are only 1-2 inches long and come in many colors ranging from gray, brown, red, cream, and green. They can change from dark to light, but their color hue stays the same. They are found in a variety of moist habitats and require standing water to reproduce. The skin is smooth and the legs are proportionally longer than the body. Males have a dark patch at their throat that will stretch when they vocalize. They hide in aquatic vegetation, cattails, under rotten logs, leaf litter, rocks, or on leaves. Males lure females to water with their call, where they mate. Females lay eggs in the water. Tadpoles eat algae, diatoms, and even pollen that float on the water. During metamorphosis from a tadpole to a frog, their digestive systems transform them from herbivorous to carnivorous animals. Adults eat insects and their larva.

The first mile is up a sometimes steep grade, but eventually you reach a grassy, boulder-strewn ridge with easy hiking as you proceed over a series of low rolling hills. Two

other trails branch off Boulder Loop. The first one is the single track Rock Ridge Trail that veers to the right, and the other is the Cougar Ridge Trail, branching off to the left. These are well marked. Stay on the Boulder Loop Trail as it goes back down to the Ranch House Road, rejoining it 3.2 miles from the trailhead. At this point there are two options. Going left up the Ranch House Road leads to the historic Ranch House in less than 0.5 mile, which is well worth a visit. Alternatively, turning right takes you back to your vehicle in 0.8 mile via the same Ranch House Road you came in on.

Walter Konopka

Pacific treefrog

Distance:	5 miles, loop
Difficulty:	🚶🚶
Elevation gain/loss:	Minimal
Hiking time:	3 hours
Agency:	City of Escondido
Trail use:	Bicycles, dogs, horses
Notes:	Hours posted dawn to dusk
Trailhead GPS:	N33.16675, W117.05202
Optional map:	USGS 7.5-min *Valley Center*
Atlas square:	I11
Directions:	(Escondido) From I-15 go east on El Norte Parkway for 3.1 miles. Turn left on La Honda Drive. Go 1.3 miles. Parking lot is on the left..

Habitat(s):

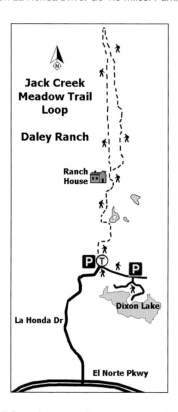

This hike is a step back in time to California's ranching past and includes a reconstructed ranch house from this early period. Hike through a meadow with bunch grasses taller than most people and see an array of native birds including California quail, mourning doves, common ravens, red-tailed hawks, western scrub-jays, and woodpeckers. Depending on the season of your visit, the hillsides may be painted a deep blue by thousands of blooming *Ceanothus* or you may be greeted by an array of colors from bush monkey flowers, blue-eyed-grass, or hundreds of other wildflowers. The cobbled stream has seasonal water and is bordered by small clumps of chaparral plants. Blue-eyed-grass (*Sisyrinchium bellum*) is a purplish-blue iris with a yellow center that grows in clumps on a long stem and is from 1 to 2 feet in height and has grass-like leaves. The six radial tepals of this perennial are double notched at the tip. It will grow in several habitats but not in the desert.

Daley Ranch has over 20 miles of named and signed trails. Many of these are loops that

Blue-eyed-grass

quito fern (*Azolla filiculoides*), can be found in stagnant pools—the kind that mosquitoes breed in. It is a very small plant, but often it is found in floating mats made up of hundreds of individual plants. In fact, though it is a native California plant, it is found practically world-wide and is considered to be highly invasive.

The trail goes through a meadow and through a field of amazingly tall perennial bunch grasses, including deergrass (***Muhlenbergia rigens***) and three-awn (***Aristida purpurea***), a native bunch grass that grows to 3 feet tall and has a striking purple inflorescence. Three-awn refers to the three bristle-like appendages at the end of the grass spikelet. Deergrass, on the other hand, has a single awnless floret. Both deergrass and purple three-awn are character-istic of the open prairies. Deergrass's extensive roots, dense stands, and its ability to remove chemicals from agricultural runoff has made it a restoration plant used when invasive plants are removed.

After hiking 1 mile through the meadow, the trail goes up a short hill and into chaparral. The ranch and the trail both end at a fence a 0.5 mile ahead. Once you reach the fence, go right, across the stream, which may be dry, and then head south on the east leg of the loop trail. This route goes through patches of oak woodland, alternating with chaparral and grassland, and it looks out over the meadow instead of pass-ing through it. Return to the Ranch House af-ter completing the 3-mile Jack Creek Meadow Loop Trail and return to your vehicle.

explore a particular ranch feature. The trails interconnect so there are a variety of ways to get to the Jack Creek Meadow Loop Trail. The route described here is the most direct. From the dirt parking lot off La Honda Drive, go through the Daley Ranch gate and continue north on the paved Ranch House Road. The pavement continues until you reach the Ranch House, which is open to monthly ranger-lead tours. Some of the best displays of chaparral wildflowers on the ranch can be found along the roadsides. The road also goes through an Engelmann and coast live oak woodland with views of ponds. The Ranch House is in an oak grove with picnic tables and benches. It is a good place to rest, have a picnic, and to water your horse if you brought one.

The Jack Creek Meadow Trail begins just beyond the Ranch House after the pavement ends, about 1 mile from the parking area. The west branch of this loop trail goes straight up the meadow, more or less paralleling Jack Creek, which it crosses twice. Look for the aquatic hairy clover fern (***Marsilea vestita***) floating in the stream as you cross it. Like all ferns, it does not produce flowers, but rather spores that are formed in a structure called a sporangium found on the underside of the leaves. When you first come across this plant you may think you found a four-leaf clover as its leaves have four leaflets. The small leaves float on the surface of the water and are at-tached by thin stems to roots (actually rhi-zomes, or underground stems) buried in the mud. Another aquatic fern, the Pacific mos-

Deergrass

Distance:	4 miles, loop
Difficulty:	🚶🚶
Elevation gain/loss:	Up to 600 feet
Hiking time:	2 hours
Agency:	City of Escondido
Trail use:	Bicycles, dogs, horses
Notes:	Hours posted dawn to dusk
Trailhead GPS:	N33.16667, W117.05206
Optional map:	USGS 7.5-min *Valley Center*
Atlas square:	I11
Directions:	(Escondido) From I-15 go east on El Norte Parkway for 3.1 miles. Turn left on La Honda Drive. Go 1.3 miles. Parking lot is on the left.

Habitat(s):

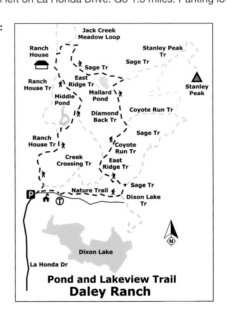

Pond and Lakeview Trail
Daley Ranch

The Daley Ranch has six ponds in addition to its 20 miles of trails that wind through the ranch's chaparral-covered hills and tree-shaded valleys. Only the larger ponds have water year-round. The ponds were all man-made to provide water for livestock and now are a haven for waterfowl and other wild animals.

This hike goes by the two largest ponds as well as some of the ephemeral ponds. Start the hike by walking down the Dixon Lake entrance road, east of the ranch parking lot. Shortly after passing the entrance kiosk, a nature trail begins on the left. Take it through a shady oak and willow riparian corridor. The nature trail continues 0.4 mile to the Dixon Lake Trail. Go left and in a short distance find the intersection of the Sage, East Ridge, and Dixon Lake trails. A small seasonal pond is just a few yards northwest of this junction and, if it has water,

the heavy vegetation surrounding it will be filled with noisy red-winged blackbirds (*Agelaius phoeniceus*). In 1975 it was estimated that there were nearly 200 million red-winged blackbirds in the US, making the species one of the most common in the nation. Within San Diego County, however, it has a limited presence. It is most seen or heard in the cattails and reeds of marshes, ponds, and lakes, but it also can be seen in open areas foraging for insects and seeds. The adult males are glossy black with red shoulder patches bordered in yellow. Females are brown and look like large dark sparrows.

Turn left at the triple junction and hike up the rather steep East Ridge Trail. In 0.25 mile is the junction with the single track Coyote Run Trail on the right. Take it and in 0.3 mile is another junction with the Diamond Back

Don Fosket

Pond view

Trail on the left. This trail goes up a low ridge from which the Mallard Pond comes into view to the north. Continue on the Diamond Back Trail until it intersects with the Sage Trail. Going left down the Sage Trail leads past the Mallard Pond, and the intersection with the Mallard Trail is in 0.25 mile. The Mallard Trail traverses the top of the dam that created the pond and is a good place to watch for migratory waterfowl as well as some year-round water birds.

Leaving the pond, continue north on the Sage Trail to its junction with the Jack Creek Meadow Loop Trail. From this point the historic Daley Ranch House and out buildings are visible under magnificent old coast live oaks. Ranger-lead tours of the Ranch House are given on the second Sunday of each month, from 11 a.m. to 2 p.m., but the buildings are not otherwise open to the public. The Ranch House, built in 1928 and restored to its original condition, is well worth a visit.

To continue the hike, walk south down the Ranch House Trail a short distance to its junction with the East Ridge Trail on the left. In 0.4 mile it will take you to the Middle Pond Trail junction. The Middle Pond is a second perennial body of water and another good place to view waterfowl. The Middle Pond Trail continues beyond the pond leading back to the recently paved Ranch House Trail with interpretative signs identifying common native plants. Follow the Ranch House Trail south back to your vehicle.

Wendy Esterly

Female red-winged blackbird

Wendy Esterly

Male red-winged blackbird

Distance:	5.5 miles, out-and-back
Difficulty:	🚶🚶🚶
Elevation gain/loss:	Up to 1000 feet
Hiking time:	4 hours
Agency:	City of Escondido
Trail use:	Bicycles, dogs, horses
Notes:	Hours posted dawn to dusk
Trailhead GPS:	N33.15941, W117.03292
Optional map:	USGS 7.5-min *Valley Center*
Atlas square:	I11
Directions:	From I-15 (Escondido) go east on El Norte Parkway for 4.5 miles. Turn a left on Valley Parkway, go 0.4 mile. Turn left on Beven Drive. Go 0.2 mile. Turn right on Save-a-Life Way. Go 0.1 mile. There will be signs for both the Humane Society and for the Caballo Trail. Parking lot is on the left.

Habitat(s):

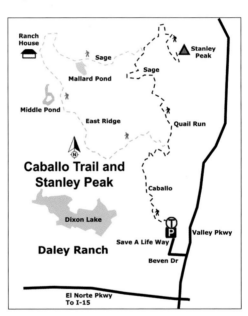

Although surrounded by suburban and semi-rural developments, the Daley Ranch is sufficiently large and diverse that one can feel detached from civilization and enjoy the experience of the native San Diego inland environment.

There are four entrances to the network of ranch trails that all interconnect. Most people enter the park from the main entrance off El Norte Parkway, near the end of La Honda Drive, but for the hike described here, use the entrance off Valley Parkway. It takes you directly to the Caballo trailhead.

The Caballo Trail starts near an abandoned avocado grove and then goes up the east-facing slope of an unnamed canyon through which an intermittent stream flows. A dense growth of coastal sage scrub and chaparral covers the hillsides. Depending on the year and season, there may be a colorful display of blooming annuals and shrubs.

The Ramona-lilac (*Ceanothus tomentosus*) with its bluish-purple flowers in season is common here. It is one of 17 species of *Ceanothus* listed in the 5th edition of the *Checklist of the Vascular Plants of San Diego County*. *Ceanothus* species (*Ceanothus spp.*) are found in almost all types of chaparral, but a given location may have only one or a few of these species. Each species has its own ecological requirements.

Stanley Peak in the distance

Some have a limited distribution, such as the Lakeside-lilac (*Ceanothus cyaneus*), which is found only in the foothills between Dehesa and Ramona, where it is endemic, while the Palmer's-lilac (*Ceanothus palmeri*) is confined to the mountains where it is abundant. Nine of the local *Ceanothus* species are called lilacs because they superficially resemble the cultivated lilac. Cultivated lilacs are deciduous shrubs or small trees adapted to cold climates with severe winters. They are in the genus *Syringa* and the family Oleaceae. However, both *Syringa* spp. and *Ceanothus* spp., that are called lilacs, have masses of small blue to purple flowers in showy panicles (a cluster of flowers on a branch) and are sweet smelling.

The roots of *Ceanothus* species develop gall-like nodules containing a bacterium called frankia (**Frankia sp.**). The relationship between frankia and *Ceanothus* roots is symbiotic. Biologically inert atmospheric nitrogen is converted to an essential nutrient by the bacterium in a process known as nitrogen fixation while carbohydrates resulting from the plant's leaves feed the bacterium. As a result, *Ceanothus* plays a vital part in the chaparral ecosystem. This symbiotic relationship allows *Ceanothus* to grow in nitrogen-poor soils. Mountain-mahogany (**Cerocarpus spp.**) is another nitrogen-fixing chaparral plant whose roots have a symbiotic relationship with frankia. A similar relationship exists with members of the birch (white alder) and legume or pea families.

The trail forks at about 1 mile. The Caballo Trail continues off to the left while the Quail Run Trail begins here towards the right. Take the Quail Run Trail and continue up the ridge for a little over 0.5 mile until it connects with the Sage Trail. Go right on the Sage Trail, which actually is a dirt road, badly eroded in spots, but easily navigated on foot. After traveling about 0.75 mile on the Sage Trail, the Stanley Peak Trail is visible. Initially this is an easy walk along the edge of a meadow, with a scattering of small Engelmann oaks. However, as you get closer to your goal, the trail begins to climb steeply to the top of boulder covered Stanley Peak (1983'), the high point of the Daley Ranch. After taking in the view you may reverse your steps to return to your vehicle or explore some of the other interesting nearby parts of the preserve, such as Mallard Pond or the old historic Ranch House, before returning to your vehicle.

Ramona-lilac

Distance:	14 miles, out-and-back
Difficulty:	🚶🚶🚶🚶🚶
Elevation gain/loss:	Up to 3000 feet
Hiking time:	9 hours
Agency:	USFS/CNF-PRD
Trail use:	Dogs
Trailhead GPS:	N33.14043, W116.85007
Optional map:	USGS 7.5-min *Mesa Grande*
Atlas square:	I15
Directions:	(Ramona) From CA-67 go north on 7th Street for 0.2 mile. Turn right on Elm Street. Go 1.4 miles. Turn right on West Haverford Road. Go 0.1 mile. Turn left on Pamo Road. Go 5.4 miles. Park on shoulder, but do not block gate. Trailhead is on the right and is designated Forest Route 12S07/Upper Santa Ysabel Road/Truck Trail.

Habitat(s):

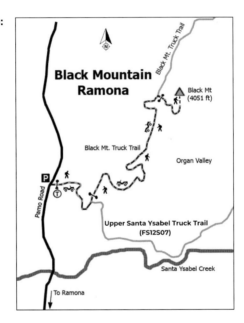

There are two Black Mountains in San Diego County. One is in Carmel Valley and the other is near Ramona. At an elevation of 4051 feet, the one near Ramona is by far the larger. As the most prominent mountain in this remote area, it provides an excellent panoramic view of the surrounding wild territory. Its unusual geology makes it a good place to find rare plants. Black Mountain is mostly composed of the dark gabbro rocks, covered with dark chaparral vegetation, that have given the mountain its name.

The trail is a dirt road that takes you through chaparral with little or no shade, making this a strenuous 14.2-mile out-and-back hike with about 3000 feet of elevation gain. It also can be an easy 2-mile stroll to the top of the moun-

tain. If you have a sturdy 4WD vehicle, you can drive 12 of these 14 miles.

If you elect to hike to the top, park at the junction of Pamo Road and Forest Road 12S07. This will give you a chance to explore the area, perhaps find and identify some of the rare plants growing here, and see some wildlife. Although the entire area burned during the Witch Creek Fire in 2007, the vegetation is recovering and there is a lot to see, particularly in the spring. Wildflowers often appear a few years after a fire.

Forest Road 12S07 meets the Black Mountain Truck Trail (Forest Road 11S04) 1.5 miles from the trailhead, as it goes off to the left. The gate here is usually open. Continuing up For-

Don Fosket

Sutherland Dam view from the peak

est Road 11S04, you will pass near the Organ Valley Research Natural Area, 4.6 miles from Pamo Valley.

This study area was established to protect rare species and to learn more about Engelmann oaks, which are common here and elsewhere in inland cismontane San Diego, but relatively rare outside of San Diego County. Gabbro rock is abundant in the more than 500-acre research natural area. Gabbro is a medium to coarse-grained, dark gray to dark green-colored, intrusive igneous rock that is low in silica and contains no quartz or alkali feldspar. It is chemically equivalent to basalt. It also contains heavy metals, which may be toxic to many plants while supporting others. Soils derived from gabbro rock support many rare and sensitive plants and are high in magnesium and iron and relatively low in calcium. Some plant species are mostly found on gabbro-derived soil.

These include Orcutt's brodiaea (*Brodiaea orcuttii*) and Laguna or Orcutt's linanthus (*Linanthus orcuttii*). Both are endemic to southern California and rare. It is possible that the chemical composition of gabbro soils is responsible for their limited distribution. Orcutt's brodiaea is a monocot with a perennial underground corm from which strap-like basal leaves emerge in the spring followed by a 10-inch floral stalk bearing flowers with six shiny dark blue tepals—three petals and three sepals—in spring. Orcutt's linanthus is an annual dicot, rarely rising above 4 inches, with small flowers having five white or pink edged petals that also appear in spring. It also grows in the Laguna Mountain meadows and on Garnet Peak. Charles Orcutt, for whom these species are named, was an early San Diego

explorer. He collected many plants throughout San Diego County and donated his collection to the San Diego Natural History Museum.

A small grove of Coulter pines also grows on the upper portion of Black Mountain. A number of other pines were planted on the slopes below under the Penny Pines program, but most were killed in the fire. Few are reproducing.

Continue on Forest Road 11S04 to within about 1 mile of the top of the mountain, where you will encounter another gate. This one will be locked. Park here and hike up the road to the right. The road does not go all the way to the top, but you will find an improvised path for the last 0.2 mile to the summit. There was a lookout tower on the peak until the 1970s. A solar powered weather station now stands on the concrete foundation of the former fire lookout. After taking in the extraordinary 360-degree view, which may extend out to the Pacific, return the way you came.

Don Fosket

Monkey flower on the trail

Distance:	5, 8, 10, or 15 miles, one-way or out-and-back
Difficulty:	🚶🚶🚶 or 🚶🚶🚶🚶
Elevation gain/loss:	1000 ft. to 1700 ft.
Hiking time:	3 to 8 hours
Agency:	CNF-PRD
Trail use:	Dogs, bicycles
Notes:	High clearance 4WD vehicles are essential if you plan to drive. Hiking is best. The Pamo Valley Trail segment of the Coast to Crest Trail heading south will open in 2019.
Trailhead GPS:	N33.14027, W116.84931
Optional map:	USGS 7.5-min *Mesa Grande*, *Ramona*
Atlas square:	J15, J16, I15, I16
Directions:	(Ramona) From CA-67 go north on 7th Street for 0.2 mile. Turn right on Elm Street. Go 1.4 miles. Turn right on West Haverford Road. Go 0.1 mile. Turn left on Pamo Road. Go 5.4 miles. Trailhead is at Forest Route 12S07/Upper Santa Ysabel Road/Truck Trail on the right.

Habitat(s):

Santa Ysabel Creek is a major tributary of the San Dieguito River. As it flows near Ramona, it is separated into upper and lower branches by the Pamo Valley. The Upper Santa Ysabel Truck Trail is a segment of the Coast to Crest Trail that will extend from Volcan Mountain to the ocean in Del Mar. The Upper Santa Ysabel Truck Trail follows Upper Santa Ysabel Creek from Pamo Valley to its intersection with Black Canyon Road near Sutherland Dam. The hike described can be extended from Black Canyon to Sutherland Dam to complete this part of the Coast to Crest Trail.

This is a great cool season hike with expansive views and a chance to experience most of the diverse habitat types found in San Diego County. The hike can be done as a one-way trip with shuttle arrangement or as a much

longer, all day out-and-back journey. It can be done from either end, but the description here assumes a Pamo Valley beginning.

Try to arrive at the trailhead early in the morning to experience the spectacular descent into Pamo Valley from the Ramona plateau. Shortly after you pass the Ramona Land Fill, the Pamo Road begins a surprisingly sharp descent of more than 600 feet into the valley. The broad oak-forested valley floor extends 6 miles north and sits between Orosco Ridge to the west and Black Mountain to the east. In the 1880s, J.M. Woods bought land here with the idea of constructing a dam to provide water for agriculture. This idea was slow to die. In 1925, the City of San Diego bought property in the valley with the same idea. In 1950, the City obtained a permit to build a 264-foot high dam that would

Pamo Valley view from the truck trail

have converted 4300 acres of Pamo Valley into a reservoir. However, in 1986 the Environmental Protection Agency ruled against the dam. The City of San Diego continues to own the valley, but it is now part of the San Dieguito River Park and is leased to cattle ranchers.

Start the hike where the Upper Santa Ysabel Truck Trail (FR12S07) begins from Pamo Road. Although it is a truck trail, it gets relatively little vehicle traffic. The trail rises steadily about 700 feet up a ridge and through first grassland, then chaparral. At the crest of the ridge, Black Mountain Truck Trail splits off to the left while the Upper Santa Ysabel Truck Trail heads east, but it never reaches Santa Ysabel Creek. From here to Black Canyon the truck trail undulates but remains substantially above the creek. It is easy walking along the road and you can enjoy the views down to Pamo Valley. A little further on, the trail passes into a tributary canyon where Engelmann oaks and western sycamores provide welcome shade and a good place to rest. At 2.3 miles there is a view down into Santa Ysabel Creek where western cottonwoods, western sycamores, willows, and oaks line the stream. In the fall the cottonwoods and sycamores turn a brilliant shade of yellow.

At 5 miles is Black Canyon with its oak forest with lush riparian vegetation. A camp-

ground was here until it was destroyed by a flash flood and never rebuilt. From here you can either end your hike or continue up the Sutherland Dam road, adding another 0.7 mile to your hike. You can arrange to be picked up at either place, but if you are doing an out-and-back, you are only halfway. Turn around and go back the way you came.

Truck trail enters a tributary canyon

Distance:	2 miles, out-and-back
Difficulty:	🚶
Elevation gain/loss:	Up to 100 feet
Hiking time:	1 hour
Agency:	CNF-PRD
Trail use:	Dogs
Trailhead GPS:	N33.1241, W116.80191
Optional map:	USGS 7.5-min *Ramona*; *Mesa Grande*
Atlas square:	I16
Directions:	(Ramona) From CA-78 east of Ramona go north on Sutherland Dam Road for 3.9 miles. Turn right on Black Canyon Road and cross over the new bridge. Go 0.1 mile. Park on left but do not block gate. Trailhead is on the left and is designated Forest Route 12S07/Upper Santa Ysabel Road/Truck Trail.

Habitat(s):

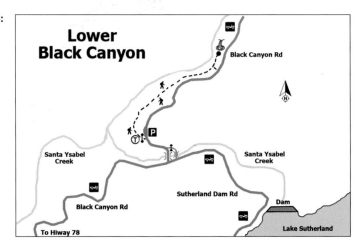

An intermittent stream flows through Black Canyon, providing seasonal water for a lush riparian habitat that includes coast live oaks, western cottonwood trees, arroyo willows, white alders, and even a few native black walnut trees. There are also waterfalls cascading down polished rock faces into pools of cool water. Water flowing through this canyon can become a torrent during a storm, moving large boulders through the canyon. It slows to a trickle in the summer and times of drought.

Begin hiking down the Santa Ysabel Truck Trail. It is 0.2 mile to Black Creek and the former US Forest Service's Black Canyon Campground that was closed in the 1980s after flood damage. It is set in a coast live oak, western sycamore, and arroyo willow forest. The trail follows Black Creek northeast. Initially the trail is the remains of a paved road that ran from the truck trail through the campground. Watch for interesting plants, including stream

orchid (*Epipactis gigantea*) and California peony (*Paeonia californica*).

Most orchids are tropical, but the stream orchid is common in much of the western states. It is a perennial herb common in wetlands and beside streams. It has typical orchid flowers, with brownish-yellow purple-veined petals that emerge from tall slender stalks. The California peony, in contrast to the stream orchid, is usually found in dry chaparral and coastal sage scrub. There are about 30 species of peony worldwide. Most are from Asia or southern Europe. They are relatively large, herbaceous perennials or trees. While they occur in the wild, we know them for their many horticultural cultivars, which lack drought tolerance. This is where our native California peony differs greatly from their European and Asian ancestors. The California peony prefers dry chaparral and coastal sage habitats. Its tuber-like roots go dormant in May and remain

Stream orchid

dormant through the summer. If given water during the summer, the roots will rot. However, with the onset of cooler fall temperatures and rain, the roots sprout leaves and grow to a height of one foot, to be followed from February through April by large drooping red flowers. It is endemic to California and northern Baja California, Mexico.

After 0.6 mile, the canyon narrows somewhat, and it becomes necessary to climb over and/or around some huge boulders. Don't become discouraged and turn around at this point because a sight worthy of the struggle to get here will be visible in another 0.25 mile. The reward is a beautiful waterfall cascading, or in dry months trickling into a large pool surrounded by tall granite walls. Further travel up the canyon from this point is not advised as it leads onto the Mesa Grande Indian Reservation.

The Black Canyon Road Bridge, built in 1913, was one of 18 three-hinged arch bridges built between 1909 and 1917 by Thomas and Post using the Thomas method of pre-cast, reinforced concrete sections. The design allowed movement in two opposite directions by two hinges at the base and one at mid-span, thus compensating for thermal and seismic expansion and contraction. It is now closed to vehicular traffic, while the new concrete and steel bridge looks as though it belongs in a city. Although the new bridge is somewhat incongruous in this setting, Black Canyon Road is a major route in and out of the Mesa Grande Indian Reservation. Black Canyon burned in the Witch Creek Fire in 2007.

California peony

Distance:	4.7 miles, out-and-back; 5 miles, point-to-point; or 10.2 miles, out-and-back
Difficulty:	🚶🚶 or 🚶🚶🚶, depending on length
Elevation gain/loss:	up to 1500 feet
Hiking time:	3 or 7 hours
Agency:	USFS/CNF-PRD; City of San Diego; San Diego County; CDFW
Trail use:	Horses
Notes:	A driver is needed to drop off and pick up hikers for trip option 2. See last paragraph for map name conflicts.
Trailhead GPS:	N33.10340, W116.85732
Optional map:	USGS 7.5-min *Ramona*; *San Pasqual*
Atlas square:	J15
Directions:	(Ramona) From CA-67 go north on 7th Street for 0.2 mile. Turn right on Elm Street. Go 1.4 miles. Turn right on West Haverford Road. Go 0.1 mile. Turn left on Pamo Road. Go 2.4 miles. Trailhead is on the left and is designated Forest Route 12S04/Lower Santa Ysabel Truck Trail. Park here, being careful to not block the gate, or drop off hikers for eventual pick up on CA-78 for trip option 2.

Habitat(s):

Coast to Crest Trail
Lower Santa Ysabel Truck Trail
San Dieguito River Park
With Side Trip to Boden Canyon

The Lower Santa Ysabel Truck Trail takes you beside a lush riparian forest of towering western sycamores, arroyo willows, western cottonwoods, and spreading oaks, draped with native grape vines, as it travels beside or above Santa Ysabel Creek. Then it climbs into patches of grassland and chaparral before descending into Boden Canyon. Depending on the season and rainfall, you may find a display of wildflowers.

Begin hiking north on FS12S04 to Santa Ysabel Creek where there is a fork. The road to the right becomes the Orosco Ridge Truck Trail. The Lower Santa Ysabel Truck Trail is on the left. At this point, the trail is a dirt road and

open to motorized vehicles, but a locked gate 0.25 mile from Pamo Road prevents further vehicle access. The trail is an easy hike in and out of the shady forest for nearly 1 mile. Take some time to explore the riparian habitat near the trail where southern California wild grapes (*Vitis girdiana*) grow profusely. This grape is a close relative of the concord grape and a more distant relative of wine grapes. Most people find the fruit too bitter to be enjoyable. It has a higher concentration of tartaric acid than most other grapes, which accounts for its bitterness. If the tartaric acid is removed from the juice, the bitterness is gone, and the flavor is quite good. This grape is a climbing woody vine with heart-

Lower Santa Ysabel Creek

shaped serrated pale-green, velvety leaves with a pointy tip. The leaves are fuzzy underneath and turn dark red in the fall, signaling to various species when the pea-size purplish-black grapes are ripe and ready to eat.

The trail then begins to climb up the side of the mountain, reaching an elevation about 200 feet above the creek. After coming to another locked gate, 1.29 miles from Pamo Valley, the trail levels off and continues through mixed *Ceanothus* chaparral until it reaches Boden Canyon, 2.25 miles further on. Although vehicles are prohibited, the canyon is used to pasture cattle.

There are at least 3 different ways to complete this hike.

Option 1 is an easy 4.7-mile out-and-back hike. Continue down the trail from the second locked gate to an unnamed tributary canyon leading to Santa Ysabel Creek, 2.35 miles from Pamo Valley. It is a heavily wooded tributary with a dense forest of grape-festooned coast live oaks, western sycamores, and western cottonwoods. A bubbling creek with seasonal water runs through it making it a cool, shady place for lunch or a picnic. Go back the way you came to complete this hike.

Option 2 is a moderate 5-mile point-to-point hike. Continue on to Boden Canyon, 3.4 miles from Pamo Road. Go left, descending to a truck trail. Continue west on this dirt road for 1.6 miles until you reach the turnout on CA-78. If

you elect this option, you must arrange to have someone pick you up on CA-78. Since parking is no longer permitted at this turn out, you need to get the timing right to make this work. This option follows the Coast to Crest Trail.

Option 3 is a more strenuous 10.2-mile hike. This option takes you into the Boden Canyon Ecological Reserve, a 1200-acre preserve managed by the California Department of Fish and Wildlife. Upon reaching Boden Canyon, instead of going west or left, turn right and go north. The dirt road crosses Santa Ysabel Creek and becomes a hiking trail, leading up a short hill and then through a delightful oak woodland and riparian wilderness. After hiking 1.8 miles through the reserve, another trail branches off to the right. This goes east and connects with another truck trail. This is a good place to turn around and go back the way you came for a moderately strenuous 10.2-mile out-and-back hike. Game bird and deer hunting are allowed in the Cleveland National Forest and shooting may occur during the hunting season.

Note: Routes are checked from multiple sources where name differences may occur. An example of this is Forest Road (FR) 12504 verses FS12S04. FS12S04 is correct and describes location: Forest Service (FS), Township (12) Section (S), and Road number (04). Boden Canyon, Drasco (misspelling of Orosco), and Guejito Truck Trails were labeled only as truck trails due to map source conflicts.

Distance:	3 miles, out-and-back
Difficulty:	🚶🚶🚶
Elevation gain/loss:	Up to 1500 feet
Hiking time:	3 hours
Agency:	City of San Diego
Trail use:	Dogs
Notes:	Hours posted dawn to dusk
Trailhead GPS:	N33.08472, W116.91655
Optional map:	USGS 7.5-min *San Pasqual*
Atlas square:	J14
Directions:	(Escondido) From CA-78, east of Escondido, turn north into the Clevenger North trailhead parking, 14 miles east of I-15 and 5.5 miles west of CA-67.

Habitat(s):

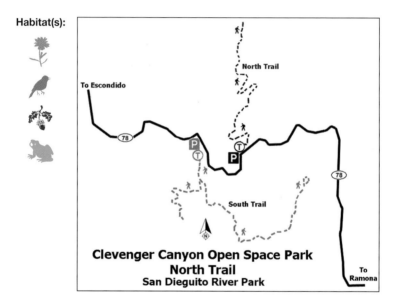

Clevenger Canyon Open Space Park
North Trail
San Dieguito River Park

Clevenger Canyon Open Space is a City of San Diego park that is part of the San Dieguito River Park. The North Trail within this open space park has suffered from frequent fires and vandalism. Despite these degradations, it retains a number of attractions that make it worth a visit. Take the short hike down to and along Santa Ysabel Creek. It is rich in wildflowers and blooming chaparral shrubs in season. The stream is lined with oaks, willows, and western sycamore and provides cool shade on hot days. The trail from the stream up the side of the canyon is a challenge some hikers will avoid, but if you do it, you will be rewarded with amazing views.

The trail descends quickly from the parking area. After passing through a short rock-framed tunnel and going down some stone steps, the descent becomes more gradual, reaching Santa Ysabel Creek in about 0.25 mile. This is a good place to look for several climbing and twining plants such as honeysuckle (*Lonicera* **spp.**) that may be draped on a variety of shrubs. The name comes from the sweet edible nectar that can be sucked from the reddish- to yellow-colored tubular flower that attracts hummingbirds.

Other climbing vines found here are manroot or wild-cucumber and the white yerba de chiva, sometimes called old-man's beard or virgin's bower (*Clematis ligusticifolia*) for its woolly appearance. Old-man's beard has oils that can irritate the skin and mucous membranes. Despite its toxicity, it was used medic-

Cryptogamic soil

inally by Native Americans to treat headaches and skin infections.

You may find a bubbling stream when you reach the canyon bottom, depending on the year and season. Even during drought years, there is still enough moisture in the ground to support a green ribbon of trees running through the canyon up to the San Pasqual Valley Agriculture Preserve that begins just to the west.

The trail stays only briefly in the canyon before climbing up the bank and following the creek along a bench about 50 feet above the woody area before ascending the south-facing slope of the canyon. It continues up this steep hillside through a series of switchbacks that can be strenuous and a good place to turn around, if hiking on a hot day. It is 1.25 miles to the top of a ridge with about a 1200-foot gain in elevation. There is no shade. Also, the trail becomes progressively indistinct and hard to follow near the top. Be sure to check your back trail as you proceed to the top so that you can easily find the return trail. It is well worth the climb to the top of the ridge for the inspiring views of the San Pasqual Valley and the surrounding hills. Enjoy the view before retracing your steps to your vehicle.

In years past, the ridge trail continued on to three viewpoints, but wildfires led to the abandonment of this part of the trail. Coastal sage scrub and chaparral are often called fire toler-

ant, or even fire dependent ecotypes. However, this is only partially true. Many species found in these habitats can survive fires, but if the fires occur too frequently these brushy habitats are converted to grasslands. The Kumey-aay Indians knew this and frequently set fires to promote the growth of the perennial native grasses whose seeds they collected and ate. Early ranchers also used fire to spread grass for their cattle. Today, all too frequent fires may result in converting some areas to weedy grasslands with highly flammable non-native annual grasses.

Honeysuckle

Distance:	6 miles, out-and-back
Difficulty:	🚶🚶🚶
Elevation gain/loss:	Up to 1250 feet
Hiking time:	3 hours
Agency:	San Diego County
Trail use:	Bicycles, dogs, horses
Trailhead GPS:	N33.10262, W116.69644
Optional map:	USGS 7.5-min *Santa Ysabel*
Atlas square:	J18
Directions:	(Santa Ysabel) From CA-78 turn north into the Santa Ysabel Preserve West trailhead parking, 1.4 miles west of Santa Ysabel.

Habitat(s):

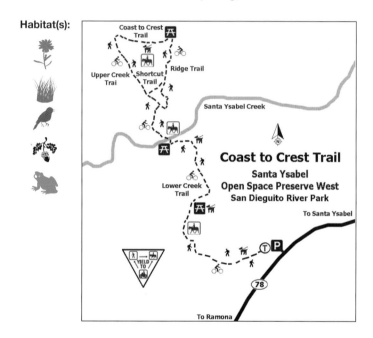

Santa Ysabel Preserve is within the San Dieguito River watershed, the drainage area from the river's headwaters near Volcan Mountain that discharges into the Pacific Ocean at the San Dieguito Lagoon in Del Mar. The land on both sides of CA-79, just north of Santa Ysabel, was acquired by The Nature Conservancy in 1999 to protect the various habitats and large animals, such as deer and mountain lions.

In 2001, San Diego County's Department of Parks and Recreation acquired 5322 acres of The Nature Conservancy lands to create both the east and west sections of the Santa Ysabel Preserve. The acreage has grown, with the latest acquisition of another 175 acres in June 2015 that connects the east and west sections for a total of 5881 acres. The preserve is part of the San Dieguito River Park and includes a por-

tion of the 71-mile Coast to Crest Trail from Volcan Mountain to the San Dieguito Lagoon.

Well before it became a preserve, the area was the home to Kumeyaay Indians who lived here for generations with cultural traditions that enabled them to thrive. With the coming of the Spanish colonists, Mission San Diego de Alcalá established Santa Ysabel Asistencia in 1818 to serve the Indian community. This small outlying mission still stands along CA-79 near the preserve. The locale then became part of Rancho Santa Ysabel, an 1844 Mexican land grant that belonged to José Joaquín Ortega and Eduardo Stokes. The town of Santa Ysabel is within the former rancho lands. It began with a store owned by C.R. Wellington and later grew to include a hotel and blacksmith shop. By 1889, the town even had its own post of-

Lark sparrow

fice—today the Santa Ysabel General Store. The primary use of the preserve lands in those days was for cattle grazing, as it is today. Hikers may encounter free range cattle. Don't approach young calves as their mothers are very protective.

One of the key attractions of this hike is to walk through grasslands to get a glimpse into the backcountry world of San Diego almost 200 years ago. The preserve has many oak trees—both Engelmann and coast live. Within the grasslands may be fields of flowers, especially in spring, with patches of coastal sage scrub accompanied by buzzing bees. Numerous bird species are also present. It also has expansive views of the mountains off in the distance where turkey vultures may be seen in the sky.

A number of colorful smaller birds also make their home in the open grasslands. Some just migrate through the area; others are winter only residents; and still others can be found here year-round. The latter includes Say's phoebe and the lark sparrow (*Chondestes grammacus*), which is a bird with a harlequin patterned head of reddish, black, and white stripes. Among the winter visitors are mountain bluebirds (*Sialia currucoides*). They are irregular visitors. In some years few or none arrive, while in other years several hundred may be found in the tall grass. Also look for greater roadrunners that may be seen in open areas.

From the trailhead, follow the Lower Creek Trail 1.84 miles to a junction with the Upper Creek Trail and the Ridge Trail. This is a loop trail. Both trails lead to the east-west connection with the Coast to Crest Trail. Right now this segment of the Coast to Crest Trail is isolated as the connecting routes have not yet been established. Bicycles, leashed dogs, and horses also have access to this small segment of the trail.

All trails within the preserve are well marked and signed. Shortcut Trail connects the Ridge Trail and the Upper Creek Trail, making a short loop. Santa Ysabel Creek runs through the middle of the preserve near the Coast to Crest Trail.

As you near the creek, look for two amphibian members of the Bufonidae or true toad family. They differ from other frogs in that they hop or walk instead of jump due to their stocky body shape and short legs. They have horizontal pupils, warty-dry skin with no tail or teeth, and for protection they have a raised mass behind their eyes called a parotoid gland. When harassed by a potential predator, the glands secrete a milky poisonous substance known as bufotoxin. The toxin affects both the cardiovascular and respiratory systems, which can lead to death, but does not normally bother humans, although it can irritate the skin, eyes, and mucous membranes. The arroyo toad (*Anaxyrus californicus*) and western toad (*Anaxyrus boreas*) look different. The western toad is larger and has a light dorsal stripe. The arroyo toad is on the federally endangered species list.

Arroyo toad

Distance:	3.25 miles, loop
Difficulty:	🚶🚶
Elevation gain/loss:	Up to 100 feet
Hiking time:	2 hours
Agency:	City of Carlsbad, City of Oceanside
Trail use:	Bicycles, dogs
Notes:	Good birding area; visitor center open 9 a.m.- 3 p.m.
Trailhead GPS:	N33.17632, W117.26990
Optional map:	USGS 7.5-min *San Luis Rey*
Atlas square:	H7
Directions:	(Oceanside) From CA-78 go south on Emerald Dr. for 0.2 mile. Continue onto Sunset Drive for 0.4 mile. Turn right on Emerald Drive. Go 0.4 mile. Turn left on Lake Boulevard. Go 0.3 mile. Turn right on Ridge Road and go to the Oak Riparian Park parking lot.

Habitat(s):

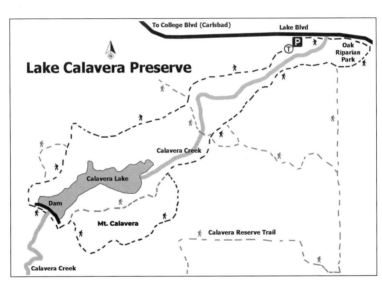

Lake Calavera Preserve is a hidden gem within the City of Carlsbad that contains the remnants of a 22 million-year-old volcano. It also has a lake created by a dam constructed in 1940. The name *calavera* means skull in Spanish and refers to the shape of Mount Calavera, which is the plug or the solidified volcanic magma that was once within the vent of the volcano. The actual volcano eroded away long ago, leaving behind only the plug with its six-sided columnar joints of basalt. It is only one of three volcanic plugs found in southern California. Today the preserve is a popular recreation area and an important wildlife corridor that is part of the Agua Hedionda watershed.

There are many ways to enter the preserve, but most lack adequate parking and toilet facilities. However, the nearby Oak Riparian Park in Oceanside does have off-street parking and restrooms. Although not part of the preserve, the park is adjacent to the northeast corner of the preserve and a short connecting trail leads from the park to the preserve. The trail passes through coast live oaks and riparian habitat before it enters the preserve and adds to your enjoyment of this trip. The hike described here uses well-traveled mostly marked trails, though it can be a challenge not to veer off on one of the many informal, heavily used side trails. Do not worry about getting lost. That would be almost impossible as your goals are usually within sight.

From the parking lot at Oak Riparian Park, walk to the southwest and take the concrete path leading west and then south toward the

Bush monkey flower

At 1.2 miles into the hike, you will find yourself on the nearly flat of Cerro de la Calavera—the volcanic plug composed of fine-grained basalt that clogged the volcano's throat. After the volcano erupted for the last time, its cone slowly eroded away leaving only the plug. In recent times, people helped this process along as the western face of the plug was mined for close to 25 years to produce gravel.

On a clear winter's day, you will be able to see the ocean to the west and spot San Clemente and Catalina Islands. Look northeast to see the snowcapped San Gorgonio and San Jacinto mountains, east to Palomar Mountain, and southeast to Double Peak.

Find the trail on the southwest side and keep to the right as you descend to a nearly flat trail leading north and then east around the mountain. When you reach the northwest side of the hill, follow a trail down to the dam that impounds Calavera Creek creating the lake. Cross the dam and take the trail leading to the right just beyond the end of the dam. This trail will take you back to Oak Riparian Park as it proceeds through several areas undergoing habitat restoration. Posters provide information on the work being done to restore the habitat. After 2.75 miles into the hike there is a junction with Creek Crossing Trail. The southern choice intersects the trail coming out from Oak Riparian Park. The eastern choice leads to Lake Street and back to the park.

oak-lined stream, where the concrete ends and a well-used dirt trail begins. Cross the stream and proceed west, following the trail on the south side of the stream, passing under huge live oak trees. In 0.12 mile, pick up the signed Lake Calavera Preserve trail. Continue walking west through the riparian ecosystem with more coast live oaks and riparian species. For the first 0.5 mile, the trail follows and crosses the stream several times before leaving the stream and entering an open grassland of mainly non-native grasses. At this point, Mount Calavera or Cerro de la Calavera, also known by its unofficial name of Skull Hill, visibly rises up to a height of 513 feet.

In another 0.6 mile, there is a well-marked fork in the trail. Choose the trail marked "Peak" passing through coastal sage scrub where you will find the yellow-flowered bush monkey flower (***Diplacus longiflorus*** replaces the earlier name of *Mimulus aurantiacus* var. *pubescens*). The colors of monkey flower range from more red on the coast to more yellow inland with species hybridizing. Hummingbirds prefer the red flowers over other colors, and inland, most pollination is done by sphinx moths. Deerweed (***Acmispon glaber***) is also special in the coastal sage community as it is a legume, which makes it a nitrogen-fixing plant. Legumes, which are able to grow in nutritive poor soils, play an important ecological role within plant communities. Other nitrogen-fixing plants include *Ceanothus* species, mountain-mahogany, and white alder.

Deerweed

Distance:	2.5 miles, out-and-back
Difficulty:	🚶🚶
Elevation gain/loss:	Minimal
Hiking time:	2 hours
Agency:	City of Vista
Trail use:	Bicycles, dogs
Notes:	Dog park located at South Buena Vista Park
Trailhead GPS:	N33.15697, W117.24671
Optional map:	USGS 7.5-min *San Marcos*; *San Luis Rey*
Atlas square:	I7
Directions:	(Vista) From CA-78 go south on Sycamore Avenue for 0.2 mile. Turn right on Shadowridge Drive. Go 1.9 miles. Turn left at Antigua Drive and go to the parking lot.

Habitat(s):

Buena Vista Park is a typical urban park, with manicured grass, ball fields, a man-made pond, and picnic tables. The Arroyo Vista Trail leads from the south end of the manicured park into a semi-wild, natural area along Agua Hedionda Creek and passes near or through a dense riparian forest consisting of coast live oaks, arroyo willows, and western sycamores, with an occasional toyon or sugar bush.

In places the forest is heavily infested with non-native plants, particularly eucalyptus and Mexican fan palms. Despite this, it is a dense, overarching forest dominated by huge, beautiful oaks and western sycamores. There is some water in Hedionda Creek year-round, fed by urban runoff. The creek also flows through a marshy area. Over 80 species of birds, both

year-round residents and migratory visitors, can be seen here.

While urban runoff has a few benefits, principally in providing needed water for meadows and riparian vegetation, it also causes major problems. As more of the areas surrounding parks, preserves, and wild areas become urbanized, storm runoff can significantly damage stream environments. There are several reasons for this. First, houses, driveways, and streets are largely impermeable to rain so it rapidly runs off into streams instead of percolating down into the soil and rocks below. The sudden rush of water into steams can cause major bank erosion, cutting deep channels in the streambed and destroying the characteristic riparian vegetation of the banks. You

Crossing Hedionda Creek

will be able to see the results of urban runoff here as you hike along Agua Hedionda Creek. The fact that storm water doesn't percolate into the ground also reduces the subsequent slow discharge of underground water into streams during intervals between storms, causing streams to dry up sooner. Urban runoff also washes pollutants from streets and houses into streams and ultimately into the ocean. These pollutants include bacteria and toxic chemicals that can sicken swimmers and kill fish.

Most of the surrounding hillsides are covered with typical inland coastal sage scrub vegetation, dominated by coastal sagebrush, black sage, and California buckwheat. These shrubs react to summer drought by losing most of their leaves. However, once the winter rains appear they come to life, producing new leaves and flowers. If sufficient rain falls, a large assortment of annual flowering plants appears.

After the first winter rains, the initial green-up may be caused by the early germination of non-native, invasive grasses such as brome and oats (***Bromus* spp., *Avena* spp.**). These grasses from the Mediterranean region in Europe were introduced into California along with the cattle that first arrived, beginning with Spanish settlers in the late 1700s. After rainfall, they germinate faster than native grasses and forbs. The exotic species co-opt light, nutrients, water, and space resources, displacing native grass and flower species.

Walk to the south end of the parking area and cross the pond dam on the paved road. The trailhead for the Arroyo Vista Trail is signed and begins on the left at the end of the road. The trail is obvious and easily followed with very little elevation gain or loss. The only drawback is that mountain bikers and cross-country runners make extensive use of the park and this trail. As a result, the trail is eroded in places, and there are many unofficial trails leading from the main trail. However, you cannot get lost.

Passing through an oak woodland

Distance:	1, 4.5 or 7.5 miles, out-and-back and loops
Difficulty:	🚶, 🚶🚶🚶 or 🚶🚶🚶🚶, depending on distance chosen
Elevation gain/loss:	Minimal, up to 900 or 1932 feet
Hiking time:	1, 3, or 4 hours
Agency:	City of San Marcos
Trail use:	Bicycles, dogs
Notes:	Paved near Discovery Lake
Trailhead GPS:	N33.12472, W117.17888
Optional map:	USGS 7.5-min *San Marcos*; *Rancho Santa Fe*
Atlas square:	I9
Directions:	(San Marcos) From CA-78 go south on Twin Oaks Valley Road for 0.6 mile. Turn right on Craven Road. Go 0.6 mile. Turn left on Foxhall Road. Go 0.3 mile. Parking lot on the right.

Habitat(s):

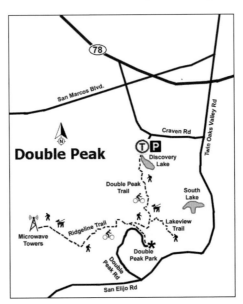

Something is always blooming nearly every month of the year on this network of trails to and around Double Peak in San Marcos' Cerro de la Posas Hills. About 80% of the trails are fire or service roads, some paved and up to 10 feet wide, while others are dirt.

The trail from the parking area crosses Discovery Lake dam and forks. The trail to the left proceeds around Discovery Lake. It is flat and about 1 mile long. The trail to the peak is the one on the right, which proceeds rather sharply up a hillside, reaching a housing development in about 0.5 mile. The trail continues through the housing development on Stoneridge Way for 0.1 mile. When Stoneridge turns right, the trail goes left, leaving the houses behind as it passes a large water tank, then resumes the climb up the mountain. At

1.15 miles into the hike, there is a brass plaque set in concrete marking the start of the San Elijo Hills 10K. The trail forks here. Go right to take the direct route to the peak. However, the trail to the left, known as the Lakeview Trail, is an interesting short easy addition to the hike to the peak. It is almost level as it contours around the chaparral covered ridges, providing views of South Lake in one of the canyons below and of the more distant state university campus, set in the rapidly urbanizing City of San Marcos. Unfortunately, this part of the Cerro de la Posas Hills was devastated by a deliberately set wildfire on May 14, 2014. While this makes for a less that inspiring look at the chaparral now, if you come during the spring in the next few years, you will be greeted by numerous colorful fire-following annuals.

Don Fosket

A field of canchalagua on the trail—only grows in undisturbed areas

To reach the peak, come back to the brass 10K marker and follow the trail to the right to Double Peak Drive, a newly built road that leads from the community of San Elijo Hills to Double Peak Park. After reaching the road, turn left on the trail that parallels this road and continue for about 0.25 mile to reach Double Peak Park where you will find water and restroom facilities. On a clear winter day, the ocean view from the peak includes Catalina Island, while to the north the snowcapped summits of the San Gabriel and San Bernardino mountains will be visible.

Listen for the northern mockingbird (*Mimus polyglottos*), whose gray plumage is varied with white wing patches and white outer tail feathers. You will hear it mimic other birds, car alarms, lawnmowers, etcetera, and even your whistles and chirps. Each call is repeated, often in a series of three, before it moves on to the next. Males can learn up to 200 calls, and in the spring, females are attracted to mates with the largest vocabulary.

After taking in the views from the peak, go back down the trail, alongside Double Peak Drive, to another trail going off to the right. After going less than 0.1 mile on this trail, there is a dirt path leading off to the right. This leads back down to Discovery Lake and, if you take it, you will have gone 4.6 miles when you reach

the lake. However, you could take the Ridgeline Trail leading off to the left that follows the spine of the ridge to the microwave relay towers. This will add another 3 miles, out-and-back, to the hike. This side trail is popular with mountain bikers and runners as well as fitness walkers, but it also passes through interesting coastal sage scrub. Look for mariposa lilies, roadrunners, and western meadowlarks as the trail passes a new San Elijo Hills development. These open areas are rapidly disappearing as housing development progresses.

Wendy Esterly

Northern mockingbird

Distance:	4 miles, loop
Difficulty:	🥾🥾
Elevation gain/loss:	up to 200 feet
Hiking time:	2 hours
Agency:	City of Carlsbad
Trail use:	Bicycles, dogs not in park but allowed on surrounding Leo Carrillo trails
Notes:	Hours posted Tuesday-Saturday, 9 a.m. to 5 p.m., and Sunday from 11 a.m. to 5 p.m., closed holidays
Trailhead GPS:	N33.11861, W117.23645
Optional map:	USGS 7.5-min *Rancho Santa Fe*
Atlas square:	J8
Directions:	(Carlsbad) From I-5 go east on Palomar Airport Road for 4.7 miles. Turn right on Melrose Drive. Go 1.1 miles. Turn right on Carrillo Way, then right again on Flying Carrillo Lane and go to the parking lot. From CA-78 go south on Sycamore Avenue for 2.3 miles. Turn left on South Melrose Drive. Go 2.2 miles. Turn right on Carrillo Way, then right again on Flying Leo Carrillo Lane, and go to the parking lot.

Habitat(s):

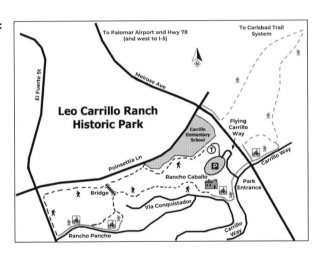

Leo Carrillo was a well-known film and television actor during the middle of the last century—best known as Pancho, the sidekick to the Cisco Kid, from the 1950's television series. He had deep roots in Alta California. He was the great-great grandson of José Raimundo Carrillo, one of the original Spanish settlers of San Diego and a member of the 1769 Portolá Expedition. In 1937 Carrillo purchased 1700 acres that had been part of the original Spanish land grant given to Juan Marron, then known as Rancho Agua Hedionda, and now a major part of the City of Carlsbad. Between 1937 and 1939, Carrillo built a large hacienda, carriage house, and barn, as well as a deep pool with a white sand beach and a cantina on his newly acquired property. In addition to his prominence as an actor he was a noted conservationist and served on the California Beaches and Parks Commission, the predecessor of today's California State Park Commission. Leo Carrillo State Park was named in his honor. Carrillo was instrumental in the establishment of the Anza-Borrego Desert State Park.

Eventually Carrillo's Rancho de los Quiotes, as it was called, became a mecca for Hollywood actors and other notables, but it was also a working cattle ranch that ultimately included over 2500 acres. Carrillo died in 1961, and over the years much of the ranch land was sold off for development. However, 27 acres, containing most of the historic buildings, were acquired by the City of Carlsbad and are now the Leo Carrillo Ranch Historic Park. The ranch is

Cultivars along the ranch road

a designated California Historical Landmark that was opened to the public in August 2003. It is also listed on the National Register of Historical Places. The buildings and grounds are continuing to be restored and preserved. The roads and trails connecting the historic buildings and parts of the ranchlands are now incorporated into the Carlsbad trail system. It has become a great place to learn about the area history and to get some exercise on the trails.

Approximately 4 miles of trails are available for easy hiking through the open space around the historic park. The city hiking trails are connected to those within the park and are open for hiking even when the park is closed. A high wall surrounds the 27-acre historic park. Peacocks patrol the grounds while its roads and trails are lined with non-native cultivars like blue agave, pyracantha, eucalyptus, and Peruvian pepper trees. Trails on both sides of an intermittent stream contain an abundance of native western sycamores, arroyo willows, and a few oaks, but they also have many non-native, highly invasive species, particularly selloa pampas grass (*Cortaderia selloana*) and the giant reed (*Arundo donax*), both in the grass family.

Selloa pampas grass, a native from the Pampas of Argentina, is an attractive ornamental grass that grows in clumps and has densely-tufted plumes atop upright stalks

that can reach a height of 10 feet. The silver, white, cream, or pinkish-colored plumes can be 1-3 feet long. Unfortunately each pampas grass plant can produce a million seeds in its lifetime, and the seeds can be carried long distances into native plant areas by the wind. The seeds readily germinate and can grow in virtually any habitat where they compete very successfully with native species for water, nutrients, and space. Although it is on California's list of invasive species, it is still commonly grown as an ornamental in other states.

The giant reed or Arundo, unlike pampas grass, is sterile and reproduces only vegeta-

Peacocks on the property

Alan King

Selloa pampas grass

tively. Even so, it can form dense thickets that can grow to a height of 20 feet along streams that choke out native riparian species and modify river hydrology. It reduces wildlife habitat and contributes to higher fire frequency. Giant reed is a Mediterranean plant.

One of the birds that you might see on the ranch, besides the many domesticated peacocks that freely roam the property, is the very small Allen's hummingbird (*Selasphorus sasin*). It nests only along a small strip of coastal California and Oregon and is a recent colonist of San Diego County. It was first discovered breeding at San Onofre in 2001 and has since spread south and increased spectacularly. The male has an iridescent scarlet-red throat and a green back contrasting with rufous on the crown, rump, and tail. The chest is white and the belly is rusty. The female's underparts are mostly white, with rufous on the sides and in the tail. Despite its diminutive size, Allen's hummingbird is even more aggressive than Anna's, with males chasing away other males, different hummingbird species, and even predatory birds like kestrels and hawks. Courtship involves some amazing flight logistics with the male frantically flying back and forth like a pendulum or making high-speed dives from 100 feet.

Clearly, this is not pristine native California habitat, but it is a pleasant place to walk, par-

ticularly if you can incorporate your hike on the city trails with a visit to the historic park. The park has limited hours for visitors, but the surrounding hiking trails have no restrictions and can be visited even if the historic park is closed. Guided tours of the park are given on weekends. Call (760) 476-1042 to verify hours and the time for weekend tours.

John Hopper

Giant reed

Distance:	4.5 miles, loop
Difficulty:	🏃🏃
Elevation gain/loss:	Up to 500 feet
Hiking time:	3 hours
Agency:	City of Carlsbad; CNLM
Trail use:	Bicycles, dogs
Trailhead GPS:	N33.08332, W117.22158
Optional map:	USGS 7.5-min
Atlas square:	J8
Directions:	(Carlsbad) From I-5 and go east on Leucadia Boulevard for 1.8 miles. Continue onto Olivenhain Road. Go 1 mile. Continue onto Rancho Santa Fe Road. Go 1.9 miles. Turn right on Camino Junipero. Go 0.3 mile. Turn right on Avenida Maravilla and park. The trailhead is on the north side of Camino Junipero where the powerlines cross the road. From CA-78 go west on San Marcos Boulevard for 2.1 miles. Turn left on Rancho Santa Fe Road. Go 3.6 miles. Turn left on Camino Junipero, and go 0.3 mile. Turn right on Avenida Maravilla and park. The trailhead is on the north side of Camino Junipero where the powerlines cross the road.

Habitat(s):

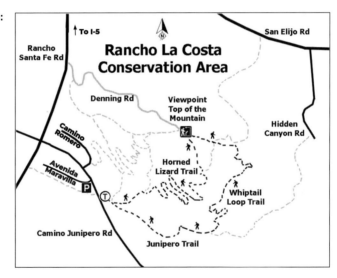

The Rancho La Costa Habitat Conservation Area was created in 2005 to protect the coastal sage scrub habitat that has been threatened by urban development. The Center for Natural Lands Management regularly monitors key rare or endangered plants within this area that include thornmint, Del Mar manzanita, Orcutt's brodiaea, and Orcutt's goldenbush. They also remove non-native species from the conservation area. Wildlife corridors are monitored with digital cameras, and there is an ongoing program to install and replace signage and fencing as needed. This is an example of a program that can protect sensitive habits within urban areas.

The goal of this hike is to climb to the top of the unnamed mountain that rises steeply to Carlsbad's highest point, where the view will be your reward. It offers a 360-degree, panoramic view of the North Coast, nearby Batiquitos Lagoon, and beyond to the Pacific and its islands. On a clear day the view to the south extends to Mount Soledad and the tall buildings of downtown San Diego. Other clearly visible landmarks include Iron Mountain, Mt. Woodson, Bernardo Peak, and Palomar Mountain.

View from the top

There are eight different trails that lead to the top of the mountain. These trails go through terrain cloaked with coastal sage scrub vegetation. The best route up is the Horned Lizard Trail. For the return take Denning Road, a dirt road to the Whiptail Loop Trail, which will lead down. There may be a good reason why this trail is named Whiptail Loop. Be on the lookout for a colorful and very energetic lizard with a very long tail—the diurnal orange-throated whiptail.

The slopes of this mountain have several large patches of crust called cryptogamic soil. Cryptogams are plants that reproduce without flowers or seeds but rather through spores. The name refers to a hidden marriage where sexual reproduction is not obvious. Examples of cryptogamic plants include ferns, mosses, algae, and fungi. Here lichens are the dominant cryptogam. Lichens can also reproduce asexually.

Spineshrub (*Adolphia californica*) is common in this coastal sage habitat. It is also found in Baja California southward to near El Rosario. Though abundant in this location it is relatively uncommon elsewhere and is considered endangered in California. It is a drought deciduous spreading shrub with rigid branches and stiff twigs that are thorn-tipped. Both leaves and flowers are small and inconspicuous. The flowers are followed by small tan to reddish fruits, technically known as spherical capsules.

Begin by hiking east on the dirt road that parallels the powerline that crosses Camino Junipero Road. Follow the powerline for about 0.4 mile and look for the start of the signed Horned Lizard Trail that leads off to the left. The trail goes all the way to the top through a series of switchbacks that make this an easy climb. At 1.6 miles into the hike the trail crosses a firebreak, and at 1.68 miles the trail forks. Go straight ahead to the Viewpoint, the term used to designate the top of the mountain. When you reach the broad almost flat high point you will have hiked 2 miles.

After taking in the view, go east on the dirt trail designated Denning Road that crosses the northeast shoulder of the peak. Continue east on Denning Road for 0.33 mile until you reach a sign where the Whiptail Loop Trail crosses the road. Go right on the Whiptail Loop Trail and follow it for approximately 2 miles down to a powerline access road. Go right and follow it west back to Camino Junipero Road and your vehicle.

Spineshrub

116 CHAPTER 6

Distance:	3.75 miles, out-and-back
Difficulty:	🚶🚶🚶
Elevation gain/loss:	Up to 1000 feet
Hiking time:	3 hours
Agency:	San Diego County
Trailhead GPS:	N33.06845, W117.26775
Optional map:	USGS 7.5-min *Encinitas*
Atlas square:	K7
Directions:	(Encinitas) From I-5 go east on Leucadia Boulevard for 1.6 miles. Turn left on Town Center Place. Find a place to park near REI in the large lot serving the numerous surrounding businesses and restaurants.

Habitat(s):

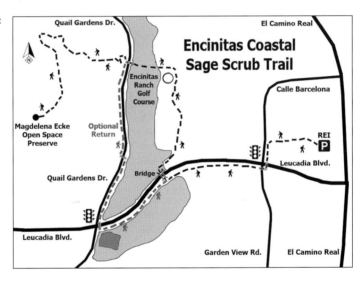

The coastal sage plant community has been substantially reduced in San Diego County, being replaced by housing developments, shopping centers, business centers, and golf courses. However, remnants remain in some of our coastal canyons and in special reserves. One such remnant, on the Encinitas Ranch, is on a public trail on a coastal ridge. The trail has stunning views of sandstone cliffs and the ocean beyond, as it goes past a golf course and to the Magdalena Ecke Open Space Preserve.

Coastal sage scrub is not chaparral. Summer dormant shrubs, especially coastal sagebrush and black sage, dominate coastal sage scrub habitat. Most shrubs within this habitat are rarely more than 4.5 feet tall, with relatively soft, easily bent branches. In contrast, chaparral shrubs are evergreen and have stiff, often thorny branches, which grow together to form an impenetrable thicket. Coastal sage scrub is sometimes called soft chaparral. You will

see many chaparral species growing on the north-facing slope, on your left, as you walk up the trail paralleling Leucadia Boulevard. This is a good example of the intermixture of chaparral and coastal sage scrub species.

Parts of this trail are on sidewalks along high traffic volume city streets. From Town Center Place, begin walking west up the street past a Walmart to Calle Barcelona. Turn left at Calle Barcelona and head to the signal light on Leucadia Boulevard, crossing to the south side of this busy road, which then becomes Garden View Road to the south of Leucadia Boulevard. A paved trail begins at the southwest corner intersection of Garden View Road and Leucadia Boulevard. The elevation of this paved trail gradually increases as the ridge is climbed. The vegetation on either side of the trail is restored habitat consisting of coastal sage scrub species. There are also a few large scrub oaks and numerous Torrey pines, which may predate the restoration.

View toward the golf course

After walking roughly 0.5 mile, there will be a bridge crossing Leucadia Boulevard. The bridge is primarily for golf carts, but pedestrians can legally walk across the bridge, taking care not to obstruct traffic. Unless you are a member of the Encinitas Ranch Golf Club, do not turn left or enter the course. Instead, immediately turn right once across the bridge, and go up the trail to the top of the ridge. Turn left upon reaching the ridge crest. The trail continues through coastal sage scrub with the golf course and scattered eucalyptus trees on the left and rust-colored sandstone cliffs on the right. There are outstanding views to the east, encompassing the extensive housing developments of Encinitas and Carlsbad, as well as west to the ocean. A little over 0.25 mile ahead, the trail crosses the golf course (stay on the trail) and reaches Quail Gardens Drive.

The trail continues on the other side of Quail Gardens Drive, dropping into the Magdalena Ecke Open Space Preserve and passing down a canyon through coastal sage scrub and riparian habitats. Although managed by the City of Encinitas, the trails are not well marked or maintained. However, these trails present an opportunity for a more extensive exploration of coastal sage scrub habitat, and a chance to see how it adapts to an infestation of invasive species, particularly eucalyptus. Return to Quail Gardens Drive after exploring this area and either return the way you came or follow Quail Gardens Drive south to Leucadia Bouvelard. Cross the boulevard and follow it east back to your vehicle.

View toward Leucadia Boulevard

Distance:	2 miles, out-and-back
Difficulty:	🥾🥾
Elevation gain/loss:	Up to 100 feet
Hiking time:	1 hour
Agency:	City of Encinitas
Trail use:	Bicycles, dogs
Trailhead GPS:	N33.05446, W117.27369
Optional map:	USGS 7.5-min *Encinitas*
Atlas square:	K7
Directions:	(Encinitas) From I-5 go east on Encinitas Boulevard for 0.8 mile. Turn left on Rosebay Drive and continue to the end. Park on the street. The trail is to your right and goes up the hill.

Habitat(s):

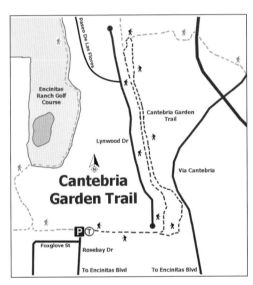

The Cantebria Garden Trail is part of the 9.5-mile Encinitas Ranch trail system that was included in the design of the 850-acre development in 1994. Previously, the property was part of the Paul Ecke Ranch known for its world-famous poinsettias. The Eckes moved to Encinitas in 1923, originally growing their poinsettias outdoors and then propagating them in greenhouses. In the 1990s, faced with intense competition, they began growing their poinsettias in Guatemala and sold part of their ranch holdings, which were developed into the Encinitas Ranch. The land surrounding the Cantebria Garden Trail was left undisturbed.

You will be pleasantly surprised to discover so many varieties of California native plants along this short urban canyon walk. The trail is popular with neighbors and their leashed dogs, yet is never crowded. Bikes are rarely encountered. There are mature laurel sumac, mis-

sion and Del Mar manzanita, lemonadeberry, mountain-mahogany, and yerba santa along the trail. Large *Ceanothus* and Torrey pines are easily spotted a short distance from the trail.

While coastal breezes keep Cantebria Garden Trail pleasant year-round, the best time for color is March and April. Deerweed shows off spectacularly, and the scent of sagebrush fills the air. In summer and fall, there may be San Diego wreath-plant (***Stephanomeria diegensis***), a highly drought resistant aster whose small flowers have serrated petal tips. San Diego mountain-mahogany (***Cercocarpus minutiflorus***), a tall shrub adorned with a blanket of feathery-plumed fruits, also is eye catching in the fall.

The rabbit that may be seen darting across the trail in twilight hours is the brush rabbit (***Sylvilagus bachmani***), the rabbit most associated with dense chaparral. It is smaller

Torrey pines atop the ridgeline

but similar to the desert cottontail and much smaller than the black-tailed jackrabbit. The brush rabbit is largely crepuscular, active at dusk and dawn. It rarely leaves the protection of scrub cover for long and may be difficult to spot. The fur is a finely grizzled mix of gray and brown, and the underside of the tail is white. When a threat approaches, it will dart directly into the brush where it will sit motionless and blend into the dark background. A common predator is the coyote, whose scat often reveals the remains of a rabbit it had for dinner.

Birds that may be seen or heard include finches that chatter away as they forage among the sagebrush, chamise, and black sage. California towhees are nearly always visible. Wrentits and bushtits keep in touch with each other. In the spring, you will hear, and possibly see black-headed grosbeaks calling to each other.

Begin the walk by going up the hill from the end of Rosebay Drive, and at the top of the hill, take the path to the right at the Y-junction to descend. It's a bit steep, but levels off shortly. To make this a loop walk turn left at the T-junction and walk up the hill. At the end of the canyon trail are Torrey pines on a flat trail abutting the Encinitas Ranch houses. From here, views of the San Bernardino Mountains can be particularly exhilarating on a clear day after snowfall in the higher altitudes. Otherwise, turn around to retrace your steps where there may be plants not noticed on the way out.

San Diego wreath plant

San Diego mountain-mahogany

Distance:	2-4 miles, loop
Difficulty:	🏃🏃 or 🏃🏃🏃
Elevation gain/loss:	Up to 550 feet
Hiking time:	2 hours
Agency:	City of Encinitas
Trail use:	Bicycles, dogs
Notes:	Good birding area; visitor center open 9 a.m.- 3 p.m.
Trailhead GPS:	N33.03056, W117.25116
Optional map:	USGS 7.5-min *Encinitas*; *Rancho Santa Fe*
Atlas square:	L7
Directions:	(Encinitas) From I-5 go east on Manchester Avenue for 1 mile. Continue onto South El Camino Real for 0.7 mile. Turn right on Calle Ryan and park at the end of the road.

Habitat(s):

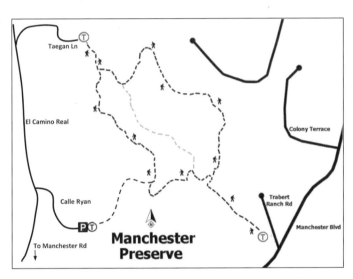

The Manchester Preserve is an island in an urban-suburban setting where endangered species such as the California gnatcatcher, Del Mar manzanita, thornmint, and Orcutt's goldenbush can thrive. Since the Center for Natural Lands Management took title to Manchester Preserve in 1998, it has striven to keep the area free of invasive non-native plants that might compete with native species. It encourages public access and understanding of why it is important to stay on the trails to protect the endangered species found there. That includes keeping dogs on a leash to protect both the plants and the dogs. The ongoing challenge is to prevent extirpation of these endangered species. Preserves such as these help researchers to identify the best management practices to keep them viable.

This hike begins at the entrance off Calle Ryan where endangered thornmint and Orcutt's goldenbush (*Hazardia orcuttii*) grow. Orcutt's goldenbush is an aster and a native of Baja California and this location in San Diego County. It is a 1.5-3 feet tall perennial evergreen with small yellow flowers. The leaves are leathery and pointed. Both grow in coastal sage scrub and chaparral communities.

The trails pass through coastal sage scrub and chaparral. For an easier excursion, stay on the interior loop trail, which passes a willow woodland shortly beyond the stone steps. The trails wander among steep, eroded canyon cliffs, and provide some fine vistas. The vegetation is dense and gives the feeling of being farther afield than its suburban setting.

The spur off the loop that goes up the wooden steps near the Taegan Lane entrance is well worth taking. Note a magnificent mission manzanita (*Xylococcus bicolor*) on the left as the trail starts to gain in elevation. The berries

Maggie Thompson

Del Mar manzanita

are visible in spring and summer and have a rich and shiny color, from red to black. They are preceded by small urn-shaped flowers in the winter months. There are other mission manzanitas and Del Mar manzanitas (*Arcto-staphylos glandulosa* subsp. *crassifolia*) in the immediate area. Although both manzanitas are members of the heath family, the two are distinct. Look at the leaves and bark to tell the difference. The leaves of the mission manzanita are oblong, glossy, and dark green on top while the undersides are lighter and have a velvety texture with edges that curl under when they age. The bark is red-gray and smooth and lighter colored than the Del Mar manzanita, which has red bark and thick leathery, dark gray-green leaves. The berries of all manzanitas were collected by Native Americans and used to make a tea that was rich in vitamin C. Manzanitas were also wild game indicators as many animals were attracted to the berries, including squirrels, rodents, deer, and birds. Hunters would wait in thickets to catch or trap game.

Continue to the top of the stairs and pause again to take in the view. On a clear day you can see neighboring hills and mountains. Farther along, the fences are a reminder that you are in a preserve. Continue up the rise on a utility easement for a great view of the preserve and beyond. Return to the loop trail to complete the hike.

Keir Morse

Orcutt's goldenbush

Diana Lindsay

Mission manzanita

Distance:	3 miles, out-and-back
Difficulty:	🚶🚶🚶
Elevation gain/loss:	Up to 800 feet
Hiking time:	2 hours
Agency:	OMWD
Trail use:	Dogs; bicycles and horses limited to designated trails
Notes:	Hours posted 8 a.m. to sunset.
Trailhead GPS:	N33.08656, W117.14526
Optional map:	USGS 7.5-min *Rancho Santa Fe*; *Escondido*
Atlas square:	J9
Directions:	(Escondido) From I-15 go west on Valley Parkway for 1 mile. Turn right on Avenida Del Diablo. Go 0.6 mile. Turn right on Citracado Parkway. Go 0.1 mile. Turn left on Harmony Grove Village Parkway. Go 0.4 mile. Turn left on Harmony Grove Road. Go 2.2 miles to the reserve staging area on the left.

Habitat(s):

With about 11 miles of trails, the Elfin Forest Recreational Reserve presents many different hiking possibilities, including a leisurely stroll along an oak-shaded stream, an easy hike along a nature trail, or a heart-pumping, multi-hour workout. Native plant communities in the reserve include oak riparian, oak woodland, coastal sage scrub, and chaparral. The best time to visit is from January through May when the landscape awakens, the shrubs and trees produce a fresh set of leaves, and flowers greet you wherever you hike. The reserve also is home to the Elfin Forest Interpretive Center housed in a newly built green building. It is shaped somewhat like a large mushroom with a living roof making the building alone worth a visit. The center has an

exhibit that changes every four months. They also hold lectures and field trips for children in grades 3-6. The center was established and is managed by the Escondido Creek Conservancy, an organization that owns and/or manages several properties in the Escondido Creek area, including the reserve.

The Way Up Trail is the most heavily used trail in the reserve, not only by hikers, but also by equestrians and mountain bikers. After leaving the staging area, the trail crosses Escondido Creek on a concrete bridge and then proceeds sharply up through a shady coast live oak forest. With increased elevation, the trail transitions into lush chaparral, the elfin forest for which the reserve is named. Chaparral plants are woody shrubs, adapted to dryer con-

View of Lake Hodges

ditions and are generally shorter, smaller, and more compact than forest trees.

In a little over 1 mile, the trail levels out on a coastal sage shrub covered plateau, and your efforts are rewarded by an inspiring view off to the northeast. Continue another 0.5 mile to the Ridgetop Picnic Area where there is drinking water, portable toilets, picnic tables, and a view of the Olivenhain Reservoir.

After taking in the view, return to the Ridgeline Maintenance Road and go right up another steep hill. Just over the top of the hill is another shade structure and the beginning of the Lake Hodges Overlook Trail. From the overlook, a hike down a steep gravel road will take you to Lake Hodges, but getting back up is strenuous. You can return to your vehicle the way you came or explore the many other trails in the reserve.

The southwest trail goes to the dam that formed the Olivenhain Reservoir. Although you are not allowed go to the dam itself or into the water, there is an exhibit just above the dam describing how it was built. The Olivenhain Dam is a storage facility capable of holding almost eight billion gallons of water (24,000 acre-feet). Instead of impounding a river, the dam was built in a dry box canyon and is used as an emergency water storage facility. The water is imported from the Colorado River and the Metropolitan Water District. The reservoir is also used for hydroelectric generation.

One highly recommended alternative hike is the Botanical Trail. The Botanical Trail will be on your right as you descend the Way Up Trail. It has 24 numbered posts to identify chaparral plants. To translate the numbers to names, you must pick up the Botanical Trail Guide before you leave the staging area. One caution: if you take the Botanical Trail, you must ford Escondido Creek to get back to your vehicle. Escondido Creek, which flows from Lake Wohlford to San Elijo Lagoon, has a perennial flow that could be treacherous after a big rain storm.

Olivenhain reservoir and dam

Distance:	1.75 miles, 3 loops
Difficulty:	🚶
Elevation gain/loss:	Minimal
Hiking time:	1 hour
Agency:	SDRP
Trail use:	Dogs
Notes:	Hours posted dawn to dusk
Trailhead GPS:	N32.97001, W117.23969
Optional map:	USGS 7.5-min *Del Mar*
Atlas square:	M7
Directions:	(Del Mar) From I-5 go east on Via De La Valle for 1.3 miles. Turn right on El Camino Real. Go 1.2 miles to the parking lot on the right.

Habitat(s):

Dust Devil
Nature Trail
San Dieguito River Park

The Dust Devil Nature Trail was named in honor of the Dust Devils, a dedicated group of volunteers who work regularly with the San Dieguito River Park Rangers, building and maintaining trails within the San Dieguito River Park. The trail has three loops and is popular with local residents who use the trails to walk their dogs, stroll, and jog. The trail was built on a mesa created from excavated soils when the lagoon underwent an extensive restoration starting in 2005. The mesa tops were eventually replanted with native scrub that is slowly taking hold. There is no shade, but a fresh sea breeze often keeps the area cool, allowing this to be hiked during all times of the year.

All three loops can be accessed from the parking area with the north trail the longest. It begins at the trailhead and trends north through areas of saltbush. Portions of intact coastal sage scrub can be seen to the east. The trail turns west and hikers can enjoy a view of

the restored San Dieguito Lagoon. The valley was part of an ancient seafloor that was uplifted by tectonic action. The San Dieguito River, which originates near Volcan Mountain, has carved a 1-mile-wide valley and deposited sediments near the mouth of the river. This eventually created a bay that later turned to marshland as sediments continued to build up near the river mouth. A seasonal pond from the river can be seen to the northwest. The trail turns southeast and follows the lagoon access road back to the trailhead.

The west trail branches from the north loop just after it turns east onto the access road. It features a great view of a seasonal pond to the north teeming with migratory waterfowl during the winter months, when wood ducks, ring-necked ducks, mallards, and buffleheads (*Bucephala albeola*) visit. The bufflehead is a small compact duck. The male is mostly white with a black back. The head is mostly dark and

Andrew Currie

Eucalyptus

iridescent, glossed with purple and green, contrasting with a large white patch on the nape. Females are gray with an oval white cheek patch. Bufflehead refers to their large bulbous head (buffalo and head). The bufflehead's small size allows it to nest in tree cavities dug by the northern flicker, a member of the woodpecker family. Buffleheads spend most of their time on the water diving for food. Shorebirds such as herons, curlew, and willits are frequent visitors to the pond, though fewer birds are visible during the summer months.

The east loop is a short, level walk that begins at the south side of the trailhead. A stand of eucalyptus trees (**Eucalyptus spp.**) can be seen on the southwest side. Eucalyptus trees are native to Australia. They were introduced to southern California in the 1850s, initially because the straight trunks were thought to have great potential for shade and for lumber used in shipbuilding and railroad ties. Unfortunately the wood splits and curls. However, once introduced, they became a significant problem because they invaded native habitats, successfully competing for space and water, thus disrupting ecological relationships. Many species of eucalyptus are now considered invasive. Also, branches can be lost with little warning, often causing hazards to pedes-

trians or cars under trees. Fortunately many local conservancies now have restoration plans in place and are removing eucalyptus in order to restore native ecosystems, especially riparian.

Donna Zoll

Vegetation restoration

Distance:	4 miles, out-and-back
Difficulty:	🚶🚶
Elevation gain/loss:	Up to 200 feet
Hiking time:	2 hours
Agency:	SDRP
Trail use:	Bicycles, dogs, horses
Notes:	Hours posted dawn to dusk
Trailhead GPS:	N33.03819, W117.15683
Optional map:	USGS 7.5-min *Rancho Santa Fe*
Atlas square:	K9
Directions:	(Del Mar) From I-5 go east on Via de la Valle (S-6) for 5.3 miles. Turn right on Paseo Delicias (S-6). Go 1 mile. Continue onto Del Dios Highway (S-6) for 1.9 miles. After passing Calle Ambiente, turn in at the fruit stand on the right. There is a road marked with a San Dieguito River Park sign that leads to the parking area. (Escondido) From I-15 go west on Via Rancho Parkway for 3.3 miles. Turn left on Del Dios Highway (S-6). Go 5.2 miles. Turn in at the fruit stand on the left. There is a road marked with a San Dieguito River Park sign that leads to the parking area. If you reach Calle Ambiente you have gone too far.

Habitat(s):

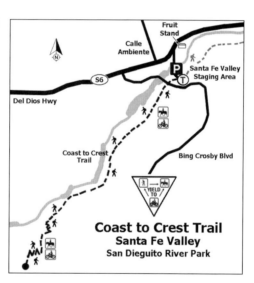

This is part of the 71-mile San Dieguito River Park's Coast to Crest Trail that will one day extend from Volcan Mountain near Julian to the shore at Del Mar. About 45 miles of the trail are now open. Both the Del Dios Gorge and Santa Fe Valley trail segments of the Coast to Crest Trail begin from the same parking area and follow the San Dieguito River. The Del Dios Gorge Trail heads northeast while the Santa Fe Valley Trail goes southwest.

The beginning of the Santa Fe Valley trail is a flat, well-groomed pathway, which crosses over seven wooden bridges. Initially the left

side of the trail abuts one of Rancho Santa Fe's golf courses with the San Dieguito River on the right. Water along the river can only be seen in the guise of three ponds along the route. There is a bit of a surrealistic feeling as one hikes and gazes right and communes with nature and then gazes left to observe golfers traversing the golf course in their golf carts.

Once completed, the Coast to Crest Trail will provide habitat connectivity as a wildlife corridor allowing vertebrate species to move through spaces that were once isolated. It also will reduce genetic isolation of plants. However, the

Alan King

Mexican fan palm

stark contrast between man-made and natural features will continue to be a dominant feature.

Along the right side of the trail going out are common coastal sage scrub plants including lemonadeberry, laurel sumac, coastal sagebrush, and chaparral bushmallow. The California poppy (***Eschscholzia californica***) also occurs here sporadically. It is the California state flower. The bright orange blooms dot the landscape here and throughout much of the county during the spring months. Its native range extends from western Oregon to Baja California, Mexico. While a pleasant sight here in California and throughout its native range, it is a problematic invader in Chile and elsewhere in the world.

Unfortunately, the area was burned in the Witch Creek fire of 2007 and is only slowly recovering. Riparian plants occurring along the river include arroyo willow, various species of grass, and Mexican fan palm (***Washingtonia robusta***), a non-native species. The Mexican fan palm is a native of Sonora and Baja California, Mexico. It was first introduced to the US as an ornamental in preparation for the 1932 Summer Olympics in Los Angeles. The palms were planted along streets to help beautify the area. Mexican fan palms grow much faster than native California fan palms and can reach heights of 80-100 feet. Mexican fan palms are topped by tuft of fronds. The leaves do not droop. It is the most commonly grown palm in the world because it is hardy and adaptable. They are in-vasive in coastal canyons. They often grow from the seeds of horticultural plantings in gardens surrounding the coastal canyons. Small animals and birds eat palm fruits and distribute the seeds in their scat.

Hiking the first 1.25 miles is easy, but the remaining 0.75 mile has a series of switchbacks bounded by railings as one climbs about 200 feet in altitude, eventually to the base of a powerline. The plan is to continue the trail further west at a later date. The end of the trail gives views of the golf course, a pond created by damming the San Dieguito River, and the path back towards the trailhead. Given the variety of flora along this route, the hike would be most impressive in the spring when plants are flowering.

Diana Lindsay

California poppy

Distance:	4.5 miles, out-and-back
Difficulty:	🚶🚶
Elevation gain/loss:	Up to 200 feet
Hiking time:	2.5 hours
Agency:	SDRP
Trail use:	Bicycles, dogs, horses
Notes:	Hours posted dawn to dusk
Trailhead GPS:	N33.03832, W117.15675
Optional map:	USGS 7.5-min *Rancho Santa Fe*
Atlas square:	K9
Directions:	(Escondido) From I-5 go east on Via de la Valle (S-6) for 5.3 miles. Turn right on Paseo Delicias (S-6). Go 1.1 mile. Continue onto Del Dios Highway (S-6) for 1.9 miles. After passing Calle Ambiente, turn in at the fruit stand on the right. There is a road marked with a San Diego River Park sign that leads to the parking area. From I-15 go west on Via Rancho Parkway for 3.3 miles. Turn left on Del Dios Highway (S-6). Go 5.2 miles. Turn in at the fruit stand on the left. There is a road marked with a San Diego River Park sign that leads to the parking area. If you reach Calle Ambiente you have gone too far.

Habitat(s):

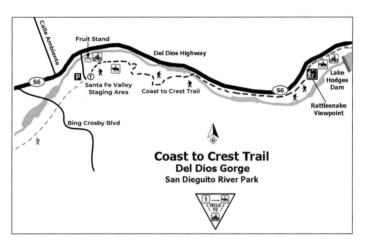

This trail is another part of the Coast to Crest Trail of the San Dieguito River Park. Del Dios Gorge is within this planned area, but only part of it is accessible. Del Dios Gorge is partly inundated by the Lake Hodges Reservoir created in 1918 on completion of the Lake Hodges Dam.

From the parking area, head east toward the dam. The plants found on the early part of the trail are common to the coastal sage scrub habitat. Several interpretive panels along the route describe the history and fauna of the area, including bats. Twenty-two species of bats, all nocturnal, live in San Diego County. Most live on insects, which they can locate and catch in flight through echolocation or sonar. The Mex-ican free-tailed bat (*Tadarida brasiliensis*) is among the most numerous bats in the Del Dios Gorge area and one of the most abundant bats in North America. It is called a free-tailed bat because the tail extends beyond the uropatagium—the membrane that stretches between the legs of flying animals like some bats and flying squirrels. The Mexican free-tailed is a medium-sized bat with brown fur, a short snout, and a wrinkled upper lip. These bats leave their roosts at sunset and forage through the night, eating moths, dragonflies, beetles, wasps, bees, and true bugs. They in turn are preyed upon by great horned owls, Cooper's hawks, Virginia opossums, skunks, and snakes that enter their roosts. They are social and live

Henry Geffroy

Overlook to Lake Hodges Dam

in large colonies. Females usually give birth to a single offspring while hanging upside down. Newborns crawl down the mother's body to find a nipple for feeding.

At about the 1-mile mark, the trail descends to a steel-railed bridge that crosses the San Dieguito River and enters a riparian area paralleling the riverbed. When the water level is low, there will be clear or stagnant pools among the many large granitic boulders, depending on the season. There is enough water, however, to support coast live oaks and various species of willow. Subsurface water also is demonstrated by the presence of cattails throughout the river corridor.

One of the historic highlights of the trail is the Hodges Flume along the north side of the gorge, to the left as you proceed to the dam. It is not used today but was once a gravity water transporter to the San Dieguito Reservoir, 4 miles to the west.

The Rattlesnake Viewing Platform is the turnaround point and a good spot for lunch or a snack. In 2010 the California State Resources Agency provided a $1 million grant for the removal of eucalyptus trees in Del Dios Gorge and for the construction of the interpretive viewing platform that was designed by architect/builder Scott Stevenson. The Rattlesnake Viewing Platform was named

not for any rattlesnakes in the area but rather for the native rock wall that was shaped into the form of a rattlesnake. The viewing platform has an interpretive panel that explains the place of rattlesnakes in the ecosystem. A burned, black, dead oak tree is on the platform and addresses the impacts of wildfires. A sculpture with a pipe ring scope lines up features at the dam, including the spillway, the bulwarks, and the river below. The view from this point is the concrete-arch Lake Hodges Dam, which impounds the San Dieguito River. After taking in the views, return to the trailhead along the same route.

Iron bridge

Distance:	4 or 6 miles, out-and-back
Difficulty:	🚶🚶
Elevation gain/loss:	Minimal
Hiking time:	up to 3 hours
Agency:	City of San Diego; SDRP
Trail use:	Bicycles, dogs, horses
Notes:	Hours posted dawn to dusk; keep dogs 50 feet from water
Trailhead GPS:	N33.07768, W117.11586
Optional map:	USGS 7.5-min *Escondido*; *Rancho Santa Fe*
Atlas square:	K10
Directions:	(Escondido) From I-15 go west on Via Rancho Parkway for 3.3 miles. Turn left on Lake Drive. Go 0.8 mile. For the longer walk starting at Del Dios Community Park, turn left into the Lake Hodges parking lot, just past Ash Lane. For the shorter walk, go another 1.2 miles to the parking lot across from the Hernandez Hideaway near the junction of Lake Drive and Rancho Drive and begin your walk there.

Habitat(s):

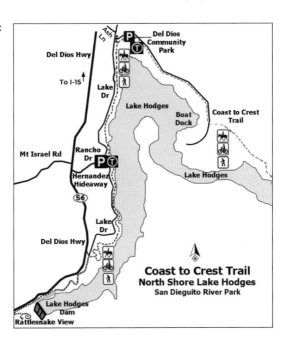

The San Dieguito River watershed is made up of three tributaries, beginning from runoff on the southern slope of Volcan Mountain that flows west as Santa Ysabel Creek. Temescal Creek rises in the Cleveland National Forest near Lake Henshaw and flows south, joining Santa Ysabel Creek. Santa Maria Creek rises near Ramona and flows north through Ramona Grasslands and Bandy Canyon, joining Santa Ysabel Creek in San Pasqual Valley where it becomes the San Dieguito River that flows to the ocean via the San Dieguito Lagoon in Del Mar. The watershed contains four reservoirs, including Lakes Sutherland, Ramona, Poway, and Hodges. Lake Hodges with its maximum depth of 115 feet and 27 miles of shoreline is contained within the 92,000-acre San Dieguito River Park.

Most of the fish that live in the San Dieguito River and Lake Hodges are non-native species. One exception is the southern California steelhead, which is also known as coastal rainbow trout. It is a distinct population of rainbow trout that is native to California and adapted to living in intermittently dry streams and rivers. There are two different populations of south-

Black-necked stilt

ern California steelhead. One population is an inland trout that spends its whole life in inland waters, while the anadromous steelheads are ocean-going fish that spawn in fresh water streams with gravelly bottoms. If the eggs hatch in streams with intermittent water they may spend only a few months in fresh water before migrating to the ocean. Others in more reliable streams may spend 1–3 years in fresh water before they undergo smoltification, the physiological process that enables them to live in salt water and head for the sea. They live in the ocean for several years as they increase in size. At some point they will return to their natal stream to spawn. However, unlike salmon, steelhead trout don't die after spawning, but return to the ocean. They can make three or four such round trips before they die. While they formerly existed in all of the major tributaries in San Diego County, the numbers of steelheads in our streams and rivers is greatly diminished due to dam building, pollution, urban development, and overfishing. A few may remain in the San Luis Rey River and San Mateo Creek.

There is a 7.65 mile trail commonly used by equestrians and bicycles, as well as hikers, starting at Sikes Adobe Staging Area just east of I-15 and continues to the dam. The two hikes described here are shorter. One begins at the Del Dios Community Park and continues on a dirt path paralleling Lake Drive to the dam. For a shorter hike, park at the lot across from the Hernandez Hideaway and join the route to the Lake Hodges Dam south of Hernandez Hideaway. Follow the trail signs as it parallels the Del Dios Highway. You will see a rusting car at the side of the trail that looks like it may have missed a turn. Continue on the path to the end of the parking area where there is a break in the fence. The trail turns left and down to the Rattlesnake Viewpoint.

Take a break before returning. Look through the pipe scope to points A and B at the 1918 Hodges multiple-arch dam funded by the

California gnatcatcher

American avocet

Looking through the pipe scope

Santa Fe Railroad. The reservoir was purchased by the City of San Diego in 1925, and the main customers today are the Santa Fe Irrigation and San Dieguito Water districts. Point C is the San Dieguito River continuing its journey to the Pacific Ocean.

Bring your binoculars to enjoy the birding in California's first site formally recognized in 1999 as a Globally Important Bird Area. This was mainly due to the California gnatcatchers (*Polioptila californica californica*) found in the coastal sage scrub habitat. The gnatcatcher is a small songbird that eats small insects and spiders and has a call like a kitten's meow. Both the bill and tail are thin and black, the tail with narrow white edges and corners. The gnatcatcher's underparts are medium gray, and its upperparts are mostly dark gray. Females have a dark brown saddle on the back, while males sport a black cap during the spring and summer. The bird's habitat is limited to the coastal sage scrub community that has been reduced in size by urban development.

Two of the most beautiful birds to be seen at Lake Hodges are the American avocet (*Recurvirostra americana*) and the black-necked stilt (*Himantopus mexicanus*). Both are large shore birds with long legs for wading in shallow water. The American avocet has a rusty-orange head and neck, white underparts, black and white upperparts, and a long up-turned bill that it sweeps through the water as it searches for invertebrates. The black-necked stilt has white underparts and black upperparts, varied by a white patch above the eye. The very long thin legs are red, and the bill is long, black, and straight. It also eats invertebrates.

The pipe scope

Distance:	6.5 miles, out-and-back.
Difficulty:	🚶🚶🚶🚶
Elevation gain/loss:	Up to 1000 feet
Hiking time:	4 hours
Agency:	SDRP
Trail use:	Bicycles, dogs
Notes:	Hours posted dawn to dusk
Trailhead GPS:	N33.05201, W117.07662
Optional map:	USGS 7.5-min *Escondido*
Atlas square:	K11
Directions:	(Escondido) From I-15 go west on West Bernardo Drive for 0.5 mile. Parking lot is on the right.

Habitat(s):

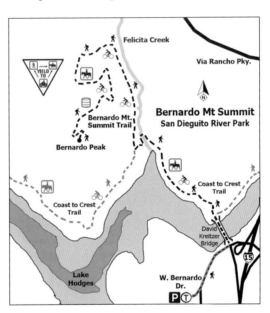

Bernardo Mountain (1150') rises steeply from the north shore of Lake Hodges. It offers a relatively short, vigorous hike to the peak for dramatic views of the rapid development of North County as well as Lake Hodges. Birding opportunities are extraordinary in non-drought years when the Lake Hodges east arm has open water. It is a popular weekend trail and is within the San Dieguito River Park.

The name is attributed to Saint Bernard, a French mystic, and was first noted on maps drawn by mission priests in the early 1800s. After independence from Spain, the Mexican government granted 17,763 acres to English sea captain Joseph Snook after he became a Catholic and a Mexican citizen in order to acquire land. He chose the baptismal name of José Francisco de Sales Snook. The historic Battle of San Pasqual took place on his Rancho Bernardo. During the American period and after subdivision of the rancho, a small settlement developed 4 miles southeast of Escondido called Bernardo. In 1961, a consortium of Texas oil men developed the community of Rancho Bernardo, one of the first of San Diego's outlying developments.

From the Piedras Pintadas parking lot, walk down the sidewalk on the north side of West Bernardo Drive to the David Kreitzer Bicycle/ Pedestrian Bridge crossing for the east arm of Lake Hodges. The bridge provides easy viewing of the colorful array of migratory waterfowl in spring and fall when there is water under the bridge. In low rainfall years, when the water may be at a distance, birds may still be viewed from the bridge while in flight or while perched on vegetation.

Lake Hodges and pedestrian bridge

From the bridge look along the water's edge for a green heron (**Butorides virescens**) that might be hunting for fish, amphibians, or invertebrates. This bird has a greenish-black cap, greenish-gray back, chestnut face and chest, and orangey-yellow legs that are short compared to other herons. The green heron is one of the few birds that will use tools to help capture prey. It will drop breadcrumbs or insects or perhaps a feather or twig into the water to entice fish. It will either stab or grab prey with its long sharp bill while wading or standing in water. It can also dive and swim.

The western grebe (**Aechmophorus occidentalis**) is another bird that you will see near the bridge. It is a black and white bird with a neck like a swan and red eyes. It is the bird most associated with Lake Hodges as it is visible year-round in great numbers and is known for its rushing choreographed courtship display in which a pair will race across the water in synchronicity with their long necks extended. The grebe builds fragile floating nest structures made from willow branches and detritus material that it collects while diving. It also nests on a floating wood platform in the lake.

Once across the bridge, go left on the well-trod dirt trail along the north shore. In about 0.5 mile, the trail turns to the north as it crosses Felicita Creek, a perennial stream largely due to urban runoff. Although it has some of the attributes of a native San Diego watercourse, the canyon has an abundance of water-loving non-native plants, especially Mexican fan palms, Canary Island date palms, and the notorious and highly invasive saltcedar or tamarisk. Coast live oaks, western sycamores, arroyo willows, and western poison-oak are still abundant here. Native wild grape vines also hang from some of the trees. The trip along the verdant riparian habitat is short, and in another 0.2 mile, the Bernardo Mountain Summit Trail splits off to the right and begins its fairly gentle ascent through coastal sage scrub up to the peak. For nearly 1 mile the trail is above Felicita Creek but not under the shady trees along the stream. Then the trail turns west, and with a few switchbacks, the trail goes past a water storage tank and up to the peak. Whenever another trail splits off from the Bernardo Mountain Trail, stay to the left. After enjoying the extraordinary views from the top, return the way you came.

Green heron

Distance:	3.8 miles, loops
Difficulty:	🚶🚶
Elevation gain/loss:	Up to 200 feet
Hiking time:	2 hours
Agency:	SDRP
Trail use:	Bicycles, dogs
Notes:	Hours posted dawn to dusk; keep dogs 50 feet from water
Trailhead GPS:	N33.05112, W117.07654
Optional map:	USGS 7.5-min *Escondido*
Atlas square:	K11
Directions:	(Escondido) From I-15 go west on West Bernardo Drive for 0.5 mile. Parking lot is on the right.

Habitat(s):

The aptly named Piedras Pintadas or painted rocks trail in Ranch Bernardo explores a small part of the rich San Diego County Kumeyaay Indian culture by following a well-marked trail with interpretive plaques. The interpretive signs along the trail provide fascinating insights into Kumeyaay culture and daily life, including information about edible and medicinal plants, use of natural resources, and the technologies they developed to survive in this harsh environment. The trail wraps around Bernardo Bay on Lake Hodges, which is an important habitat refuge for many native and migratory animal species, especially birds. Walking through the boulder-strewn hills that encircle Lake Hodges, it's easy to see why the native Kumeyaay people were inspired to live in this area. Look for a large boulder that was used as a food processing cen-

ter that still contains depressions or morteros where acorns and other grains were ground by a hand-held pestle. Many of the most important Kumeyaay plant species are still abundant along the trail as well.

Lake Hodges was not originally part of this Kumeyaay landscape. There was once a river before it was impounded by Lake Hodges Dam to the west. The upland habitat has since become a crucial habitat for the endangered California gnatcatcher and coast cactus wren, in addition to supporting raptors, wetland birds, and many other species. A visit in the winter months should provide great birding opportunities as many winter residents and stop-over migrating species may be seen. One of the birds that will be seen here is both a visitor and a resident—the American coot or mud hen (*Fulica*

Trail along the lake

americana), which is in the rail family. This chicken-like bird is more closely related to the sandhill crane than it is to a duck, although it is usually found in association with ducks swimming in ponds, marshes, reservoirs, and lakes. It is easily distinguished by its short, thick, white bill that extends onto the forehead and small red eyes on an otherwise dark-gray bird with a black head. If you see a coot on land, look at the feet. That is your clue that the coot is not related to a duck. Instead of webbed feet, it has yellow-green lobes of skin on each toe that aid the bird in swimming and standing on mud without sinking. Conveniently, this flap of skin folds back when the bird lifts its leg, minimizing water resistance on the upstroke. Coots eat aquatic plants and algae primarily, small vertebrates and invertebrates secondarily. They build floating nests on water.

This 3.8 mile looping trail is just off I-15 on the south side of Lake Hodges. Depart from the southwest corner of the parking lot off West Bernardo Road, directly across the street from a large retirement complex. Pick up a map at the trailhead information center and work your way south and west, circling south of Bernardo Bay. Enjoy the wetland plants and wildlife and

notice the changing vegetation as you climb a short but steep section into the coastal sage scrub on the hills overlooking the lake. After passing a small waterfall, go through a gate and work to the right to climb the scenic Ridge Loop Trail before returning to the trailhead. If time permits, try one of the other loop trails around Bernardo Bay.

American coot

Distance:	4 miles, out-and-back
Difficulty:	🏃🏃🏃
Elevation gain/loss:	Up to 500 feet
Hiking time:	3 hours
Agency:	City of San Diego
Trail use:	Bicycles, dogs, horses
Notes:	Hours posted dawn to dusk
Trailhead GPS:	N32.99264, W117.11636
Optional map:	USGS 7.5-min *Poway*; *Del Mar*
Atlas square:	M10
Directions:	(Rancho Peñasquitos) From CA-56 go north on Black Mountain Road for 2.3 miles. Turn right on Carmel Valley Road. Go 0.9 mile. Turn right into the Black Mountain Open Space Park, and drive to the end of road.

Habitat(s):

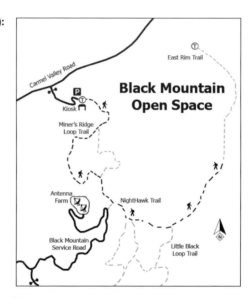

If the cool wet weather has kept you indoors, it is time to shake off the cabin fever and explore the Black Mountain Open Space Park. Cool weather is a perfect time to hike the shade-free slopes. Decomposed granite stones line the Miner's Ridge Loop Trail. It is moderately steep, so hiking boots are advised and trekking poles can be useful. Black sage (*Salvia mellifera*) is the dominant plant in the park, although the trail features many native plants such as mission manzanita, lilac, lemonadeberry, laurel sumac, chamise, monkey flower, chaparral broom, and bedstraw (*Galium* spp.).

Black sage is a highly aromatic evergreen shrub that stands 3-6 feet in height and is abundant in coastal sage scrub and lower chaparral communities. It has wrinkled green leaves and white to light blue flowers. Native Americans ate black sage seeds and used the leaves to spice foods. They also brewed a tea from the leaves to relieve symptoms of a cold. Be sure to smell the plant's rich aroma. Bedstraw is a herbaceous plant that often can be found in shady locations. It has tiny hooks making it slightly sticky and reminiscent of Velcro. Historically, it was a preferred bedding material because it stuck together. There are many species of bedstraw in the county.

There are spots along the trail with great views of the surrounding areas including Lake Hodges, Carmel Mountain, Palomar Mountain, and Mount Woodson. Keep following the trail past the Glider Point Marker, near the rail fence, in order to stay on the Miner's Loop. If the views inspire you for a longer hike, turn

Bedstraw species

right at the next fork. Turning left will lead back toward the entrance. If you turn right, other trails such as the Nighthawk Trail and the Little Black Loop Trail can be accessed.

On rainy days, the cutoff from Miner's Loop to Nighthawk can be very wet with a slick clay surface. Use caution. On wet days it is easy to spot spider webs glistening with diamond-like raindrops. For the most part the junctions are well marked, but keep an eye on your back trail to avoid getting lost. If you opted for the right turn, from then on keep following left forks to hike a short section of the Nighthawk and Little Black Loop trails. Eventually you will hook up to the East Rim Trail. The views along the East Rim are grand, with numerous small trails splitting off into private lands.

A good place to end the hike before turning around would be at a wooden bench at elevation 905 feet with a great view of Carmel Mountain Road and Rancho Bernardo. Looking in the other direction, Point Loma is visible. Beyond the bench, the trail gets steep again with old burned manzanita branches peeking up among the new growth. Near the peak, the left fork narrows down with an overgrowth of fragrant black sage. The right fork keeps going indefinitely through an elfin forest without views. A mountain lion was

seen in this portion of the trail and the territorial markings of scat piles indicate a regular presence. If hiking this route, it may be best to do so in a group. Hikers will also share the trail with mountain bikers. Look around and above to spot quail, red-tailed hawks, coyotes, and other wildlife that share the space.

Black sage

Distance:	3.5 miles, loop
Difficulty:	𝝠𝝠𝝠
Elevation gain/loss:	Up to 500 feet
Hiking time:	2 hours
Agency:	City of San Diego
Trail use:	Bicycles, dogs, horses
Notes:	Hours posted dawn to dusk
Trailhead GPS:	N32.9599, W117.22142
Optional map:	USGS 7.5-min *Del Mar*
Atlas square:	M8
Directions:	(La Jolla) From I-5 go east on Del Mar Heights Road for 1.4 miles. Turn left on Lansdale Drive. Go 0.1 mile. Turn left into Torrey Highland Park, and park near the dog park.

Habitat(s):

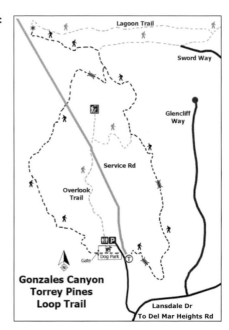

Gonzales Canyon is named for Levi Gonzales, a Portuguese immigrant who constructed an adobe home and farmed near here in the late 1800s. Gonzales Canyon Open Space became part of the City of San Diego's Multiple Species Conservation Program in the 1980s. This countywide program was developed to preserve a network of habitat and open space that would protect the biodiversity of the region. The program conserves approximately 900 square miles from the Mexican border to the San Dieguito River Valley and from the Cleveland National Forest to the Pacific Ocean.

The walk described here starts on the east side of the road, just south of the dog park, where there is a break in the shrubs allowing access to the powerline dirt road. Go left at the Torrey Pines Loop Trail sign. The trail parallels the road for a short distance before descending to the bottom of the canyon while passing through typical coastal sage scrub vegetation, including coast spice bush or bush-rue (*Cneoridium dumosum*), a California native of the citrus family. Coast spice bush is endemic to the southern California coast and northern Mexico. It can be identified by its white flowers and dimpled reddish fruit that matures to a black color. Before turning black, the fruit has texture like a miniature orange. Coast spice bush also is aromatic with a strong spicy odor. Take care touching the leaves, however, as they can cause a rash.

Coast spice bush or bush-rue

Continue over one bridge to the base of the canyon. Before coming to a second bridge, the trail crosses a small section of white cliffs that is composed of sandstone. Note the smell of licorice or anise from sweet fennel growing at the bridge.

Further, down the trail the plants are sparser and it may be easier to spot reptiles. One reptile that you might see on the trail is the common side-blotched lizard (*Uta stansburiana*). A dark bluish-black mark on each side of its chest, behind its front limbs, gives this lizard its name. Females have a less well-defined blotch on their sides. Color and patterns can vary from brown to gray to yellowish or even black with blotches or stripes. The underside is white to gray and usually unmarked. The tail is long and slender, and the body from snout to vent is 1.5-2.5 inches. The unusual thing about this lizard is polymorphism, or different forms, in the males.

Males can have orange, yellow, or blue throats, and each color demonstrates different patterns of behavior. Orange-throated side-blotched lizards are dominant, territorial, and aggressive, and mate with many females. Yellow-throated males are not territorial. They mimic females and sneak by the orange-throated males to mate with their females. The blue-throated males have one mate that they guard against yellow-throated males, but they will run off if confronted by an orange-throated male. When blue-throated males cooperate with each other to defend their mates, they can successfully defend them against yellow-throated and orange-throated males.

Past a stand of blue elderberry trees is a sandy service road. Turn left and continue walking through riparian habitat with some western poison-oak. Turning right onto the Lagoon Trail will lead a short distance to an intermittent creek. Retrace your steps by turning left onto the service road then go right for a short distance before taking the next right to return to the Torrey Pines Loop Trail. Take the right turn at the signed Y-junction.

Follow the trail to loop around the mesa, crossing another bridge before turning left at the loop trail sign and continuing south past multiple blocked trails that lead to the next mesa. The trail then starts an incline towards a football field, passing by Torrey pine trees. At the football field fence, turn left and pass through the dog park gate to return to your vehicle.

Common side-blotched lizard

Distance:	4 miles, out-and-back
Difficulty:	🚶🚶
Elevation gain/loss:	Up to 100 feet
Hiking time:	2 hours
Agency:	SDRP
Trail use:	Bicycles, dogs, horses
Notes:	Hours posted dawn to dusk
Trailhead GPS:	N33.05263, W117.06567
Optional map:	USGS 7.5-min *Escondido*
Atlas square:	K11
Directions:	(Escondido) From I-15 go east on Pomerado Road for 0.2 mile. Turn left on Highland Valley Road. The Highland Valley Trail staging area is on the right, about 400 feet from the traffic light.

Habitat(s):

The Highland Valley Trail is part of the San Dieguito River Park trail system. It is, however, not part of the backbone Coast to Crest Trail that will eventually extend 71 miles from Volcan Mountain near Julian to the Pacific Ocean at Del Mar. It is a subsidiary trail that extends into a scenic part of the San Pasqual Valley Agricultural Preserve.

The trail contours along the hillside, just above Highland Valley Road for three-quarters of its length. It is well maintained, not too long, and with little elevation gain or loss. It is an easy stroll through grassland interspersed with periodic oak woodland, riparian habitat, or patches of coastal sage scrub. The oaks include not only coast live oak but also the occasional Engelmann oak. The riparian habitat includes mule-fat and arroyo willows, occasionally festooned with

western poison-oak or native grapevines. Wildflowers in season add to your enjoyment of this hike. Pastoral vistas of farms, hills, and the river valley are frequent while hiking the trail.

About 0.5 mile into the hike, the trail crosses a bridge spanning an intermittent stream that flows through an oak forest. Then 1.46 miles from the trailhead, the trail turns south up Sycamore Creek and follows a gravel road for another 0.5 mile. It ends in an oak grove where there is a picnic table and a few benches. It is a shady respite where you can enjoy lunch or a snack before heading back to your vehicle.

This hike crosses several different habitats. The place where two habitats meet is called an ecotone. It is a particularly rich area because the plants and animals of different hab-

Don Fosket

View of river valley

itats are sharing the same space as one habitat transforms into another. As you move from coastal sage scrub to riparian, or from riparian to oak woodland, take note of that place called an ecotone.

This is a great hike to do with children. From the San Dieguito River Park website, download the brochure named the Ruth Merrill Children's Interpretive Walk. There are 15 Discovery Posts, numbered 1 to 15, scattered along the first mile of the 2-mile-long trail. The posts have only numbers. You need the guide to discover the natural feature you are asked to consider. For example, Discovery Post No. 2 focuses attention on water and the river, emphasizing its importance for wildlife. It also asks us to stop and look for evidence of wild animals, such as footprints, scat, or bird calls, and it illustrates the tracks of several animals that can be found here.

One of the interesting things you can see in the river is a water penny beetle (**family Psephenidae**). You might not notice the adult, but you can identify the beetle in its larval stage. It looks like a small copper penny underwater with its round, flattened copper-tan to black body with plate-like segments, somewhat similar in shape to a marine mollusk called a chiton. The adult beetle is not aquatic.

In its larval stage it eats algae, phytoplankton and feces. It is often attached to rocks or wood in fast-moving water. The larvae are sensitive to pollution.

Don Fosket
Trail through grasslands

Distance:	6.7 miles, out-and-back
Difficulty:	🚶🚶🚶
Elevation gain/loss:	Minimal
Hiking time:	4 hours
Agency:	SDRP
Trail use:	Bicycles, dogs, horses
Notes:	Hours posted dawn to dusk; Sikes Adobe is also the westbound trailhead for the Lake Hodges Trail.
Trailhead GPS:	N33.06657, W117.06781
Optional map:	USGS 7.5-min *Escondido*
Atlas square:	K11
Directions:	(Escondido) From I-15 go east on Via Rancho Parkway for 0.25 mile. Turn right on Sunset Drive and go to end of street to park. Sikes Farmstead is on the left where the Mule Hill Trail begins.

Habitat(s):

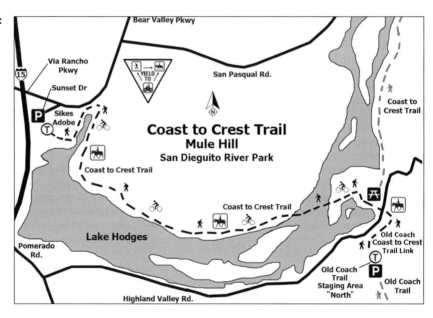

Part of San Dieguito River Park's Coast to Crest Trail is within the 11,000-acre San Pasqual Agricultural Preserve owned by the City of San Diego. The Coast to Crest Trail within this preserve is also called the San Pasqual Valley Trail. This portion of the Coast to Crest Trail has four staging areas that go through natural and historical areas where significant events of American and San Diego's history occurred. The staging areas include Sikes, Old Coach, Ysabel Creek, and San Pasqual Valley at Bandy Canyon Road. Some of the segments are very long in distance. The best way to explore this area by foot is through a series of out-and-back hikes starting from one of the various staging areas.

Bicyclists and equestrians can cover greater distances.

The Mule Hill Trail explores a colorful part of San Diego's history. The hike begins at the Sikes Adobe Historic Farmstead, built by the Sikes family in 1872 and recently reconstructed after it was almost destroyed by the Witch Creek Fire in 2007, shortly after the adobe's first restoration was completed. The farmstead has a small museum dedicated to the history of the American pioneer. The Sikes Farmstead is also a great place to learn more about nature, with docent-led walks and/or talks on the birds of the area and the lagoon, as well as many other topics. The San Dieguito River Park Staff (or rangers) orga-

Mule Hill battle site

nize these events with help from volunteers. For information on current events at the Farmstead, see: http://www.sdrp.org/wordpress/sikes-adobe/. They also host a Sunday farmers market where local produce can be purchased.

The hike continues on into the San Pasqual Valley Agricultural Preserve where some of San Diego's local vegetables are grown as well as acres of turf grass. After curving around the west side of the Sikes Farmstead, the trail doubles back toward Via Rancho Parkway, skirting a marshy area, then turns away from the road and proceeds almost due south. Look for a monument and informational posters telling about the hill on your left where a battle was fought in the Mexican–American War of 1846. The American soldiers under General Stephen Watts Kearny retreated to this hill, which was later called Mule Hill because the starving Americans captured a wayward mule that wandered away from the Californios, shot it, cooked it, and ate it.

Further down the trail, just before it turns toward the east, another monument marks the site of the town Bernardo that existed here from 1872 until the Lake Hodges dam was completed and the reservoir was filled in 1916. Bernardo was a small town, but it had a general store that served ranchers and farm-

ers from Valley Center to Poway for 40 years.

At this point the trail turns east and continues for another 0.5 mile. The vegetation here has struggled to come back after the 2007 Witch Creek Fire, as there are only a few scattered patches of golden bush and broom baccharis plants, with sparse non-native annual grasses. Seasonal rains will help the recovery.

Black phoebe

Dan Fosket

Sikes Adobe. Additions to the one-room Sikes Adobe were made of wood

At 1.4 miles from the Sikes Farmstead, the Mule Hill Trail joins the San Pasqual Valley Agricultural Trail. For the next mile the trail threads the border between the San Dieguito River floodplain, on the right, with carefully cultivated agricultural fields on the left. The floodplain vegetation is highly varied, with thick pockets of willow and mule-fat with a mixture of native and non-native species.

One of the birds that you will see here is a black phoebe (*Sayornis nigricans*), a small flycatcher with a big head that is colored dusty black and a white belly. There is a slight peak at the back of the crown, and the square-tipped tail bobs up and down constantly while the bird is perched on low limbs or out in the open, scanning for insects. The phoebe chirps while it waits, then catches an insect in a short flight.

It is always found near water and uses mud to build a distinctive cup-shaped nest attached to ledges, overhangs, and eaves. The male gives the female a tour of potential nest sites, and the female chooses the actual site and builds the nest. Except for the barn swallow, no other California bird makes a nest like that of the black phoebe. Nests are protected overhead, preventing disintegration during storms. Before bridges and buildings offered many new opportunities, sites suitable for black phoebe nests along creeks were rare, so the birds often reused the same site year after year.

At 2.6 miles from the Sikes Adobe, the trail starts across the floodplain, now completely dry, and clothed with sparse vegetation composed mostly of non-native annual grasses with widely scattered native shrubs. Up ahead is a lush green wall of vegetation marking the channel of the San Dieguito River. The river, while lacking surface water, must maintain a substantial flow of subterranean water to support this abundance of large native trees.

Just after crossing the river, the trail splits with the San Pasqual Valley Trail continuing on the left. The trail on your right that is signed "Old Coach—Coast to Crest Trail Link" leads to the City of Poway's trail network. In about 0.1 mile after crossing Highland Valley Road is the Old Coach Staging Area. This is the turnaround point for this hike.

Distance:	4.7 miles, out-and-back
Difficulty:	🚶🚶
Elevation gain/loss:	Up to 400 feet
Hiking time:	3 hours
Agency:	SDRP
Trail use:	Bicycles, dogs, horses
Trailhead GPS:	N33.05846, W117.03042
Optional map:	USGS 7.5-min *Escondido*; *San Pasqual*
Atlas square:	K12
Directions:	(Escondido) From I-15 go east on Pomerado Road for 0.2 mile. Turn left on Highland Valley Road. Go 2.4 miles. Parking lot is on right. Trailhead is well marked.

Habitat(s):

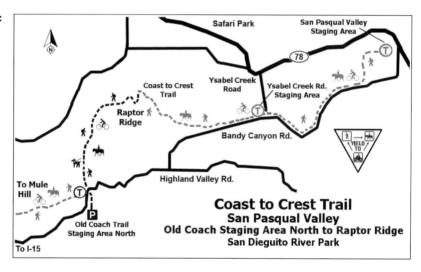

Coast to Crest Trail
San Pasqual Valley
Old Coach Staging Area North to Raptor Ridge
San Dieguito River Park

The Old Coach Staging Area is the starting point for two trails—one to Poway on the Old Coach Trail and the other to the Coast to Crest/San Pasqual Valley Trail. The hike described here goes north from the staging area and connects to the Coast to Crest/San Pasqual Valley Trail and to the 700-foot high Raptor Ridge overlooking the San Pasqual Valley.

Walk north from the parking area, along the Highland Valley road through the nursery growing grounds for about 200 yards until the marked crossing of Highland Valley Road is encountered. Carefully cross the road and the path will shortly tie into the Coast to Crest Trail. To the left will take you to the Mule Hill Historical Trail. Go to the right to follow along an old road for 1.5 miles. There is riparian habitat to the left and coastal sage scrub to the right. This part of the trail is mostly level. Depending on the time of year, many wild-

flowers can be in bloom. The trail has several benches located under trees that are inviting stops to contemplate the views.

The old road ends in 1.5 miles. There is a picnic table and information kiosk at this point. From here, start the 0.85-mile climb on a north-facing slope that has a mix of large boulders and chaparral. The trail is not difficult but does gain about 350 feet in elevation. The wildflower bloom here in the spring can be spectacular. At the top of the ridge, there is a wide spot with a couple of benches where there is a nice view of the San Pasqual Valley to the north and west. Continue for another 50 feet to a viewpoint overlooking the San Pasqual Valley Agricultural Preserve.

Remember to bring binoculars. Raptor Ridge is aptly named. In earlier days when the Kumeyaay and early settlers lived here, the San Pasqual Valley was known as the valley of eagles. Raptors that will be seen here include

Wendy Esterly

White-tailed kite

Wendy Esterly

American kestrel

the red-tailed hawk, American kestrel, and white-tailed kite.

Red-tailed hawks (***Buteo jamaicensis***) are large and usually seen soaring with broad rounded wings and a short, wide reddish tail. They vary widely in color and pattern but are usually brown with a light-colored underside. This is the most common hawk of North America. Its raspy cry is the sound most associated with raptors, as Hollywood usually uses the cry in films no matter what kind of raptor the film may show. The American kestrel (***Falco sparverius***) is North America's smallest falcon, about the size of a mourning dove. Males have a slate-blue crown and wings, a rust-colored back and tail, and a dark, long, vertical tear slash under their eyes. Females have the wings as well as the back barred with rust and black. Kestrels eat insects, small rodents, and birds and stash surplus food to retrieve in lean times. The white-tailed kite (***Elanus leucurus***) is a medium-sized raptor that hunts small mammals and roosts communally. Like the kestrel, it hovers while searching for small animals. It has a gray back, black and gray wings, and a white face, underside, and tail.

There are also numerous other birds, including ostriches at a couple of farms in the valley. If you are lucky, you may be able to pick out a giraffe or rhinoceros at the San Diego Zoo Safari Park as you look North and East from the overlook.

The return trip is via the same trail unless arrangements were made to park a second vehicle at the Ysabel Creek Road Staging Area, about 2.5 miles from the viewpoint (see Trip 4).

Paula Knoll

Trail

Distance:	4.6 or 8 miles, out-and-back
Difficulty:	🧍🧍🧍 or 🧍🧍🧍🧍, depending on length
Elevation gain/loss:	Up to 900 feet
Hiking time:	3 or 5 hours
Agency:	SDRP
Trail use:	Bicycles, dogs, horses
Notes:	Hours posted dawn to dusk
Trailhead GPS:	N33.07717, W116.98773
Optional map:	USGS 7.5-min *San Pasqual*; *Escondido*
Atlas square:	K12
Directions:	(Escondido) From CA-78 go south on Ysabel Creek Road for 0.6 mile. Parking lot is on left and is marked with a San Dieguito River Park/Ysabel Creek Road Staging Area sign. Caution: the Ysabel Creek Road bridge can wash out after rain. In that event or to avoid the chance of a washout, the trailhead on Ysabel Creek Road can be reached by continuing another 2.3 miles east on CA-78, past Ysabel Creek Road. Turn right on Bandy Canyon Road. Go 2.8 miles. Turn right on Ysabel Creek Road. Parking lot is on the right.

Habitat(s):

Coast to Crest Trail
San Pasqual Valley
Ysabel Creek Rd. Staging Area to Raptor Ridge
San Dieguito River Park

This segment of the Coast to Crest Trail explores the area between Ysabel Creek Road Staging Area and the Old Coach Trail Staging Area, with the turn-around at Raptor Ridge for a shorter out-and-back hike. The hike can also be a longer out-and-back hike between the two staging areas.

From the perspective of a naturalist, this is the wildest, most interesting segment of the San Pasqual Valley Trails. It is also the most challenging as it climbs the shoulder of the coastal sage-covered Raptor Ridge, and if continued to the Old Coach Trail Staging Area, will then proceed through an oak woodland before descending down to the San Dieguito River and passing into a rich riparian habitat. (See the previous trip if you're interested in

hiking to Raptor Ridge from the Old Coach Trail Staging Area.)

The first 0.5 mile going west from the parking lot/Ysabel trailhead is on the shoulder of Bandy Canyon Road. Few cars use this road, so traffic isn't a problem. The trail initially passes through coastal sage scrub vegetation heavily infused with non-native invasive species, particularly annual grasses, mustards, horehound, and tamarisk. Broad-leaf peppergrass (*Lepidium latifolium*) in the mustard family is a native of the Mediterranean, southern Europe, and Asia. It is the most invasive in wetlands and riparian areas, although this perennial spreads easily to other ecosystems. It is thought to have been brought over in a shipment of sugar beets from southern Europe. Each plant

Don Fosket

Trail paralleling the road

has the capability of producing thousands of seeds. It is insect pollinated and can reproduce from seeds, roots, and the semi-woody crown. Seeds can be dispersed by the wind. It has deep roots and easily displaces native plants. Leaves are bright green and the four flower petals are white. It can reach a height of 6 feet.

Horehound (*Marrubium vulgare*) is an exotic plant in the family Lamiaceae with the square-shaped stems characteristic of the mint family plants. Horehound has a whitish or hoary appearance and was a favorite of early Europeans who made the plant into a candy. Horehound candy can still be found today in Old Town's old-fashioned candy shops. It also has a medicinal value, and has long been used to relieve cough symptoms. A more serious invader is tamarisk or saltcedar, which chokes out native vegetation.

The trail gradually leaves the road as it heads west, encountering more native coastal sage scrub species. The trail also climbs gradually after leaving the road, reaching its highest point on Raptor Ridge, 2.3 miles from the Ysabel trailhead. Benches on Raptor Ridge provide views across the agricultural preserve and up the San Pasqual Valley. Turn back at this point unless a longer hike is desired.

The trail continues on through an open oak woodland as it descends to the riverbed. Once the trail reaches the riverbed, it passes in and out of oak woodland and dense riparian vegetation as it bends south, ultimately arriving at Highland Valley Road and the Old Coach Trail Staging Area, the turn-around point for the longer out-and-back hike.

Alan King

Horehound

Distance:	6 miles, out-and-back
Difficulty:	character icons
Elevation gain/loss:	Minimal
Hiking time:	3 hours
Agency:	SDRP
Trail use:	Bicycles, dogs, horses
Notes:	Hours posted 6 a.m. to 6 p.m.
Trailhead GPS:	N33.09208, W116.95681
Optional map:	USGS 7.5-min *San Pasqual*
Atlas square:	J13
Directions:	(Escondido) From CA-78 go south on Bandy Canyon Road and then make an almost immediate right turn onto a gravel road with a San Dieguito River Park sign. Go to the parking lot and the San Pasqual Valley Trailhead.

Habitat(s):

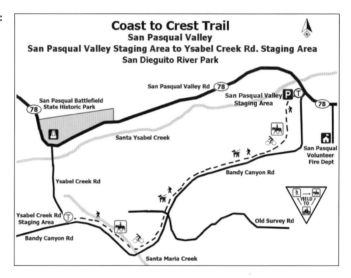

Coast to Crest Trail
San Pasqual Valley
San Pasqual Valley Staging Area to Ysabel Creek Rd. Staging Area
San Dieguito River Park

This segment of the Coast to Crest Trail within the San Pasqual Agricultural Preserve explores the eastern end of the San Pasqual Valley beginning at the San Pasqual Valley Staging Area.

Begin hiking west from the trailhead, with Santa Ysabel Creek on your right and a large citrus grove on your left. The creek bed is thick with typical riparian vegetation, including arroyo and other species of willows, western cottonwoods, mule-fat, and scattered western sycamore. The creek is a haven for wildlife, particularly birds. In 0.5 mile the trail makes a sharp turn south, leaving the creek. As it continues along the western boarder of the citrus grove, the view on the right is of a large turf grass farm. After walking another 0.5 mile, the

trail turns west again and now follows Bandy Canyon Road. You will pass abandoned buildings and a recently closed dairy, all signs of the rapidly changing nature of farming in this agricultural preserve. Once the source of milk for most of San Diego, now only one dairy remains operational in the preserve. Today the principle crop of the agricultural preserve is lawn grass. Huge expanses of flat land are covered with lawn grass and irrigated with overhead sprinklers, which may come to life, giving you a short shower. With recent drought conditions and limits on using water, growing grass may not continue to be profitable.

There are many non-native invasive species on this segment of the hike, including eucalyptus, Mexican fan palms, mission prickly-pear

Salt heliotrope

or Indian-fig, and saltcedar. Non-native invasive species are plants we either accidentally brought with us when the area was settled or were deliberately introduced for their beauty or economic value. They became established for a variety of reasons and often out-compete native species. Mission prickly-pear (**Opuntia ficus-indica**) was originally imported as a food crop. It is important for both its fruit, called a tuna, and its pad, which is considered a vegetable and is called nopal. Culinary dishes referring to prickly-pear usually mean this plant. It is also an important fodder food for domesticated animals. However, it has escaped from cultivated fields and has aggressively spread to other areas, displacing native species.

There are also many native species in this segment of the hike, including climbing milkweed, wild grape, California buckwheat, black sage, and salt heliotrope (**Heliotropium curassavicum**). Salt heliotrope is a succulent more commonly found in moist growing conditions. It is a sprawling perennial herb with small white flowers with a yellow throat that uncoil as the plant continues to bloom. The flowers turn purple-white as they are pollinated. As a member of the borage family, this plant has five fused petals with stamens attached and five separate sepals. This plant contains a class of alkaloids that cause liver damage to

vertebrates. Because of this, certain insects eat these plants in order to alter their flavor so that predators will learn to avoid them. More important for humans, some honey bees gather nectar from plants that have alkaloids toxic to humans, which also can make their honey hazardous to our health.

When you reach the Ysabel Creek Road Staging Area, turn around and head back to complete the hike.

Mission prickly-pear or Indian-fig

Distance:	2.8 or 4.4 miles, out-and-back
Difficulty:	🚶🚶🚶🚶 or 🚶🚶🚶🚶🚶
Elevation gain/loss:	Up to 1000 feet
Hiking time:	2 or 4 hours
Agency:	City of San Diego
Trail use:	Dogs
Notes:	Good birding area; visitor center open 9 a.m.- 3 p.m.
Trailhead GPS:	N33.08503, W116.92209
Optional map:	USGS 7.5-min *San Pasqual*
Atlas square:	J14
Directions:	(Escondido) From CA-78 turn south into the San Pasqual Clevenger Trails South parking lot, 5.5 miles east of Safari Park and 5.9 miles west of Main Street in Ramona.

Habitat(s):

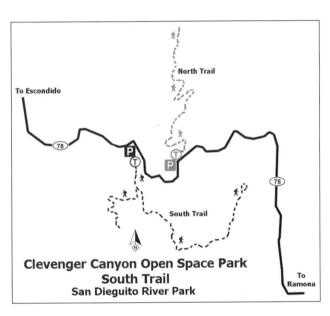

Clevenger Canyon Open Space Park
South Trail
San Dieguito River Park

San Diego City's Clevenger Canyon Open Space Park is known for its peaks and steeply-slopped canyons. It is one of many preserves and parks that are part of the San Dieguito River Park, and one day portions of the canyon's trails may be part of the final alignment for the river park's Coast to Crest Trail. The canyon is named for an early migrant to the San Diego area, John Clevenger, who established a farm near here in the latter part of the 19th century.

The Clevenger Canyon South Trail offers impressive views not only of the canyon and the San Pasqual Agricultural Preserve but also of the ocean to the west and mountains to the east, especially on clear winter days. It also gives one a chance to sit in the "cat bird's" seat

and watch the world drive by a thousand feet below. There are actually two wire-mesh seats side-by-side. It is unknown who took the time to carry them up and bolt them to the top of a large boulder. The trail up to the viewpoint can have spectacular displays of wildflowers in late winter and spring.

Clevenger Canyon is situated on a local fault. The coarse reddish sandy loam can be seen on the hillsides where the exposed batholith has weathered. Look for the rare Engelmann oak in the canyon among the mixed chaparral that includes chamise, *Ceanothus*, scrub oak, and red shank, which is rare this close to the coast. Clevenger Canyon chaparral was scorched in the 2007 Guejito Fire, but it is making a beautiful comeback.

Bushtit

The single trail begins from the parking area and forks about 0.5 mile from the trailhead into an east and west branch. The shorter West Trail leads off to the right and provides a relatively short hike to a 1550-foot knoll, via a series of switchbacks. The view west from the top of the knoll is the San Pasqual Agriculture Preserve and beyond to the ocean that can be seen on clear winter days. The East Trail, going off to the left, provides a longer, more interesting hike, gaining 1000 feet of elevation before ending on a ridge that is over 1600 feet in elevation. The ridge overlooks the San Pasqual Valley to the west, Boden Canyon to the north, and Santa Ysabel Creek to the east.

Shortly after the trails diverge, the East Trail goes into a small side canyon, crossing a small wooden bridge over an intermittent stream lined with riparian vegetation and bordered by large coast live oaks. Neither trail is particularly steep, but both climb steadily for most of their length. There is very little shade. Although both are considered strenuous, they are well maintained and easily negotiated. A variation of this hike can be made by hiking only 0.75 mile to the intermittent steam crossed by the small wooden bridge on the East Trail. The best time to go is February through May.

Two birds that will be seen here are the bushtit and the house finch. The bushtit (***Psal-***

triparus minimus) is a very small gray-brown songbird with a large head and lighter-tan underparts. Bushtits usually feed in large flocks moving from bush to bush looking for small insects and spiders. As they move, they make twittering sounds and frequently hang upside down as they search through leaves. They build large hanging nests made from soft grasses and spider webs that resemble dirty socks hanging on a line. Several family members may sleep in a nest during the breeding season. A nesting pair may have assistance in raising the young from other adult males in the group.

The house finch (***Haemorhous mexicanus***) is one of the most widespread year-round residents of the county that is equally at home in several habitats, including backyard feeders. They are also widespread across North America with an estimated population of about 1 billion birds. Males are easily recognized by their splashes of red. The red coloring comes from pigments in the food they eat. Females do not exhibit this coloring and are streaked grayish-brown. House finches are herbivores, eating seeds, fruits, and other parts of plants, but they will feed their young insects. Except when breeding, house finches forage in flocks.

Male house finch

154 CHAPTER 7

Distance:	3.5 miles, loop
Difficulty:	🚶🚶
Elevation gain/loss:	Up to 300 feet
Hiking time:	2 hours
Agency:	San Diego County
Trail use:	Bicycles, dogs, horses
Notes:	Hours posted 8 a.m. to 5 p.m. in winter, 8 a.m. to 7 p.m. in summer; locked after heavy rain
Trailhead GPS:	N33.03423, W116.95022
Optional map:	USGS 7.5-min *San Pasqual*
Atlas square:	L13
Directions:	(Ramona) From CA-67 go north on Highland Valley Road for 2.3 miles. Turn left to stay on Highland Valley Road. Go 0.8 mile. Parking lot for the Ramona Grasslands Preserve is on the right.

Habitat(s):

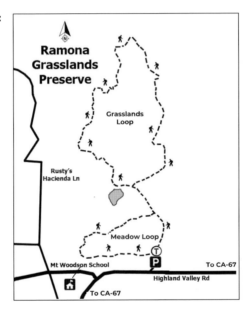

Between Interstate 15 and the town of Ramona lies a new gem for San Diego outdoor enthusiasts. Only recently opened to the public, the Ramona Grasslands Preserve allows hikers, joggers, and horseback riders to explore oak woodland, grasslands, chaparral, and wetland habitats.

The preserve is in the Santa Maria Valley, south of Ramona and north of Mount Woodson, set in rolling pasturelands. At 3521 acres, the preserve protects a large portion of a diverse ecosystem that is elsewhere at risk from residential development and other human encroachments. A 4-mile trail system allows visitors to explore approximately 480 acres that include vernal pools, alkali playas, and

riparian areas along the Santa Maria Creek, as well as chaparral and grassland. Additional trails are planned for the future. The preserve has San Diego County's largest population of the California large-leaf filaree (*California macrophylla*), an uncommon native filaree in the geranium family that is on the California Native Plant inventory of rare and endangered plants. Look for an annual herb that grows no more than a few centimeters high with round-leaves and white flowers with five petals. The sword-shaped fruit is typical of storksbill.

Particularly popular with birders, the preserve is a safe haven for large raptors, such as the red-tailed hawk and even golden eagle. Winter is optimal for spotting these magnifi-

Joe Fader

The trail

cent birds as several species overwinter in the area. Throughout the month of January and February, the Wildlife Research Institute, Inc., hosts a free public Hawk Watch every Saturday morning. Check the website for dates and information: www.wildlife-research.org. Large congregations of turkey vultures (*Cathartes aura*) can also be seen.

Turkey vultures are bigger than other raptors except for eagles and condors, and they have dark forewings with light gray flight feathers. They are scavengers with a keen sense of smell that leads them to carrion. The name vulture comes from the Latin *vellere*, meaning to tear. There are no feathers on a Turkey vulture's red head, which minimizes soiling as it eats carrion. Vultures have a very strong immune system that prevents them from getting sick from botulism, salmonella, or anthrax. They soar in groups and roost together. Their characteristic teetering flight with wings held raised in a shallow V helps them maintain stability and lift at low altitudes. They have a wingspread of 63-72 inches. Another name for them is the Peace Bird, since they do not kill. They do not follow weak or dying animals, but they do follow the scent of animals that are already dead. Their superior sense of smell can detect one drop of blood in an Olympic-sized pool. They

mate for life, or at least for many years, are social and not aggressive.

Many types of earthbound wildlife find their homes in the preserve. With even a short walk you will see large populations of California ground squirrels. Their furry heads are regularly seen emerging from the entrances to extensive burrow systems. There is little doubt that at such high numbers they play an integral part in this ecosystem, supporting not only birds of prey but other predators such as snakes, coyotes, and bobcats. Even if the coyote isn't seen, its stirring vocalizations reveal its presence in the late afternoon and evening.

Two main loops constitute the trail system at Ramona Grasslands Preserve. The 1.0-mile Meadow Loop explores some typical grassland habitat and can be reached by taking an immediate left at the preserve entrance on Highland Valley Road. Take another left at the intersection with the main trail from the parking lot to reach the Grasslands Loop where a few more habitat types can be explored. Begin by turning right at the fork and meander along a small creek and some low lying grasslands. Look for birds in the various trees lining the broad dirt trail.

The trail soon begins a small climb into classic chaparral habitat for the most challenging part of the hike, although still relatively easy at only about 200 feet of elevation gain. Descend back down towards the grasslands where you will find a pleasant lake with a picnic table before making your way back to the parking lot.

Wendy Esterly

Turkey vulture

Distance:	3.75 miles, out-and-back; or 5.5 miles, loop
Difficulty:	🚶🚶🚶🚶
Elevation gain/loss:	Up to 1100 feet
Hiking time:	up to 5 hours
Agency:	San Diego County
Trail use:	Bicycles, dogs
Trailhead GPS:	N33.00826, W116.95539
Optional map:	USGS 7.5-min *San Pasqual*
Atlas square:	L13
Directions:	(Ramona) From CA-67 park on the north side of road by the Cal Fire Station sign, 3 miles north of Poway Road and 0.3 mile south of Archie Moore Road.

Habitat(s):

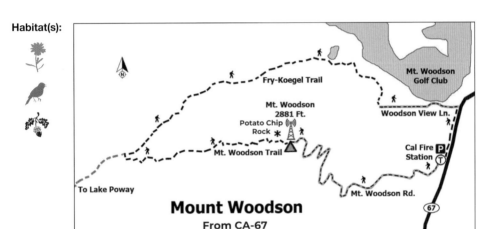

Mount Woodson has become one of the most popular hikes in San Diego County since the Potato Chip Rock made its appearance in YouTube videos. On a typical weekend, there may be a hundred or more people hiking up from Lake Poway, milling around this famed rock, waiting for their turn to scamper out on the ledge and capture a photo of their adventure. But Mount Woodson has many other things to offer.

If the hike is extended to Potato Chip Rock, it adds 1 mile to the journey to the peak. An even more interesting possibility is the 5.5-mile loop hike described here that includes the experience of the diverse terrain and life of this unique area.

The well-marked trailhead is on the south side of the Cal Fire station access road, a few feet from CA-67. The hike begins as a short trail through a live oak and sycamore woodland leading to the paved road that will be the route to the top. Live oaks and occasional Coulter pines periodically shade the road

during the steep ascent along with enormous boulders composed of Woodson Mountain granodiorite, a light-colored intrusive rock that weathers into rounded shapes, such as Potato Chip Rock. The abundance of these huge boulders has made this a popular place for rock climbers.

More than 50 common chaparral shrubs and wildflowers have been found growing beside the road on the way to the top. These include three kinds of manzanita, laurel sumac, yerba santa, California buckwheat, coastal sagebrush, white sage, chamise, and cardinal or scarlet larkspur (*Delphinium cardinale*). The cardinal larkspur is a showy plant that grows in coastal, inland, and desert chaparral slopes. The flowers grow on erect stems as high as 6 feet. The flower is red and tubular, attracting hummingbirds. Two of the red petals have yellow blotches on them.

The top of Mount Woodson is 1.75 miles from the CA-67 trailhead. The pines, huge boulders, and a forest of communication

The road to the summit from CA-67

towers tend to obscure views from Mount Woodson's summit from the trail. This is the turn-around point for the out-and-back hike. For the longer loop hike, continue west down the ridge from the summit, leaving the asphalt road, and continuing on a well-traveled dirt trail where, weather permitting, there are outstanding views of San Diego, Point Loma, and the ocean. Most likely there will also be a crowd waiting to climb out onto the Potato Chip Rock, particularly on weekends. On down the ridge, past Potato Chip Rock, there will be the signed junction for the Fry-Koegel (F-K) Trail, 1.3 miles from the summit.

The F-K Trail is the 2.7-mile route back to your parked vehicle on the loop hike. Initially the F-K Trail passes through lush chaparral now fully recovered from the 2007 Witch Creek fire. Continuing down this well-maintained trail, there is a transition to a cool, shady, coast live oak woodland before reaching the western boundary of Mount Woodson Estates, a suburban development. Follow the trail to the right to CA-67. Upon reaching CA-67, walk south beside the highway to the Cal Fire Ramona station.

The best time to go is when the chaparral shrubs and wildflowers are in bloom, from March through June. If going during the warmer days of summer or fall, plan to hike in the early morning, before the heat of the midday.

The City of Poway and San Diego County have future plans to extend a trail from Iron Mountain either over or under CA-67 to Mount Woodson and Potato Chip Rock, eventually connecting to Boulder Oaks.

Cardinal or scarlet larkspur

Distance:	2 miles, out-and-back
Difficulty:	🚶🚶
Elevation gain/loss:	Up to 200 feet
Hiking time:	1 hour
Agency:	City of Poway; CDFW
Trail use:	Dogs, horses
Notes:	Parking lot hours posted November to May sunrise to sunset, June to October 6:30 a.m. to sunset
Trailhead GPS:	N33.01602, W117.02366
Optional map:	USGS 7.5-min *Escondido*
Atlas square:	L12
Directions:	(Poway) From I-15 go east on Rancho Bernardo Road for 1.5 miles. Continue onto Espola Road. Go 1.6 miles. Turn left into the Blue Sky parking lot and drive to the end.

Habitat(s):

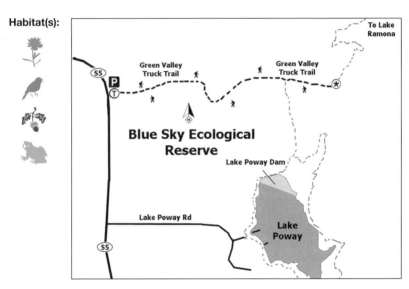

The rolling hills in and around Poway create a unique mix of habitat types and climatic conditions. These varied ecosystems, in turn, foster an incredible amount of plant and animal diversity and are examples of the reason why San Diego, and much of southern California for that matter, are world-famous biodiversity hotspots. Several of these habitat types are easily explored via a comfortable and accessible walking tour through Blue Sky Ecological Reserve. This reserve is one of 119 reserves owned and managed by the California Department of Fish and Wildlife, but it is the only one with a full time naturalist. During the weekends, the naturalist and volunteer docents lead free walks that educate the public about the plants and animals living here. See their website for details (http://www.blueskyreserve.

org/). The 700-acre reserve provides a perfect opportunity to experience and learn about the natural surroundings first-hand. The purpose of the reserve is habitat conservation. Bicycles are not allowed.

A largely flat, gravel and dirt path departs from the parking lot on Espola Road, first dropping into an oak canyon/riparian corridor. This part of the trail is mostly shaded, thanks to the stream on the north side of the trail that provides enough water for relatively tall coast live oaks and western sycamores to thrive. Go left onto the Oak Canyon Trail to descend into a cool oak grotto, where these beautiful trees and a wide section of the stream can be explored up close, but watch out for poison-oak. Keep an ear out for the songs of frogs as you near the cool water, and look for birds, one

Don Fosket

An Oak woodland at Blue Sky Ecological Reserve

of which is the yellow-rumped warbler (*Setophaga coronata*), one of the county's most widespread winter visitors, found in most habitats. It is the only warbler in the county with a distinct yellow patch on its rump. The plumage varies greatly by the bird's age, sex, and season. Through the winter, the birds are dull brownish or grayish, softly streaked darker, with some degree of yellow on the throat. Before departing in the spring, the birds grow in their breeding plumage, in which the males are strikingly patterned in black, gray, white, and yellow. They forage in trees, shrubs, and on the ground, looking for insects and berries, or flit out from the foliage to chase an insect.

Upon exiting the oak grotto, the trail continues to follow through the oak woodland above the stream until a fork is reached just under 1 mile from the parking lot. One branch continues parallel to the stream (stay left at the fork), eventually reaching the Ramona Dam after an additional 1.5 miles. There is a small outdoor classroom for educational programs and a pit toilet on the right side of this trail, just after the fork. A right turn at the fork will lead to the Lake Poway Dam in a little over 1 mile. For further distance and/or challenge, a number of additional trails can be reached from here including the Lake Poway Loop and the Mount Woodson Trail.

Whether you choose to turn back at the fork or explore one or all of the trail extensions, be

sure to find a break in the shelter of the oaks lining the trail to catch the view of the surrounding rocky hills covered with coastal sage scrub, a habitat characterized by aromatic, drought-resistant plants. Now try to gain a little elevation to view another habitat—the cool, shaded corridor you walked through from the parking lot. The importance of water and gravity becomes abundantly clear when the green vein of oaks is seen snaking along the valley floor below much drier hillsides.

Wendy Esterly

Yellow-rumped warbler

Distance:	11 miles, out-and-back
Difficulty:	🥾🥾🥾🥾
Elevation gain/loss:	Up to 2200 feet
Hiking time:	7 hours
Agency:	City of Poway; CDFW
Trail use:	Dogs
Notes:	Parking lot hours posted November to May sunrise to sunset, June to October 6:30 a.m. to sunset
Trailhead GPS:	N33.01603, W117.02366
Optional map:	USGS 7.5-min *Escondido*; *San Pasqual*
Atlas square:	L12
Directions:	(Poway) From I-15 go east on Rancho Bernardo Road for 1.5 miles. Continue onto Espola Road. Go 1.6 miles. Turn left into the Blue Sky parking lot and drive to the end.

Habitat(s):

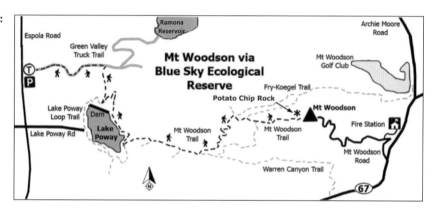

Mount Woodson is one of San Diego's favorite places for a dayhike. Many people make the climb on the asphalt-paved road that rises steeply to the top off of CA-67, on the east side of the mountain. Other hikers take the somewhat longer but more scenic west side trail that starts from Lake Poway. A less traveled option, presented here, is to start your ascent at the Blue Sky Reserve, adding a few more miles, but giving you a chance to stroll through one of San Diego County's more scenic oak woodlands while experiencing a diversity of vegetation types on your way up. The Blue Sky Reserve directly connects to Poway's extensive network of hiking trails.

This strenuous 11-mile round-trip hike is on well-marked and maintained trails. Start hiking on the Blue Sky Reserve Trail, at the south end of the parking lot. Although this trail continues 2.4 miles to the Ramona Dam, turn south or right 0.9 mile from the trailhead onto the Lake Poway Recreational Area trail. Much of both of these trails pass through a beautiful

coast live oak forest and near a lush riparian community with mature western sycamore, mule-fat, and Goodding's black willow (*Salix gooddingii*), as well as oaks and a dense thicket of western poison-oak along the stream. Be assured that the trail doesn't go through the western poison-oak but does allow you to enjoy the brilliant red color of its leaves in the fall in relative safety.

Goodding's black willow, which is a fast-growing, tall (20-60 feet), deciduous tree, is common in riparian areas. The tree is dioecious. Flowers are catkins with the female flower longer than the male flower. The bark is thick, furrowed, and shedding, and the branches are thin. Leaves are shiny-green on both sides, lance-shaped, and serrated along the edges. Both fires and floods create good seedbed conditions. It has high flood tolerance and low shade tolerance. It sprouts vigorously from the root crown after a fire. In some areas of the southwest it is planted for stream bank stabilization and erosion control. It provides browse and cover for animals

Mt. Woodson boulders

and was a plant valued by Native Americans for medicinal purposes. The bark contains salicin, a precursor of aspirin.

In another 0.25 mile is the Poway Wilderness Picnic Area with picnic tables, water, and toilet facilities. From there, the trail switchbacks up a coastal sage scrub-covered hillside to take you over the east side of the Lake Poway Dam and into the recreation area.

The Lake Poway Trail loops around the lake, but leaves the lake when the Mount Woodson Trail branches off to the left, 0.4 mile ahead. For the first mile, the trail is a nearly straight, somewhat steep, dirt road whose saving grace is the view behind of the lake that recedes as you climb. A little over 1 mile from the lake is the Warren Canyon–Mount Woodson Trail junction. From this point on the trail is more interesting, extending up the chaparral-covered hillside, initially through a series of switchbacks, but then straightening out to climb up a ridge to the top of Mount Woodson, 1.9 miles ahead. On your way are some amazing well-weathered boulders, including the famous Potato Chip Rock. Do not forget to check out the vegetation, including several

species of *Ceanothus* and big-berry manzanita that add interest and color to the hike.

A forest of tall metal communications towers will become visible long before reaching the peak and will guide you to the summit. After exploring the summit area, return the way you came.

Goodding's black willow

Distance:	5.6 miles, out-and-back
Difficulty:	🚶🚶🚶
Elevation gain/loss:	Up to 1750 feet
Hiking time:	up to 4 hours
Agency:	City of Poway; RMWD
Trail use:	Bicycles, dogs, horses
Notes:	Hours posted 6 a.m. to sunset, parking fee for non-Poway residents
Trailhead GPS:	N33.00714, W117.01396
Optional map:	USGS 7.5-min *Escondido*; *San Pasqual*
Atlas square:	L12
Directions:	(Poway) From I-15 go east on Rancho Bernardo Road for 1.5 miles. Continue onto Espola Road. Go 2.3 miles. Turn left on Lake Poway Road. Go 0.6 mile to the entrance of the recreation area. Park in the northeast lot near the landscaping building.

Habitat(s):

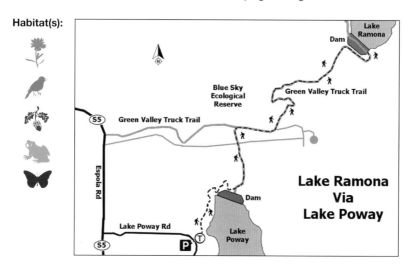

Lake Poway Recreation Area is a convenient starting point for a hike to Lake Ramona, since it provides abundant parking and numerous additional recreational opportunities. The hike to Lake Ramona takes you through a variety of habitats, including coastal sage scrub, shady oak woodlands, and riparian habitat with a great ocean view, including a peek at San Clemente Island if clear. The trails are all heavily used and well signed, making navigation easy with the view of Lake Ramona dam as well as much of the trail visible from Lake Poway.

Lake Ramona is a reservoir created by an earthen dam built in 1988 by the Ramona Municipal Water District to supply water for agriculture and as an emergency storage facility. Its water is purchased from the San Diego Water Authority. Boating and swimming are not permitted, but fishing from the shore is allowed with a valid fishing license. The lake is not stocked, but it does contain a population of largemouth bass.

To reach the lake, find the Lake Poway Trail entrance on the left side of the landscaped building near the northeast parking lot and head north. Lake Poway's dam was built in the early 1970s many years before the Lake Ramona dam was completed. The trail completely circles Lake Poway, but you will be on it for less than 1 mile as it winds up and over a hill northwest of the lake and down the front side of the dam. The trail forks 0.87 mile from the parking lot. The circumferential Lake Poway Trail continues to the right. A sign on the trail to the left indicates that Lake Ramona is 2 miles ahead. The trail is a dirt road, but without motorized vehicles, and follows an oak-forested canyon. It joins the Blue Sky Ecological Reserve Trail, also a dirt road.

Bill Howell

Bill Howell

Male monarch with two black dots on back wings *Female monarch with no black dots on back wings*

Before reaching this junction, you will pass what was once the Lake Poway Campground. Camping is no longer permitted here, but it is an attractive, well-maintained area, set in a dense coast live oak forest with picnic tables, running water, and toilet facilities.

The hike continues near or through the oak woodland as you go north to the Blue Sky Ecological Reserve Trail, labeled on many maps as the Green Valley Truck Trail. Once you reach this trail, go right or east. The oak woodland now begins to blend with a lush riparian habitat that includes western sycamores, arroyo willows, and of course, abundant western poison-oak. Mule-fat, another common resident of riparian habitat, also is abundant here.

Mule-fat flowers are attractive to the queen butterfly (*Danaus gilippus*), which is a close relative of the monarch (*Danaus plexippus*). Both are milkweed butterflies whose larvae exclusively eat a species of milkweed for food. Adults, on the other hand, seek nectar from flowers. The adult queen, living in mule-fat territory, is strongly attracted to the nectar of mule-fat blooms. Adult queens living in other areas are attracted to other species of plants, similar to milkweed, that also contain the alkaloid lycopsamine, which they convert to a pheromone, a secreted chemical that makes them more attractive to males. The queen can mate up to 15 times in a day, a number that is significantly higher than any other species of

Don Fosket

Lake Ramona

View of Lake Poway

moths and butterflies. After queens mate, the female will lay a single egg on the leaf, stem, or flower bud of a milkweed plant (***Asclepias* spp.**). All milkweed species contain a toxic alkaloid in their leaves and stems. The milky sap found in all milkweed plants is the reason for their common name. By consuming milkweed, queen and monarch larvae absorb the leaf toxins into their systems, making them unpalatable to prey.

Adult queens and monarchs are also unpalatable to prey as adults, but the queen is not as toxic as the monarch. Queen's coloration mimicry of monarchs offers them extra protection from predators. Although they closely resemble monarchs, queens are smaller and do not undertake as dramatic migrations but rather do short-distance flights to tropical areas where there are distinct dry seasons. Despite the alkaloid toxicity of milkweeds, Native Americans harvested the young buds and immature seed pods. They usually parboiled the blooms and young seedpods before consuming them.

In another 0.25 mile is a signed junction. The road to the right leads to a pumping station and is closed to the public. Take the trail to the left. From this point it is 1.2 miles to

Lake Ramona up a steep but well-graded dirt road. Lake Ramona offers few recreational opportunities other than fishing from the shore in season (license required), but the view to the west is outstanding, extending out to the ocean. San Clemente Island can be seen on the clear days. After exploring the lake and enjoying the view, return to Lake Poway the way you came.

Queen butterfly

Distance:	3 miles, loop
Difficulty:	🚶🚶🚶
Elevation gain/loss:	400 feet
Hiking time:	2 hours
Agency:	City of Poway
Trail use:	Bicycles, dogs, horses
Notes:	Hours posted 6 a.m. to sunset; parking fee for non-Poway residents
Trailhead GPS:	N33.00728, W117.01377
Optional map:	USGS 7.5-min *Escondido*
Atlas square:	L12
Directions:	(Poway) From I-15 go east on Rancho Bernardo Road for 1.5 miles. Continue onto Espola Road. Go 2.3 miles. Turn left on Lake Poway Road. Go 0.6 mile to the entrance of the recreation area. Park in the northeast lot near the landscaping building.

Habitat(s):

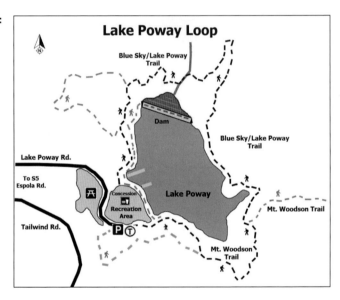

The Lake Poway Recreational Area is a great place to enjoy your favorite outdoor activities from fishing, boating, camping, and picnicking to hiking on one of the many trails that radiate from its grassy, manicured core. The trail described here is a loop that goes around the lake, passing through varied native habitats while offering outstanding views. The lake is a reservoir, holding drinking water for the City of Poway, and swimming is not permitted.

Begin the hike leaving from the most southeasterly part of the parking area, and head in a counterclockwise direction around the lake. The first trail segment is on a bluff overlooking the lake along a north-facing canyon through fairly dense chaparral that includes broom baccharis (***Baccharis sarothroides***). Native Americans used this perennial evergreen shrub to make brooms by tying the long green stalks together to clean out living areas. This plant is dioecious with separate male and female plants. Can you tell which plants are which? (Hint: the flowers of the male plants have pollen.) The flowers are cream- to white-colored and are pollinated by insects. If it is autumn or winter, check out the small flowers on the broom baccharis. Broom baccharis provides nectar to insects during the time when little else is in bloom. The western blue pygmy butterfly (***Brephidium exilis***) is particularly attracted to the nectar. Males will patrol the area around the flowers looking for receptive females. This butterfly is

Broom baccharis

the smallest butterfly in North America, and possibly in the world, with a total wingspan less than 0.75 inches. They are copper-brown in color with blue markings on the upperside of the wings and flecks of white on the underside and on the wing edges.

Western blue pygmy butterfly

After about 0.5 mile the trail makes a nearly 90-degree turn toward the north and continues along the eastern side of the lake. This southwest-facing slope receives more direct sunlight and is hotter and dryer as a result. The vegetation now is typical of coastal sage scrub with abundant coastal sagebrush (*Artemisia californica*), California buckwheat (*Eriogonum fasciculatum*), and telegraph weed (*Heterotheca grandiflora*). These are all drought resistant plants able to survive our typically rainless summers, but they differ in how they are able to do so. Coastal sagebrush loses all of its leaves and enters a type of dormancy. California buckwheat survives and even thrives under drought conditions due to its deep roots and small leaves with a thick cuticle to reduce water loss. Telegraph weed also has deep roots, but instead of small leaves, they are much larger and thicker and stay green through most of the summer drought because they are covered densely with trichomes or hairs that reduce water loss.

The trail forks at slightly less than 1 mile into the hike. Keep to the left to continue your hike around the lake but avoid descend-

Don Fosket

Trail leaves Lake Poway

ing to the shoreline fisherman's trail, which is not continuous. The right branch leads up to Potato Chip Rock and the top of Mount Woodson, which you could explore, but it will add about 5 strenuous miles to the hike.

The Lake Poway Loop Trail heads northwest toward the dam, cresting as it rounds the restricted area near the dam. It then descends through a series of switchbacks to the canyon bottom near the foot of the dam. The trail again forks. The trail to the left will go back up the hillside on the west side of the dam and on to the recreation area's concession stands, not far from the parking area. Before returning to the parking area, however, take a short hike down the trail on the right, heading toward the Blue Sky Reserve. The Lake Poway Picnic Area is about 0.1 mile down this path. Camping is not permitted. It is strictly a day-use area. However, it offers cool shade amongst coast live oaks, as well as picnic tables, drinking water, and restroom facilities. It is a good place to rest before climbing up the hill back to your vehicle.

Jim Varnell

Telegraph weed

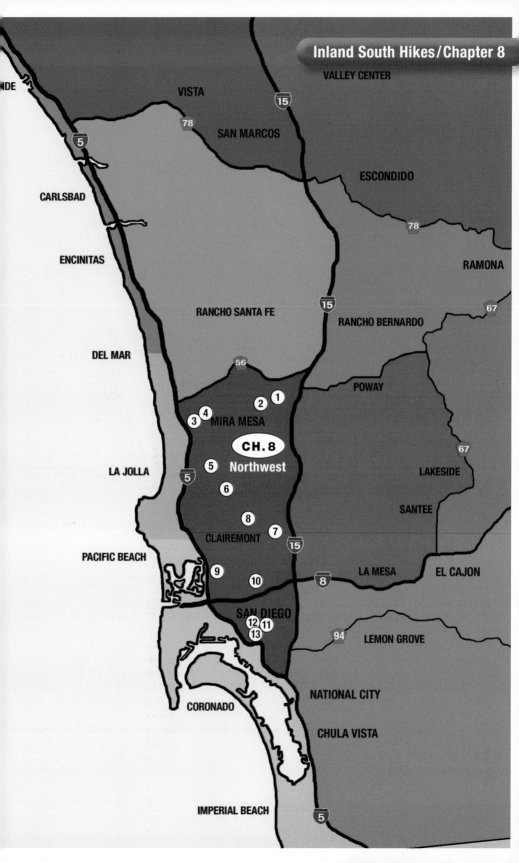

Distance:	3 or 5 miles, out-and-back
Difficulty:	🚶 or 🚶🚶
Elevation gain/loss:	Up to 100 feet
Hiking time:	2 or 3 hours
Agency:	San Diego County
Trail use:	Bicycles, dogs, horses
Notes:	Hours posted 8 a.m. to sunset; parking fee
Trailhead GPS:	N32.93867, W117.13004
Optional map:	USGS 7.5-min *Del Mar*; *Poway*
Atlas square:	N10
Directions:	(Rancho Peñasquitos) From I-15 turn west on Mercy Road. Go 1.4 miles to Black Mountain Road. Cross Black Mountain Road to the entrance of Los Peñasquitos Canyon Preserve and park. From CA-56 go south on Black Mountain Road for 1.1 miles. Turn right at Mercy Road and into the entrance of Los Peñasquitos Canyon Preserve and park.

Habitat(s):

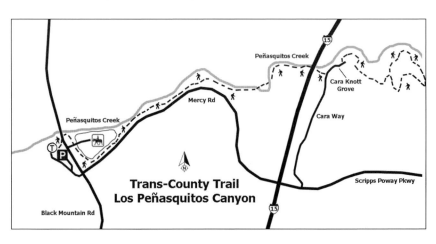

The Trans-County Trail is one of several regional trail systems being developed in San Diego County. It runs east to west over approximately 110 miles from Anza-Borrego Desert State Park to the ocean at Torrey Pines. About 70% of the trail is over existing trails in the county and is currently open to the public. This section of the trail follows along the Peñasquitos Creek riparian zone from Black Mountain Road east, crosses under I-15, and continues on for a short distance. This hike includes a scenic loop with great views and diverse chaparral species.

From the parking area, walk down towards the creek and follow the trail that crosses under Black Mountain Road and continues east toward Mercy Road. This well-marked trail is signed Trans-County Trail. For the first 0.25 mile, the trail passes some stables on the left. Once past the stables, the trail will drop

down along the riparian zone of Peñasquitos Creek. From this point until crossing under I-15, there will be a profusion of wildflowers in spring and early summer. If hiking during this time, look for an impressive display of the fuchsia-flower gooseberry (***Ribes speciosum***) with its purplish-red elongate flowers hanging from spiny stems. The leaves are leathery and shiny green, somewhat dividing into several lobes. It is a spreading shrub found in coastal sage scrub and chaparral areas that can grow up to 9 feet in height. Hummingbirds are attracted to this plant.

Much of the trail is shaded by western sycamores, coast live oaks, and willows and crosses the creek a couple of times on well-constructed foot bridges. Just past the first bridge on the right is a pool that is home to fish, crayfish, and other aquatic animals. Look for the common water strider that is

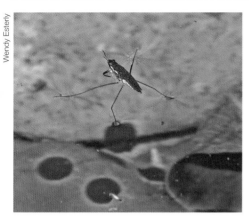

Wendy Esterly

Common water strider

also called a pond skater (**Aquarius remijis**). It is a true bug in the family Gerridae. It will be flitting around on the surface of the pond. These are delicate water-based insects that can literally walk on water. Because of this ability, they have also been called Jesus bugs. Their toes have velvety oil hairs which allow them to stay afloat using surface tension. Notice the smallest pair of legs tucked under their chin for hunting or defense. They walk with their middle legs and steer with their hind legs. Males attract females by tapping the surface of the water. If the rhythm is seductive enough, there might be six girlfriends in an hour. They wait for other insects to fall in the water that will become their prey. They also feed on mosquito larvae.

Once you pass the second crossing, there are fewer trees close to the trail and more open space that provide many opportunities throughout the season to view flowering

Pauline Jimenez

Fuchsia-flower gooseberry in fruit

plants such as monkey flowers, goldenbush, California buckwheat, and jimson weed. Ahead will be the undercrossing at I-15. Once on the other end, you will cross under the Los Peñasquitos Arch Bridge that was in use until I-15 was completed. It is now used only as a bike trail. In 1995 the new bridge was renamed the Cara Knott Memorial Bridge in memory of a university student who was killed in the area in 1986. This is where the 3-mile hike ends by turning back and retracing your steps to your vehicle.

For the longer loop hike, continue down this road and skirt around the City of Poway's pump station. The trail climbs for a short distance to an old roadbed on the back side of the pump station. It then continues with a gradual uphill climb through many common

Mary Lueking

Crossing Peñasquitos Creek

chaparral species. After about 0.5 mile, there is an unmarked trail off to the right that heads up a fairly steep but short climb to a saddle on the ridge. This is the high point on the trip where there is a good view of the east end of Los Peñasquitos Canyon. Continue on down the trail to the east to join the main trail close to the creek. When you meet up with the main trail, turn to the left to begin the loop and the return trip. Since this is now on the north-facing slope, there are many flowering plants including toyon and dudleyas. This is a great place to get a good view of the old highway bridge with the much larger I-15 bridge looming overhead. After completing the loop, return to the main trail and go left or west to return to your vehicle.

Distance:	5 miles, out-and-back
Difficulty:	🚶🚶
Elevation gain/loss:	Up to 200 feet
Hiking time:	3 hours
Agency:	City of San Diego; San Diego County
Trail use:	Bicycles on designated trails only, dogs, horses
Notes:	Hours posted 8 a.m. to sunset
Trailhead GPS:	N32.93325, W117.14579
Optional map:	USGS 7.5-min *Del Mar*
Atlas square:	N9
Directions:	(Mira Mesa) From I-15 go west on Mira Mesa Boulevard for 1.8 miles. Turn right on Camino Ruiz. Go 1.4 miles to the entrance of Camino Ruiz Neighborhood Park. The trailhead is on the left after the first few parking spaces

Habitat(s):

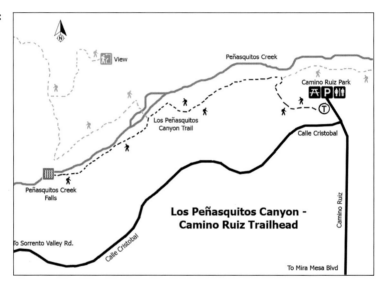

Los Peñasquitos Canyon Preserve is a 4000-acre open space area that stretches 7 miles in length from I-15 to the I-5 and I-805 merge. It has 37 miles of multi-use trails. Natural resources include over 500 plant species (nearly 20% of the species in the county), more than 175 species of birds (more than 1/3 of the species ever spotted in the county), and a great variety of reptiles and mammals. Peñasquitos Creek, which flows year-round, runs through the heart of the preserve.

The Camino Ruiz Trailhead is the only trail that accesses Los Peñasquitos Canyon Preserve from the south rim between Black Mountain Road and West End parking lot off Sorrento Valley Boulevard. Before the Camino Ruiz Trailhead was established in 2009, it was very difficult to access the canyon from the south

side. The upper portion of the trail is steep with loose cobbles. Western poison-oak is prevalent. Rattlesnakes are common, although the trails are wide enough that you can easily avoid them.

This trail is unique in that it gives you a chance to hike under a canopy of scrub oaks that provide a tunnel-like experience. The majority of the trail is in the shade. The Camino Ruiz Trail terminates at 0.6 mile when you reach the canyon bottom near Los Peñasquitos Creek and enter the canyon's riparian zone. Note how greater moisture and water availability associated with the stream has given rise to a lush growth and more water-intensive species, such as western sycamores and willows.

Go left or west, 1.9 miles on the main south side trail, to reach the waterfall on Los Peñasquitos Creek. The round trip from the trailhead

Granary in dead sycamore

Mosses (***phylum Bryophyta***) are bryophytes or plants that do not have vascular tissue that transports water and nutrients to plant cells. They produce spores rather than flowers and seeds. Mosses grow in damp or shady areas and tend to form mats. The plant has a simple, one-cell-thick leaf attached to a non-vascular stem and absorbs water and nutrients mainly through its leaves. Mosses can grow on rocks, trees, soil, downed logs, and in cracks. They help break up rocks to make soil. They can absorb water very quickly.

Moss on rock

to the waterfall is about 5 miles. Alternately, you can go right to reach the Los Peñasquitos Creek crossing 0.25 mile ahead. There is also a single-track trail on the south side of the creek that is shared with equestrians. The waterfall is a delightful location to enjoy the sound of the water, get your feet wet, or have a picnic. Water is found here year-round, and crossing the creek can be a challenge at times.

Wildlife is plentiful all year long in the Los Peñasquitos Canyon riparian zone, where you may see acorn woodpeckers, red-shouldered hawks, and kites. It is not uncommon to see a bobcat, coyote, raccoon, rabbit, or a southern mule deer. An early morning or late afternoon hike provides the best opportunities for seeing or photographing the wildlife, as many species are largely crepuscular, active early morning and at dusk.

The trail is accessible year-round and offers different sensory experiences based on phenology or timing of life-cycle events associated with the seasons. Late summer flowers include those of California buckwheat and goldenbush. Winter brings red fruit to toyon shrubs, which attracts birds. The oaks are evergreen, providing shade all year. In the spring, there is a profusion of mushrooms, lichens, mosses, and other species that like the dampness. The spring flower bloom is spectacular from March through June with blue-eyed-grass, fuchsia-flower gooseberry, and milkmaids, along with many other typical chaparral plants.

Moss sporophytes

Distance:	6 miles, out-and-back
Difficulty:	🥾🥾
Elevation gain/loss:	Up to 200 feet
Hiking time:	3 hours
Agency:	City of San Diego; San Diego County
Trail use:	Bicycles on designated trails only, dogs, horses
Notes:	Hours posted 8 a.m. to sunset
Trailhead GPS:	N32.90648, W117.20610
Optional map:	USGS 7.5-min *Del Mar*
Atlas square:	N8
Directions:	(Mira Mesa) From I-5 N exit on Sorrento Valley Road and then turn left on Roselle Street. Go 0.1 mile. Turn right on Sorrento Valley Boulevard. Go 1.1 miles. Parking lot is on the right. From I-5 S take the I-5 Local Bypass then go east on Carmel Mountain Road for 0.3 mile. Turn right on Vista Sorrento Parkway. Go 1.4 miles. Turn left on Sorrento Valley Boulevard and go 0.9 mile. Parking lot is on the right. From I-805 exit on Sorrento Valley Road and turn left on Vista Sorrento Parkway. Go 1.1 miles. Turn right on Sorrento Valley Boulevard. Go 0.9 mile. Parking lot is on the right.

Habitat(s):

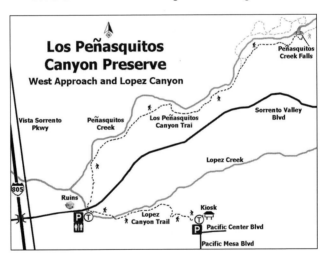

Los Peñasquitos Canyon Preserve encompasses both Los Peñasquitos Canyon and Lopez Canyon. Both canyons may be accessed from a western approach. The canyon walls are responsible for the preserve's name (little cliffs in Spanish) and the name of the first Mexican land grant in California—Santa Maria de los Peñasquitos—granted to Francisco de María Ruíz in 1823. Ruíz was unhappy with his grant because he felt the land was not good for cattle grazing, so he requested additional land to the west called El Cuervo, which was granted to him in 1834. He built an adobe home near the confluence of Lopez Creek and Peñasquitos Creek that later became known as the El Cuervo adobe, possibly because crows (*cuervo* in Spanish)

roosted there. The Ruíz heirs abandoned the adobe when they built a new elaborate home at the east end of the canyon around 1860. The newer home is open for tours on weekends.

The highlight of the hike from the canyon's western approach is the visit to the Peñasquitos Creek Falls, a waterfall and associated ponds carved in volcanic rocks at the midpoint of Los Peñasquitos Canyon, one of many large canyons in San Diego that cut through mesas from the foothills of the mountains to the coast. The rocky ledges overlooking the pools makes a great place to rest before turning back.

The trail begins amid dense vegetation along Lopez Creek which opens up into a clearing with a choice of continuing east along Lopez

Relaxing around the pools

Creek into Lopez Canyon or heading north underneath Sorrento Valley Boulevard to explore Peñasquitos Canyon.

Once in Los Peñasquitos Canyon turn west for a short side trip, of about 1500 feet, to see the historic El Cuervo adobe ruin which lies between Peñasquitos Creek and Sorrento Valley Boulevard under a protective roof. Cattle continued to graze these lands for hundreds of years, first with the Ruíz family and then, beginning in the 1840s, with the Lopez family who had their operation in the adjacent canyon southeast of the boulevard.

The waterfall is 3 miles northeast from the adobe. The trail follows the creek at varying distances. Near Peñasquitos Creek are riparian woodlands that consist of trees such as the western sycamore, arroyo willow, western cottonwood, mule-fat, coast live oak, and other oak species. Away from the creek are grassy meadows, rolling hills, steep canyon walls, and chaparral and coastal sage scrub plant communities.

Chaparral and sage scrub species include the usual suspects—lemonadeberry, laurel sumac, toyon, mission manzanita, blue elderberry, fuchsia-flower gooseberry, chamise, coastal sagebrush, California buckwheat, black and white sage, chaparral broom, goldenbush, wild-cucumber, monkey flower, and Ramona-lilac. On a typical daytime hike, you can see (or hear) many bird species along with butterflies and other insects. Birds commonly sighted in and about the canyon include various hawks, common ravens, American crows, coots, mallards, quail, mourning doves, egrets, herons, hummingbirds, black phoebes, blue-

birds, mockingbirds, thrashers, blackbirds, bushtits, wrentits, finches, and towhees. Watch along the trail for scat that has fur, berries, and or seeds, most likely evidence of coyotes, and small mounds of dirt indicating the presence of gophers. Fish, frogs, and crayfish can be found in the creek.

Much of the route is lined with rounded, ancient river-borne rock deposited during the Eocene 45 million years ago in a volcanic region of Sonora, Mexico. The rocks moved northward via tectonic plate movement beginning some 10 million years ago. As you near the junction to the waterfall, looking to the right up the hill will reveal a red shelf-like structure capping lighter colored rock. This is a Lindavista Formation originating about a million years ago from iron-rich shoreline deposits. Wend your way carefully over the rocks to get down to the water. Return via the same trail.

The waterfall

Distance:	2, 5 or 7.5 miles, out-and-back
Difficulty:	🏃🏃 or 🏃🏃🏃
Elevation gain/loss:	Up to 200 feet
Hiking time:	2 or 4 hours
Agency:	City of San Diego; San Diego County
Trail use:	Bicycles on designated trails only, dogs, horses
Notes:	Hours posted 8 a.m. to sunset
Trailhead GPS:	N32.90648, W117.20617
Optional map:	USGS 7.5-min *Del Mar*
Atlas square:	N8
Directions:	(Mira Mesa) From I-5 N exit on Sorrento Valley Road and then turn left on Roselle Street. Go 0.1 mile. Turn right on Sorrento Valley Boulevard. Go 1.1 miles. Parking lot is on the right. From I-5 S take the I-5 Local Bypass then go east on Carmel Mountain Road for 0.3 mile. Turn right on Vista Sorrento Parkway. Go 1.4 miles. Turn left on Sorrento Valley Boulevard and go 0.9 mile. Parking lot is on the right. From I-805 exit on Sorrento Valley Road and turn left on Vista Sorrento Parkway. Go 1.1 miles. Turn right on Sorrento Valley Boulevard. Go 0.9 mile. Parking lot is on the right.

Habitat(s):

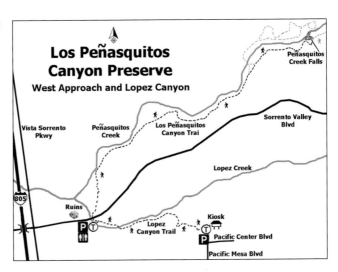

Lopez Canyon is named for the family that had a cattle operation in the canyon in the 1840s. Although it is next to the highly visited Peñasquitos Canyon, it gets little traffic, which makes it attractive.

The hike begins with a pleasant canopy of western sycamore, mule-fat, willow, and other riparian plants that line Lopez Creek. The trail sometimes crosses the creek, so watch your balance on wet rocks. Western poison-oak thrives here in large stands and up on western sycamore trees. Be sure you know how to identify it before you hike here.

There is a mix of native and non-native plants in the canyon. Native plants include blue elderberry, black sage, lemonadeberry, laurel sumac, monkey flower, and wild-cucumber. The wild-cucumber (*Marah macrocarpa*) has a green, prickly fruit scattered throughout the branches. The prickles are derived from a plant's epidermis, or skin layer, while spines are modified leaves, and thorns are from shoots. This is a perennial vine whose leaves and stems die after the fruits have matured. It is perennial because of its enormous underground tuber from which green shoots emerge in the spring or after a fire. The tuber can weigh up to 220 pounds and have lateral arm-like extensions making it look like a man, leading to the common name of manroot. The tuber

Wild cucumber fruit

contains chemical compounds called saponins with soap-like properties. The Kumeyaay used the tubers for soap and for fishing. Tubers were crushed and thrown into pools, releasing saponins into the water. The saponins paralyzed the fish causing them to float where they could be easily collected. Wild-cucumber belongs to the Cucurbitaceae or squash family. This family of plants is primarily pollinated by two genera of bees commonly referred to as squash bees (*Peponapis* spp. and *Xenoglossa* spp.).

The most common squash bee in San Diego County is (*Peponapis pruinosa*), a name that means dusty-looking pumpkin bee. These native squash bees are specialist pollinators, foraging only on squash family members. Although they evolved to live exclusively on wild members of the squash family, farmers encourage them in their fields as they are efficient pollinators of crop pumpkins, squash, and cucumbers. The squash bees also have evolved to forage very efficiently and early in the morning when the squash blossoms are open. On the other hand, generalist pollinators such as the European honeybee, forage later during the day when many of the squash blossoms have closed, and hence, they pollinate these plants with lower effectiveness. Squash bees are about the size of small bumblebees and nest up to a foot underground. They generally can be distinguished from honeybees based upon the time of day when foraging and on their robust body shape.

Plants such as plantains, blackberry, jimson weed, and thistles, also found here, can be either native or non-native depending on the species. Non-natives, many of which were introduced into the area through the cattle industry, include perennial rye grass, wild oat, black mustard, horehound, curly dock, pineapple-weed, plus various filaree species.

There are many gopher holes lining the trail. Pay attention and you may see a gopher poking its head out of a hole. Funnel weaver spiders (**family Agelenidae**) take advantage of vacant gopher holes to set up their nests as well as dotting the hillsides with their funnel-shaped webs. If you go early in the morning, the webs glisten with dew and create a fairy-like setting. These spiders are very sensitive to vibrations, and once they sense that an insect has become tangled in their web, they will dart out into the web and deliver a paralyzing bite to the victim before consuming or dragging their prey back to their lair.

The trail ends to the right of the kiosk and uphill to the Pacific Mesa Boulevard cul-de-sac near the intersection with Pacific Center Boulevard, where limited parking and some seating areas provide for a leisurely lunch before returning to the west entrance. An alternate option is to add an additional 5 miles by then following the trail under the Sorrento Valley Boulevard bridge to the Peñasquitos waterfalls.

Funnel weaver spider

Distance:	3 miles, out-and-back
Difficulty:	🚶🚶
Elevation gain/loss:	Up to 200 feet
Hiking time:	2 hours
Agency:	City of San Diego
Trail use:	Bicycles, dogs
Trailhead GPS:	N32.86037, W117.20880
Optional map:	USGS 7.5-min *La Jolla*
Atlas square:	P8
Directions:	(University City) From I-5 go east on La Jolla Village Drive for 1 mile. Turn right on Genesee Avenue. Go 0.6 mile. Turn right on Decoro Street and park. From I-805 go west on La Jolla Village Drive for 0.8 mile. Turn left on Genesee Avenue. Go 0.6 mile. Turn right on Decoro Street and park. From CA-52 go north on Genesee Avenue for 1.6 miles. Turn left on Decoro Street and park. Walk south on Genesee Avenue back to the trailhead.

Habitat(s):

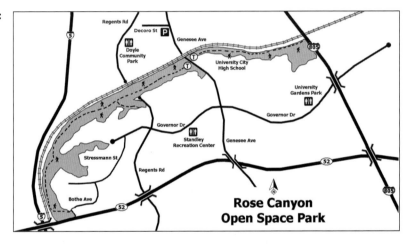

**Rose Canyon
Open Space Park**

Rose Canyon is one of the many local canyons set aside for walking, jogging, and bike riding. Views of the canyon from the bridge show its diversity, with four different habitats easily distinguished: chaparral, coastal sage scrub, riparian, and oak woodlands. The canyon was named for Louis Rose who purchased over 600 acres to ranch and run a tannery in 1853. Until his death in 1888, Rose advanced the interests of the county through his active participation in city government as a trustee, postmaster, and land speculator who developed Roseville in Pt. Loma. Later in 1913, George Sawday's cattle operation included Rose Canyon with the last of the ranch structures evident until the 1960s.

In winter months, frost covers the south side where shaded areas are slow to warm and cold air pools at the canyon's base. Rose Creek, visible in small glimpses from the wide trail, centers the riparian plants that include willows, toyon, and western sycamore trees that provide sporadic shade. The 23,427-acre Rose Canyon Watershed starts from runoff on the western slopes of Scripps Ranch through MCAS Miramar, joining with San Clemente and Stevenson canyons and their tributaries while Rose Creek enters Mission Bay at the Kendall Frost Marsh.

Nature trails put in by the La Jolla Rotary Club start near the bridge and are an interesting side trip through an elfin forest—an area thick with compact, shorter, and smaller plants as one would find in chaparral. Coastal sagebrush, currants, and toyon are among the native plants found here.

Garland daisy (***Glebionis coronaria***) is often seen in Rose Canyon. This attractive annual flower has either yellow petals or white pet-

Trail crosses a bridge

als with yellow near the disk. It can reach to a height of 3 feet. After flowering, the plant is not very attractive. A native of southern Europe, the garland daisy is non-native to southern California having escaped cultivation and establishing readily in disturbed soils. Belonging to the Asteraceae or sunflower family, this daisy is a good visual example of a radiate flower head, clearly showing the difference between ray and disk florets. Each flower head is comprised of many individual flowers, either ray florets or disk florets. Ray florets have the characteristic long, petal-like lobe and ring the inner disk. The inner disk florets are small and tubular and it may be a surprise to learn that each is an individual flower. Think of a sunflower head and recall that the center becomes filled with many individual sunflower seeds. The location of each seed marks a single fertilized disk flower. Members of the family Asteraceae may have both disk and ray florets, only disk florets, or they may consist entirely of liguliflorus florets, meaning they resemble ray florets only.

A good turn-around point is after crossing a bridge at 1.5 miles when the trail veers along railroad tracks, I-5, and the Rose Can-

yon fault. Evidence of the Scripps Formation and Bay Point Formation margin can be viewed after a 15-minute drive south to West Tecolote Canyon.

Trees arch over the trail

Distance:	2.5 miles, out-and-back
Difficulty:	🚶
Elevation gain/loss:	Minimal
Hiking time:	2 hours
Agency:	City of San Diego
Trail use:	Bicycles, dogs
Trailhead GPS:	N32.84562, W117.19982
Optional map:	USGS 7.5-min *La Jolla*
Atlas square:	P8
Directions:	(Clairemont) From CA-52 E turn right on Genesee Avenue. Go 0.1 mile. Turn right into Marion Bear Memorial Park parking lot. From CA-52 W go south on Genesee Avenue for 0.3 mile. Make a U-turn and go 0.1 mile. Turn right into Marion Bear Memorial Park parking lot.

Habitat(s):

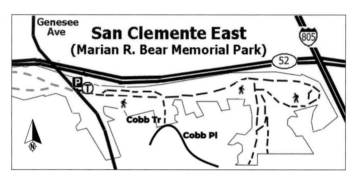

In 1971, San Clemente Canyon became San Diego's first officially dedicated natural park. It was rededicated as Marian R. Bear Memorial Park in 1979 for her role in preventing Highway 52 from being built in the San Clemente Creek bed. She also helped preserve Tecolote Canyon and worked for the passage of Proposition C, a $65 million open space preservation plan for the acquisition of major parcels of park preserves within the City of San Diego. Mrs. Bear was one of the city's most active and persistent defenders of open space preservation.

San Clemente East is centrally located with easy access to a riparian woodland habitat. This scarce environment is only meters in width, but with vegetation that is both dense and diverse. This is one of the most productive for wildlife, due to relatively abundant water and cold air drainage.

Start walking eastward on the dirt road towards I-805, crossing the creek bed that can be impassable during significant rain. Stay on the trail as there is an abundance of western poison-oak growing amongst the riparian indicator species of western sycamore, mule-fat, and willows.

There are two south side trips to lengthen your walk. The first is Cobb Trail, an interesting shaded trail that ends with steps up to Cobb Drive. Walking up the steps and back adds exercise before returning to the main trail. Another side trip follows high-voltage powerlines up along an open trail to Conrad Avenue. Return to the main trail and continue east until arriving at I-805. Then retrace your steps to the parking lot.

Binoculars can help you differentiate the two most common hawks found in the area. The red-tailed hawk (***Buteo jamaicensis***) can be seen soaring on large broad wings or perched in sycamore trees. It hunts primarily while in a soaring position, scanning the ground for rodents, small mammals, snakes, and rarely a bird. Its nest, a platform of sticks and twigs 3 feet in diameter, tends to be in more exposed sites and is often reused by common ravens, great horned owls, and other hawks. Adult red-tailed hawks have uniformly-colored tails with a terminal band, light pink below and rusty red above. Juvenile red-tailed hawks have finely barred tails so are more easily confused with the other com-

Red-shouldered hawk

Red-tailed hawk

mon hawk, the red-shouldered hawk (**Buteo lineatus**).

The red-shouldered hawk is a medium-sized hawk, smaller than the red-tailed. Adults have the tail strongly banded with black and white and the underparts rufous. Red-shouldered hawks hunt mostly from a perch, catching reptiles, rodents, insects, and small birds. They return to the same nesting area year after year, and they are highly vocal, especially when compared to a red-tailed hawk.

San Clemente Canyon joins the Rose Creek tributary near I-5 on its route to Mission Bay near the Kendall Frost Marsh. The 23,427-acre

Rose Canyon Watershed starts from runoff on the western slopes of Scripps Ranch, runs through MCAS Miramar, and joins with Rose and Stevenson canyons and their tributaries.

Mileage can be extended on this hike a number of ways: walk the three sections of San Clemente Canyon, add Rose Canyon, add a side trip to Standley Park, or even add Tecolote Canyon by combining other trails and some streets.

The trail

Distance:	Choice of 2 trails, each 2.5 miles, out-and-back
Difficulty:	🚶🚶🚶
Elevation gain/loss:	Up to 200 feet
Hiking time:	2 hours per trail
Agency:	City of San Diego
Trail use:	Dogs
Trailhead GPS:	N32.80139, W117.12931
Optional map:	USGS 7.5-min *La Jolla*
Atlas square:	Q10
Directions:	(Serra Mesa) From I-15 go west on Aero Drive for 1.1 miles. Turn left on Ruffin Road. Go 0.6 mile. Cross Gramercy Drive and park on the east side of Taft Middle School. From I-805 go north on Murray Ridge Road for 1.3 miles. Turn right on Sandrock Road. Go 0.1 mile. Turn left on Gramercy Drive. Go 0.6 mile. Turn right on Ruffin Road and park on the east side of Taft Middle School.

Habitat(s):

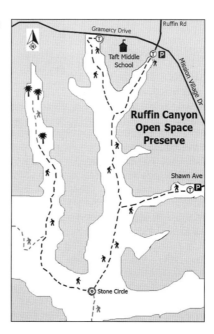

Ruffin Canyon is a pleasant escape amidst the bustle of downtown San Diego, which is located only 8 miles away. This 84-acre natural open space preserve extends from the end of Ruffin Road into Mission Valley and has three major entry points. The two northern entry points are on the east and west side of Taft Middle School on Gramercy Drive, with those two trails joining just south of the school. The third entry is at the west end of Shawn Avenue just past Mission Village Drive. There are some steep embankments, but a number of wooden stairs help make the 100-foot drop in elevation to the canyon bottom a little easier.

The Friends of Ruffin Canyon keep the primitive trails clean.

The Ruffin Road Trailhead on the east side of the middle school has a kiosk. The school has a special relationship to the canyon and helped put together a native plant garden at this entrance with individual coastal sage scrub plants named on colorfully-painted rocks placed next to the plants. After viewing the garden, follow the canyon down to the bottom via some steps to where the other northern entrance joins in from the west side of the middle school. Some discovery is needed at the end of the dirt trail to find the streambed to continue south.

Pipestem virgin's bower

After a rain, look for water in this streambed but note that the water can be easily missed in this seasonal stream. Along this riparian corridor are wetland plants that include various rushes, sedges, and willows.

Hiding under some of the rocks will be some bizarre-looking Jerusalem crickets (**Stenopelmatus spp.**) that come out at night to feed. Spanish speakers call this wingless, cricket-like insect *niña de la tierra* (child of the earth) because its bald head and expressive "face" look almost human. Although it will bite if provoked, this 2-inch nocturnal predator is relatively harmless to humans. It communicates with other members of its kind by drumming its body against the ground. It is parasitized by the horsehair worm (**phylum Nematomorpha**), which lives on the plants that the cricket eats. Once inside the cricket's digestive system, the worm burrows out into the body cavity to feed, but doesn't harm its host enough to kill it outright. When the worm matures, the cricket is motivated toward a wet site. The worm exits the cricket's body, enters the water, and finds a mate. The mutilated Jerusalem cricket dies in short order. Perhaps this was inspiration for the movie *Alien*?

The Shawn Avenue Trailhead follows a wide section past a group of cattails before merging to the main section of Ruffin Canyon. Evergreen plants and seasonal blooms found here include Pipestem virgin's bower (**Clematis lasiantha**), which is a woody vine that has a very distinctive fruit. The fruit is a cluster of seeds with curly and fuzzy styles that form large white tufts decorating the vine.

Roads and trails can be a challenge to follow at this seasonal tributary of the San Diego River. Be sure and check your back trail and the canyon rim for landmarks for the return to the original starting point. Use trekking poles to stabilize on the round cobbles for an enjoyable walk.

Jerusalem cricket

Distance:	4 miles, out-and-back
Difficulty:	🚶🚶
Elevation gain/loss:	Up to 400 feet
Hiking time:	2 hours
Agency:	City of San Diego
Trail use:	Bicycles, dogs
Trailhead GPS:	N32.80366, W117.18000
Optional map:	USGS 7.5-min *La Jolla*
Atlas square:	Q9
Directions:	(Clairemont) From I-5 go east on Clairemont Drive for 0.8 mile. Turn right on Burgener Boulevard. Go 0.1 mile. Turn left on Field Street. Go 0.1 mile. Continue onto Mount Acadia Boulevard. Go 1.3 mile. Turn right on Acworth Avenue. Go 0.3 mile. Parking lot is on the right. From I-805 go west on Balboa Avenue for 1.1 miles. Turn left on Genesse Avenue. Go 0.7 mile. Turn right on Boyd Avenue. Go 0.5 mile. Continue onto Acworth Avenue. Go 0.2 mile. Parking lot is on left.

Habitat(s):

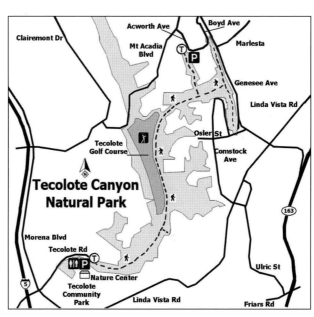

Tecolote Canyon Natural Park is one of San Diego's earliest designated open space parks. At around 900 acres, it is a relatively large canyon park near downtown San Diego. This eastern approach to the canyon is less crowded than the one farther south.

The name *tecolote* (owl) comes from the Nahuatl language of Mexico. There are two species of owls found in the canyon: the great horned owl (**Bubo virginianus**) and the barn owl (**Tyto alba**). The great horned owl has ear-like tufts and yellow eyes and is a powerful predator that can kill birds and mammals larger than itself. It often uses the abandoned nests of large birds like hawks and ravens. The female is larger than the male. It is common and has a wide distribution in the Western Hemisphere.

The barn owl is smaller with a distinct heart-shaped white face. Occurring in the Old World as well as the New World, it is the most widely distributed species of owl and one of the most widespread of all birds. In some parts of its range, however, it has been declining because of habitat loss. (For more about owls, see page 188.)

Barn owl

Although the route turns right or west, there is the option of adding an extra mile by going left or east towards Genesee Avenue to explore that area before proceeding east and descending towards Tecolote Canyon Golf Course. At approximately 0.75 mile, the trail crosses a wide dirt access road for the north-south running high power transmission line and the end of the Tecolote Golf Driving Range. The appearance of golf ball mushrooms will make this apparent. Proceed another 0.25 mile and the trail turns south to parallel the golf course fairways. The physically driven may wish to proceed another mile to the end of the southern tip of the golf course, but the trail and vegetation here pales in richness compared to what you have just experienced.

The east-west portion of the canyon trail varies between clearly defined 8-foot wide straight runways with open spaces to winding, shoulder-width paths that are densely vegetated on either side. At some points the trail merges with the cobble-filled streambed and at times there may be momentary delays as the hiker is forced to try alternate routes, some of which quickly dead end and require additional scout-

The trail begins with a nearly level broad path running due south. Keep to the left at the Y-junction, passing near the trees towards the east side of the canyon. Gradually descend along a cobblestone, narrow dirt path until arriving at the main trail junction with an east-west running canyon at approximately 0.4 mile.

Trees on trail

Wendy Esterly

American crow

ing to locate the continuing path. Fortunately, none of this is a problem because the scenery is so attractive. This section of the canyon leaves the visitor hiking under well-matured riparian habitat with century-old coast live oaks and western sycamores amidst many western cottonwoods and willows.

Take your time sauntering through the filtered sunlight that creates a pointillist landscape of multi-shaded green and yellow dabbled light. Bird and wind sounds murmur in the background. It is very easy to forget the presence of the surrounding city environment. Signs of deer, coyotes, fox, and northern raccoon can be found, and even the occasional appearance of a rabbit, ground squirrel, lizard, or, if lucky, a sunning snake. Where there is leaf litter, look for the resident California thrashers, both the California and spotted towhees, and overhead the usual western scrub-jays, woodpeckers, Anna's and Allen's hummingbirds, seasonal yellow-rumped warblers, and hawks. Also present are common ravens (*Corvus corax*) with their v-shaped tails or American crows (*Corvus brachyrhynchos*) with their blunt-cut or rounded c-shaped fan tails (c for crow, to remember whose tail is rounded or cut).

The common raven is much larger than the American crow, but scruffier, with a large thick black beak like a Roman nose and shaggy throat feathers. Ravens are among the smartest of all birds. They are not as social as crows and usually fly alone or in pairs. They live in all of San Diego County's habitats and, being scavengers, do well around people. They are acrobatic

flyers, and the young like to play games with sticks. Common ravens can mimic the calls of other birds. They will eat anything, including garbage and carrion.

American crows with their black glossy coats prefer areas with some trees. Agriculture or grasslands are ideal for foraging, as well as urban parks and neighborhoods. Like the raven, the crow is an omnivore but more social, sleeping in communal roosts that could have thousands of birds. Family members may help raise the young, and they harass and chase predators in a group. Though the crow also makes diverse sounds, its typical "caw" distinguishes it from the raven, which makes a throaty croak at a lower pitch.

Tecolote Canyon's mix of chaparral, coastal sage scrub, and riparian habitat lends itself to considerable biodiversity. To learn more, visit the Tecolote Canyon Nature Center where they have educational exhibits and a volunteer group that leads regular hikes for the public.

Wendy Esterly

Common raven

Distance:	4 or 6 miles, out-and-back
Difficulty:	🚶🚶
Elevation gain/loss:	Up to 400 feet
Hiking time:	2 hours
Agency:	City of San Diego
Trail use:	Bicycles, dogs
Trailhead GPS:	N32.77573, W117.19747
Optional map:	USGS 7.5-min *La Jolla*
Atlas square:	Q8
Directions:	(Clairemont) From I-5 go east on Tecolote Road for 0.6 mile. Park at the Tecolote Nature Center.

Habitat(s):

Tecolote Canyon Natural Park was created in 1978 after residents of Linda Vista and Clairemont joined forces to oppose a plan to turn the canyon into a sanitary landfill and a city operations yard. It had previously been used for grazing cattle until 1953 and then as a gravel pit for the construction of I-5. The 900-acre park today has a nature center with information about the canyon and the various plants and animals found there.

The canyon is located 1 mile north of the San Diego River and generally runs north and south for a distance of about 6 miles and varies from a quarter-mile to about a half-mile wide. The geology of the park consists primarily of marine and non-marine sedimentary rocks of the Scripps and Friars formations dating back to about 45-50 million years ago, capped with sedimentary rocks on the mesas that are more recent at about 1.8 million years of age. Rocks at the canyon mouth consist of sediments from the Bay Point Formation that are only 200,000 years of age.

Four faults have been mapped in the park, all located near the mouth. Behind the fence at center field of the upper baseball field, the Rose Canyon fault can be seen where the margins show 50 million-year-old sandstone of the Scripps Formation against red-stippled Pleistocene conglomerate of only 500,000 years. The Rose Canyon Fault parallels the San Andreas Fault, extending north through La Jolla Shores.

After visiting the nature center, follow the access road or trails that parallel the water channel, and then follow in the direction of the powerlines to the end of the golf course.

Paula Knoll

The trail

The turnaround point for the 4-mile out-and-back option is at the peak of the hill under the powerlines that overlook the golf course. The longer hike follows the trail closest to the golf course. At the end of the course, turn east to Genesee Avenue and then head back.

Along the trail, look for evidence of owls for which the canyon is named. Listen for their hoots, and look for owl pellets in the leaf litter under the larger trees. The pellets are a sure sign that an owl or tecolote lives in this canyon. Owls usually swallow their prey whole. Pellets contain material from prey that the owl's stomach acid cannot break down. Rather than being passed through the rest of the digestive tract, it is regurgitated in the form of a pellet. Skulls, bones, teeth, feathers, and fur are commonly seen in dissected owl pellets. Owls create this compacted pellet after eating, but need not regurgitate it immediately after formation—the pellet can remain stored for many hours, but must be expelled before the owl can eat again.

Owls constitute the order Strigiformes, birds of prey characterized by an upright stance, talons, binocular vision, usually solitary habits, hunting usually at night, and feathers modified to allow them to fly silently. The eyes of an owl do not move in its sockets, but the owl can swivel its head more than 180 degrees to see in any direction. This order has two families: the Tytonidae or barn owls and the Strigidae, comprising all the other owls. Both families are represented in the canyon. The owl that is most commonly seen in Tecolote Canyon is the great horned owl. Other birds that might

be seen include the California thrasher, house wren, hawk, towhee, and common raven. The walk is through three different habitats that include coastal sage scrub, chaparral, and riparian areas.

Tecolote Creek, north of the golf course, can run to a depth of 6-8 feet during the rainy season. In the summertime, the creek is normally dry, except for runoff from the course greens. The creek empties into Mission Bay at the Pacific Passage side of Fiesta Island. The creek also contributes to the groundwater table in the lower end of the canyon.

Wendy Esterly

Great horned owl

Distance:	2 miles, loop
Difficulty:	🚶
Elevation gain/loss:	Minimal
Hiking time:	1 hour
Agency:	City of San Diego
Trail use:	Bicycles, dogs
Trailhead GPS:	N32.77073, W117.15458
Optional map:	USGS 7.5-min *La Jolla*
Atlas square:	R9
Directions:	(Mission Valley) From CA-163 go east on Friars Road for 0.3 mile. Turn right on Frazee Road. Go 0.1 mile. Turn right on Hazard Center Drive and park. Walk 0.2 mile east to the intersection at Mission Center Drive and Hazard Center Drive, taking care when crossing the road. Or, take the Green Line Trolley to Hazard Station. Walk 0.2 mile east to the intersection at Mission Center Drive and Hazard Center Drive, taking care when crossing the road.

Habitat(s):

The San Diego River Trail is a network of paths found along the San Diego River. The river extends from the mountains near Julian to the ocean at Mission Bay for a distance of 52 miles. The trail highlights the importance of the river. It was first used as a water source by the Kumeyaay, then later for Mission San Diego de Alcalá, 19th century European settlers, and currently the City of San Diego, through San Vicente and El Capitan reservoirs. The river also has a history of flooding since record keeping began in 1914. The biggest recorded flood occurred in January of 1916, when the river grew to be 1-mile-wide with a flow rate of 70,200 cubic feet of water per second, damaging roads, tracks, and telephone/telegraph lines that took over a month to repair.

Although this segment of the San Diego River is located in the midst of metropolitan San Diego, the river itself meanders along a lush wooded watercourse that includes toyon or Christmas berry, lemonadeberry, and blue elderberry as it makes its way to the Pacific Ocean. A kiosk along the river path gives a brief overview of the area, including a map and a description of plants and animals found along the river trail.

The walk begins at North Marker 4 at the entrance of the parking lot. Along the path are native plants, such as rushes, mule-fat, arroyo willow, chaparral broom, white patchy western sycamore trees, and coast live oaks. Look for gulls, ducks, and American coots that splash and feed down the banks and islands in the river.

At North Marker 5, the river view opens looking south. Native pink California roses and California encelia (*Encelia californica*) line the river pathway. California encelia is an evergreen shrub varying in height from 1.5 to 5 feet with daisy-like yellow flowers. It is also known as bush sunflower. The blooms fore-

Joan Doad

City view from the river trail

tell the approach of spring. Birds that might be seen peeking out of the bushes include the black phoebe, bushtit, and white-crowned sparrow. Laurel sumac, an indicator plant of a frost-free area, provides shelter and food.

Around these flowers, you may observe bees foraging. Bees are attracted to flowers for a number of reasons including their color and scent, but also for their electric field. Flowers are slightly negatively charged relative to the surrounding air, and bees are positively charged relative to the air. This property helps pollen stick to the pollinator, and in some instances, it has even been observed jumping off the flower to the bee. Once a bee visits a flower and charged pollen has moved onto the bee, the flower's electrical field is somewhat neutralized and remains changed for about 100 seconds. This indicates to other bees that recent foraging has occurred, and is less attractive to the other pollinators. This may be a method that bees use to communicate with each other to avoid using excess energy foraging on flowers depleted in nectar.

Along the trail, near North Marker 6, is an overlook for observing river life. To continue east along the river, turn north on Camino del Estes for a short distance to a crosswalk. Carefully cross the street, then immediately turn south back down to the river and turn east on the path until Qualcomm Way. The path turns south and crosses over the San Diego River at Qualcomm Way. Looking westward,

the river eventually empties into the ocean between Mission Beach and Ocean Beach via an estuary.

Turning west, the path runs parallel to the trolley tracks. Passengers on the trolley have a fabulous view of the river as they speed along the line. There are benches and picnic tables along the trail. Sugar bush that is not usually found at this low of an elevation is a reminder that banks of the river have been replanted after the channel was straightened. Following the path west to the end, turn north and return to your vehicle or the trolley station.

Don Fosket

California encelia

Distance:	1 to 5 miles, out-and-back
Difficulty:	🚶 to 🚶🚶🚶
Elevation gain/loss:	up to 200 feet
Hiking time:	1 to 3 hours
Agency:	City of San Diego
Trail use:	Bicycles, dogs
Trailhead GPS:	N32.73903, W117.14244
Optional map:	USGS 7.5-min *Point Loma*
Atlas square:	R9
Directions:	(Balboa Park) From CA-163 go east on Washington Street for 0.3 mile. Turn right on Lincoln Avenue. Go 0.2 mile. Turn right on Park Boulevard. Go 0.7 mile. Turn left on Morley Field Drive. Go 0.2 mile. Cross Florida Drive and continue uphill for 0.1 mile. Turn right and then take another immediate right. Park in the California Native Plant Garden lot.

Habitat(s):

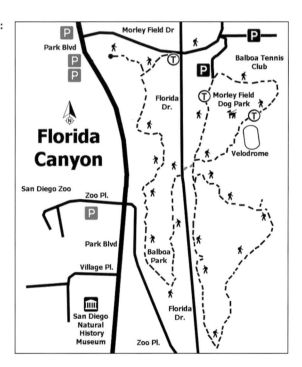

When thinking of Balboa Park, images of the world famous San Diego Zoo, world class museums and theatres, and acres of gardens with lush exotic vegetation come to mind. Relatively few are aware of the eastern portion of the park consisting of Morley Field with 25 tennis courts, the Balboa Park Golf Course, several multi-purpose fields, a disc golf course, a velodrome, a parcourse, plus acres of open space that hint of the park's original landscape. One needs to walk only a short distance to discover the relatively untouched expanse of Florida Canyon. The 150 acres of coastal sage scrub provides an important habitat for wildlife. Here are found many native chaparral plants and animals plus miles of interconnected trails that may be used for walking, jogging, and bicycling, all within easy reach of a major metropolitan area.

The hiking trails traverse the east and west sides of Florida Canyon and are bisected at the bottom of the canyon by Florida Drive. The Florida Canyon trail complex can be accessed through several entrances, but the most frequently used and conveniently located access

Looking west

point is a 40 vehicle parking area just west of the tennis courts off of Morley Field Drive. From this trailhead, nature lovers may choose to initially take a short loop walk through the California Native Plant Garden comprised of native San Diego plants, some with identification tags to acquaint visitors and help them to identify the flora that may be found along the trail.

There are three starting points to enter the trail complex, two of which begin at the parking area. Due south across a grassy field used as a dog run is a gradually descending path that soon divides into several optional routes allowing either an in-and-out approach or a loop hike. A second option is to start the hike by heading southeast from the parking lot through a towering eucalyptus grove and then turn due south past a velodrome and along the eastern rim of Florida Canyon. This route is a combination of graded dirt roads and foot paths which are connected at various points to the trail complex below in the canyon bottom. Finally, visitors also have the option to head west down Morley Drive, across Florida Drive at a four-way stop, and beginning walking uphill on the left or south side of the street, and then turn south on a trail which parallels the roadway and allows the quick-footed to cross the street further south, without the assistance of cross walks or stop signs, to make their way back on the trail complex on the east side of the canyon. Be sure to take adequate water and sun protection on the hike since there is little shade along the trails.

Among the native plants to be discovered along the trails are laurel sumac, black sage, scrub oak, coastal and short-wing deerweeds, broom baccharis, Mojave yucca, blue elderberry, and Hairy matilija poppy (***Romneya trichocalyx***), which is also known as the fried-egg plant because of its distinct yellow yolk center and surrounding large white petals. Birds frequently seen are the black phoebe, red-tailed hawk, California towhee, Anna's hummingbird, bushtit, and wrentit.

Keep an eye out for coyote scat left in the middle of the trail. You can often tell what the coyote had for dinner from the presence of rabbit fur and seeds. If your wanderings take you down to the canyon floor, you'll discover many riparian plants by the small streambed. Look for western fence lizards, spotted and striped harlequin bugs, cochineal scale insects with their red

Argiope spider—top view

stain, and argiope spiders (*Argiope aurantia*) with striking markings on their abdomen. The black and yellow argiope spider is a common garden spider that is sometimes known as the yellow garden spider or the writing spider. It is an orb weaver and a member of the family Araneidae, one of the three largest spider groups. Orb weavers build spiral wheel-shaped webs. Like all orb weaver spiders, it has three claws per foot, which is one more than most spiders. The third claw is used to handle the threads while spinning. It also has eight similar eyes arranged in two rows of four eyes each.

Also look for ground squirrels and cottontails. Some of the non-native plants that will be encountered are the eucalyptus and various palm species.

It was during the summer of 1973 that Helen Vallejo Chamlee, Nancy Inman, and Betty Robinson began the FIorida Canyoneers by training 27 volunteers, associated with the nearby San Diego Natural History Museum, in the plants, animals, geology, history, and Native American uses of the canyon area. In November of that year, the Florida Canyon Nature Trails formally opened. Some 5000 people participated in the hiking program led by the trained trail guides. When a series of fires greatly diminished the dense and diverse chaparral shrubs and other flora found there, the volunteers decided to find other areas in which to guide and renamed

Argiope spider—bottom view

themselves simply the Canyoneers. Today the Canyoneers lead weekly hikes throughout San Diego County from the coast to the desert, providing the public with opportunities to visit some 70 different trails every year. For information on how to participate in these free outings, visit http://sdnat.org/canyoneers.

While Florida Canyon may not appear as it once was some 40 year ago, more than 200 plants have been identified in the canyon at various times of the year. The other inhabitants of this diverse floral community reflect a corresponding biodiversity with the many species of birds, reptiles, insects, and mammals. The canyon continues to delight visitors after all these years.

The native garden

Distance:	3 miles, loop
Difficulty:	
Elevation gain/loss:	Minimal
Hiking time:	2 hours
Agency:	City of San Diego
Trail use:	Bicycles, dogs
Trailhead GPS:	N32.73244, W117.14739
Optional map:	USGS 7.5-min *Point Loma*
Atlas square:	R9
Directions:	(Balboa Park) From CA-163 go east on Washington Street for 0.3 mile. Turn right on Lincoln Avenue. Go 0.2 mile. Turn right on Park Boulevard. Go 1.2 miles. Turn right onto Village Place and park. Parking is free in the lots in front of the museum and across the way by the carousel. This hike begins and ends at the San Diego Natural History Museum.

Habitat(s):

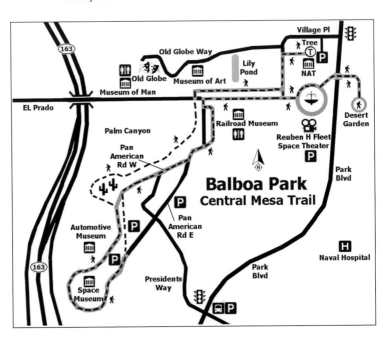

This hike explores key areas in Balboa Park that were part of the 1915 Panama-California Exposition. As you walk, consider the fact that visitors were enjoying much of the same sights 100 years ago.

Start your hike by the Moreton Bay fig tree in front of the San Diego Natural History Museum. The 80-foot tall giant is over 100 years old and has a trunk 42 feet around and a canopy spanning 145 feet. The tree, native to eastern Australia, was planted in 1910 as the focal point of a formal garden for the exposition. It has grown so well that today it is considered among the champion trees of Cal-

ifornia and is listed in the California Registry of Big Trees. The Moreton Bay fig is a strangler tree, although this particular tree never used this option as it was planted. In the wild, seed germination takes place in the canopy of a host tree with the seedling growing as an epiphyte on the host until its roots can be established in the ground. As an epiphyte, it does not harm the host tree, getting its nutrients and moisture from the air and rain. However, once its roots are established, the Moreton Bay fig will strangle and kill the host tree and become a free-standing tree.

Fig trees have a mutualistic relationship

The lily pond

with fig wasps, a relationship that has co-evolved over the last 70-90 million years, and the Moreton Bay fig is no exception. Female fig wasps enter the immature fig fruit through a tiny hole called the ostiole. Once inside, the female lays her eggs, and also fertilizes the tiny flowers on the inside of the fig fruit with pollen she has picked up on other trees. Once the eggs have been laid, the female dies inside the fig. The eggs hatch, the larvae mature, and mating occurs all inside the fruit. Finally, the males bore an exit hole and die shortly thereafter. The females leave the fig fruit through this exit hole, and begin the lifecycle over once again.

Begin walking down Village Place on the west side of the Natural History Museum, past the Casa Del Prado Theatre. Turn right onto El Prado past Casa De Balboa on the left, which houses the San Diego History Center, the Model Railroad Museum, and the Museum of Photographic Arts. Casa Del Prado on the right houses a variety of arts groups. Do not forget to look up and around at the Spanish-Moorish architectural features of the buildings, which are exquisitely detailed. Feel free at any point to visit any museum that attracts your interest. If you have taken advantage of the Balboa Park Explorer annual pass,

one pass will get you into 17 different museums that normally charge individual general admission fees.

Continue down El Prado to the lily pond on your right in front of the botanical building. The pond has an interesting collection of lotus and water lilies, with colorful koi swimming in the water. You may see a family of ducks swimming among the lily pads. If the botanical building is open, take a walk through this free arboretum as a side excursion.

Next, the path curves left in front of Mingei Museum marked by colorful statues. Pass the museum and walk down the steps into the lush, green Palm Canyon. Abruptly, it feels as though you have stepped in the midst of a tropical forest, dropping below the level of the main promenade. Follow the path until the first fork then head to the left to join up with the main Palm Canyon Trail. At this point, either walk up the steps and follow the sidewalk next to the Houses of Hospitality or continue to follow the Palm Canyon Trail along a parallel lower path. The path will eventually rise up to the left, back to street level with some easy riser steps marked by wooden rails.

Back at street level, pass the Balboa Park Club. Walk around the back of the club to find a xeriscape garden. Although the garden is not

Janine Kardokus

Moreton Bay fig

exclusive to native plants, it is quite beautiful with artistically arranged planters of cacti and succulents at the back of the building. For a rest stop, pause at the benches and tables behind the club next to the cactus garden overlooking the canyon. The garden contains a wide variety of cacti, succulents, acacias, creosote, agave, and South African protea.

After coming back out of the xeriscape garden, pass the Margaret Hitchcock Puppet Theatre and the Recital Hall on your right and head back toward the museums. The San Diego Air & Space Museum is next. Be sure to circle around the back of the museum to see a spectacular cityscape view. Then pass the Starlight Musical Theatre, followed by the San Diego Hall of Champions Sports Museum. Cut back through the courtyard of the Houses of Hospitality. Visit the international houses representing different countries on a Sunday when local cuisines may be featured.

After exiting the Houses of Hospitality courtyard, walk to the Organ Pavilion. There are usually free organ concerts on Sunday mornings, as well as many other special events. The Japanese Friendship Garden is on the other side of the Organ Pavilion.

For a refreshment break, stop by The Prado at Balboa Park restaurant. Afterwards, return to El Prado and walk toward the fountain between the San Diego Natural History Mu-

seum and the Reuben H. Fleet Science Center. Cross the bridge over Park Boulevard to get to the rose garden. After admiring the roses, enter the larger cactus garden. When you view the spectacular and fanciful shapes of the cacti and succulents, it will suddenly become apparent where Theodore Geisel might have found his inspiration for the fanciful tree drawings in the Dr. Seuss books. Finish the hike by crossing back over the bridge and returning to the Natural History Museum.

Janine Kardokus

A flowering lily

Distance:	5.5 miles, out-and-back
Difficulty:	🚶🚶
Elevation gain/loss:	up to 200 feet
Hiking time:	3 hours
Agency:	City of San Diego
Trail use:	Bicycles, dogs
Notes:	Sidewalks with Quince and Spruce streets; bridges have steps
Trailhead GPS:	N32.73158, W117.14572
Optional map:	USGS 7.5-min *Point Loma*
Atlas square:	R9
Directions:	(Balboa Park) From CA-163 go east on Washington Street for 0.3 mile. Turn right on Lincoln Avenue. Go 0.2 mile. Turn right on Park Boulevard. Go 1.2 miles. Park on the east side of Park Boulevard and Village Place, across from the San Diego Natural History Museum.

Habitat(s):

This walking tour through Balboa Park, Banker's Hill, and Hillcrest is a way to really get to experience a bit of early San Diego history. The tour begins on the east side of Park Boulevard and Village Place at the Inez Grant Parker Memorial Rose Garden, one of only 10 US gardens (as of 2015) to receive an Award of Excellence from the World Federation of Rose Societies. The rose garden won this award in 2003, and in 2014 was named to the World Hall of Fame of the Great Rosarians. For peak color, visit the garden in April and May, though blooms can be seen on the more than 2400 rose bushes in 180 varieties nearly year-round. Be sure to also view the adjacent xeriscape garden before crossing the first pedestrian bridge towards the Natural

History Museum—home of the Canyoneers.

Head west along El Prado through the middle of Balboa Park, passing museums and the lily pond, continuing across the 1914 Cabrillo or Laurel Street Bridge, the first multiple-arched cantilever bridge built in California. During the 1915 Panama-California Exposition, the bridge spanned a small lake in Cabrillo Canyon. Continue west, now on Laurel Street, crossing 2nd Avenue to view one of the 10 churches Irving Gill designed on the southwest corner. Turn north on 2nd Avenue, then left on Maple to Albatross Street, where there is a plaque commemorating Waldo Waterman's flight of a biplane hang glider launched by auto-tow in 1909. Retrace your steps east for two blocks,

Paula Knoll

1st Avenue bridge

turning north or left onto 1st Avenue for the third bridge.

The First Avenue Bridge was built in 1931, shipped to San Diego to be reassembled in place. It is still the only steel-arch bridge in the city. It was reopened in 2010 after a 15-month refurbishment that included actions to meet California earthquake standards plus removal of lead paint. After viewing Maple Canyon, continue on 1st Avenue and then turn right on Quince Street to reach the Quince Street Bridge entrance. The wooden trestle bridge was built in 1905 with a construction cost of less than $1,000. The trestle bridge allowed easier access to the 4th Avenue trolley station. After crossing to 4th Avenue retrace your steps to 2nd Avenue and turn right or north for two blocks.

Turn left or west on Spruce Street to the 1912 Spruce Street Suspension Bridge. Enjoy the movement when crossing over Kate Sessions Canyon, the fifth bridge on this tour. Turn right on both Brant and Upas streets. Turn left on Albatross Street, right on Walnut Avenue, and then left on 1st Avenue for four blocks to a right turn on University Avenue.

As you walk past 10th Avenue notice the large mural painted on the west side of the Ace Hardware building on the southeast corner. "The Loading Dock" was created by muralist Linda Churchill in 1999. Turn left at Vermont Street and cross the Vermont Street Bridge, stopping every few feet to read the inspiring quotes on panels that span the bridge. This bridge, built in 1995, replaced a 1916 wooden trestle bridge that allowed residents to access the University Avenue trolley line that was the primary transportation corridor in San Diego from 1888-1949.

After crossing the sixth bridge, turn east on Lincoln, taking a right or south turn down Georgia Street, one block to the seventh and final bridge on this tour. In 1907 a redwood truss bridge was built after the ridge was cut to allow the streetcar line to extend eastward to Fairmont Avenue, opening North Park and other surrounding areas to development. In 1914, the current concrete bridge was built and is now designated as a local, state, and national landmark. Turn right or west on Robinson Avenue and then left or south again on Park Boulevard to return to the start.

Quince Street bridge

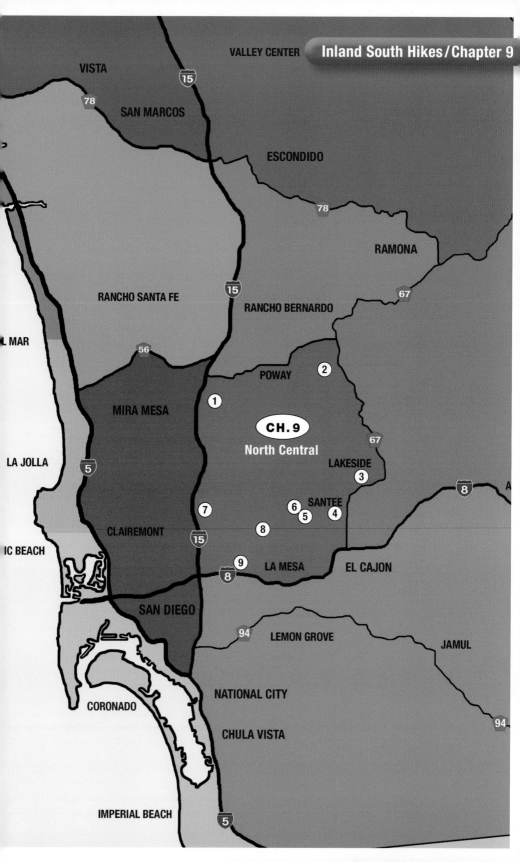

Distance:	4.9 miles, loop
Difficulty:	🚶🚶
Elevation gain/loss:	Minimal
Hiking time:	3 hours
Agency:	City of San Diego
Trail use:	Bicycles, dogs at least 50 feet away from the water
Notes:	Hours posted 5:30 a.m. to sunset
Trailhead GPS:	N32.91453, W117.09678
Optional map:	USGS 7.5-min *Poway*
Atlas square:	N10
Directions:	(Mira Mesa) From I-15 go east on Mira Mesa Boulevard for 0.3 mile. Turn right on Scripps Ranch Boulevard. Go 0.3 mile. Turn left on Scripps Lake Drive. Go 0.5 mile. Turn left into the parking lot.

Habitat(s):

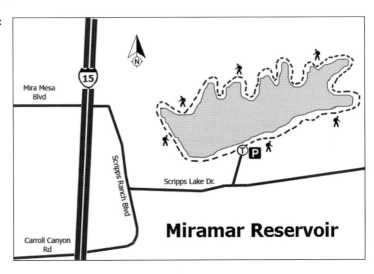

Lake Miramar Reservoir was created with the construction of a dam in 1960 as part of a San Diego Aqueduct project with water from both the Colorado River Aqueduct and the California Aqueduct. This City of San Diego facility can store 6682-acre feet of water while providing recreational opportunities that include fishing, boating, birding, walking, jogging, or cycling around the 4.92-mile paved service road around the man-made lake. The reservoir is open seven days a week with cars allowed on the road Saturday through Tuesday. Leashed dogs are permitted on the service road but must remain 50 feet or more from the water at all times.

The lake is part of the Scripps Ranch area that was once owned by newspaper publisher E.W. Scripps and his philanthropist wife, Ellen Browning Scripps. When the property was purchased in 1890, there were no build-

ings to obstruct the view of Mount Soledad and the Pacific Ocean, so it was named Miramar, Spanish for sea view. Ellen Browning Scripps generously supported a multitude of institutions in southern California that included schools, parks, and hospitals.

Bring your binoculars to view cormorants or pelicans competing with anglers for bass, bluegill, or sunfish. Mallards, lesser scaups, redhead, gadwall, northern shovelers, and ruddy ducks are found on the lake, depending on the season. The ruddy duck (*Oxyura jamaicensis*) is a small duck most commonly seen in San Diego from October to April, though it is more easily recognized during the breeding season, when the males have a sky-blue bill and mostly ruddy plumage. In the nonbreeding season when mostly brown, the ruddy duck can still be recognized by the white cheek patch of the male or brown bar

Spineshrub

Canchalagua

across the cheek of the female, as well as by the short tail held in a raised position. Turkey vultures or hawks can be seen catching the wind currents while the sounds of the California quail and wrentit can be heard in the chaparral.

Chaparral plants include chamise, black sage, manzanita, monkey flower, and coastal sagebrush, plus some species that are either difficult to spot or rare. These include canchalagua (*Zeltnera venusta*), which is a low-growing common annual with five pink petals and white centers with yellow anthers—the pollen producing part of the stamen. Look closely after pollen is harvested and note that the anthers are shaped like corkscrews. Another species called spineshrub (*Adolphia californica*) is listed as a rare, threatened, or endangered shrub in California by the California Native Plant Society but is considered more common elsewhere. The cream-colored flower has five triangular petals with small folded petals between each triangular-shaped ones. The center of the flower is yellow. The dark green twigs are stiff and sharp-pointed like a spine but are thorns or modified stems. On these plants look for webs of tangle-web spiders. Potentially the most well-known tangle-web spider in the county is the black widow (*Latrodectus hesperus*) recognized by the red hourglass shape on the underside of the abdomen and the messy, irregular web. Some researchers think that the black widow is being displaced by non-native brown widows (*Latrodectus geometricus*) who outcompete the black widows for space, food, and other resources in much of the county. The brown widow is thought to have originally evolved in Africa, though it is now found in many tropical and subtropical areas. Many other species of spiders are present in the county too, continuously providing insect control services.

Miramar Reservoir is open to fishing and private boats and kayaks from a half hour before sunrise to sunset. For current information about permits and lake usage, check the website.

Black widow on buckwheat

Distance:	6 miles, out-and-back
Difficulty:	🚶🚶🚶
Elevation gain/loss:	Up to 500 feet
Hiking time:	3 hours
Agency:	San Diego County
Trail use:	Bicycles, dogs, horses
Notes:	Hours posted 8 a.m. to sunset
Trailhead GPS:	N32.92997, W116.96995
Optional map:	USGS 7.5-min *San Vicente Reservoir*
Atlas square:	N13
Directions:	((Poway) From CA-67 turn west into the entrance of the Sycamore Canyon Open Space Preserve, 6.8 miles north of Mapleview Street in Lakeside and 0.7 mile south of Scripps Poway Parkway. Drive 1.4 miles over a well-maintained dirt road to the trailhead.

Habitat(s):

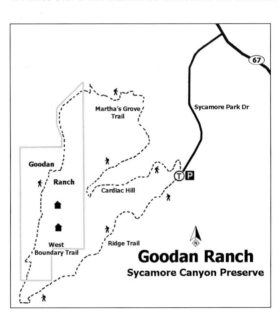

The 2272-acre Sycamore Canyon Preserve is owned by San Diego County Parks and Recreation while the 325-acre Goodan Ranch that is within the preserve is jointly owned by the county, the cities of Poway and Santee, and the California Department of Fish and Wildlife. Together they offer over 10 miles of hiking through coastal sage scrub, chaparral, oak woodland, riparian, and grassland habitats.

The 2003 Cedar Fire burned over 95% of the preserve, but it has come back beautifully. Look for the fragrant coast spice bush or bushrue in the citrus family as well as chamise, *Ceanothus*, mission manzanita, California buckwheat, laurel sumac, bush monkey flower, and other common chaparral species bloom-

ing in the spring. Note the interesting rounded and polished rocks on the top of the ridge that appear to have been tumbled in water.

There are outstanding views of rolling, chaparral covered hills and of Sycamore Canyon below on the Ridge Trail. It is best to bring at least a quart of water and start early at the west end of the staging area since there is no shade. At 1.2 miles, look for a wooden sign and a trail leading off the ridge on your right, continuing just a little over 0.5 mile to the bottom of Sycamore Canyon to the historic Stowe Trail. In the latter part of the 19th century a town named Stowe was established in Sycamore Canyon and a dirt road went up Sycamore Canyon from Santee to Stowe. Although the town of

Sycamore Canyon from Cardiac Hill

Stowe has long since vanished, the road still exists, although it is an illegal entry into the preserve from Mission Trails.

Once you reach the canyon, follow the trail or dirt road north approximately 0.25 mile to a trail leading off to the left. Follow it, cross the stream, and join the West Boundary Trail which parallels the road. Continue north on the edge of lush riparian vegetation with western sycamore trees, arroyo willows, coast live oaks, western cottonwoods, and, in the winter and spring, a flowing stream. About 0.5 mile up this trail, cross over onto the road and visit the Goodan Ranch Center, a newly constructed building where there are toilets, drinking water, a small museum, and a place to sit in welcome shade and relax. It is just west of the ruins of the Goodan Ranch House that was destroyed in the 2003 Cedar Fire.

After resting and imagining what it must have been like to live in this isolated setting, continue north on the West Boundary Trail for 0.5 mile where you have the option of going east up Cardiac Hill to the staging area to finish the hike in a little over 1.3 miles, but if you do, you will miss a highlight of the preserve. Instead, continue north on the road for less than 1 mile to the Goodan Staging Area and the preserve's Poway north entrance to the Martha's Grove Trailhead. A good part of this well-maintained trail traverses a shady, coast

live oak woodland and, at about 0.75 mile, you will come to the Martha Harville Memorial Oak Grove where there is a cool, verdant, shady oasis with picnic tables and benches that honor this park ranger who died too young.

After resting in Martha's Grove, continue walking south and west. The trail again becomes a dirt road taking you back into the grassland. At about 1.75 miles from the trailhead, there is a junction. The road to the left goes up Cardiac Hill leading to your parked vehicle. Despite its name, Cardiac Hill is not very challenging. In a little over 1 mile is the junction with Sycamore Park Drive.

Martha's Grove trailhead

Distance:	2 miles, out-and-back
Difficulty:	🚶
Elevation gain/loss:	Up to 100 feet
Hiking time:	1 hour
Agency:	LRPC
Trail use:	Bicycles, dogs, horses
Notes:	ADA accessible; hours posted sunrise to sunset
Trailhead GPS:	N32.86307, W116.94097
Optional map:	USGS 7.5-min *El Cajon*
Atlas square:	O13
Directions:	(Lakeside) From CA-67 go north on Riverford Road for 0.4 mile. Turn right on Riverside Drive. Go 0.4 mile. Entrance is on the right where Rio Camino intersects. The north trailhead sign is located next to River Run Business Park. There is also a single accessible parking space at the east trailhead on Channel Road. To reach it, continue another 1 mile east on Riverside Drive, just past Lakeside Avenue. Parking is on the right. There is also parking at the west trailhead at the south end of Marathon Parkway near Lakeside Baseball Fields. Park on the street and not in the baseball fields parking lot.

Habitat(s):

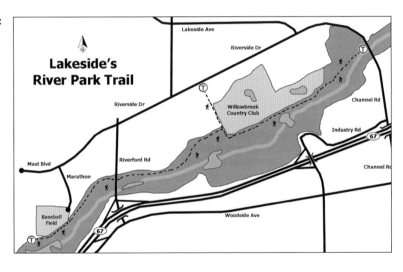

Lakeside's River Park Conservancy was formed in 2001 to acquire lands along the San Diego River through purchase or donation and to restore the habitat and develop trails for the benefit of Lakeside residents. Lakeside's 100-acre preserve used to be a highly channelized river with a surrounding sand mine. It is now becoming a beautiful riparian willow forest and flood plain. In early 2008, the first phase of a three-mile trail was opened to the public along the river from Channel Road to Riverford Road. Visible is the difference that native plants can make as one compares the restored preserve area with the section that is still being used for sand mining and is covered in predominately non-native mustard. The current mine will one day become additional park space, once the mining operations are complete. Hanson Heidelberg Cement Group will be donating 22 acres off Channel Road for parking and recreational/educational use. The property currently has a monument on it constructed by artist James Hubbell. The monument will become one of the entrances to the river park.

The section that is currently opened to the public is generally flat and accessible to all hiking abilities. It is open seven days a week to hikers, runners, cyclists, and horses between dawn and dusk. Dogs are allowed on a leash. Visitors will note several small memorial name plates

Liz Tymkiw

Viewing deck

This is a wonderful area for birdwatching. Several of California's threatened and endangered bird species, such as the southwestern willow flycatcher and the least Bell's vireo (*Vireo bellii pusillus*), are dependent on riparian willow thickets like those found here. Preservation of this type of habitat needed for these species is the reason funding was made available to restore and preserve these lands. Besides the general loss of needed riparian habitat for these species, they also suffer from nest parasitism from the brown-headed cowbird (*Molothrus ater*), a blackbird that searches for nests of other birds in which to lay her eggs, then abandons them to be raised by the host bird at the expense of the host's own brood. Keep your eyes open in spring and summer here for the least Bell's vireo. It is a small gray songbird with lighter underparts that eats spiders and insects. Among other birds, expect to see the gadwall, American coot, herons, egrets, and osprey, which fishes in the pond.

For more information about Lakeside's River Park Conservancy and their restoration and conservation efforts, see their website: www.lakesideriverpark.org.

along the trail, paid by donors who helped to pay for the restoration and river trail.

There are three possible trailheads that include both an east or west entrance with a 4-mile out-and-back or a north entrance that has two out-and-back options for either a 2-mile or 4-mile trip. The trip described here starts at the north trailhead on Riverside Drive, known as the Lakeside Land Reach, which heads south along the west side of Willowbrook Country Club. It then turns abruptly east along the section known as the Willowbrook Reach that has the country club on the north side and the river on the south side. This section has a deck overlook where wildlife can be viewed in the pond below. The last section of trail is known as the Hanson Reach, which is adjacent to Hanson Aggregates who donated this section of trail to the conservancy. After reaching the east entrance, retrace your steps back to the southwest corner of Willowbrook Country Club. Either complete the 2-mile out-and-back by retracing your steps back up the Lakeside Land Reach to your vehicle, or continue west toward the Lakeside Baseball Fields to complete the second out-and-back portion of this trip. Plants to be seen along the entire length of this trail include willow, mule-fat, black sage, monkey flower, toyon, and laurel sumac. Non-native eucalyptus is gradually being thinned as native oaks and western sycamores are maturing.

Wendy Esterly

Brown-headed cowbird

Wendy Esterly

Least Bell's vireo

Distance:	2.6 miles, out-and-back
Difficulty:	🚶🚶
Elevation gain/loss:	Minimal
Hiking time:	2 hours
Agency:	City of Santee
Trail use:	Bicycles, dogs, horses
Notes:	Hours posted sunrise to sunset
Trailhead GPS:	N32.84936, W116.96955
Optional map:	USGS 7.5-min *El Cajon*
Atlas square:	P13
Directions:	(Santee) From CA-52 go north on Magnolia Avenue for 1.2 miles. Entrance is on the right. Park on the street. From CA-67 N go west on Prospect Avenue for 0.2 mile. Turn right on Magnolia Avenue. Go 1.3 miles. Entrance is on the right. Park on the street. From CA-67 S go south on Woodside Avenue for 0.4 mile. Turn right on Magnolia Avenue. Go 0.8 mile. Entrance is on the right. Park on the street.

Habitat(s):

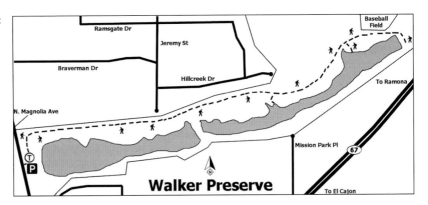

Walker Preserve

This trail adds another segment to the San Diego River Trail, which will eventually stretch more than 50 miles from the river headwaters to the Pacific Ocean. The property that makes up the preserve was most recently the site of a sand-mining operation and was not open to the public. Previously, the parcel was part of the Walker family dairy farm that was in operation from 1926 until 1971.

The Walker Preserve is a 107-acre parcel which goes from Magnolia Avenue to the eastern city limits of Santee near the Lakeside Baseball Park at Marathon Parkway. East of Marathon Parkway, the trail continues as part of the Lakeside River Park Trail, ending at Channel Road. Different sections of the trail are completed along its future path into the mountains. Work continues to complete the gaps. To the west, the trail continues through Mast Park with segments further west to be completed until it is a through route to the Pacific Ocean.

The Walker Preserve segment opened in April 2015. It is a 14-foot wide trail that has a decomposed granite surface and lodge-pole fencing on both sides of the trail. Historical artifacts are present along the trail, which represent the previous uses of the land. There's a dragline dredge bucket that was once used to mine sand, as well as an original horse-drawn plow from the Walker farm. Interpretive panels describing the history and the natural features of the area are found along the trail as well as several outlooks with benches facing toward the river. The trailhead has a shaded area, picnic tables, a bicycle repair work station, and a water fountain for dogs.

Three species of designated threatened or endangered birds, identified by the US Fish and Wildlife Service, require the type of high quality habitat that is found here: the southwestern willow flycatcher, the California gnatcatcher, and the least Bell's vireo. It is the hoped that

Frass trail on laurel sumac

by providing this type of protected habitat that these particular species will be attracted to the area and thrive. Overall, the river is home to about 25 rare and endangered species of plants and animals.

In addition to the riparian and wetland habitats along the river on the south side of the trail, there is coastal sage scrub habitat on the hillsides to the north. Willow trees, cattails, mulefat, and other typical riparian vegetation grow near the river. Birds seen here include the great blue heron, wood duck, red-winged blackbird, double-crested cormorant, American coot, western scrub-jay, and black phoebe. Plants on the hillsides include California buckwheat, broom baccharis, white sage, coast live oak, and laurel sumac (*Malosma laurina*).

Laurel sumac is a large evergreen shrub that is sometimes called the taco plant because of its folded taco-shaped leaves that help funnel water to the roots and stems preventing water loss through evaporation. The leaves are very sensitive to frost, and will turn pinkish if they get too cold. To this end, some California avocado and citrus growers use this as an indicator plant in their orchards. Model railroad toy sets included paint-sprayed laurel sumac blossoms as trees. This tree is important in chaparral habitat, providing both food and cover for a variety of birds and animals. The stigmella moth (*Stigmella* **sp.**) lays her tiny

eggs between the linings of young laurel sumac leaves. As they eat and mature, her young leaf miner caterpillars tunnel their way out, leaving tiny brown waste trails called frass as the only evidence that they were there.

Laurel sumac in bloom

Distance:	3 or 6 miles, out-and-back
Difficulty:	🚶 or 🚶🚶
Elevation gain/loss:	Minimal
Hiking time:	2or 3 hours
Agency:	City of Santee
Trail use:	Bicycles, dogs, horses
Trailhead GPS:	N32.84405, W116.99761
Optional map:	USGS 7.5-min *El Cajon*
Atlas square:	P12
Directions:	(Santee) From CA-52 W go north on Fanita Drive for 0.1 mile. Turn right on Mission Gorge Road. Go 0.3 mile. Turn left on Carlton Hills Boulevard. Go 0.4 mile. Parking is on right just beyond the San Diego River. From CA-52 E go east on Mission Gorge Road for 0.8 mile. Turn left on Carlton Hills Boulevard. Go 0.4 mile. Parking is on right just beyond the San Diego River. From CA-125 turn right on Mission Gorge Road. Go 0.4 mile. Turn left on Carlton Hills Boulevard. Go 0.4 mile. Parking is on right just beyond the San Diego River.

Habitat(s):

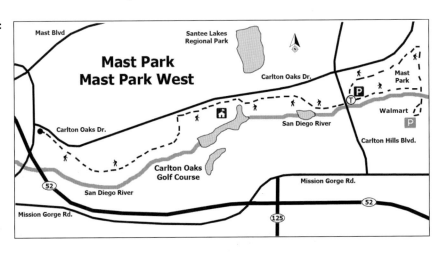

Mast Park and Mast Park West are trail segments along the San Diego River Trail, a regional multi-use trail that will someday make it possible to trek from Ocean Beach to the mountains near Julian. Each trail segment has its own management jurisdiction and works with the nonprofit San Diego River Park Foundation and the State of California's San Diego River Conservancy for the common goal of preserving riparian habitat and completing this contiguous regional trail of over 50 miles. This segment of the trail offers an easy stroll under trees and by waterways and follows the San Diego River through the community of Santee, currently ending at a local golf course. There are benches to sit on, a native plant garden to explore, and spots to look out on the river. There are interpretive signs telling about the river ecosystem and enough open space to forget about busy city life.

There are numerous bird species to observe along the waterway. It is home to the endangered least Bell's vireo and the California gnatcatcher, as well as providing habitat to attract the southwest willow flycatcher. Birds to note include the great blue heron, great egret, Cooper's hawk, red-shouldered hawk, mallard, American coot, acorn and Nuttall's woodpeckers, belted kingfisher, and black phoebe. Anna's hummingbird can be observed year-round. During the spring and summer, numerous species stop here including the lazuli bunting, black-chinned hummingbird, cliff swallow, and Bullock's oriole (***Icterus bull-***

Eva McCuatty

Golf course trail

ockii), which prefers tall trees in open woodlands along streams. Look for a brilliant orange bird with a black stripe through its eye, a black crown, throat, and back, and dark wings with a white patch. Females, mostly pale gray and dull yellow, build a hanging nest in trees, weaving them from fibers, grasses, hair, and litter, like balloon ribbons, and line the nests with willow cotton and feathers. Bullock's oriole forages for caterpillars, other insects, and flower nectar. Watch out for other animals too, like the western pond turtle, the two-striped gartersnake, western fence lizard, and butterflies, including the tiger swallowtail, mourning cloak, and monarch.

Although invasive and non-native plants grow here, there are ongoing efforts to restore the native habitat. The riparian habitat along the river contains cattails and bulrushes that filter the river water. It also has tall western sycamores, willows, and western cottonwoods with an understory of mule-fat and yerba mansa. Toyon and blue elderberry grow by the trail as well as coyote melon, wild grape, wild-cucumber, and western jimson weed (***Datura wrightii***).

Western jimson weed is in the nightshade family, containing several plants that are toxic to both herbivores and humans, including henbane, deadly nightshade, tobacco, and mandrake. They contain alkaloids, such as tropane, belladonna, and atropine that are not only potentially lethal but can have medicinal or hallucinogenic effects, depending on the specific chemical and dose. These alkaloids affect the central nervous system including cells of the brain and spinal cord. Chinese traditional medicine uses tropane alkaloid-containing plants to treat a variety of ailments while Kumeyaay shamans prepared toloache or jimson weed, containing scopolamine—a highly poisonous hallucinogenic

Alan King

Bullock's oriole

Donna Zoll

Western jimson weed

drug, for use in their initiation ceremonies. Local Kumeyaay, Luiseño, and Cahuilla Indians also used jimson weed for medicinal use to mitigate the pain of childbirth, as a general painkiller for setting bones and toothache, to cure hemorrhoids, and for making a paste to treat venomous bites of snakes, tarantulas, spiders, and insects. The plant was made famous by artist Georgia O'Keeffe.

There are two native species of jimson weed in the county. Western jimson weed, which is found in this area, has a wide distribution that includes desert areas. It is a large herbaceous perennial that is 2 to 3 feet tall. It has a large,

white, and lavender-tinged, trumpet-shaped flower with a white throat, and it smells like peanut butter. Desert thornapple (*Datura discolor*), on the otherhand, is a monsoonal annual found only in the desert and typically under 1000 feet in elevation. It is 1 to 2 feet tall. It has a striking purple patch in the throat of the trumpet-shaped white flower. Thornapple refers to the prickly fruit of Datura species.

Loop trails for both Mast Park and Mast Park West begin at the welcome sign off the parking lot. Facing the sign, there is a road off to your right that descends to another lot where the walk to Mast Park West begins by going under the Carlton Hills Boulevard bridge, where you will encounter murals painted in 2011 by a local Boy Scout troop. The Mast Park West Trail also begins on the other side of Carlton Hills Boulevard at a kiosk and small picnic area near a small shopping center. The trail follows the river west and then runs alongside a golf course. Along here the trail becomes the San Diego River Trail and winds around near CA-52. This is a longer trek than Mast Park to the east.

Beginning at the same welcome sign, the Mast Park trails are off to the left. A portion of the trail is concrete and blacktop surfaces, but another portion of the trail leads down to the river where there is a bridge to walk over. This same portion of the trail can be entered from the nearby Walmart parking lot. Expect to see dog walkers and possibly equestrians riding along the river.

Eva McCatty

Murals on the underpass

Distance:	0.6, 1.8, or 3.1 miles, loop
Difficulty:	🚶 or 🚶🚶
Elevation gain/loss:	Minimal
Hiking time:	1 or 2 hours
Agency:	SLRP
Trail use:	Bicycles, dogs
Notes:	Parking fee; open 6 a.m. Friday-Sunday and 8 a.m. Monday-Thursday
Trailhead GPS:	N32.84914, W117.00505
Optional map:	USGS 7.5-min *La Mesa*, *El Cajon*
Atlas square:	P12
Directions:	((Santee) From CA-52 go east on Mast Boulevard for 1.3 miles. Turn right on Fanita Parkway. Go 0.3 mile. The entrance to Santee Lakes will be on the right.

Habitat(s):

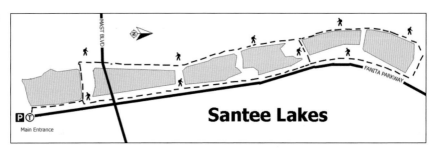

The 190-acre Santee Lakes Recreational Preserve evolved out of the need for Padre Dam Municipal Water District to handle the wastewater disposal issues of a growing suburban community. The problem was handled in a unique and creative way. What started as a wastewater treatment facility in the 1960s became a series of seven man-made lakes that are clean enough and attractive enough for a public park and campground with resort-like activities and amenities that include boating, fishing, picnicking, playgrounds, cabin rentals, and a general store. The lakes are regularly stocked with rainbow trout and channel catfish, while bluegill and bass are residents and regularly caught here. You do not need a California fishing license to fish in these lakes, but you need the daily fishing permit sold at the preserve's general store. There is a fee for vehicles to enter, but no charge to pedestrians or bicycles. Dogs must be on a leash. Check the website for special events.

The recreational facilities found here probably draw the largest number of visitors, but Santee Lakes also is a great place for walking and birding. The terrain is flat and paved around the lakes. A total of 175 species of birds, both native and non-native have been observed. American coots, mallards, wood ducks, great blue herons, great egrets, cinnamon teals, and many other water birds can be easily spotted in the lakes. The cinnamon teal (*Anas cyanoptera*) is considered one of the most beautiful ducks as well as the best tasting. It prefers shallow natural wetlands and feeds mainly on plants. Its small size and erratic flight pattern make it a difficult target for hunters. The coots and mallards are particularly tame and approach people since the park office/general store sells bird food. The mallard (*Anas platyrhynchos*) is San Diego County's most widespread duck and among the few that nest locally. The herons and egrets are slightly less approachable, but good opportunities for photography abound, even for those without a telephoto lens. Great blue herons (*Ardea herodias*) nest in treetops, laying their eggs from January to March. You are more likely to spot a great blue heron flying or stalking prey. They are able to curl their neck into an S-shape and strike prey with shocking quickness, thanks to the shape of the vertebrae at the kink in the neck. Seeing a great blue heron hunting at dusk or night is not uncommon. With a high percentage of rods in their eyes, these birds are able to see quite

Peula Knoll

Santee Lakes

well even in low light levels. Fish are common prey, but small mammals (especially gophers), reptiles, amphibians, crustaceans, and insects are also eaten.

Take time to view the trees as well as the water for birds, such as the western scrub-jay, finches, hummingbirds, woodpeckers, goldfinches, swallows, and many others. Bring binoculars for a close up view of the birds. The best time for viewing birds is early in the morning, so arrive as soon as the park opens for the most

bird activity. Birds also call more frequently in the morning, offering the possibility for identification through sound as well as enjoyment of their pleasant melodies. Food and drinks are sold at the general store, and there are restroom facilities throughout the park.

Be on the lookout for native plants as well. The north end of the park sports a native plant garden, but both native and non-native species can be found throughout the park. Santee Lakes is part of the San Diego River Park.

Wendy Esterly

Great blue heron

Wendy Esterly

Mallard ducks

Distance:	3 miles, out-and-back
Difficulty:	🚶🚶
Elevation gain/loss:	Up to 200 feet
Hiking time:	2 hours
Agency:	City of San Diego
Trail use:	Bicycles, dogs
Trailhead GPS:	N32.83164, W117.10234
Optional map:	USGS 7.5-min *La Mesa*
Atlas square:	P10
Directions:	((Tierrasanta) From I-15 go east on Clairemont Mesa Boulevard for 0.9 mile. Turn left on Santo Road. Go 0.1 mile. Turn right on Remora Street and park. Walk north on Santo Road to the trailhead. From CA-52 go south on Santo Road for 0.9 mile. Turn left on Remora Street and park. Walk north on Santo Road to the trailhead.

Habitat(s):

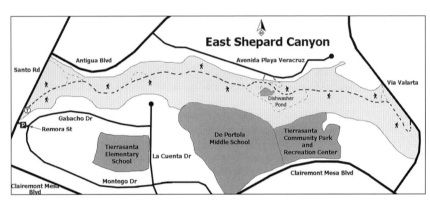

East Shepherd Canyon is interesting in all seasons with a combination of native coastal sage scrub and non-native plants in the canyon. Walk north on Santo Road for about 160 feet where the trail starts just past the signed gate that separates traffic by a non-native hedge on the left. This canyon is also known to locals as Greenbelt Canyon. The beginning of this hike is a good place to contemplate the history of the area.

The area was first inhabited by the Kumeyaay and then was managed from 1769 to 1833 by the Mission San Diego de Alcalá Franciscans. Under the Decree of Confiscation in 1834, the mission lands were divided into ranchos and given to officers who fought in the War of Independence against Spain. The mission was not restored to the Catholic Church until 1862 by President Abraham Lincoln. In the 1940s, the old mission lands fell under the use of the US military.

In 1941, Camp Elliot was comprised of a roughly parallelogram shape within the confines of I-15 northeast to Pomerado Road/

Beeler Canyon to Sycamore Canyon, before going south to Mission Gorge Road and before returning to just west of I-15. Use of the area included tank and artillery training plus communications training for the WWII Navajo Code Talkers (see www.navajocodetalkers.org).

Later in 1960, 13,277 acres were annexed into San Diego with different land use plans finally evolving into East Shepherd Canyon, which became one of San Diego County's first community parks in the 1980s. Take seriously the warning sign at each point of entry stating there is a possibility of unexploded shells that might still surface in the park.

Just past the entrance gate to the right are laurel sumac, coastal sagebrush, prickly-pear cactus, and black sage. To the left is an example of a dioecious species that exhibits separate male and female plants with distinct differences in their flowers. The chaparral broom or coyote brush (*Baccharis pilularis*) male flowers are cupped and cream-colored, and when the wind blows, a great amount of pollen is blown into the air (wind dispersal) with

Female chaparral broom or coyote brush

some of the pollen falling into receiving female flowers that are white with long slender hairs. Wind again plays a role with the dispersal of the mature seeds months later that can be seen when the plant branches are lightly shaken. Wind pollinated plants do not have to put out extra energy to attract pollinators through smell, color, or reward of food (nectar).

Follow the trail to the right along a small creek, then over a fallen tree trunk to continue. There are a couple of crossings where a board has been placed to keep your feet dry. Look along the trail and redwood fence for toyon (*Heteromeles arbutifolia*), a tall evergreen shrub or small tree found in coastal sage scrub and chaparral communities that is a member of the rose family that includes apples, cherries, peaches, almonds, and strawberries. It has serrated holly-leaf edges and, white flowers in spring. It is easily noticed during the winter months when the pulp carbohydrate levels increase, turning berries from green to a vivid red. The ripened fruit are an attractive meal to robins, mockingbirds, and cedar waxwings that assist in seed disbursal when feasting. The winter berries are the reason why it is also known as Christmas berry. A common misconception is that the Los Angeles community of Hollywood was named for the toyon berry. In fact, there is no connection whatsoever. The name was coined by rich landowners, Harvey

and Daeida Wilcox who subdivided the land and named it Hollywood simply because they liked the name. Native American inhabitants are reported to have used the plant for a variety of purposes including the fruits for food and leaves for tea. The fruits are acidic and contain low levels of toxic cyanogenic glycosides that can be broken down by cooking.

The trail leads to Dishwasher Pond, originally created in the 1960s by building an earthen dam across an ephemeral stream. A concrete spillway was added in 1980. The pond is a small body of aerated water where sometimes ducks, dragonflies, and damselflies can be seen amongst the willows and cattails. Local residents use it for bird watching and fishing. Continue hiking under eucalyptus trees to Via Valarta, then return.

Toyon or Christmas berry

Distance:	2 miles, one-way or 4 miles, out-and-back
Difficulty:	
Elevation gain/loss:	Up to 200 feet
Hiking time:	1 or 2 hours
Agency:	City of San Diego
Trail use:	Bicycles, dogs
Trailhead GPS:	N32.81344, W117.05596
Optional map:	USGS 7.5-min *La Mesa*
Atlas square:	Q11
Directions:	(San Carlos) From I-8 go north on College Avenue for 1.3 miles. Turn right onto Navajo Road. Go 0.3 mile. Turn left on Margerum Avenue. Go 0.9 mile. Parking lot is on the right. From CA-52 go east on Mast Boulevard for 0.2 mile. Turn right on West Hills Parkway. Go 0.7 mile. Turn right on Mission Gorge Road. Go 3.4 miles. Turn left on Margerum Avenue. Go 0.3 mile. Parking lot is on the left.

Habitat(s):

A hike through Rancho Mission Canyon Open Space is an opportunity to experience one of the many urban canyon parks we are so fortunate to have access to in San Diego. The winding trail traverses through a section of urban canyon just outside of Mission Trails Regional Park. This is part of the over 24,000 acres of open space canyons and parklands managed by the City of San Diego Park and Recreation Department's Open Space Division.

This hike may be done as either a 4-mile out-and-back trail starting at either Rancho Mission Canyon Park or from the other end at Hemingway Drive. If able to carpool with a friend, this trail can become a leisurely 2-mile one-way stroll from either end. To do the easiest route, heading downhill, park a car at Rancho Mission

Canyon Park and drive the other car to Hemingway Drive by heading north on Margerum Avenue, turning right into Mission Gorge Road, right onto Jackson Drive, then right onto Hemingway Drive, and keep bearing right. Park at the end of Hemingway Drive.

The trail is a wide and well-maintained path that makes its way up the side of a hill perched below homes on the ridgetop. Soon forgotten is the proximity to civilization when walking among the abundance of native vegetation found along the way. One of the plants that you will encounter is lemonadeberry (***Rhus integrifolia***), which sports pink buds in the winter and into the spring. The name *rhus* is Greek for sumac, which is the name for the family of this plant. It is an aromatic evergreen shrub

Jim Varnell

View toward Mt. Woodson

or small tree from 3-15 feet in height that is typically found in coastal and inland canyons, north-facing slopes, and chaparral areas below 2500 feet elevation. The species name (*integ-* is Latin for whole or entire) is a reference to the shape of the leaf, which is broad and nearly flat, leathery with a waxy appearance and slightly toothed edges. The flower is white to rose in color while the sticky berry—a stone fruit or drupe—is red. The berry has a tart citrus flavor that was used by both Native Americans and early pioneers to make a drink similar to lemonade. The fruit is eaten by a variety of birds. Be wary though, lemonadeberry is closely related to western poison-oak, and some people may have an allergic reaction.

Be sure to notice some of the spring and summer-flowering wildflowers either around or below the larger plants. One of the most common will be the multi-colored bush monkey flower in either its red, orange, or yellow splendor. Another likely springtime bloomer is the purple and yellow blue-eyed-grass, which is often found in stunning clusters. However, do not forget to look up to likely spot red-tailed hawks and turkey vultures soaring overhead, riding leisurely on thermal updrafts. Smaller birds also abound, such as towhees, both the brown California and the more colorful spotted.

If hiking down from Hemingway Drive, there will be a kiosk where the trail splits after about 1.25 miles. While either direction leads to Rancho Mission Canyon Park and your vehicle if it was left there, the trail to the right is a direct walk through the park. The trail to the left allows a bit longer stay in the canyon. If this is an out-and-back hike from either direction, do a short loop here before retracing your route to complete your 4-mile trek.

Lemonadeberry

Distance:	2.6 miles, out-and-back
Difficulty:	🚶🚶
Elevation gain/loss:	Up to 400 feet
Hiking time:	2 hours
Agency:	City of San Diego
Trail use:	Dogs
Trailhead GPS:	N32.78292, W117.08637
Optional map:	USGS 7.5-min *La Mesa*
Atlas square:	Q10
Directions:	(Del Cerro) From I-8 go north on Waring Road for 0.3 mile. Turn right on Adobe Falls Road at the first signal light. Go 0.1 mile. Park where Adobe Falls Road turns left.

Habitat(s):

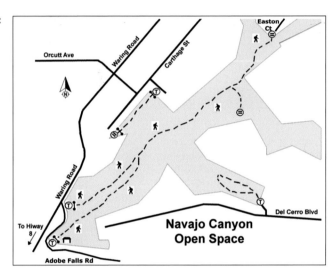

Navajo Canyon is one of 18 open space and canyon parklands within the City of San Diego that is maintained by the City's Department of Park and Recreation. Open space areas are free from development or have low intensity uses that respect natural environmental characteristics. Natural resources are preserved in these open areas and canyons.

The trail for Navajo Canyon begins on Adobe Falls Road and works its way up-canyon with several intermittent creek crossings. There are over 100 Mexican fan palms in this canyon and a variety of coastal sage scrub, chaparral, and riparian plants. It also has western poison-oak. Large shrubs include lemonadeberry, laurel sumac, scrub oak, *Ceanothus*, toyon, and arroyo willow. Cattails, sedges, and rushes (*Juncus* **spp.**) also are found along the watercourse. Rushes have linear leaves, usually spine tipped, often reduced to a basal sheath and a small blade. Flowers are inconspicuous and the fruit

is a capsule. The genus name *Juncus* is Latin for rush. Rush is a food plant of the larvae of many butterfly and moth species. It is an important Indian basket-making plant.

We usually think of the desert when we think about cholla. However, there are two species of cholla common in coastal sage scrub habitat, and you will find them growing here. The first is coast cholla (***Cylindropuntia prolifera***), which grows in coastal San Diego County inland as far as Lakeside and south into Baja California. The canyon's second cholla species is snake-cholla (***Cylindropuntia californica***), so named because its sprawling stems look like fighting snakes. Unlike coast cholla, it is not restricted to the coast.

Another plant associated with the desert that has a coastal species found here is coast prickly-pear (***Opuntia littoralis***). Look for small balls of white that may appear on some of the prickly-pear leaves. This is not part of

Pauline Jimenez

Coast cholla

Cyndy Cordle

Coast prickly-pear

the leaf but rather a scale insect called cochineal (*Dactylopius coccus*) that feeds on Opuntia leaves. Use a pencil or pocketknife to remove one of these white balls and spread it on a piece of white paper. You will notice that a crimson-colored dye oozes out of the squashed insect. These insects contain a red dye also known as cochineal. It is commonly used today as a food-coloring agent, either as cochineal or a processed form of the dye known as carmine. You undoubtedly have eaten it as it is very widely used to color food. Peru collects

and sells approximately 200 tons of cochineal each year. The red dye was used in 15th century Mexico as a fabric dye.

At about 0.9 mile the trail forks. Take the left trail that leads to the third intermittent creek crossing. After crossing over the creek rocks, the trail has a steep climb that leads to an overview of Navajo Canyon at 1.15 miles. The trail ends at about 1.25 miles at a parking lot for Prince of Peace Lutheran Church on Easton Court. Turn around and head back down the canyon to Adobe Falls Road and the trailhead.

Diana Lindsay

Rush

Walter Konopka

Cochineal on Indian-fig cactus

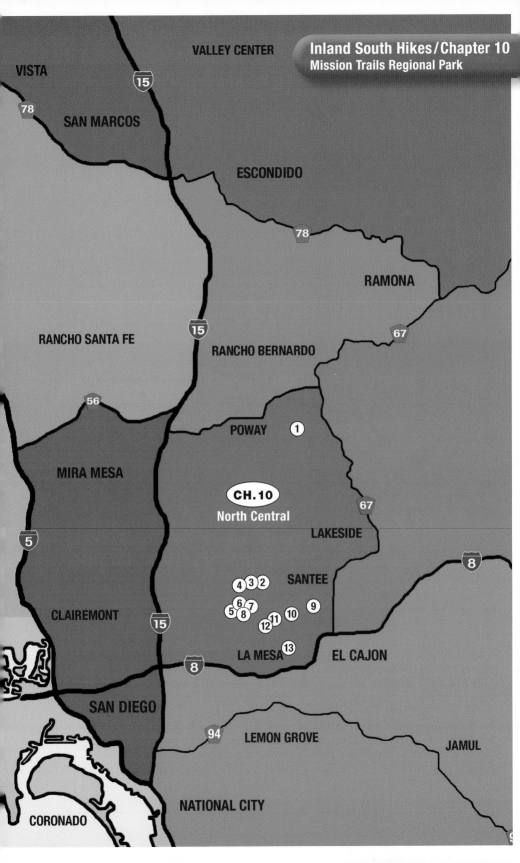

Distance:	5.9 miles, out-and-back
Difficulty:	🚶🚶🚶
Elevation gain/loss:	Up to 1000 feet
Hiking time:	4 hours
Agency:	City of San Diego
Trail use:	Bicycles, dogs, horses
Notes:	Trails to the south stop abruptly at MCAS Miramar property line where entry is prohibited.
Trailhead GPS:	N32.92983, W117.00162
Optional map:	USGS 7.5-min *Poway*
Atlas square:	N12
Directions:	(Poway) From I-15 go east on Scripps Poway Parkway for 0.8 mile. Turn right on Spring Canyon Road. Go 2.6 miles. Continue onto Pomerado Road for 0.2 mile. Turn right on Stonebridge Parkway. Go 3.7 miles. Drive to the end of the road and into the West Sycamore Staging Area straight ahead. From CA-67 go west on Scripps Poway Parkway for 5.7 miles. Turn left on Pomerado Road. Go 1 mile. Turn left on Stonebridge Parkway. Go 3.7 miles. Drive to the end of the road and into the West Sycamore Staging Area straight ahead.

Habitat(s):

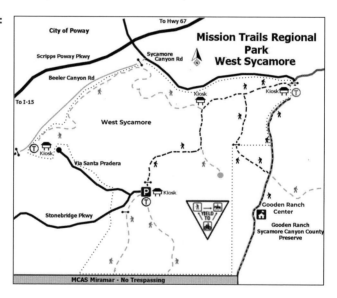

West Sycamore Open Space is an extension of Mission Trails Regional Park that was opened to the public in December 2014. It is adjacent to the San Diego County's Goodan Ranch and Sycamore Canyon Preserve and has interconnecting trails with the preserve but not to the remainder of Mission Trails Regional Park at this time. There are long-term plans to acquire land for a direct connection.

West Sycamore is located in Scripps Ranch. There are 7 miles of trails in this 1372-acre park that offer easy strolling with views of La Jolla, Mount Woodson, Iron Mountain, Cowles Mountain, and the Cuyamaca Mountains. You can stay on the ridgetop service roads for little elevation change or plunge down into one of the canyons for a more challenging hike, as described here, with spectacular views, a variety of vegetation, and historical/educational experiences.

The habitat on the ridgeline is chaparral while the deep valleys below are a mix of coastal sage scrub and chaparral. Stand still on the ridgeline to see turkey vultures sweep-

East entrance

steep at times, but do not despair when there is a major climb in front of you. Look to the left for a narrow-track trail that goes around the hill. Continue north to another kiosk. An alternate hike to the left of this kiosk is the Beeler Canyon Trail, a 2.45-mile narrow-track trail that skirts down the valley's wall to Beeler Canyon Road. If you park a second car at Beeler Canyon Road Trailhead before the hike, you won't have to climb the steeply-paved fire road and Via Santa Pradera back to the West Sycamore Staging Area, which will make a 4.7-mile loop.

Continuing east from the kiosk on the service road, views of Mount Woodson and Iron Mountain will fill the sky. During the rainy season one can experience strong weather up close as there is no cover from the elements up here. At the next intersection take the powerline road to the right that is marked Goodan Ranch Preserve. It plunges down into a side canyon away from the elements to a valley on Goodan Ranch when it levels out. From here go right to visit the Goodan Ranch Center with information, picnic tables, and water. After a rest, return to the last intersection. Look around the valley for wildlife—roadrunners, hares, and birds. Continue north up to the Goodan Ranch Staging Area.

In the parking lot take the narrow-track trail to the west/North Ridge Trail. This is the east entrance to West Sycamore. Enjoy the gradual climb through thick laurel sumac, coastal sagebrush, and broom baccharis. At the service road, head right or west for the return hike back to the trailhead.

ing up from below to catch thermals only a few feet away from the ridgeline. Look for tracks in puddles after an evening rain, and you may find those of southern mule deer, coyote, fox, and possibly mountain lion. There are many nocturnal animals here, and during the day you may see southern mule deer, horned lizards, western rattlesnakes, and California ground squirrels (*Otospermophilus beecheyi*). Some populations of adult California ground squirrels are partially immune to rattlesnake venom, unlike other small mammals.

The California ground squirrel is the most common member of the squirrel family found in San Diego County. They have strong front paws and incisors that never stop growing, as do all members of the order Rodentia. Foraging on tough plant matter wears the teeth of rodents down, so continuous growth is needed in order to maintain functionality.

From the West Sycamore Staging Area, take the trailhead on the north side of the parking lot. There are maps on the side of the kiosk. Follow the service road for 1 mile through revegetated habitat. Soon the landscape turns to undisturbed vegetation. The road can be

California ground squirrel

Distance:	1 to 2 miles, out-and-back
Difficulty:	🚶
Elevation gain/loss:	Minimal
Hiking time:	1 hour
Agency:	City of San Diego
Trail use:	Bicycles, dogs
Trailhead GPS:	N32.83975, W117.03320
Optional map:	USGS 7.5-min *La Mesa*
Atlas square:	P11
Directions:	(Santee) From CA-52 go east on Mast Boulevard for 0.2 mile. Turn right on West Hills Parkway. Go 0.7 mile. Turn right on Mission Gorge Road. Go 0.2 mile. Turn right on Father Junipero Serra Trail. Go 0.2 mile. The entrance to Kumeyaay Lake is on the right at Bushy Hill Drive. Parking for day-use is on the right.

Habitat(s):

Kumeyaay Lake Campground is part of the over 7219-acre Mission Trails Regional Park, owned and operated by the City of San Diego. The lake was part of a sand and gravel mining operation until the early 1970s. The H.G. Fenton Material Company's Monarch Plant produced concrete, plaster, and gunite sand. After the lake was mined out, it was turned into a camping and fishing facility called Hollins Lake Fish Farm and Lake Recreational Facility, named for Mary Hollins who was instrumental in creating a facility where seniors could fish. The restored habitat area was planted with riparian vegetation, especially willow. The willows along the streams and lakeshore grew into thickets attracting the endangered least Bell's vireo.

The facility was closed in 1985, and the area north of the lake became a least Bell's vireo mitigation site for the California Department of Transportation CA-52 freeway project. Today, the lake can no longer be circumnavigated because the north side of the lake is closed off by locked gates to protect areas where the least Bell's vireo nests. Listen for its song, a fast, nasal, angry-sounding "don't-you-tell-me-what-to-do."

Now renamed Kumeyaay Lake, the lush vegetation has created a first-class botanical and wildlife habitat with both riparian and chaparral plants. In December 2000, Mission Trails Regional Park opened the campground with 46 primitive sites for tent camping and recreational vehicles. With budget cuts, the camp-

North Fortuna Mountain reflection

ground is open for camping only Friday and Saturday, while the rest of the week it is open only to day-use.

From the parking area, walk north toward the lakeshore, past restrooms and picnic areas, where short paths lead either left or right. Interpretive signs here depict many of the birds that can be found around the lake, including the blue-gray gnatcatcher, California quail, great blue heron, great egret, Anna's humming-bird, western scrub-jay, red-winged blackbird, and the least Bell's vireo, among others. Also watch for birds of prey including the osprey, various hawks, and the great horned owl. The sounds of birds and running water are joined in the late afternoon with the sounds of crickets and bullfrogs. Waterfowl glide across the lake surface making hypnotic kinetic ripples.

The trail to the left or west leads to an outdoor amphitheater and crosses over a cement bridge that allows water from the San Diego River to flow through the lake. This is a good place to observe waterfowl. Mallards are typical birds seen here. Beyond the amphitheater there is a locked gate beyond which there is no entry. However, just to the south of the gate is a 0.1 mile shaded trail that leads to a view from the center of the lake. Shade trees around the lake include western cottonwoods, western sycamores, willows, and mule-fat. From this point retrace your steps back to the interpre-

tive signs, which completes 1 mile. For a second mile, explore the route to the right or east until you reach the second locked gate on the north side of the lake. Some native plants that may be in bloom include the yellow Hooker's evening primrose, the pink California wild rose, whitish-pink California buckwheat, prickly-pear, and the white blooming yerba mansa or lizard tail.

Signs around the lake indicate sensitive habitat. Bicycles are allowed only on paved roads and not on the paths around the lake. Fishing is allowed, but those ages 16 and older must possess a California state fishing license; catch and release is highly recommended. Dogs are allowed only on a leash and must be picked up after.

Mallard ducks in lake overflow

Distance:	2.2 miles, out-and-back
Difficulty:	👥👥👥
Elevation gain/loss:	Up to 1000 feet
Hiking time:	2 hours
Agency:	City of San Diego
Trail use:	Dogs
Trailhead GPS:	N32.84020, W117.03700
Optional map:	USGS 7.5-min *La Mesa*
Atlas square:	P11
Directions:	(Santee) From CA-52 go east on Mast Boulevard for 0.2 mile. Turn right on West Hills Parkway. Go 0.7 mile. Turn right on Mission Gorge Road. Go 0.2 mile. Turn right on Father Junipero Serra Trail. Go 0.2 mile. There is a dirt parking lot on the corner of Father Junipero Serra Trail and Bushy Hill Drive. The trailhead is 0.2 miles further, past the entrance to the park and to Kumeyaay Lake and Campground, on the left side of Father Junipero Serra Trail.

Habitat(s):

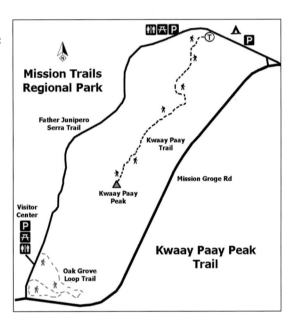

Kwaay Paay Peak is a good alternative to Cowles Mountain for anyone who wants a good climbing hike without a crowd. It is the fourth highest peak in Mission Trails Regional Park at an elevation of 1194 feet. The name of the peak is from the local Kumeyaay Indian word referring to a leader, perhaps for its upright position. The trail to the peak is challenging because of the vertical climb and elevation gain. The top of the peak is a large level area with many flat-topped rocks that make nice seats to rest and take in the panoramic view extending out to Miramar, Point Loma, and Coronado. Santee and La Mesa are below the peak.

The Kwaay Paay Peak Trail begins off of Father Junipero Serra Trail, 0.2 miles west of Bushy Hill Drive and the Kumeyaay Lake and Campground. In 0.3 mile you will come across a junction with a trail from the west (which is being closed for habitat restoration), but continue straight. The trail passes through some coastal sage scrub and grassland habitats and continues to the peak through typical chaparral. Plants encountered en route to the peak include laurel sumac, *Ceanothus* species, chaparral broom, black sage, manzanita, chamise (***Adenostoma fasciculatum***), and California buckwheat (***Eriogonum fasciculatum***).

Wendy Esterly

European honey bee

Alan King

California buckwheat bloom

By comparing the leaves of chamise and buckwheat, you can gain insight into the Latin species name *fasciculatum*. Notice that the leaves of both species come out of the stems in little bunches, or fascicles. A fasces or bundled sticks was a symbol of power in Imperial Rome, and was later symbolically used by the Italian Fascist Party. Buckwheat was used by local Native Americans. The seeds of the buckwheat were ground and used in times of famine as a filler food. Be sure to examine any flowering buckwheat closely to view its characteristic pink pollen and listen for the sound of bees, which can often be found in great numbers on the flowers. While San Diego County is home to over 650 species of native bees, the introduced European honeybee (**Apis mellifera**) will likely be the most conspicuous pollinator. It is an important agricultural pollinator and is the bee usually kept by beekeepers for its honey product. Its Latin name means honey-bearing bee. This bee has a strict caste system and a complex way of communicating to other honeybees where food is located, which can best be described as a dance routine. Honeybees are threatened by colony collapse disorder, the cause of which has not been agreed upon in the scientific community.

At 0.75 mile, the steep trail reaches a small flat crest where there is a view of the gorge dropping down toward the MTRP Visitor Center. Two peaks are visible from here as is the trail that heads straight up. Kwaay Paay is the second peak. Now begins the really steep part that does not level off until mile 1.0. The return through this section is very challenging, and this is where trekking poles really make a difference. The peak is only 0.1 mile ahead

from this point. Take time to enjoy the expansive view from this peak. Head back down the same way, ignoring the trail junction on the left at 0.3 mile. This trail is closed for habitat restoration. Continue down the trail, taking extra care on the steep sections, and return to Father Junipero Serra Trail where you began.

Alan King

California buckwheat leaf bundles and dried blooms

Alan King

Chamise leaf bundles and dried blooms

Distance:	5.3 miles, loop
Difficulty:	🚶🚶🚶🚶
Elevation gain/loss:	Up to 2000 feet
Hiking time:	4 hours
Agency:	City of San Diego
Trail use:	Dogs; horses only on Perimeter and Saddle Trails; no bicycles on Oak Canyon Trail
Trailhead GPS:	N32.83964, W117.04180
Optional map:	USGS 7.5-min *La Mesa*
Atlas square:	P11
Directions:	(Santee) From CA-52 go east on Mast Boulevard for 0.2 mile. Turn right on West Hills Parkway. Go 0.7 mile. Turn right on Mission Gorge Road. Go 0.2 mile. Turn right on Father Junipero Serra Trail. Go 0.4 mile to the small parking lot for Mission Dam on the right. If the lot is full, park along the road.

Habitat(s):

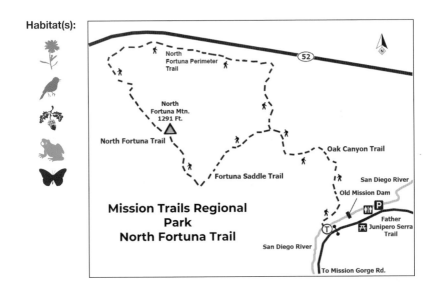

North Fortuna Mountain (1291') is the third tallest mountain in Mission Trails Regional Park after Cowles Mountain and Pyles Peak, but it is the most challenging to climb because of the steep ascent and descent. The route described includes views of Mission Dam, with a quick side trip possible, a shaded oak canyon with views to the open grasslands, riparian areas, and plenty of coastal sage scrub and chaparral areas with a variety of plants.

North Fortuna is part of a long-arced mountain with two peaks that was once called Long Mountain on century-old maps. North Fortuna is separated from South Fortuna by a 910-foot saddle. This area has a long military history, beginning in 1917 when Fortuna was used as an artillery target for training during WWI by the

US Army based at Camp Kearny, a few miles to the west. The area was reactivated in 1934 by the US Marines when it became part of Camp Elliott during WWII, and 10 years later, it was transferred to the US Navy. Fortuna was used for tank, artillery, and infantry training for both WWII and the Korean War. After a cleanup for live ordnance, the land was transferred to the City of San Diego in the 1960s, and by the late 1970s, a master plan was created for Mission Trails Regional Park. On rare occasions live ordnance may surface after heavy rainfall and should be reported and never handled.

Hike west from the parking area past the turnoff to Mission Dam to a sign and a small footbridge over the San Diego River that leads into Oak Canyon. Several interpretive signs are

View from the summit

found along this section of the trail. A wood fence separates the trail from the grasslands area to the east from the shaded oak woodland and riparian areas. Be careful of western poison-oak found under the coast live oaks. Other trees to note in this area include western sycamores and western cottonwoods. At 1.1 miles is the junction with the Fortuna Saddle Trail to the left. Head up this very steep service road, gaining close to 500 feet in elevation in 0.5 mile to the 910-foot saddle. Take the trail to the right to head to the summit of North Fortuna. The first peak is not the true peak; continue to the second peak at mile 2.3, which is the true summit. Look for several ammo cans nestled in the summit rocks. Write a note in one of the log books and/or read some of the entries written by hikers. Plants to note on the top include laurel sumac, mission manzanita, broom baccharis, and California buckwheat.

After taking in the view, which includes the flight runways for MCAS Miramar, traffic on CA-52, and the other peaks and trails in MTRP, begin the descent from the summit. At mile 2.8 is a junction with the North Fortuna Perimeter Trail; take the trail on your right, heading east down the very steep "rollercoaster" that parallels CA-52. Extra care should be taken on this steep descent, best done with trekking poles. At mile 3.8 is the junction with the Oak Canyon Trail on your right and the trail to the

Grasslands Loop Trail; turn right onto the Oak Canyon Trail, which is especially delightful when water is running and there are pools of cool water. At mile 4.2 is another junction with the Grasslands Loop Trail and the close of the loop hike; turn right and return to your vehicle following the original trail to this point.

Trail to the summit

Distance:	3.6 miles, out-and-back with several optional hikes to extend the trek
Difficulty:	🚶🚶
Elevation gain/loss:	Up to 100 feet
Hiking time:	2 hours
Agency:	City of San Diego
Trail use:	Dogs, no bicycles on Grinding Rocks Trail, Climber's Loop, Mission Dam Trail, or Oak Canyon Trail
Trailhead GPS:	N32.81948, W117.05582
Optional map:	USGS 7.5-min *La Mesa*
Atlas square:	P11
Directions:	(Santee) From CA-52 go east on Mast Boulevard for 0.2 mile. Turn right on West Hills Parkway. Go 0.7 mile. Turn right on Mission Gorge Road. Go 2.4 miles. Turn right onto Father Junipero Serra Trail at a large wooden sign for Mission Trails Regional Park. Continue a short distance following the signs to the Visitor Center parking lot.

Habitat(s):

This hike goes through scenic Mission Gorge and leads to the Old Mission Dam that impounded the San Diego River to provide water for the Spanish Mission San Diego de Alcalá. The dam is listed in the National Register of Historic Places and is a California Historical Landmark. It is composed of large boulders and handmade kiln-fired clay tiles that have been cemented together with crushed seashells and lime. It was an impressive engineering feat in its day, given its size and available tools. Construction took six years (1809-1815) and was done by Kumeyaay laborers with hand tools, working under the direction of the padres. An aqueduct was completed simultaneously to carry the water 6 miles from the dam to the mission.

Begin the hike from the Visitor Center and head toward Father Junipero Serra Trail. Just before reaching the paved trail is a sign for the Visitor Center Loop Trail. This is the first possibility for extending the length of the hike by 1.5 miles to follow this loop trail down near the San Diego River and through the shade of the dense riparian growth along the river. If not interested in extending the trip here, just continue to the Father Junipero Serra Trail and go left.

The right side of the Father Junipero Serra Trail is a 15 mph, one-way vehicular road that parallels the San Diego River as it makes its way through Mission Gorge. One could drive a vehicle the 1.8 miles to the Old Mission Dam parking lot from the visitor center. However, if you do, you will miss many of the sights and

Wall of the old dam

sounds of this remarkable rugged canyon. The left side of the Father Junipero Serra Trail is reserved for pedestrians and bicyclists. Use it as your path to the dam.

At mile 0.4 after leaving the Visitor Center, there is another opportunity to take a brief side excursion by following the trail marked Grinding Rocks Trail on the left. The trail leads to a place where the Kumeyaay people processed acorns for food. Look for the deep mortero holes found on boulders, which are evidence of their life and long presence in this area. After harvesting, the acorns were ground and then the tannins were leached out by repeated soakings in running water. When the acorn meal was ready, it was cooked with water to make a mush called *shawii*. After it cooled, it solidified. It was cut in squares and eaten cold. San Diego County Indians still make *shawii* today.

On the right side of the paved trail is the beginning of the Climber's Loop, at nearly the same point where the Grinding Rocks Trail departs. It is another loop trail, 1 mile in length that rises several hundred feet to the base of huge boulders providing some of the best rock climbing in the County. Even if not interested in rock climbing, the views of the city from this loop trail are worth the extra effort.

Even if not taking one or more of the optional detours going up the paved trail, take time to examine the diverse vegetation beside the trail. This includes typical chaparral and coastal sage scrub plants such as mission manzanita, black sage, fuchsia-flower gooseberry, chaparral candle, lemonadeberry, and many others. A full-color guide, entitled "Flowering Plants of Mission Trails Regional Park," is available at the Visitor Center to help identify the many plants.

At 1.8 miles is the parking area for the Old Mission Dam and the short trail leading to the dam. After exploring this engineering marvel, consider continuing the hike up the Oak Canyon Trail. This area was devastated by the 2003 Cedar Fire, but the shrubs and trees that line the canyon have almost completely recovered. There won't be any flowing water in the canyon unless it has rained recently.

Paved trail from the Visitor Center

Distance:	2 miles, loop, including short side trip
Difficulty:	🚶🚶
Elevation gain/loss:	Up to 600 feet
Hiking time:	1 hour
Agency:	City of San Diego
Trail use:	Bicycles, dogs
Trailhead GPS:	N32.81956, W117.05592
Optional map:	USGS 7.5-min *La Mesa*
Atlas square:	P11
Directions:	(San Carlos)) From CA-52 go east on Mast Boulevard for 0.2 mile. Turn right on West Hills Parkway. Go 0.7 mile. Turn right on Mission Gorge Road. Go 2.4 miles. Turn right on Father Junipero Serra Trail at a large wooden sign for Mission Trails Regional Park. Continue a short distance following the signs to the Visitor Center parking lot.

Habitat(s):

The Mission Trails Visitor Center Loop Trail is a great hike for those who want an introduction to San Diego outdoors. It has it all, including the 14,575-square-feet, award-winning Visitor and Interpretive Center with both audio and visual displays that help you understand the resources in this over 7000-acre park. Mission Trails Regional Park purports to be one of the nation's largest urban natural parks. The loop trail is great for trail runners, mountain bikers, and dog owners. For those who want a guide, park naturalists lead free interpretive walks on the loop trail every Wednesday, Saturday, and Sunday morning at 9:30 a.m.

Before you begin your hike, take time to enjoy the many displays at the Visitor Center. Learn how water was first transported to San Diego

and how in the early days of this park it was part of the military's Camp Elliott from 1917-1961. The Visitor Center is open daily 9 a.m.-5 p.m.

One of the amazing things about this loop is how quickly one can leave the noise of a major street and crowds and step into a natural environment. While we enjoy the quiet and hear the wind as it moves through the plants, the call of a wrentit, or the buzz of an insect, think about how the quiet is much more fundamental for many of the animals calling the chaparral, coastal sage scrub, and riparian woodland ecosystems home. Noise pollution is of concern to these animals since their hearing is so sensitive, having evolved in areas without the roar of freeways or of a jet flying above. A mouse for instance, may be temporarily deafened with a

Trail heads toward Fortuna Mountain

loud noise, leaving it more susceptible to predation, whereas in a quiet location, the mouse may have picked up on subtle clues giving away the presence of a predator.

The hike begins at the parking entrance to the Visitor Center off Father Junipero Serra Trail. The trailhead is signed Visitor Center Loop. The loop trail ends on the other side of the drive entrance. Begin walking north, noting common chaparral plants encountered at the beginning of the loop that include laurel sumac, California buckwheat, and chaparral candle. The large peak straight ahead is South Fortuna Mountain.

As you approach the San Diego River, cottonwoods will come into view. At 0.3 mile there is a turnoff to the Grinding Rocks Trail which leads to the Riverside Grinding Site where bedrock morteros may be seen. It was here that early-day Kumeyaay would grind their collected seeds and acorns to prepare them for meals. Take this short jaunt if you want to see this grinding area and then return to the junction to continue the loop.

As the trail begins to follow the river, more riparian plants become visible, including mulefat, western sycamore, arroyo willow, and rush that was used by the Kumeyaay for making collection baskets. Watch out for western poison-oak near the trail. At about 0.9 mile, you approach the San Diego River Crossing from which you can go right to head to the Fortuna Mountains. Go left and head uphill passing a

small stream to your right. Note the blocks of ancient granite that rise above the streambed where cattails are visible. The green material floating in the pond eddies is a freshwater green alga known as pond scum or pond-moss (*Spirogyra* spp.), although it is not really a moss. The alga is photosynthetic—a chlorophyte that typically forms greenish mats on the water's surface, especially during dryer months when water is stagnant.

The loop continues past the Jackson Staging Area. As the route parallels Mission Gorge, the quiet is interrupted with the sounds of street traffic and soon the parking area comes into view.

Pond scum or pond-moss

Distance:	1 or 1.6 miles, loop
Difficulty:	🏃
Elevation gain/loss:	Up to 100 feet
Hiking time:	1 hour
Agency:	City of San Diego
Trail use:	Bicycles, dogs
Trailhead GPS:	N32.81934, W117.05569
Optional map:	USGS 7.5-min *La Mesa*
Atlas square:	P11
Directions:	(San Carlos) From CA-52 go east on Mast Boulevard for 0.2 mile. Turn right on West Hills Parkway. Go 0.7 mile. Turn right on Mission Gorge Road. Go 2.4 miles. Turn right on Father Junipero Serra Trail at a large wooden sign for Mission Trails Regional Park. Continue a short distance following the signs to the Visitor Center parking lot.

Habitat(s):

The highlight of this short hike is the transition from grasslands and coastal sage scrub habitats to shaded oak woodland with majestic coast live oaks and rare Engelmann oaks found along a stream where a replica of a Kumeyaay home is found. The inviting shady area also has benches where one can sit and enjoy the butterflies and dragonflies that often visit this area. Interpretive panels tell about the Kumeyaay that once called this area home.

The hike begins across from the entrance to the parking area for the Mission Trails Regional Park Visitor Center at the kiosk. There are three complete loops—a larger north loop, a smaller south loop, and a much smaller east loop. This hike does not close the east loop but incorporates it as a finger of the north loop.

The best direction to do the loops is to begin by first turning left at the kiosk and then taking the trail to the right, heading southeast, to complete the south loop, which is 0.5 mile in length. Halfway through this loop there is a T-junction. Go right to return to the start. The habitat is coastal sage scrub. Back at the start again, hike to the T-junction once more, bringing the total mileage completed to about 0.75 mile. Turn left this time, and hike a short distance to the next junction. The left or north turn continues the larger north loop but will miss the east loop. Go right to do the east loop and rejoin the larger loop after about 0.25 mile. While on the east loop, look for sweet fennel (*Foeniculum vulgare*).

Sweet fennel is an invasive plant that origi-

Sweet fennel

They end up squeezing native plants out of their own niche. Harmful invasives include giant reed, artichoke thistle, pampas grass, and saltcedar or tamarisk. All are found within MTRP, but park staff work with volunteers to keep them under control.

At the junction with the larger north loop, turn right. Notice that almost immediately there is a transition from the coastal sage scrub to a thick oak woodland as the elevation descends toward a small stream. Just over 1 mile into the hike, a Kumeyaay 'ewaa or house appears beneath the shaded oak canopy. Typically, the frame for the dome-shaped dwellings was made from strong arroyo willow or western sycamore branches lashed together with strips of bark. Slimmer leaved willow branches were then woven into the framework. Benches are located along this shady path and make a good place to sit and enjoy the area and to contemplate the early Native Americans who lived and thrived in this environment. The trail joins the paved path at about 1.5 miles. Turn left and walk back toward the start of the hike where the loop began.

nally comes from the Mediterranean area and thrives in coastal sage scrub and grasslands. It is an erect tall herb with a characteristic licorice or anise smell, feathery leaves, and yellow flowers that are clustered in a large (up to 4 inches) umbel—an umbrella-like arrangement. It is in the carrot family and related to cumin, dill, and caraway. In the Mediterranean region, it has been used as a spice for centuries and is an ingredient in Italian sausage. It was used by the ancient Egyptians as both a food and a medicine. In ancient China it was used as a snake-bite remedy, and in the Middle Ages, it was hung in doorways to fend off evil spirits. The Greek Pheidippides ran through a fennel field in his 26.2-mile run from Marathon to Athens. Here it is an invasive species that impacts habitat. Do not mistake common poison hemlock, a naturalized weed in San Diego, for fennel. Common poison hemlock (*Conium maculata*) does not smell of licorice, has purple streaks on the stems, and is very poisonous.

Invasive, non-native plants are generally a problem as they compete for resources and are often more aggressive than the native plants.

Entering the oak grove

Distance:	5.5 miles, loop
Difficulty:	🚶🚶🚶
Elevation gain/loss:	Up to 1800 feet
Hiking time:	4 hours
Agency:	City of San Diego
Trail use:	Dogs, horses only on Fortuna Saddle Trail; no bicycles on South Fortuna Trail south of the peak
Notes:	Bicycles can access South Fortuna only from Fortuna Saddle
Trailhead GPS:	N32.81787, W117.06012
Optional map:	USGS 7.5-min *La Mesa*
Atlas square:	P11
Directions:	(San Carlos) From CA-52 go east on Mast Boulevard for 0.2 mile. Turn right on West Hills Parkway. Go 0.7 mile. Turn right on Mission Gorge Road. Go 2.7 miles. Turn right on Jackson Drive and into the Mission Trails Regional Park parking lot. From I-8 go north on Mission Gorge Road for 4 miles. Turn left on Jackson Drive and into the Mission Trails Regional Park parking lot.

Habitat(s):

The top of South Fortuna Mountain (1094') has sweeping views of all of the major peaks found in San Diego's largest regional park. It was used for physical fitness training by US Marines when Camp Elliott was active, and it is still a great place for a workout. Although not as tall as North Fortuna (1291'), it has one of the best views and is the most challenging when approached from the south ridge.

From the trailhead, follow the wide path to the northwest. Less than 0.5 mile is a trail to the right or east heading to the Visitor Center. Straight ahead is the San Diego River Crossing. Flowing water here fluctuates seasonally.

To avoid getting wet if the flow is high, take a tree-covered path to the left near the junction with the Visitor Center Loop Trail. Walk across a cement piling to a concrete slab path reconnecting on the opposite side of the river. The riparian area has a variety of plants associated with this habitat. Watch out for western poison-oak near the trail.

Begin looking for junctions and take all right turns. At about 1 mile into the hike, go right to head down toward Suycott Wash, and then take another right immediately at 1.05 miles heading toward South Fortuna Trail. Follow the trail to yet another junction

A bridge crossing on the South Fortuna Trail

at the Suycott Valley Trail; go right to begin the South Fortuna Trail that will lead across a small bridge through nice oak woodland with old growth oaks.

While walking through the oaks, look for galls formed by the plant as a chemical reaction to the cynipid oak gall wasp (**family Cynipidae**). There is a great diversity in the type of galls, but the variety called an apple gall is the easiest to identify as it is round, brown or red, and looks like a small apple. The tiny adult female wasp makes a gall by ovipositing its eggs into young oak twigs with an organ called an ovipositor that is designed to direct the egg where it needs to be deposited. The wasp has a plant growth regulating hormone that it injects into the plant along with its eggs. The chemical causes the tree to produce abnormal tissue that becomes the gall. The galls provide food for the larvae and also protect them from predators and parasites. Most galls don't hurt the tree. If you were to look inside a gall, you might see the wasp larvae that have hatched, larvae from parasites of the wasp that have consumed the larvae of the gall maker, or nothing, provided the larvae of either the wasp or parasitoid (a parasite that ultimately sterilizes, kills, or eats the host) have successfully exited the gall. There are over 500 species of cynipid oak gall wasps that use various oak trees for hosts.

The trail will turn to the left to approach the south ridge of South Fortuna. As elevation increases the surrounding habitat changes from oak woodland to grassland to coastal sage scrub as the steep wood staircase climbs close to 560 vertical feet in little over 0.5 mile to reach the top. There are more than 350 steps. Enjoy the view at the top of the staircase at the marked viewpoint at 1000 feet above Mission Gorge. To the southeast are three tall peaks within Mission Trails Regional Park, beginning with the closest that include Kwaay Paay Peak (1194'), Pyles Peak (1379'), and lastly, Cowles Mountain (1592'), which is easily recognized by the radio antenna towers. North Fortuna is in the opposite direction. After taking in the view, follow the trail to the real summit.

From the summit, hikers can backtrack to the start or continue following the trail to the Fortuna Saddle for about 0.5 mile. From the saddle, take the steep trail down that leads back to Suycott Wash and the Suycott Valley Trail. At the junction, turn left and hike past the picnic area to complete the loop. Follow the trail back to the trailhead at Jackson Drive.

Wood steps lead to summit

Distance:	3.6 miles, loop
Difficulty:	🚶🚶🚶
Elevation gain/loss:	Up to 600 feet
Hiking time:	2 hours
Agency:	City of San Diego
Trail use:	Bicycles, dogs
Notes:	Add 5 miles to include summit climb; deduct 1.4 miles if loop begins at Big Rock Park
Trailhead GPS:	N32.81545, W117.01010
Optional map:	USGS 7.5-min *La Mesa*
Atlas square:	Q12
Directions:	(San Carlos) From CA-125 go west on Grossmont College Drive for 0.2 mile. Turn left on Highwood Drive. Go 0.2 mile. Turn right on Lake Murray Boulevard. Go 0.3 miles to the end of the road and park.

Habitat(s):

On any given day, the main route up Cowles Mountain, the highest point in the City of San Diego, is busy. A route with less traffic and easy parking is the Mesa Trail route that may be accessed via Mesa Road in Santee, south of Big Rock Park, or from Lake Murray Boulevard on the western side of El Cajon near Grossmont College. This route offers a loop on the eastern shoulder of Cowles Mountain that can be extended to include a trek to the top of Cowles Mountain by connecting to the Cowles Mountain Service Road, which begins off of Barker Way Road. The advantage of this route, besides being less traveled, is greater variety in the landscape, including creek crossings with

riparian plants, chaparral-shaded trails, and grasslands. In this area of Mission Trails Regional Park it is easy to stay on-trail as it is so well signed.

This hike begins at the Lake Murray Boulevard Trailhead by following an old service road down the hill, which is an extension of Mesa Road in Santee. After 0.57 mile, look to the west for the beginning of the Mesa Trail that is signed. Cross the small bridge over the creek and begin the hike up the mountain noting a variety of typical chaparral plants that include laurel sumac, scrub oak, chaparral broom, chamise, California buckwheat, *Ceanothus*, curly dock, and San Diego gold-

View north toward CA-52

enbush. During spring, blooms of monkey flower and California poppy can be seen. The red-flowered coast monkey flower (***Diplacus puniceus***) and the other species of monkey flower have a very interesting, touch-sensitive stigma—part of the pistil or ovary producing part of the flower that receives pollen and where pollen germinates. The small white stigma is in the middle of the flower petals. On an open flower, look closely and see the white stigma with two lobes. When the stigma is gently touched by a hummingbird or other pollinator, the two lobes close. Upon realizing no pollen has been deposited, the lobes will reopen after a few minutes. If pollen has been deposited, then the lobes will stay closed. You may gently touch an open stigma to see for yourself.

The trail is rocky and uneven. As you increase in elevation, red-barked manzanita will provide shade and the odor of black sage will be in the air. At 1.36 miles will be the signed junction of Big Rock Trail, which will lead down to Big Rock Park in Santee. This is the highpoint of this hike at 890 feet. Big Rock Trail continues up the mountain to the Cowles Mountain Service Road and to the summit, a distance of about 2.5 miles. To do the peak in this loop will add 5 miles to the overall trip and an additional elevation gain of 700 feet.

Take the trail down and notice the great view toward CA-52 and Santee as the trail descends toward a grassland. At 2.31 miles is a small intermittent creek crossing that may be dry during summer. Western sycamores and mule-fat are found here.

After crossing the creek, Big Rock Park will soon be visible where there are restrooms and water. The trail entrance to Big Rock Trail is at 2.46 miles. This is the lowest elevation on the hike at 370 feet. At the trail entrance turn right and begin south on Mesa Road to return to your vehicle. No vehicles are allowed on the road past 2.91 miles. The route will pass the entrance to Mesa Trail at 3.05 miles, and 0.5 mile further will be the top of Lake Murray Boulevard.

Coast monkey flower

Distance:	3 miles, out-and-back
Difficulty:	🚶🚶🚶
Elevation gain/loss:	Up to 1000 feet
Hiking time:	2 hours
Agency:	City of San Diego
Trail use:	Dogs
Trailhead GPS:	N32.80998, W117.02093
Optional map:	USGS 7.5-min *La Mesa*
Atlas square:	Q12
Directions:	(San Carlos) From CA-125 go west on Navajo Road for 0.7 mile. Turn right on Boulder Lake Avenue. Go 0.5 mile. Turn right on Barker Way and park on the street. Trailhead is on the left.

Habitat(s):

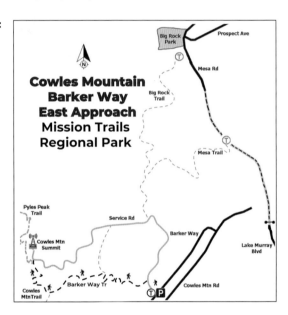

As both the highest peak in the City of San Diego and one of the most popular hiking destinations in the county, Cowles Mountain (1592') is better known for spectacular views of southern California than quiet, wilderness solitude. Indeed, the popular southern route that begins near the corner of Navajo Road and Golfcrest Drive accommodates at least several hundred hikers daily. But start your hike just a little more than 1 mile to the east, and you can have the same superb hiking and sweeping vistas that make Cowles so popular with a fraction of the south-route crowds, not to mention an easier time finding a parking spot.

From Barker Way, enter through the gate on the northwest side of the road to find a small kiosk with park and safety information. Continue up the road 150 yards and turn left onto

the Barker Way Trail to the summit of Cowles Mountain. Stay to your right as you begin your ascent to avoid a southern offshoot trail that returns to the San Carlos neighborhood. A string of consecutive switchbacks and an escalating heart rate are good clues that you are going the right way.

Continue climbing for about 1 mile until the trail intersects with the popular southern route, and then turn right to finish the trek to the summit. Although the relative solitude of the east trail is lost at this point, there are good reasons for Cowles' popularity. The 360-degree views at the top are well worth another grueling 0.5 mile of switchbacks, even on a crowded weekend day. The summit offers panoramic views of southern California and northern Baja California, Mexico, with interpretive

Barker Way Trail meets Cowles Mountain Trail

signs to help hikers identify natural and man-made landmarks throughout the region.

Looking from the summit into the urban landscape of the greater San Diego and Tijuana region, this trail offers a sharp contrast between natural and built landscapes. If focusing on the hike just completed and the sweeping vistas, one can nearly imagine what the landscape might have looked like centuries ago when it was dominated primarily by coastal sage scrub and chaparral ecosystems. Humans have fundamentally altered our surroundings, and natural systems and public health have been major casualties. Missing are well-connected landscapes allowing for robust animal populations; more often we have to check the air-quality index. Human-induced change has had negative consequences on ecosystem integrity, but recent research into the understanding of our impact on global climate and natural systems is increasing awareness of what can be done to reverse negative trends. Visit the San Diego Natural History Museum to learn more about global change and how each of us can make individual changes, collectively adding up to create more sustainability, thereby helping to protect our natural spaces for our children and grandchildren.

Return to Barker Way via the same trail or make a loop by turning right or east onto the Cowles Mountain Service Road that passes just north of the peak and winds its way down

to the entrance at Barker Way. Either option provides a 3-mile round trip hike with a nearly 1000-foot elevation gain. Shade is scarce on the exposed southern slope, so this is a great hike for winter or spring when temperatures are milder. Consider early morning or evening hikes in the summer, and always bring plenty of water. If it is hot, leave your dog at home, as many dogs have suffered heat-related illness (including death) on the trails.

Starting up the trail

Distance:	3 miles, out-and-back
Difficulty:	🏃🏃🏃
Elevation gain/loss:	Up to 1000 feet
Hiking time:	2 hours
Agency:	City of San Diego
Trail use:	Dogs
Trailhead GPS:	N32.80462, W117.03714
Optional map:	USGS 7.5-min *La Mesa*
Atlas square:	Q11
Directions:	(San Carlos) From I-8 go north on College Avenue for 1.3 miles. Turn right onto Navajo Road. Go 2 miles. Turn left on Golfcrest Drive and park in the lot on right. From CA-125 go west on Navajo Road for 2 miles. Turn right on Golfcrest Drive and park in the lot on the right.
Habitat(s):	

If popularity is any indication of quality, then the Cowles Mountain trail from the staging area at the intersection of Golfcrest Drive and Navajo Road is among the best, if not the best, in San Diego. First and foremost, it offers one of the best workouts in San Diego, with a moderately steep climb of almost 1000 feet over 1.5 miles. It also offers spectacular views, interesting natural history, and a significant Kumeyaay archeological site.

Begin the hike at the Cowles Mountain staging area, which is a great place to hang out and wait for your hiking party to assemble or to start a solo hike with the assurance of others on the trail if needed. The staging area has shade trees, which is in short supply on the trail. The staging area also has many native plants, which is a great place to familiarize yourself with the plants that may be encountered on the trail. If it is spring, be sure to compare the California encelia with the San Diego sunflower (*Bahiopsis laciniata*). The San Diego sunflower is found in coastal sage scrub and chaparral and is an evergreen perennial shrub that reaches a height of 3 to 4 feet. It has smaller and has more wrinkled leaves than California encelia, and the ray flowers are more oval and folded back.

As you start up the trail, look south for views of Lake Murray, also part of Mission Trails Regional Park. The rock around Lake Murray is volcanic or tuff-breccia, unlike the rock of Cowles Mountain, which is plutonic or

Cowles Mountain summit view

granitic. However, both rocks are of the same age, somewhat over 100 million years old, and of more-or-less the same chemical composition. Cowles Mountain is most likely part of the core of what was once an island arc volcano and the rock around Lake Murray formed from the ash ejected from that volcano, or other similar volcanoes nearby.

If you brought a hand lens, examine the rocks on the trail. The rocks are granitic, containing grains of black hornblende, whitish plagioclase feldspar, pinkish alkali feldspar, and gray quartz. The hornblende and feldspar weather out, staining the rock red from the iron in the hornblende and leaving small rectangular holes. Note the size of these holes at around 2 mm or about 0.08 inch.

A little past the halfway point, the trail reaches the top of the prominent south shoulder of Cowles Mountain, near what was a Kumeyaay site for observing the winter solstice. The observatory site is on the shoulder, a little south of the trail. This area is closed off except for a few days around the solstice when a number of organizations lead early morning hikes to observe the double-sun visual effect at sunrise that indicates the solstice.

Just past this area, at the north end of the shoulder, is the junction with a trail that leads to

Barker Way. The Barker Way Trail has junctions with two side trails (West and East spur trails) that traverse the east side of Cowles Mountain lower down and ultimately join up with the Cowles Mountain Service Road on the north ridge. The Barker Way Trail and these side trails are far less crowded than the Cowles Mountain Trail and offer alternatives for future hikes (see previous hike).

San Diego sunflower

Cowles Mountain orientation

Above the shoulder, the trail switches back and forth to the summit. This area was extensively renovated in spring 2013 to repair damage from hikers cutting switchbacks. Fences were added in an attempt to prevent future damage.

After reaching the summit of Cowles Mountain, look again at the grains in the rocks. The grain size, in particular the size of the rectangular holes, is larger now, more like 3 to 4 mm or closer to 0.16 inch. This indicates that the rock cooled more slowly and was, therefore, closer to the heart of the volcano that is now Cowles Mountain. Slower cooling gives time for like minerals to come together.

The view from the top of San Diego city's highest summit is spectacular. On clear days, usually sometime in late autumn or winter, it is even possible to see two of the Channel Islands, San Clemente and Santa Catalina. The Coronado Islands, in Mexico, are often visible to the southwest.

If the summit area is overly crowded or hot, cross the service road to the flat rocky area just north of the summit, where it is usually less crowded, and there is often a cool breeze by the cliff. This is a good place to rest and have a snack before returning back down the trail. However, if not tired yet, head west a few feet down the service road, towards the antenna station, to the Pyles Peak trail for an extra 3 miles out-and-back and an additional 834-foot gain/loss of elevation.

The best time to hike Cowles Mountain is in spring to see the diverse wildflowers and blooms on most of the shrubs. Cowles Mountain can be excessively hot in the summer, and the heat can be especially dangerous for dogs. In summer, either go early or late or even bring a headlamp to hike after dark. Late autumn and winter are good times to hike Cowles Mountain, and foggy autumn mornings can be spectacular when the summit protrudes above the clouds. The trail is good immediately after rainstorms, as its decomposed granite drains well and does not become particularly muddy.

This trip can become a low-carbon-footprint adventure by taking public transportation. The San Diego Metropolitan Transit System No. 115 bus stops at the corner of Golfcrest Drive and Jackson Drive, a block away from the staging area, and has hourly service on weekends.

Distance:	6.2 miles, out-and-back
Difficulty:	🚶🚶🚶🚶
Elevation gain/loss:	Up to 2000 feet
Hiking time:	4 hours
Agency:	City of San Diego
Trail use:	Dogs
Notes:	Bicycles can only access Pyles Peak from the service road
Trailhead GPS:	N32.80460, W117.03722
Optional map:	USGS 7.5-min *La Mesa*
Atlas square:	Q11
Directions:	(San Carlos) From I-8 go north on College Avenue for 1.3 miles. Turn right onto Navajo Road. Go 2 miles. Turn left on Golfcrest Drive and park in the lot on the right. From CA-125 go west on Navajo Road for 2 miles. Turn right on Golfcrest Drive. Park in the lot on the right.

Habitat(s):

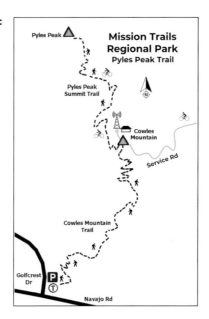

Pyles Peak (1379') is mid-way between Cowles Mountain and Fortuna Mountain and is part of a series of peaks that was called Long Mountain on some older maps. It has some unrestricted views of the north, east, and west sections of San Diego. In the early 1970s, after realizing the peak was unnamed, the Chief Cartographer for the San Diego County Planning Department, Kenneth Pyle, took the liberty of naming the peak after himself.

Pyles Peak is accessed through Cowles Mountain, which has three approaches. The most common is the south approach on the corner of Golfcrest and Navajo Road in San Carlos, which is the recommended approach. The trail to the top of Cowles Mountain is well marked and is regularly used by nearby residents and, at times, with their dogs. It is 1.5 miles to the top of Cowles Mountain via multiple switchbacks. Upon summiting Cowles Mountain from any of its three approaches, face north and walk onto the service road that hugs the downside of the summit. Turn left and walk briefly to its western end where the Pyles Peak Trailhead is found on the left. This trail is less traveled.

The Pyles Peak trail is generally well marked and maintained, making for a leisurely and occasionally challenging hike. The trail descends into the chaparral in a northerly direction followed with multiple ascents and descents along the ridgeline before reaching its destination.

Pyles Peak Trail

The chaparral is low and sparse, dominated by chamise, mission manzanita, and laurel sumac. While walking, look around you for signs of fires in previous years.

Chaparral is not adapted to fire per se, but to a particular fire pattern. If fire returns too frequently, burns the wrong time of year, or fails to burn at high intensity, the chaparral can be eliminated. The natural fire return interval for chaparral is 30 to 150 years or more. Late summer and fall, when lightning storms occur, were the seasons chaparral fires historically ignited. Most fires today are human-caused, increasing both fire frequency and unseasonal burning periods. If chaparral communities burn more frequently than every 30 or so years, post-fire recovery of the vegetative community is often incomplete. A type-conversion of ecosystems from a native, shrub-dominated landscape to an exotic, grass-dominated landscape is a common result of increased fire frequency. Exotic grasses are annuals, dying every year, while shrubs are perennial and maintain some greenness throughout the entire year. As such, the ignition thresholds can be much lower for grasses. Therefore, they are dubbed flashy fuels and can feedback into reduced fire return intervals and further dominance of exotic grasses.

The elevation, distance from habitation, and the dearth of hikers provide quiet and clean air, making the call of the occasional

wrentit stand out. Western scrub-jays and Anna's hummingbirds are frequent companions on this hike. Nearing Pyles Peak, the trail drifts westerly for a bit, where a well-marked, lookout spot on the lower western corner of the peak is visible. The final ascent to the summit begins here and is fairly straight up to the top. The trail narrows with a loose gravel base, which will challenge even experienced hikers. The reward is an unobstructed view to the north and east with the Cuyamacas and Lagunas as backdrops.

The return is just over 3 miles with the first leg to Cowles Mountain a mostly upward hike of 1.6 miles, then descending for about 1.5 miles back to the trailhead on Golfcrest and Navajo Road.

The trail

Distance:	6.4 miles, out-and-back
Difficulty:	👤👤👤
Elevation gain/loss:	Minimal
Hiking time:	4 hours
Agency:	City of San Diego
Trail use:	Bicycles, dogs
Notes:	Gates open at 5:30 a.m. and close at 8 p.m. during Daylight Savings Time and 6:30 p.m. September-February
Trailhead GPS:	N32.78576, W117.03905
Optional map:	USGS 7.5-min *La Mesa*
Atlas square:	Q11
Directions:	(La Mesa) From I-8 go north on Lake Murray Boulevard for 0.5 mile. Turn left on Kiowa Drive. Go 0.5 mile to the parking lot.

Habitat(s):

The southern end of Mission Trails Regional Park is a great place to enjoy chaparral and coastal sage scrub with its easy access path along Lake Murray's lakeshore. You will know you are in coastal sage scrub when you can find typical indicator plants of this habitat, which include coastal sagebrush, California buckwheat, and black sage. Lake Murray is also a great place to think about water and its role in the county's history.

Water was essential to the growth of early San Diego County, beginning with the formation of the San Diego Water Company in 1873 that served a population of 2000. Between 1887 and 1897, six major dams were constructed in the county to keep pace with rapid growth, one of which was the La Mesa hydraulic fill dam constructed in 1895 by the San Diego Flume

Company. Water was diverted from the San Diego River via canal, and then by an innovative process, pumped with silt to the dam site for a pond, creating a compacted core by allowing the water to seep into the ground. The upstream side was strengthened by two layers of wood planks that were caulked and swabbed with asphalt, thus having controlled leakage estimated to be 100,000 gallons per day.

After the great floods of 1916, a new dam was needed to replace the La Mesa Dam. Lake Murray's hollow, gravity multi-arch dam was built by the Cuyamaca Water Company downstream of the old dam and completed in 1918 at a cost of $1.21 million. It was named for James Murray, the project engineer who operated the dam along with Col. Ed Fletcher until 1926 when they sold it to the forerunner of the Helix

Paula Knoll

View of paved path and lake

Water District. In 1961 it was transferred to the City of San Diego. The 198-acre Lake Murray reservoir, which is able to hold 4818-acre feet of water, is the last stop for fresh water coming from the California Water Project before it is filtered at the adjacent Alvarado filtration plant to serve 400,000 users. The filtration plant with its Spanish colonial-style bell tower was open for tours until the September 11, 2001, terrorist attack. For security reasons, it is no longer open to the public.

Lake Murray today is a popular recreation destination for boating, fishing, jogging, bicycling, walking, and birding. Cormorants, ducks, sparrows, and wrentits are among the more than 140 species of birds sighted at the lake or in the coastal sage scrub that surrounds the lake. Bring your binoculars and camera as the wind currents along the edge of the lake allow great viewing of turkey vultures and hawks as they soar or hover. Near the softball fields is an osprey (***Pandion haliaetus***) nest overhead, easily found by the guano sprayed on the road. The osprey is an unusual raptor in that it dives for fish. Its dramatic dives begin from 30-100 feet above the water's surface. Once they snag a wriggling fish in their curved claws, they will quickly use gripping pads on their feet to orient the fish headfirst to ease wind resistance as they fly away with their reward. The osprey has blackish upperparts, a white head and underparts, and a distinctive black eye-stripe.

Don Endicott

Female osprey in her nest

Don Endicott

An osprey with a fish

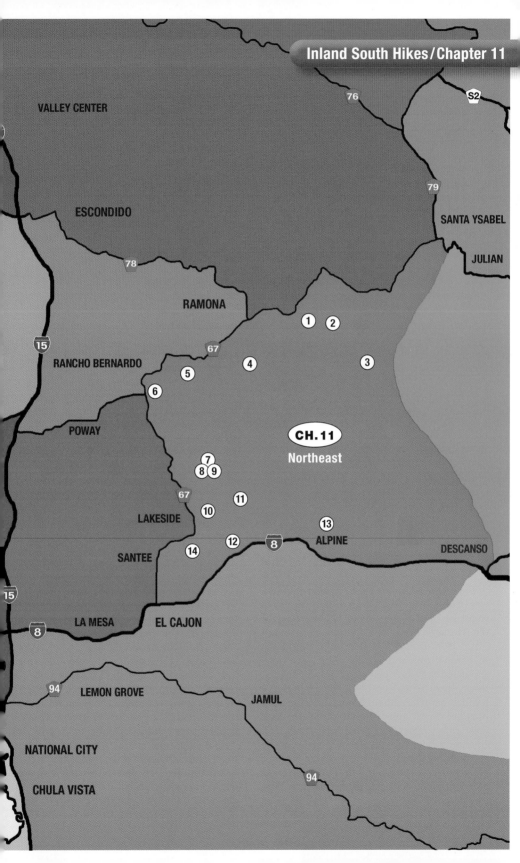

Distance:	4.4 to 6.2 miles, out-and-back
Difficulty:	🚶🚶🚶 or 🚶🚶🚶🚶
Elevation gain/loss:	Up to 1100 feet
Hiking time:	3 to 4 hours
Agency:	San Diego County
Trail use:	Bicycles, dogs, horses
Trailhead GPS:	N33.02732, W116.82038
Optional map:	USGS 7.5-min *Ramona*
Atlas square:	L16
Directions:	(Ramona) From CA-67 in Ramona continue straight onto CA-78 for 0.7 mile. Turn right on Third Street. Go 0.7 mile. Continue onto Old Julian Highway for 1.4 miles. Continue onto Vista Ramona Road for 1.2 miles. Turn right on Calle Andrea and park. The unmarked trailhead is to the north side of Vista Ramona Road, just south of Calle Andrea.

Habitat(s):

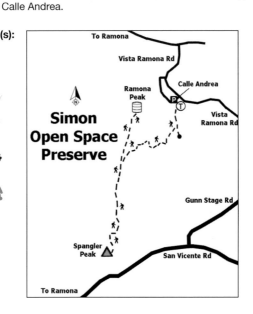

The 650-acre Simon Preserve near Ramona was acquired by San Diego County in 1995 from the sons of the former US Secretary of the Treasury William E. Simon who served from 1974 to 1977 under both Presidents Richard Nixon and Gerald Ford. The sons stipulated that the open space area be named the William E. and Carol G. Simon Preserve for their parents. Although small, this preserve provides over 6 miles of hiking trails through grasslands, chaparral, coastal sage scrub, and riparian habitat with outstanding views of the surrounding mountains. Many different routes are possible as there is a web of looping trails covering the lower parts of the preserve. The trail described here goes to the top of the ridge and to both Spangler and Ramona peaks.

From Vista Ramona, near Calle Andrea, a well-groomed trail leads west with houses to the north and chaparral and coastal sage scrub on the left. The trail is slightly above but near an intermittent stream flanked by oak woodland and riparian habitat. The trail forks in 0.3 mile. Going off to the right takes you up the ridge to Spangler and Ramona peaks. However, consider going another 0.1 mile on the trail to the left, bringing you to the stream where it bubbles over polished granite slabs, provided it is flowing. After enjoying the stream, return to the fork and head up the trail to the ridge.

Initially the trail passes through chaparral where you will hear, but may not see, the endangered California gnatcatcher with its series of hoarse whines and cat-like mews. After hik-

Mt. Gower and the Cuyamacas

ing 1.3 miles and ascending 500 feet, you will arrive at the ridgetop in the middle of a grassy field. Large patches of grassland extend over much of the ridgetop and the land to the north. Here wild oats and other non-native grasses dominate, along with several species of non-native filaree (***Erodium* sp.**). Filarees or storksbills come from Eurasia and were introduced to North America in the 18th century. The long seedpod of these herbaceous plants resemble the bill of a stork, hence one of its common names. After the arrival of this weed into North America, Native Americans reportedly picked the leaves before flowers appeared and cooked them as greens or ate them raw. It has the taste of spinach. Another non-native that is unfortunately common here is the highly invasive cheat grass (***Bromus tectorum***). Cheat grass is a winter annual that sprouts after a rain and rapidly reaches maturity before native annuals have even germinated, choking them out. It produces arching spikes bearing numerous seeds that can stick tenaciously to fur or socks, and can damage the eyes and lips of cattle. After it matures and sets seed, the plant dies, forming a highly flammable mat of tinder dry grass that can rapidly spread a wildfire.

Meadowlarks can be seen, or at least their melodious songs heard, in the grasslands while hawks soar above looking for an incautious mouse. There are also some beautiful native herbaceous species, including blue dicks, and soap-plants.

There is a three-way junction of trails at the top of the ridge. The trail straight ahead continues to follow the powerline, while the trail on the left or west goes to Spangler Peak. The trail to the right or east goes to Ramona Peak. It is about 3.7 miles out-and-back to Spangler Peak while Ramona Peak is about 1.2 miles out-and-back from the trail junction.

Equestrians must use the Mount Gower Preserve staging area as there is limited parking on Calle Andrea. The Rutherford Trail leads west from the Mount Gower staging area and connects to the trail at the start of the Simon Preserve near Calle Andrea.

Red-stem filaree or storksbill

Distance:	12 miles, out-and-back
Difficulty:	🚶🚶🚶🚶🚶
Elevation gain/loss:	Up to 1000 feet
Hiking time:	7 hours
Agency:	San Diego County; USFS/CNF-PRD
Trail use:	Bicycles, dogs, horses
Notes:	Hours 8 a.m. to sunset; closed the month of August due to extreme heat
Trailhead GPS:	N33.02667, W116.79251
Optional map:	USGS 7.5-min *Ramona*
Atlas square:	L16
Directions:	(Ramona) From CA-67 in Ramona go south on 10th Street for 0.4 mile. Continue onto San Vicente Road for 5.5 miles. Turn left on Gunn Stage Road. Go 1.9 miles and continue 0.3 mile on well-maintained dirt road. Park at end of road in the staging area.

Habitat(s):

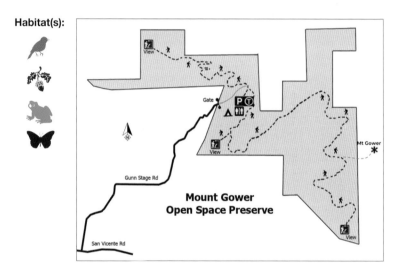

Mount Gower Open Space Preserve (1574 acres) has recovered nicely from the 2003 Cedar Fire and remains a pristine wilderness with a variety of habitats including oak woodlands with seasonal steams, isolated mountain meadows, and chaparral-covered hillsides. There is also the challenge of climbing to the summit of Mount Gower (3103') that can be an alternate to hiking to the southernmost viewpoint in the preserve. Mount Gower is actually east of the preserve in the Cleveland National Forest, but accessible from the preserve trail.

Note that the county map for this open space advertises 8 miles of trails within the preserve. However, the actual mileage on these hikes is much more. The map does not accurately reflect the distance to the southern viewpoint. Plan on a long hike of about 12 miles

round trip from your car to the southernmost viewpoint or shorten the hike by turning back after viewing the hoodoo rock formations on the granite slabs below Mount Gower.

From the information kiosk, follow the trail and at the junction head right or south. At 0.93 mile from the junction are two large boulders leaning against each other forming a teepee-like structure known as Teepee Rock. The short trail from Teepee Rock to the view point will add 0.5 mile to your hike. From this peaklet are views of San Vicente Valley and the San Diego Country Estates. From Teepee Rock, the trail dips into Swartz Canyon where coast live oak, willow, and western sycamore trees provide shade.

There is plenty of coyote (*Canis latrans*) scat visible along the trail. The coyote is om-

Coyote

Alice did the cooking, but their marriage is now on the rocks.

The fungus determines the lichen shape and houses the single celled alga within its mass. Lichens vary in appearance, and most belong in one of three groups. Crustose lichens are closely attached to a substrate such as tree bark, rocks, or soil, and appears crust-like. Foliose lichens have a leafy appearance. Fruiticose lichens can grow erect or are found hanging from trees. The fungus also protects the alga from harmful ultraviolet light. Lichens are extremely hardy and can be found in the harshest environments. However, they are very sensitive to sulfur dioxide pollution in the air and are good indicators of air quality. They are ecologically important as they are one of the first plants to appear after a glacier has receded or a landslide has exposed bare rock. They are able to grow on the bare rock where they secrete acids that help break down the rock, forming the soil that permits the growth of other plants.

Reach the top of Mount Gower either by climbing east across the granite slabs and scramble to the top of the southernmost ridge or continue following the trail for another 1.5 miles to the peak for another overview of San Diego Country Estates. Follow the trail back to the parking area.

nivorous and will eat whatever is available, which includes rodents, frogs, lizards, birds, fruit, or manzanita berries. Coyote scat gives an indication of the animal's last meal. Coyotes can live in any habitat. Other mammals that live in the preserve include the southern mule deer, northern raccoon, gray fox, and bobcat. Common birds include the common raven, California thrasher, western scrub-jay, lesser goldfinch, and red-tailed hawk.

The trail continues along the ridges and comes to the first of two meadows. Cross the meadow climbing up to a rock shelf to the upper meadow. The real attraction here is the unusual rock formations. Note the great variety of lichen and moss found on the rock slabs. Lichens (**phylum Ascomycota**) are organisms in which a mutualistic symbiotic association has evolved between a fungus that provides the organism's structure and a photosynthesizing partner, usually a green alga (*Trebouxia* **spp.**) or a cyanobacterium. The alga produces food that both organisms share. An easy way to remember this relationship is with this anecdote: Freddy Fungus took a liking to Alice Algae, and they got married. Freddy provided the housing and

Lichen on a rock

Distance:	6 miles, out-and-back
Difficulty:	🚶🚶🚶🚶🚶
Elevation gain/loss:	Up to 1000 feet
Hiking time:	4 hours
Agency:	USFS/CNF-PRD
Trail use:	Dogs not advised due to heat
Notes:	Permit required; no shade on trail
Trailhead GPS:	N32.99522, W116.75630
Optional map:	USGS 7.5-min *El Cajon Mtn*, *Tule Springs*
Atlas square:	L17
Directions:	(Ramona) From CA-67 in Ramona go east on 10th Street for 0.4 mile. Continue onto San Vicente Road for 6.4 miles. Turn left on Ramona Oaks Road. Go 2.9 miles. Turn right on Thornbush Road. Continue to the trailhead and park in the lot on right.

Habitat(s):

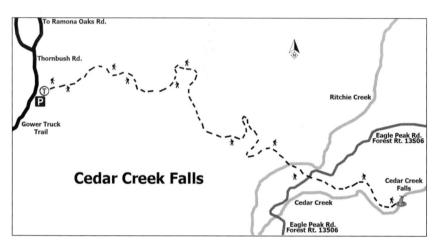

As anyone acquainted with San Diego County knows, free flowing water is a scarce commodity and a substantial waterfall is an even rarer occurrence. At almost 90 feet, Cedar Creek Falls in the Cleveland National Forest is one of the highest waterfalls in San Diego County and arguably the most visited and photographed. Heavy use of this area has led to a permit system to protect the area from overuse. Visitors must have proof of permit in their possession while in the permit area and must carry photo identification. Permits are available from the US Forest Service. Cedar Creek Falls is on Cedar Creek just before it enters the San Diego River and one of the segments included in the San Diego River Park.

Popular as a hike destination since the 1930s, Cedar Creek Falls has developed a reputation as one of the most spectacular waterfalls in San Diego County. While the beauty of the falls is without question, the difficulty of this 6-mile out-and-back hike is largely determined by the planning and preparation of the hiker. A multitude of signs at the start of the trail cautions hikers to carry at least one gallon of water per person, warns that the temperature at the canyon floor may be up to 15 degrees higher than at the trailhead, and strongly discourages bringing dogs due to the heat. While the trek down seems easy, the shadeless climb back in the heat of the day has caused many emergency rescues. Start early on this hike to beat rising temperatures.

There are two approaches to Cedar Creek Falls. For those willing to make an 8-mile drive over a County-maintained dirt road, access can be gained from Julian via Eagle Peak Road. There is limited parking at this trailhead. The primary route is via the Thornbush Trailhead from the Ramona side, which has an upgraded staging and parking area.

The falls in a low rainfall year

The trail itself is well maintained and clearly marked, making it easy to follow.

On the way to the falls, the descent is steady at a little over 1000 feet in the 2.5 miles to Cedar Creek. Look to the north on the descent to see a high sheer cliff where ephemeral Mildred Falls will appear immediately after a rainfall. Mildred Falls, at 100 feet, is one of the tallest waterfalls in the county. Other waterfalls are also in the area.

Watch for the aptly named catclaw acacia (*Senegalia greggii*) beside the trail. Another common name of this plant is wait-a-minute, referencing the fact that if caught in the shrub, one should slowly disentangle himself rather than hastily ripping away, which is often the cause of bloodied fingers, arms, and legs. At the bottom of the creek, cross the Eagle Peak Trail and enter the required permit area where a lone sign points towards the Cedar Creek Waterfall.

Water along the streambed allows for a variety of riparian trees, including coast live oaks, western cottonwoods, western sycamores, and willows. Their welcome shade provides relief on a warm day. Beyond the trees there is some boulder scrambling for 0.5 mile between the steep walls of the narrowing canyon. At the end of the canyon, forward progress is halted by the granitic rock face of Cedar Creek Falls. The pool is 50 feet across and as deep as 20 feet during the rainy season. While diving from surrounding rocks is not permitted and many have been injured doing it, the cool water makes for a refreshing plunge.

While enjoying the scenery, watch for side-blotched lizards sunning on the rocks and black phoebes displaying their elegant black and white tuxedo as they snap up insects over the pool. Have a good drink of the water you carried before starting your uphill return.

The trail to the falls

Distance:	2.5 or 5 miles if combined, out-and-back
Difficulty:	🚶 or 🚶🚶
Elevation gain/loss:	Up to 200 feet
Hiking time:	2 or 3 hours
Agency:	San Diego County
Trail use:	Bicycles, dogs, horses
Notes:	Hours posted 8 a.m. to sunset
Trailhead GPS:	N33.00076, W116.86448
Optional map:	USGS 7.5-min *Ramona*
Atlas square:	L15
Directions:	(Ramona) From CA-67 in Ramon ago east 10th Street for 0.4 mile. Continue onto San Vicente Road for 2.6 miles. Turn right onto Deviney Lane. Park in the staging area on the left.

Habitat(s):

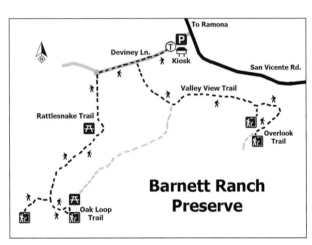

Wide open space abounds at Barnett Ranch, the 728-acre preserve that once was a cattle ranch owned by Augustus and Martha Barnett. Their adobe ranch house still stands today. This was a working ranch from the early 1800s until recently. The County purchased part of the property in 2002, and it is now part of its Multiple Species Conservation Program. The goal of this program is to maintain and enhance biological diversity in the region and maintain viable populations of endangered, threatened, and key sensitive species and their habitats. These habitats include oak woodland, coastal sage scrub, chaparral, and native grassland. There are also several small ponds that fill up after the rains adding interest to this hike. A variety of birds can be found here.

Be sure to listen for the melodious song of the western meadowlark (**Sturnella neglecta**). This robin-size bird with a dark V on its bright yellow chest is especially vulnerable to urbanization, as it requires wide open areas with low grass and few shrubs or trees. This bird was once common over much of San Diego County, but with low conservation value assigned to grasslands along with rapid development and fragmentation of these areas, relatively little habitat remains. As a ground-nesting and ground-foraging bird, it needs such open areas. Fortunately, the effect on the meadowlark of the proliferation of exotic plants in our grasslands appears to be rather slight.

There are plans to link the ranch to lands owned by the Nature Conservancy and Monte Vista Ranch to the south, which will create large trail loops. Further proposed connections will link these trails to Lakeside's proposed community trails, go along San Vicente Reservoir, and connect to Boulder Oaks and San Vicente Highlands trails. Ultimately, the system would connect to the Cuyamaca Mountains and the Anza-Borrego Desert. Each new county preserve open to the public is a step toward riding, hiking, and biking uninterrupted for miles.

A trail on the ranch

This hike is actually two separate hikes going in opposite directions that begin from the same point. At the staging area, head west on the trail next to the paved road, then at 0.2 mile there is a choice of turning left for the Valley View Trail or going straight to connect with the Rattlesnake Trail. If there is time only for one hike, the Rattlesnake Trail is the more scenic.

When turning left at the gate and onto the Valley View Trail, there will be a low wooden fence in 0.25 mile where the trail splits. Go left. The trail to the right is not an official trail. At a little over 1 mile and a slight elevation gain, there will be another fork, go left again. The right trail is a short 0.06 mile to a picnic table. The left fork gradually descends for about 0.3 mile to an overlook into the rural San Vicente Creek Valley and Stagecoach Road.

Reverse your trek and return to the paved road and either turn right to return to your vehicle or turn left and walk 0.1 mile to the start of the Rattlesnake Trail. This trail has gently rolling grasslands and stands of live oak. In the spring, the multitude of wildflowers is a delight. In 1 mile is the Oak Loop Trail for a 0.2 mile loop to a picnic table under an oak tree. This is a good place to stop for a snack or lunch and enjoy some birdwatching or perhaps catch sight of an early morning or evening coyote out hunting for its own meal. From here, reverse directions and return 1 mile to the paved road, from where it's 0.3 mile to the staging area.

Western meadowlark

Distance:	1 mile, loop
Difficulty:	🚶
Elevation gain/loss:	Minimal
Hiking time:	1 hour
Agency:	San Diego County
Trail use:	Dogs
Notes:	Hours posted 9:30 a.m. to sunset; day-use fee
Trailhead GPS:	N32.99914, W116.93927
Optional map:	USGS 7.5-min *San Vicente Reservoir*
Atlas square:	L13
Directions:	(Ramona) From CA-67 in Ramona go south on Mussey Grade Road for 1.1 miles. Turn right on Dos Picos Park Road. Go 0.6 mile. Parking lot is on the left.

Habitat(s):

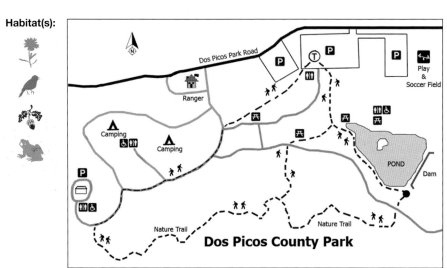

Dos Picos County Park

The Dos Picos Regional Park is a bit of a hidden treasure tucked in the heart of Ramona. The 78-acre park, named for two prominent mountains nearby, features a large, well-maintained picnic area, a campgrounds with good facilities nestled within shady oak woodlands and boulders, and a stream-fed pond. The nature trail is a special treat with beautiful views of the park and surrounding hills and an abundance of unusually large and healthy native plant species.

Animals seen here include the northern raccoon, Virginia opossum, gray fox, and striped skunk (*Mephitis mephitis*). The striped skunk is an omnivore whose main natural predators are birds of prey, especially the great horned owl. It has two scent glands on each side of its anus that each contain about a half-ounce of an oily sulfur-alcohol compound that it can spray up to several feet if threatened. Skunks

are polygamous. A male may have several females in a harem during the mating season.

There are two ways to enter the Ernie Pantoja Memorial Trail, named for an employee of the California Conservation Corps who lived in Ramona. The official trailhead is located between camping site Nos. 48 and 49 and is marked with a sign, a memorial plaque and a low brick wall backed by large, dramatic boulders. However, the other end of the trail is easier to access from the picnic area parking lot.

Starting from the map kiosk in the parking lot, walk to your left until you see a wooden bridge leading you into a shady area with oak trees and rocks. The bridge spans an intermittent stream that is usually dry part of the year. This leads past many picnic tables and a pond with ducks, grackles, great blue herons, great egrets, and other birds. Walk to your right, al-

Ramona-lilac

most to the southeast corner of the pond, and you will reach the back of the Ernie Pantoja Memorial Trail. This part of the path leads up the hill and is less shady, but the path is wide, terraced, and very well maintained, so it is not a difficult climb.

This path packs a large number of native plants into a short 1-mile trail. There are both coast live oak and Engelmann oak, with coast live oak predominant. Usually one finds a few scattered small plants of bush monkey flower or penstemon on hikes in the East County. Here, however, large stands of these plants make a surprising and beautiful display in the late spring. Many plants found along this trail show unusually large leaves and tall growth, suggesting a good amount of precipitation. The Ramona-lilac (*Ceanothus tomentosus*) in particular may be hard to recognize in an almost tree-like form. Look at the alternating oval, dark green leaves that are hairy on top and woolly underneath. The species name is related to the adjective tomentous that means covered with short matted, woolly hair. This is the reason for this plant also being called woollyleaf ceanothus. Look at the leaf margins and see the glandular structures found there that are characteristic of this species. Young stems are reddish and the inflorescence cluster can be white to deep blue. When in full bloom, the plant is stunning.

Look for the large ceanothus silk moth (*Hyalophora euryalus*) with an impressive 3- to 5-inch wingspan. The moth larvae, or caterpillars, can be found feeding on the Ramona-lilac. Also check the Ramona-lilac for possible moth cocoons that hang like teardrops from the leaves. The ceanothus silk moth has brown to reddish-brown wings with characteristic crescent-shaped slashes on its wings and an eye-spot on the corner of its upper wings. Members of the silk moth family Saturniidae are among the largest and most spectacular moths in the world. The ceanothus silk moth is the largest on the Pacific coast. This moth also will use manzanita, San Diego mountain-mahogany, and laurel sumac as host plants.

Beware of western poison-oak found here. It grows vigorously and can be beautiful when the leaves are mixed red and green. Other plants to look for include black mustard (non-native) with yellow flowers, blue elderberry, yellow-flowered chamise, holly-leaf redberry, and mountain-mahogany with its feathery seeds. A surprising find is the mission manzanita. It has a limited range and is usually found closer to the coast where it is a common component of coastal sage scrub habitat.

There is a good view of Mount Woodson about halfway through the trail, and the intermittent shade makes the hike suitable for anytime of year. If you are interested in camping or in reserving portions of the large picnic areas, contact the park directly for reservations and fee information.

On the trail

Distance:	5.8 miles, loop
Difficulty:	🏃🏃🏃🏃
Elevation gain/loss:	Up to 1600 feet
Hiking time:	4 or 6 hours
Agency:	City of Poway
Trail use:	Bicycles, dogs
Trailhead GPS:	N32.98768, W116.97694
Optional map:	USGS 7.5-min *San Vicente Reservoir*
Atlas square:	M13
Directions:	(Poway) From CA-67 turn east on Ellie Lane, 0.7 mile north of Poway Road and the main Iron Mountain Trailhead. Parking lot is on the right.

Habitat(s):

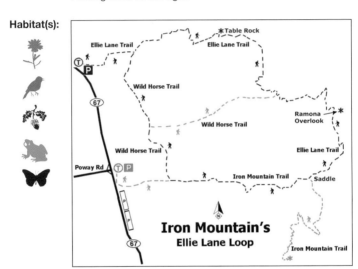

If you want to take a hike on Iron Mountain and find the trailhead parking lot looking like Qualcomm Stadium on a day when the Chargers played the Raiders at home, and the trail is churning like a sea of people, don't lose heart. There is a nearby alternative—the Ellie Lane Trail. It offers a loop hike with almost the same challenges and scenery as the 5.5 miles out-and-back hike up Iron Mountain from the CA-67/Poway Road trailhead. The Ellie Lane parking lot and most of the route is less crowded. From the parking lot a pastoral vista awaits you, often containing grazing sheep in a large grassy field.

In the first mile the trail goes up a hillside littered with huge weathered granite boulders that will remind you of Mount Woodson, which you can see looming up to the north. These boulders were not transported here, but were formed in place by chemical weathering, a process in which groundwater reacts with the

minerals in the rock causing it to decompose, a process that takes many thousands of years. Surface erosion then strips off the rotten rock, leaving the more resistant cores as boulders. The eroded material is mainly quartz, which the streams will carry to our beaches as sand. Iron Mountain itself is composed of granodiorite containing reddish deposits of iron, which may be the reason the mountain was named this. An old iron mine is found on the south side of the peak.

As you near the top of the ridge, at mile 1.1, there is a feature known as Table Rock, which not too surprisingly, looks like a stone table. This is a good place to rest for a while as you take in the excellent view west to the ocean on a clear day.

From Table Rock, follow the signed Ellie Lane Trail east and south for about another mile. Although the trail is reasonably well marked and maintained, some of the signs have

Passing huge boulders

disappeared. This is not usually a problem except at the unmarked junction of the Ellie Lane Trail and an extension of the Wild Horse Trail, about 2 miles from the staging area. If you go right, down the canyon, on the Wild Horse Trail extension, you will come to a T of the main Wild Horse Trail. Taking a right there will lead back to the Ellie Lane staging area, having hiked a shorter loop of about 3.5 miles. Instead, go left, staying on the Ellie Lane Trail. Go uphill via a series of switchbacks to the Ramona Overlook. A 0.1 mile side trail will bring you to a viewpoint with vistas of Ramona to the east.

Return to the Ellie Lane Trail as it descends an east-facing slope and ends at 3.6 miles from the Ellie Lane staging area. Here you connect with the Iron Mountain Trail coming up from the Iron Mountain staging area. This trail junction is known as the Saddle and sits 600 feet lower than the top of Iron Mountain (2696'). On a clear day enjoy the ocean views to the west.

At this point you could hike up to Iron Mountain, which is slightly less than 1.5 miles away, adding nearly 3 miles to your hike. Instead, go about 1 mile down the Iron Mountain Trail, toward the CA-67/Poway Road staging area and turn right or north on Wild Horse Trail, which leads back to the Ellie Lane staging area and your vehicle. As you will discover, this is a branch of the Wild Horse Trail. On your right as you head toward the Ellie Lane Trailhead, you will pass an ephemeral pond. If it has water, look for ducks and American coots.

While taking this hike, look for chaparral bushmallow (*Malacothamnus fasciculatus*), a pink/lavender-flowered shrub in the mallow family that is common on dry slopes in chaparral and coast sage scrub habitats. It is an evergreen that stands up to 15 feet, usually blooms from April to October, and has multibranched stems and leaves that are coated with white or brownish star-shaped hairs. The flowers have five cup-shaped petals that are about 1 inch in diameter, and they attract butterflies. It is the larval food for the northern white skipper (*Heliopetes ericetorum*), a predominately white butterfly with brown markings on the wing tips.

Chaparral bushmallow

Northern white skipper

Distance:	2 miles, loop
Difficulty:	🚶🚶
Elevation gain/loss:	Up to 1000 feet
Hiking time:	2 hours
Agency:	SD Audubon
Notes:	Hours posted Sundays only 9 a.m. to 4 p.m.
Trailhead GPS:	N32.91936, W116.88130
Optional map:	USGS 7.5-min *San Vicente Reservoir*
Atlas square:	N14
Directions:	(Lakeside) From CA-67 turn east on Willow Road for 0.9 mile. Turn left on Wildcat Canyon Road. Go 3.8 miles. Turn right on Cienga Trail and Silverwood Wildlife Sanctuary. Parking lot is on the left.

Habitat(s):

There is something for every nature lover and even those who only want to get a bit of exercise at Silverwood Wildlife Sanctuary. With a network of nearly 5 miles of trails, there are both easy walking paths through shady oak woodlands and more extensive paths through the chaparral where there are many wild-flowers that bloom here in late winter and spring. Hiking up to the ridgeline provides outstanding views of the surrounding mountains and out to the ocean. It is also a great place to learn about birds at the Sanctuary's Observation Area and Nature Center, which is to be expected since the sanctuary is owned and operated by the San Diego Audubon Society. Tours are available on Sunday, when you also are free to explore on your own.

From the parking area, start hiking southeast on the Harry Woodward Trail, named for the man who gave 85 of these acres as a gift to the Audubon Society to start Silverwood. This is an easy self-guided trip through chaparral with many shrubs identified with signs. Currently this area is dominated by chaparral whitethorn (*Ceanothus leucodermis*), a tall lilac or *Ceanothus* species that forms dense, almost impenetrable thickets after a fire, a reminder that Silverwood was completely destroyed in the 2003 Cedar Fire. This species has an extensive root system that helps stabilize the soil and prevent erosion. The roots usually develop nodules containing the nitrogen-fixing bacterium Frankia, which adds this essential plant nutrient to the soil. It also produces a

Bird observation area

prodigious amount of seeds whose germinations are stimulated by fire. This and the fact that it can readily sprout from a basal burl accounts for the fact that the habitat here and in other burned areas can make a rapid recovery after a fire.

Turn right at the Chaparral Trail to continue the self-guided tour where more chaparral shrubs are identified with signs. Up ahead, across a bridge over an intermittent creek, is the bird observation area, a place to get acquainted with some of the more than 100 species of birds that visit or live in the sanctuary. After exploring the bird observation area, return to the Chaparral Trail and continue east to the Spring Trail. Go right on the trail where it will soon cross an open grassy area with very few chaparral shrubs. In a normal rainfall year, this will be a marsh, or cienaga. At the marsh, listen for sounds of grasshoppers (**family Acrididae**) and other insects. Grasshoppers make their characteristic sound through stridulation, or the act of rubbing their hind leg against their forewing. Grasshoppers can also produce sound by snapping their wings as they fly. A common species seen in the county is the very large gray bird grasshopper (*Schistocerca nitens*).

Continuing on beyond the cienaga, the Spring Trail intersects with the Circuit Trail. Go left on the Circuit Trail, which continues up to the backbone of the ridge and crosses

the Big Rock Slab, a large granite outcropping nearly devoid of plants, except for mosses and lichens. Silver-leaf lotus and a few dudleyas grow in the cracks. The Circuit Trail loops around the sanctuary, eventually returning to the entrance. As it does so, it will intersect with six other trails that could be explored if time permits. One highly recommended for outstanding views is the Howie Wier-Rady's View Trail up to the sanctuary's high point at 2100 feet. There is also a self-guiding Geology Trail that is compelling and informative.

Chaparral whitethorn

Distance:	3.4 miles, loop
Difficulty:	🚶🚶
Elevation gain/loss:	Up to 700 feet
Hiking time:	2 hours
Agency:	San Diego County
Trail use:	Dogs, horses
Notes:	Hours posted 7 a.m. to sunset
Trailhead GPS:	N32.91267, W116.88723
Optional map:	USGS 7.5-min *San Vicente Reservoir*
Atlas square:	N14
Directions:	(Lakeside) From CA-67 turn east on Willow Road for 0.9 mile. Turn left on Wildcat Canyon Road. Go 3.3 miles. Turn left into the entrance for Oakoasis Preserve, immediately opposite Blue Sky Ranch Road and the El Capital Preserve. Go 0.1 mile on paved road to parking lot.

Habitat(s):

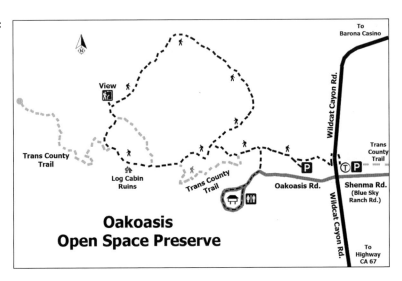

The 397 acres of chaparral and oak woodlands that are included in this preserve were gifted to the County by the Margaret Minshall family in the 1980s. Minshall was a Hoover High School physical education teacher who built a cabin on her property in 1936 and later, during the 1940s, operated a summer camp there for girls. Almost 95% of the preserve was consumed in the 2003 Cedar Fire, including the original Minshall cabin. Today, the preserve is nicely recovering with young chaparral vegetation.

Oakoasis has boulder-studded hillsides, acres of woods, multi-use trails, and sweeping views of the surrounding area and San Vicente Reservoir. Part of the preserve trail system is included in the 110-mile Trans-County Trail (TCT) that is being developed between Torrey

Pines State Natural Reserve and Anza-Borrego Desert State Park. Over 70% of the TCT will utilize existing trails found within parks and preserves in the county. The Oakoasis parking area will be one of the staging areas for this trail when it officially opens some years from now.

The double loop-trail starts from the parking lot and is a large clockwise loop followed by a smaller counter-clockwise loop. Begin the hike by descending on the TCT towards the west. Follow signs marked trail and not TCT, as the loop will depart from the TCT, which will continue to the west. The trail marked TCT will be the return trail.

Take all right turns at trail junctions until arriving at a T in the trail at an old dirt road near the bottom of an oak-lined ravine. Turn left, and go through the shady oak grove, passing

Grasslands and chaparral

what is left of the Minshall cabin at 0.7 mile from the trailhead. After passing the cabin ruins, there will be a sign for the Upper Meadow Trail to the right. Go to the right or north, following the Upper Meadow Trail signs, where the first site of San Vicente Reservoir will be visible to the west. Take a short side trail to the west to the scenic overlook, where there are good views of San Vicente Reservoir some 800 feet below. Return to the main trail and turn left for the steepest part of this hike, up and over a 1480-foot saddle. Note how different the habitat is here from the riparian woodland below.

Pass an upper grassy meadow where there is a sign indicating halfway and continue circling right until finally descending again to the oak oasis ravine. In the grassy meadow, look for native forbs and a variety of insects. You may see grasshoppers flying around, and perhaps ants and other ground dwelling species if you kneel and explore a small portion of the area at a different height. There is the option of retracing steps from here to the trailhead, and saving about 0.5 mile on the hike, but if doing this, some of the more scenic areas of the preserve will be missed.

To continue, go through the oak oasis again about 300 yards until seeing a trail to the left marked TCT. Follow it as it loops counter-clockwise around the wooded area. Note the riparian vegetation that includes coast live oak,

toyon, skunkbrush or basket bush, bush monkey flower, horehound, and watch out for western poison-oak. On the oak, look for evidence of galls, which are made when tiny wasps oviposit into plants and cause the plant to produce a small, ball like structure around the eggs. At the junction with the main trail, turn right and retrace your steps back to the trailhead.

The trail

Distance:	11 miles, out-and-back
Difficulty:	🚶🚶🚶🚶🚶
Elevation gain/loss:	Up to 2100 feet
Hiking time:	7 hours
Agency:	San Diego County
Trail use:	Bicycles, dogs, horses
Notes:	Hours posted 7 a.m. to sunset; closed in August because of extreme heat.
Trailhead GPS:	N32.91167, W116.87766
Optional map:	USGS 7.5-min *San Vicente Reservoir*
Atlas square:	N14
Directions:	(Lakeside) From CA-67 turn east on Willow Road for 0.9 mile. Turn left on Wildcat Canyon Road. Go 3.3 miles. Turn right on Blue Sky Ranch Road. Parking lot is on the left.

Habitat(s):

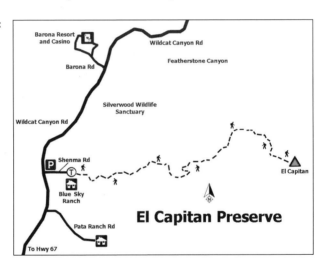

Standing sentinel above the community of Lakeside is the imposing, boulder-strewn peak of El Capitan (3648'). Most locals recognize the mountain and its surrounding preserve by this name, which was inspired by its resemblance to the famous rock face in the Yosemite Valley. Whether it is called El Capitan or by its official title of El Cajon Mountain, the journey to its summit will leave hikers breathless from both wonder and exhaustion. Referred to lovingly by many writers as the hike that goes "uphill both ways," El Capitan Preserve is one of San Diego County's most physically challenging and rewarding, offering views from mountains to ocean and bragging rights to those who summit its noble, granite peak. It is also a testament to the powers of uplift, weathering, and time.

The main attraction of the El Capitan Preserve is the trail to El Cajon Mountain's peak. Making it to the top not only feels like a great physical feat, but on clear days one can see from the Cuyamaca Mountains to the Coronado Islands. The sheer length of the trail, along with its constant changes in elevation and occasional dips into valleys, ensures that travelers will enjoy a wide variety of habitats—from chaparral to oak woodlands and riparian stands. Chamise, scrub oak, and deep cyan-blue Lakeside-lilac (*Ceanothus cyaneus*) dominate the landscape, complemented in the spring by bursts of red, yellow, and violet from canyon larkspur, heart-leafed penstemon, mariposa lilies, fragrant or Cleveland sage, and blue-eyed-grass.

Lakeside-lilac is a large shrub, up to 15 feet tall when mature, with bright green leaves and plumes of dark blue flowers in the spring. The flowers bloom two to three months later than the other *Ceanothus* species. Another distinguishing feature is the deep blue color of the small flowers that are clustered on the stems,

Lakeside-lilac

Common side-blotched lizard and El Capitan

the trailhead. Just beyond the restrooms, be certain to follow the trail to the left up a zig-zag of switchbacks. The remainder of the trail provides obvious signage, and paths are well maintained, although sometimes very slippery due to erosion. Despite this, precaution must be taken if bringing along a bike or animal because of how rutted, rocky, and steep the road can become; pets can easily overheat.

Should El Capitan's challenge be met, hikers will enjoy its place in history both distant and recent. They will travel the greatest length of their journey along a wide and abandoned mining road. The rusted shell of a Jeep, free of tires and occasionally housing an active bee hive, remains as a relic of the preserve's dance with industry.

Now that El Cajon Mountain is enjoying the protected status of a preserve, plans for the 110-mile Trans-County Trail, from Borrego Springs to Torrey Pines State Natural Reserve, continue to move forward utilizing many existing trails that include those running down the length of El Cajon Mountain, across Wildcat Canyon Road, and into neighboring Oakoasis Preserve.

Because the trail is largely shade free, bring at least two liters of water per person and remain aware of your surroundings, as this is mountain lion territory.

Granitic rock at summit

with many stems on branches that appear so thick from a distance that the branches and leaves are almost not visible. Insects that visit the blooms include bees, beetles, flies, bugs, butterflies, and moths. It is near endemic to San Diego County with a few from northern Baja California, Mexico. Its fruit is a capsule that explodes with a loud pop when ripe, scattering its seeds far from the mother plant.

The official trailhead begins 0.5 mile from the parking area up Blue Sky Ranch Road. Mile markers consider this the start of a hiker's journey, so be sure to add 1 mile total for the very steep ascent to and from the lot to

Distance:	3 miles, out-and-back
Difficulty:	🚶🚶 or 🚶🚶🚶 if reaching the peak
Elevation gain/loss:	Up to 600 feet
Hiking time:	2 hours
Agency:	San Diego County
Trail use:	Bicycles on designated trail, dogs
Notes:	Hours posted 9 a.m. to sunset; ADA compliant; day-use fee
Trailhead GPS:	N32.88287, W116.89689
Optional map:	USGS 7.5-min *San Vicente Reservoir*
Atlas square:	O14
Directions:	(Lakeside) From CA-67 turn east on Willow Road for 0.9 mile. Turn left on Wildcat Canyon Road. Go 1 mile. Turn right into entrance for Louis A. Stelzer County Park. Take care in exiting the park due to heavy traffic in both directions on Wildcat Canyon Road.

Habitat(s):

The varied topography and ecosystems of Louis A. Stelzer County Park make this 420-acre reserve a delight to visit. It is situated along Wildcat Canyon Creek and includes the rocky hillsides, ridgeline, and a peak with 360-degree views of the surrounding area. The topography also includes a series of small meadows. A narrow granite-lined passage follows the creek bed where gabbro is the dominate rock. Plant communities found in the park include coastal sage scrub, chaparral, and oak riparian woodland.

This park provides a good example of fire recovery. In October 2003, the Cedar Fire raged, burning 15% of San Diego County and charring 273,246 acres. Over 15,000 acres of county parklands burned, including 95% of Stelzer County Park. Many of the oaks in the park survived, as they are adapted to fire, with thick bark that does not readily burn.

The hike begins at the entrance gate following the Riparian Trail. The first interpretive panel warns hikers to be on the lookout for western poison-oak and has illustrations showing what it looks like. The trail is shaded by a variety of trees including coast live oaks, western sycamore, and western cottonwoods. The oaks are festooned with wild grape.

A series of small wooden bridges crosses the creek. Note the colorful lichens adhering to the blocks of gabbro found on the trail. The trail abruptly turns to the left as the Wooten Loop begins and climbs up the hillside into the chaparral and surrounding meadows. At the junction with the Stelzer Trail, hikers have the choice of either cutting their hike short

Shaded riparian trail

by turning to the left and heading 0.3 mile to the campground area or going to the right 0.24 mile up a zigzag trail to meet the Summit Trail. At the top of the Summit Trail there are two options. Follow the service road to the left 0.4 mile to the top of Stelzer Summit, the highest point in the park at 1179 feet. The climb is very steep, and the view is worth the effort. The service road to the right leads to Kumeyaay Promontory, which is covered with power-line towers. Retrace steps back to the junction with the Stelzer Trail and follow it to the campground. Cross the campground area to return to the trailhead.

One of the harmless snakes that you might see in this park is the rosy boa (*Lichanura trivirgata*) that can grow to a maximum length of a little more than 3 feet. This docile, slow-moving snake, which can come in many colors, is usually the preferred snake sold in pet shops. It is also not prone to bite. The species name refers to the three stripes found on the length of their body—one on top and one on each side. The color of the snake and its stripes will vary with stripes on some individuals being barely visible but still there and an identifier for this species. Stripe colors can be rose, maroon, orange, rust gray, bluish-gray, brown, or black. The name rosy refers to a pink coloration on the ventral side of some individuals. Rosy boas are constrictors that hunt for small mammals. Because they are slow, they lay in ambush waiting for prey and then quickly bite and hold

them with sharp teeth. They coil around the prey's body and squeeze, leading to circulatory arrest. Rosy boas usually hide in rocks and crevices and prefer habitats near water.

Louis Alexander Stelzer purchased the property as a private retreat in the 1940s calling it Shadow Mountain Ranch. Upon his death in 1972, he deeded the land to the County so that children would have a place for outdoor education and recreational opportunities. The park is named in his honor and was dedicated in 1982. It became the first recreational facility in southern California designed to accommodate visitors of all abilities. Interpretive panels are found on the trails. There is also a large camping area reserved for the use of sanctioned youth groups.

Rosy boa

Distance:	2 to 8 miles, out-and-back depending on options
Difficulty:	🏃🏃 to 🏃🏃🏃🏃
Elevation gain/loss:	Up to 1200 feet
Hiking time:	1 to 5 hours
Agency:	San Diego County
Trail use:	Bicycles, dogs, horses
Notes:	Open daily from 9:30 a.m. to sunset; day-use fee
Trailhead GPS:	N32.88879, W116.85004
Optional map:	USGS 7.5-min *El Cajon Mtn*
Atlas square:	O15
Directions:	(Lakeside) From I-8 go north on Lake Jennings Park Road for 1.8 miles. Turn right on El Monte Road. Go 3.8 miles to the park entrance. From CA-67 go east on Mapleview Street for 0.8 mile. Continue onto Lake Jennings Park Road. Go 0.6 mile. Turn left onto El Monte Road. Go 3.8 miles to park entrance. Alternatively, there may also be free parking across the street in the equestrian staging area.

Habitat(s):

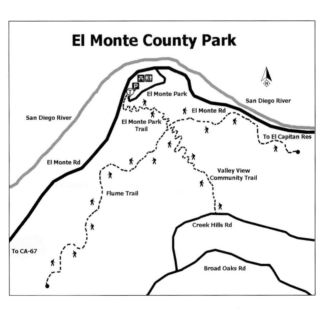

The 88-acre El Monte County Park was one of the first areas set aside for a park in the county but it was not until February 2011 that an official trail was opened to the public in El Monte Valley. The County Park is opened for day-use only. On the north side of El Monte Road, the rocky face of El Cajon Mountain glistens over a pastoral scene of green grass, coast live oaks, and picnic areas. There may be sightings of heron, wild turkeys, and southern mule deer that come in to feed on the grass. Soak in the view before heading out on the trail.

Many have mistakenly identified the trail beginning in El Monte County Park as the Flume Trail. It is actually the El Monte Park Trail that climbs the ridge to meet the Flume Trail, which crosses it. The El Monte Park Trail ends where it meets the Flume Trail on the ridge. The route after crossing the Flume Trail is called the Valley View Community Trail, which begins at the Flume Trail crossing and ends at Creek Hills Road in Blossom Valley. The El Monte County Park portion of the Flume Trail follows the ridge east for 1 mile and west for 1.5 miles where it ends at a fence and private property begins.

The trails are subtly marked with the El Monte Park/Blossom Valley Trailhead at the

View of El Cajon Mountain

edge of a fence near picnic area No. 8, at the far side of the park. The first 0.6 mile of the narrow trail has an initial climb of about 1100 feet, and then descends to a trail intersection. On the way down, look to the left of the trail where there is a flume grade, a historic feature of the trail. Hidden between the two hillsides is an old tunnel that is a remnant of a flume installed by the San Diego Flume Company in 1889. The San Diego Flume ran from Boulder Creek down the south side of the San Diego River to the La Mesa Reservoir. The tunnel is closed, but it invites a look through to the other end via openings that a camera lens can fit. Today, El Monte County Park is one of several parks and open spaces along the San Diego River that are included in the San Diego River Park.

San Diego flume tunnel

Pamela Weinisch

Zig-zag switchbacks on the trail

At the trail intersection, the options include returning directly to the starting point or continuing to ascend south on the Valley View Community trail for another 1200 feet before descending to Creek Hills Road in Blossom Valley. This combination will give the best workout over the many steep switchbacks that look like they were carved into the mountainside. The top of the ridge offers panoramic views of homes, ranches, and orchards in the valley below. Earlier in history, this valley was a homeland for bands of the Kumeyaay Indian nation.

Another hike option is to go west on the Flume Trail, a wide, somewhat level trail running both east and west. Going west, the trail leads about 1.5 miles towards Lake Jennings where there is interpretive information about the San Diego Flume. Look off to the western side of the trail to see large animal-like rock formations. The last hike option is to go east for 1 mile. Return to the trail intersection to finish the hike and descend north to the parking area where a rest under the trees is well earned.

Many native coast sage scrub species are clustered along the north-facing cliff of the Flume Trail. Unfortunately, the invasive non-native black mustard (**Brassica nigra**) is the predom-

inant plant in the area. One of the reasons for its prevalence is that it was used to seed burned areas to prevent subsequent soil erosion. It no longer is used for this purpose as it is too invasive. Some of the additional invasive plants intermixed with the native plants include saltcedar (tamarisk), castor bean, and tree tobacco.

Possible wildlife sightings include a coyote that may run across the trail and up into the hills, or lizards and birds that pop in and out of the chaparral. Easier to see are American crows and hummingbirds that do not bother to hide from hikers. What you can count on seeing are various holes and burrows belonging to a variety of small mammals. You can be assured that some of them belong to Botta's pocket gopher (*Thomomys bottae*). This medium-sized pocket gopher inhabits a wide range of habitats. It is an herbivore that eats a variety of plant material including roots, tubers, and bulbs. The gopher can eat in safety by excavating a tunnel under a plant, then pulling down the entire plant by its roots to eat. In the process of excavating, the gopher aerates the soil, sometimes up to a depth of 8 inches. In urban and agricultural areas, gophers are considered a pest because of their burrowing and garden consuming habits. Botta's pocket gopher can dig in a wide variety of soils because it digs primarily with its strong, large teeth rather than its claws. Gophers that dig primarily with their claws are limited to digging in softer soils. Major predators include badgers, coyotes, weasels, and snakes—carnivores that can easily dig into or crawl into the burrows.

Jon Rebman

Black mustard

Distance:	5.5 miles possible, loop and out-and-back
Difficulty:	🚶🚶 or 🚶🚶🚶, depending on length
Elevation gain/loss:	Minimal
Hiking time:	2 to 4 hours
Agency:	HWD
Trail use:	Bicycles
Notes:	Day-use fee; open Friday-Sunday for recreational use and daily for campers.
Trailhead GPS:	N32.85328, W116.88568
Optional map:	USGS 7.5-min *El Cajon*
Atlas square:	P14
Directions:	(Lakeside) From I-8 go north on Lake Jennings Park Road for 0.3 mile. Turn right on Harritt Road. Go 0.3 mile. Turn right at sign to Lake Jennings recreation area picnic/fishing entrance and park. From CA-67 go east on Mapleview Street for 0.8 mile. Continue onto Lake Jennings Park Road. Go 2.1 miles. Turn left on Harritt Road. Go 0.3 mile. Turn right at sign to Lake Jennings recreation area picnic/fishing entrance and park.

Habitat(s):

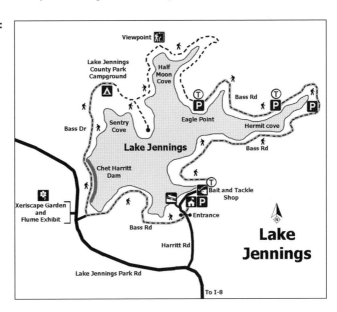

Lake Jennings is a man-made 9800-acre-foot capacity reservoir owned by the Helix Water District. In 1962 the Helix Irrigation District built Chet Harritt Dam, which forms the reservoir, storing water that is treated and used by more than 260,000 people in the San Diego region today. The lake is named for Bill Jennings who served on the California Water Commission and was legal counsel for the district. Harritt was the district's first manager. The water district operates the recreational facilities at the lake that include fishing, camping, picnicking, boating, and hiking activities.

The hike begins from any point you choose. A nice stroll around the lake starting from the bait shop and hugging the shore is a great way to watch for waterfowl. This 5.5-mile route includes the paved road and a dirt trail. Another starting point is to drive to the end parking area by Eagle Point and take the dirt road northwest about 1.5 miles that eventually goes through the camping area. Halfway along this trail overlooking Half Moon Cove is a low ridge and saddle to the north. Climb the ridge for a view of the lake and El Cajon Mountain in the distance. From the camping area, continue on the road

View of the lake

back down to the bait shop and around the rest of the lake to where you parked or turn around on the dirt trail to complete a 3-mile out-and-back hike.

The area around the lake was once part of the 48,800-acre Mexican land grant known as Rancho El Cajon. The terrain that surrounds the lake is a nice mix of coastal sage scrub, native chaparral, and riparian plants.

Keep an eye out for any birds, including the American white pelican (*Pelecanus erythrorhynchos*). Preferring fresh water, this species breeds inland in lakes of the Great Basin and Great Plains but visits the San Diego area only in winter. The American white pelican is among the largest of North American birds with a wingspan of up to 9 feet. It is a magnificent sight in flight with its outstretched black-edged white wings. Unlike the brown pelican, the white pelican does not dive for food, but scoops up fish while swimming with its large bill. White pelicans often feed in groups, cornering a school of fish, then scooping them up in unison.

Many butterflies can be found here. One of the most commonly encountered butterfly is the painted lady (*Vanessa cardui*). It can be found on every continent except Antarctica. Although individuals only live for 3-4 weeks they can mate 5-7 days after emerging from their cocoons and up to eight times in their short lives. They occasionally undertake mass migrations and may go through several generations during these migrations.

The trail offers no real shade, so it is best to hike in the early mornings before the heat of the day sets in or to keep close to the shore where there are more trees. Enjoy a nice picnic while taking in the splendid scenery. If there is time, stop by the water treatment facility on Lake Jennings Park Road south of the campground. A xeriscape garden is found there demonstrating plants that can best survive in a dry climate with little water. Across from the garden is a display of part of the old redwood flume that once carried water from the Cuyamaca Mountains to San Diego. The 25-mile flume officially opened in 1889 and was officially retired in November 1937 after El Capitan Dam and Reservoir were completed in 1935.

Painted lady

American white pelican

Distance:	3 miles, out-and-back
Difficulty:	𝑿𝑿𝑿
Elevation gain/loss:	Up to 1500 feet
Hiking time:	3 hours
Agency:	USFS/CNF-DRD
Trail use:	Dogs
Trailhead GPS:	N32.85664, W116.74212
Optional map:	USGS 7.5-min *Viejas Mountain*
Atlas square:	P17
Directions:	(Alpine) From I-8 go north on Tavern Road and onto Victoria Park Terrace. Go 0.9 mile. Turn left on West Victoria Drive. Go 1.5 miles. Turn left on Anderson Road. Go 0.4 mile. Pass water towers on right where Anderson Road veers to the left onto Boundary Truck Trail West. Go 0.3 mile on dirt road and park. Trailhead on right through a break in the Fence with a small brown "hiker" sticker on a post.

Habitat(s):

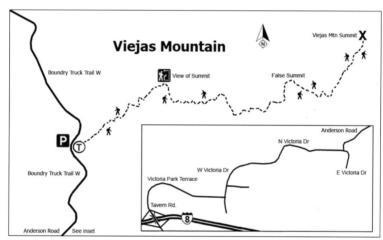

Viejas Mountain (4187') near Alpine rises steeply. It is sacred to the Kumeyaay Indians who made a pilgrimage to its summit to hold ceremonies at sunrise on the winter solstice. In the 1970s hikers constructed a windbreak of rocks they found on the peak. Unfortunately the rocks they used were those placed there by the Kumeyaay, which had pointed to Buckman Peak (4641'), 16 miles to the southeast, the precise place where the sun would rise on the winter solstice.

Flowers abound in the spring, including chaparral candle and *Ceanothus*, with hummingbirds and swallowtail butterflies flitting around. On the lower slopes, look for the Hermes copper butterfly (*Lycaena hermes*), a small rare butterfly endemic to San Diego County and northern Baja California, Mexico. Although not officially listed as endangered, it is rare and threatened by loss of

suitable habitat and wildfires. Only about 15 colonies are now known to exist. Many were lost in the 2003 Cedar Fire. This species is totally dependent on the spiny redberry (*Rhamnus crocea*) for its existence, found in coastal sage scrub and chaparral communities. The female lays her eggs on the branches of this relatively uncommon chaparral shrub. After overwintering, larvae emerge and feed on the plant for 10 to 14 days before undergoing metamorphosis. Adults emerge and will be present from mid-May to mid-July when they feed on the nectar of buckwheat flowers. The upper forewings are brown and yellow with brown spots, while the undersides are yellow with brown spots.

The 2003 Cedar Fire burned the vegetation here. More than 10 years have passed since the fire, and these hills are green again. Scrub oak, felt-leafed yerba santa, chamise,

Annie Hoppe

Boulders at the summit

and manzanita blanket the mountain. Are the Hermes copper butterflies back? You will have to find out.

Starting at 2700 feet, the trail begins with a gentle slope and then starts to climb relentlessly at an average grade of 20%. Stop and look at the amazing views of San Diego County's valleys and mountains as you climb. El Cajon Mountain in its vast granite glory is behind you. As 3000 feet is reached, Palomar and San Jacinto mountains come into view with San Gorgonio Mountain visible at 3300 feet. The views just keep getting better as you climb.

At 3840 feet you can take a climbing break with an inviting flat stretch of the trail. This is a good place to look for El Capitan Reservoir, name the peaks that are visible, or find the Coronado Islands or even the Rosarito plateau in Baja California, Mexico! When you reach the saddle at 4100 feet, Cuyamaca Peak, the second highest mountain in San Diego County, comes into view along with the desert peaks to the east and the Viejas Casino at your feet. From the saddle, reaching the summit is a short walk north with 80 feet of vertical gain. If a Santa Ana wind is blowing, it may get windy but the visibility is best. At the 4187-foot summit, there is a rock wind shelter with a boulder in the center. Sit and enjoy the beauty of the granitic peaks of San Diego County before returning on the same trail.

The hike is enjoyable all year long, but it can be very hot in the summer months, so start early. Look back along the trail climbing to the summit and know your comfort level for the return, as the descent is on those same loose rocks, washouts, and slick areas. The chance of having the mountain to yourself is very high, as this is a trail less traveled. If the hike is started in the cooler part of the evening, let a friend know what time you plan to return and bring strong headlamps to use on the trail as it is pitch black when the sun sets if the moon is not up.

Jim Varnell

Spiny redberry

Bill Howell

Hermes copper butterfly

Distance:	2.8 miles, out-and-back
Difficulty:	🚶🚶
Elevation gain/loss:	up to 800 feet
Hiking time:	2 hours
Agency:	San Diego County
Trail use:	Dogs
Notes:	Open from dawn to dusk
Trailhead GPS:	N32.84218, W116.91528
Optional map:	USGS 7.5-min *El Cajon*
Atlas square:	P14
Directions:	(Lakeside) From I-8 go north on Los Coches Road for 1.4 miles. Park on street, just past Ha Hana Road and just before Los Coches Court. The trailhead is on the right. From CA-67 go east on Mapleview Street and make an immediate right turn onto Maine Avenue. Go 0.5 mile. Continue onto Los Coches Road. Go 1.1 miles. Park on the street, just past Los Coches Court and just before Ha Hana Road. The trailhead is on the left.

Habitat(s):

Nationally known master architect Mary Jane Coulter (1869-1958), who designed and constructed buildings for the Harvey House in Grand Canyon National Park, inspired the design of the hilltop house that was later donated to the County in 1992, so "that it never be broken or cut up, but it be recognized as God's Hill" for all to enjoy. Hale and Mildred Whitaker built their house in what is known as National Park Service rustic style. The Whitakers built the stone house over a five-year period from 1935-1940 using stones found locally on the property. Hale Whitaker broke the rocks into building blocks with a sledgehammer.

The house is surrounded by trees and shrubs planted by Mildred Whitaker.

When the Whitakers donated their 7.5-acre hilltop and 1500-square foot stone home to the County it created a problem. The only road to the property was a single-track steeply paved road to the top that was unsafe to open to the public. For years, the property languished until 2008 when the County designated it as an historic site allowing improvements and then designating adjoining open space areas as a preserve under the Multiple Species Conservation Program. The Lakeside Linkage Open Space Preserve is 100 acres in size and has a

Diana Lindsay

View of Lindo Lake

trail that now links to the historic site, making it available to hikers.

The preserve is a good example of the endangered coastal sage scrub habitat native to the coastal and inland hillsides of southern California. Up to 85% of this habitat has been lost to development. Sensitive species in this habitat include the coastal cactus wren and the orange-throated whiptail lizard (*Aspidoscelis hyperythra*). The orange-throated whiptail lizard is still fairly common where coastal sage scrub exists, ranging from southern California to northern Baja California. However, the population is declining along with the habitat. This lizard is brown, gray, or black with five or six whitish-stripes down its back and sides and an orange-colored throat and belly. It has a long tail, and the tail of the juvenile is blue. This whiptail is active during the day in spring and summer when it feeds on insects and spiders. It also likes termites.

Begin the well-signed hike to the Whitaker house from the trailhead on Los Coches Road. The first 0.25 mile winds up the ridge and then follows it to the north. The trail joins a dirt road for one small section and then breaks off to the left skirting several houses along the ridge. The best views are at the Whitaker house. At 1.29 miles, the trail appears to end at the steep paved road leading up to the Whitaker house, which can be seen above. However, the trail does continue to the left around the property leading to stone steps up to the driveway area. Several benches are located around the house. Visible from the top are Lindo Lake and El Capitan. Follow the same route to return to the trailhead.

The Whitakers and Mildred's mother are buried on the property. The County has hired a caretaker, who lives in a trailer on the premises. The house is open for public viewing only on special occasions.

Diana Lindsay

The Whitaker home

Alan King

Orange-thoated whiptail

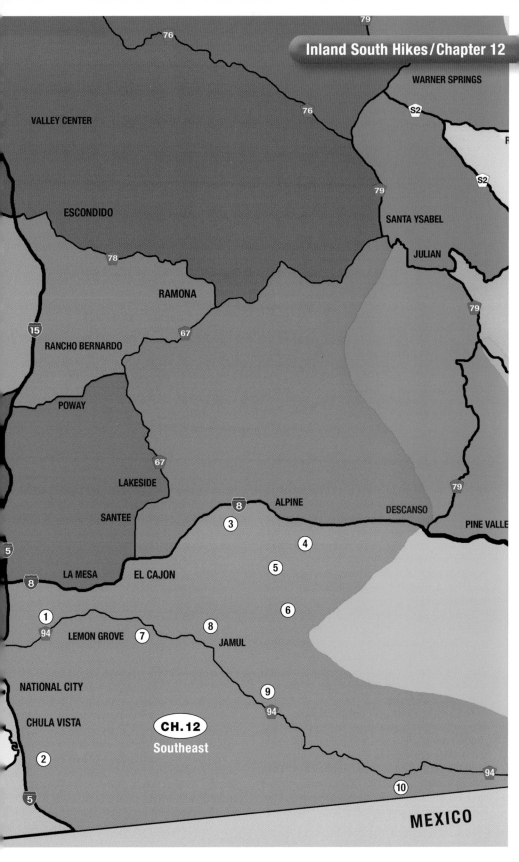

Distance:	1 or 3 miles, loop or out-and-back
Difficulty:	🚶 or 🚶🚶
Elevation gain/loss:	up to 200 feet
Hiking time:	1 or 2 hours
Agency:	City of San Diego
Trail use:	Bicycles, dogs
Notes:	Hours posted 6:30 a.m. to sunset
Trailhead GPS:	N32.73828, W117.06100
Optional map:	USGS 7.5-min *National City*
Atlas square:	R11
Directions:	(Oak Park) From CA-94 go north on College Avenue for 0.3 mile. Turn left on College Grove Drive. Go 0.7 mile. Turn right into the main park entrance, just past College Grove Way. There are 3 parking lots with 2 farther west of the main entrance.

Habitat(s):

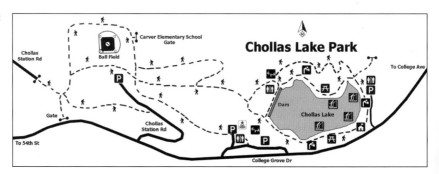

Chollas Lake Reservoir was built in 1901 to serve as San Diego's water supply. The 16-acre lake was turned over to the City's Department of Park and Recreation for management in 1966, and in 1971 was designated a youth fishing lake. The lake was named for the cholla cactus found in the area. There are many recreational activities that are within the 60-acre preserve. All this is within easy freeway accessibility right in the heart of a relatively densely built-out urban/suburban area.

From the main entrance parking lot, the first visitor impressions will be of the lake, its many water-loving birds, and a surrounding forest of towering eucalyptus. These trees provide abundant shade on a warm summer day while still allowing nearly unimpeded views of the lake from nearly all places.

A 0.8 mile, a dirt path circles the lake where dragonflies and damselflies (**order Odonata**) can be seen at the water's edge. Dragonflies and damselflies are easy to distinguish, once you know what to look for. Dragonflies have large bodies, strong, rapid, and deliberate flight, and they cannot fold their wings when still. They hold their wings out to the side parallel to the ground—whether flying or sitting on a branch. They hunt the muddy edges of lakes and ponds, holding their legs like baskets to capture smaller flying insects that they can eat on the wing. Dragonflies used to be called devil's darning needles. Folk stories say they could sew up the lips of lying children.

Damselflies are slender and more delicate than dragonflies, having a weaker, slower, and more fluttering flight. While at rest they angle their wings back toward their abdomen, folded over their body. They can be found on stems of plants that grow near ponds. Dragonflies are ancient insects evolving over 300 million years. Both dragonflies and damselflies are predators.

North of the lake loop is a designated nature trail, which meanders along a hillside filled with more eucalyptus plus an assortment of native and non-native plants. There is also a small garden of mixed, mostly non-native, succulents.

At the western end of the lake the more adventuresome can descend a hill and exit a back gate for a longer walk in the park. The eastern section of the park consists of several trails, which can be combined into a variety of lengths

East side lakeview

from 1 to 3 miles. The most straight-forward route has very little elevation gain/loss, but other routes might total a few hundred feet.

This western area of the park has obviously seen considerable human influence and is now awash in disturbed soils that provide a great breeding ground for non-native mustards, crown daisies, European grasses, and various escaped landscape plants like Brazilian and Peruvian pepper trees, cyclops acacia, Perez's marsh-rosemary, and jade plant. However, there are also the usual native coastal sage scrub species. While there is considerable plant life to observe, the biodiversity is not high. Those interested in an unspoiled environment with more species variation are advised to seek out other areas.

The major wildlife attraction is undoubtedly the birds at the lake. There are the usual urban denizens, but there is also a large collection of lake birds including the mallard, American coot, pied-billed grebe, great egret, and lesser scaup, beside the domesticated Muscovy duck and geese.

Damselfly wings straight back

Dragonfly wings perpendicular to body

Distance:	4.5 miles, loop
Difficulty:	🏃🏃
Elevation gain/loss:	Up to 200 feet
Hiking time:	3 hours
Agency:	San Diego County
Trail use:	Bicycles, dogs, horses
Notes:	Good birding area; visitor center open 9 a.m.- 3 p.m.
Trailhead GPS:	N32.58828, W117.07161
Optional map:	USGS 7.5-min *Imperial Beach*
Atlas square:	V11
Directions:	(Chula Vista) From I-5 go east on Main Street for 0.9 mile. Turn right on Broadway. Go 0.3 mile. Continue onto Beyer Boulevard. Go 0.2 mile. Park at ranger station on right. Trailhead is across the street. From I-805 go west on Main Street for 2.3 miles. Turn left on Broadway. Go 0.3 mile. Continue onto Beyer Boulevard. Go 0.2 mile. Park at ranger station on right. Trailhead is across the street.

Habitat(s):

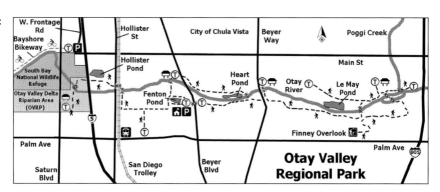

Otay Valley Regional Park (OVRP) is an open space preserve with plans to link the San Diego Wildlife Refuge on San Diego Bay to the Otay River Valley and its headwaters in Otay Lakes and the San Miguel, Jamul, and Otay Mountains, a distance of 13 miles. The planning area encompasses 8869 acres.

The trails of OVRP pass through riparian woodland, marsh, coastal sage scrub, and chaparral habitats, presenting many opportunities for birdwatching and observing nature. Here one will find rare plants such as Orcutt's bird's beak (*Dicranostegia orcuttiana*) and endangered birds such as the least Bell's vireo, the coastal California gnatcatcher, and the southwestern willow flycatcher, although only a single individual flycatcher was seen here in recent years. Orcutt's bird's beak, on the northern edge of its distribution here, is an annual herb with 15-20 flowers on a spikelet that is seriously threatened because of urbanization, trail widening, and non-native plants.

The area has been continuously inhabited by humans for 9000 years, beginning with the earliest bands of Native Americans that settled into the area. Lands today that include National City, Chula Vista, and Bonita were later included in Rancho del Rey during the Spanish period and then as Rancho de la Nación under the Mexican period. Frank Kimball and his brothers acquired the entire rancho in 1868 and retained the name National with their purchase. Today, this area is under multi-jurisdictional planning control of San Diego County and the Cities of San Diego and Chula Vista.

The early use of the area for cattle grazing probably led to the introduction of many invasive species while others have invaded the area since that time. One of the most problematic species is saltcedar found in the riparian areas. Other invasive plants include the extremely allergenic castor bean plant with its toxic castor beans, artichoke thistle, Canary

Northern raccoon

Island date palms, crown daisies, and Peruvian pepper trees.

There are numerous official trailheads to this park with about 10 miles of trails that crisscross, but the best place to start a hike is at the ranger station on Beyer Boulevard. From here, you can do a short 2-mile loop up one side of the river to Heart Pond and back, crossing the watercourse to Fenton Pond and the ranger station, or a longer 5-mile hike. A map is helpful because of the many intersecting trails. However, any choice is a delight for all hikers—novices will enjoy the wide, flat, meandering trails through the valley floor while all will enjoy the diverse plant varieties.

Some of the more common plants encountered include western poison-oak and broom baccharis along the trails; mule-fat, western cottonwoods, and western sycamores in riparian areas; and California buckwheat, coast prickly-pear cactus, coastal sagebrush, black sage, chaparral-pea, and jimson weed in the chaparral and coastal sage scrub communities.

Use caution when wandering near the trail's edge due to the heavy proliferation of western poison-oak throughout the area. It will be encountered almost immediately upon leaving the ranger station on Beyer Boulevard. Staying on the trails keeps one safe and affords rare glimpse of wetlands, ponds, and streams.

The Otay River is one of only three rivers that discharge into San Diego Bay. It empties at the southern end of the Bay while Sweetwater and San Diego river watersheds discharge further north.

Watch for northern raccoon (*Procyon lotor*) tracks with marks from five long toes in the soft mud in riparian areas. This 12- to 35-pound mammalian Lone Ranger with its distinctive black mask walks with plantigrade locomotion, with the entire sole of its foot, like bears, humans, and rabbits, rather than just on its toes as do many mammals. It is primarily a nocturnal species that survives well in urban and suburban areas by using its deft hands to pry off garbage can lids. In the wild it will eat almost anything, including crayfish, lizards, birds and nestlings, small rodents, frogs, fish, mollusks, insects, fruits, and nuts. Raccoons have a reputation for using their forepaws or hands to wash their food before eating, although they may be simply holding the food underwater while they examine it by touch. These secretive bandits are adapted to a variety of habitats but prefer areas near water, trees, and wooded swamps. In April or May, females typically have 3-8 furry babies that are born with their eyes closed. The mothers raise them in a hollow log, rock crevice, cave, or an abandoned building, sometimes carrying them about in feline fashion.

Orcutt's bird's beak

Distance:	1 to 15 miles, loops or out-and-back
Difficulty:	🥾 to 🥾🥾🥾🥾🥾
Elevation gain/loss:	Varies according to route
Hiking time:	1 to 8 hours
Agency:	CDFW
Trail use:	Bicycles, dogs, horses
Trailhead GPS:	N32.82823, W116.85637
Optional map:	USGS 7.5-min *Alpine*
Atlas square:	P15
Directions:	(El Cajon) From I-8 go south on Greenfield Drive for 0.5 mile. Turn left on La Cresta Road. Go 3.1 miles. Turn left onto Mountain View Road. Go 1.2 miles. Turn left on Horsemill Road. Go 0.6 mile. Park at end of street at signed entry to the reserve.

Habitat(s):

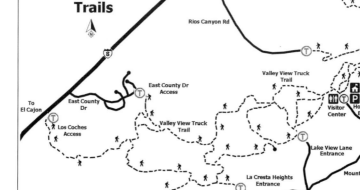

The Crestridge Ecological Reserve is one of 16 California Department of Fish and Wildlife Ecological Reserves in San Diego County. The current 136 statewide ecological reserves provide habitat for a wide diversity of plant and animal species and preserve habitats from every major ecosystem. Crestridge has close to 3000 acres that preserves a core block of habitats identified by the San Diego Multiple Species Conservation Program (MSCP) that serve as a link between the northern and southern parts of the county. The purpose of the MSCP is not only to preserve San Diego's native habitats and wildlife for future generations, but also to protect federally listed endangered species.

Vegetation types found within the reserve include coastal sage scrub, chaparral, oak woodlands, riparian, and grassland. Two rare plant species, Lakeside-lilac and thornmint,

plus insects of concern that include Hermes copper butterfly and Harbison's dun skipper are within the reserve. It is also home to hawks, owls, woodpeckers, gnatcatchers, southern mule deer, coyotes, bobcats, foxes, mountain lions, horned lizards, and rattlesnakes.

Thornmint (*Acanthomintha ilicifolia*) is a small, California-listed endangered and federally-listed threatened mint found where there is gabbro or calcareous (clay-like) soil openings in coastal sage scrub, chaparral, grasslands, and occasionally near vernal pools. This annual herb is endemic to coastal San Diego and northern Baja California. It is less than 1.5 feet tall with funnel-shaped white flowers tinted purple to pink with two lips, with the upper lip smaller than the lower lip. It has small oval serrate leaves and blooms April through June. It is an unusual member of the mint family because

View north

it has conspicuous spines on the floral bracts or leaflike structures at the base of the flower, hence its common name. It has lost 90% of its habitat, mainly due to development. Of the 32 remaining populations, 28 are on private lands and only four are covered by the Multiple Species Conservation Program. This reserve is one of those four.

There are many access points to Crestridge in the surrounding urban interface, so please be considerate of the neighbors and avoid access to their homes and private property by using the official entrance at Horsemill Road. Trails leading east and west radiate like the wings of a bird from the hub of the reserve at the official Horsemill Road entrance.

When you first arrive, examine the map on the kiosk, and if available, pick up a trail map. The trails zigzag, climb, and loop for miles throughout much of the reserve. It is possible to hike over 20 miles and seldom travel the same route. Trails are made up of fire roads, truck trails, and hiking and horseback riding paths with some of the trails eroded to the point of decommission. Earth Discovery Institute, Endangered Habitats Conservancy, and the San Diego Mountain Biking Association have partnered to reroute and repair many of the trails to reduce erosion.

A popular route is the 3-mile Valley View Truck Trail that has less than 500 feet of elevation gain. From the Horsemill Road entrance, follow the dirt road northwest or left through a riparian woodland of coast live oaks and Engelmann oaks. As you exit the woods, take the north-most trail to the right, up and into the coastal sage scrub/chaparral habitat. This fire road runs along the north edge of the reserve where there are private avocado orchards that grow down to the urban interface with I-8. This route is popular with runners and equestrians and can be followed out of the reserve and all the way to the shopping center parking lot on Los Coches Road. Distance markers are placed along the route every 0.5 mile within the reserve. At the western edge of the reserve is a heavy, yellow-painted metal gate that is about 3.5 miles from the Horsemill entrance.

To make this a loop hike, turn left or south at mile 1.8 onto a single track and climb. Stay right at forks until you reach a boulder-studded high point at 2.8 miles with stunning views. The view includes El Cajon, Lake Jennings, and glimpses of the Pacific Ocean on a clear day. This also can be an out-and-back or, for the more adventurous, a 4-mile loop. Head east down the single-track trail from the highpoint, taking an old roadway north to

Mary Duffy

Oaks near the Horsemill Road entrance

a T-junction. To the right the trail eventually leads to the Valley View Truck Trail, heading east and back to the Horsemill Road entrance to complete the loop.

For a simple mile-long hike, start east of the James Hubbell straw-bale-built shelter and head northeast up a signed trail. Climbing past the blackened woody remains of the 2003 Cedar Fire, you will find Engelmann oak among the sumac, California buckwheat, and chamise along the trail. At the top, head left or west at the Y-junction to an overlook of east El Cajon and the San Diego River watershed to the north. The trail loops back down to the southwest past a large-scale native grassland restoration project with hundreds of protective plant cones. This is a multi-year habitat restoration effort that has included over 20,000 school students. They have visited on science/service-learning field trips coordinated by the Endangered Habitats Conservancy's education/outreach partner, Earth Discovery Institute. The trail ends at the oak grove. From here there is a path leading through the oaks to boulders that have morteros where the Kumeyaay ground acorns into meal.

Jessie Vinje

Thornmint

Distance:	1 or 2 miles, out-and-back
Difficulty:	🚶 or 🚶🚶
Elevation gain/loss:	Up to 100 feet
Hiking time:	1 hour
Agency:	USFS/CNF-DRD; Sweetwater Authority
Trail use:	Dogs
Notes:	Hours posted sunrise to sunset
Trailhead GPS:	N32.79961, W116.76013
Optional map:	USGS 7.5-min *Alpine*
Atlas square:	Q17
Directions:	((Alpine) From I-8 go south on Tavern Road for 2.8 mile. Continue onto Japatul Road. Go 1 mile. Parking lot is on right.

Habitat(s):

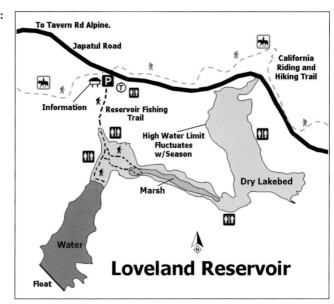

Loveland Dam, also known as Sweetwater Falls Dam, is a concrete thin arch design built in 1945. Loveland Reservoir is one of the two man-made lakes made by dams along the Sweetwater River. It is used for flood control and drinking water for Chula Vista, National City, and Bonita residents. Until 1966 the reservoir was used solely for water storage. A land exchange between the Sweetwater Authority and the US Forest Service gave the Sweetwater Authority control over land adjacent to the reservoir. The Authority constructed a parking lot and trail and opened the reservoir to the public for shoreline fishing on January 14, 1997. No boats, swimming, or use of live bait is allowed. Largemouth bass, channel and bullhead catfish, bluegill, red-eared sunfish, and crappie can all be caught at Loveland

with a fishing license and in the posted fishing areas only. Trails offer little to no shade, so it is best to hike in the early mornings before the heat of the day sets in.

The trailhead is at the parking lot. The trail quickly descends to the reservoir by way of a flight of wooden steps. Drought conditions have greatly reduced the size of this reservoir. Depending on the current water level, which fluctuates throughout the year, the easternmost, shallow arm can turn into a soggy meadow that is difficult to traverse. Trails are found to the left and right along the lakeshore but aren't always obvious and may be difficult to follow. Trails are also found at different levels as the water has fluctuated.

The trails to the east or left can be explored for a short distance but are not recommended

View from the steps

The trail to the west or right from the staircase and bridge leads down to the metal fishing pier that is totally surround by cattails and other thick vegetation in drought conditions. Red-winged blackbirds flit around the cattails. A fisherman's trail leads through a thicket of plants past the pier to the shoreline of the reservoir where waterfowl may be seen. The water lapping on the shore can be mesmerizing, and the view from the shore is very peaceful.

One of the birds that you might see in the reservoir is the lesser scaup (*Aythya affinis*). The widespread lesser scaup is a medium-sized duck with a bluish bill with a black tip. Males have a black head, neck, chest, and tail, a gray back, and white sides. Females are mostly brown with a contrasting white face. Scaups eat clams, crustaceans, snails, and aquatic plants. The chicks can dive on the same day they are hatched but can only stay under for a moment because they are so buoyant. Adults can dive up to 60 feet and stay under for up to 25 seconds.

The chaparral terrain above the lake is dominated by chamise and California buckwheat. For those who might want to explore more in this area, a portion of the California Riding and Hiking Trail is accessible from the west side of the parking area. About 12 miles of this trail, established statewide in 1945, winds through Alpine between Crest and Dehesa.

with low water conditions that have left most of the area dry or with patches of marshy areas thick with riparian growth such as cattails and willows.

Lesser scaup male

Lesser scaup female

Distance:	4 miles, out-and-back
Difficulty:	🚶🚶🚶
Elevation gain/loss:	Up to 1000 feet
Hiking time:	3 hours
Agency:	Sweetwater Authority
Trail use:	Bicycles, dogs, horses
Trailhead GPS:	N32.78416, W116.80481
Optional map:	USGS 7.5-min *Alpine*
Atlas square:	Q16
Directions:	(Dehesa) From I-8 go south on Tavern Road for 2.8 mile. Continue onto Japatul Road. Go 0.3 mile. Turn right on Sequan Truck Trail. Go 3.1 miles. The last 0.2 mile is on a dirt road. Park in turnout where road makes a sharp right turn to the south. Trailhead is 0.2 mile farther south on left.

Habitat(s):

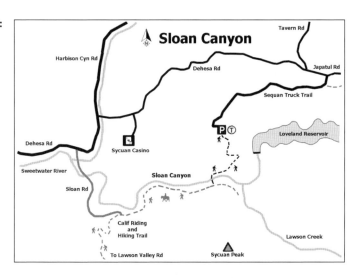

The hike along Sloan Canyon is on a portion of the California Riding and Hiking Trail that offers views of Loveland Reservoir and surrounding mountains before descending into a rich riparian area along the Sweetwater River. The hike begins in an unshaded chaparral area with exposed large granitic slabs that gradually transitions to an inviting shaded, riparian woodland at the canyon bottom. One can truly experience the difference that water can make for the surrounding habitat on this hike. The canyon's sensitive habitat supports several rare or endangered plants and animals. It also has great views and provides a deep peacefulness that is a welcome change from the hustle of the city. The canyon itself was named for Hampton Sloane, a rancher who lived in the Dehesa area in the 1890s. Through time, the e was dropped from the name.

Sturdy shoes are necessary as the trail is steep and eroded in places for about 0.25 mile as you head south. Follow the sign to the California Riding and Hiking Trail on the left. Before descending into Sloan Canyon, take a moment to view Sycuan Peak directly to the south with Lyons and Lawson peaks slightly southeast and a bit higher in elevation. At just under 1.35 miles, the trail continues down into the canyon passing a few scattered houses to the west.

On the hillsides you can see fine examples of exfoliated granite slabs. Exfoliation is the process in which rocks weather by peeling off in sheets rather than eroding grain by grain. Exfoliation can happen in thin layers on individual boulders, or it can take place in thick slabs as it does here in Sloan Canyon as evidenced by the large, smooth granite pieces poking through the chaparral.

Wendy Esterly

California towhee

Paula Knoll

Dodder bloom

Along the way, keep your eyes out for flowers blooming amongst the laurel sumac, *Ceanothus*, and chamise that line the road, which may include lilies and dodder (*Cuscuta* **spp.**). Dodder looks like orangey-yellow spaghetti strands that twine around a host plant. Dodder is a parasitic plant that contains no chlorophyll and absorbs food and water from its host plant through haustoria, root-like organs that penetrate the cells on the stems of the host plant. The severity of the attack on the host plant depends on whether the plant is already stressed, if the dodder carries disease, and on how much of the dodder is growing on the plant. Dodder flowers are tiny yellow-white, bell-like lobed clusters that are easily overlooked.

You'll likely spot one of the chaparral's signature birds in this canyon, the California towhee (*Melozone crissalis*). Found only on the Pacific seaboard from Oregon to Baja California, Mexico, this brown bird can be seen challenging its reflection in your car's review mirror or doing the classic towhee double-scratch, a foraging maneuver of lunging forward and quickly scratching back with both feet. During breeding season, the male sings a series of metallic chip notes from a high perch in the chaparral, rapidly accelerating into a trill and then stopping abruptly. Towhees can also be seen darting in and out of the western poison-oak in Sloan Canyon's riparian understory. Many towhees build their nests in poison-oak and feast on the plant's pale white berries.

As you descend further into the canyon, note that the vegetation changes from chaparral to riparian woodland. The Sweetwater River runs through the bottom of the canyon and the chaparral gives way to western sycamore, oak, western cottonwoods, and willow trees as you approach an old bridge crossing the river. Even in drought when the river might be dry, the riparian growth will be healthy as it taps into underground sources of water. The various trees still provide a nice shaded spot to rest and eat lunch or a quick snack before heading back up the hill to your vehicle.

Stacey Vielma

Riparian area

Distance:	2 miles, out-and-back
Difficulty:	𝕏𝕏𝕏
Elevation gain/loss:	Up to 800 feet
Hiking time:	2 hours
Agency:	CDFW
Trail use:	Dogs
Trailhead GPS:	N32.74682, W116.79920
Optional map:	USGS 7.5-min *Alpine, Dulzura*
Atlas square:	R16
Directions:	(Jamul) From CA-94 go east on Lyons Valley Road for 1.6 miles. Continue onto Skyline Truck Trail. Go 2.2 miles. Turn left on Lawson Valley Road. Go 2.2 miles. Park on the side of road near the trailhead on the left.

Habitat(s):

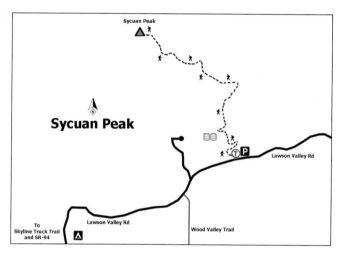

Sycuan Peak (2801') is the high point of the 2300-acre Sycuan Peak Ecological Reserve managed by the California Department of Fish and Wildlife. This area was acquired to protect endangered and sensitive wildlife, special habitats, and native plants. It was designated an ecological reserve in 2000. The area has a unique form of chaparral vegetation that is confined to soils rich in ferromagnesian minerals. Sycuan Peak had a designated National Geodetic Survey Airway Beacon west of the summit until modern radar and radio communication made ground-based landmarks obsolete for helping pilots navigate US transcontinental flights at night.

The climb to the peak is on a steep eroded dirt road. Be sure to wear sturdy hiking shoes and consider trekking poles for the trip down as there are several slick, gravelly areas. The vegetation on the sides of the path is colored a rusty pink in late summer with California buckwheat and browned chamise tips that accent the

red soil of the gabbro rock. This rock is a black granitic rock that cooled slowly with high concentration of magnesium and iron. Also providing reddish color is Eastwood's manzanita, which is prevalent in this area.

Several towering plants, commonly known as chaparral candle (*Hesperoyucca whipplei*), accent the path. Take a look at the six-chambered seed pods littering the path with small, flat black seeds. The chaparral candle has a symbiotic relationship with the female yucca or pronuba moth (*Tegeticula maculata*), the only known pollinator for this plant. This small black moth collects yucca pollen and deposits it on the stigma to fertilize the flower's eggs while laying her eggs near the yucca's ovules. As seeds develop, the moth's eggs hatch to become larvae, which will burrow into the ovules and feed on the seeds, their only food source. They rarely eat all the seeds, leaving some for the next generation of yucca. Each species of yucca has its

Tarantula hawk wasp

Tarantula

burrow the following season. Adult tarantula hawk wasps feed on nectar as bees do.

At dusk, you may be able to see a tarantula crossing a trail. Tarantulas are the largest of arachnids, and they come in various colors and live in various habitats. Most are black or brown and have hairy bodies. Tarantulas eat grasshoppers, beetles, and other spiders. Most use ambush strategies to catch prey, injecting them with venom. Males will wander great distances to find females, and these are the individuals you usually see on roads and trails. While sexual cannibalism is reported in some species of tarantulas, males almost always survive encounters with females. Males do not live as long as females. Some female species can live up to 35 years.

Near the top, the panoramic views begin to unfold, including Loveland Reservoir below. Cliff swallows and white butterflies make their home here. Sit at the boulder on top, and enjoy the surrounding hills in solitude. Carefully make your way back down.

own species of yucca moth that pollinates it. The two are totally dependent on each other for reproduction of its own species. The chaparral candle is found in coastal sage scrub, chaparral, and in oak woodland communities. It was used and processed by Native Americans very much like the desert agave. Every part was used. The flower stalk, the purple-tinged white flowers, immature pods, and seeds were all eaten. It was, and still is, an important fiber plant. The leaves were used to make rope, sandals, and fiber baskets. Once the plant blooms and produces seeds, it dies. Hummingbirds are attracted to the flower's nectar.

Smell the air that is perfumed with coastal sagebrush, white sage, and laurel sumac with its green-apple-scented, taco-shaped leaves, and the sweet soapy scent of fragrant sage. Torrey's scrub oak is also abundant along the path. Dragonflies and June bugs can be present. Listen also for the piercing, bouncing song of the wrentit.

In summer, you might also see a tarantula hawk wasp (*Pepsis* **sp.**) that uses a tarantula (*Aphonopelma* **sp.**) to feed its young. The tarantula hawk wasp has one of the most painful stings of any North American insect. When the female is ready to lay an egg, she will hunt for a tarantula, sting it, and drag it into a burrow and lay a single egg on top of the paralyzed tarantula. The hatched maggot-like larva will eat on the still living paralyzed spider for about a month. An adult wasp will emerge from the

Chaparral candle

Distance:	1 mile, loop with longer options available
Difficulty:	🚶 to 🚶🚶🚶🚶, depending on option taken
Elevation gain/loss:	Up to 200 feet
Hiking time:	1 or 5 hours depending on option
Agency:	NWR
Trail use:	Bicycles, dogs, horses
Trailhead GPS:	N32.73239, W116.94028
Optional map:	USGS 7.5-min *Jamul Mountains*
Atlas square:	R13
Directions:	(Spring Valley) From CA-94, south of the Steel Bridge, go south on Millar Ranch Road, then take an immediate right into the parking area. Limited parking is also found north of the Steel Bridge off Singer Lane, west of CA-94. The trailhead is at the south end of the historic Sweetwater Steel Bridge.

Habitat(s):

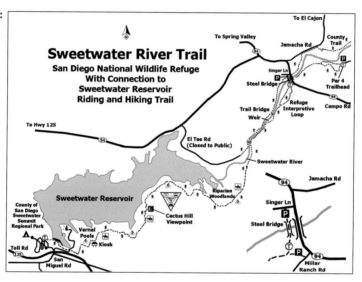

The Sweetwater River is the main artery of the Sweetwater watershed. Its headwaters are in the Cuyamaca Mountains. After flowing into Sweetwater Reservoir, its waters empty into San Diego Bay at the Sweetwater Marsh. The Sweetwater Interpretive Loop is on the south side of the river corridor. The trail is within the San Diego National Wildlife Refuge.

The trailhead is south of the historic Sweetwater Steel Bridge constructed in 1929 using Parker Truss triangular steel girders. Turn west on the trailhead. The refuge property doesn't start until you reach the wooden informational kiosk. Continue into the wooded riparian area, where a small bridge goes over the creek bed. Beware of western poison-oak as it is common here.

There are many side trails. The interpretive loop follows the fence along the riparian area as

the river flows southwest. The riparian and oak woodland habitats provide nesting sites and habitat for many resident and migrating birds making this a favorite area for birdwatching. One of the more striking birds that may be seen is the spotted towhee (***Pipilo maculatus***), a large sparrow with, in the male, a jet-black throat, head, and back, black and white spotted wings, rufous flanks, and a white belly. The female has the same pattern except she is slaty-gray instead of black. The spotted towhee forages on the ground beneath tangled shrubbery, scratching through leaf litter looking for insects, seeds, and fruit.

There is signage along the interpretive loop describing many of the rare and endangered plant and animal species found in this refuge, including the least Bell's vireo, California gnatcatcher, Quino checkerspot butterfly, and San

The trail

Diego ambrosia (*Ambrosia pumila*). San Diego ambrosia is a small herbaceous perennial in the sunflower family that grows in grasslands and close to wetlands and vernal pools. It is threatened by urban development and agriculture. It reproduces vegetatively through a rhizome or underground stem, sending up sprouts. It rarely produces seeds.

At 0.64 mile the trail continues straight, or makes a sharp turn back along the flank of the hillside, traveling through coastal sage scrub and offering a panoramic view of the watershed. Living along this section of the trail are Blainville's horned lizards, red diamond rattlesnakes, roadrunners, and California and spotted towhees. The trail wraps back around to the north, eventually bringing you to the steel bridge crossing the creek.

An alternative loop can be made by going straight along the river corridor at the 0.64 mile mark. In another 0.2 mile, there is a wooden bridge that crosses the riverbed to the north side. The trail eventually connects to a service road that is not as scenic. A turn to the right makes this a nice 2-mile loop back to the Singer Lane parking area. Or, if looking for a longer challenge (6 miles one-way), head south on the trail at the bridge and eventually connect to the

Sweetwater River Riding and Hiking Trail on San Diego County land before returning. Access to this trail from the south can be found at Sweetwater Summit Regional Park, which has 15 miles of multiuse trails and campground facilities at this 500-acre County park.

If you are starting at the County park, be aware that the gates close at 4 p.m. Day parking is free just southwest of the entry to the campgrounds on Summit Meadow Road. The trailhead is just past the entry and to the right, where there is a wooden fence. Turn right and descend, and continue walking south on the west side of a dike. At the end of the dike, walk past the intersection; north goes to the fishing area while south exists on Summit Meadow Road. Continue east parallel to CA-125, and take an abrupt left turn, then a right turn. There are vernal pools along here, mostly across the wooden fence. If there is water in the pools, Canadian geese may be in the area. There is no sign for the Sweetwater River Riding and Hiking Trail until 2 miles into the walk near the Cactus Hill Viewpoint, where there is an engraved wooden post. Continue on the south of the lakebed and riparian section until you cross the Steele Canyon Bridge to Singer Lane.

There is also a trail in the San Diego Wildlife Refuge on the north side of CA-94 along the Sweetwater River flood plain. This 1.4-mile section is best reached by parking at the trailhead at the end of Par 4 Drive, accessed from Steele Canyon Road off CA-94. There is no parking lot in this residential neighborhood, so please be respectful of driveways and access.

Spotted towhee

Distance:	4.7 miles, out-and-back
Difficulty:	🚶🚶🚶
Elevation gain/loss:	Up to 1300 feet
Hiking time:	3 hours
Agency:	CDFW; USFW; TNC
Trail use:	Bicycles, dogs, horses
Notes:	Beginning of trail and peak not recommended for horses
Trailhead GPS:	N32.72952, W116.87243
Optional map:	USGS 7.5-min *Jamul Mountains*, *Dulzura*
Atlas square:	S15
Directions:	(Jamul) From CA-94 go east on Lyons Valley Road for 0.7 mile. Turn left on Jamul Drive. Go 0.4 mile. Parking lot is on the right.

Habitat(s):

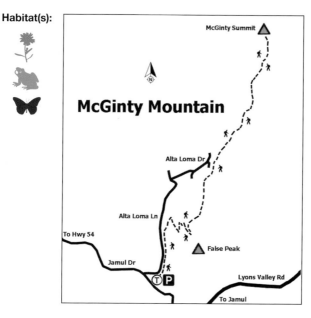

McGinty Mountain lies within a collective ecological preserve managed by The Nature Conservancy, the California Department of Fish and Wildlife, and the US Fish and Wildlife Service's San Diego National Wildlife Refuge. Several rare and endangered plant species make their home here on a relatively uncommon type of soil known as Las Posas soil that is derived from gabbro or black granite rock. This rock type occurs in the Peninsular Range Batholith along with other granitic rock in San Diego County. The soil derived from gabbro is characterized by having low levels of calcium, phosphorus, and potassium, major nutrients usually required by plants. In addition, they also contain high levels of iron, magnesium, and heavy metals such as nickel, chromium, and cobalt that are toxic to most plants.

Among the plants living here are thornmint and San Miguel savory (***Clinopodium chandleri***), an especially rare native in California, listed by the California Native Plant Society as endangered in our state. San Miguel savory is an aromatic, low shrub with small white flowers that appear in the spring and summer. Its leaves have a smell like mint, which is one of its relatives. Also in the area is the similarly rare Parry's tetracoccus (***Tetracoccus dioicus***), a shrub with springtime clusters of small red flowers found within the chaparral plant community. It has a distinct four-lobed fruit. These are plants to look for on this hike.

The trailhead leaves from the rear of the parking lot next to the refuge information kiosk. The view from the lot may look short

Jim Varnell

View toward Mt. Miguel.

and easy to the peak, as the summit does not seem that far away. In actuality, you are looking up at a bluff that is acting as a false summit and is far from the final destination. The first segment of the trail starts out as a wide road, but at 0.25 mile, it bears right and becomes a single-track switchback trail.

After about 0.5 mile of chaparral-lined trail and some elevation gain, the trail is at the false summit seen from below. The correct trail will now ascend to the north. Do not take the path going south and downhill towards Jamul as it crosses onto private property. However, before continuing the uphill climb to the summit, investigate this area for the remains of an old mine. However, do not enter any mine openings as they are unsafe—danger of collapse, vertical shafts that you could fall into, and noxious gas—and their cool recesses are a favorite haunt for rattlesnakes during the heat of the day. They can also be maternity roosts for bats (**order Chiroptera**). If disturbed, female bats may abandon their young to save themselves from a perceived threat.

If you happen to be on the trail around dusk, you may be lucky enough to see a bat.

While bats are common in San Diego County, they frequently escape notice because of their nocturnal habits. The order name Chiroptera means hand-wing and refers to the arm and four elongated fingers supporting the wing membrane. Bats find prey by echolocation—high-frequency sound waves are sent out, and the speed and sound at which they return enable bats to gauge the location and type of insect. Except for one nectar-sipping species, local bats feed entirely on insects.

In the early 1900s, silicified alaskite aplite was mined for use in porcelain-ware manufacturing. The miner's name was McGinty. Nothing more is known about him except for his mining operation and that the mountain was named for him. Alaskite is a general term for rocks consisting essentially of quartz and alkali feldspar without regard to texture. Aplites at this location are fine-grained sugary-textured white rocks. Look for rocks on the grounds that are characterized by the absence or scarcity of dark-colored minerals that have a granular habit. Several other mines and scrapings can be seen along the way, but this is the only opening readily visible.

Dehesa nolina

After continuing northward 0.1 mile, the trail will crest the bluffs and for the first time McGinty Mountain (2183') can be seen another 1.5 miles ahead. Look for Dehesa nolina (*Nolina interrata*) on the way to the summit. With its showy blue-gray foliage, it roughly resembles another member of the agave family—the far more common chaparral candle—though it does not have the same supportive structure in its leaves. Over half of California's remaining 9000 specimens of Dehesa nolina are found along McGinty's ridgeline.

Be sure to note the many less-traveled trails branching off the main trail so you can find the proper path on your way back down. Atop the summit you will have views of most of eastern San Diego County and many of the county's peaks, such as Cowles, North Fortuna, Otay, Jamul, Lyons, Tecate, El Capitan, and Viejas. On a clear day you even can see all the way to the Pacific Ocean. Once taking a well-deserved rest on the summit, return the same way to the parking lot. As you make your way down, be sure to smell the Cleveland or fragrant sage that is found along the trail and on the hillsides.

Parry's tetracoccus

Distance:	6.4 miles, loop
Difficulty:	🚶🚶🚶🚶
Elevation gain/loss:	Up to 1000 feet
Hiking time:	4 hours
Agency:	CDFW
Trail use:	Bicycles, dogs, horses
Trailhead GPS:	N32.67081, W116.82319
Optional map:	USGS 7.5-min *Dulzura*
Atlas square:	T15
Directions:	(Jamul) From CA-94 go east on Honey Springs Road for 0.1 mile. Parking lot is on the left.

Habitat(s):

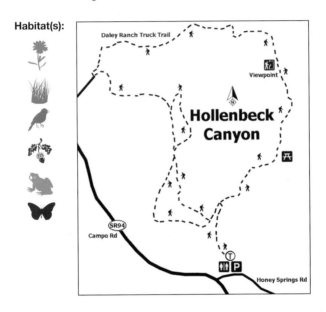

The 6065-acre Hollenbeck Canyon Wildlife Area was once part of a Mexican land grant given in 1831 to Pio Pico, the last Mexican governor of California. It was known as Rancho Jamul. The property went through several ownerships and was eventually sold to a former San Diego mayor in 1916 and then to the Daley family in 1929. The Daleys used the property as a truck farm and cattle ranch until they, in turn, sold the property to the California Department of Fish and Wildlife in 2001. The property was designated as a wildlife area that same year. It is important as a wildlife corridor and for the variety of habitats found on the property that includes coastal sage scrub, chaparral, oak woodlands, riparian forests, freshwater marshes, and grasslands.

From the trailhead it is 0.3 mile to Hollenbeck Canyon and the magnificent old oaks that establish its riparian corridor. A seasonal stream runs through the wide-mouthed canyon from Lyons Valley. A complete loop can be hiked by crossing the streambed and taking the trail at the T to the left or right. The trail's right fork goes up Hollenbeck Canyon along the wooded stream corridor of coast live oaks, western sycamore, willow, mule-fat, western poison-oak, and other riparian vegetation. Engelmann oak and coastal sage scrub communities grow on the hillsides above the canyon. Except in severe drought, there are a few places where standing water can always be found in the creek bed.

Large clumps of San Diego sedge (*Carex spissa*) are found here. Look for a large grass tussock-like plant that has stems with edges, characteristic of all sedges. This type of sedge is the host plant to the rare Harbison's dun skipper (*Euphyes vestris harbisonii*) found here, a small skipper butterfly that has yellow-orange

Mary Duffy

San Diego sedge

undersides and brown-black wings. The species name *vestris* refers to an Italian dancing master in the court of Louis XVI who was considered the greatest dancer of his day. The skipper's quick, darting flight patterns call to mind the master's intricate dance patterns.

Where the trail forks, at about 1.5 miles, one can climb to the left to complete the loop, or continue straight along the trail as it hugs the canyon side for about 0.25 mile. Eventually the canyon opens up onto an oak-shaded meadow. Cross the creek bed to the right (a step trail climbs out of the canyon on the left) and follow the trail through the oaks. If you look carefully, you will find large granitic boulders partially buried in leaf litter with several Kumeyaay grinding holes or morteros—evidence that Native Americans once harvested and processed acorns in the canyon.

The understory is also home to Gilbert's (***Plestiodon gilberti***) and western skinks (***Plestiodon skiltonianus***). Skinks are lizards with thick necks, short legs, and smooth, shiny scales. These diurnal lizards are found under rocks or other debris. The juveniles are striped with either a bright blue (western skink) or pink (Gilbert's skink) tail. Both species are small to medium-sized lizards with snake-like

movements. Adults are usually striped (western skink) or solid colored (Gilbert's). The two species are difficult to tell apart.

Several trails lead east and south out of this valley but don't connect to exit points. Your best bet is to return the way you came, down the canyon, and either continue on the loop by turning right and climbing up at the fork or returning to the parking area at the Hollenbeck Trailhead.

If you take the fork north or left when coming up the canyon at the1.5 mile point, you climb to a high vantage point. From here look south to Otay Mountains and east to Lyons Peak (3722'). At 1.9 miles, the trail forks again, the right fork follows an old truck trail onto private property. Stay left and hike the fire road/trail down to Jamul Creek, another seasonal drainage hosting coast live oak and western sycamore. Within 1 mile, there will be fences and holding pens—relics of days gone by. Stay on the trail, crossing the streambed and cutting back east to catch the dirt road up and across large fields of non-native pasture grass. The trail crosses the open, rolling foothills for 2 miles before returning to the pleasant shade of Hollenbeck's mother oaks to complete the loop.

In spring, this can be a luscious green hike with waterfalls and wildflowers. If it has rained, be prepared for creek crossings. In summertime, the exposed sections of the trail can be hot and dry. The trail is best hiked between October and June. Wear a hat and bring plenty of water.

Stacey Vielma

Harbison's dun skipper

Distance:	10 miles, out-and-back
Difficulty:	🚶🚶🚶🚶🚶
Elevation gain/loss:	Up to 1500 feet
Hiking time:	6 hours
Agency:	BLM-CDD
Trail use:	Bicycles, dogs
Notes:	Good birding area; since peak is considered sacred, some people voluntarily do not climb it. If choosing to climb it, do so with reverence for the peak
Trailhead GPS:	N32.57833, W116.66849
Optional map:	USGS 7.5-min *Tecate*
Atlas square:	V19
Directions:	(Tecate) From CA-94 go south on CA-188 for 1.6 miles. Turn right and onto a dirt road (Tecate Mission Road) just before sign saying "International Border 150 feet." Go 2.8 miles. It is easy to get onto the wrong track due to a maze of roads in the area. The road goes along the corrugated-metal border fence before turning northwest and beginning the climb up Tecate Peak. Park along road shoulder above or below gate, but parking above the gate runs the risk of returning to a locked gate.

Habitat(s):

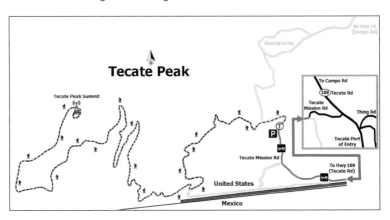

Tecate Peak (3885') is a border sentinel visible from both Baja California, Mexico, and from southern California. The actual summit is less than 1 mile north of the border in California with a service road that winds to expansive vistas of both countries and the Pacific Ocean.

Known as *Kuuchamaa* to the Kumeyaay, it remains a sacred site for the Kumeyaay people of southern California and northern Baja California, as it has been for hundreds of years. When the peak was threatened by nearby development, Kumeyaay people came forward to talk about their sacred religious beliefs in order to protect their sacred mountain. It was revealed that shamans would go there to acquire power for an individual or group's spiritual and religious well-being. In

1992 as a result of their disclosures and effort, *Kuuchamaa* was placed on the National Register of Historic Places.

The peak and much of the land surrounding it have been designated an area of critical environmental concern by the Bureau of Land Management, the managing agency. There is no official trail to the summit. From the gate, hike up the service road, which can have restricted vehicle access because of road conditions or to protect the local environment. Constructed in 1958, the road is a long series of switchbacks with a steep 15% grade. Without the road, the hike would be difficult on the unmaintained use-trail through boulders mixed with chaparral and coastal sage scrub.

The vegetation on the north side of the mountain near Highway 94 reflects the na-

Tecate cypress

ture of the Peninsular Ranges, with alkaline clay soils derived from gabbro, a dark-colored plutonic rock rich in iron and magnesium. However, here the rock is more typical granodiorite. Huge boulders hug the side of the road, many still bearing the red stains of fire retardant dropped during the 2007 Harris Fire, which burned most of the Tecate cypress (*Hesperocyparis forbesii*) stands on the mountain. A mature Tecate cypress forest will have about 32 trees per acre, with about 35% ground cover and no seedling trees. It is serotinous, meaning that fire releases the seeds from the cones. Because of the 2007 fire, there is new growth of Tecate cypress seedlings on the mountain. Look for their scale-like leaves.

There is an unsightly array of towers, chain-link fences, and concrete foundations on the summit. A fire lookout station was once located here. Now, there are TV relay towers, but the views make up for the intrusion. On a clear day, you will get a good view of the divide between the US and Mexico, the town of Tecate, mountains in Baja California, the Pacific Ocean, and the sparsely populated landscape of southeast San Diego County. Return the same way.

To learn more about the Kumeyaay, take an optional side trip to the town of Tecate, Mexico, for a visit to the El Museo Comunitaria Kumiai (Kumiai Community Museum). It is a charming structure designed and built by James Hubbell, a noted San Diego artist and architect. The museum is open from 10 a.m. to 5 p.m., Wednesday through Saturday, and charges a small fee (see www.carem.org/museokumiai/). If you go, be sure you take the needed current documentation necessary to exit and re-enter to the US. See www.baja bound.com/before/permits/usreentry.php for the documents required. You can park in the lot on the US side of the border for a small fee, then take a 15-minute walk from the border into Tecate, Mexico.

Tecate cypress cones

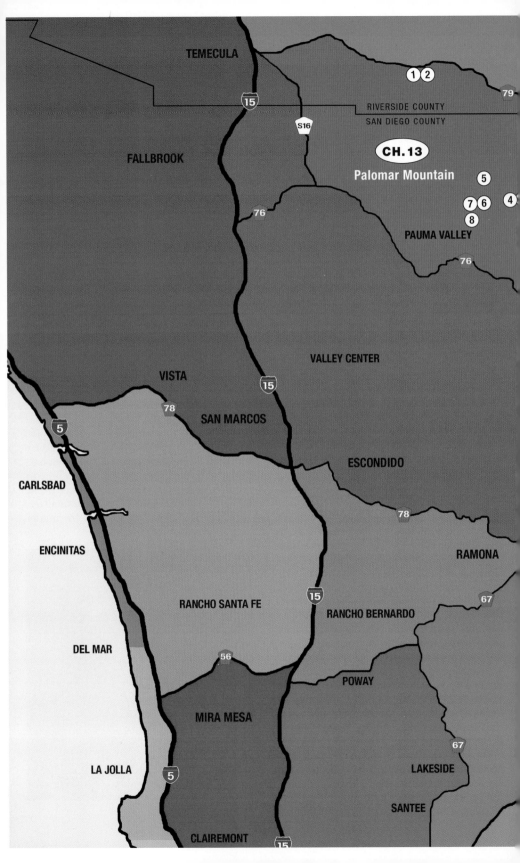

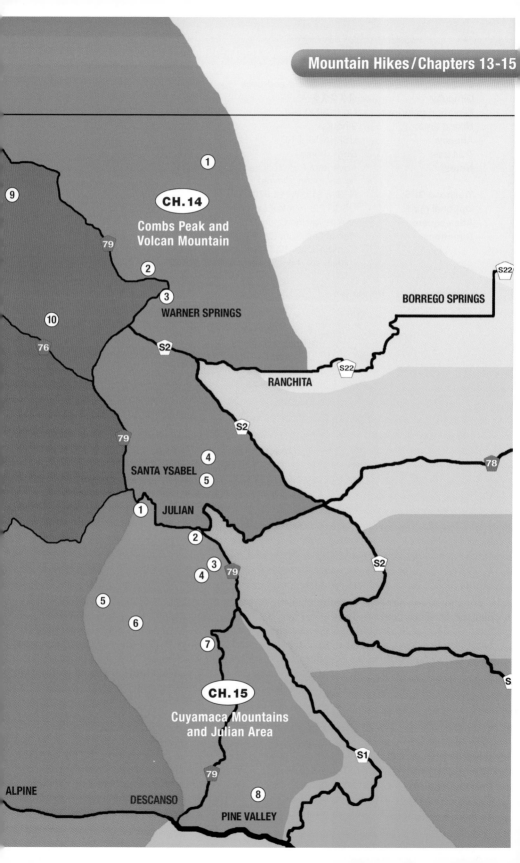

CH. 14

Combs Peak and
Volcan Mountain

WARNER SPRINGS

BORREGO SPRINGS

RANCHITA

SANTA YSABEL

JULIAN

CH. 15

Cuyamaca Mountains
and Julian Area

ALPINE

DESCANSO

PINE VALLEY

Distance:	13.8 miles, out-and-back
Difficulty:	🚶🚶🚶🚶🚶
Elevation gain/loss:	Up to 3000 feet
Hiking time:	9 hours
Agency:	USFS/CNF-PRD
Trail use:	Dogs, horses
Notes:	Adventure Pass required; wilderness permit required to backpack; no campfires allowed
Trailhead GPS:	N33.45815, W116.97082
Optional map:	USGS 7.5-min *Vail Lake, Boucher Hill*
Atlas square:	N/A (Riverside County)
Directions:	(Temecula) From CA-79 go south into the Dripping Springs Campground, 10.5 miles east of I-15 and 7.4 miles west of CA-371. Park in the day-use area near the entrance.

Habitat(s):

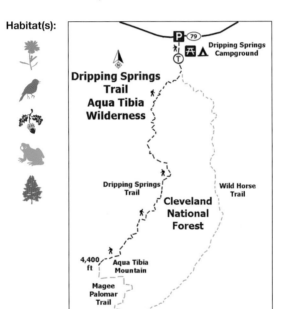

For those looking for something challenging, the Dripping Springs Trail is perfect. It not only offers a chance for vigorous exercise, but it also presents a series of dramatic vistas stretching as far north as the San Bernardino Mountains. And, most of the major southern California vegetation habitats are encountered while hiking here.

Dripping Springs Trail begins among granite boulders in a seasonal stream lined with coast live oaks, sycamores, and willows at an elevation of 1600 feet. Initially the route goes up a ridge covered with inland sage scrub and then through dense chaparral with big-berry manzanita and chaparral whitethorn thickets. Finally the route leads to the Coulter pine, big-

cone Douglas fir, and black oak-forested Agua Tibia Mountain at an elevation of 4400 feet. Agua Tibia Mountain is not a distinct peak but a broad ridge that is the northern most high point in the Palomar Mountain range.

The Dripping Springs Trailhead is at the far end of the Dripping Springs Campground, about 0.5 mile from the campground entrance. Proceed south along the dry Arroyo Seco Creek bed for a short distance after leaving the campground before entering the wilderness area. There is a junction on the left with the Wild Horse Trail 0.1 mile from the trailhead. The Wild Horse Trail continues up the Arroyo Seco and is another way to reach the summit, but not part of the hike described here. The

Vail Lake and Mt. San Jacinto

Dripping Springs Trail soon leaves the creek and begins a series of switchbacks up the dry side of the canyon onto a broad ridge.

During the first mile, the trail passes through typical coastal sage scrub vegetation. Many of these shrubs bloom in spring. The slope can look bleak in summer after the rains have stopped and the sagebrush has dropped its leaves. In a short distance a panoramic view opens up to include vineyards and Vail Lake below along CA-79, with Mount San Jacinto and Mount San Gorgonio in the distance to the north. Further along the trail as the elevation increases, typical chaparral species begin to appear.

In addition to the common big-berry manzanita and chaparral whitethorn, red shank (*Adenostoma sparsifolium*) is a dominant plant within this chaparral community. It can grow up to 15 feet in height, is multi-trunked, can be readily identified by its shredding, ribbon-like red bark, and has an abundance of cream-colored flowers. It is closely related to chamise (*Adenostoma fasciculatum*)—they are the only two species in their genus in the rose family—and often coexist, although red shank is numerous only in small local areas. Chamise's high drought-tolerance and adaptability allows it to be much more widely distributed than red shank. The leaves of both species are similar in size, but chamise leaves are close to the stem and conspicuously resinous. Like red shank, chamise will have an abundance of cream-colored flowers in spring and early summer. Chamise is much-branched and is an erect to spreading evergreen shrub that can grow up to 12 feet tall. Note the new growth on the chamise. It grows straight in order to provide less surface area to the sun and helps to conserve water. Because it grows straight, Native Americans used it to make the foreshaft of arrows for hunting. They would also use branches in the construction of houses, ramadas, granaries, and fences. The large roots were used for firewood and the coals were used for roasting agave.

Both red shank and chamise are highly flammable, but rapidly recover from wildfires and regrow quickly from basal burls, which begin

Red shank and manzanita

Red shank

Chamise

to sprout new growth as soon as the ground has cooled. Chamise's Spanish name *chamizo* translates as half-burned log or tree and refers to its often fire-scarred branches. Another name is greasewood, which refers to its high resin content that burns intensely. The natural resin found in chamise is a necessary part of the plant's drought strategy for water retention. Chamise's rapid growth after a fire, including germination of new seedlings, outcompetes surrounding plants for space, therefore making it one of the most abundant of chaparral species, occasionally blanketing entire hillsides with a uniform of olive green.

The Dripping Springs Trail ends on the shoulder of Agua Tibia Mountain, where it intersects with the Magee–Palomar Trail, 6.9 miles from the trailhead, in a beautiful grove

of Coulter pines, coast live oaks, and big-cone Douglas firs (**Pseudotsuga macrocarpa**), which are well-adapted to fire with their thick trunk and ability to sprout new crowns and branches. The fir is a medium-size tree, related to the tall Douglas fir covering much of the Pacific Northwest, but it is a smaller tree, reaching a height of up to 98 feet, but with much larger cones that are 4 to 6 inches long. It has long sweeping branches and reddish-brown twigs that are often drooping. The bark is dark, reddish-brown and deeply furrowed with rounded ridges. It is an evergreen with flat, single needles that are sharp pointed. It has a limited range in southern California, and this is near its southern limit. It rarely forms dense stands as its northern brother does.

Take a little time to walk to the top of the ridge for a view west into the Pauma Valley many thousands of feet below. The big-cone Douglas fir forest you passed is a place where backpackers and equestrians frequently camp. If considering this for an overnight backpack trip, plan on a dry camp and pack plenty of water. There are no springs on the Dripping Springs Trail; the campground and trail are named for springs that lie on the other side of CA-79. Also remember that no campfires are permitted. If not camping, retrace your steps back down to the campground and your vehicle.

Check on permits needed for access to Agua Tibia and Pine Creek, the two National Wilderness Preservation System areas in the San Diego portion of the Cleveland National Forest.

Big-cone Douglas fir

Distance:	8 miles, out-and-back
Difficulty:	🚶🚶🚶🚶
Elevation gain/loss:	Up to 1000 feet
Hiking time:	5 hours
Agency:	USFS/CNF-PRD
Trail use:	Dogs, horses
Notes:	Adventure Pass required; wilderness permit required to backpack; no campfires allowed
Trailhead GPS:	N33.45813, W116.97095
Optional map:	USGS 7.5-min *Vail Lake, Boucher Hill*
Atlas square:	N/A (Riverside County)
Directions:	(Temecula) From CA-79 go south into the Dripping Springs Campground, 10.5 miles east of I-15 and 7.4 miles west of CA-371. Park in the day-use area near the entrance.

Habitat(s):

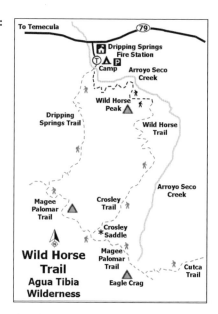

You are unlikely to encounter any horses on this trail, but it offers a chance to hike through shady oak and sycamore canyons and lush chaparral, which can be ablaze with the color of wildflowers from late winter to spring.

The trailhead is at the south end of the campground, 0.5 mile from the day-use parking area. It is well marked and easily found by walking south through the linear campground. Start hiking on the Dripping Springs Trail. Almost immediately you will cross the Arroyo Seco streambed. It is dry much of the year, as its name would suggest, but it can be a roaring river after a rainstorm; if so, cross it with care. After entering the Agua Tibia Wilderness, there is a trail fork with the Dripping Springs

Trail continuing straight ahead, while the Wild Horse Trail takes off to the left.

Wild Horse Trail rises steeply for about 0.5 mile, then levels off, gaining elevation more slowly as it undulates a couple of hundred feet above the Arroyo Seco streambed and passes in and out of its tributaries. Chaparral vegetation includes chamise and its tall, colorful relative, red shank, as well as the relatively rare rainbow manzanita.

Rainbow manzanita (*Arctostaphylos rainbowensis*) is endemic in the Peninsular Ranges in northern San Diego County (Fallbrook and Camp Pendleton areas) and the south end of Riverside County. It was named for Rainbow, a community just east of Fallbrook where it is

Wilderness area

Wrentit on laurel sumac

should be classified, as it is neither a wren nor a bushtit. It is the only species in its genus, and its closest relatives are in Asia. It is very sedentary, mates for life, and usually moves less than a quarter mile from the nest where it hatched to the first nest it builds itself.

On more moist and shady sites, the chaparral flora arches thickly over the trail, often reaching a height of 20 feet or more. Dense oak woodlands and riparian vegetation cloth some of the tributary canyons, especially the unnamed canyon at 1.75 miles from the starting point. The canyon's seasonal stream bubbles over rocks, flanked by mossy banks lined with ferns all under tall canyon oaks and western sycamores.

As the trail gradually climbs, the Arroyo Seco streambed grows more distant and views open up to the north and east to the San Jacinto and San Bernardino mountains. At about mile 4, the trail crosses a ridge and turns south. At this point there is a view to the east of a large vineyard nestled in a valley named Devils Hole. In the fall, you may hear periodic explosions as the farmers set off carbide cannons to scare birds away from the ripening grapes. This is a good place to turn around and head back. The Wild Horse Trail extends another 6 miles to the Crosley Saddle, overlooking the Pauma Valley and out to the Pacific, making that option a long 20-mile round trip.

prominent. It is endangered throughout most of its range due to loss of habitat. The Rainbow manzanita can grow to just over 10 feet in height and has a burl at its base from which new growth can appear after a fire. The flowers are white and the fruit is dark purple-brown in color.

A common bird that you might hear in the chaparral is the wrentit (*Chamaea fasciata*). Listen for its tell-tale song known as the voice of the chaparral. This small, dull, grayish brown song bird may be difficult to see among the thick chaparral, but its song is easily recognized and sometimes described as the sound of a ping-pong ball falling on a table. The wrentit is a year-round resident of the chaparral of western Oregon, California, and northwestern Baja and is also found in coastal sage scrub. Its name reflects some of the controversy of how it

Manzanita

Distance:	1.8 miles, loop
Difficulty:	
Elevation gain/loss:	Up to 400 feet
Hiking time:	1 hour
Agency:	USFS/CNF-PRD
Trail use:	Dogs
Notes:	Adventure Pass required
Trailhead GPS:	N33.34454, W116.88007
Optional map:	USGS 7.5-min *Boucher Hill*
Atlas square:	D14
Directions:	(Palomar Mountain) From CA-76 go east on S-6 (South Grade Road/Palomar Mountain Road) for 6.7 miles until the intersection. Turn left to stay on S-6 (Canfield Road/South Grade Road). Go 2.6 miles. Turn left into the Fry Creek Campground, just past Observatory Campground. The campground is closed from December 1 through March 31, but remains open to hikers. Park on the right side of the highway, and enter the campground on foot.

Habitat(s):

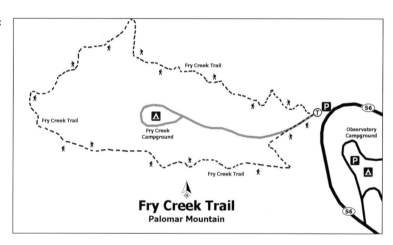

Fry Creek Trail
Palomar Mountain

The Fry Creek Trail is one of the few places to hike on public lands on Palomar Mountain, other than the trails of Palomar Mountain State Park. The Fry Creek trail climbs through a magnificent dense mixed montane forest that is reminiscent of forests much further north. Since it receives around 40 inches of rain each year, it has a lush growth of conifers and oaks, as well as an understory of manzanita, *Ceanothus*, coffeeberry, and other shrubs.

Coffeeberry (*Frangula californica*) is a shrub in the buckthorn family that is usually 3-6 feet tall but can grow up to 12 feet tall. Branches have a reddish tinge and new twigs are red. It has small greenish flowers. A hand lens is needed to see its five sepals and five petals that are characteristic of plants in the rose family. It is easily identified by consistently spaced par-

allel leaf veins that are prominent both visually and by touch on the leaf underside that is lighter green in color than the top. It derives its name from the fruit, a drupe, containing two seeds that resemble coffee beans. The fruit is edible and the beans have been used at times as a coffee substitute. The bark was used as a laxative by Native Americans.

Palomar Mountain was once called *Paauw* by the local Luiseño Indians. Santa Ysabel Kumeyaay Stan Rodriguez said it was called *'epal omarr*, which translates as, to win with arrows. The Spaniards gave it its current name, but for half a century, until 1920, it was called Smith Mountain after one of the early pioneers. Palomar means pigeon roost or pigeon home in Spanish. Palomar Mountain is home to the native band-tailed pigeon as well as the

Grassy saddle

acorn woodpecker, Steller's jay, golden eagle, and mountain quail. This is a good place to look for birds that may not be seen or rarely seen in the chaparral or desert environments.

The trail begins near the information boards about 100 feet from the campground entrance. After climbing up a small hill, the trail turns to the east, passing near campsite No. 1, and continues above the entrance road. Soon the trail makes a hairpin turn and proceeds up the south-facing Fry Creek slope, leaving the campground behind. From this point the hike is through a dense forest of canyon oak, coast live oak, Jeffrey pine, Coulter pine, white fir, big-cone Douglas fir, and California black oak.

After hiking about 0.8 mile, cross a dirt road with the trail continuing on the other side. This will go up to the high point of this trail, which is a saddle (5240'). The saddle is the divide between Fry Creek and an unnamed canyon leading down to Upper Doane Valley in the state park. There used to be a trail leading to the state park from near here, but now it is completely overgrown and is not recommended. An area of planted Coulter pines, known as Penny Pines, lies just off the trail.

After passing the high point, the trail begins its descent down the north-facing Fry Creek slope. The north-facing slope is steeper than the south-facing slope, so the forest is somewhat less dense, allowing occasional views beyond the immediate trees, including outlooks

to the white dome of the Palomar Observatory. A few short switchbacks will head down to the campground, near campsite No. 9, not far from the campground entrance.

Coffeeberry leaf

Coffeeberry

Distance:	4.4 miles, out-and-back
Difficulty:	🚶🚶🚶
Elevation gain/loss:	Up to 800 feet
Hiking time:	3 hours
Agency:	USFS/CNF-PRD
Trail use:	Dogs
Notes:	Adventure Pass required
Trailhead GPS:	N33.34313, W116.87758
Optional map:	USGS 7.5-min Boucher Hill, *Palomar Observatory*
Atlas square:	D14
Directions:	(Palomar Mountain) From CA-76 go east on S-6 (South Grade Road/ Palomar Mountain Road) for 6.7 miles until the intersection. Turn left to stay on S-6 (Canfield Road/South Grade Road). Go 2.3 miles. Turn right into the Observatory Campground. Follow signs for the Observatory trailhead parking.

Habitat(s):

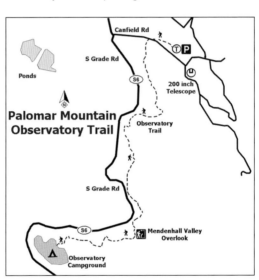

The Palomar Mountain Observatory Trail is one of only four National Recreation Trails in San Diego County. From the tree-shaded, well-maintained trail, there are bucolic vistas of grassy meadows with grazing cattle. It also provides a chance to visit the world class Palomar Observatory. It is easily accessible and is a rewarding hike year-round, but it could get snow in winter storms.

Palomar Mountain rises steeply from the Pauma Valley in the west and from the Temecula Valley in the east, but the mountain itself consists of gentle rolling hills blanketed by a lush mixed forest of conifers and oaks with scattered patches of chaparral. The hills are interspersed with broad, grassy valleys, possibly reminding one of Vermont. There is not one specific peak that can be said to be Palomar Mountain. The highest point, called simply High Point (6140'), can be reached by car from the town of Oak Grove on the east side, but is not often visited by the thousands of visitors who flock to Palomar Mountain to frolic in the winter snow or camp at one of the campgrounds. Palomar Mountain also is the home of the 200-inch Hale Telescope, only 2 miles from the Palomar Observatory Campground and the trailhead.

The Palomar Mountain Observatory, operated by Caltech and open to the public, has made fundamental discoveries about some of the most distant points of the universe and continues to be an important contributor to astronomy. The telescope and a small nearby museum are open to visitors daily. For more information, see www. astro.caltech.edu/palomar.

Mendenhall Valley

While Palomar Mountain is a delightful place to visit or for car camping, it has relatively few public trails. In part this is because much of the mountain is in private ownership. Mendenhall and Dyche valleys have working cattle ranches without public access. There are 14 miles of hiking trails within Palomar Mountain State Park, and only this hike and the Fry Creek Trail are within the Cleveland National Forest.

The Observatory Trail leaves the campground and parallels the road leading to Palomar Observatory, although the road can hardly be seen or heard from the trail. The trail passes through a highly varied forest, at times consisting of dense stands of coast live oak and scrub oak, interspersed with ponderosa and Jeffrey pines, while at other times it passes through glades of California incense cedar. Deciduous California black oaks provide autumn color as their leaves become golden, but they reemerge in the spring in a delicate pink before assuming the deep green of summer.

Palomar Mountain is a great place to compare the various three-needle pine trees found on the mountain. The easiest way is to compare the pine cones. Jeffrey or yellow pine (*Pinus Jeffreyi*) cones are smooth to the touch. Pacific ponderosa pines (*Pinus ponderosa*) are prickly, and Coulter pines (*Pinus coulteri*) are huge. This ditty helps: gentle Jeffrey, prickly ponderosa, and killer Coulter (if it falls on your head). The bark on the Jeffrey pine smells like vanilla, although some say it smells more like lemon, apple, pineapple, or even butterscotch, while that of the Ponderosa smells like pitch. The longest needles are on the Coulter pine.

As you hike, look for deep blue and rusty-colored western bluebirds (***Sialia mexicana***) that swoop to the ground from low perches to catch insects. They also eat berries. They nest in cavities in trees, often dead trees, made by woodpeckers or natural processes. In the nonbreeding season they are social and gather in flocks.

Western bluebird

Distance:	3 miles, out-and-back
Difficulty:	🚶🚶
Elevation gain/loss:	Up to 200 feet
Hiking time:	2 hours
Agency:	CSP-CDD
Notes:	Day-use fee; no bicycles or dogs allowed on trails at PMSP
Trailhead GPS:	N33.34147, W116.90155
Optional map:	USGS 7.5-min *Boucher Hill*
Atlas square:	E14
Directions:	(Palomar Mountain) From CA-76 go east on S-6 (South Grade Road/ Palomar Mountain Road) for 6.7 miles until the intersection. Turn left to stay on S-6. Turn left again immediately on S-7 (State Park Road), just before the store and restaurant. Go 3.1 miles. After Park entrance go 0.2 mile. Turn right at stop sign. Go 1.4 miles following signs to School Camp and Doane Pond. Parking lot on right.

Habitat(s):

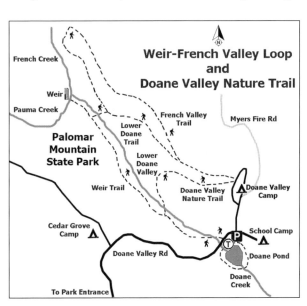

Palomar Mountain is one of the few places in San Diego County where you can go for a four-season experience. At over 5000 feet in elevation, it has a Sierra Nevada feel to it with a mixed conifer forest environment and a diversity of plant life, including western dogwood, ocellated lilies, and very small orchids. Wildlife includes the southern mule deer, bobcat, mountain quail, and Steller's jay.

At the parking lot, start on the Doane Valley Nature Trail, then head left on the Weir Trail to head to the stone weir that was constructed to control the flow of water. Rainbow trout can be spotted in the creeks. Many are escapees from Doane Pond, where they were stocked by the California Department of Fish and Wildlife. Watch for Pacific banana slugs (*Ariolimax columbianus*) along Doane Creek where there is an isolated population.

Banana slugs are usually yellowish in color, giving rise to their name, but here they are mostly brown. They are typically associated with the Pacific Northwest coastal coniferous rainforest areas, ranging as far south as Santa Cruz with isolated populations as far south as Palomar Mountain State Park. Palomar Mountain has a Sierra Nevada-like coniferous forest that can support the banana slugs, which are thought to be a relic of the Pleistocene epoch. The Pacific banana slug is the second largest species of terrestrial slugs in the world. They may grow up to 10 inches

Pacific banana slug

in length and weigh several ounces. Banana slugs are able to estivate, a type of hibernation, in hot dry weather. They bury themselves in the forest duff and excrete a layer of slime around themselves. While estivating they remain inactive until the rains come.

Doane Creek and French Creek merge just above the weir. There is a small pool of water next to the weir where volumetric flow rate was measured when the water flowed over a low barrier in hopes that power could be brought to the area. Turn back after a rest at the pond and continue up the trail until a spur crosses Doane Creek, turning left towards French Creek. Then loop back on the French Valley Trail until you reach the Doane Valley Campground. Find and take the Doane Valley Nature Trail, which will take you to the parking lot to retrieve your car. There is a restroom behind trees at the kiosk after crossing a small bridge with a view of the pond.

The loop trail can also be accessed at the Doane Valley Nature Trail and Doane Valley Trail intersection, starting at the corner of the Doane Valley parking lot or by walking from the parking lot to the campground trailhead, just beyond campsite No. 25. The trail from the campground peeks in and out of the pines, oaks, firs, and shrubs. If you stay to the right, you will remain on the French Valley Trail. Here, note the ancient oaks, some of which have grown over large granitic boulders for support. There is evidence of acorn woodpecker granaries in enormous pines. However, many pines have succumbed to

fire and bark beetle infestation. There is also a large group of deep morteros as you head down valley on the left hand side of the trail.

After about 1 mile, the trail loops back to the left and follows the edge of a meadow before merging with the Lower Doane Trail. A right turn will head you in the direction of Doane Creek. If you turn right again just before Doane Creek, a spur trail will take you out and back to the weir. Use caution when stepping on the rocks surrounding the pool of water in front of the weir, as they are well-worn and very slick, making it easy to take a plunge! After returning on the spur trail, continue across Doane Creek, and turn left to head back up valley toward the Doane parking lot. This portion of trail has some exposure, and then disappears under tall firs. The trail ends with a short steep section up stone steps and a shallow creek crossing with stepping-stones. Cross the main park road to a short bridge crossing, and the trail will end at the parking lot.

The weir

Distance:	1 mile, loop
Difficulty:	🚶🚶
Elevation gain/loss:	Up to 300 feet
Hiking time:	1 hour
Agency:	CSP-CDD
Notes:	Parking fee; two stream crossings; no bicycles or dogs allowed on trails at PMSP
Trailhead GPS:	N33.34147, W116.90155
Optional map:	USGS 7.5-min *Boucher Hill*
Atlas square:	E14
Directions:	(Palomar Mountain) From CA-76 go east on S-6 (South Grade Road/Palomar Mountain Road) for 6.7 miles until the intersection. Turn left to stay on S-6. Turn left again immediately on S-7 (State Park Road), just before the store and restaurant. Go 3.1 miles. After Park entrance go 0.2 mile. Turn right at stop sign. Go 1.4 miles following signs to School Camp and Doane Pond. Parking lot on right.

Habitat(s):

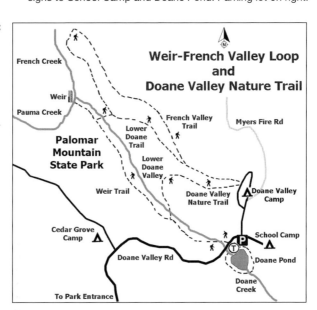

The Doane Valley Nature Trail provides a sampling of the many plants and shrubs that can be found at Palomar Mountain State Park. Taking a hike on this trail is a great way to learn about those plants. If you enjoy nature trails with interpretive stations, you will be delighted with this trail. There are 30 stations, each giving a brief description of the plant, shrub, tree, or item featured. Be sure to pick up a trail guide at the trailhead. There is a small fee charged for the guide, and it is well worth it as the rangers of Palomar Mountain State Park have done a wonderful job putting it together.

The nature trail runs alongside Doane Creek, and the brochure highlights many of

the plants and shrubs found here and provides information on how the Luiseño tribe of Native Americans used them for food, housing, and/or clothing. A Luiseño band has lived on or near Palomar Mountain since pre-Hispanic times—before 1769. Luiseños are related to the Cupeños, who once lived at Warner Springs before being marched down the Cupeño Trail of Tears to the Pala Reservation. They are also related to the Cahuillas who live today at Agua Caliente and further north in the Santa Rosa Mountains, Palm Springs area, and east to the Coachella Valley. They speak a Uto-Aztecan Shoshoni language, while the Kumeyaay, who live to the

Andrew Currie

California rose

Enrique Medina

Thimbleberry

south and in northern Baja California, Mexico, speak a Yuman language. The Luiseño and Kumeyaay have different customs, but their use of plants is similar.

At the first station is a hoary or stinging nettle (*Urtica dioica*) with beautiful green leaves. The recommendation is to look but not touch this plant as it has chemicals in its trichomes or hairs that will cause a mildly painful sting if touched. Some Native American tribes in southern California used the stem and leaves as a threat to whip misbehaving children. The Luiseño would collect the younger leaves, boil them, and eat them as greens. The stems were gathered in fall and used as a fiber for basket making or to make twine used to make fishing nets and slings. The stems and leaves were also gathered to treat rheumatism or arthritic joints and as a bath for poison-oak and other skin irritations. It continues to be used by some modern-day medical practitioners to treat prostate enlargement and other illnesses. You can buy powered stinging nettle in many health food stores today.

The five-petaled California rose (*Rosa californica*) is at the second station. This is the wild rose of much of California. Notice the placement of the thorns, which are correctly called prickles as these modified hairs occur randomly on the plant. Thorns are modified branches that occur at nodes in an axillary position with leaves below, while spines are modified leaves or stipules and may have a bud or a portion of the leaf above. The hooked thorns or prickles of the California rose act like a thorny Velcro. Rose hips, the fruit of the plant,

are edible and high in vitamin C. Rose hip jam is commonly prepared and eaten by rural families, but has never been commercialized. In addition to being a food, it had many uses both medicinal and religious in Native American culture.

Landscape features are also pointed out along the trail. For instance, station No. 8 highlights where a landslide took place during the winter of 1992-93 when approximately 80 inches of rain fell on the mountain. You will also learn about various mountain wildflowers, such as the thimbleberry (*Rubus parviflorus*) that grows in abundance alongside the creek. It is not a true berry and is like a raspberry with an aggregate of fruit drupelets around a core. When the fruit is removed from the central core, it resembles a thimble. Thimbleberry fruits are too soft to be sold in stores, but they are collected and made into a jam sold as a local delicacy. It is also in the rose family.

After following the stream for about 0.25 mile, the trail climbs a little into an open meadow where grassland shrubs and flowers can be seen. The trail continues to rise into a wooded hillside where there is white alder, California incense cedar, white fir, Jeffrey pine, and California black oak. The trail ends on the access road to the Doane Valley Campground where you can either turn around and go back down the same trail to see the things missed on the way up or traverse the campground and return to Doane Pond via the road.

Be sure to check at the entrance station whether any guided nature walks or campfire programs are scheduled while you are there.

Distance:	4 miles, loop
Difficulty:	🚶🚶🚶
Elevation gain/loss:	Up to 900 feet
Hiking time:	3 hours
Agency:	CSP-CDD
Notes:	Parking fee; trekking poles recommended; no bicycles or dogs allowed on trails at PMSP
Trailhead GPS:	N33.34140, W116.90129
Optional map:	USGS 7.5-min *Boucher Hill*
Atlas square:	E14
Directions:	(Palomar Mountain) From CA-76 go east on S-6 (South Grade Road/Palomar Mountain Road) for 6.7 miles until the intersection. Turn left to stay on S-6. Turn left again immediately on S-7 (State Park Road), just before the store and restaurant. Go 3.1 miles. After Park entrance go 0.2 mile. Turn right at stop sign. Go 1.4 miles following signs to School Camp and Doane Pond. Parking lot on right.

Habitat(s):

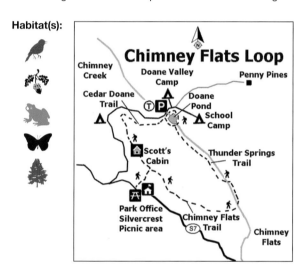

Thanks to the efforts of volunteer organizations such as Friends of Palomar Mountain and the Palomar Mountain Trail Maintenance Unit, plus the State Park rangers, the park has well-maintained trails, restrooms, and camping facilities. Simply put, Palomar is beautiful. The old growth cedars and oak trees might make you feel as if you were magically transported into the middle of a northwest forest. Whether you visit the park on a warm, sunny day or on a misty, overcast one, stunning vistas abound.

A recommended route with great views is the steep Cedar Trail past Doane Pond up to the Silvercrest picnic area along the Scott's Cabin Trail, and then along the Chimney Flats Trail until it loops back to Doane Pond via the Thunder Spring Trail.

The parking area near Doane Pond offers access to Cedar Trail once past the facilities and over the small bridge next to the pond's edge. The trail is steep, so come prepared with good footwear and trekking poles if you use them. Watch out for western poison-oak, which in October is surprisingly beautiful with brilliant red color that glows with light shining through the leaves. The contrast of red against yellow ferns, the green of the cedar, yellow of California black oak, and the gray-greens of lichen and moss on the tree trunks create a perfect fall palette. New healthy growth or, in the winter, leafless twigs ring the base of old, fire-scarred tree trunks and line portions of the Cedar Trail. Early morning provides the best opportunity for viewing deer and non-native turkeys. Predators that are there but are less likely to be seen

Ladybug or ladybird beetles

include the mountain lion, bobcat, coyote, and gray fox (*Urocyon cinereoargenteus*).

The gray fox is considered the most primitive of the living canids. Because it has hooked claws, it has the ability, unusual among canids, to climb trees, by which it avoids other predators. The gray fox is grizzled-gray on top, reddish on the sides, and has a bushy tail that is one-third of its body length with a dark stripe and tip. The vixen or female gray fox may use a hollow tree for a den. The gray fox is active primarily at night.

Follow the Scott's Cabin Trail to the cabin site. Just past the site is a spur trail that leads to Silvercrest and park headquarters where picnic tables are available. Return to Scott's Cabin Trail and continue along the trail, which becomes Chimney Flats Trail as it curves back toward Doane Pond. At the intersection with Upper Doane Valley Trail, go left on Thunder Spring Trail to close the loop at Doane Pond.

One of the highlights on this hike is Chimney Creek with its small waterfall and the thick growth of western azaleas. Hike in May and June to see and smell them in bloom.

On cold winter days, ladybug or ladybird beetles (**family Coccinellidae** with over 5000 species) sometimes can be found in great numbers in the deergrass (bunchgrass) or other low foliage. Despite being commonly referred to as ladybugs, they are true beetles with parallel hard wing covers creating a centerline down their back and chewing mouthparts. True bugs (**order Hemiptera**) have needle-like stylets that pierce plants for liquid and have wings that look like an X. Bugs have incomplete metamorphosis with the juveniles lacking wings and are smaller than adults. Ladybug beetles have complete metamorphosis with the larvae being voracious predators of aphids, more so than in the adult stage. The lady for whom they were named is the Virgin Mary. In German, they are also known as the Mary beetle. The red is said to represent her cloak and the black spots her sorrow. This lady can be foul smelling. When threatened, this beetle excretes a fluid from the knee joints that is both toxic and rank smelling that can repulse potential predators. It also leaves a yellow stain on leaf surfaces. The red and black coloration also signals potential toxicity to predators. This lady is not nice. If hungry, it will cannibalize its own siblings or larvae.

Check the park website (www.parks.ca.gov) for campsite reservations, maps, and other useful information.

Harlequin bug: note X wings

Distance:	2 miles, out-and-back
Difficulty:	🏃
Elevation gain/loss:	Up to 200 feet
Hiking time:	1 hour
Agency:	CSP-CDD
Notes:	Parking fee; no bicycles or dogs allowed on trails at PMSP
Trailhead GPS:	N33.33204, W116.90710
Optional map:	USGS 7.5-min *Boucher Hill*
Atlas square:	E14
Directions:	(Palomar Mountain) From CA-76 go east on S-6 (South Grade Road/ Palomar Mountain Road) for 6.7 miles until the intersection. Turn left to stay on S-6. Turn left again immediately on S-7 (State Park Road), just before the store and restaurant. Go 3.1 miles. After the park entrance, turn left into the Silvercrest Picnic Area and park.

Habitat(s):

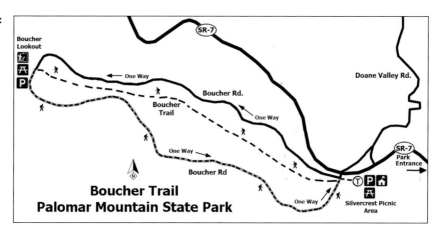

Boucher Trail
Palomar Mountain State Park

Palomar Mountain is known for its wide diversity of plants and wildlife. There is plenty to investigate on the Boucher Loop while hiking among tall trees, chaparral, and meadow communities. This short scenic hike includes local and natural history.

From the Silvercrest parking area, walk back out to the parking entrance and turn left. Alternatively, walk through the Silvercrest Picnic Area, where there is a trail sign leading to the park road. Go downhill along the main paved road while keeping to the right side of the road to avoid any traffic along the blind curve. Along the road, begin enjoying the diversity of plant life. Proceed past the ranger's house to the junction of Nate Harrison Road and the Campground Road. At the junction there is a stone plaque on the left that commemorates those that served in the Civilian Conservation Corps (CCC) on Palomar Mountain and across the United States. The

CCC was responsible for building structures and trails in the park.

Ahead on the left is the narrow trailhead, which is located on a one-way paved loop road. The Boucher Trail parallels the paved one-way road to Boucher Lookout. This trail maintains a gentle ascent through partly shaded and open mixed conifer forest. The hike is ideal in the fall when the California black oaks are changing color. Southern mule deer are frequently seen along this portion of the trail.

The trail begins on a moderate slope with partially open areas. Along the trail there is evidence of past fires that include hollow logs and burnt tree sculptures. Palomar has sustained several fires over the years, including a severe firestorm in the 1980s. Continuing uphill, the trail will eventually become more level and shady, and there will be views through the trees on both sides of the trail. To

California incense cedar

California incense cedar granary

the right, Lower French Valley is visible below in the distance, and to the left are views down the mountain. The trail will drop downhill briefly and join the paved loop road. Stay on the dirt trail to the right for now in order to enjoy the left side views more fully upon your return trip via the paved loop road.

Along the route, look for several massive California incense cedar trees (**Calocedrus decurrens**) covered with acorn caches. The trees are used by many generations of acorn woodpeckers. California incense cedars typically reach heights of 130-200 feet and are only found at the higher mountain elevations. The bright green foliage is in flattened sprays of scale-like leaves. When crushed, the aroma is reminiscent of shoe polish. California incense cedar is one of the most fire and drought tolerant of plants. Indians used the bark of the tree to make temporary shelters while gathering acorns in the mountains.

At the top of the trail, there is an historical fire lookout tower, viewing deck, and picnic area. The current fire tower is the third lookout structure built on this location. This tower was transported here in 1948 and was in use until 1983. It was reopened in 2012 and is often manned with volunteers who will invite you to come up the tower for a visit. The top of the tower provides a magnificent 360-degree view. The volunteers will share information about how to determine the direction and distance of a smoke plume or fire.

The viewing deck is a separate structure at ground level, looks out over the edge of the point, and provides a panoramic view to the north, west, and southeast. On clear days, it is possible to view as far as the Coronado Islands and Baja California with the naked eye. However, there is also a scope available for your use. The deck includes informative panels on the history of the area. A parking lot at the top provides easy access for visitors, making summer weekends and holidays a busy time to visit.

Return to the park entrance by following the paved road to the left from the fire tower

Viewpoint

picnic area. This road circles around the hill while hugging the edge of the mountain, providing outstanding views. The road is not used frequently by motorized vehicles, but be aware of the possibility of downhill traffic. Look for band-tailed pigeons (**Patagioenas fasciata**) roosting in the trees. The local native band-tailed pigeon is much larger than a city pigeon. It is the closest genetic relative to the extinct passenger pigeon. The gray band-tailed pigeon forms large flocks and feeds on acorns, seeds, buds, and fruits, such as elderberry. It can be recognized by its yellow bill, a white crescent on its nape, and a long tail with a dark band across the middle and a wide pale band at the end. Nesting pairs can travel up to 3 miles from their nest to hunt for food for their young. Like other doves, parents feed their young with a secretion from their esophagus called crop milk.

On the descent back to the starting point, the route will merge with the main park road. A right turn will lead back uphill to the Silvercrest parking lot. While at Silvercrest, take the time to walk the path from the parking lot along the left side of the picnic area. There you will find morteros used by the Luiseño Indians and a 400-year-old California incense cedar. Look for overlapping scale-leaves that hang down on this tree.

The trail

Distance:	7 miles
Difficulty:	🚶🚶🚶🚶
Elevation gain/loss:	Up to 1000 feet
Hiking time:	4 hours
Agency:	USFS/CNF-PRD
Trail use:	Dogs, horses
Notes:	Adventure Pass required
Trailhead GPS:	N33.33966, W116.78794
Optional map:	USGS 7.5-min *Palomar Observatory*
Atlas square:	E16
Directions:	(Palomar Mountain) From CA-79 go west on Palomar Divide Road (S907), 10 miles north of S-2 and 13.2 miles south of CA-371, for 7.8 miles. Park on side of road. Trailhead on the left.

Habitat(s):

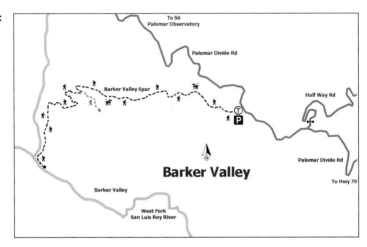

Barker Valley, at the southern end of Palomar Mountain and between the peak of Palomar Mountain to the north and Lake Henshaw to the south, is one of the most remote and least visited locations in the area. Whether for a dayhike or an overnight backpacking adventure, you may have this secluded little valley to yourself.

The hike starts with a scenic, winding 7.8-mile drive to the trailhead. After passing the entrance gate just off the CA-79, continue on a well-maintained dirt road. At 1.4 miles there will be a segment of paved, but deteriorating, asphalt road. There is an access control gate at 3.6 miles which may be closed after bad weather to prevent road damage. At 6.2 miles, the pavement ends, and the dirt road becomes increasingly rough with the last mile possibly requiring a higher clearance vehicle. Note that at 6.8 miles there is an intersection with Half Way Road (9S06). Make sure you don't take this road on the return drive; a locked

gate might prevent you from reaching the highway. At 7.8 miles from the highway, there will be a wide section in the road and the sign for Barker Valley. Park and do not block the road. In spring, there may be roadside displays of showy penstemon (***Penstemon spectabilis var. spectabilis***) with their long stalks of light purple, trumpet-like flowers and spiny, prickly poppy (***Argemone munita***), reminiscent of a sunny side up fried egg. The showy penstemon is a perennial herb with a wide-mouthed tubular flower that is purplish-blue in color. It is pollinated by hummingbirds and wasps. The species name for prickly poppy, meaning armed, is a reference to its spiny stems and prickly leaves. The dark pistil in the center of the yellow stamens, surrounded by six white crinkly petals, looks like a speck of pepper on a fried egg.

The Barker Valley trail is well-maintained and easily followed with the first section gradually descending down the old roadbed of the

Showy penstemon

Barker Valley Spur for 1.7 miles. Then, after a sharp bend to the left, the trail narrows and winds its way to the valley floor, 3.1 miles and 1000 feet below the starting point. The trail is lined with manzanita, the ubiquitous chamise, and the closely related red shank. Depending on the time of the year, the sides of the trail can host a wide variety of wildflowers.

Glance down, as there may be a horned lizard, which resembles a miniature dinosaur, or tracks of southern mule deer on the trail. Look up, as there are often red-tailed hawks or other raptors soaring on the valley's thermals. The lucky observer may also spot a bald eagle (*Haliaeetus leucocephalus*), a species that winters at Lake Henshaw and, since 2004, roosts there sometimes. The bald eagle has been the national emblem of the US since 1782. These heavy-bodied birds have, in adult plumage, white heads and tails, and dark brown bodies and wings, and they engage in piracy. Rather than doing their own hunting, they often harass another raptor in mid-air until it drops its catch and the eagle can swoop in and grab it. The bald eagle is notorious for forcing an osprey to drop a fish so it can steal it. Bald eagles even steal prey from fishing mammals. Benjamin Franklin opposed the selection of the bald eagle as the emblem of the US because he felt it was of "bad moral character" by not earning an honest living.

Across the valley on the ridge to the north are the white domes of several of the Caltech's Palomar Observatory telescopes, including the famous 200-inch Hale Telescope—for decades the largest telescope in the world. To the right on the ridge is the High Point fire lookout tower. Built in 1967, at 67 feet it is the tallest remaining forest service lookout in California.

Once on the valley floor you will soon reach the bed of the west fork of the San Luis Rey River. Here, there are several choices. Rest in the shade of one of the large coast live oaks and then return uphill for a 7-mile out-and-back trip. Alternatively, if time and energy allow, turn upstream and follow the trail to an open clearing, a nice spot if setting up camp for the night. In picking a spot for your tent and sleeping bag, be careful to avoid areas where California harvester ants (**Pogonomyrmex californious**) are active. These large red ants form colonies in sandy open areas that may seem ideal for a tent. But beware, these ants are aggressive and a have very painful bite. While you don't want them for campmates, they are interesting to observe. The nest may have a single entrance, but it may extend several meters underground with many branches and cavities. A colony may occupy the same nest for many years and house a large number of successive generations. A clear area usually surrounds the nest entrance, but there will be a ring of seed husks on its periphery. The ants eat seeds, depositing the husks neatly out of their living area.

Another option is turning south to follow the trail downstream for about 1 mile to discover a rocky area with pools, waterfalls, and more potential campsites where granitic rocks with holes for grinding acorns, called morteros, can be found by the observant hiker.

California harvester ant

Distance:	2 or 4 miles, out-and-back
Difficulty:	🚶 or 🚶🚶
Elevation gain/loss:	Up to 300 feet
Hiking time:	1 or 2 hours
Agency:	USFS/CNF-PRD
Trail use:	Bicycles, dogs, horses
Notes:	Adventure Pass required
Trailhead GPS:	N33.26379, W116.77376
Optional map:	USGS 7.5-min *Palomar Observatory*
Atlas square:	F16
Directions:	(Palomar Mountain) From CA-76 go north on S7 (East Grade Road) for 3.3 miles. Parking and trailhead on left.

Habitat(s):

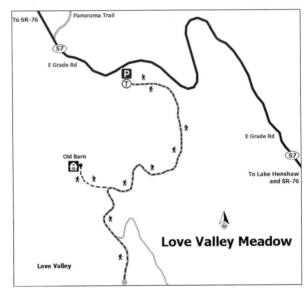

The trailhead for Love Valley Meadow can be easily missed when driving up the East Grade Road/S-7 into Palomar Mountain, as it begins from the back of a deep turn-out alongside the road. While not a particularly long or challenging trail, it offers the opportunity to spend a few hours enjoying the views and solitude of this pocket-sized mountain valley. Once owned by the Mendenhall family who settled on Palomar Mountain in 1869, Love Valley has been part of the Cleveland National Forest since the 1980s. The Mendenhalls did, and still do, use Love Valley for winter grazing of cattle that summer in nearby French Valley.

The entrance gate to the trail is found at the rear of the turnout. The trail is on a wide dirt road, which is a former segment of East Grade Road. Before leaving the turnout, look

for the small light blue, sometimes almost white, displays of baby blue eyes and the dark purple pea-like flowers of winter vetch.

As you descend into Love Valley, you will be rewarded with spectacular views of Lake Henshaw in San Felipe Valley. The lake came into being in 1923 with the construction of Henshaw Dam, an earthen dam 123 feet tall and 650 feet long. It is owned by the Vista Irrigation District, and its waters are used primarily for agricultural irrigation. It fills what is termed a sag basin caused by downward land movements beside the Elsinore fault.

If hiking in spring, look for the purple blooms of *Ceanothus* and the hot pink flowers of the four-petal California rock-cress (***Boechera californica***) sprouting from their long slender stalks along the trail. Even the California black oak will have color in spring.

View of Lake Henshaw

Although not a flower, the pinkish red hue of new black oak leaves put on a colorful show before they turn to their summer green. While parts of this area were burned in the 1999 La Jolla Indian Reservation fire, the chaparral has recovered well.

At the valley floor, the trail may be taken either to the right or left. Going right for a short distance (0.2 mile) will bring you to a dilapidated barn and corral. You may spot red-winged blackbirds atop the wooden fence. Look for the flash of the red on their wings as they move from perch to perch. After visiting the barn, retrace your steps to the trail junction and continue south along the meadow while walking among stands of blue-gray leaved Engelmann oaks and their cousins, the coast live oaks with darker green, cup-shaped, often spiny leaves.

The meadow hosts a variety of San Diego County wildflowers, depending on the season. Purple bouquets of lupine, seas of yellow buttercups, and the pink cup-shaped flowers of checkerbloom cover the meadow floor. There may also be seasonal ponds after the showers of winter and spring. You may choose to turn around at any point or continue along the meadow's edge and eventu-

ally loop back to the old barn. In either case, retrace your steps back up the road to return to your vehicle.

California rock-cress

Distance:	4.6 miles, out-and-back
Difficulty:	🚶🚶🚶
Elevation gain/loss:	Up to 1200 feet
Hiking time:	3 hours
Agency:	CSP-CDD
Notes:	Trekking poles recommended
Trailhead GPS:	N33.38155, W116.59513
Optional map:	USGS 7.5-min *Bucksnort Mtn*
Atlas square:	C20
Directions:	(Warner Springs) From CA-79 go east on Chihuahua Valley Road for 6.3 miles. At this point, Chihuahua Valley Road makes a ninety-degree right turn. Don't turn. Continue straight ahead onto the unpaved Lost Valley Road. Almost immediately the road seems to split, with a well-graded road leading off to the left while a rougher dirt road goes off to the right. Take the road to the right to stay on Lost Valley Road and continue for 5 miles. The Pacific Crest Trail (PCT) crosses Lost Valley Road near this point. Park on the left. Trailhead is on the left.

Habitat(s):

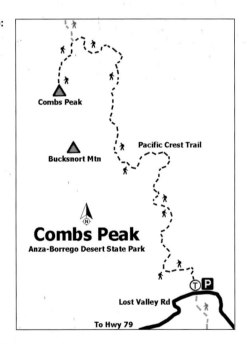

Combs Peak on Bucksnort Mountain is the fifth highest peak in San Diego County and also one of the most remote. Surprisingly, it is in the Anza-Borrego Desert State Park. From this lofty summit there are views of the two highest peaks in southern California—San Gorgonio and San Jacinto. There is also a view of the second lowest point on the North American continent—the Salton Sea. The sea's surface is 227 feet below sea level, 55 feet higher than Death Valley.

A sign designating the Pacific Crest Trail (PCT) marks the trailhead. It indicates that it is 6 miles to the Riverside County line and 24 miles to the nearest facility at Paradise Café. Start hiking north on the PCT as it makes its way up a relatively gradual slope from Lost Valley Road to an unnamed saddle, gaining about 600 feet of elevation in 1.8 miles. The Coyote Fire struck this area in 2003, killing the scattered Coulter pines that grew with red shank and chamise in this chaparral domi-

Don Fosket

View toward Salton Sea

nated habitat. Since the 2003 fire, the chaparral shrubs have made a comeback, particularly on the lower and east-facing slopes. Numerous seedling Coulter pines make an appearance near the saddle, but there are no mature pines until the peak, where a single, relatively large pine managed to avoid death by wildfire.

Watch for western poison-oak on this hike and check for ticks (**Dermacentor sp.**), which are arachnids and spider relatives that are parasites and blood feeders. Humans, pets, and wild animals are all suitable hosts for ticks. Unlike a mosquito that bites, sucks, and quickly leaves, the tick bites and feeds for days. It attaches itself very firmly so that it can't be easily dislodged. It does this with curved teeth and spines on its mouthparts and by burying them deeply. The tick may also have a parasite living in it, like the spirochete bacteria that causes Lyme disease. As the tick feeds, it releases anticoagulants that keep blood from clotting. Feeding stimulates the spirochete bacteria that lives in the gut of the tick and causes it to begin moving into the tick's bloodstream and saliva so that it can enter a new host. The process takes several days. Immediate removal of ticks can help prevent the spread of Lyme disease that is passed from the saliva of the very small deer tick into the host's bloodstream.

Once at the saddle, leave the PCT and begin a more arduous, but shorter journey from the saddle to the peak over a rarely trod trail, gaining another 600 feet of elevation in only 0.5 mile. Many PCT thru-hikers camp at this saddle as it is one of the few relatively flat areas for

many miles. Look for an obvious camping spot on the left as you cross the saddle. The trail starts just west of this camping spot and goes up the ridge. The trail is not always obvious, but is well marked with small stacks of three or more rocks, called either a cairn or duck to point the way. Once on the peak the reward will be some amazing views. Return the same way taking care when descending.

Note: Trail angels may provide a drinking water stash for PCT thru-hikers who may not have another source. Please do not use this water unless you are a PCT thru-hiker. Bring your own water for this outing, at least two liters.

Don Fosket

PCT signage

Distance:	8 miles, out-and-back
Difficulty:	🚶🚶🚶🚶
Elevation gain/loss:	Up to 1000 feet
Hiking time:	5 hours
Agency:	USFS/CNF-PRD
Trail use:	Horses
Notes:	Treat stream water before drinking
Trailhead GPS:	N33.28854, W116.65571
Optional map:	USGS 7.5-min *Warner Springs*
Atlas square:	F19
Directions:	(Warner Springs) From CA-79 turn south into turnout, 4.9 miles north of S-2 and 18.5 miles south of CA-371, and park. The trailhead is across the road.

Habitat(s):

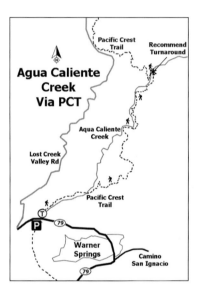

This section of the Pacific Crest Trail (PCT) is a welcome sight for thru-hikers on their way to Canada after spending many days in waterless stretches of the desert. Dayhikers will also enjoy the oaks and sycamores alongside a stream as well as chaparral and wildflower habitat. In most years, water flows beside several miles of the trail as Agua Caliente Creek descends from the San Ysidro Mountains. It is best not to count on water being present since in some years the creek goes dry by late summer.

Initially, the trail is just above or on a broad sandy wash studded with towering coast and Engelmann oaks, interspersed with sagebrush and non-native grasses. The trail here is on Warner Ranch property that the PCT legally crosses as a result of an easement. Numerous horse tracks and a dirt road intertwine, but the PCT is well marked and easily followed. After trudging through the sand for about 1 mile, the trail crosses the stream and begins a gradual climb up a chaparral covered hillside, leaving Warner Ranch property and entering the Cleveland National Forest.

Chamise dominates the chaparral at first, but as the trail climbs, red shank or ribbonwood, a chamise cousin, becomes more abundant, forming a nearly 20-foot canopy over the trail. When the red shank is in bloom in October, it casts a golden glow over the entire chaparral-covered hillsides. Holly-leaf redberry (***Rhamnus ilicifolia***) is less frequently encountered but easily identified with its serrated, holly-like, thick oval leaves that curve under in concave fashion. If you are lucky enough to see it in fruit, the bright, translucent scarlet berries seem to glow in the sun-

The creek flows in summer

chaparral candle, and Mojave yucca. A late winter or spring visit has an additional reward with numerous blooming herbaceous plants, including paintbrush, showy penstemon, scarlet monkey flower, and purple owl's-clover (*Castilleja exserta*) that is related to paintbrush. This annual herb in the broom-rape family is a hemiparasite sending out modified roots called haustoria that penetrate the cells of a host plant to extract water and nutrients from it. It can also photosynthesize. Examples of other hemiparasites are desert mistletoe and *Krameria*. Purple owl's-clover is a tubular flower surrounded by colorful purple to lavender bracts or modified leaves, which give the appearance of being the flower, much like a poinsettia.

After hiking about 3 miles listen for the sound of water flowing over rocks as you descend toward the stream. The trail then follows the stream for almost 1 mile, crossing it several times. The stream passes through a riparian forest dominated by coast live oaks, western sycamores, arroyo willow, western cottonwoods, and Coulter pines. The trees here are not as large as those encountered in the first part of the hike, but they are much more numerous and provide almost constant shade.

After nearly 4 miles, the trail leaves the stream and begins to switchback up the hillside. This may be a good point to turn around and retrace your steps. If you were focused on the trail ahead on the way to this point, the journey back is an opportunity to enjoy the views to the west toward Lake Henshaw and Palomar Mountain.

light. The Native Americans used the roots and bark of this plant to alleviate pain, but it is unclear if they ate the berries. There are a few reports of modern-day people eating the berries and finding them flavorful. However, until their potential toxicity has been investigated, it is best to leave these berries for the wildlife. The beauty of this plant has led it to its wide use in horticulture.

Other plants to look for in this area include mountain-mahogany, big-berry manzanita, white sage, toyon, *Ceanothus*, sugar bush,

Holly-leaf redberry

Purple Owl's clover

Distance:	6.5 miles, out-and-back
Difficulty:	🚶🚶🚶🚶
Elevation gain/loss:	Up to 1600 feet
Hiking time:	5 hours
Agency:	USFS/CNF-PRD
Trail use:	Horses
Trailhead GPS:	N33.27342, W116.64496
Optional map:	USGS 7.5-min *Warner Springs*
Atlas square:	F19
Directions:	(Warner Springs) From CA-79 park next to the Cal Fire station, 2.5 miles north of S-2 and 21 miles south of CA-371. The trailhead is about 10 yards south of the fire station on the east side of CA-79. Look for a gate and the Pacific Crest Trail sign.

Habitat(s):

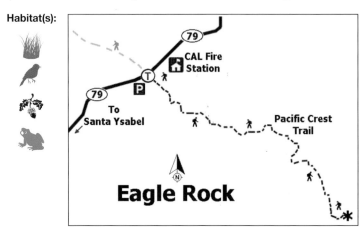

The trail to the Eagle Rock formation passes by huge old live oaks and what may be San Diego's oldest and largest sugar bush. From March to May there can be fields of wildflowers. It is also an opportunity to hike a little over a 3-mile segment of the Pacific Crest Trail (PCT), named a National Scenic Trail by Congress in 1968. The trail stretches 2627 miles from Mexico to the Canadian border.

From the trailhead, follow the well-marked PCT signs south and east up Canada Verde Creek as it passes through open oak woodland with huge old coast live oaks. Notice that some of the oaks are marked as bee trees. The creek runs strong after rains and is lined with dense riparian vegetation. The trail follows the creek, but it is largely out of the creek. At intervals the oak woodland is interspersed with chaparral shrubs.

Look for the old, large sugar bush (*Rhus ovata*). It is more a tree than a shrub. The sugar bush generally is an evergreen shrub or small tree, found on dry slopes and foothills. Leaves are broad, leathery, and folded along the midrib with smooth edges. The fruit is a red sticky drupe that was gathered June through August by local Indians and eaten fresh, cooked, or dried and then ground into a flour for mush. It was also made into a lemonade-like drink. The leaves of sugar bush were used in a tea as an aid during childbirth or to cure coughs, colds, and chest pain. As a member of the sumac family, it is related to western poison-oak.

After about 1.25 miles, the trail leaves the oak woodland and begins a gradual climb up a hillside sparsely covered with chaparral. In an exceptional year this area can put on a stunning display of annual wildflowers. As this is the west side of the San Ysidro Mountains, the display will come a little later than on the hotter, dryer east side.

After 2 miles, the trail goes over a gentle rise and crosses open grassland with much evidence of cattle. Here in this open rangeland are sporadic occurrences of annual wildflowers along with the non-native grasses. At the peak of the

The backside of Eagle Rock

season, whole hillsides may be painted blue, yellow, red, or golden with wildflowers. While walking through the grasslands, be on the lookout for a low-gliding and possibly weaving northern harrier (***Circus cyaneus***) that may be looking and listening for a tasty meal of a small mammal. The northern harrier is a slender, medium-sized hawk with a long rounded tail and broad wings that are held in a V-shape when gliding. Males are white below and gray above with black wingtips. Females are brown with white below that is streaked in brown. The northern harrier has an owl-like face and a hooked bill, and like an owl, it relies on hearing as well as vision to find prey. It nests on the ground usually in clumps of willow, grasses, reeds, sedges, or cattails.

At about 3.4 miles, an outcropping of boulders on the hill up ahead will become visible. Here there is a fork in the trail with the PCT going to the right. Take the spur trail to the left or east that heads for the rocky outcrop and circles around it. Eagle Rock is among these rocks. For a startling view, walk around the backside of the outcrop, about 30 to 40 feet beyond the formation, before turning around to view the eagle. From this vantage point there is no doubt why it is named Eagle Rock. After viewing the eagle and having lunch or a snack, return to your vehicle via the same route.

Sugar bush

Northern harrier

Distance:	3.3 or 4.8 miles, loop (different staging areas); 7.4 or 11.1 miles, one-way
Difficulty:	🚶🚶 or 🚶🚶🚶🚶
Elevation gain/loss:	Up to 300 or 800 feet; 1000 or 1300 feet
Hiking time:	2 or 3 hours; 4 or 6 hours
Agency:	San Diego County
Trail use:	Bicycles, dogs, horses
Notes:	Open from 8 a.m. to 5 p.m. fall and winter, 8 a.m. to 7 p.m. summer; may be closed after inclement weather; a 3-mile trail connects the loops; longer hike options available
Trailhead GPS:	N33.12009, W116.60296
Optional map:	USGS 7.5-min *Julian*
Atlas square:	J20
Directions:	There are two trailheads. CA-79 Trailhead: (Santa Ysabel) From CA-79 drive 1.5 miles north of Santa Ysabel and just south of the Santa Ysabel Mission. Park along side of road. Farmer Road Staging Area: (Julian) From CA-78/79 take Main Street north out of Julian for 2.2 miles (Main Street becomes Farmer Road). Turn right on Wynola Road. Go 100 yards and then take the first left, which is a continuation of Farmer Road. Go 1.3 miles. Parking lot is on left.

Habitat(s):

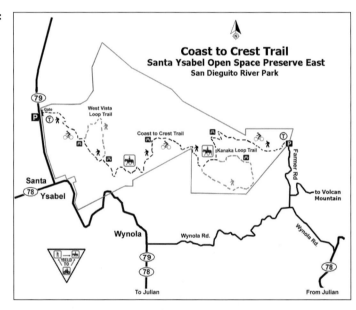

Santa Ysabel Open Space Preserve is one of the best-kept secrets of San Diego County. The preserve offers hikers a little over 11 miles of oak woodlands, riparian, chaparral, and grassland habitats. With 3800 acres of wilderness, this preserve offers something for everyone and is well worth a day trip.

The Nature Conservancy bought the land in 1999 from its longtime owners, the Edwards family of Julian. The State of California purchased the land from the Conservancy, and in 2001, San Diego County acquired it with help from the state Wildlife Conservation Board. The County continues to provide land for grazing cattle and opened the area to the public in 2006.

Agricultural and grazed lands often attract ground squirrels, which are a favorite food of the badger (*Taxidea taxus*), found here. Badgers frequent dry open grasslands, fields, and pastures where they can hunt for gophers, squirrels, and mice. They will also eat what-

Rolling hillsides

ever else they can catch including birds, lizards, fish, insects, and amphibians. They are seldom seen, but their dens, which are commonly 6-10 inches high and slightly broader, can be easily identified if seen. The badger has a distinctive patterned head, with the throat and chin whitish, black patches on the face, and a long white dorsal stripe running from the nose back. Badgers are solitary, nocturnal, weigh from 10 to 26 pounds, and have powerful forearms enabling them to dig rapidly, especially in pursuit of prey.

Santa Ysabel Open Space Preserve East straddles two of San Diego County's major watersheds. The headwaters for the San Diego River are located in the southern section of this preserve. Santa Ysabel Creek, with its origin in the Volcan Mountains, flows through the northern section of the preserve and is the source for the San Dieguito River watershed that flows down toward Del Mar. San Dieguito River Park's Coast to Crest Trail crosses the preserve.

Begin at either the Highway 79 Trailhead or the Farmer Road staging area. Both entrances start with an easy hike through grasslands and wildflower meadows on a wide firmly-packed dirt trail. The best time to visit the preserve is March through June after winter rainfalls welcome an assortment of wildflowers and 4-8 feet tall chaparral candles with purple-tinged

white flowers. Visitors will be surprised to meet a herd of cattle and their calves grazing along the trail. Do not approach or spook the cows as they are overprotective when their calves are near.

Seasonal rainfalls feed the Santa Ysabel Creek that flows through the Kanaka Loop Trail. There are also several perennial springs and cattle ponds along the hike. The inclines can be steep and challenging, but once you reach the top of a hill, the view is spectacular.

A pond in the open range

Entrance sign

Gnarled oak tree

Hikers on the trail

The landscape is dotted with giant sycamores and several varieties of oak trees, some majestic in size: coast live, Engelmann, scrub, California black, and the occasional hybridized mixed oak.

Look among the tree crevices, under the bark of dead trees, or in the soil for nests with long foraging trails of California velvety tree ants (*Liometopum occidentale*) that can extend 200 feet or longer. House ants also are found here. House ants (*Tapimona sessile*) often protect and tend aphid and scale insects and harvest the honeydew, a sugary, sticky liquid these insects produce as they suck sugars from plants. In other words, the ants are harvesting the poop of those insects!

The most common ant found here is the big-headed ant (*Pheidole hyatti*), which has a distinct worker cast polymorphism (different body types within the species) with major workers being considerably larger than minor workers and having disproportionately large

heads. Big-headed ants seem to move randomly in large groups. They nest under stones or in soil with abundant rocks and will try to escape instead of protecting the nest from outside harassment. They are nocturnal.

After 3.3 miles on the West Vista Loop Trail, you can continue another 3 miles on the Coast to Crest Trail to meet up with the 4.8-mile Kanaka Loop Trail at the end of the Farmer Staging Area Trailhead. Be sure to position another vehicle at the second trailhead if you are planning a 11.1-mile hike that includes both loops or a 7.4-mile hike from one trailhead to the other, point-to-point, on the Coast to Crest Trail. Alternatively, you can take a leisurely 2- to 4-hour hike through one of the loops. The trailhead and trails are all well marked, including points of interest along the way.

If you continue on the Coast to Crest Trail, the habitat abruptly changes from grassland and oak woodland to chaparral. Plants in this part of the preserve are dense and shrubby.

The preserve is closed after rain or snow to prevent damage to the trails and reopened when the trails dry out. Be sure to carry plenty of water as Santa Ysabel can be hot and dry during the summer, and there is no water available on the trails.

Distance:	3.2 miles or 5.4 miles, out-and-back
Difficulty:	🚶🚶🚶 or 🚶🚶🚶🚶
Elevation gain/loss:	Up to 1000 feet or 1300 feet
Hiking time:	2 or 4 hours
Agency:	San Diego County
Trail use:	Bicycles, dogs
Trailhead GPS:	N33.10511, W116.60242
Optional map:	USGS 7.5-min *Julian*
Atlas square:	J20
Directions:	(Julian) From CA-78/79 take Main Street north out of Julian for 2.2 miles (Main Street becomes Farmer Road). Turn right on Wynola Road. Go 100 yards and then take the first left, which is a continuation of Farmer Road. The preserve entrance is on the right, park on the shoulder of the road.

Habitat(s):

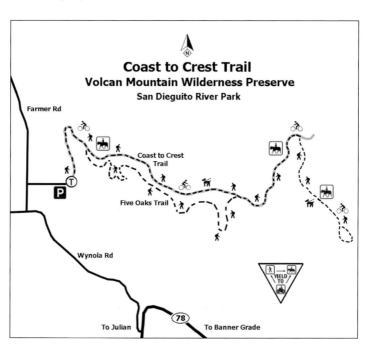

Volcan Mountain is part of the Peninsular Ranges. These include the Palomar, Cuyamaca, Santa Rosa, and Laguna mountains in San Diego. These ranges are generally westerly-tilted fault blocks composed of granitic rock that was originally created by plutonic activity.

The Volcan Mountain land mass extends in a northwest direction from Banner Grade to the Santa Ysabel Valley. The mountain is the fountainhead for two of the county's primary waterways: the San Dieguito and the San Diego river basins. Ironside Spring at 4600 feet

is the fountainhead for San Dieguito with a pumping rate of about 15 gallons per minute. The headwaters of the San Diego River begin about 2 miles northwest of the Wynola Valley on the mountain's lower south slope with its waters flowing through the dramatic San Diego Canyon before emptying into El Capitan Dam.

The San Diego gold rush started in 1870 on the southern flank of Volcan Mountain, south of the Elsinore Fault. A cowboy named Fred Coleman noticed yellow flakes in a small creek while watering his horse. The total out-

The Hubbell entrance gate

put of San Diego County gold mines was less than $5 million. Adjusted for inflation, the $200 million was enough to fuel a full-scale gold rush and to create the town of Julian that for years was the largest in the county. However, the county is better known for gems and minerals, especially tourmaline and garnet.

Cream cups

The 2900-acre Volcan Mountain Wilderness Preserve offers a mid-summit hike of 3.2 miles and a summit hike of 5.4 miles, both with viewpoints following multi-use trails. The Elsinore fault passes under the staging area for the preserve trail and is responsible for the northwest-southeast trending mountain. Julian artist James Hubbell designed the entrance gateway, building the rock wall using white pegmatite and black tourmaline, obsidian, limestone, and Julian schist, a layered shale-like rock.

Follow the fire road for 0.33 mile. Then turn right onto the Five Oaks Trail, named for the number of oak species once found on this trail. There are now at least seven species in the area, including coast life oak, canyon live oak, California black oak, Engelmann oak, scrub oak, interior coast live oak, and interior live oak (**Quercus wislizeni**). Volcan Mountain is at the right elevation for oak species that have both lower and higher elevation requirements, making this a great area to compare these oak species. Interior live oak is a rounded evergreen that is endemic to California and Baja California, Mexico. It can be a large shrub or a small tree. Leaf surfaces are shiny green and darker on top. It grows only

Entrance gate detail

Hubbell rock compass

in climates characterized by mild wet winters and hot dry summers. It grows best in dry valleys and canyons and on foothill slopes. The bark is smooth when young. Acorns were collected and processed by local Indians.

The trail climbs in mostly shaded areas until meeting the fire road after taking in the mid-summit view of the surrounding area. Either turn left on the fire road to complete the 3.2-mile hike or turn right on the fire road to continue 1.2 miles to the summit, with an elevation gain of 1253 feet from the parking area to the 5353-foot summit. En route to the summit is a lone chimney—all that is left of an observation outpost from 1928-1932 when astronomers were evaluating areas for placement of the Hale telescope that now sits on Palomar Mountain. The climb to the summit area is particularly stunning in spring when cream cups (**Platystemon californicus**) are in bloom and drape the area in a blanket of whitish-yellow blossoms. Cream cups have six petals, are slightly hairy and are in the poppy family.

The view from the top is amazing simply because of the mountain's location. From the top you can see features in five counties, two states, two countries, and on two tec-

tonic plates. You can see two major bodies of water and an aerial view of at least seven habitats! The remains of an Airway Light Beacon System are found at the summit. Originally developed by the US Post Office Department, it was used by air mail pilots to direct them along major flight paths across the United States. By 1946, over 2000 beacons were in operation serving 24 airways across the US. By 1972 the light beacons had become obsolete because of the rapid change in technology.

As you walk back down the trail, take note of masses of mistletoe on some of the oak trees, reminiscent of Dr. Seuss' truffula trees in *The Lorax*. Also look for acorn woodpecker granary trees that literally have no more room for acorn storage. Chances are good that you will also see a woodpecker somewhere near the tree.

If time allows, be sure and stop by the Volcan Mountain Nature Center manned by volunteers of the Volcan Mountain Foundation. The foundation owns 400 acres adjacent to the preserve at 22850 Volcan Road in Julian. For information about the foundation, the nature center, and activities that it sponsors, go to www.volcanmt.org.

Distance:	1 mile
Difficulty:	🏃
Elevation gain/loss:	Up to 100 feet
Hiking time:	1 hour
Agency:	USFS/CNF-PRD
Trailhead GPS:	N33.09834, W116.66456
Optional map:	USGS 7.5-min *Santa Ysabel*
Atlas square:	J19
Directions:	(Wynola) From CA-78/79 turn south into the Inaja Memorial Picnic Ground parking lot, 1 mile south of Santa Ysabel and 6 miles west of Julian.

Habitat(s):

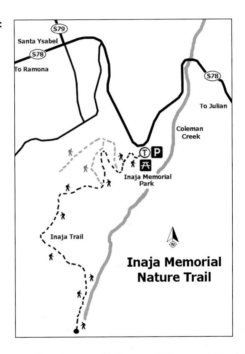

There are many reasons to stop and explore the Inaja Memorial Picnic Ground and Trail. First, it is a great place for a picnic, with tables under shady ramadas or old coast live oaks. Second, it is one of the four National Recreation Trails in San Diego County. The nature trail circles the hill behind the picnic area and provides great views down into the rugged San Diego River Gorge to the southeast, a spectacular contrast to the pastoral view of the Santa Ysabel Valley off to the southwest. Finally, this is a great place to learn about the transition zone where chaparral gives way to forest.

This area is a memorial to 11 firefighters who died here in on November 25, 1956, when the wildfire they were combating suddenly turned and shot up-canyon before they could escape.

It is one of the worst firefighting disasters in the nation. This tragedy changed forever how wildfires are fought in America. The deaths of the firefighters—three trained forest service firefighters, seven Viejas Honor Camp volunteers and their correctional officer—led to a new determination to understand wildfires and to develop new rules for engagement. The original 10 Standard Firefighting Orders were developed in 1957 and have successfully been used by thousands of firefighters.

The hiking trail begins on the west side of the restroom and extends in a loop up to the high point on the ridge before returning to the picnic area. In the past it was a nature trail with numbered stops and a brochure providing information on some plant or fea-

View toward Santa Ysabel

ture at each stop, but most of the numbered posts have disappeared and brochures are no longer provided.

Although the trail starts out in oak woodland, it soon takes you out onto a southwest-facing hillside covered with vigorous chaparral. The principal shrubs found here include two species of *Ceanothus*, big-berry manzanita, mountain-mahogany, scrub oak, and chamise. In the spring, wild hyacinths and winter currents provide colorful accents while blooming *Ceanothus* scents the air with a wonderful aroma. The trail also passes massive granite boulders that have been eroded into dramatic shapes.

Several viewpoints are found off the main trail. One near the halfway point looks down into the rugged San Diego River Gorge and the upper portion of the San Diego River watershed. Inaja Memorial Picnic Ground is one of several preserves found along the San Diego River that is part of a river-long system of parks and open spaces supported by The San Diego River Park Foundation.

The dense vegetation carpeting the steep canyon walls is testimony to the ability of the chaparral to regenerate, if it does not burn too frequently. High intensity fires in the chaparral are natural and consume all living matter above ground. The plants have developed various adaptations in order to recover from these events, and chaparral plants need ideally 30 or

more years to replenish the seed banks to insure plant viability.

Another viewpoint looks northwest to pastoral Santa Ysabel Valley where black cattle graze in verdant grasslands dotted with scattered live oaks. The elevation at the top of the overlook is 3440 feet. Completing the loop returns to the parking area where there is also an inner loop to explore before leaving.

Trail begins under shady live oaks

Distance:	3.25 miles, out-and-back
Difficulty:	🚶🚶
Elevation gain/loss:	Up to 800 feet
Hiking time:	2 hours
Agency:	BLM-CDD
Trail use:	Bicycles, dogs, horses
Trailhead GPS:	N33.07851, W116.58398
Optional map:	USGS 7.5-min *Julian*
Atlas square:	K20
Directions:	(Julian) From CA-78/Banner Road go east on Whispering Pines Drive for 0.2 miles. Turn right on Gold Dust Lane then turn left onto Woodland Road. Park in the cul-de-sac at the end of the public road.

Habitat(s):

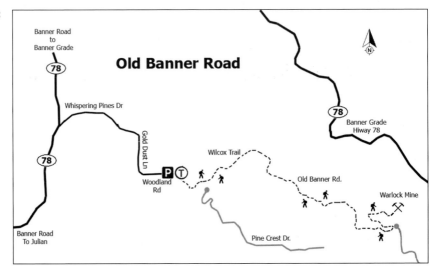

Julian's Old Banner Road, now a hiking trail, starts in a suburban-like setting among Coulter pines and California black oaks and descends through lush chaparral, providing a chance to explore a fascinating bit of San Diego's history on this old wagon road. Horace Wilcox built the first road connecting Julian with Banner in 1871 and operated it as a toll road for several years for both livestock and vehicles. San Diego County purchased the road in 1874 and eliminated the toll. For the next 51 years the Wilcox Road was the way to get from Julian to Banner, only to be replaced with the present Banner Grade Road in 1925. Today the Wilcox Road is a well-maintained hiking trail for about 1.5 miles. This portion of the historic road has been closed to motorized vehicles since 1980. Although it continues on to Banner as a gravel road after the

Warlock Mine site, it is signed "No Trespassing" beyond the end of the hiking trail.

Start hiking down the signed private road extending east from the cul-de-sac. The public has permission to travel on this and other private roads in this area, but there is no place to park further on. The pavement ends in 0.17 mile as you reach a dry creek bed. Three roads branch off near this point, all with signs saying "Private Road." The road on the left with the yellow sign is the road to take. Immediately below the yellow sign is a crude, easy to miss sign saying only "Trail" and pointing to the left. The road loops around to someone's house while the trail continues down the canyon. The hike from here is on an excellent trail going through a verdant canyon surrounded by Coulter pines, California black oaks, and tall manzanitas.

Looking down into Banner Canyon

Banner Canyon begins in about 0.25 mile. There is a faded sign on the left providing a brief history of the Wilcox Road. As you proceed down the trail, look for the Elsinore Fault trace on the west-facing slope of Banner Canyon across from the trail. The more distant, dramatic views also include Granite Mountain, Earthquake Valley, and other features of the Anza-Borrego Desert area, as well as CA-78 now far below, snaking its way down the canyon.

The town of Julian got its start as a result of the discovery of gold by a former slave, Fred Coleman, in 1869. The Warlock Mine site is just one of several former mines in the vicinity of the Wilcox Road, but it is the only one that can be easily reached by the trail. The mine was first worked in 1870. It has the distinction of having the longest tunnel in the Cuyamacas. It ran 1660 feet and intercepted seven different veins. It yielded up to $50,000 in gold, which is close to $1 million adjusted for inflation. Mining operations were suspended in 1957. Not much remains except a rusting hulk and other bits of mining machinery. The mine recently collapsed. The trail to the mine site adds another 0.5 mile to the hike. Take care exploring around mines as they are both very dangerous and biologically important. Mines are often important roost sites for bats as well as ringtails who are both extremely susceptible to disturbance.

Also be aware of the danger of trespassing on mining property, especially in the vicinity of Banner Canyon. In 1989 two men were killed on Memorial Day weekend over trespassing issues on mining property. Their deaths have been called the Chariot Canyon Massacre.

Turn around here at the mine. The old road continuing on down toward Banner is now on private property.

Warlock Mine ruins

Distance:	2.3 or 4 miles, out-and-back or loop
Difficulty:	🚶🚶 or 🚶🚶🚶
Elevation gain/loss:	Up to 900 feet
Hiking time:	2 or 3 hours
Agency:	San Diego County
Trail use:	Bicycles, dogs, horses
Notes:	Parking fee; check for snow in winter
Trailhead GPS:	N33.04465, W116.58263
Optional map:	USGS 7.5-min *Julian*
Atlas square:	K20
Directions:	(Julian) From CA-78/79 go south on Pine Hills Road for 2.3 miles. Turn left on Frisius Drive. Go 2 miles. Once past the park entrance follow the road about 0.5 mile to the Canyon Oak day-use area, by Campsite area 2, and park.

Habitat(s):

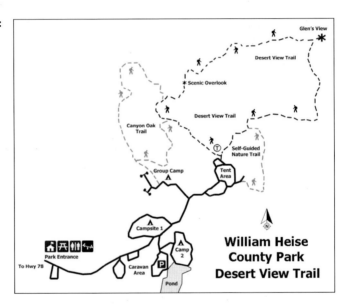

William Heise County Park Desert View Trail

The next time you visit Julian and find you need to work off that extra serving of apple pie you could not resist, consider taking a hike in William Heise County Park, located just a few miles south of the town. It is a well-maintained public campground located in a beautiful forested setting. Over 10 miles of hiking trails, ranging from short and easy to moderately challenging, lie within or originate from this approximately 1000-acre park. There are picnic tables for day-use and separate camping areas for RVs and tents. This county park also has equestrian trails, and mountain bikers are allowed on the trails as well as leashed dogs. Lands for this park were donated to the County in 1968 by successful businessman William Heise who wanted to preserve an area

where families could gather, picnic, and hike as a retreat from city life.

The Desert View Trail leads to Glen's View at the northeastern corner of the park. It is well worth the time and effort required to reach it for the dramatic views from here out to the Anza-Borrego Desert area, as well as a view down into the town of Julian and west out to the ocean. The Desert View Trail leaves the forested slopes and valleys of the campground to take you through chaparral rapidly recovering from the 2003 Cedar Fire. Much of the park burned in the Cedar Fire. There is little evidence of the fire in the developed part of the park. However, once you get into the chaparral covered hillsides, the bleached white skeletons of California black oaks and manzanitas

Glen's view and scope

are stark reminders of that fire. In the case of the manzanita species that can resprout, white dead branches protrude from a base of healthy green shoots that are sprouting from the underground burls that were not killed by the fire. The oaks and pines are making a much slower recovery, largely from seedlings that germinated since the fire. It will be many years before anyone will find shade under these trees. For several seasons after the 2003 fire, especially the first year, spectacular displays of wildflowers occurred.

The California black oaks and live oaks that are in the campground area have another challenge, however. The goldspotted oak borer (*Agrilus auroguttatus*) is killing many of them here and throughout the forested areas of Cuyamaca Rancho State Park and Cleveland National Forest. Although oak mortality was first noted in 2002, it was not until 2004 that it was attributed to this wood-boring jewel beetle. The beetle likely originated in southeastern Arizona and southward and has relatives in Central America. It may have been introduced on firewood. The larva of this beetle feeds on the tree. Researchers estimate that over 80,000 trees have been killed, which increases the likelihood of fires in fire-prone areas. The beetle is metallic green with yellow spots on its forewings. The larva is white and legless.

The Desert View Trail is one of three loop trails that intersect at the upper end of the park, so the distance covered depends on how much of these other trails one may want to incorporate into a hike. If Glen's View is your only goal, you will hike a minimum of 2.3 miles with 900 feet of elevation gain, but this could be extended to about a 4-mile hike by approaching the Desert View Trail from the Canyon Oak Trail.

Both southern mule deer and large flocks of non-native turkeys are frequently seen in the area. This is the same area that the turkeys were inadvertently released in 1993. Both bobcat and mountain lion live here. The higher elevation allows a variety of seasonal changes including spring wildflowers, fall colors, and winter snow.

Wild turkey

Distance:	5.6 miles out-and-back; 5.6 miles 1-way; or 11.2 miles out-and-back
Difficulty:	🚶🚶🚶🚶 or 🚶🚶🚶🚶🚶, depending on hike undertaken
Elevation gain/loss:	Up to 1000 feet
Hiking time:	4 or 6 hours
Agency:	San Diego County
Trail use:	Bicycles on multi-use trails only; horses on designated trails only
Notes:	Parking fee; check for snow in winter
Trailhead GPS:	N33.03907, W116.59272
Optional map:	USGS 7.5-min *Julian*
Atlas square:	K20
Directions:	(Julian) From CA-78/79 go south on Pine Hills Road for 2.3 miles. Turn left on Frisius Drive. Go 2 miles. Park in the day-use lot on right, just before the Park entrance.

Habitat(s):

The Kelly Ditch Trail is a 5.6-mile hiking path extending from William Heise County Park to Lake Cuyamaca. Prior to 2003, it passed through one of the most magnificent oak and coniferous forest in San Diego County. The 2003 Cedar fire burned many of the trees, especially the California black oaks and conifers. Their bleached white skeletons continue to tower over the now green understory where the vegetation has made a remarkable comeback. Palmer's-lilac, the dominant tall shrub that is found in dense stands along the trail, plays a critical role in the post-fire habitat by returning nitrogen to the soil. Trail crews cleared most of the brush and piles of dead, fallen trees blocking the trail, and the Kelly Ditch Trail is now open all the way through for hikers. Mountain bikers and horses may have difficulty getting around downed dead trees,

which continue to fall across the trail. The part of the trail within William Heise County Park currently presents the most scenic hiking opportunity, but spectacular views and beautiful wildflowers can be found throughout the route.

There are actually three possibilities for hiking the Kelly Ditch Trail. The first option is a 5.6-mile one-way hike that assumes there will be a vehicle at Cuyamaca Lake to pick up the hiker, or the one-way hike could begin at the lake and end at William Heise County Park. If the latter, then arrange for a drop-off at the lake or purchase a lake parking pass if one vehicle is left there. The second option is an 11.2-mile out-and-back hike for more ambitious hikers. The third option is the one recommended here—a more moderate 5.6-mile out-and-back that goes 2.8 miles before turning back at the trail's

Don Fosket

New growth after the fire

high point. This is also a hike recommended for the future if the *Ceanothus* thicket grows back, blocking the trail to Lake Cuyamaca as you enter state park land. If riding a bicycle or horse, pay attention to trail signs.

The northern end of the Kelly Ditch Trail begins at the southern terminus of the Heise Park day-use parking area. Follow the signs and begin hiking down the trail through towering inland coast live oaks and Coulter pines. The Fern Trail goes off to the right at 0.4 mile from the start, while the Kelly Ditch Trail continues straight ahead up a dirt road, passing through an abundance of chaparral species which are especially attractive when in flower. The live oaks are fire scarred, but most survived. California black oaks typically were burned to the ground, but many have stump sprouted and now show considerable growth.

At 0.75 mile into the hike, the Kelly Ditch Trail leaves the road, branching off to the right and heading over a ridge and down to Cedar Creek, a perennial stream flowing even in most drought years. At 1 mile you reach a junction with the other end of the Fern Trail, which goes off to the right, while Kelly's Ditch Trail goes to the left and crosses Cedar Creek to begin a gradual ascent up the northwest side of North Peak. You reach the Heise Park boundary and cross into state park land 1.85 miles from the trailhead.

Some of the tallest thickets of *Ceanothus* are ahead. Trail crews have worked hard to establish

the path through this fragile, post-fire habitat. Enjoy the beautiful *Ceanothus* canopy. Look behind you to see the view that stretches to the top of Granite Mountain peaking over the ridge to the east in the Anza-Borrego Desert. At about 2.8 miles from the start, you reach an unused dirt road coming up from Engineer's Road. This would be the place to turn around if you are planning a 5.6 mile out-and-back hike. However, if you intend to complete either the 5.6 mile one-way or the 11.2 mile out-and-back hike, continue on. The dirt road is now the trail, crossing grass and bracken fern carpeted meadows, permitting views to the west extending to the ocean and south to Cuyamaca Mountain. In less than 1 mile, the trail leaves the road, going off to the left. In another 0.3 mile the trail crosses Engineer's Road and begins its descent to the remnants of the actual Kelly's Ditch, constructed in the 19th century to channel runoff from North Peak into the then newly constructed Cuyamaca Reservoir. On the way, keep an eye out for the ocellated lily (*Lilium humboldtii*), a spectacular lily that may be as much as 8 feet tall with large brilliant orange-yellow flowers spattered with maroon spots with long stamens. It looks like an escapee from someone's garden. In fact, it is often used horticulturally and looks somewhat like a tiger lily and is sometimes called leopard lily. However, this is a native, though rarely seen plant in our mountains and foothills. Ocellated lilies bloom soon after Memorial Day.

The trail ends just west of where Highway 79 curves around the Cuyamaca Reservoir dam. The trail sign is currently missing. This last segment of the trail may be closed to mountain bikers.

Paula Knoll

Ocellated lily

Distance:	4 miles, out-and-back
Difficulty:	🚶🚶🚶
Elevation gain/loss:	up to 1000 feet
Hiking time:	3 hours
Agency:	SDRPF
Trail use:	Bicycles, dogs, horses
Notes:	Possible bushwhacking if you lose the trail
Trailhead GPS:	N33.01155, W116.71287
Optional map:	USGS 7.5 min *Santa Ysabel*
Atlas square:	L18
Directions:	(Julian) From CA-78/79 turn south on Pine Hills Road. Go 1.6 miles. Turn right on Eagle Peak Road. Go 8.7 miles. The Eagle Peak Preserve South Staging Area is on the left. If the gates are open there is adequate off road parking. If the gates are closed, park on the roadside without blocking traffic.

Habitat(s):

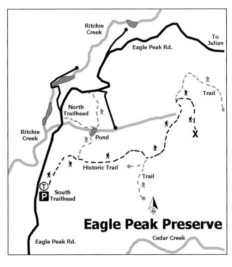

The Eagle Peak Preserve, located about 4.5 miles north of Eagle Peak, is a conservation area owned and managed by The San Diego River Park Foundation (SDRPF). It does not include Eagle Peak itself, but is on Eagle Peak Road. The preserve is one of the most biologically diverse areas of the county.

The Foundation began a program in 2003 to raise funds to purchase this privately-held inholding within the Cleveland National Forest. SDRPF now manages over 700 acres of the preserve and keeps it open for the public. This is only one of various reserves and parks managed by several agencies and cities that will eventually connect to the 52-mile-long San Diego River. The San Diego River has its source in the mountains near Julian and flows through this remote, rugged canyon before entering populous Mission Val-

ley, ultimately emptying into the ocean near Pacific Beach.

William Marcks, as a recent immigrant from Germany, homesteaded the land that became the preserve in 1899. He and his family lived there his whole life raising bees and cattle. Since SDRPF acquired most of the former ranch, it has begun to revert back to its natural state. Few relics of its life as a ranch remain.

The trail leaves the south staging area on an old unused dirt road in an area that once was a homesite. Eucalyptus trees were planted here and are thriving. After passing a water tank, the road becomes a single-track trail that heads up the side of a hill covered with typical coastal sage scrub. Shortly, it joins another dirt road, labeled the "Historic Trail" on preserve maps. The Historic Trail crosses the preserve, leaving it at about 2 miles from the south staging area.

Don Fosket

The "Historic Trail"

sensitive to any threats and will quickly bolt if threatened. Coachwhips are among the largest and fastest moving snakes of North America. They are long and thin, capable of traveling up to 4 miles per hour. They actively chase their prey, have sharp teeth, and they hunt during the day. Their overlapping scales resemble the braiding of a whip. There is a large color variation depending on the subspecies with colors ranging from black, brown, pinkish brown, yellowish brown, to red. There are many myths associated with coachwhips, one of which is that they will chase people.

A few words of caution for this hike: there is little shade except for a ramada that covers a picnic table near a usually dry stock pond, and the trails are not signed and frequently overgrown with brush. Take care to always be aware of your location relative to obvious landmarks. The best time to visit is in the spring after the rains have brought this area back to life. After adequate rain you can expect an abundance of wildflowers and flowering shrubs. The stock ponds will fill with water and waterfalls can be seen cascading down the preserve's many ravines and canyons. Southern California steelhead or rainbow trout has been recorded in the creek adjacent to the preserve.

Gene markers indicate that inland rainbow trout could be descendants of an early southern California steelhead population that has become isolated and can no longer travel down to the ocean to smolt and become steelhead. There is also a lot of discussion as to whether trout found in San Diego streams are the result of fish plantings or natural occurrences. Since the 2003 fires, many of the fish have been eliminated through a combination of low water levels and the heat from the fires.

The road was the original route between San Diego and Julian in the early part of the 20th century. A great deal of hand labor must have been needed to construct the stone walls that line its downslope side.

The trail goes north, up along the west-facing slope of a mountain with the peculiar name of Mount Son 2, reaching the ridge after 0.5 mile of easy upslope hiking. It turns east after crossing the ridge, where the vegetation continues to be coastal sage scrub with scattered Engelmann or mesa blue oaks and blue elderberry.

In about 0.25 mile there is a branch trail off to the left that goes down to a seasonal stock pond and some scattered ranching artifacts. If you have the time and energy, you might consider a side trip down to the ramada and picnic table near the pond basin.

The goal of this hike is to reach the top of the unnamed peak at elevation 3200 feet. Although it is just outside the preserve, peak 3200 offers a spectacular nearly 360-degree view of the surrounding mountains and the San Diego River Gorge. To reach the peak, continue up the Historic Trail from its junction with the Pond Trail. After it curves north and begins to climb up the west-facing slope of peak 3200, the trail may become difficult to follow. Before the trail crosses a low divide and begins to curve in a southeasterly direction, leave the trail and start your cross-country ascent to the peak. It is open country and relatively easy going.

As you cross the grasslands, you might be surprised by a nonvenomous coachwhip (*Coluber flagellum*) that may stretch his head up above the grass to look at you. They are curious snakes with good eyesight that are

Diana Lindsay

Coachwhip

Distance:	4.2 miles, out-and-back
Difficulty:	🚶🚶🚶
Elevation gain/loss:	Up to 1000 feet
Hiking time:	3 hours
Agency:	USFS/CNF-PRD
Notes:	Adventure Pass required
Trailhead GPS:	N32.98454, W116.67711
Optional map:	USGS 7.5-min *Tule Springs*
Atlas square:	M18
Directions:	(Descanso) From CA-79 go north on Riverside Drive for 1 mile. Turn left on Viejas Grade Road, then make an immediate right past the store onto Oak Grove Drive. Go 1.6 miles. Turn right on Boulder Creek Road. Go 13 miles (the last 7 miles is on a well-kept dirt road) to a hairpin turn that intersects Cedar Creek Road and the trailhead. The trailhead is for both Three Sisters Falls and Eagle Peak with Cedar Creek Fire Road slightly to the north. Park near the hairpin turn. The Boulder Creek Road trailhead also can be accessed via Engineers Road from Lake Cuyamaca. It is a shorter route but has many hairpin turns.

Habitat(s):

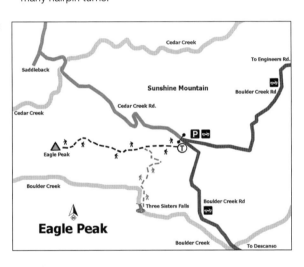

Eagle Peak

Eagle Peak is south of the 711-acre Eagle Peak Conservation Area that includes the upper portion of the San Diego River acquired by The San Diego River Park Foundation in 2006. The peak is not the highest in the area, but it has a commanding 360-degree view of the San Diego River Canyon, the river's main tributaries, and all of the surrounding peaks. It is a popular destination for local area rock climbers. The trip described here does not require any special climbing skills. Much of the hike goes through grassy fields with scattered Engelmann oaks or relatively open chaparral. When *Ceanothus* is in bloom, the shrubs will be covered with a mist of blue flowers with a wonderful fragrance. Wildflowers are

abundant here in the spring and include the shy mariposa lily, caterpillar phacelia, woolly Indian paintbrush, and four-spot clarkia (*Clarkia purpurea* subsp. *quadrivulnera*). It is for a reason that another common name for four-spot clarkia is wine-cup clarkia. This member of the evening-primrose family has a side silhouette that resembles a long-stemmed glass filled with a pink to lavender-purple-colored wine. Look for a small cup-like annual herb with four fan-shaped petals. It is one of the last flowers to bloom in spring.

The trail to the peak leads straight ahead from the trailhead, passing through chaparral dominated by chamise with a scattering of interesting shrubs and vines. The trail begins to

Don Fosket

View of San Diego River canyon

rise and goes to the top of a hill under a few Engelmann oaks set in non-native grassland. They managed to survive the 2003 Cedar Fire that scorched this whole area. From the top of the hill, the trail declines to a saddle 0.66 mile from the trailhead with the left trail going to Boulder Creek's Three Sisters Waterfall. The trail to Eagle Peak goes straight ahead or west from this point and continues up the side of a south-facing slope vegetated with a mixture of foothill chaparral shrubs, including scrub oaks, *Ceanothus*, and coastal sagebrush as well as chamise.

Beyond the Three Sisters Falls split, the trail is less traveled and can be narrow in places, so there is a chance of ticks hitching a ride on your clothing. Wear light colored long pants and sleeves. At 1.35 miles from the parking area, the trail crosses a saddle and begins a slow descent into a shallow valley, while staying on its north-facing slope. The aspect of this slope protects it from the sun's direct rays, permitting the growth of a lusher coast live oak woodland with an understory of chaparral.

There is a second fork in the trail 1.7 miles from the start. The trail to the left goes about 0.2 mile to a lookout with spectacular views of the rugged Boulder Creek and Eagle Peak cliffs. The trail straight ahead continues 0.4 mile with about 300 feet of elevation gain to the peak. The trail becomes increasingly difficult to fol-

low before reaching Eagle Peak itself, and care is needed due to the sharp drop off. However, the climb is worth it for the perspective it gives you on this whole area. Return to your vehicle the way you came.

The shear portion of Eagle Peak is closed to rock climbers during raptor nesting season. A map is available at www.fs.usda.gov/detail/cleveland/home.

Don Fosket

Four-spot clarkia

Distance:	5 miles, loop
Difficulty:	🏃🏃
Elevation gain/loss:	Up to 100 feet
Hiking time:	3 hours
Agency:	LCR&PD
Trail use:	Dogs, horses
Notes:	Hours posted dawn to dusk; access fee payable at Tackle Shop
Trailhead GPS:	N32.97661, W116.58125
Optional map:	USGS 7.5-min *Cuyamaca Peak*
Atlas square:	M20
Directions:	(Julian) From CA-79 turn north into the Trout Pond parking area, 9.5 miles south of Julian and 13.4 miles north of I-8, where the road makes a 90-degree turn.

Habitat(s):

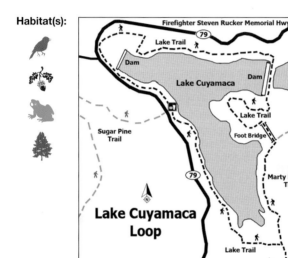

Lake Cuyamaca sits at an elevation of 4600 feet in an oak and pine forest, surrounded on three sides by the 26,000-acre Cuyamaca Rancho State Park. The dam that forms this 110-acre lake is the second oldest in California and was completed in 1888. A long vanished 33-mile wooden flume transported its water to the growing population of San Diego County. Now owned by the Helix Water District, the lake provides a multitude of recreational activities including fishing, camping, and hiking. The name Cuyamaca is a Spanish corruption of the Kumeyaay phrase *ekwiiyemak* which has been translated to mean behind the clouds or as the place where it rains, alluding to the higher than average rainfall experienced here as compared to the dryer coastal regions of the county.

This area has a variety of large mammals including southern mule deer, mountain lion, bobcat, and coyote. A host of smaller mammals are also found such as ground squirrel, vole, pocket mice, and bat. The western gray squirrel (*Sciurus griseus*), once plentiful, has been on the decline in recent years due to mange, a skin disease caused by mites that are specific to rodents. The western gray squirrel is active during the day, feeding primarily on seeds and nuts. Pine nuts and acorns are especially critical because they provide carbohydrates and oil needed for body fat. The gray squirrel is a scatter hoarder, depositing several small caches of nuts and seeds within its territory. Sometimes it forgets where all the caches are, which helps with seed dispersal. It spends most of its time

Jim Varnell

Paintbrush growing at the lake

in trees, coming to the ground for foraging. The western gray squirrel is prey for coyotes, bobcats, mountain lions, hawks, and raccoons.

Over 220 species of birds have been reported here. Red-winged blackbirds can usually be found in the cattails along the edge of the lake. Caspian terns, great and snowy egrets, and great blue herons may be patrolling the lake for a fish dinner. There is a thriving population of wild turkey, not native to the area but introduced in 1993. The turkey is now a common sight in the meadows or crossing the trail. Other bird species likely to be seen are the acorn woodpecker, western bluebird, and northern flicker.

Begin the hike at the Trout Pond Trailhead where there are actually three trails beginning at or near this location (Minshall, Los Vaqueros, and Los Caballos). In a dry year, when the lake's level is low, a loop completely around the lake is feasible and very rewarding and is described here. Start on the Marty Minshall/Los Vaqueros Trail that skirts to the south of a large meadow at the edge of the lake. Much of this meadow will be submerged in wetter years. This is also the northern boundary of the Cuyamaca Meadows Natural Preserve, which was established to protect a number of sensitive and/or endangered plants including Parish's meadowfoam, Cuyamaca larkspur, and Cuyamaca Lake downingia (*Downingia concolor*), an attractive blue-flowered annual. The downingia is an endemic species found only in about 20 sites, all of which are meadows within the Cuyamaca watershed. Its most

unusual trait is that its seeds can germinate only when submerged in cold water.

Keep straight on the Minshall Trail as it intersects with the Los Caballos Trail (heading towards the Los Caballos Horse Camp) at about 0.4 mile. At just under 1 mile there will be a trail marker on the right for the Stonewall Mine. In a wet year this would make a fine alternative hike over to the mine. For now, however, look to the left. Look for a narrow opening through the fence that leads toward the lake and onto the Lake Trail. Cross over a bridge and begin the loop around the lake. Turn right after the bridge for a slightly shorter walk or turn left for an additional 0.4 mile to walk under the shade of mature oak and pine trees. Keep alert for an imposing wooden sculpture of a bear (a photo op must). After crossing over the eastern boundary of the lake, the trail will follow along the northern shore and past Chambers Park and Lone-Pine Camp. As the restricted area of the dam is approached, turn right and follow the trail north and then west to CA-79. Walk about 300 yards beside the road until the dam is passed, and then drop down to the shore to continue the hike. This is a good section of the lake to pause for a snack or lunch before continuing on to the east and passing through the meadow once again to arrive back at the Minshall Trail. Retrace your route for 0.5 mile to return to your vehicle at the trailhead.

Michele Hernandez

Cuyamaca Lake downingia

Distance:	5 miles, out-and-back
Difficulty:	🧍🧍🧍
Elevation gain/loss:	Up to 1600 feet
Hiking time:	3 hours
Agency:	USFS/CNF-DRD
Notes:	Adventure Pass required; GPS or map and compass recommended
Trailhead GPS:	N32.83964, W116.54208
Optional map:	USGS 7.5-min *Descanso*
Atlas square:	O20
Directions:	(Pine Valley) From I-8 go north on Pine Valley Road for 0.3 mile. Turn left on Old Highway 80. Go 1.6 miles. Turn left at the Pine Creek Trailhead sign on Pine Valley-Las Bancas Road. Go 0.5 mile to the parking area.

Habitat(s):

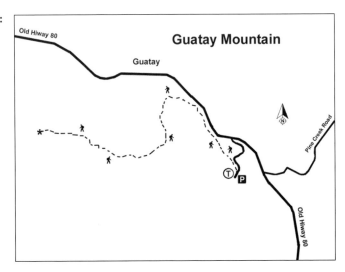

The first challenge of this hike will be finding the trailhead. It starts at the same parking lot that serves the better known Pine Valley and Secret Canyon trailheads in the Cleveland National Forest. Bringing a GPS or compass and map is a prudent precaution if you are hiking there for the first time.

The easiest way to find the trailhead is to walk from the parking lot back toward the main road keeping an eye to your left for a sign reading, "Welcome, Entering National Forest Recreation Fee Area." From this sign, walk about 50 feet more to a bend in the road, and look to the left. Under a stand of oak trees there is a gate marking the start of the trailhead. Follow the trail through the gate, down to a grassy low area. From here, the trail moves again to the left. Continue up the trail, which becomes increasingly rocky and steep. About halfway up to the summit, there will

be a rail to your left. Turn left and continue beyond the rail up the slope. Keep an eye on your back trail to help find your way back, and do not forget to enjoy the many native plant species along the way.

As you near the crest just before the summit you will see a number of Tecate cypress trees (***Hesperocyparis forbesii***) growing on the north side of the slope. This evergreen multi-trunked bushy conifer is native to southern California and Baja California, Mexico. It is generally about 20 feet tall but its height varies. It can grow on rocky, clay, or sandy soils. Come prepared with gaiters or long sturdy pants so that you can pick your way through the chaparral to view the trees up close. Many of these trees are more than 100 years old. The cones resemble gray soccer balls the size of a golf ball. These hard, impenetrable-looking cones take up to two

Guatay Mountain

years to mature and open only in response to high heat. Fire is the primary means of opening up the cones to disperse the seeds, and the tree propagates solely from seeds. There are four groves of Tecate cypress in southern California, and three of them are in San Diego County: here on Guatay Mountain, Otay Mountain, and on Tecate Peak. The fourth is on Sierra Peak in the Santa Ana Mountains of Orange County.

Watch out for Pacific velvet ants (**Dasymutilla aureola**) as you make your way through the chaparral and rocks to the trees. These colorful ant-like insects actually are a species of wasp. The females' wingless bodies are covered with long red hairs, making it look as though they were wearing velvet coats. The males have wings and are seldom seen. Their sting is very painful. This insect is also known as a cow killer. Yet they are solitary and mainly eat nectar.

The most comfortable times of year to do this hike are spring and fall. Going in mid-June offers a gorgeous abundance of wildflower blooms, but the heat and the biting flies will both be intense at that time. Bring insect repellant, sunscreen, and lots of water. Early summer will also bring opportunities to view horned lizards and other reptiles. Be alert for mountain lions that could roam this area as well.

Female Pacific velvet ant is wingless

Male Pacific velvet ant has wings

Distance:	2.7 miles, out-and-back
Difficulty:	🚶🚶
Elevation gain/loss:	Up to 300 feet
Hiking time:	2 hours
Agency:	LCR&PD; CSP-CDD
Trail use:	Bicycles on paved road only, horses
Notes:	Crosses a muddy marsh
Trailhead GPS:	N32.97666, W116.58134
Optional map:	USGS 7.5-min *Cuyamaca Peak*
Atlas square:	M20
Directions:	(Julian) From CA-79 turn north into the Trout Pond parking area, 9.5 miles south of Julian and 13.4 miles north of I-8, where the road makes a 90-degree turn.

Habitat(s):

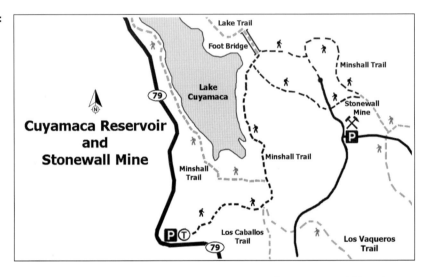

Unlike most of Cuyamaca Rancho State Park, mature trees that enhance Cuyamaca Lake's peninsula were not heavily damaged or destroyed by the 2003 Cedar Fire. As a result, this area is a reminder of the Cuyamaca Mountains' past glory. The best time to visit is late March through June when wildflowers are in bloom, but there is something here to enjoy throughout the year. The California black oaks can provide a splash of color in autumn, and there may be snow in winter.

The area is steeped in history. It was in the early 1870s that gold was discovered in a quartz outcrop near Julian, and it sparked a gold rush that lasted over 20 years. Stonewall Mine was the most productive mine in the Cuyamaca Mountains throughout that time. During San Diego's booming rapid growth in 1887, a dam was constructed to form the Cuyamaca Lake Reservoir, the first dam built

in southern California and the fifth in the state. Although no longer used as San Diego's water source, the lake is still popular for its many recreational opportunities including fishing, boating, camping, and hiking.

Begin the hike at the Trout Pond Trailhead, where there are actually three trails beginning at or near this location (Minshall, Los Vaqueros, and Los Caballos). Take the Minshall Trail east through a marsh, crossing two small streams and walk past a small puddle that could be what has been called the Trout Pond. The pond may have had trout at one time, but there are none now. Muddy places such as stream banks, ponds, and seeps are great places to look for hot spots where butterflies, especially whites and sulphurs, love to probe the damp soil. Common yearround whites and sulphurs include the cabbage white (***Pieris rapae***) and dainty sulphur

Trail to the mine

(*Nathalis iole*). As its name suggests, the small to medium-sized cabbage white butterfly is white with small black dots on its wings. It is a widespread common butterfly that is considered a pest for commercial agriculture because the larvae or cabbage worms eat cabbage and other members of the mustard family including kale and broccoli.

The dainty sulphur larvae are not agricultural pests and are not as common. Look for a butterfly that has a yellow upperside with black tips on the forewings and black bars at the bottom of the forewings and at the top of the hind wings. The underside has a yellow-orange spot at the base of the forewings and black dots on the hind wings.

Once out of the marsh, the trail curves north and passes through grassland at the base of a hill. In 0.4 mile there is a signed junction of the Los Caballos/Los Vaqueros Trails on the right and the continuation of the Minshall Trail straight ahead. Continue straight ahead on

Cabbage white butterfly

Dainty surphur

Don Fosket

Stonewall Museum

the Minshall Trail. This trail, formerly known as the Lake Loop Trail, was renamed to honor Margaret Minshall, owner of a ranch between the horse camp and the Stonewall Mine and a dedicated park volunteer who donated land to CRSP and to Oakoasis Preserve. This trail follows the lake's former shoreline around a peninsula that during heavy rainfall seasons has been surrounded on three sides by water. With the recent drought much of this area has dried to become marsh or grassland. If visiting in the spring, and especially in wetter years, look for a riot of blooming wildflowers.

In another 0.1 mile the trail crosses a causeway that currently has grassland on both sides, although water can be seen to the northwest. The land beyond the causeway is more heavily forested and eventually follows the contours of the lake, but slightly above it. The most abundant trees are California black oaks and Jeffrey pines with a dense understory of shrubs.

About one mile into the hike, look for a bridge on the left leading to Fletcher Island. It is an island only in El Niño years when the water level is much higher; otherwise it remains a peninsula. Access to the bridge and island is blocked by a fence. Private events are sometimes held there.

Continue straight ahead on the Minshall Trail. Shortly you will pass the Stonewall Mine Trail on your right, but for now, continue ahead on the Minshall Trail where expansive views of grassland and meadows open up to the northeast and extend to the Sunrise Highway and southeast to the Soapstone Grade. Soon there will be another fence and another right turn that leads to the Stonewall Mine. A hard rock mineshaft once went over 600 feet down, from which $2 million of gold was extracted, as recorded in 1880. Adjusted for inflation, that would be close to $100 million. A company town grew up here and housed about 500 workers at its peak. Not much remains today other than a number of mining artifacts. There is a small museum in a separate building that tells much of the mine's history. It is worth a visit. The Stonewall Mine site can be reached by car from CA-79, making it accessible to non-hikers. There is a parking lot and restroom facilities here for mine visitors.

After exploring the mine, walk down the paved road to the north, past a service area, and find a trail leading down to an equestrian picnic area. Though not signed at this end, it connects with the Minshall Trail beyond the picnic area. Turn left on the Minshall and follow it back to your vehicle.

Distance:	6 or 8 miles, out-and-back
Difficulty:	🏃🏃🏃🏃 or 🏃🏃🏃🏃🏃
Elevation gain/loss:	Up to 1100 feet
Hiking time:	4 or 5 hours
Agency:	CSP-CDD
Trail use:	Bicycles on fire roads only, horses
Notes:	Snow possible in winter
Trailhead GPS:	N32.97652, W116.58179
Optional map:	USGS 7.5-min *Cuyamaca Peak*
Atlas square:	M20
Directions:	(Julian) From CA-79 turn north into the Trout Pond parking area, 9.5 miles south of Julian and 13.4 miles north of I-8, where the road makes a 90-degree turn.

Habitat(s):

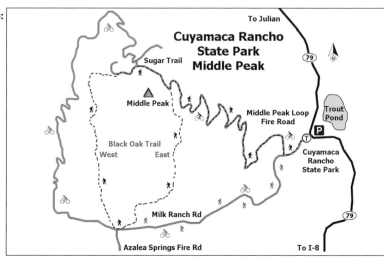

In 1907, General Land Office survey records note "Mid Peak" as the peak between North and Cuyamaca peaks. It was not until 1970 that "Middle" Peak first appeared on forest maps. This peak used to feature Cuyamaca's big trees until the Cedar Fire of 2003. Open, expansive views at nearly every level on the slopes are now the unexpected gift.

From the Trout Pond parking area, cross CA-79N and continue up Milk Ranch Road to a gate. Keep to the right, and walk through the gate. The left road goes to the burned remainder of Camp Hual-Cu-Cuish, Kumeyaay wording for tough or strong but flexible. It was built by the California Conservation Corps in the 1930s and then used by the Boy Scouts from 1940 to 1998 as a camp. The camp burned in the 2003 Cedar Fire, along with 90% of Cuyamaca Rancho State Park. The fire roared over 280,000 acres, burning desert and moun-

tain areas, and extended west into San Diego suburbs as far as I-805. San Diego's remaining coniferous forest habitat is critical to a wide variety of native mammal and bird species. In 2007, California State Parks began a restoration project to plant 2,530 acres in a patch mosaic of saplings that are hoped to become centers for seed dispersal.

Once past the gate and at approximately 0.3 mile from the parking area, turn right onto Middle Peak Loop Fire Road that climbs along multiple switchbacks. Catch your breath as you look over your shoulder at the clear views of Paso Picacho Campground, Lake Cuyamaca, and Stonewall and Cuyamaca peaks. With such wide vistas, this is a great place to look for soaring birds such as the turkey vulture, bald eagle, common raven, and red-tailed hawk.

Turn left after 2.2 miles onto the east section of Black Oak Trail, descending through

Paula Knoll

View from the peak

burned trunks of pines and oaks to return to Milk Ranch Road. Turn right and go a short distance of 0.1 mile to the log-blocked crossroads of Azalea Spring Fire Road/Milk Ranch Road/Black Oak Trail (west). Notice that the dead logs and trees are important in every stage of their decay because they provide shelter for birds and bats and storage places for squirrels and woodpeckers. They provide a food source because they attract insects, mosses, lichens, and fungi which also help to replenish soil nutrients, and act as nurse logs for new seedlings. The higher snags are look-out points that raptors use to discover their next meal.

Ascend back to the Middle Peak Loop Fire Road by crossing Milk Ranch Road onto the west section of the Black Oak Trail. On a clear day, the view to the west includes Mount Woodson with its multiple antennas, Viejas Mountain, and El Cajon Mountain. A section of the trail is bordered by *Ceanothus*. Among the Jeffrey pine skeletons are a few trees with tall, wide trunks and snaggled crowns. These are the remnants of a mature population of sugar pines.

The trail ends at the Middle Peak Loop Fire Road. Turn right, pass the Sugar Pine Trail on the left, then hike the east Black Oak Trail on the right to return to the Trout Pond parking area. As an alternative, a shorter hiking route is to stay on Milk Ranch Road, then ascend

the west Black Oak Trail. You would return to Trout Pond on the Middle Peak Loop Fire Road or by descending east Black Oak Trail and turning left on Milk Ranch Road.

Burned Jeffrey and sugar pines

Distance:	7.7 or 8.7 miles, loop
Difficulty:	🚶🚶🚶🚶🚶
Elevation gain/loss:	Up to 1500 or 1850 feet
Hiking time:	5 or 6 hours
Agency:	CSP-CDD
Trail use:	Bicycles on fire roads only, no horses on Lookout Fire Road
Trailhead GPS:	N32.97646, W116.58224
Optional map:	USGS 7.5-min *Cuyamaca Peak*
Atlas square:	M20
Directions:	(Julian) From CA-79 turn north into the Trout Pond parking area, 9.5 miles south of Julian and 13.4 miles north of I-8, where the road makes a 90-degree turn.

Habitat(s):

The Conejos Trail is a beautiful, less-traveled trail with a striking view of Lake Cuyamaca to the northeast, Middle Peak, and North Peak to the north, and El Capitan Reservoir to the west. The trail provides the option of climbing Cuyamaca Rancho State Park's highest and San Diego County's second highest peak, Cuyamaca Peak (6512'), from a new direction. On a clear winter day, the view from the antenna-clustered summit stretches into six counties—San Diego, Imperial, Riverside, San Bernardino, Orange, and Los Angeles—plus northern Baja California, Mexico. Look for Hale Telescope's white dome on Palomar Mountain, 30-40 miles to the northwest. To really enjoy it all, bring along a good map and some binoculars.

The Conejos Trail looks down on lands that once belonged to the Los Conejos Band of Mission Indians who lived on Capitan Grande Indian Reservation. *Conejos*, which means rabbits in Spanish, is actually a partial translation of a Kumeyaay word meaning rabbit house, referring to the name of the Indian village where the Los Conejos band lived. Conejos is also the name of one of the most destructive fires that burned in the Cuyamaca Mountains in the 1950s. The fire actually began 4000 feet below Cuyamaca Peak on the Capitan Grande Reservation. A hot, dry wind propelled the fire toward the Cuyamacas and past Conejos Creek, eventually burning 10,000 acres of parkland.

Goldenbush and view of the Cuyamacas

Begin the hike at the Trout Pond near Hual-Cu-Cuish equestrian staging area. Look for tiny Quino checkerspot butterflies (***Euphydryas editha quino***). Their wingspan is only about 3 centimeters (1.18 inches), with a bright checkerboard of brown, red, and yellow spots. This butterfly was federally listed as endangered in 1997, and the species has already been extirpated from Los Angeles and Orange counties. Urban sprawl, grazing, and human-caused accidental invasion of exotic plants are responsible for the destruction of most of this butterfly's habitat. The range for the Quino checkerspot is now limited to a few populations in Riverside and San Diego counties. Adult Quino checkerspot butterflies will visit a variety of wildflowers for their nectar. The primary host plant for the larvae is dot-seed plantain (***Plantago erecta***) but it will also use a species of paintbrush. Dot-seed plantain is a pale green annual herb less than 12 inches in height with very small flowers clustered on a stalk. Leaves grow from the base of the plant. The plant has a hairy surface and looks like grass when it grows in dense clusters. The seeds of this plant were formerly harvested by Native Americans who considered it a grain plant. The plant used to be common on coastal bluffs and around the Los Angeles basin.

Quino checkerspot on quartz top view

Follow the Milk Ranch Road past well-developed oak trees, mountain-mahogany, and spicebush, to where Azalea Spring Fire Road branches off on the left and continues for a 1000 feet before branching to the right onto the Conejos Trail. Mountain bikers are permitted on the fire roads and may be encountered up to this point, but not beyond where the Conejos Trail begins. The trail is rough in spots, with challenging switchbacks, narrow spots, steps, stumps, and boulders strewn across the path. You will pass a graveyard of bone-white trees

The Conejos Trail

from the 2003 Cedar Fire, but the cleared vegetation does leave a few nice viewpoints.

The trail will continue to rise in elevation until an area of new growth of pine and fir is encountered. Plants in the pine family (pines, spruces, firs, cedars, larches, etc.) bear cones that have overlapping scales, typically arranged in organized Fibonacci number ratios (1, 1, 2, 3, 5, 8, 13, 21, 34, 55…). It is interesting to note that the familiar woody cone on a pine is the female reproductive part, which produces seeds. Female cones usually grow on the tips of the higher branches toward the top of the plant. The pollen-producing male cones are harder to spot because they are smaller and grow at the base of the branches. Since the male cones are positioned below the female cones on each tree, wind-dispersed pollen usually blows toward other trees. This tends to promote species diversity because self-pollination becomes less likely. To ensure the widest seed dispersal, the cone of fertilized seeds will go through a cycle of opening when dry and closing when wet, going through many cycles in its life span even after it matures and falls to the ground. The condition of fallen pine cones is an indicator of the forest floor's moisture content, which helps to assess wildlife risk. Open cones indicate that the forest floor is dry.

Finally the trail will meet the Lookout Road and a decision needs to be made whether to take the trail up to the peak, which means climbing another 382 feet over 0.5 mile, or skipping the peak and beginning the hike back down. Lookout Road is wide and smooth, but steep. Azalea Spring Fire Road meets up with Lookout Road on the left or north after 1.1 miles. Follow this trail a little over 1 mile to meet the Milk Ranch Road, and turn right or east to return to the trailhead.

Quino checkerspot on paintbrush bottom view

Distance:	5.6 miles, loop
Difficulty:	🚶🚶🚶🚶
Elevation gain/loss:	Up to 900 feet
Hiking time:	3 hours
Agency:	CSP-CDD
Notes:	Parking fee
Trailhead GPS:	N32.95965, W116.57915
Optional map:	USGS 7.5-min *Cuyamaca Peak*
Atlas square:	M20
Directions:	(Descanso) From CA-79 turn west into the Paso Picacho Campground, 11 miles south of Julian and 12 miles north of I-8. Park in the day-use area. The trailhead is across CA-79.

Habitat(s):

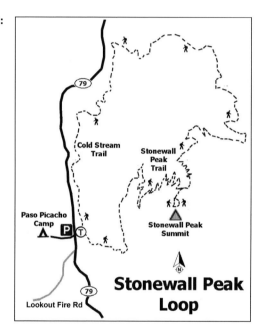

Stonewall's white granitic summit is a striking landmark. Its southern exposure and position among neighboring peaks provide some of the best views in Cuyamaca Rancho State Park. This hike is best taken in the early morning or late afternoon to enjoy the lighting on the panoramic scenery of Cuyamaca Peak (6512'), Middle Peak (5883'), North Peak (5993'), and Lake Cuyamaca.

The drive to Paso Picacho Campground and the views of Stonewall Peak and the Vern Whitaker and Cold Stream trails show both the impact of the 2003 Cedar Fire and the inspiring signs of recovery. On October 25, 2003, this human-started fire burned more than 270,000 acres. Labeled as the 2003 Firestorm, it was the second largest wildfire in recorded southern

California history. The largest fire was the 1889 Santiago Canyon Fire that burned more than 300,000 acres in San Diego, Orange, and Riverside Counties. You will also notice evidence of later prescribed burns and pine tree plantings starting their new lives among the fire-follower plants and dead oaks. It makes for a contemplative hike.

Fire followers, also known as fire annuals, are non-woody, soft-leaf plants with seeds that remain in the soil for years until they are cured to germinate after a fire. This strategy allows them to take advantage of enhanced conditions when the canopy is opened to more sunlight and most of the area's herbivores have been killed or displaced. These plants will bloom for several years until the surrounding

Paula Knoll

Fire damage

species return to compete for water and nutrients and ultimately to crowd out their sunlight. Then they will wait to germinate again following a fire. Common fire followers include the fire poppy (***Papaver californicum***), an annual with naked stalks bearing 1.5-inch diameter flowers with green-based orange petals, and purple-spot gilia (***Gilia clivorum***), a small annual whose five-petaled flowers are a pale violet with a deep purple center.

Begin the hike by carefully crossing CA-79 at the kiosk to intersect Cold Stream Trail and Stonewall Peak Trail. Turn right on Stonewall Peak Trail and follow it to the 5700-foot peak, past the northeast spur on the left near the summit. At the end of the dirt trail, walk over the sloped boulder and behind another before veering to the left where, after a few feet, you will see the pipe handrail and steps to reach the summit.

Depending on whether the summit is crowded, this is a good spot for a snack or, for more shelter, come down to boulders where

the wind is warmer and not as strong. Watch violet-green swallows and white-throated swifts do their daring, high-speed flight maneuvers. Swallows (**family Hirundinidae**) have a shuffling, waddling gait on the ground because their legs are so short, but their streamlined bodies and long, pointed wings make them the most efficient fliers of any passerine their size. Hunting insects on the wing, they are supreme acrobats with athletic endurance. Swifts (**family Apodidae**) are superficially similar to swallows in their quick acrobatic movements, but they are totally unrelated. Swifts are in the same order as hummingbirds. They look dissimilar, but internal anatomy, such as a unique shape of the humerus, reveals the relationship.

You also may see larger birds wheeling and soaring in the sky, such as the common raven or a hawk. Especially in winter, look north toward the Cuyamaca Reservoir and use binoculars to watch for the egrets, herons, ospreys, and bald eagles that may be attracted to its shoreline.

Poodle-dog bush

When you have had your fill of the summit, return to the dirt trail and follow the northeast spur of the Stonewall Peak Trail, now on the right. After a 20-foot walk onto the spur, there is a pipe rail and signage stating, "STAY ON TRAIL CRR 4326 to Los Caballos Horse Camp in 1.5 miles." If you are hiking in early spring, on the way down the mountain you may step on crunchy snow patches that are shaded by *Ceanothus*. Listen to busy acorn woodpeckers caching their newest treasures, use your binoculars to find northern flickers looking for ants,

Fire poppy

admire soaring hawks commanding the sky, and watch for southern mule deer that may be eyeing you from a safe distance among the downed trees.

Continue on the trail until it ends, then turn left along the California Riding and Hiking Trail to another left on the Cold Stream Trail to return to Paso Picacho's parking area. Beware of the poodle-dog bush or sticky nama (***Eriodictyon parryi***), another fire follower with showy purple flowers that is on both sides of the Cold Stream Trail. Poodle-dog bush is a tall shrub in the same genus as yerba santa. Although the poodle-dog's flowers are attractive, avoid touching the plant because the leaves and other plant parts can cause painful blistering. Within a few months following the Cedar Fire, poodle-dog plants germinated and began to grow vigorously near the Stonewall Peak Trail. They can be expected to become less common here as other chaparral species become established.

If you drive one mile further north on CA-79, you can take the exit to Stonewall Mine. Parking is about 1 mile away. Along the way, look closely in the meadow for herds of southern mule deer. Your destination is an old miner's cabin with a history of the mine found inside. In 1870 gold was discovered in Julian. A fenced area now encloses some historic mining equipment. These artifacts were used in the mine's production until it closed in 1892.

Distance:	3 miles, loop
Difficulty:	𝅷𝅷
Elevation gain/loss:	Up to 500 feet
Hiking time:	2 hours
Agency:	CSP-CDD
Trail use:	Bicycles on fire road only, horses
Notes:	Parking fee
Trailhead GPS:	N32.95932, W116.58048
Optional map:	USGS 7.5-min *Cuyamaca Peak*
Atlas square:	M20
Directions:	(Descanso) From CA-79 turn west into the Paso Picacho Campground, 11 miles south of Julian and 12 miles north of I-8. Park in the day-use area and find the Azalea Glen Trailhead, visible just southwest of the parking lot.

Habitat(s):

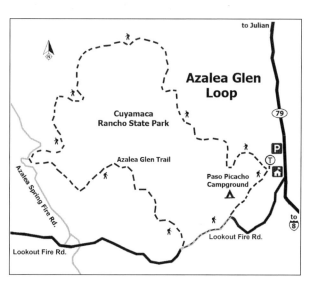

The Azalea Glen Loop Trail is on the slopes of Cuyamaca Mountain, the second highest peak in San Diego County. Although the area is still recovering from the 2003 Cedar Fire that devastated most of Cuyamaca Rancho State Park, there is a wealth of fascinating things here to see and experience.

From the trailhead, begin hiking through a mixed conifer forest, with a shrub understory of montane chaparral. A prescribed burn occurred here in 2011 that was part of the Cuyamaca Rancho State Park's reforestation project. The 2003 Cedar Fire burned much of the forest throughout the park. The 1889 Santiago Canyon Fire was similar in that it too burned much of the forest. In an effort to speed up reforestation, the park is in the process of replanting conifers in key locations in order to establish sources for conifer

regrowth. Reforestation is a long and sometimes aesthetically challenging process. Treatments and prescribed burns have removed large areas of post-fire habitat in an attempt to increase the number of pines. However, opening the land for conifer seedling planting can also lead to the invasion of non-native species such as cheat grass. Many of the large shrubs you see in the area are part of the natural process of succession after a fire. These species, mostly Palmer's-lilac, build up new habitat and restore the soil's nitrogen.

There are several trails branching off in other directions, but always with an instructive sign; just note the directions on the sign and continue the Azalea Glen Loop Trail. At about 0.7 mile from the trailhead, the Azalea Glen Loop Trail merges with a California Riding and Hiking Trail as it approaches Azalea Creek. Even under

Don Fosket

Trailhead

and is typically 4 inches long. Yellow to orange blotches appear on the flower typically in April and May.

In spring also look for western redbud (*Cercis occindentalis*) in bloom. Calliope hummingbirds (*Selasphorus calliope*) may be feeding on its nectar. The calliope hummingbird is the smallest American bird with a weight about equal to that of a penny. Despite its diminutive size, it is here only in spring and early summer, leaving in July to spend winters in Mexico. It is one of six species of hummingbird found in San Diego County and the only one commonly found in our mountains. Almost everything about hummingbirds is unusual. They have an exceptionally high rate of metabolism and must eat up to 1.5 times their weight each day to support it. Most of the calories necessary for this high metabolic rate come from the sugar in nectar, but they also eat flying insects to provide other nutrients. Their wings beat up to 70 times per second and they can vary their wings' pitch so that they are able to change direction in less than a second, hover and fly backwards.

Further ahead the trail leaves the creek and rises more rapidly as it passes through tall, dense growths of white-flowered (in May and June) Palmer's-lilacs. The Azalea Spring Fire Road is 1.7 miles from the trailhead, with the Azalea Spring just beyond. Here are interesting views off to the east of the desert as well as of Lake Cuyamaca and Stonewall Peak. Go left, down the fire road, perhaps 0.2 mile, and watch for the continuation of the Azalea Glen Trail branching off to the left. Take it back to your vehicle at the campground.

drought conditions, this is perhaps the most delightful part of the trail as it enters the lush riparian vegetation bordering a flowing stream with dogwoods, western azaleas, willows, rushes, and horsetails lining the banks of the stream, shaded by towering California incense cedars, white firs, western cottonwoods, and California black oaks. The trail was named for the western azalea (*Rhododendron occidentale*) that occurs here. It is a showy shrub occasionally found along streams in mountainous areas. If it is in bloom when you pass by, stop to enjoy its captivating sweet and spicy clove scent. It is one of the most fragrant of azalea species. It is also one of only two native species of rhododendron found on the west coast of North America. The white to deep pink flower is funnel-shaped

Don Fosket

Western azalea

Alan King

Western redbud

Distance:	1 mile, loop
Difficulty:	🚶
Elevation gain/loss:	Up to 100 feet
Hiking time:	1 hour
Agency:	CSP-CDD
Trail use:	Bicycles on fire road only
Notes:	Parking fee
Trailhead GPS:	N32.95709, W116.58049
Optional map:	USGS 7.5-min *Cuyamaca Peak*
Atlas square:	M21
Directions:	(Descanso) From CA-79 turn west into the Paso Picacho Campground, 11 miles south of Julian and 12 miles north of I-8. Park in the day-use area and walk to the trailhead at campsite No. 7.

Habitat(s):

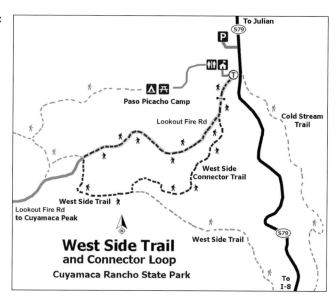

West Side Trail
and Connector Loop
Cuyamaca Rancho State Park

This short walk has an array of different habitats, many insects, and countless plant species. The loop is a triangle of three different routes, beginning just south of campsite No. 7, on the Lookout Fire Road, opposite the West Side Connector Trail (also named Paso Trail on some maps). The loop goes counterclockwise from the trailhead up the paved Lookout Fire Road, 0.5 mile before turning left on the West Side Trail, which then heads east for a short distance of about 0.2 mile. Turn left again onto the West Side Connector Trail for about 0.3 mile to return to campsite No. 7.

Begin walking west on the Lookout Fire Road, paralleling the campground for 0.5 mile. It's an easy walk on pavement except for the last 100 yards that becomes a little steep, but not difficult. Because of the devastating fire

in 2003, there will be little shade. Some of the trees seen in the distance are the pine and oak survivors of the fire.

In this locale will be three major San Diego County oak trees. Covering the hillsides and along the trail are interior coast live oak (*Quercus agrifolia* var. *oxyadenia*). They can be identified by their downward cup-shaped, prickly leaves. Coming back after the devastating fires is the California black oak (*Quercus kelloggii*) that can be identified by its large-lobed leaves. It is the county's only deciduous oak, dropping its leaves in winter. Less conspicuous and harder to find will be canyon live oak (*Quercus chrysolepis*), an evergreen with flat thin leaves that have a golden fuzz on their undersides and with large caps on their acorns.

Bill Howell

Grape soda lupine and scarlet bugler

The forest has an understory of montane chaparral shrubs. Spring wildflowers will enhance the experience. Look for a large roadside plant with elongated leaves in threes branching from the stems. This is Indian milkweed (*Asclepias eriocarpa*). Its flowers have a unique look and no dusty pollen. Instead, they have little packets (pollinia) of pollen that hitchhike on the spiky legs of the bees and wasps. On the sunny part of this road is grape soda lupine, which has an aroma of grape soda from the new buds.

At 0.5 mile on the fire road, you will find the turnoff to the left or southeast for the dirt path of the West Side Trail. No longer traveling uphill, the route is now a gentle descent. On your right is a huge block of igneous rock. The Kumeyaay Indians, who inhabited this area for many years, used similar slabs nearby to grind acorns and other materials. The milling of acorns was an important part of food preparation for the local people.

The rocks on Cuyamaca Peak are a plutonic rock called gabbro. It is dark colored and weathers without forming huge boulders. Stonewall Peak is a different plutonic rock

called quartz diorite, with lighter minerals and giant crags exposed during weathering. Note the difference as you view both mountains on your walk.

The trail here narrows and becomes overgrown. Look at the stumps of downed Jeffrey pines and study the tree rings to see their life history. A tree's history is reflected in the width of the rings. If widely spaced, then the tree grew under optimum conditions whereas narrow rings most likely indicate drought, crowding, or even an insect infestation. There is some western poison-oak on the left of this path. Be alert, but not overly concerned. This stretch of trail is more than 90% damp shade in most places. You can find the large Parish's stream lupine (*Lupinus latifolius*) in this dank environment. It is one of the largest lupine species in the state.

After 0.2 mile on this trail, turn left (northeast at the marker sign for the West Side Trail Connector) and continue through a tunnel of shrubs. Continue on the last leg of the walk for 0.3 mile, where there is hoary or stinging

Bill Howell

Parish's stream lupine

California or round-hood milkweed

nettle that can be 9 feet tall. Look, but don't touch, and press on.

A fast flying butterfly in the shade might be the unusual Satyr angelwing (***Polygonia satyrus***). Their caterpillars dine only on nettle. When the adults are flying, they display their upper wings of orange with black dots. At rest with their wings folded, only the mottled-tan underwings are visible, blending in with leaf litter and tree bark. As you skirt an open meadow and leave the thicketed area, notice sun-loving flowers and butterflies hovering with their proboscis while feeding on nectar. Flitting in the flower fields will be many species of tiny blues (**family Lycaenidae**), usually around buckwheat or members of the pea family.

Satyr angelwing bottom

In the sunshine of the meadow area you may find the tubular flowered scarlet bugler (*Penstemon centranthifolius*), and the only specimen on the hike of showy penstemon (*Penstemon spectabilis* **var.** *spectabilis*). These penstemon species are very different. Scarlet bugler has elongated red flowers, while showy penstemons have asymmetrical flower petals with a fusion of red, blue, and purple. Also along the meadow trail will be California milkweed (*Asclepias californica*), with maroon-tinged flowers and opposite long soft leaves. It differs from Indian milkweed which has white or creamy flowers; both have the same insect companions.

Satyr angelwing top

Distance:	5.6 miles, out-and-back
Difficulty:	🚶🚶🚶🚶
Elevation gain/loss:	Up to 1500 feet
Hiking time:	4 hours
Agency:	CSP-CDD
Trail use:	Bicycles, dogs
Notes:	Parking fee
Trailhead GPS:	N32.95653, W116.58368
Optional map:	USGS 7.5-min *Cuyamaca Peak*
Atlas square:	M20
Directions:	(Descanso) From CA-79 turn west into the Paso Picacho Campground, 11 miles south of Julian and 12 miles north of I-8. Park in the day-use area and walk to the trailhead at campsite No. 69.

Habitat(s):

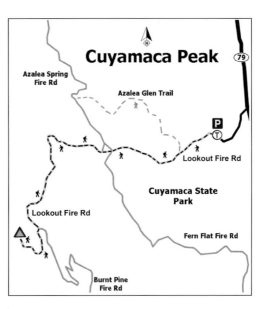

Cuyamaca Peak (6512') is the second highest peak in the county. Its location and height gives it an unsurpassed 360-degree view that is hard to beat, extending from the Coronado Islands in Mexico to desert mountains in Arizona, as well as to the tallest southern California mountains in Los Angeles and San Bernardino counties. The trek to the top of the peak is one of the most popular hikes at Cuyamaca Rancho State Park. There is always something interesting to see, but for best views, come after a rainstorm.

From the day-use parking area, walk through the campground to campsite No. 69, where there is a short trail heading to the Lookout Fire Road. Both the peak and the fire road are visible from the campsite. Follow the paved trail. Every possible trail junction is ad-

equately signed so it is difficult to get lost or make a wrong turn.

A paved road can become monotonous. However, there is an abundance of interesting plants and animals living beside the road. Take frequent detours into the vegetation lining the road to explore the life found there. When in bloom, *Ceanothus* can put on a colorful floral display, as can the pink-bract manzanita that grows here. Annual wildflowers, including lupines, are abundant near the road. Later in the spring and summer, several kinds of ragweed and goldenrod lend color to the journey. Depending on when you go, you may find monarch butterflies visiting Indian milkweed plants (***Asclepias eriocarpa***), commonly found growing here. Milkweed sap contains a toxic

View to Middle and North Peaks

cyanide chemical that, while poisonous to vertebrates, does not bother these butterflies or several other kinds of insects that feed on these plants. In fact, this toxin is adsorbed into the insects' tissues protecting them from predators, which soon learn to avoid them.

Deer Spring is on your left, approximately 2 miles into the hike, flowing even in a drought year. Here, look for western blue flag (*Iris missouriensis*) as well as rushes, willows, and other water-loving plants. The iris is bluish, as its name indicates. This hardy plant likes high elevations and alpine meadows. It is an erect herbaceous perennial with leafless 7- to10- inch long unbranched stems and basal linear leaves. The flower has three large recessed blue to purplish-striped sepals with yellow nectar guides for bees. The three petals are solid col- ored from light to dark blue or purple. It is con- sidered a weed and a nuisance in pasture lands because livestock find its bitterness distasteful.

Most large trees in the area were killed in the 2003 Cedar Fire. There are a few unburned areas that were either protected by firefighters from the 2003 devastation, such as the Paso Picacho Campground itself, or were just for- tunate and escaped the capricious flames. In addition to the campground, a small patch of forest at the top of Cuyamaca did not burn. So once you reach the peak, there will be some shade. Explore the mountaintop to be certain that the extraordinary views are not missed. The best viewing usually is after a winter storm when there is no difficulty seeing 100 miles in all directions, if not further. After exploring the peak area, return the way you came.

Indian milkweed bloom

Indian milkweed seed pod

Distance:	6.9 miles
Difficulty:	🚶🚶🚶🚶
Elevation gain/loss:	Up to 1000 feet
Hiking time:	4 hours
Agency:	CSP-CDD
Trail use:	Bicycles on fire roads only, horses
Notes:	Best time October through June
Trailhead GPS:	N32.94025, W116.56606
Optional map:	USGS 7.5-min *Cuyamaca Peak*
Atlas square:	N20
Directions:	(Descanso) From CA-79 turn east into the West Mesa parking area, 13 miles south of Julian and 10 miles north of I-8. This parking area serves other trails in addition to this one. The trailhead is across the road.

Habitat(s):

Before the 2003 Cedar Fire, this area in particular had a beautiful forest of mature shady oaks and tall pines, with occasional openings of luxurious grassy meadows. The area is no longer what it was before the fire, but there is still much to see and experience in this large wilderness area. A visit here provides an opportunity to see the forest's remarkable level of recovery from the fire, though it is still a work in progress. Also, there are spectacular views of distant ridges and grasslands from this rolling plateau, perched on the flanks of Cuyamaca and Japacha peaks. In the spring you will find a spectacular array of wildflowers, including grape soda lupine (Yes, it does smell like grape soda), four-spot or winecup clarkia, splendid mariposa, yarrow, and scarlet larkspur.

Cross the highway from the parking area and find a locked gate crossing a dirt road leading uphill from CA-79. This is the West Mesa Fire Road—Google Maps shows it as the Japacha Fire Road. There is a sign on the right for the West Side Trail, but it is not part of this hike. Go around the gate and continue up the fire road for 0.6 mile to its junction with the Fern Flat Fire Road. At this point you have completed the stem of the loop. Go either left or right to complete the loop, but this description recommends a right turn up the Fern Flat Fire Road, where you will return to this point on the last leg of the hike.

Although evidence of the fire remains in the ghostly dead trees, they stand above the bright green of montane chaparral shrubs and

Start of the trail

grasses that now cover the hillsides. Periodically the trail passes through dense stands of tall Palmer's-lilac (**Ceanothus palmeri**) that appeared and have grown vigorously in response to the fire. It regenerates via seeds and germinates soon after a fire. Palmer's-lilac is an erect evergreen shrub that is 5-12 feet high and has bark that is green to gray. Leaves are alternate and oval in shape and are covered with a powdery white covering that can be rubbed off. The flowers are clustered on a long stalk and are mostly white in color. The fruit of this plant is eaten by small mammals, insects, and birds. Larger animals like bighorn sheep and southern mule deer browse on Palmer's-lilac.

Almost all of the pines were killed by the 2003 fire and are now either blackened or silver spears rising into the sky or fallen logs. Many interior live oaks were killed, but those that survived, though badly scarred, are now recovering. Seedling black oaks have appeared while fire casualties, with dead branches, have new growth sprouting from roots that survived the fire. Assisting this natural reforestation, the park has planted numerous pine seedlings, some of which are now several feet high.

Go northwest on the Fern Flat Fire Road for 0.8 mile, then find the single-track West Mesa Trail, branching off to the left, and take it. At this point you enter the designated wilderness area where mountain bikes are not permit-

ted. The West Mesa Trail goes through grassy meadows, dense patches of chaparral, and recovering black and live oak forest. At 1.4 miles pass the Burnt Pine Trail to Cuyamaca Peak on the right, and continue straight ahead on the West Mesa Trail for another 1.5 miles. Pass the Arroyo Seco Trail junction, and continue east along Airplane Ridge to the Monument Trail coming up from Green Valley. The West Mesa Trail takes a sharp left turn at this point, descending down to Japacha Creek. You might consider a short but steep detour to the Airplane Monument off to the right that is a memorial for two aviators who were killed when their plane crashed here in 1922.

Come back to the West Mesa Trail and descend another 0.2 mile into the dense riparian growth along Japacha Creek, with thickets of native azaleas, wild rose, and ferns under tall willows and sycamores. The trail goes northeast after it leaves the creek, following the contours of the canyon, but is 40 to 80 feet above it. In about 0.5 mile, the trail will pass Japacha Spring on the right. This is another opportunity for a short detour, though the spring is often only a wet spot. Just ahead is the junction of the West Mesa Trail with the Japacha Fire Road, also on the right. Your path is straight ahead in a northeasterly direction on the trail now signed "West Mesa Fire Road." In another mile will be the junction of the West Mesa Fire Road with the Fern Flat Fire Road, on your left. Continue down the West Mesa Fire Road to reach CA-79 and your vehicle.

Palmer's-lilac

Distance:	7.8 miles, loop
Difficulty:	🚶🚶🚶🚶🚶
Elevation gain/loss:	Up to 1500 feet
Hiking time:	5 hours
Agency:	CSP-CDD
Trail use:	Bicycles on fire roads only, horses
Notes:	Best October through June; best wildflowers March through June
Trailhead GPS:	N32.94025, W116.56583
Optional map:	USGS 7.5-min *Cuyamaca Peak*
Atlas square:	N21
Directions:	(Descanso) From CA-79 turn east into the West Mesa parking area, 13 miles south of Julian and 10 miles north of I-8. This parking area serves other trails in addition to this one. The trail begins at the south end of the parking area.

Habitat(s):

This hike offers an opportunity to experience the great beauty and diversity of the Cuyamaca Mountains. This loop travels along Cold Stream Creek under shady, ancient oaks with the sound of water gently flowing over rocks, then continues up to Stonewall Creek before ascending through chaparral, where a wide variety of flowering shrubs and wildflowers can be seen in spring and early summer. The route then continues to the Soapstone Grade grasslands with views down to the large meadow east of Lake Cuyamaca and North Peak beyond. At the top of the loop, it crosses a chaparral-covered ridge before descending to the Sweetwater River in Upper Green Valley, where tall Jeffrey pines, interior live oaks, and more wildflowers may be seen.

Start at the south end of West Mesa Parking area and walk east a short distance across Cold Stream to the Cold Stream Trail. Turn left and continue northwest through black and interior live oak trees for about 0.2 mile to Cold Spring. The trees were only slightly damaged by the 2003 Cedar Fire in this section of the park, where Cold Spring fills a barrel designated as a watering spot for horses.

See if you can identify some sedge plants (*Cyperus* **spp.**) near water areas. Sedges, rushes (*Juncus* **spp.**), and grasses (**family Poaceae**) may all look similar but are different. Look to the stems to tell the difference by using the mnemonic "Sedges have edges, rushes are round, grasses have knees that bend to the ground—or are hollow right up from the

Field of rancher's fiddleneck

ground—or have nodes from their tips to the ground." The stems of sedges tend to have a triangular shape with edges, and the stems are also solid, not hollow like grasses. The knees on grasses are joint-like nodes on the round, hollow stems where leaves have attached. The edges of sedges are where leaf attachments are found on that plant. Sedges, rushes, and grasses are all wind-pollinated plants. A well-known sedge is papyrus, from which a paper-like material was made from the pith. The sedges most likely seen on this trail are various species of flatsedges.

Leave Cold Stream Spring, turning right on to the Cold Spring Trail and continue northeast for 1.4 miles, over a ridge and down to Stonewall Creek. The creek flows intermittently during the rainy season, but is likely to be dry by early spring. Cross the creek bed and just beyond it find the Stonewall Creek Fire Road. Turn left or north for 1.46 miles along the west-facing slope of the canyon, passing the signed Vern Whitaker Trail and continuing on the Stonewall Creek Fire Road as it follows a low ridge above a large expanse of grassland, sloping down to the meadows east of Lake Cuyamaca. Continue to the Soapstone Grade Fire Road. Turn right or east on to Soapstone as it gradually climbs toward a more distant chaparral-covered ridge.

Notice the white streak on this ridge, an outcropping of metamorphic rock extending for about 1 mile, just under the ridgeline. This is the soapstone for which this grade was named. Soapstone is a very soft rock, easily scratched and often used for sculpture. Some Native Americans carved bowls from soapstone. More recently soapstone is mined in some areas such as the northeastern United States and France for its talc content—baby powder and talcum powder are both composed of talc, and it has industrial uses as well.

A penstemon species on the trail

Don Fosket

Passing a field of boulders

At 0.9 mile from its junction with the Stonewall Creek Fire Road, the California Riding and Hiking Trail branches off to the left of the Soapstone Grade Fire Road. Ignore it. Continue straight ahead on the Soapstone Grade Fire Road as it begins to descend into Upper Green Valley. In about 0.3 mile you will cross the soapstone outcropping noticed earlier. Here the road goes over whitish-gray soapstone rocks, embedded in the roadway.

At the bottom of the grade will be the Sweetwater River and the Upper Green Valley Fire Road. Go right or south on the Upper Green Valley road, and continue for 2.9 miles. Thick riparian vegetation hides the river initially, with the river valley gradually widening to become rolling grassland with scattered inland live oaks and nearly mature Jeffrey pines. Usually there is a grand display of wildflowers in late May and early June.

After traveling 2.5 miles on the Upper Green Valley road, you reach the southern end of the Soapstone Creek Fire Road branching off to the right. Walk past and continue straight ahead on the Upper Green Valley road for another 0.4 mile and find the Hill Trail on your right that takes you west, a short cut, back to the Cold Stream Trail. Turn right going north and after another 0.7 mile, the loop is completed and you re-cross Cold Stream to arrive back at the West Mesa parking area trailhead.

Mountain bike route: from the visitor center ride north on the Upper Green Valley Fire Road and turn left or northwest on the Stonewall Creek Fire Road. Turn right or east on the Soapstone Grade Fire Road, then right or south on the Upper Green Valley Fire Road to return to the visitor center while avoiding the trails.

Don Fosket

Descending into the canyon

Distance:	3 miles, out-and-back
Difficulty:	🚶
Elevation gain/loss:	Up to 200 feet
Hiking time:	2 hours
Agency:	CSP-CDD
Trail use:	Bicycles on fire road only, horses
Notes:	Parking fee
Trailhead GPS:	N32.92792, W116.56020
Optional map:	USGS 7.5-min *Cuyamaca Peak*
Atlas square:	N21
Directions:	(Descanso) From CA-79 turn east into the Cuyamaca Rancho State Park Visitor Center parking area, 14 miles south of Julian and 9 miles north of I-8. Trailhead parking is just south of the visitor center.

Habitat(s):

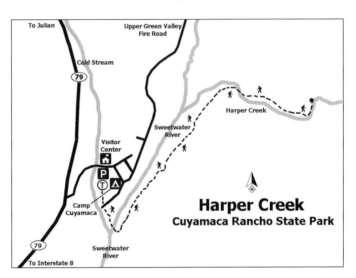

Harper Creek has a series of shallow bathing pools, making it a popular place to enjoy dipping your toes or jumping into this cool mountain stream on hot days. Although both Harper Creek and the Sweetwater River were dry in August 2014, in a normal year both the river and its tributary creek have abundant flowing water, at least in the spring and early summer. The best time to enjoy wildflowers on this hike is from February through June, although there is something blooming practically throughout the year.

The Harper Creek pools are about 1.5 miles from the Cuyamaca Rancho State Park Visitor Center. Go south on the Cold Stream Trail from the visitor center day-use parking lot through a forest of Jeffrey and Coulter pines interspersed with huge inland live oaks. In about 0.5 mile, the trail crosses the Sweetwater River and ascends the bank to join the East Side Trail. Turn left on the East Side Trail and head northeast as it crosses the grassy meadow that flanks the Sweetwater River. Among the non-native annual grasses that cover the meadow, there may be numerous annual wildflowers, often forming a massive colorful blanket across the valley floor.

In about 0.75 mile, the East Side Trail enters Harper Creek drainage and continues for 0.25 mile on the west side of the creek before crossing it. The well-trod Harvey Moore Trail leads to the pools that are about 0.1 mile up the creek from that point. The Harvey Moore Trail passes through an oak woodland with scattered inland live oaks mixed with numerous chaparral shrubs, including chaparral whitethorn, holly-leaf redberry, California rose, Palmer's-lilac, and mountain-mahogany. These can put on a colorful show even in the absence of flowing water in the creek.

Don Fosket

View toward Stonewall

This is where you may see large-eared woodrat (*Neotoma macrotis*) nests made from large sticks, shrubs, and plant material. Archaeologists often excavate these nests as they often contain artifacts collected by the woodrat. Nests can be several feet high and decades old as they are passed down through generations. The nests are divided into various chambers, one of which is a debris pile that is often decorated with treasures, such as pebbles, bones, and human artifacts. Woodrats can eat the bark and foliage from coast live oaks. The species' metabolism is adapted to allow digestion of phenolic compounds like tannins found in oak trees. These dark brown woodrats have blunt noses, long whiskers, and very large round ears.

Be on the lookout for and avoid western poison-oak (*Toxicodendron diversilobum*) that might be present near the water; it has an oil urushiol or resin on all surfaces. The extremely variable plant can fool people in that it can look like a small tree, a climbing vine, or it can grow in thickets, but it can be identified by its leaves, mostly in threes with the terminating leaflet having a short stem. The leaves can be glossy or matte finished with the color ranging from bright green to luminescent red in the fall. There are small white flowers that, when fertilized, develop cream-colored berries in spring. No matter how attractive, do not touch, as the urushiol oil can cause rashes or dermatitis upon contact in many people. A safe habit for any age is to follow "leaves of three, let it be" until you can identify this plant. Once you enjoy the pools, return the way you came.

Alan King

Poison-oak

Distance:	5 miles, out-and-back
Difficulty:	🚶🚶🚶🚶
Elevation gain/loss:	Up to 1000 feet
Hiking time:	3 hours
Agency:	CSP-CDD
Trail use:	Bicycles on fire roads only, horses
Notes:	Trekking poles recommended; trail steep and rocky in places
Trailhead GPS:	N32.91140, W116.57413
Optional map:	USGS 7.5-min *Cuyamaca Peak*
Atlas square:	N20
Directions:	(Descanso) From CA-79 turn east into the large parking area, 15.3 miles south of Julian and 7.5 miles north of I-8. This parking area serves other trails in addition to this one. The trail begins across the road just north of the Sweetwater Bridge.

Habitat(s):

Spring is the optimal time to visit the Airplane Monument. Chaparral and coastal sage scrub brighten the landscape with an array of beautiful flowering plants. Checker-blooms and golden yarrow are prevalent wild flowers during spring and another attractive feature on this hike. Majestic granitic rocks dot the landscape with chunks of white and black stones, making it a difficult landscape to navigate in spots on the trail.

The trek to the Airplane Monument begins on the north side of CA-79, immediately after crossing Sweetwater Bridge. Go north then left to the southwest on the West Mesa Trail, paralleling CA-79, in a beautiful oak-forested area of Cuyamaca Rancho State Park. Just short of

0.5 mile into the hike, turn right to take the Monument Trail. Summer snow (*Leptosiphon floribundus*), in the phlox family, decorates the walk with beautiful white flowers in late May and early June. Be sure to listen for Steller's jays, scrub jays, and acorn woodpeckers. A flashy bird seen on this hike is the black-headed grosbeak (*Pheucticus melanocephalus*), the male of which has a largely cinnamon-orange body, black head, and black and white wings. They are one of the few birds that prey upon monarch butterflies (*Danaus plexippus*), despite the toxins found in the monarch. Black-headed grosbeaks eat the monarchs in eight-day cycles to allow their systems to rid themselves of the toxins. The male black-

Male black-headed grosbeak

headed grosbeak shares equal time with his partner incubating the eggs and feeding the young. Monarchs winter in the San Diego region between November and February. They migrate during the day and often gather in clusters at night called a roost or bivouac.

The scenery changes from oak woodland to dense chaparral as you ascend. Evergreen shrubs become the dominant scenery. After a winding 2.5 miles through various habitats, you arrive at Airplane Monument. The 1000 feet of elevation gain provides a panoramic view of the surrounding Cuyamaca Rancho State Park. Be certain to bring binoculars so you can see the geologic beauty of Stonewall

Peak from the monument. The monument is a Liberty 12-cylinder aircraft engine mounted in stone. The engine is from a DH-4B biplane that crashed on December 7, 1922. Army pilot Charles Webber volunteered to fly Colonel Francis Marshall to Arizona from San Diego for military business. Inclement weather forced them to head back to San Diego. Engine trouble caused the plane to crash with no survivors. Search teams failed to find the men or plane. Five months later, a local rancher found the burned remains and the wreckage. The engine block was mounted in stone as a memorial for these World War I veterans. Beware of bees that have taken residence inside this historical landmark.

You can either return by the same trails or extend 0.5 mile as a loop by continuing north from the engine where the Monument Trail continues as the West Mesa Loop Fire Road. Turn south on Japacha Fire Road (or Pipeline, depending on the reference map used) after crossing Japacha Creek, continuing south on West Side Trail. Just north of the Sweetwater Bridge, turn left to cross CA-79 to the parking lot. Note that trails may have multiple names as they merge, e.g., Japacha and Pipeline Fire Road. Neither route is recommended to hike in winter. However, the trail is well defined and can be navigated by advanced hikers when snow covered.

Large cluster of monarch butterflies

Distance:	9.8 miles, loop
Difficulty:	🚶🚶🚶🚶🚶
Elevation gain/loss:	Up to 1100 feet
Hiking time:	6 hours
Agency:	CSP-CDD
Trail use:	Horses
Notes:	Untreated water at Granite Spring—reservations needed to camp; trails are rocky
Trailhead GPS:	N32.91042, W116.57412
Optional map:	USGS 7.5-min *Cuyamaca Peak*
Atlas square:	N20
Directions:	(Descanso) From CA-79 turn east into the large parking area just south of the Sweetwater Bridge,15.3 miles south of Julian and 7.5 miles north of I-8. This parking area serves other trails in addition to this one.

Habitat(s):

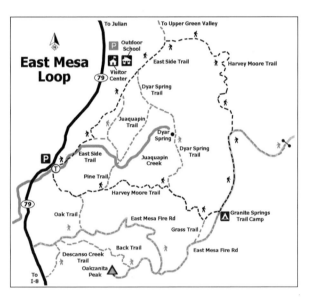

This trail has it all—views of the mountains in the park and the Laguna Mountains to the east, rolling grasslands, dense pine forests, shaded streams, and a steep descent into a rocky gorge, but it is not a hike for beginners. The hike can be done in one long day or with an overnight at the Granite Spring backcountry campground. There is also the option of two smaller loops for less mileage. To stay overnight at Granite Spring campground, contact Reserve America for reservations at www.reserveamerica.com or call (800) 444-7275.

The trailhead is at the parking area. Look for the signed Harvey Moore Trail that starts off to the southeast and ascends steeply up

400 feet to a saddle with a nice view of Oakzanita Peak to the south. A trail branches off left or northeast after 1.6 miles. Continue on the Harvey More Trail through an oak forest to the lovely rolling grassland of the East Mesa. Pass the Dyar Spring Trail on the left or north, 1.1 miles after the last junction. (The Dyar Trail links back to the Juaquapin Trail for another loop back to the trailhead.) Continue up the grassy slopes to the saddle where you are rewarded with a sweeping view of the Laguna Mountains off to the east.

The trail curves down and north, joining the East Mesa Fire Road, reaching the Granite Spring campground 1.6 miles past the Dyar Trail junction. Here you will find

Canyon view

pit toilets, tent sites, horse corrals, and non-potable water.

From the campground head north up a hill back onto East Mesa, most of which is in a state wilderness area. The trail follows along an old fence to a grove of pine trees where, about 1 mile after the campground, it takes a sharp bend right or east. At this point, take the Harvey Moore Trail on the left at the junction. The trail soon takes a steep dive into the Harper Creek drainage along rocky switchbacks. Cross the creek then travel parallel to it as it hugs the northern slope of this steep rocky gorge. After 2.2 miles the trail emerges back into the flat lush Sweetwater River valley. Follow the East Side Trail past the park headquarters 2.2 miles back to the trailhead.

As you are hiking, you may see wild turkeys (*Meleagris gallopavo*). About 300 of this non-native species were introduced into the county by state officials and members of Safari Club International and the Wild Turkey Federation in 1993. Safari Club International paid to have the turkeys hauled to San Diego County from Kansas. With no major predator and abundant food, the turkeys have thrived with a population today estimated to be over 10,000, ranging from Riverside County to the Mexican border in rural areas. The turkeys are a hybrid mix of two subspecies, the Texas Rio Grande and Eastern, common also in the Midwest. They roost in trees at night and eat nuts, leaves, and insects, including acorns and maybe a few rare butterflies. Far from being wild, they have accumulated in parks and around human settlements, domesticating themselves. Cuyamaca Rancho State Park is a turkey hotspot, despite some attempts to eradicate them from the park. Safe from hunters, they are free to breed within the state park's protected borders.

Summer snow

Distance:	3.3 miles or 6.2 miles, loop
Difficulty:	🏃🏃 or 🏃🏃🏃
Elevation gain/loss:	Up to 500 feet
Hiking time:	2 or 3 hours
Agency:	CSP-CDD
Trail use:	Bicycles on fire road only, horses
Notes:	Parking fee at campground
Trailhead GPS:	N32.90356, W116.58494
Optional map:	USGS 7.5-min *Cuyamaca Peak*
Atlas square:	N20
Directions:	(Descanso) From CA-79 turn west into the Green Valley Campground, 16 miles south of Julian and 7 miles north of I-8. Follow the signs to the Arroyo Seco Picnic Area or continue another 0.6-mile to the Sweetwater Bridge parking area.

Habitat(s):

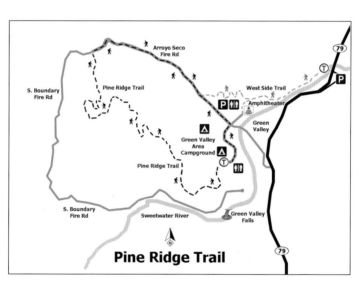

The Pine Ridge Trail has some delightful views of the Cuyamaca Mountains and the Sweetwater River watershed as it reaches the crest of the ridge at an elevation of 4573 feet. There is much of interest year-round on this short trip. In addition to a shady oak woodland and a mixed conifer forest, there can be an abundance of wildflowers, depending on rainfall and the season.

The Green Valley Campground is a central location for a number of hikes, including this one, and a good place for an extended visit with campsites set in among mature live oaks, Jeffrey and Coulter pines and, if water is flowing in the Sweetwater River, the opportunity of visiting the nearby falls.

Begin the 3.3-mile Pine Ridge loop just north of the Arroyo Seco Picnic Area near the kiosk by the restrooms. Walk north on the Arroyo Seco Fire Road through tall inland live oaks showing fire scars from the recent wildfire. Continue north on the fire road for 0.8-mile to its junction with the South Boundary Fire Road that is also signed as the California Riding and Hiking Trail. Go left on the South Boundary Fire Road for 0.1 mile to where it joins the Pine Ridge Trail on the left. The Pine Ridge Trail proceeds up the north-facing slope of Pine Ridge through a series of switchbacks to the top of the ridge. Be sure to pause for the views of the valley's peaks that include Japacha and Cuyamaca to the north.

The trail continues along the ridge, passing through typical montane chaparral with occasional Coulter pines and California black oaks. Be on the lookout for numerous wildflowers

Don Fosket

Live oaks and Coulter pines

that may be in bloom, depending on the season and recent rainfall. These can include Nuttall's snapdragon, Parry's phacelia, California everlasting, scarlet bugler, the ocellated and mariposa lilies, and chaparral bushmallow. The area is still recovering from wildfire, so the blackened stems of fire-killed shrubs are apparent, but there is almost complete coverage of the soil with new, living, burl-sprouted and seedling Eastwood's manzanita, Palmer's-lilac, chamise, scrub oak, sugar bush, and bush-rue. One of the colorful birds that may be seen on this hike is the male lazuli bunting (***Passerina amoena***), distinguished by its glossy sky-blue head and upperparts, rusty chest, and white-belly. It has a thick bill allowing it to crack seeds, though it also eats many insects. Each male has its own distinct series of warbled phrases that it develops around one-year of age, which it repeats after a brief pause. Females build the cup-like nest in shrubs close to the ground, using leaves, grasses, strips of bark, and animal hairs. The lazuli bunting was one of the greatest beneficiaries of the Cedar Fire of 2003. Previously uncommon before the fire, the population of this bird will gradually decrease as the mature forest returns.

Continue south on the Pine Ridge trail as it descends 2 miles down the ridge to reach the Green Valley Campground between campsites No. 37 and No. 38. Go north on the paved campground road to the Arroyo Seco Picnic Area to complete the loop. If parked at the Sweetwater

Bridge lot, return via the West Side Trail, turning right just north of the bridge.

To extend the hike mileage another 3 miles with an elevation gain of an additional 500 feet, park your vehicle in the large parking lot on the east side of CA-79N where there are three entrances to the lot just before the bridge that crosses Sweetwater River. If starting from this location, carefully cross to the west side of CA-79 where, just north of the bridge, it is a very short distance to the West Side Trail. Turn south and continue past the Monument Trail until passing the Arroyo Seco Picnic Area amphitheater to the fire road.

Jim Varnell

Lazuli bunting

Distance:	6.25 miles, loop
Difficulty:	𝍇𝍇𝍇
Elevation gain/loss:	Up to 700 feet
Hiking time:	4 hours
Agency:	CSP-CDD
Trail use:	Bicycles on fire roads only
Notes:	Parking fee at campground; trekking poles useful for crossing the river
Trailhead GPS:	N32.90241, W116.58235
Optional map:	USGS 7.5-min *Cuyamaca Peak*
Atlas square:	N20
Directions:	(Descanso) From CA-79 turn west into the Green Valley Campground, 16 miles south of Julian and 7 miles north of I-8. Follow the signs to the day-use parking lot/picnic area past campsite No. 76, or park at the upper lot for Green Valley Falls Trail off the campground exit road.

Habitat(s):

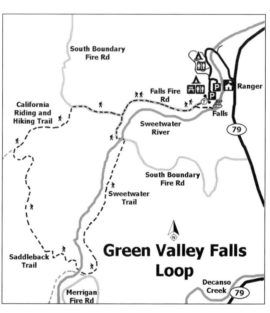

A hike to the Green Valley Falls is one of the more popular outings at Cuyamaca Rancho State Park. An early morning start is recommended because of the limited amount of day-use parking near the falls. Follow the signs to the Green Valley Falls Trail, taking time to explore the cascading falls from the top by traveling down the trail while making forays to the ponds involving some boulder scrambling for the best pictures. The Sweetwater River water flows over granitic boulders with the longest drop at 15 feet. The pools are at different depths and sizes, with rock slabs and boulders creating people magnets for sunning spots after wading in the cold water.

Towards the base of the falls, find the Green Valley Falls Trail signpost and follow directions 0.1 mile to the Falls Fire Road. Turn left at the Falls Fire Road, which heads first west and then south, stopping for a view at the Tom Crandall Memorial Bird Station bench and panel. This is one of the four Birds of Cuyamaca Rancho State Park identification stations in the park that honors volunteer interpreters. Look for northern flickers, Anna's hummingbirds, Steller's jays, and western flycatchers among the hawks and other birds found in the riparian, chaparral, and meadow habitats.

Continue south on the Falls Fire Road for a total of 0.8 mile, passing the right or west

Green Valley Falls pool

branch of the South Boundary Fire Road. You are now on the South Boundary Fire Road heading south for a short distance to the Sweetwater River crossing. Cross to the east side of Sweetwater River. Check on both sides of the trail for logs or stones to walk on or wading may be needed depending on the water depth. There is then an abrupt turn to the right onto the Sweetwater Trail to continue in a south direction on the east side of the river.

Watch for hawks over the river gorge. Chaparral plants found here include mountain-mahogany, sugar bush, and southern pink (***Silene laciniata***), a plant with many names including Indian pink, Mexican-pink, campion, and cardinal catchfly. This is a good example of why scientific names are so important to plant identification. There can be many common names for a plant, and sometimes the same common name is used for more than one plant, but each plant has only one distinct scientific name with both the genus and species name that could be further broken down to the subspecies or variety level. Southern pink is a herbaceous perennial almost a foot-tall with flowers that have five fringed orange-red petals.

The trail descends to a meadow where various signs will guide you on this loop. The trail passes a Sweetwater Trail sign. Continue to the right as you pass a Merrigan Fire Road post. Continuing to the right will be a Saddleback

Trail sign that will lead back to the Falls Fire Road. There are signs marking the State Wilderness Boundary and others prohibiting bicycles. The trail along the west side of the creek is a good place to stop for a snack or to enjoy the Indian paintbrush. Continue on the Saddleback Trail through the meadow where a large fallen oak and sections lined with juncus lead to another T-crossing for a right turn towards Green Valley Falls. Turn right again after approximately 0.5 mile onto the South Boundary Fire Road, then turn left on the Falls Fire Road to complete the loop.

Southern pink

384 CHAPTER 16

Distance:	8 miles, loop
Difficulty:	🚶🚶🚶🚶
Elevation gain/loss:	Up to 1000 feet
Hiking time:	5 hours
Agency:	CSP-CDD
Trail use:	Horses
Trailhead GPS:	N32.88954, W116.57596
Optional map:	USGS 7.5-min *Cuyamaca Peak*
Atlas square:	O20
Directions:	(Descanso) From CA-79 turn east into the dirt parking area immediately after entering Cuyamaca Rancho State Park, 17 miles south of Julian and 6 miles north of I-8.

Habitat(s):

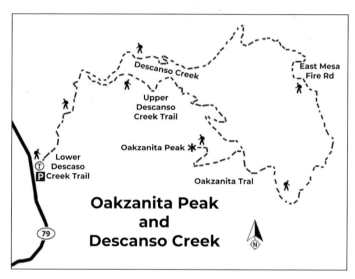

Oakzanita Peak and Descanso Creek

The 2003 Cedar Fire took its toll in this area, but the chaparral is coming back. Visitors in late March into June will be met with a multi-hued display of both perennial and annual wildflowers. Also the view from the peak on a clear day is inspiring.

The Lower Descanso Creek Trailhead is about 10 yards from the Oakzanita sign, just off the highway. The name is a give-away as to what you will be seeing in this area—lots of oaks and manzanita. Begin hiking south, to the right as you face the sign. The trail soon turns east and follows Descanso Creek, taking you past an abundance of arroyo willow, skunkbrush or basket bush, Eastwood's manzanita, and chaparral whitethorn, with occasional sycamores and oaks in various stages of recovery.

Shortly after crossing the creek and passing through an oak grove will be the East Mesa Fire Road, which is 0.8 mile from the trailhead. Go right on the fire road for a short distance and find the Upper Descanso Creek Trail on your right, just less than 1 mile from the trailhead. The Upper Descanso Creek Trail gradually, but steadily, goes away from the creek and up the northwest-facing slope of the canyon through vigorously growing species of *Ceanothus*, mountain-mahogany, and scrub oak. The skeletons of the pre-fire manzanitas protrude above the living chaparral but are only sparsely represented among the living here. After about 1.6 miles, the Upper Descanso Creek Trail ends at a low saddle where the Oakzanita Trail begins.

Go to the right on the Oakzanita Trail for an easy 0.6 mile to reach the boulder strewn, 5054-foot peak. Look for the peak register at the top if you want to sign your name. On a clear day, you can expect dramatic vistas in

Overlooking meadowlands

every direction. Note both Cuyamaca and Stonewall peaks in the distance. There is even a hitching post to tie up your horse, if you brought one.

After descending from the peak via the Oakzanita Trail, continue east, past the junction with the Upper Descanso Creek Trail and through what must have been a stand of massive oaks and pines. Most of the pines are now charred stumps. Some scattered Jeffrey and Coulter pines survived, so the area may eventually recover. Seedlings have been planted to help this recovery.

A healthy pine and oak forest is critical to animals that are dependent on it for food and shelter. Woodpeckers like the soft wood of pine trees for storing nuts, and their nest holes later become homes for a host of animals. Squirrels and chipmunks find shelter and food in the trees. Southern mule deer find cover in the trees. The tiny but large-headed mountain chickadees (*Poecile gambeli*) live in the holes of pine trees and eat the pine cone seeds, sometimes hanging upside down to pluck seeds from the cones or insects that are on the cones. Listen for their "dee dee—do do" call. The spotted owl (*Strix occidentalis*) roosts in oak trees and builds nests in tree holes or abandoned raptor nests. The owl's range is limited to the availability of forest lands.

Follow the Oakzanita Trail 1.5 miles from the peak to East Mesa Fire Road. Go left down the fire road, and after 2.5 miles of easy downhill walking on this narrow dirt road, you will come to the well-marked Lower Descanso Creek Trail off to the left. Take it to return to your vehicle.

View from the peak

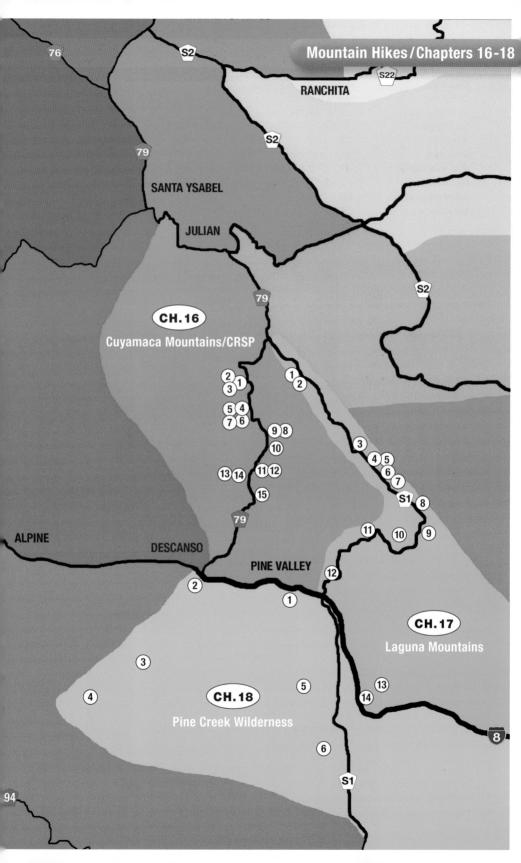

76

S2

RANCHITA

S22

S2

79

SANTA YSABEL

JULIAN

79

S2

CH. 16

Cuyamaca Mountains/CRSP

2 1
3

1
2

5 4
7 6

9 8
10

3
4 5
6
7

13 14 11 12

15

S1 8

79

11

10 9

ALPINE

DESCANSO

PINE VALLEY

12

2

1

CH. 17

Laguna Mountains

3

5

13

4

CH. 18

Pine Creek Wilderness

14

8

6

S1

94

Distance:	9 miles, loop
Difficulty:	🏃🏃🏃🏃
Elevation gain/loss:	Up to 700 feet
Hiking time:	5 hours
Agency:	CSP-CDD
Trail use:	Bicycles, horses
Trailhead GPS:	N32.97802, W116.52497
Optional map:	USGS 7.5-min *Cuyamaca Peak*
Atlas square:	M21
Directions:	(Mount Laguna) From the Sunrise Highway (S-1) turn west into the Sunrise Trailhead staging area, 20.6 miles north of I-8 and 3.3 miles south of CA-79. The trailhead is at north end of the staging area.

Habitat(s):

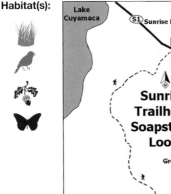

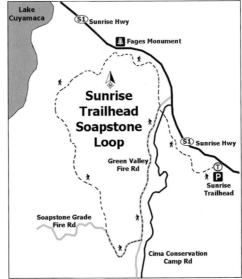

It may be a surprise to many that some areas of Anza-Borrego Desert State Park can be enjoyed during the summer months. This hike allows you to explore one such area. The higher elevations are cooler with trails open to various recreationalists. Because the trails have only recently opened, few take advantage of this great area.

In 2001, California State Parks and the Anza-Borrego Foundation acquired the initial portion of the Lucky 5 Ranch along the Sunrise Highway as an addition to the desert park. The ranch lands are adjacent to Cuyamaca Lake and connect the desert park to Cuyamaca Rancho State Park, providing a wildlife corridor between the mountains and the desert. There is also an equestrian staging area.

Two trails lead out from the Sunrise Trailhead staging area. The Lucky 5 Trail heads

south toward Kwaaymii Point while the short La Cima Trail connects to the recommended loop that heads west toward Upper Green Valley. The trail is well-maintained and signed, passing through oak woodlands, chaparral, and meadowlands.

The trail crosses the Cima Conservation Camp paved road and then parallels the road on the north side. At 1.37 mile, there is a junction with the Upper Green Valley Trail. Turn left, and at 2 miles, there will be a boundary sign indicating that you are leaving Anza-Borrego Desert State Park and entering Cuyamaca Rancho State Park. Large oak and sycamore trees shade the trail. At 3 miles there is a junction with the Soapstone Grade Fire Road. Turn right to leave the Upper Green Valley Trail and head up the fire road. At 3.7 miles there will be another junction and a sign pointing

Lake view with juncus

to the right for the California Riding and Hiking Trail, indicating that the Sunrise Highway is 2.4 miles ahead. Go right. At 4.5 miles a boundary sign indicates that you are reentering Anza-Borrego Desert State Park.

As you begin heading back to the trailhead, look at the sweeping views of the meadow below and get a glimpse of Lake Cuyamaca. At about 6.2 miles there is a junction leading to Sunrise Highway and the Fages Monument. It's only a few hundred yards over to the monument and well worth a detour to learn about Pedro Fages, who discovered the desert while chasing deserters east from the San Diego Presidio in 1772. Then come back to the junction.

As you continue along the trail you will soon pass under large California black oak trees (***Quercus kelloggii***). Various species of oaks are found at different elevations. California black oaks are found at the highest elevations (above 3500'). They have been a favorite of the Kumeyaay and other California Indian bands because the nutritious acorns are large in size and have relatively low tannin content that requires less rinsing and processing. Besides its use as food, unhusked acorns were used in children's games, similar to jacks, and for juggling, or to be made into spinning tops or even strung together to make necklaces. Acorns were used as bait in snares and traps, and the oak was used to make wooden mortars. California black oak is fall deciduous, but before the leaves fall, they turn a rusty orange yellow, a sight worthy of a fall visit.

At mile 7.7 the large loop will be completed. Turn left and follow the trail back to the trailhead and the parked vehicles. Camping is allowed near the trailhead, without charge. The water in the trough is for horses and not potable. Corrals are available for horses. Ground fires are prohibited because of the surrounding grass and potential fire danger. From the Sunrise Trailhead, equestrians can ride to Los Vaqueros Group Horse Camp in Cuyamaca Rancho State Park, or they can ride on the California Riding and Hiking Trail.

California black oak acorns and leaves

Distance:	4 miles, loop
Difficulty:	🏃🏃
Elevation gain/loss:	Up to 400 feet
Hiking time:	2 hours
Agency:	CSP-CDD
Trail use:	Horses on PCT section only
Notes:	Good birding area; visitor center open 9 a.m.- 3 p.m.
Trailhead GPS:	N32.97742, W116.52408
Optional map:	USGS 7.5-min *Cuyamaca Peak*
Atlas square:	M21
Directions:	(Mount Laguna) From the Sunrise Highway (S-1) turn west into the Sunrise Trailhead staging area, 20.6 miles north of I-8 and 3.3 miles south of CA-79. The trailhead is at south end of the staging area.

Habitat(s):

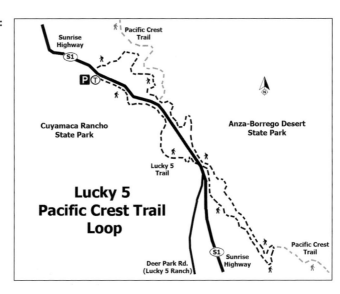

The Anza-Borrego Foundation played a crucial role in creating a wildlife corridor from the desert floor to the Laguna Mountains when they purchased 2675 acres or 63% of the Lucky 5 Ranch in 2001 and transferred it to the State, thereby connecting Anza-Borrego Desert State Park to Cuyamaca Rancho State Park and the Cleveland National Forest. An additional purchase of almost 2100 acres of the adjacent Rancho Cuyamaca/Tulloch Ranch in 2005 by the Nature Conservancy and the State Water Resources Control Board expanded a sizable portion of the desert park in the Laguna Mountains, straddling both sides of the Sunrise Highway. Further inclusion of 1130 acres of the Lucky 5 Ranch at the end of 2015 resulted in a total area of 3805 acres. The Daley family has retained only 400 acres of the Lucky 5 Ranch for private use.

Conservation of all of these ranch lands means an expanded wildlife corridor between desert and mountains in addition to an expansion of outdoor recreation for county residents and visitors.

The Lucky 5 Ranch was originally homesteaded in the 1860s by the Harper family who built a home and some ranch buildings in Rattlesnake Valley. Charles Luckman purchased the ranch in 1940 as a summer home. Luckman, his wife, and three sons made five, so he changed the name of the ranch to the Lucky 5. The ranch supports mature oaks and sycamores and abundant wildlife such as golden eagle, mountain lion, bobcat, gray fox, southern mule deer, and numerous species of reptiles and birds. It is an important transition between chaparral and mixed conifer forest habitats. The elevation on the ranch

Following the PCT

The trailhead

varies from 4600 to 5400 feet above sea level and includes rolling grasslands and mountainous areas. The views to the desert below from the top of the escarpment are spectacular. It is also an important cultural area associated with the Kwaaymii Laguna Band of Mission Indians.

The trailhead is behind the vault toilets and is signed. Follow the trail 1.18 miles south to the highway crossing and the entrance to the Lucky 5 Ranch, which is currently gated and closed to the public until a management plan is in place. Cross the highway to continue following the trail on the other side of the road. Note the exposed rock on the trail. It is Julian schist, a metamorphosed sedimentary rock layer that is one of the oldest in the county, well over 200 million years old. The best exposures of this rock are found along the Sunrise Highway.

At 1.82 miles from the Sunrise parking area is the junction with the Pacific Crest Trail

(PCT). Turn left on the PCT to head north, paralleling the Sunrise Highway. Vegetation along the trail includes sugar bush, chamise, California buckwheat, *Ceanothus* species, manzanita, and California thistle (***Cirsium occidentale* var. *californicum***), a perennial herb native and limited or endemic to the state, recognized by its purple inflorescence.

The desert view from the PCT includes Mason, Vallecito, and Blair valleys backed up by Ghost Mountain and the Pinyon, Vallecito, and the distant Santa Rosa mountains. At 3.77 miles there is a signed junction to the west with the PCT continuing north to the right. Turn left to return to the Sunrise Highway and the parking area.

California thistle

Distance:	1.4 miles, out-and-back
Difficulty:	🚶🚶
Elevation gain/loss:	Up to 200 feet
Hiking time:	1 hour
Agency:	USFS/CNF-DRD; CSP-CDD
Trail use:	Dogs, horses
Notes:	Adventure Pass required; non-potable water for horses
Trailhead GPS:	N32.92476, W116.48215
Optional map:	USGS 7.5-min *Monument Peak*
Atlas square:	N22
Directions:	(Mount Laguna) From the Sunrise Highway (S-1) turn north into the Pioneer Mail Trailhead staging area, 15.6 miles north of I-8 and 8.3 miles south of CA-79. Drive to end of road and park.

Habitat(s):

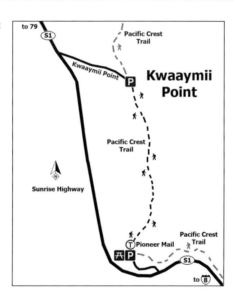

This short segment of the Pacific Crest Trail (PCT) follows a wide ledge that was hacked out of the nearby cliff that was once part of the original Sunrise Highway. The drop from the ledge is a few thousand feet to the Anza-Borrego Desert below. This old road was difficult to maintain and dangerous for motorists, especially with extremely high winds. The highway was rerouted to a safer, though less spectacular location, on the other side of a nameless hill in the 1970s. This trail segment is one of the most spectacular places to view the transition from mountains to desert.

If interested in visiting only Kwaaymii Point and not going on this short hike, instead of starting at the Pioneer Mail Trailhead, drive to milepost 30.3 on the Sunrise Highway and turn onto Kwaaymii Road on your right. Drive 0.3 mile down the paved road to its end to arrive at

Kwaaymii Point. Parking here doesn't require an Adventure Pass because it is in the Anza-Borrego Desert State Park rather than in Cleveland National Forest.

The hike begins at the Pioneer Mail Trailhead, which is actually a misnomer. It was named in the 1930s when it was thought that the 1857-1861 Jackass Mail Line between Vallecito and San Diego came through this area. It actually came up from the desert through Oriflamme Canyon. From the Pioneer Mail Trailhead, head north on the trail, which has all the characteristics of a dirt road as it leads up the slope through low growing chaparral consisting of shiny-leaf yerba santa, manzanita, buckwheat, chamise, mountain-mahogany, and scattered scrub oaks. Continuing up the trail, the drop off on the right becomes more dramatic and a sense of appreciation begins to grow for the ef-

High above the desert

fort necessary to chisel a road into this increasingly steep slope. Soon you will be gazing over a cliff with an unbroken 3000-foot drop to the floor of Cottonwood Canyon and Mason Valley. The Pinyon Mountains rise on the other side of the valley and, in the hazy distance, the massive Santa Rosa Mountains loom over the horizon. After a fall or winter storm, the view will be even more spectacular as you will be able to see much further.

Kwaaymii Point, named for a Kumeyaay Indian band, is an aggregate of uplifted, colorful metamorphic rocks. The Elsinore Fault Zone is visible below in Mason Valley as it runs along the mountainous southwest facing slopes towards the Volcan Mountain area. The abandoned roadway is a good place to examine the Cuyamaca-Laguna Mountain Shear Zone. Exposed rocks visible here include quartz, feldspars, and biotite. Look for inclusions of Julian schist in Jurassic gneiss and pegmatite dikes cutting across the Jurassic gneiss.

While taking in the view from the point, look for islay or holly-leaf cherry (**Prunus ilicifolia** subsp. *ilicifolia*), an evergreen shrub or small tree with thick, dark green, dense leaves with spiny margins similar in appearance to those of holly. The leaves have an odor of almonds when crushed. The small white flowers grow in clusters in spring. The fruit is a small red or purple drupe that has a thin sweetish pulp surrounding a boney seed. The fruit is an important food source for songbirds. Rodents and other small mammals eat the seeds. Islay is a browse plant for mule deer and desert bighorn sheep. The fruit was considered a delicacy by the Cahuilla Indians. The Kumeyaay ate the fruit and also ground the seeds into a meal, made them into patties, and roasted them. An infusion of leaves was used by the Kumeyaay for coughs. After exploring the point and considering the importance of islay, retrace your steps back to the Pioneer Mail Picnic Area.

Islay or holly-leaf cherry

Laguna Mountain aster

393 LAGUNA MOUNTAINS

Distance:	2.4 miles, out-and-back
Difficulty:	🚶🚶
Elevation gain/loss:	Up to 500 feet
Hiking time:	2 hours
Agency:	USFS/CNF-DRD
Notes:	Adventure Pass required
Trailhead GPS:	N32.91149, W116.46121
Optional map:	USGS 7.5-min *Monument Peak*
Atlas square:	N23
Directions:	(Mounta Laguna) From the Sunrise Highway (S-1) park on the east side of the road, 14.1 miles north of I-8 and 9.8 miles south of CA-79.

Habitat(s):

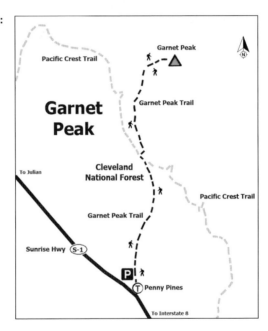

A wildfire swept over Garnet Peak not long ago. Some of the grandest views of any peak in San Diego County can be seen from this point. From the top, views extend east to the Salton Sea, south into Mexico, west to the Pacific Ocean, and north to Mounts San Jacinto and San Gorgonio.

The fire promoted subsequent growth of wildflowers. Some of the unusual or rare plants growing here include the Laguna Mountain aster (*Dieteria asteroides* var. *lagunensis*), a rare variety of aster with pale violet flowers, and Wallace's woolly daisy (*Eriophyllum wallacei*). The yellow-flowered Wallace's woolly daisy grows low to the ground in desert transition areas, achieving a height of about 6 inches. It has a woolly appearance and yellow daisy-like flowers.

You may also find Laguna or Orcutt's linanthus.

The trail proceeds north from the Sunrise Highway, crossing the rolling hills burned by the fire. The scene immediately seems bleak, with charred downed tree trunks and blackened shrub branches everywhere. A closer look reveals abundant signs of renewed life. Many of the blackened shrub branches show vigorous shoots sprouting from their base. Chaparral plants capable of crown sprouting include manzanita, mountain-mahogany, chamise, and some species of *Ceanothus*. Some chaparral species produce abundant seeds that remain dormant in the soil until after a fire. Chemicals released by fire stimulate these seeds to germinate and begin growth. Frequently the greatest profusion of wildflowers can be found the first

Whale Peak above Mason Valley

few years after a fire. Even during a drought year, at least 50 different wildflowers will bloom after a fire. Several of the shrub species germinate seeds only following a fire.

Cross the Pacific Crest Trail at 0.65 mile and follow the Garnet Peak Trail as it continues its northern direction up the slope of Garnet Peak. Note the bright red swellings on the leaves of many of the Eastwood's manzanitas. These are wasp galls. In another 0.65 mile, you will be on the top of the peak. Western tiger swallowtail butterflies (*Papilio rutulus*) and other insects may be seen hilltopping. This is thought to be a mate-location behavior that happens once the temperature warms up in spring. The western tiger swallowtail is the most common swallowtail of North America. It is so named because the tail on its hindwings resembles the long tail feathers of swallows. The wings are pale yellow with black tiger stripes and black on the edges. Look for orange spots on the inner wing margins and blue spots on the outer margins.

You may also see the elusive horned lizard (*Phrynosoma sp.*), aka horny toad. There are 14 species of horned lizards in the western US. Those found in San Diego's mountains are Blainville's horned lizards (*Phrynosoma blainvillii*). All horned lizards are striking in appearance with a crown of horns protruding from their heads and neck. They are somewhat flattened with short tails and a fringe of scales along the edge of their abdomen. A fearsome looking animal, almost like a miniature dinosaur, it is quite harmless, feeding mainly on ants.

After contemplating the views in all directions, return the way you came.

Note: Parking at the turnout is limited with alternative starting points to Garnet Peak at Penny Pines or just south of Penny Pines at a turnout. Bring a map that shows the Pacific Crest Trail in relationship to S-1 and Garnet Peak. One option is a 5.8-mile walk to the peak from Pioneer Mail Picnic area and back.

Western tiger swallowtail

Wallace's woolly daisy

Distance:	7.8 miles
Difficulty:	🚶🚶🚶🚶
Elevation gain/loss:	Up to 1500 feet
Hiking time:	5 hours
Agency:	USFS/CNF-DRD
Trail use:	Bicycles, horses
Notes:	Adventure Pass required
Trailhead GPS:	N32.90579, W116.45766
Optional map:	USGS 7.5-min *Monument Peak*
Atlas square:	N23
Directions:	(There are two trailheads. (Pine Valley) From I-8 go north on Pine Valley Road for 0.4 mile. Turn left on Old Highway 80. Go 1.2 miles. Turn right on Pine Creek Road. Go 1.6 miles. Turn right at the Noble Canyon Trailhead sign and go 0.2 mile. Park one vehicle here. Shuttle hikers to the trailhead at Penny Pines. (Mount Laguna) From Sunrise Highway (S-1) turn east into the Penny Pines parking area, 13.7 miles north of I-8 and 10.2 miles south of CA-79. With the shuttle, allow 0.5 hours of driving time between trailheads.

Habitat(s):

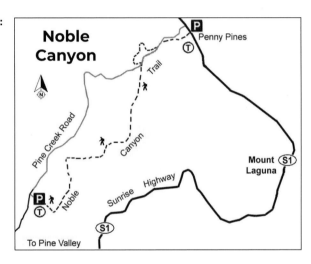

About 200 yards from the east side of the Penny Pines parking area is a view overlooking the Anza-Borrego Desert. Take a look before you enter the forest canopy. The Noble Canyon hike, one of the four National Recreation Trails in San Diego County, begins in an alpine forest and descends to an open chaparral and has water crossings and a variety of rocky landscapes and open views. Oak-lined trails along mountain cliffs are a highlight of hiking through the Laguna Mountains in this part of the Cleveland National Forest.

Immediately upon entering the top of the trail at Penny Pines, hikers are surrounded by a dense forest of canyon live oak oaks (*Quercus chrysolepis*), which are highly variable in form.

They can be shrub-like or among the tallest of oaks, depending on their location. It grows under more variable conditions than any other oak tree. A defining characteristic of this species is their flat leaves with golden hairs on the underside and large thick caps on the acorns. It has exceptionally hard wood, giving it the name maul oak, as wedges of its wood were used to split redwood. Some of the trees found here may be over 300 years old with canopies that spread for 100 feet. This plant is wind pollinated, and acorn production varies from year to year and among individual trees.

Look for some rare plants, including the ocellated lily and the white globe lily (*Calochortus albus*), a close relative of mariposa

Giant canyon live oak

lilies with delicate nodding white flowers. Further down the trail are showy penstemon and mountain bluecurls.

Note the vegetation changes as you descend. After leaving the oak woodland and riparian habitats, the trail opens to arid chaparral with yucca and various species of cacti. Within the last mile of the trail you will enter a section of red shank. At first glance you might think you have found another species of manzanita, given the red bark; but this is a cousin of the nearby chamise. Both are in the rose family.

The route crosses Pine Creek Road a couple of times during the descent as you head down to the Indian Creek Trail junction. The area burned in the 2003 Cedar Fire but is recovering. Along the trail there is evidence of old mining activity and the remnants of a homestead. Look for an abandon mine shaft with the tailings spread around the opening.

Be alert to the sounds and sights of many bird species. One of the more brightly colored is the male western tanager (***Piranga ludoviciana***) with his red head, yellow breast, and black wings. Most birds with red feathers get the color from carotenoid pigments in their food. Plants with this pigment include tomatoes, carrots, apricots, and cantaloupes. However, the western tanager gets his red head from eating insects that have consumed plants containing the pigment rhodoxanthin, responsible for showy fall colors in many trees. As showy as the western tanager is, he can easily disappear into the dense foliage. Also be alert for mountain bikers on the trail.

Canyon live oak acorns and leaves

White globe lily

Distance:	10.6 miles, loop
Difficulty:	🚶🚶🚶🚶🚶
Elevation gain/loss:	Up to 2000 feet
Hiking time:	7 hours
Agency:	USFS/CNF-DRD
Trail use:	Bicycles, horses
Notes:	Adventure Pass required
Trailhead GPS:	N32.90574, W116.45772
Optional map:	USGS 7.5-min *Monument Peak*
Atlas square:	N23
Directions:	(Mount Laguna) From Sunrise Highway (S-1) turn east into the Penny Pines parking area, 13.7 miles north of I-8 and 10.2 miles south of CA-79.

Habitat(s):

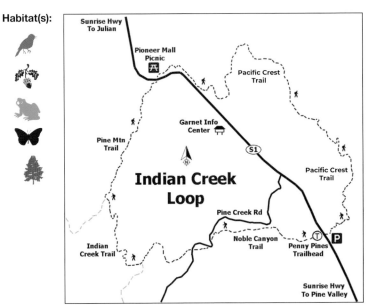

The Indian Creek Trail is full of surprises but does not give them up easily. The trail wanders through oak woodlands and down narrow canyons to streamside meadows, then climbs up to the chaparral, ending with magnificent views of the desert below. A trail for all seasons, it is best in the spring for wildflowers, in the fall for the changing leaf colors, in summer for bracing workouts, and magical after a winter snowfall. Plan your gear accordingly. It is also a great place for birdwatchers who can look for the black-headed grosbeak, Nashville warbler, and several flycatchers, along with the Steller's jay, western bluebird, and red-tailed hawk.

This description begins from the western (clockwise) approach. The trail and junctions are well marked with Cleveland National Forest signposts and distance markers. Parts of the trail are multi-purpose, so keep an eye out for mountain bikes and horses. From Penny Pines take the Noble Canyon Trailhead west for approximately 2 miles to reach the Indian Creek Trail junction towards Champagne Pass. Go right at the Indian Creek Trail down a series of switchbacks for about 1 mile to reach a stream crossing reminiscent of an alpine meadow with soft grasses and colorful wildflowers. This makes a good resting spot before embarking on the steepest climb of the trail— or as a turnaround point. At the top of a steep 0.25 mile climb is Champagne Pass. This is the junction with Pine Mountain Trail on the right and straight for the continuation of Indian Creek Trail.

Hikers on the trail

An unmarked narrow trail on the left, across from the Pine Mountain Trailhead, goes uphill to the Champagne Pass Viewpoint barely 100 yards away. After catching your breath, it is worth the detour for a great 360-degree view of the surrounding peaks.

From the junction, take the well-marked Pine Mountain Trail heading north, climbing towards Pioneer Mail, approximately 1.5 miles away, across from the Sunrise Highway. The Pioneer Mail picnic area has restrooms but no water. Here you will join the Pacific Crest Trail (PCT) heading right or south for a 4-mile hike back to Penny Pines. The PCT runs parallel to and behind the picnic area. The signpost is on the far edge of the dirt parking area. Be sure to head south towards Garnet Peak and not in the direction of Kwaaymii Point. The trail continues to climb to the highest point on the hike at almost 5600 feet. Several spots offer great views of the Anza-Borrego Desert and the Salton Sea to the east. Hardy folks can take the short side trip to Garnet Peak for a panoramic view of the desert and mountains. It is a great place to contemplate how the rise of the Laguna Mountains 1.5 million years ago created the rain shadow that resulted in the desert to the east.

This hike crosses several plant communities in close proximity, from mixed conifer-oak woodlands to riparian (streamside) habitats, and from chaparral transitioning into desert.

Among notable trees found here are Jeffrey pine, California black oak, and western choke cherry (**Prunus virginiana var. demissa**), which is a small tree or large shrub in the rose family with purplish-gray bark and reddish-brown twigs. It produces an abundance of small white flowers that have a sweet, almond-like smell. The fruit varies in color from dark red to purple-black. Native Americans ate the fruit raw or sun dried them for later use. The pit was ground into a meal. A tonic was made from the inner bark that was taken for indigestion, diarrhea, and stomach upsets. The fruit is also used in jellies, jams, and wine.

Western choke cherry

Distance:	3 miles, out-and-back
Difficulty:	🚶🚶
Elevation gain/loss:	Up to 500 feet
Hiking time:	2 hours
Agency:	USFS/CNF-DRD
Trail use:	Dogs, horses
Notes:	Adventure Pass required
Trailhead GPS:	N32.89651, W116.44869
Optional map:	USGS 7.5-min *Monument Peak*
Atlas square:	O23
Directions:	(Mount Laguna) From the Sunrise Highway (S-1) turn east into the viewpoint parking lot, 12.8 miles north of I-8 and 11.1 miles south of CA-79.

Habitat(s):

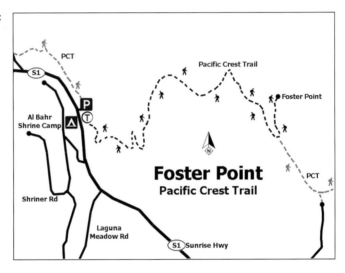

In 1968 the San Diego chapter of the Sierra Club built a small trail east of its Guymon Lodge to an overlook that they named Foster Point in honor of the chapter's founders, Loris and Ivy Foster. There they built a monument consisting of a waist-high pedestal of rocks with a flat plate bearing arrows with the names and distances of 17 peaks and points of interest.

The trail to Foster Point mostly follows the Pacific Crest Trail (PCT), which has excellent views. Most of this area burned in the 2003 Cedar Fire, and all of it burned again in the 2013 Chariot Fire, opening grand vistas. Here you will see fire-following wildflowers that are rarely seen, only for a few years after a fire. Typically seed germination in fire-following species requires substances released by burning. Burning also opens up the area, reducing competition for water, sunlight, and minerals.

Begin the hike at the stairs by the observation deck. Walk down a connecting path of about 50 feet and turn right onto the PCT where there are Jeffrey pines that survived the 2013 fire. Older, larger pines are more apt to survive a fire since their insulating bark is thicker and their lower branches are often high enough to avoid the flames. Note that most of these pines have green crowns, but the needles on the lower branches are brown, killed by the fire but not ignited. Here and along the more wooded parts of the trail you will probably see and hear Steller's jays (***Cyanocitta stelleri***), which are fairly large blue birds with dark gray, almost black, head and back and a notable crest. They have raucous cries and are anything but shy. They are also generalists and will eat whatever is available, including unattended lunches.

Along this stretch, look for resprouting birch-leaf mountain-mahogany (***Cercocarpus***

Walter Konopka

Short-lobe phacelia

betuloides) root-crowns at the base of burned branches. In the spring living mountain-mahogany will be covered with white flowers, and in the fall they are again white, this time with their long-plumed seeds.

Where the trail comes to a hairpin turn in a gully at 0.2 mile, there are burned California black oaks sending out large-leaved new growth from their roots. Oaks tend to be quite hardy and if just a strip of tissue survives, a branch may send out leaves a year or two after a fire. If not, then suckers, as viewed here, will come up from the roots.

Sara orangetip (*Anthocharis sara*), a small white butterfly whose wings have orange tips, may be flying up and down the gully. Each male patrols a territory in a gully, and females pass through them to pick out a mate, afterwards laying eggs on wild mustards.

The main shrub here is Palmer's-lilac (*Ceanothus palmeri*), a white-flowered wild-lilac. This shrub sprouts in large numbers in forest areas that have burned. It has nitrogen-fixing bacteria in nodules in its roots, like other members of the buckthorn family. The bacteria restore nitrogen to soils, replenishing the nitrogen lost by fire from the rotting leaf-litter. Along the way, you may also see the sierra gooseberry (*Ribes roezlii*), shrubs with three sharp spines per node and round red berries covered with prickles.

Along the trail are outcroppings of gneiss. This rock has salt and pepper crystals like granite, but the heat and pressure has metamorphosed it into rock with twisted light and dark layers. The trail loops gradually east and

southeast. Here the crown-spouting shrubs are manzanita, with 1 inch-long oval leaves, and chamise, with tiny leaves held tightly in bundles. Fire-following flowers on these exposed slopes include the pretty yellow-centered white flowers of short-lobe phacelia (*Phacelia brachyloba*) and the endemic San Diego hulsea (*Hulsea californica*), a relatively large annual sunflower (up to 4 feet tall) with its leaves and stems covered with grayish hair.

The 2003 Cedar Fire stopped at this fairly narrow section of the trail. The 2013 Chariot Fire jumped both the trail and the highway as well. As the trail slowly loops south, the monument on Foster Point becomes visible on the left, a bit over 0.1 mile from the PCT. Take time to view the near and distant peaks as identified on the monument.

Look out at Garnet Peak and the slopes below to see what appears to look like rough white walls. These are pegmatite dikes that formed when molten, light-colored minerals filled cracks in older rocks. Below is a valley labeled Earthquake Valley on topographic maps with the developed area now called Shelter Valley. The valley sits on a fault line. The abrupt steep drop-off to the valley floor is called an escarpment and is formed through faulting action. After enjoying the view, retrace your steps to the highway.

To learn more about fire succession, visit the *Coast to Cactus in Southern California* exhibition at the San Diego Natural History Museum, where there is a special display on fires in southern California.

Don Fosket

Birch-leaf mountain-mahogany in flower

Distance:	2 miles, out-and-back
Difficulty:	
Elevation gain/loss:	Up to 500 feet
Hiking time:	1 hour
Agency:	USFS/CNF-DRD
Notes:	Adventure Pass required
Trailhead GPS:	N32.88561, W116.43267
Optional map:	USGS 7.5-min *Monument Peak*
Atlas square:	O23
Directions:	(Mount Laguna) From the Sunrise Highway (S-1) turn east into pullout, 11.5 miles north of I-8 and 12.4 miles south of CA-79.

Habitat(s):

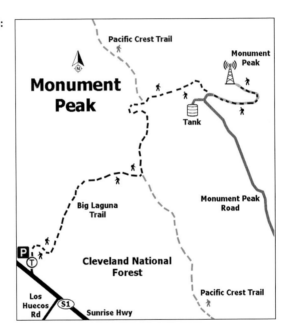

This is a short, easy stroll through an open Jeffrey pine and California black oak woodland with stands of old growth chaparral to a peaklet with outstanding views of the desert and Laguna and Cuyamaca mountains. Although Monument Peak is not very prominent when viewed from the Sunrise Highway, at 6270 feet it is the fourth highest point in San Diego County. It is especially impressive when viewed from Mason Valley in the Anza-Borrego Desert, only a few miles east but nearly 5000 feet lower.

Begin hiking on the signed Big Laguna Trail heading north, northeast, away from the Sunrise Highway as it goes through an open forest with stands of tall Jeffrey pines and large California black oaks with an occasional Pacific ponderosa pine and Coulter pine (*Pinus coul-*

teri). Coulter pine grows in drier, hotter areas than either Jeffrey or Pacific ponderosa pines, although all three may be found in mixed conifer habitat such as that found here. Unlike the other two pines, Coulter pines also grow in chaparral, down to about 2500 feet of elevation. Coulter pines have the largest cones of any pine, averaging 4-5 pounds each when fresh, but have been known to reach 12 pounds. It is for a reason that they are dubbed killer Coulter to distinguish them from the cones of gentle Jeffrey and prickly ponderosa.

The Big Laguna Trail ends in 0.5 mile when it reaches the Pacific Crest Trail (PCT). Go left or north on the PCT for another 0.38 mile. Although there has been only minor change in altitude, this short distance leads into dense chaparral with some quite large manzanita,

View west toward Mason Valley

scrub oaks, and mountain-mahogany that have grown into small trees.

At 0.9 mile from your vehicle, the PCT takes a sharp left turn. At this point a well-trod trail continues straight ahead where Monument Peak, crowned with microwave antennae, can easily be seen. Follow the trail up the shallow ravine to a firebreak bulldozed along the desert divide ridge. Continue up the firebreak toward the microwave towers to a paved road, which you can follow to the peak.

Most of the animals that live along this trail are most likely to be seen in the early morning or late afternoon. However, there is one animal you are unlikely to see unless you brought a shovel, namely earthworms (**family Lumbricidae**). California has several species of native earthworms. They are much hardier than the European earthworms (*Lumbricus rubellus*) that you find in your lawn or other cultivated areas. European earthworms require moist soil and quickly die if it becomes too dry. Native earthworms can live in the soil under chaparral, coastal sage scrub, and oaks. Like native plants, they go dormant during our long dry summers, coming back to life with the first rains. Earthworms feed on decomposing plant material, fungi, and bacteria found in soil. The soil actually passes through their digestive system as they burrow through it. In so doing they aerate and enrich the soil.

This appears to be a busy communications area. In addition to four clusters of antennae, there also is a laser facility and a helicopter pad. The road is not open to motorized vehicles other than those for the workers. While hikers can explore the peak, they must keep off the antennae and away from the laser targets. The views are the main reason to visit this peak, and they can be spectacular. Once you have finished exploring the peak, return the way you came.

Coulter pine needles and cones

Distance:	1.6 miles, loop
Difficulty:	🚶
Elevation gain/loss:	Up to 300 feet
Hiking time:	1 hour
Agency:	USFS/CNF-DRD
Notes:	Adventure Pass required
Trailhead GPS:	N32.86074, W116.41818
Optional map:	USGS 7.5-min *Mount Laguna*
Atlas square:	O23
Directions:	(Mount Laguna) From the Sunrise Highway (S-1) turn east into the Burnt Rancheria Campground, 9.3 miles north of I-8 and 14.6 miles south of CA-79. Park near the signed "Nature Trail" in the day-use parking lot near the entrance.

Habitat(s):

First time visitors to the lush green pine and oak forest covering the more than 6000-foot high Mount Laguna may be astonished to learn that the desert is only a short distance away. If you have never experienced the wonder and thrill of looking down into the arid desert lands that lie east of the mountains, here is one place to do so with a short easy hike. Additionally, the Burnt Rancheria Campground, where the Desert View Trail starts and ends, is a great place to bring your family for a weekend outing.

The trip begins at the southeastern end of the day-use parking area. Start walking on the signed Desert View Trail. For the first 0.25mile, the trail goes southeast and crosses two paved campground roads before merging with the adequately signed Pacific Crest Trail (PCT). For the next 0.2 mile, the PCT continues in a southeasterly direction before turning north.

The PCT continues under a mixed forest of Jeffrey pines and California black oaks with an understory of chaparral shrubs including Eastwood's and big-berry manzanita. If you are here in late March through early June, these could be in bloom, along with many colorful annual wildflowers. Wildflowers are not abundant in the shady oak-pine forest but are more common along this part of the trail as it goes in and out of the transition between pine forest and montane chaparral. The elevation is too high for western poison-oak. The plant you may see with three leaflets is likely

View east from PCT

to be skunkbrush (***Rhus aromatica***), also called basket bush as its branches were used by Native Americans to weave baskets. Its crushed or bruised foliage has a skunky scent. Local Indians ate the lemon-tasting berries or soaked them in water to make a beverage. The berries were also used medicinally as a restorative for inactive stomachs, according to the late Cahuilla elder Katherine Siva Saubel.

Notice the rocky outcroppings while walking north on the PCT. Millions of years ago, layers of sediment accumulated under an ocean. Subsequently, while continents moved and mountains rose, these layers were subjected to intense heat and pressure transforming them into a type of metamorphic rock. These layers tilted nearly 90 degrees from the beds in which they first formed, as the Laguna Mountains were pushed up over the last 5 million years.

The view to the east is down to chaparral-cloaked upper slopes of the La Posta Creek Valley, extending further down toward the McCain Valley and the desert hills beyond. After going about 0.5 mile, there is an unexpected drinking fountain constructed here on the PCT in 1993 to slake the thirst of hikers traveling the trail from the Mexican to the Canadian borders. However, don't count on the fountain working. Bring your own water.

Continuing for about another 0.25 mile, the trail goes up over a gentle rise with a desert view with over a 2000-foot drop within 0.5 mile. Continuing on up the PCT leads to even more spectacular desert views on Monument Peak, Garnet Peak, and especially Kwaaymii Point, near the Pioneer Mail Picnic Area, but these will add many miles to your adventure. Instead, go left on the Desert View Trail, which leaves the PCT to complete the loop back to the day-use parking lot.

Skunkbrush bloom

Distance:	0.5, 1.5, or 6 miles, loops
Difficulty:	🚶 to 🚶🚶🚶
Elevation gain/loss:	Up to 300 or 700 feet
Hiking time:	1 or 3 hours
Agency:	USFS/CNF-DRD
Trail use:	Bicycles, dogs, horses
Notes:	Adventure Pass required; logs on trail will challenge bicyclists
Trailhead GPS:	N32.85813, W116.43842
Optional map:	USGS 7.5-min *Mount Laguna*
Atlas square:	P23
Directions:	(Mount Laguna) From the Sunrise Highway (S-1) turn north into the Wooded Hills Campground, 8.1 miles north of I-8 and 15.8 miles south of CA-79. Go 0.6 mile to the Agua Dulce Trailhead parking lot on right.

Habitat(s):

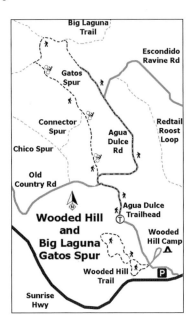

When it becomes too warm to hike in the desert but still overcast at the beach, it is time to head to the mountains. Wooded Hill in the Laguna Mountains is a lovely escape with both a short 0.5-mile loop and a longer 1.5-mile figure-eight loop along a nature trail that leads to the top of Wooded Hill Peak (6223'), the highest wooded summit in the Laguna Mountains with great surrounding views. If you are looking for a longer, less steep hike, take a loop through the Big Laguna Trail spur. This loop trail features large Jeffrey pine, California black oak, and California incense cedar, providing intermittent shade throughout the loop.

Walk north through the metal gate, continuing down the paved road. After approx-

imately 0.25 mile, you will see a barbed wire fence with wooden supports to the right of the road. Walk through the opening and turn right at the graveled road, then left as the fire road follows Agua Creek. Continue taking left turns on trails until back at this point. Then take a right turn followed by a left on Old Country Road to return to the trailhead.

Just past the left fork on Agua Dulce Road, there is an old, lichen-covered California incense cedar, dramatically tall, and a huge pine tree riddled with holes made by acorn woodpeckers with some of the holes filled with acorns. Trees with stored acorns are known as granary trees. You will hear and see many other birds among the trees. Through the

Agua Dulce Loop trail

branches you may spot red-tailed hawks and turkey vultures soaring high overhead.

With the presence of so many old, large California black oak trees, some perhaps more than 200 years old, you might expect to encounter morteros, holes worn in boulders where the Kumeyaay Indians ground acorns into flour. About 2.8 miles from the trailhead there are three large rocks with morteros worn into the surface. This shaded area is a good rest stop.

The trail now crosses fields with many colorful wildflowers in the spring. A noticeable plant is paintbrush (*Castilleja* **spp.**), a hemiparasitic plant that robs nutrients from the nearby roots of grasses and herbaceous plants. There are over 200 species in the genus with a variety of flower color. The species typically seen are orangy-red on a brush-like stalk. The species serves as a host plant for the endangered Quino checkerspot butterfly. Just past the barbed wire fence enclosure, take the left fork onto the Gatos spur.

The trail can be an aromatic experience. In addition to the aroma of Jeffrey or yellow pines and cedars, look to see if lupines are in bloom. There may be many varieties along this trail, including the large grape soda lupine (*Lupinus excubitus* **var.** *austromontanus*), which has buds that emit the aroma of grape soda. This is a small shrub with gray-green foliage, fan-shaped leaves made of five-to-seven leaflets, and purple flowers each with a bright yellow spot. This plant likes sun and is phototropic, with leaves tracking the movement of the sun.

Pay attention to what's ahead and behind you on the trail since mountain bikes and horses share this space. This loop also can be taken in the opposite direction by taking the second left once off Old Country Road.

Grape soda lupine

Distance:	3.3 or 9 miles, loop or 4 miles, one-way
Difficulty:	🏃🏃 or 🏃🏃🏃🏃
Elevation gain/loss:	Up to 500 feet
Hiking time:	2 or 5 hours
Agency:	USFS/CNF-DRD
Trail use:	Bicycles, dogs, horses on Big Laguna Trail only
Notes:	Adventure Pass required
Trailhead GPS:	N32.86093, W116.46209
Optional map:	USGS 7.5-min *Mount Laguna*
Atlas square:	N23
Directions:	(Mount Laguna) From the Sunrise Highway (S-1) park on the side of the road at the Meadows Information Station, 5.5 miles north of I-8 and 28.4 miles south of CA-79. The trailhead is on the north side of the road.

Habitat(s):

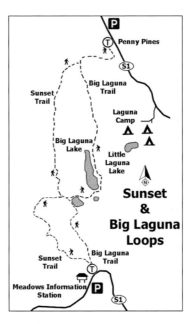

Montana is not the only state that can boast being Big Sky Country. We have the same bragging rights in our own backyard with the Laguna Mountains. Tucked in the Cleveland National Forest, the Lagunas are an impressive mountain range with the highest point at 6271 feet, high enough for snowfall during winter. One of the best hikes in the Lagunas is the lower Sunset Trail section, a 3.25-mile loop filled with vast meadows, dense pine forests, a pond, and a couple of lakes. It offers fantastic views of the mountains and, on a clear day, the Pacific Ocean and downtown San Diego.

The trailhead is off Sunrise Highway (S-1) where you can park along the highway at the Meadows Information Station at mile marker

19.1. The trailhead is located off the highway shoulder on the north side of highway. There are several trails connecting to Sunset Trail, but the route is easy to follow with trail markers at each intersection. Sunset Trail connects with the Big Laguna Trail to make for an enjoyable and easy two- to four-hour loop with about 500 feet of elevation gain/loss. You can alternately make this a one-way hike with a shuttle at Penny Pines.

After 1.5 miles into the hike, the trail heads toward the Laguna Meadows, passing through a forest of California black oaks, Engelmann oaks, and giant Jeffrey or yellow pines. In another mile, Big Laguna Trail intersects with Sunset Trail in the meadows at Water-of-the-

Big Laguna Lake

Woods, which is a good place for a snack before returning. Water-of-the-Woods is a small pond brimming with flowering water lilies and ducks during the spring and early summer. Plants that you will see in spring in the meadow areas are tidy tips (**Layia platyglossa**) and California buttercup (**Ranunculus californicus**). Tidy tips are common in damp meadows and grasslands. Look for yellow and white 2-inch-wide daisy-like flowers on long stalks. The ray flowers have three-toothed white tips with deep yellow petal bases. The California buttercup is a leafy perennial herb that is also common in chaparral and woodlands. The bright yellow bloom somewhat resembles a rose. Petals are teardrop-shaped, and flowers appear on long, green leftless stems that are from 1 to 2 feet tall. The California buttercup is one of the first flowers to bloom in spring.

One mammal found here you are unlikely to see is the California weasel (**Mustela frenata**), primarily because it is nocturnal. Weasels are a small, slender animal with a small head, short legs a long body and a tail almost as long as its body. They are solitary and live in underground burrows or dens under logs. They are carnivores with a big appetite. They consume about 40% of their body weight each day, mostly small mammals and birds. Their small heads and long thin bodies make it possible for them to follow prey—mice, rabbits, and gophers—into their dens where they quickly kill them by crushing their skulls with their strong jaws.

This is a decision point: either extend the walk via a combination of Sunset /Big Laguna trails north or take Big Laguna Trail south to leisurely finish the 3.25-mile loop. This loop hugs the Big Laguna Lake, situated in the middle of Laguna Meadows with views of the Laguna Mountains, surrounded by pine forests on all sides. Birdwatchers will have no problem spotting several types of water fowl, red-winged blackbirds, Steller's jays, and robins.

The best time to visit is either in the spring when the ponds and lakes are full of birds and flowering water plants or during the autumn when the air is crisp and mountain-fresh and the black oak leaves turn to autumn colors.

Tidy tips

California buttercup

Distance:	2 miles, out-and-back
Difficulty:	🏃🏃
Elevation gain/loss:	Up to 200 feet
Hiking time:	1 hour
Agency:	USFS/CNF-DRD
Trail use:	Dogs
Notes:	Adventure Pass required
Trailhead GPS:	N32.82743, W116.49543
Optional map:	USGS 7.5-min *Mount Laguna*
Atlas square:	P22
Directions:	(Mount Laguna) From the Sunrise Highway (S-1) turn east into the large paved turnout, 1.7 miles north of I-8 and 22.2 miles south of CA-79. Reach the trailhead by walking north past the guard rail to find the trail starting beneath the powerlines and heading southeast into the canyon.

Habitat(s):

Cottonwood Creek Falls is one of the most accessible waterfalls in San Diego County. This series of falls isn't the thundering falls of Yosemite, but it is worth the hike for its subtle beauty and restful setting.

Once parked, notice the large elongate feature in the northern parking area on the other side of the road from the trailhead. It is an exposed granitic dike. Caltrans left it there because they thought it might be an exposure of a fault surface. It is in fact a dike composed of feldspar and quartz and shows little evidence of being part of a fault movement. It is an intrusion into surrounding gneisses.

The trail starts out steeply as it generally follows a line of wooden power poles downhill through dense chaparral, characterized by *Ceanothus* species (sometimes called generically California lilac), mountain-mahogany, scrub oak, manzanita, chamise, chaparral candle, and other hardy woody species interspersed with wildflowers in the spring and early summer. Descending into the canyon beneath the overarching 10- to 12-foot shrubs, note that the sounds of the highway quickly fade away as it becomes more peaceful entering the natural world of the elfin forest.

At about 0.75 mile, where the trail reaches the junction with a larger canyon containing a grove

Wendy Esterly

Southern mule deer buck

Wendy Esterly

Southern mule deer doe

of stately old coast live oak trees, you might see the remains of a100-acre wildfire from January 2014. Don't be tempted to hike off trail at this point. The flames' destruction allows rich nutrients to regenerate the landscape. Seeds of some plant species lay dormant for years, awaiting the fire which is required for them to sprout. Don't disturb them by roaming off trail. Other plants, like some manzanita, scrub oak, and a few *Ceanothus* species, will regenerate from root crowns and quickly send up new branches.

Mountain lion tracks and scat may be encountered along this trail, as well as those belonging to coyote, gray fox, bobcat, and southern mule deer (***Odocoileus hemionus***), named for their large ears resembling those of a mule. The mule deer is adaptable and lives in a wide range of habitats. An adult has a whitish or yellow rump patch, a black tip on its tail, a white patch on its neck, gray to brown to reddish body color, weighs between 100 and 300 pounds, and its antlers branch to form two equal forks. The species is a browser, eating a wide variety of plants. It has a distinctive bounding leap called stotting, in which all four legs come down at once. Mule deer are an important source of food for the mountain lion. Young mule deer can be taken by the coyote, bobcat, and golden eagle.

While hiking, look and listen for birds. San Diego County has more species of birds than any other county in the United States. Scrub-jays, Nuttall's woodpeckers, wrentits, and California towhees are among commonly seen and heard birds along this trail.

After reaching the junction of a large canyon, turn left or northeast and walk along the creek for about 0.25 mile (five to ten minutes) until you reach a large pool and the falls. In autumn, there may be turkey or deer hunters in this area since this is the Cleveland National Forest, and a duck hunting club has land to the south of the junction. Notice how green the riparian vegetation is, in contrast to the dark gray/green hillsides.

Listen for the California treefrog (***Pseudacris cadaverina***), who may serenade you in the spring. This small 1- to 2-inch gray or brown frog with dark blotches will hide in shaded rock crevices near streams during the day. It has large toe pads and no stripe across its eyes. During the breeding season males can be very raucous. After enjoying this riparian area, retrace your steps for the return trip uphill.

Alan Marshall

Blainville's horned lizard

Distance:	6 miles, out-and-back
Difficulty:	🚶🚶🚶
Elevation gain/loss:	Up to 1400 feet
Hiking time:	4 hours
Agency:	USFS/CNF-DRD
Trail use:	Dogs
Notes:	Adventure Pass required; carry plenty of water
Trailhead GPS:	N32.74719, W116.45128
Optional map:	USGS 7.5-min *Cameron Corners*
Atlas square:	R23
Directions:	(Pine Valley) From I-8 go north on Kitchen Creek Road for 2.4 miles, and look for the signs of the Pacific Crest Trail on both sides of the road. Turn left into the pullout and park. The trailhead is across the road.

Habitat(s):

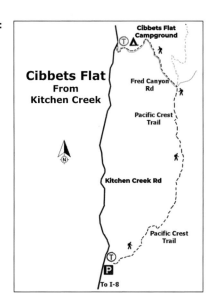

This trek is along a portion of the Pacific Crest Trail beginning at the junction with Kitchen Creek Road. It starts on a ridgeline with expansive views of backcountry and south toward Mexico and Cameron Valley as one ascends up the gentle to moderate slope composed of interesting rock formations that will delight geology enthusiasts. Foliated red-stained gneiss makes a nice contrast to seasonal blooming forget-me-nots. The trail levels out and then drops into Fred Canyon with mixed chaparral lined with chamise, mountain bluecurls, manzanita, and an occasional desert four o'clock.

Both Eastwood's manzanita (*Arctostaphylos glandulosa* subsp. *glandulosa*) and big-berry manzanita (*Arctostaphylos glauca*), found here, are well suited for southern California's climate that ranges from just under zero degrees Fahrenheit to hot Santa Ana conditions. These dense evergreen shrubs are easily identified with their bright red bark and large berries. They need little water, tolerate salty soil, and grow well in direct sun. Both tolerate wildfires, if they are not too frequent, but they have rather different mechanisms for coping with fire. Eastwood's manzanita is a stump-sprouter. It has a thick burl at its base called a lignotuber that is a protected woody swelling of the root crown/basal burl at or below the surface. The lignotuber contains buds and food reserves that allow the plant to grow new stems during a period when it is unable to photosynthesize if the plant structures above

Eastwood's manzanita

the ground are destroyed by fire. Examples of other stump-sprouters include mountain-mahogany, chamise, and various species of *Ceanothus*. In contrast, big-berry manzanita has no burl and most often is totally killed by fire. However, this species produces an abundance of fire-resistant seeds, which remain dormant in the soil and are stimulated to germinate and grow by fire.

Deer browse manzanitas extensively, while birds, coyotes, foxes, raccoons, and small mammals also are attracted to the berries that look like small apples. In fact, the Spanish name translates as little apples. Grizzly bears, once common in chaparral but now extinct, were fond of manzanita berries. The genus name Arctostaphylos is derived from the Greek words for bear, *arkto*, and grapes, *staphyle*.

California black bears (**Ursus americanus californiensis**) also consume manzanita berries. Although bear sightings in San Diego County are very infrequent, they are increasing as black bears extend their range south from the San Bernardino Mountains. There were 12 bear sightings between 1994 and 2000. The San Diego Natural History Museum has an exhibit specimen of a 200-pound bear that was shot by a concerned homeowner in the early 2000s in Ballena Valley, 8 miles east of Ramona. A more recent sighting was caught on a video taken by a border patrol agent in January 2013 and was reported in the San Diego *Union-Tribune*. The California black bear can weigh up to 200 pounds but is the smallest of bears found in North America. They are omnivores and manzanita berries are a major

component of the fall diet. Manzanita berries were also harvested by local Indians who consumed the berries and boiled the leaves to drink as a tea to treat stomach pain or to cure urinary infections.

The creek in Fred Canyon is usually dry but there is a glade of oaks. From the creek the trail ascends to a clearing where the Fred Canyon road crosses. Follow the road to the west 0.8 mile to Cibbets Flat Campground.

The reward on the trip comes at Cibbets Flat where Kitchen Creek tumbles over granitic rock and ponds among the cottonwoods and willows. This is a great place to stop and have a bite to eat and relax in this shady spot and maybe soak your feet in a cool pond. There are also vault toilets, tables, and water at the campground. After enjoying your respite at Cibbets Flat, reverse direction to return to your vehicle.

Although this hike is best in the spring when the mountain bluecurls, foothill penstemon, and wild peony are in bloom, it is also beautiful on clear days with mid-high temperatures when butterflies, such as pale swallowtail, marine blue or striped blue, and sulfurs are out.

This trail cuts through the habitat of California's largest known remaining population of the gray vireo (**Vireo vicinior**). From late March to early September listen for its song, a deliberate succession of monotonous burry phrases, often repeated in a cycle of four. Nesting in the dense chaparral, the plain gray birds are often difficult to see, though singing males may perch conspicuously atop shrubs. The dwindling population suffers from heavy predation of its nests by the western scrub-jay, as well as parasitism by the brown-headed cowbird.

Big-berry manzanita with blooms

Distance:	5 miles, out-and-back
Difficulty:	🏃🏃🏃
Elevation gain/loss:	Up to 900 feet
Hiking time:	3 hours
Agency:	USFS/CNF-DRD
Notes:	Adventure Pass required; carry plenty of water
Trailhead GPS:	N32.73231, W116.48320
Optional map:	USGS 7.5-min *Cameron Corners*
Atlas square:	S22
Directions:	(Pine Valley) From I-8 go west on Buckman Springs Road and then make an immediate left turn on Old Highway 80. Go 2 miles to the large parking area on the right. The trailhead is across the road.

Habitat(s):

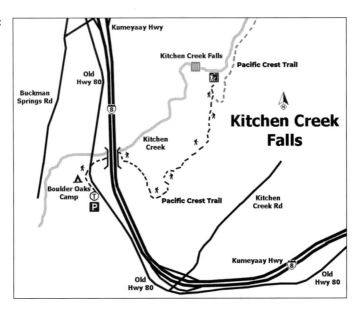

Kitchen Creek Falls is found in a remote canyon off the south flank of the Laguna Mountains that is easily accessed by the well-maintained Pacific Crest Trail (PCT). During the wet season, water from higher elevations flows into Kitchen Creek over bedrock slabs and finally falls into a small pool. The creek continues to flow south down to Lake Morena. Along the trail are abundant wildflowers in spring and early summer.

From the Boulder Oaks parking area and campground, site of a defunct store, carefully make your way across Old Highway 80, following the signs for the PCT. Follow the trail to the left and down to cross beneath I-8. At this point you are in the riparian zone along Kitchen Creek. It is dominated by western cottonwoods, which provide abundant shade during the hot summer months. This is a good spot to see many birds and other wildlife including southern mule deer.

The small California vole (***Microtus californicus***) or California meadow mouse lives in this area. A vole has small eyes and ears, a short tail, and a rounded snout. It also has a short life span, usually only a few months. Females reach reproductive maturity by an age of three weeks, males by about 25 days. The California vole is active at night and at dawn and dusk and lives in rotting fallen trees or underground in burrows connected by above-ground runways that are marked by trails scented with urine. Unfortunately for the voles, predators follow the urine scent to find them. Raptors, that can see ultraviolet light, can follow the florescent urine to their burrows.

Old manzanita on the trail

Once you pass under the twin I-8 bridges, the trail begins a sharp rise to the right, through a series of switchbacks on a north-facing slope. Spring and early summer wildflowers are abundant along this section of trail. Once to the top of the switchbacks, pass through a spring-loaded gate. (Leave it closed behind you.) Now the trail levels out a bit and will gradually rise through common chaparral species. After about 1 mile, there will be an expansive scenic view down onto this portion of the Kitchen Creek watershed. Even in a very dry year, the numerous western cottonwoods along the creek make it appear to be a green oasis.

As the trail continues to climb, the overview of the riparian zone becomes even more stunning. At about 2.2 miles into the trip, the PCT takes a turn to the right and continues up the back side of the ridge. At this point, look for a poorly marked trail off to the left. There is a split granite rock formation pointing to the sky that the trail skirts around and then starts descending. It is poorly maintained here as compared to the PCT, so be careful of loose rocks and spiny yuccas reaching out into the trail that readily impale the unobservant hiker. This trail continues to get steeper and eventually the hiker finds himself scrambling to get down to the level of the top ledge of the falls. The bedrock sheets here provide good traction when dry, but when wet, they are extremely slippery since they are polished by the running water. In dry years, the stream may dry up completely late in the season. So, the best time to visit would be in the spring or early summer when wildflowers are out and the sound of the waterfall guides you to its location. Return to your vehicle by the same trail.

A pool at Kitchen Creek

Distance:	5 miles, out-and-back or 15.6 miles, one-way
Difficulty:	𐑟𐑟 or 𐑟𐑟𐑟𐑟𐑟
Elevation gain/loss:	Up to 600 or 2200 feet
Hiking time:	3 or 9 hours
Agency:	USFS/CNF-DRD
Trail use:	Dogs
Notes:	Adventure Pass required; kiosk with map at parking area
Trailhead GPS:	N32.83713, W116.54270
Optional map:	USGS 7.5-min *Descanso*
Atlas square:	P21
Directions:	(Pine Valley) From I-8 go north on Pine Valley Road for 0.3 mile. Turn left on Old Highway 80. Go 1.6 miles. Turn left at the Pine Creek Trailhead sign on Pine Valley-Las Bancas Road. Go 0.5 mile to the parking area.

Habitat(s):

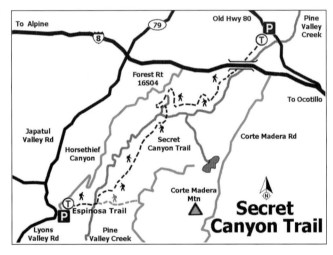

Pine Valley Creek flows from the Laguna Mountains into Barrett Reservoir, passing through Secret Canyon on its descent. Most of the 14-mile trail traverses the 13,000-acre Pine Creek Wilderness in the Cleveland National Forest. The trail is accessible from two locations: in the north from the Pine Creek Trailhead off of Old Highway 80, described here, and from the south at Horsethief Canyon trailhead.

The shorter 2.5-mile option (5 miles round trip) along Pine Creek will take you under the I-8 bridge and to the start of the flume, leaving time to cool your feet in the creek and watch the birds that favor the canyon's riparian woodland before returning.

The creek and wilderness support diverse habitats, and a few pine trees dot the canyon above the bridge, along with coast live oak, manzanita, arroyo willow, blue elderberry, and a healthy understory of California or wild rose,

skunkbrush or basket bush, honeysuckle, and yes, western poison-oak. Coastal sagebrush and California buckwheat dominate the slopes above the canyon, and the charred remains of the 2007 fires are a reminder of its impact on this environment. Along the trail you will find a variety of wildflowers in season and even prickly-pear cactus (***Opuntia*** **spp.**).

Both the young pads and the fruit of the prickly-pear were consumed by local Indians who considered it a significant food source, often encouraging their growth near their encampments and village areas. Pads were diced, boiled, and eaten or dried for later use. The fruit was also consumed and had medicinal value as a healing agent when placed on wounds. Today the cactus pads are sold in many grocery stores, especially in Mexico, where they are called nopales. The fruit or tuna is used to make jams and jellies.

Pine Creek

Pick up the trail at the south end of the Pine Creek parking lot and cross Pine Valley Creek, then climb to the oak-lined east bank. The upper section courses alongside Pine Valley Creek, passing under the more than 400-foot tall Pine Valley Bridge on I-8, and then winds above the canyon to follow a dry-laid stone flume that was constructed to transport water to a reservoir that was never built.

At 1.8 miles there is a gate. Be sure and close it after passing through to make sure that cattle do not enter the wilderness area. There will be an upward view of the lofty Pine Valley or Nello Irwin Greer Memorial Bridge. Another 0.7 mile past the bridge, the trail joins the flume line. The flume was built in 1895 and was intended to divert water from a reservoir in Pine Valley to King Creek, a tributary of the San Diego River, and then to go on to the growing San Diego metropolis. It was never completed and sections of the remaining stone flume were used in 1992 to construct the Secret Canyon Trail. This is the turnaround for the 5-mile out-and-back hike.

For those continuing on for the longer hike, at 6 miles there is an up-and-over stretch where a tunnel for the flume was to be built but never constructed. The trail leaves the flume bed at 7 miles and descends into Nelson Canyon. A few miles further the trail crosses the Pine Valley Creek again, and travels through remote Secret Canyon. The lower reaches of the trail are steep and often hard to find. Whenever the trail crosses or follows drainage, it is often overgrown with head-high western poison-oak. Be prepared if the plan is to hike the entire length of the trail. It is rugged, isolated, and hot. GPS or maps and compass, extra water, and the ability to overnight are a must for this hike.

Near Secret Canyon's confluence with Pine Valley Creek at 12.5 miles, the trail climbs and meanders above the draw until it reaches a junction with the Espinosa Trail at 13.8 miles. This is the official end of the Secret Canyon Trail, but you aren't done yet; you still have the final 1.8-mile hike out of the canyon to the Horsethief Canyon parking lot. Be sure to arrange for a pick up here or position a car ahead of time for this longer hike.

Secret Canyon can also be accessed by the Horsethief Canyon trail. From the trailhead parking lot, pass the gate and walk north about 0.25 mile, then follow the steep Espinosa Trail to the right into the canyon. The trail leads to oak-lined Horsethief Canyon, bending right toward Pine Valley Creek. Crossing the creek at 1.5 miles, you will pick up the eastward-ascending Espinosa Trail. Walk a short distance up that slope and take the left fork on the unsigned Secret Canyon Trail. A gradual climb follows the canyon above Pine Valley Creek, eventually reaching the riparian woodland of Secret Canyon.

Prickly-pear cactus

Distance:	3.5 miles, loop
Difficulty:	🥾🥾
Elevation gain/loss:	Up to 200 feet
Hiking time:	2 hours
Agency:	USFS/CNF-DRD
Trail use:	Bicycles, dogs
Notes:	Good birding area; visitor center open 9 a.m.- 3 p.m.
Trailhead GPS:	N32.82335, W116.62741
Optional map:	USGS 7.5-min *Viejas Mountain, Descanso*
Atlas square:	P19
Directions:	(Descanso) From I-8 go south on Japatul Valley Road for 0.2 miles. Park just north of the Caltrans maintenance facility on the side of the road. Entrance gate is on the left.

Habitat(s):

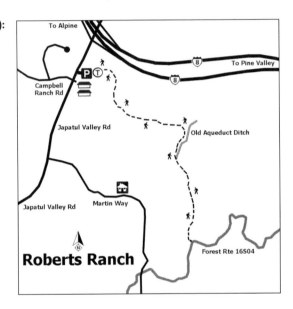

Roberts Ranch is a hidden jewel nestled on both sides of I-8 at the foot of the Cuyamaca Mountains. There is no sign announcing its presence, so this is a hike experienced only by those in the know. The land was formerly the Roberts and Ellis Ranches and was on the road to becoming a housing development. Thanks to the work of Save Our Forests and Ranchlands, the Back Country Land Trust, and concerned citizens, the development was halted in the late 1990s. Today the 714 acres of oaks, meadows, and hills are part of the Cleveland National Forest. The ranch is divided into north and south sections by I-8. Fortunately this area was spared from the devastating fires of 2003.

Begin the hike by entering at the unmarked pipe gate just north of the Caltrans mainte-

nance yard. There are no officially marked trails and no trail signs here. Instead, you are free to follow once graded, but now rutted, dirt roads, vehicle tracks, or cow paths. It is not a good idea to travel cross-country in this somewhat fragile environment. The terrain is mostly flat and provides easy walking.

The most traveled route strikes out from the gate toward the oaks to the east, keeping I-8 on the left. A deteriorating road leading through the oaks turns southward and, after about 0.5 mile, leads to a large grassland meadow surrounded by groves of Engelmann oaks. The flat, open area is filled with non-native grasses, probably brought in by grazing cattle that can be seen roaming the fields. In the spring the hillsides are dotted with clusters of California peony and some of our low

White-bresting nuthatch

and diminutive wildflowers such as baby blue eyes, red maids, and ground pink.

Keep a sharp eye out for the white-breasted nuthatch (*Sitta carolinensis*), creeping head first down the trunks of the oaks in its search for insects and large meaty seeds. It is a small songbird that gets its common name from its habit of jamming acorns or large nuts into tree trunks and then whacking them with its strong bill to crack the nut and extricate the seed.

Be listening for the raucous chattering between flocks of acorn woodpeckers. Many of the birds found here are migratory, spending only part of the year in our mountains. For example, the western or pacific-slope flycatcher (*Empidonax difficilis*) is a common summer inhabitant of riparian woodlands along the Pacific coast of North America where it breeds, but then migrates to Mexico in winter. The western wood-pewees (*Contopus sordidulus*), a drab olive gray flycatcher, is another migratory species that spends its summers with us but migrates to South America in winter. It makes a clapping sound with its bill when it chases away and attacks intruders. In contrast to the western wood-pewee, the ruby-crowned kinglet (*Regulus calendula*) breeds in the mountains of the Pacific Northwest in summer and migrates to southern California in winter. It is a tiny olive-green bird with two white wing bars. Only the adult males have the ruby crown; females and juveniles lack it. Kinglets flit through foliage and flick their wings constantly. Say's phoebe (*Sayornis saya*) is a migratory species over most of western North America but is found year-round in our mountains. This medium-sized slender flycatcher is a pale brownish bird with a rusty cinnamon-colored belly and a black tail. It flies from a low perch to pursue flying insects or snatches them from the ground.

Once in the grasslands, there are a multitude of paths from which to choose. Going east for another 0.5 mile brings one to the never completed remains of a century-old ditch designed

Western wood-pewee

Say's phoebe

Western or Pacific-slope flycatcher

as part of an aqueduct and flume to bring water from a proposed reservoir on Pine Valley Creek to King Creek, a tributary of the San Diego River on the western slopes of the Cuyamaca Mountains. Other sections of this abandoned aqueduct can be found along the Secret Canyon Trail, which runs south from Pine Valley through the Pine Valley Creek gorge.

One very common mammal found here is the San Diego pocket mouse (***Chaetodipus fallax***). This is a small brown mouse with a white belly that lives in an underground burrow. It forages at night for seeds, its principal food. If you have slept out in the open while camping, you probably had them run over your sleeping bag. They are called pocket mice because they have fur-lined pouches in their cheeks where they store seeds while foraging. The seeds are brought back to their burrows and stored there to help them get through times when few seeds are available. One unusual fact about pocket mice is that they don't need to drink water. They get all the water they need from the seeds they eat.

Continuing from the ditch, go due south for another 0.75 mile until there is a fire road, which is a continuation of the road from Horsethief Canyon. Turning right leads to a locked gate while the road left can be followed for several miles before eventually encountering another locked gate. However, for this hike, this will be the turnaround point at 1.75 miles. Return by retracing your path or choose any one of the other meandering trails heading back in the general direction from which you came.

Oak woodland

Distance:	3.2 miles, loop or 5.2 miles, out-and-back
Difficulty:	🚶🚶🚶
Elevation gain/loss:	Up to 600 feet (drop of 400 feet in 0.75 mile)
Hiking time:	2 or 3 hours
Agency:	USFS/CNF-DRD
Trail use:	Bicycles, dogs, horses
Notes:	Adventure Pass required
Trailhead GPS:	N32.74694, W116.66836
Optional map:	USGS 7.5-min *Barrett Lake*
Atlas square:	R19
Directions:	(Descanso) From I-8 go south on Japatul Valley Road for 5.5 miles. Turn left on Lyons Valley Road. Go 1.5 miles to the Japatul Fire Station. Turn left and left again into the large staging area.

Habitat(s):

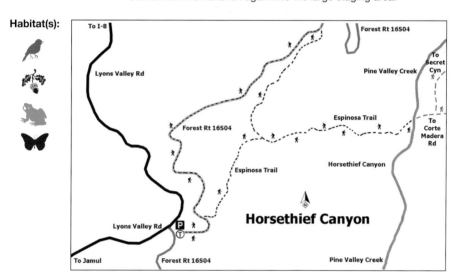

Horsethief Canyon is within the 13,480-acre Pine Creek Wilderness area that is managed by the US Forest Service. It is also part of the National Wilderness Preservation System designated by Congress in 1984. No motor vehicles or campfires are allowed. Habitats found in this wilderness area include chaparral with abundant scrub oak, riparian, and oak woodland. During the 1870s and 1880s, horse thieves discovered that the canyon was a perfect corral in which to hide their stolen horses until they were able to drive them across the border into Mexico. Today this wilderness area is valued for its natural resources, riparian zones, and small beautiful meadows.

Two hikes are described here. The first mile of the two hikes is on the same route, and then they diverge. The trailhead for both hikes is just behind the kiosk in the staging area. Enter the trail through a gate that drops down onto Las Bancas-Horsethief Road. After about 0.25 mile, just after a large bend in the road to the left, take the unnamed trail to the right. It drops down 400 feet fairly steeply into Horsethief Canyon. At the bottom of the steep part of the trail, there is a small meadow with old oak and sycamore trees. It is here that the trail splits into the two hikes.

For the 3.2-mile loop trail, take the left or northwest leg at the T-junction. The trail is narrower in this direction and is not maintained by the forest service. The trail goes through a narrow valley that parallels the dry streambed. The farther you travel, the narrower the canyon becomes. As the canyon walls close in, so does the western poison-oak. There is also an abundance of skunkbrush or basket bush mixed with western poison-oak. Make sure you can tell the difference between the two.

Jim Varnell

The pools

In a couple of places the trail is blocked by fallen debris, but there are alternate routes around the obstructions. After enjoying this trail for about 0.75 mile, it climbs up back onto Las Bancas-Horsethief Road. The 1.75 mile return trip is much gentler than climbing out of the canyon on the Espinosa Trail.

For the 5.2 mile out-and-back hike, take the Espinosa Trail, which is the right or west leg of the T-junction and is a maintained path. This trail, which leads to Secret Canyon, is fairly wide, and there is very little western poison-oak. The trail is generally flat and open with western sycamore and old oak trees interspersed with small meadows here and there.

A bird that you might see in the oak woodland is the western scrub-jay (**Aphelocoma californica**). It is a deep blue on the crown, wings, and long tail, gray-brown on the back, a lighter gray on its undersides, and white on the throat. It differs from the Steller's jay and blue jay (not found locally) in that it does not have a crest on its head. Among its calls is a repetitive screech "kweep, kweep, kweep." It is a ground forager and an omnivore eating a variety of seeds and insects. It steals acorns from woodpecker caches and robs seeds from other birds, including other jays. It is an important disperser of seeds that sometimes forgets where it has hidden the seeds. Sometimes the jays are seen on the backs of southern mule deer, picking out parasites and ticks to eat. The western scrub-jay is a frequent predator of other birds' nests, eating the eggs.

A good stopping place on this trail is the pool on Pine Valley Creek. During drought, there may be little water in the pool, but one can still enjoy the shapes and colors of the rocks that have been sculpted by water.

From the pool, the Espinosa trail ascends to the Secret Canyon Trail and continues north to Pine Valley, but that is a very strenuous hike of over 15 miles one-way. To return to the trailhead, retrace your steps and enjoy the trail from a different perspective.

Wendy Esterly

Western scrub-jay

Distance:	4.5 miles, out-and-back
Difficulty:	🚶🚶🚶🚶
Elevation gain/loss:	Up to 1600 feet
Hiking time:	3 hours
Agency:	USFS/CNF-DRD
Trail use:	Bicycles, dogs
Notes:	Adventure Pass required; summiting top boulder required rock climbing skills
Trailhead GPS:	N32.71357, W116.70567
Optional map:	USGS 7.5-min *Barrett Lake*
Atlas square:	S18
Directions:	(Descanso) From I-8 go south on Japatul Valley Road for 5.5 miles. Turn left on Lyons Valley Road. Go 4.9 miles and park at the base of a gated dirt trail, 2.8 miles east of the intersection of Honey Springs Road and Skyline Truck Trail. Limited parking is available in two small turnouts on Lyons Valley Road.

Habitat(s):

Lawson Peak (3664') is one of the 100 tallest peaks (41st) in the county as determined by the San Diego Chapter of the Sierra Club. It is also one of a series of three peaks in the Cleveland National Forest, along with Gaskill and Lyons, that help define San Diego County's eastern mountainous skyline. Lawson is popular among peak baggers and rock climbers who enjoy the challenges found on the large granite boulders that make up the summit area. Lawson Peak is named for John Lawson, a settler who had his own post office from 1890-1891.

Off-roaders are no longer allowed direct access to Lawson Peak and Pancake Rock. Private property with locked gates blocks entry from Carveacre Road and Wisecarver Road. The City of San Diego has installed a locked gate that blocks vehicle entry from Lyons Valley Road. Access via these routes is now restricted to hikers and mountain bikers. The locked gate on Carveacre Road is 2.5 miles from Japatul Road. From the gate, it is 1.8 miles to the top of Gaskill Peak. The locked gate on Wisecarver Road/Truck Trail is 1.5 miles from Skyline Truck Trail. It is 2 miles from the gate along Wisecarver Road to the junction with the trail from Lyons Valley Road.

The recommended trail to Lawson Peak starts at mile marker 13 on Lyons Valley Road at the locked gate. The first 2 miles follow the steep climb of the deeply rutted trail and then descend slightly to meet Wisecarver Road, the dirt trail coming from the left. Nearby is the large granitic slab known as Pancake Rock.

Stacey Vielma

Approaching the summit

Straight ahead is the massive granite pile that is Lawson Peak.

Along the way, look for California trapdoor spiders (***Bothriocyrtum californicum***) that are prevalent on the slopes on the side of the road. Related to tarantulas, they are ambush experts who wait in a burrow below a trapdoor. Unsuspecting insects walking on the surface are ambushed from below and whisked back into the burrow to be eaten. Their doors are closed most of the time, but the spiders usually have one leg in the door to allow their rapid response if they sense nearby prey.

Once you are past the dirt trails, the real climb begins through low brush and over boulders up to the peak. This is prime rattlesnake habitat, so keep a sharp eye out where you place your hands and feet. This area of the Cleveland National Forest is a highly sensitive wildlife area because the surrounding peaks are nesting areas for prairie and peregrine falcons. Call the office for Cleveland National Forest to see if there are any restrictions, especially in spring during raptor nesting.

Continue bushwhacking up the trail to the summit block where a narrow, vertical rock cave is found. To reach the top boulder, it will be necessary to climb up and through the cave to reach a broad shelf on the summit. It will require reaching for a ledge and pulling one's self up. This is a fouth class chimney in rock climbing terms. Be aware that while this is a popular spot for rock climbers, some of the bolts left behind might be years old and may not be secure anymore. Don't attempt the climb to the top shelf unless you have experience doing some

climbing. Once up, the chimney reaching the topmost boulder will be easier.

The view from the summit is spectacular. Surrounding peaks include Gaskill, Lyons, Tecate, Corte Madera, and beyond to Cuyamaca, Mount San Jacinto, Mount San Gorgonio, and even Mount Baldy. To the west lie the City of El Cajon and the Pacific Ocean. There can be gusty winds toward the top and it may be cooler. Dress accordingly.

For those looking for more mileage and adventure, an option would be to follow Carveacre Road north about 1 mile to find the trail up the south ridge of Gaskill Peak. This peak requires rock climbing to reach the top. Although higher in elevation than Lawson Peak, the view is not as spectacular. Retrace your steps to return to your vehicle. The best time to visit this area is between November and May when it is cooler, although it may be climbed any time during the year.

Stacey Vielma

Trapdoor spider hole

Distance:	7 miles, out-and-back
Difficulty:	🚶🚶🚶🚶🚶
Elevation gain/loss:	Up to 1800 feet
Hiking time:	5 hours
Agency:	USFS/CNF-DRD
Trail use:	Dogs
Notes:	Adventure Pass required; trekking poles recommended
Trailhead GPS:	N32.73575, W116.55740
Optional map:	USGS 7.5-min *Morena Reservoir*
Atlas square:	R21
Directions:	(Pine Valley) From I-8 go south on Buckman Springs Road for 3.3 miles. Turn right into the Corral Canyon OHV area and onto Corral Canyon Road/Morena Stokes Valley Road. Go 4.8 miles. Just past a green gate on the right (Kernan Road) and a hairpin curve, park off pavement on the left side of the road. There is room for 3 to 4 cars.

Habitat(s):

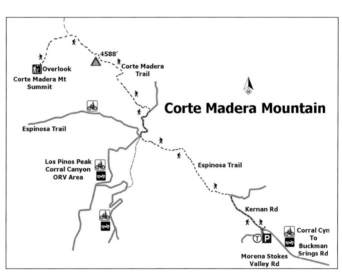

The hike up Corte Madera Mountain is for those seeking solitude and a trail less traveled. The rewards are some spectacular views and the chance to see resident golden eagles, peregrine falcons, and prairie falcons that nest on the mountain's cliffs, bluffs, or in trees on slopes. Hawks, owls, and turkey vultures are also found in this area. Check with the Cleveland National Forest for closure dates during nesting season.

There are fewer than 50 pairs of the golden eagle (*Aquila chrysaetos*) breeding in San Diego County. The species nest mainly from February to June and may reuse or alternate nests from year to year. It is sensitive to disturbance and human encroachment in the area of its nest. Golden eagles are dark brown with golden or light brown napes, brown eyes, and mostly dark beak. The feet are feathered down to the toes.

Golden eagles forage for food in grasslands, subsisting mainly on rabbits and California ground squirrels.

Peregrine falcons (*Falco peregrinus*) are fast flying—up to 69 miles per hour in pursuit of prey and up to 200 miles per hour during a downward swoop toward prey. They are specialized predators, hunting for medium-sized birds. They are making a good recovery from earlier widespread use of pesticides, such as DDT. They nest from February to June or July. They are similar in size to prairie falcons and are blue-gray above with barred underparts and a dark head.

The prairie falcon (*Falco mexicanus*) is also a scarce breeding bird with only about 20-30 pairs in San Diego County. They hunt medium-sized mammals, lizards, and birds, foraging in

Wendy Esterly

Peregrine falcon

open deserts and grasslands. They nest February through June and alternate nests, sometimes using abandoned nests of ravens, hawks, and eagles. They have a pale brown back and whitish chest with brown bars and spots. They have dark patches on their ears and in their armpits, and a dark mustache line on their face. The wings are pointed.

The route up Corte Madera Mountain averages a 7% steady climb with some steep sections before reaching the mountain's plateau. Return is by the same route, so check your back trail for points of reference. It will look different on the downhill return. The trail starts directly across from the off-pavement parking and goes up from a Birds of Prey sign. Watching for traffic, cross to the unsigned gated Kernan Road. The first 20 feet of the trail ends with a drop-off to the road and is slippery because of loose soil. Squeezing around the gate may be a better option. Enjoy the oak-shaded, dirt road for 0.5 mile, and then continue in the northwest direction behind the signed garbage can onto the Espinosa Trail.

At 1.5 miles, look back over the view of the valley at the hiker's gate before crossing the intersection of fire roads. This is the first view of the 300-foot high precipice of Corte Madera Mountain just right and beyond the sign. Clearly marked Espinosa Trail, Los Pinos Peak (closed vehicle access road), and the Corral Canyon Off-Highway Vehicle Area. An added wooden sign labeled Corte Madera Mountain points to the right where you continue on a fire road until coming to a T-junction. Directly

across and to the right of a slab of granodiorite rocks, another Birds of Prey sign marks the Corte Madera Mountain trail. The trail narrows with manzanita, sage, rocks, Coulter pines, and oaks making it easy to follow but sometimes a challenge to see at a distance.

What has been a steady uphill becomes a steep, nearly 60% grade up and over the 4588-foot peak. This is where trekking poles and/or hands help scramble up and over rocks and loose soil. There are views of Los Pinos Mountain, Long Valley Peak, Corte Madera Valley, and the Pine Valley Bridge over Secret Canyon. Continue past the split rock and start down. After descending past a huge boulder at your left shoulder, the last mile seems effortless. The trail is easy to follow with one Y-junction where you take the left choice. The right goes up to private property in Corte Madera Valley. There are a couple of granodiorite slabs where cairns point out the trail to Corte Madera Mountain peak.

Look for a peak guestbook on the highest point; it's in a coffee can that is surrounded by and weighted down by rocks. Take a camera to capture the 360-degree view of mountain ranges and valleys, which can be remarkable on a clear day. To the south in Baja California, Mexico, is the Sierra Juarez plateau. Depending on atmospheric conditions you may be able to see the Santa Catalina and San Clemente Islands. To the west and east are views of Los Pinos Mountain and the Espinosa Trail.

Paula Knoll

Granitic peak face

Distance:	6 miles, loop
Difficulty:	🚶🚶🚶
Elevation gain/loss:	Up to 400 feet
Hiking time:	3 hours
Agency:	San Diego County
Trail use:	Dogs, horses
Notes:	Parking fee
Trailhead GPS:	N32.68250, W116.51698
Optional map:	USGS 7.5-min *Morena Reservoir*
Atlas square:	T22
Directions:	(Campo) From I-8 go south on Buckman Springs Road for 5.3 miles. Turn right on Oak Drive. Go 1.6 miles. Turn right on Lake Morena Drive. Go 0.4 mile. Park in the PCT parking lot on the left just across from Lake Shore Drive.

Habitat(s):

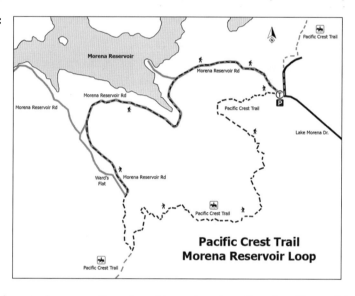

**Pacific Crest Trail
Morena Reservoir Loop**

The start of this loop is along a portion of the 2650-mile long Pacific Crest Trail (PCT) with expansive views of Lake Morena and the Laguna Mountains. Lake Morena is owned by the City of San Diego and is the highest and most remote of the City's reservoirs. It is the fourth oldest and the third largest reservoir in San Diego's water storage system and was constructed between 1897 and 1912. Drought conditions affect the level of the lake.

The six-mile walk begins from the back of the PCT parking lot just outside of the Lake Morena County Park. Parking is available on either side of the lot, but note there is a fee required for the northwest portion. A gently climbing trail leads through dense mixed chaparral. A variety of wildflowers may be seen on either side of the trail including woolly bluecurls and southern jewelflower (*Streptanthus campestris*), a perennial herb listed as rare and endangered by the California Native Plant Society. The foliage is gray and the flower is violet, blooming May through June. As a member of the mustard family, it has four petals. The calyx or leaf-like structures at the base of the flower is bell-shaped. Also, note the stands of redshank with its ribbon-like peeling bark, some growing next to chamise, a close relative. Stop at any of several overlooks to enjoy vistas of the lake and surrounding area. Ask any backpackers encountered their origin and destination. Depending on the season, they may be either starting or finishing the PCT trail that runs from the borders of Mexico to Canada.

The first half of the hike is on the PCT where the trail signs are easy to follow. At 1.8 miles,

Jim Varnell

Lake Morena view

crest a low rise and start a gradual descent. At about 2.7 miles, the trail will leave the PCT. Be on the lookout for a somewhat obscure trail, an old roadbed, going uphill on the right (N32 40.099, W116 32.016). If you get to the Morena Butte Trail, then you have gone too far and will need to retrace your steps about 0.2 mile. After a moderate walk of 0.5 mile and gaining 100 feet, there will be a dirt road that leads northwest though Ward's Flats meadow, a beautiful area underneath the massive granitic presence of Morena Butte and dotted with live oaks and Coulter pines. In season, the valley floor may be carpeted in wildflowers. Note the damage from feral pigs (*Sus scrofa*) rooting in the meadow, which extends farther west into Hauser Canyon. The feral pig, a non-native species, was introduced in 2006 near El Capitan Reservoir. A highly invasive species, it threatens native ecosystems because of its foraging by rooting, disturbing soils and associated plants and animals. Their population is declining due to a systematic campaign by various agencies to eradicate them.

Along the way, you might encounter the remains of Charles Hatfield's rainmaking tower. It is likely that his burning of chemicals was merely coincidental with the 35-plus inches of rain that fell at the lake in January 1916, causing widespread destruction and over 15 deaths in San Diego County. Stop on the steps of the ruins of an old hunting lodge for lunch before returning to the starting point by way of the Morena Reservoir's shoreline road, keeping the lake on your left for two miles.

Stacey Vielma

Southern jewelflower buds

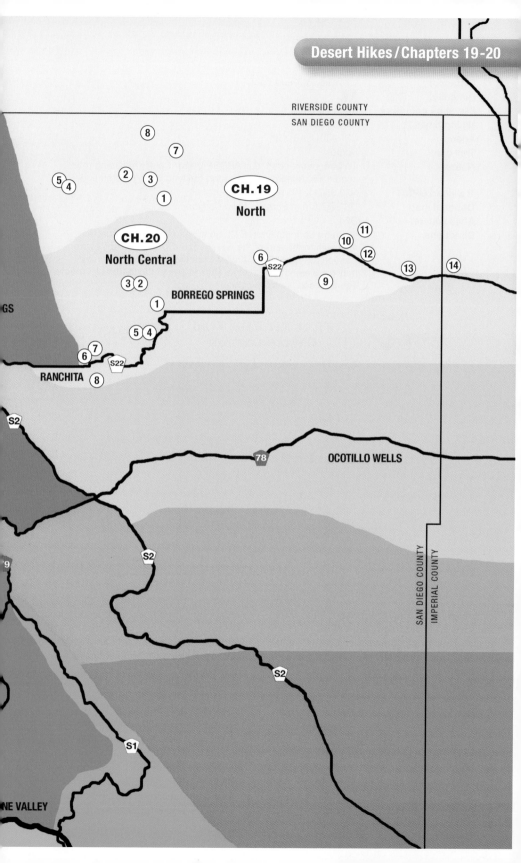

RIVERSIDE COUNTY
SAN DIEGO COUNTY

⑧

⑦

② ③

⑤④ ①

CH.19
North

⑪
⑩
⑥ ⑫
⑥ S22 ⑬ ⑭

CH.20
North Central

③②

① ⑨

BORREGO SPRINGS

⑤④

⑦
⑥
S22

RANCHITA ⑧

S2

⑨

78

OCOTILLO WELLS

S2

SAN DIEGO COUNTY
IMPERIAL COUNTY

S2

S1

NE VALLEY

GS

Distance:	1.7 miles, out-and-back
Difficulty:	🚶🚶
Elevation gain/loss:	Up to 700 feet
Hiking time:	1 hour
Agency:	CSP-CDD (ABDSP)
Trail use:	Horses
Notes:	4WD recommended; call ABDSP Visitor Center regarding road conditions; bring plenty of water; trekking poles recommended
Trailhead GPS:	N33.35311, W116.38376
Optional map:	USGS 7.5-min *Borrego Palm Canyon*
Atlas square:	D24
Directions:	(Borrego Springs) From S-22 go north on DiGiorgio Road for 4.7 miles to the end of the paved road. Continue onto Coyote Canyon dirt road. Go 2.4 miles from the pavement. The road may have areas of soft sand. Park in one of the roadside turnouts. The trailhead is on the right.

Habitat(s):

One of Anza-Borrego Desert Park's trails has an intriguing name—Alcoholic Pass. It may have been named that because of the winding trail, although one source indicates the name is a reference to the drinking habits of early settlers and cattlemen of the Clark Valley area who liked "to wet their whistles" in Borrego Springs. The steep twisting trail climbs a rocky ridge 0.8 mile up to the northwestern saddle of Coyote Mountain that connects the entrance of Coyote Canyon with Clark Valley. It saved almost 6 miles from going around Coyote Mountain to get to Clark Valley.

The trailhead is signed and the hike begins at an elevation of 900 feet. Head north-northeast

to the ridge directly ahead, only 0.15 mile. The trail is rough and rocky with loose gravel. Surrounding vegetation includes creosote bush, ocotillo, cheesebush or burrobrush, white bursage, Gander's cholla, teddy-bear cholla, and indigo bush. As the elevation increases, there is a wide view of both upper Coyote Canyon and Borrego Valley. The relatively straight line of Coyote Canyon follows the northwest-tending San Jacinto Fault Zone—one of the most active fault systems in California. Across the canyon the massive San Ysidro Mountains block the full view of Borrego Valley.

Just before reaching the crest of the saddle is a register to log your comments. From here it

The register at the pass

sepals. The five flower petals are expressed as two large oil glands and three bicolored flags sticking up. The white rhatany fruit resembles a medieval mace with a tiny barb at the tip of each prickle on the fruit. Local Indians used the root of this plant as a red dye in basket making. An infusion made from the roots was used for pain, coughs, and fevers. It contains flavonoids and a high concentration of astringent tannins. White rhatany occurs below 4,600 feet (1400 meters) in dry, rocky, or sandy places, especially on lime soils.

A similar species called Pima rhatany or purple-heather (*Krameria erecta*) is also found here. The flower color is the same but the shape of the flower is different. The easiest way to distinguish the two is to look at the shape and spines of the fruit. White rhatany's fruit is round with retrorse barbs at the tip of the spine while the fruit of Pima rhatany is cordate or heart-shaped and the barbs are scattered along the spine.

If you have time, after returning to the trailhead, follow the Coyote Canyon dirt road up another 0.6 mile to Desert Gardens. There are picnic tables and a very short trail to another viewpoint with a bench. A sign placed here in 1971 indicates that the area was once a private inholding within the park. Funds were raised by the predecessor of the Anza-Borrego Foundation to purchase the land and transfer ownership to the state park.

is only a short distance to the top of the saddle (1575'). The Coyote Mountain ridge separates the parallel Clark Mountain Fault from the Coyote Canyon Fault, which are both part of the San Jacinto Fault Zone. The high mountain range to the east on the other side of the valley is the Santa Rosas with its highpoint of Toro Peak (8716') clearly visible. Although this hike returns from here back down to the trailhead, the trail does continue down into Clark Valley and Rockhouse Canyon. The Cahuilla Indians used this route as a short cut between Borrego Valley and settlements in Rockhouse Canyon.

White rhatany (*Krameria bicolor*) is found here. This low-lying, densely branched, shrub is a root hemiparasite. Hemiparasites can both photosynthesize to make their own food and steal water and nutrients by invading a nearby host plant with specialized penetrating organs called haustoria. Another unusual characteristic of white rhatany is that its flowers produce oil instead of nectar to allure pollinators. Rhatany flowers attract oil bees (*Centris* spp.) that have specialized hind legs adapted for scraping up the oil. Although these oil bees also feed on nectar from other flowers, the oil collected from rhatany is brought back to their nests to use as larval food. If the rhatany is in flower, take a look at its bizarre composition. The five red-purple petal-looking parts are actually the

White rhatany bloom and fruit

Distance:	5 miles, loop
Difficulty:	🚶🚶🚶
Elevation gain/loss:	Up to 300 feet
Hiking time:	3 hours
Agency:	CSP-CDD (ABDSP)
Trail use:	Dogs on designated vehicle routes only, horses on designated vehicle routes or equestrian trails
Notes:	4WD recommended; call ABDSP Visitor Center regarding road conditions; bring plenty of water; no vehicle access June 1 through September 30
Trailhead GPS:	N33.37148, W116.42337
Optional map:	USGS 7.5-min *Borrego Palm Canyon*
Atlas square:	D23
Directions:	(Borrego Springs) From S-22 go north on DiGiorgio Road for 4.7 miles to the end of the paved road. Continue onto Coyote Canyon dirt road. Go 5.3 miles from the pavement. Park on the northeast side of Third Crossing (before crossing the creek).

Habitat(s):

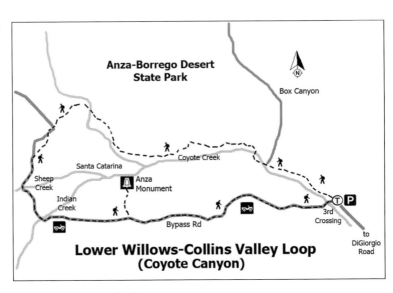

**Lower Willows-Collins Valley Loop
(Coyote Canyon)**

Lower Willows was a site of a large Cahuilla Indian village. The reliable water and plants important to desert Indians, including mesquite and agave, made this an attractive site. This village was first described by members of the Anza Expedition in 1774 and, in the following year, Juan Bautista de Anza escorted 200 settlers and 800 head of cattle through Coyote Canyon.

Today, Lower Willows is a wilderness resource that continues to support endangered wildlife, including the magnificent desert bighorn sheep (*Ovis canadensis nelsoni*). The relationship of the bighorn sheep to Anza-Borrego Desert State Park is reflected in the name—*borrego* is Spanish for lamb or sheep. Concern for the protection of the sheep has led to the closure of Coyote Canyon to vehicles during the summer to provide a safe and necessary source of water during the high summer temperatures. The sheep need wilderness to survive. They can't compete with domestic animals that may transmit diseases or pollute local water sources. That is one of the reasons that feral cattle and horses were removed from Coyote Canyon.

4WD vehicles are recommended on the Coyote Canyon dirt road, which becomes increasingly problematic as one drives upcanyon. Water levels at both First Crossing

View of Lower Willows

(mile 3.6) and at Second Crossing (mile 4.5) will vary seasonally. If concerned about the road, park before Second Crossing and begin the hike from there, which will add 1.6 miles to the total trip. Be aware that mountains lions have been encountered in Coyote Canyon. It is best not to hike alone.

A sign on the northeast side of Third Crossing identifies the start of the Lower Willows Trail, which extends northwest from this point. Follow the equestrian and hiking trail that is marked and signed northwest of Third Crossing. It is sporadically marked with small red flags. Follow the trail carefully as it meanders through this thick riparian area passing a US Geological Survey gaging station survey marker before entering a flat bench near the creek. The trail opens up in Collins Valley, beyond the last palm trees that are visible from Santa Catarina Spring. Look for the Lower Willows Trail (clearly marked) to the south that climbs out of the creek bed and leads to the vehicle road in Collins Valley and a junction with a trail going to Sheep Canyon. Follow the vehicle road southeasterly which leads back to Third Crossing.

At mile 3.5 take a short side trip to the Santa Catarina Historical Marker on a knoll overlooking Santa Catarina Spring. The marker commemorates the 1774 and 1775 Anza Expeditions' campsites at the spring, visible 0.25 mile to the west in the palm-green riparian area. This was also the site of the execution of four Cahuilla Indians who participated in the 1851 Garra Revolt. The Indian village was burned during the military encounter and never recovered from the aftermath of the revolt.

The last portion of the hike is down the rocky bypass road that was built in 1988 to divert vehicles from driving through Lower Willows. Take care walking down this road and watch for traffic. Cross over the running creek at Third Crossing to your vehicle.

Desert bighorn sheep

Distance:	7.5 miles, out-and-back
Difficulty:	🚶🚶🚶🚶🚶
Elevation gain/loss:	Up to 1500 feet
Hiking time:	5 hours
Agency:	CSP-CDD (ABDSP)
Notes:	4WD recommended; call ABDSP Visitor Center regarding road conditions; bring plenty of water; no vehicle access June 1 through September 30; trail is not obvious—bring GPS or map and compass for route finding; mountain lions are present
Trailhead GPS:	N33.37149, W116.42333
Optional map:	USGS 7.5-min *Borrego Palm Canyon*
Atlas square:	D23
Directions:	(Borrego Springs) From S-22 go north on DiGiorgio Road for 4.7 miles to the end of the paved road. Continue onto Coyote Canyon dirt road. Go 5.3 miles from pavement. Park on the northeast side of Third Crossing (before crossing the creek). The Box Canyon trail begins on the east side of Third Crossing.

Habitat(s):

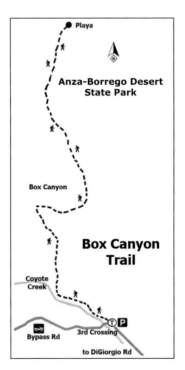

Here is your chance to walk on part of a trail that the Cahuilla Indians used to travel between villages in Coyote Canyon and those in Jackass Flat and Rockhouse Canyon. Although the trail is a little hard to follow in spots, it is still visible even more than 100 years after these Native Americans last used it. The trail also provides stunning views of the Santa Rosa Mountains to the east and the San Ysidro Mountains in the west.

If concerned about the water level at the creek crossings, park before Second Crossing and begin the hike from there, which will add 1.6 miles to the total trip. If beginning from the recommended parking area at Third Crossing, cross the creek and follow the road east a short distance until it begins to curve southeast. A sign on the northeast side of Third Crossing identifies the start of the Lower Willows Trail, which extends northwest from this point. Fol-

Bobcat

low this trail lined with desert-willows for only a short distance of about 0.2 mile, looking for the trail marked with ducks going northwest into Box Canyon. This rich riparian area is home to many animals that depend on the water resource found here, which makes it a good area for animals seeking prey, such as the bobcat (**Lynx rufus**).

The bobcat, which is named for its short, bobbed tail, is the most common wildcat in North America. It is also one of two species of lynx in North America, but the only one in California. It is secretive and primarily hunts at night for rabbits, rodents, lizards, large ground birds, and whatever else might be available, including insects. It is very adaptable and will take advantage of what the local environment has to offer. They can also be seen in the suburban-wilderness interface. Although only twice the size of a domestic cat, it is powerful enough to take down a small deer. Adult bobcats can weight up to 30 pounds. The fur is buff or brown and may have a slight orange tinge. Visible are black stripes and spots, primarily on the limbs. The tip of the short bobbed tail and the back of the ears are black. Noticeable are ear tuffs and elongated fur on the side of the face giving the appearance of sideburns. They live in dens which they make in rock crevasses or hollow logs. Bobcat kittens are preyed upon by foxes, owls, and coyotes.

As you head up the trail, the canyon quickly narrows and some scrambling over or around boulders is necessary. Continue up the main canyon for about 1.25 miles, noting the trib-

utary canyons coming into the main canyon on your right. Go about 0.25 mile up the second tributary canyon. Keep to the right as this canyon branches. Aim for the low ridge ahead. Segments of the old Cahuilla trail are found on top of the ridge. These segments are not continuously visible due to growth of cholla and other vegetation. Continue on the ridge, watching for ducks that periodically mark the trail. Agave and ocotillo are abundant in places as well as many cactus species, including beavertail cactus, hedgehog cactus, California barrel cactus, Engelmann's prickly-pear, fish-hook cactus, teddy-bear cholla, and Gander's cholla.

Plants in the cactus family have evolved a special type of photosynthesis—CAM photosynthesis—to lose less of their precious water

View into Box Canyon

Don Fosket

Borrego Valley view from the ridge

stores in the hot, dry conditions of the desert. Most plants gather the atmospheric carbon dioxide necessary for photosynthesis during the day by opening their stomata—little pores on leaves and green stems. Cacti, however, have the ability to keep these pores closed during the day and open them instead at night when temperatures are cooler and humidity higher. This results in less water evaporating out of the plant in the process of securing the necessary carbon dioxide. CAM photosynthesis allows a kind of time delay action. Cacti store the carbon dioxide overnight in an acid solution within a vacuole (a sac-like structure within the cell). In the morning, the acid is broken down and the carbon dioxide released to be used in the metabolic process of creating the plant's food (carbohydrates) just as if it had been collected during the day. CAM stands for Crassulacean Acid Metabolism, so-called because this was first discovered in the family Crassulaceae (stonecrop family) in the genus *Dudleya*. The price cacti pay for this CAM photosynthesis benefit, however, is slower growth as there is a limit to how much acid solution (and therefore, carbon dioxide) can be physically stored each night.

The destination of this hike is the Box Canyon playa which lies 3.75 miles from the trailhead. A playa is the flat-floored bottom of an undrained desert basin that at times can be a shallow lake. Rains erode sand and silt from the surrounding hills, which flow into and accumulate in this shallow depression. It is ringed with creosote bushes, but very few plants grow in the playa soil, possibly due to salt that the runoff deposits here. From this playa, you could continue on to Jackass Flat, Hidden Spring, or Rockhouse Canyon, but these are beyond the scope of a dayhike for most people. Return to your vehicle the way you came.

Vehicle access to this area is prohibited from June 1 through September 30 to protect water resources for desert bighorn sheep. They can sometimes be seen along the road or up on the slopes, so bring your binoculars!

Diana Lindsay

Engelmann's hedgehog utilizes CAM photosynthesis

Distance:	3.5 miles, out-and-back
Difficulty:	🚶🚶🚶🚶
Elevation gain/loss:	Up to 1200 feet
Hiking time:	3 hours
Agency:	CSP-CDD (ABDSP)
Trail use:	Leashed dogs allowed at campsites and on all vehicle roads; horses on roads or equestrian trails
Notes:	4WD recommended; call ABDSP Visitor Center regarding road conditions; bring plenty of water; no vehicle access June 1 to September 30 to protect desert bighorn sheep; vault toilets; treat stream water; bring GPS or map and compass for route finding; mountain lions present
Trailhead GPS:	N33.36622, W116.48129
Optional map:	USGS 7.5-min *Borrego Palm Canyon*
Atlas square:	D22
Directions:	(Borrego Springs) From S-22 go north on DiGiorgio Road for 4.7 miles to the end of the paved road. Continue onto Coyote Canyon dirt road and go 9.2 miles from pavement to the entrance of Sheep Canyon. The most difficult part of the drive is the bypass road just beyond Third Crossing at 5.3 miles. Once passed this area, it is an easy drive to the Sheep Canyon Primitive Camp. Keep to the left at road junctions in Collins Valley, except for the final leg into Sheep Canyon, which is signed and is on the right.

Habitat(s):

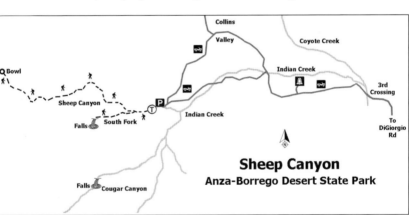

Sheep Canyon
Anza-Borrego Desert State Park

Sheep Canyon has one of the larger streams flowing east out of the San Ysidro Mountains. Its bubbling waters cascade over boulders and down waterfalls into clear pools, and its banks are lined with shady riparian vegetation, often including western sycamores (*Platanus racemosa*), narrow-leaf willows (*Salix exigua*), and western cottonwood (*Populus fremontii*). It provides a quiet, peaceful sanctuary where the desert scenery may be enjoyed in a cooler environment. In a wet year, the creek can flow throughout the year. Usually water is flowing in the canyon from November through April. The rugged hillsides and dependable water make this a safe haven for desert bighorn sheep.

Sycamores are large trees with broad leaves and a wide canopy with spreading and twisted branches. Like willows and cottonwoods, they are common in streamside canyons. Sycamores are generally monoecious (each flower is male or female and both sexes occur on each plant) with inconspicuous, wind-pollinated flowers. The fruit is a ball-shaped head on a pendent peduncle or flower stalk. The leaves resemble maple leaves, and the bark is grey and mottled. Older bark is darker and can peel away. Native Americans used the branches in house construction. The Cahuilla made wooden bowls from sycamore wood.

Don Fosket

The road to Sheep Canyon

Willows and cottonwoods are both in the willow family and are dioecious (separate male and female plants), wind-pollinated woody trees with alternate simple, unlobed leaves. The inconspicuous, greenish male and female flowers are clustered in dangling catkins (cylindrical spikes). The fruit is a capsule and the numerous seeds are dispersed by the wind. Willows and cottonwoods were important resources for the Native Americans who lived in the desert.

Lower, Middle, and Upper Willows of Coyote Canyon are named for the willows found in those riparian areas. The bark of the willow tree was used to make a breechclout (loincloth), skirting, or a belt, and fibers were used to make cordage and for padding in baby cradles. Leaves and branches were used to make storage baskets. Chemicals found in members of the willow family discouraged insects from invading the contents of storage baskets, which commonly held acorns or mesquite beans. A tea was made from the willow bark (which contains salicin, also found in aspirin) for headaches and fever. Branches were used for thatching ramadas and houses. Shredded bark was used as fire tinder.

The name cottonwood comes from the silky, cotton-like tuffs that surround mature fruits. Like willows, the inner bark provided fiber for Native Americans to use in weaving women's skirts and aprons. Wood from the trunk was made into portable mortars. Wood from branches was made into various utensils, boat paddles, war clubs, and bows. It was also used to make storage baskets. The bark and leaves of the cottonwood were used as an anti-inflammatory agent by boiling it into a poultice and placing the poultice on sore areas to relieve muscle swelling and pain from strains, breaks, and wounds. An infusion of bark and leaves soaked in a cloth and tied around the forehead was used to relieve headaches.

There is no maintained trail into Sheep Canyon beyond the primitive camp area. However, once you leave your parked vehicle, use-trails (unofficial trails created by repeated use) seem to be everywhere. You can get through the dense riparian vegetation and up the canyon by carefully choosing among these often interconnecting paths. Stay on the trails near the

Alan King

Western sycamore fruit

Don Fosket

Cottonwoods, sycamores, and willows

stream (or the sandy streambed if the creek is dry) where possible. The stream will have to be crossed frequently to avoid boulders or impenetrable thickets. Occasionally it will be necessary to get around small waterfalls by climbing up the slope on one side of the falls or the other, which ever looks most promising.

There are several tributaries that come into the main canyon. The first is the South Fork at 0.4 mile from the primitive campground, which is on the left and heads southwest. Stay in the main canyon, on the right. An unnamed tributary comes into the main canyon 1.2 miles from the campground, on the right. Going up this steep canyon and over the saddle would lead to the South Fork of Salvador Canyon, an interesting adventure that should be saved for another day. Instead, bear to the left as the main canyon continues in a westerly direction. In another 0.5 mile, the canyon opens into a broad bowl into which a third tributary flows from the left. This may be a good place to turn around and go back the way you came as dense chaparral and steep terrain is found in the upper reaches of Sheep Canyon.

The various palm groves in this rocky canyon are classic habitat for the ringtail (***Bassariscus astutus***). It is sometimes called the ringtail cat or miner's cat, although it is not related to cats but to the raccoon family. Early prospectors kept ringtails in their camps as mousers, hence one of the common names. These agile climbers have a raccoon-like tail with alternat-

ing bands of black and white. They can climb vertical walls, rocky cliffs, or even cacti, and their feet can rotate 180 degrees to give them a better grip when going up or down. Smaller than a house cat and weighing no more than three pounds, this omnivore eats insects, small mammals, lizards, birds, and fruit. It has large eyes surround by white fur and large ears that serve it well as a nocturnal animal. Its face is fox-like, its grayish-brown body cat-like, and it has short legs. It is solitary except during mating season and timid. It grooms itself like a cat. When threatened, a ringtail will bristle the hairs on its tail and arch it over its back to look larger. If captured, it releases a foul-smelling secretion from its anal glad and emits a loud, piercing scream.

Diana Lindsay

A grotto with a waterfall

Distance:	1.8, 7.6, 9, or 11.2 miles, out-and-back, depending on where you park your vehicle
Difficulty:	🚶 to 🚶🚶🚶🚶🚶
Elevation gain/loss:	Up to 1000 feet
Hiking time:	1, 4, 5, or 6 hours
Agency:	CSP-CDD (ABDSP)
Notes:	4WD recommended; call ABDSP Visitor Center regarding road conditions; bring plenty of water; no vehicle access June 1 to September 30 to protect desert bighorn sheep; treat stream water
Trailhead GPS:	N33.36488, W116.47686
Optional map:	USGS 7.5-min *Borrego Palm Canyon*
Atlas square:	D22
Directions:	(Borrego Springs) From S-22 go north on DiGiorgio Road for 4.7 miles to the end of the paved road. Continue onto Coyote Canyon dirt road and go 9.2 miles from pavement to the entrance of Sheep Canyon. The most difficult part of the drive is the bypass road just beyond Third Crossing at 5.3 miles. Once passed this area, it is an easy drive to the Sheep Canyon Primitive Camp. Keep to the left at road junctions in Collins Valley, except for the final leg into Sheep Canyon, which is signed and is on the right. At the Sheep Canyon Campground turn left on the road into Indian Canyon and park.

Habitat(s):

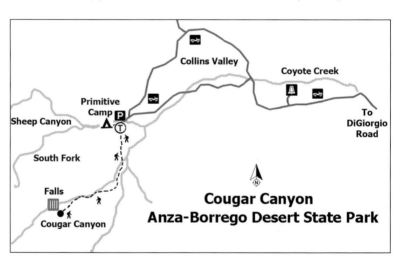

Cougar Canyon is one of the delights of Coyote Canyon. It has willows, sycamores, and cottonwood trees in a lush riparian oasis where waterfalls cascade into deep pools surrounded by huge boulders and sandy beaches. The canyon descends precipitously from the crest of the San Ysidro Mountains, near the highest peak in San Diego County, and can be relied upon to have a bubbling stream from November through April.

If uncomfortable crossing any of the Coyote Canyon creeks or going up the bouldery bypass road, you can start you hike from where you have parked your vehicle, but the extra mileage will be added to your hike. At the Sheep Canyon Campground turnoff at 9.2 miles, go left on the road into Indian Canyon, which ends in 1 mile. A well-marked trail leads south from the road's end, and in 0.6 mile heads into Cougar Canyon wash. The trail up into the canyon is rather diffuse, with numerous paths that invite exploration. About 0.5 mile into the canyon is a deep pool and a waterfall.

Cougar Canyon was a valued seasonal camp for Cahuilla Indians who found food, water, shade, and shelter nearby. The remains of an Indian sweathouse are at the entrance of

Palms, willows, and sycamores

the canyon, while several rocks and boulders in the canyon have morteros. Natural caves in the canyon provided shelter for the Cahuilla.

Cougar Canyon can be explored further, but it becomes very rugged with huge boulders and dramatic waterfalls the further one goes. Eventually there will be a point where one will need climbing skills and equipment to go further. Go as far as you feel safe, keeping a lookout for the eye, a rock painting or graffiti dating back to the 1970s when Cougar Canyon was a mecca for people on a spiritual quest. Perhaps it still is.

Cougar Canyon is named for the mountain lion (**Puma concolor**). Besides cougar, the mountain lion is also called a puma, panther, or catamount. Mountain lions are territorial and hunt alone at night, at dusk, and dawn. They are powerful animals that can leap up to 15 feet and sprint up to 50 miles an hour. They are opportunistic ambush hunters that prey on deer, desert bighorn sheep, and small mammals. A mountain lion stalks its prey until an opportunity for an attack arises, then it goes for the back of the neck to subdue the prey. It will cache a large carcass and feed on it for days. Females weigh from 80 to 130 pounds, males from 110 to 180. From nose to the tip of the tail, an adult mountain lion measures from 5-8 feet, depending on the sex. The tail is long, about two-thirds the length of the body. The head is proportionally smaller than the body. It is not uncommon to find mountain lion tracks in the Coyote Canyon area. Human encounters with mountain lions are rare, but it is best not to hike alone, especially at dusk when mountain lions may be hunting for prey.

Mountain lion track

Mountain lion

Distance:	5.2 miles, out-and-back
Difficulty:	🥾🥾🥾
Elevation gain/loss:	Up to 800 feet
Hiking time:	3 hours
Agency:	CSP-CDD (ABDSP)
Notes:	Bring plenty of water
Trailhead GPS:	N33.29541, W116.28943
Optional map:	USGS 7.5-min *Clark Lake*
Atlas square:	F26
Directions:	(Borrego Springs) From S-22 go north on Rockhouse Canyon Road for about 100 yards and park off of the road. Trailhead is on the left.

Habitat(s):

Coyote Mountain is a spur of the Santa Rosa Mountain system that may have separated from the main Santa Rosa Mountain mass through fault action. It lies astride two faults of the San Jacinto Fault system (the Clark and Coyote branches) that have caused it to be uplifted. It was named for the canyon and the people who once lived there. This adventure provides a chance to see the Borrego Valley and the Anza-Borrego Desert from a new perspective. Once you reach the top of the shoulder, the view extends east to the Santa Rosa Mountains and the Salton Sea, as well as south to the Borrego Badlands and Borrego Mountain.

Most of this hike is on a former jeep trail built over a half-century ago that has been closed to motorized vehicles for many years. The old road is visible climbing up the slope west of the area from the recommended parking on Rockhouse Canyon Road. Start hiking across the sand and rocks, heading toward the road at the base of the mountain. Once you reach it, you will see a sign saying the road is closed to motorized vehicles, but offering no further information. Although extensively eroded in places, the old road is no problem for hikers.

Shortly after climbing hundreds of feet above the valley, there is a raven's eye view of the Borrego Valley and the magnificent San Ysidro Mountains to the west of it. Continue west on the road for 1.25 miles until you see a road coming up from the valley from Pegleg Monument that crosses your trail. Go to the right on that road, continuing upslope, and staying on the upper road when it branches.

Don Fosket

View toward Borrego Springs

At 1.44 miles from Rockhouse Canyon Road, there is a well-marked trail with ducks going up the hillside. Follow it up to another former jeep road. Go left on this road. It will take you to the top of the South Shoulder, 2.59 miles from your vehicle. The views from here are dramatic on a clear day. Looking to the east, the Santa Rosa Mountains rise as a wall on the other side of Clark Valley down below. To the southeast is the blue of the Salton Sea, while the Borrego Badlands undulate like crumpled cardboard to the south. After taking in the view, return the way you came.

This route is not the easiest way to get to the top of Coyote Mountain, but it is one of the routes that could be used. The hike to the South Shoulder could be extended to include a hike either to peak 2589, which could add up to two hours to the trip, or to the top of Coyote Mountain (3192'), which might add an additional two hours. A shorter route to the top of the mountain is possible from the Clark Lake area. Desert bighorn sheep are sometimes spotted near the top. Vegetation is sparse on Coyote Mountain except for creosote bush, brittlebush, and a scattering of ocotillo.

Don Fosket

The trail follows an old jeep road

Distance:	10 miles, loop
Difficulty:	🚶🚶🚶🚶🚶
Elevation gain/loss:	Up to 1000 feet
Hiking time:	6 hours
Agency:	CSP-CDD (ABDSP); BLM-CDD (SR&SJMNM)
Notes:	4WD recommended; call ABDSP Visitor Center regarding road conditions; bring plenty of water
Trailhead GPS:	N33.38713, W116.36581
Optional map:	USGS 7.5-min *Clark Lake NE*
Atlas square:	C24
Directions:	(Borrego Springs) From S-22 go north on Rockhouse Canyon Road for 1.6 miles. Turn left at the Rockhouse Canyon sign and skirt Clark Dry Lake and the northeast wedge of Coyote Mountain. Do not attempt to cross Clark Dry Lake if it is wet or muddy—you will get stuck. Go 3.6 miles. Stay left at the road that goes right into the former Clark Lake Radio Observatory, now posted Authorized Vehicles Only. Continue 4.4 miles to the junction of Butler Canyon and Rockhouse Canyon and park.

Habitat(s):

One of the more interesting hikes in the Santa Rosa Mountains is a loop hike up Rockhouse Canyon to Jackass Flat and back down through Butler Canyon. This hike begins and ends in Anza-Borrego Desert State Park and extends into the Bureau of Land Management's Santa Rosa and San Jacinto Mountains National Monument.

Mountain Cahuilla Indians lived in a village area named Ataki in Jackass Flat until the late 1800s, and their presence is still felt and seen in many deep mortero grinding holes and slicks scattered in the area; pottery shards are also in evidence. Do not collect or move the shards as

exact location of pottery shards is important to archeologists who study Indian sites. All Indian artifacts are protected by the American Antiquities Act of 1906.

The first part of the hike follows the rough and rocky 4WD road 3.3 miles up Rockhouse Canyon. At the road end, a foot trail begins up the narrowing canyon, which is part of the Santa Rosa Wilderness. Less than 1 mile up this foot trail is Hidden Spring. Bees may be drinking at the spring if there is water. Look for a trail just before the Hidden Spring sign that leads up the ridge to Jackass Flat, where Cahuilla Indians once lived. El Toro Peak (8716'),

Indian village site in Jackass Flat

Hidden Spring

the highpoint of the Santa Rosa Mountains, will be visible to the north. The trail forks here.

Head left or west toward the head of Butler Canyon, which is the return route via a magnificent, narrow, high-walled serpentine gorge through this canyon. A long-abandoned two-wheel cart seen in Butler Canyon causes some conjecture as to how it was transported to this remote location. Perhaps it was brought in by the old prospector for whom the canyon was named.

Plants growing in the area include cheese-bush, ephedra, various cacti, desert agave, ocotillo, creosote bush, and desert baccharis (***Baccharis sergiloides***). *Baccharis* is the largest genus in the sunflower family with over 500 species. It is dioecious with male and female plants producing different flower heads, both without ray flowers. Flowers are white and not showy, but they attract a multitude of insect pollinators This erect shrub can reach a height of 6 feet. It is sometimes called a desert broom.

As the canyon begins to narrow and twist, the granite and schist walls become smooth and polished from the force of water that has swept down this canyon during occasional floods. The mouth of the canyon opens up on a boulder field that needs to be carefully negotiated down to the end of the Butler Canyon Road. It is 1 mile down this road to the

junction with Rockhouse Canyon to finish the loop.

This mountainous area was formed through fault action within the San Jacinto Fault System. The Clark Lake Fault in Rockhouse Canyon is separated from the Coyote Canyon Fault by a spur of the Santa Rosa Mountains that has slipped down, forming Coyote Mountain. Jackass Flat is a bench separating Rockhouse Canyon from Butler Canyon.

Trail through Butler Canyon gorge

Distance:	10 miles, out-and-back
Difficulty:	🚶🚶🚶🚶🚶
Elevation gain/loss:	Up to 2000 feet
Hiking time:	6 hours
Agency:	CSP-CDD (ABDSP); BLM-CDD (SR&SJMNM)
Notes:	4WD recommended; call ABDSP Visitor Center regarding road conditions; bring plenty of water
Trailhead GPS:	N33.41716, W116.38606
Optional map:	USGS 7.5-min *Collins Valley*
Atlas square:	C24
Directions:	(Borrego Springs) From S-22 go north on Rockhouse Canyon Road for 1.6 miles. Turn left at the Rockhouse Canyon sign and skirt Clark Dry Lake and the northeast wedge of Coyote Mountain. Do not attempt to cross Clark Dry Lake if it is wet or muddy—you will get stuck. Go 3.6 miles. Stay left at the road that goes right into the former Clark Lake Radio Observatory, now posted Authorized Vehicles Only. Continue 7.3 miles to end of road and park.

Habitat(s):

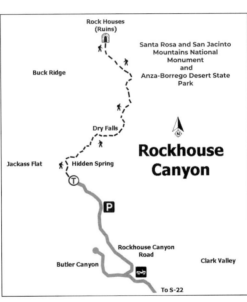

Rockhouse Canyon may be the Grand Canyon of Anza-Borrego. It is a deep, narrow gash through high cliffs connecting Rockhouse Valley with Clark Valley. The colorful rock layers tell a story about the geological events that have occurred here over the past half-billion years. The area also contains evidence of long Indian habitation with many artifacts to remind us of the thousands of years that the Cahuilla have lived here. Today it is one of the most remote, least visited places in the Anza-Borrego Desert region, a place to visit if seeking solitude. In addition, it is a place to learn some human and natural history of both the Anza-Borrego Desert State Park and the southern Santa Rosa and San Jacinto Mountains National Monument.

The jeep road ends where the Anza-Borrego Wilderness area and the 10 mile hike officially begin, at 12.5 miles from S-22. No vehicles are allowed past this point even though older maps show the road continuing. The roughest part of the 4WD route is the last 3.2 miles to the trailhead from the Butler Canyon-Rockhouse Canyon split. If starting the hike from this split, it will add about 6 miles to the trip and may be better as an overnight backpack.

Coues's cassia or desert senna

While traveling up the wash, look for smoke trees scattered among the large boulders as well as white bur-sage, desert-lavender, and the occasional brittlebush. Other shrubs to note include desert bladderpod, cheesebush or burrobrush, and desert-willow. If exploring the canyon in spring, look for occasional wildflowers, including Arizona lupine, trailing windmills, and the golden flowers of Coues's cassia (*Senna covesii*), also known as desert senna. Coues's cassia is a perennial shrub in the pea family that is leafless most of the year. In spring look for flowers with five-rounded golden petals. Another plant to look for is Greene's ground-cherry (*Physalis crassifolia*) in the nightshade family with bell-shaped yellow flowers. The base of the flower enlarges as the seed develops, reminiscent of a paper lantern. Although the fruit is not toxic, the leaves and stems are.

Pause to note the 200 feet of unconsolidated alluvium rising above you, forming a near cliff on your left. Jackass Flat is at the top of the huge pile of sand and rocks that have eroded from Buck Ridge over the past several million years. This giant pile of alluvium awaits the infrequent flash floods to carry it down into Clark Valley in a violent cataclysm. At 13 miles from S-22 is Hidden Spring, found on a hillside below Jackass Flat. Bees will be present if there is water.

Farther up the canyon is a grove of native blue palo verde trees and numerous honey mesquite trees (*Prosopis glandulosa* var. *torreyana*) are scattered throughout the canyon. The protein rich mesquite seeds were one of the main foods of the Cahuilla who had a village in Jackass Flat. In fact, every part of the tree was used by the Indians—blossoms, pods, sap, gum, limb, trunk, bark, spines, and root. Mesquites are good indicators of ground water supply. They usually grow in washes, near springs and seeps, or where there is shallow groundwater. The tap root grows down to secure a permanent source of water before the

Rockhouse ruins at valley entrance

Don Fosket

Boulders within metamorphic rock

plant grows up. Tap roots growing down 30 or 40 feet are not uncommon. Having a permanent water supply allows this winter deciduous plant to have a water source during the heat of its spring and summer major growing season.

Note the reddish-brown, desert varnished rocks that make up the walls of the canyon. These are probably the oldest rocks in the canyon, which are several hundred-million years old. Several types of metamorphic rock, including schist, quartzite, and marble are found here.

In another mile from Hidden Spring, begin looking for parts of the granitic pluton that continues elevating the Santa Rosa Mountains. The first sign of its presence is several enormous granite boulders, just before a granite outcrop that forms a dry fall, perhaps 20 feet high. It is fairly easy to climb around this massive wall, staying to the right. For the next 2.8 miles, hiking is mostly through soft sand.

To see one group of rock house ruins, keep to the west side of the valley after entering Rockhouse Valley and hike about 0.6 mile to a ridge that extends to the valley floor. Then go another 0.2 mile north to find three rockhouses on a hill overlooking the valley. Currently they are just rocks piled up to form a low circular wall, but it is likely that the

Cahuilla made roofs over these houses with branches and brush.

This may be as far as most people want to go on a dayhike, though there are several more rock houses in Rockhouse Valley as well as other interesting things to see. However, water is scarce and the distances are long. These other sites are best left for a multi-day backpack trip. After exploring the valley entrance and the rock houses, turn around and head back to your vehicle.

Don Fosket

Greene's ground-cherry

Distance:	2.6 miles, loop
Difficulty:	🚶🚶
Elevation gain/loss:	Up to 200 feet
Hiking time:	2 hours
Agency:	CSP-CDD (ABDSP)
Trail use:	Dogs on designated roads only
Notes:	4WD recommended; call ABDSP Visitor Center regarding road conditions; bring plenty of water
Trailhead GPS:	N33.27033, W116.23195
Optional map:	USGS 7.5-min *Fonts Point*
Atlas square:	F27
Directions:	(Borrego Springs) From S-22 go south onto Fonts Point Wash, 10.3 miles east of Christmas Circle in Borrego Springs. Drive 3.1 miles up Fonts Point Wash, passing the turnoff to Short Wash to the left after about 2 miles, and continuing on to the right for the last mile and park.

Habitat(s):

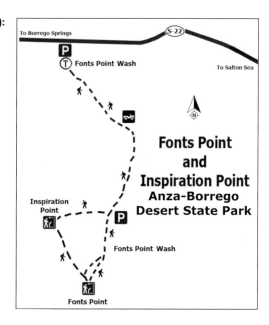

Fonts Point and Inspiration Point are two of the most scenic overlooks in the Anza-Borrego Desert. After traveling several miles through a sandy wash and hiking across a relatively flat mesa, you arrive at the top of a cliff overlooking an astounding labyrinth of multihued canyons and steep, sharp-ridged hills that extend several square miles. This contorted landscape is known as the Borrego Badlands. Inspiration Point overlooks the western part of the badlands while Fonts Point gives you views mainly to the south and east.

Fonts Point was named for Pedro Font, a Franciscan priest who was selected for the 1775 Anza Expedition for his ability to use a quadrant to navigate and record the route traveled. He kept a diary and was the first European to write in detail about the Anza-Borrego Desert and was the first to note the presence of desert bighorn sheep in the area.

As you drive to Fonts Point, take time to examine the sedimentary rock. Half a million years ago, these were part of the Santa Rosa Mountains. Over millennia, layers of sediment eroding from the rising Santa Rosa Mountains accumulated here, forming the sand and mudstone of these hills. The climate has since become much warmer and drier. Embedded

Don Fosket

The view into Borrego Badlands

within these rocks are fossils of numerous large herbivores, including camels, horses, mammoths, and ground sloths, as well as meat-eating predators such as the saber-toothed cat, the bone-eating dog, and the wolf coyote.

If you stop on the way to look at the layered sandstone for fossils, remember that if a fossil is found, it is fully protected. No excavating or taking of samples is allowed. Report any fossil finds to the park so that they might be properly studied and recorded. Also, if driving, don't stop in soft sand or you may be there for a very long time.

Drive 3.1 miles up Fonts Point wash, park, and begin hiking west cross-country to Inspiration Point. There is no official trail, but the terrain consists of rolling hills with sparse vegetation and is easily negotiated. Continue hiking west to the highest hill on the near horizon, which is Inspiration Point, 0.4 mile ahead. Your reward will be the outstanding view of the western Borrego Badlands. After taking in the view, start hiking south-southeast along the ridge above the badlands, being careful not to get too close to the edge as these cliffs are unstable. Head toward the highest hill in the near distance, which is Fonts Point itself.

As you drove south on Fonts Point Wash you were going up a gradual hill. The wash, which now flows into Clark Valley, was once tilted the other way, with sediment flowing south.

The earth's crust under Anza-Borrego is highly mobile, and Fonts Wash sits on a block that has tilted up while the block underlying Clark Dry Lake to the north is sinking. Currently, Fonts Point is about 700 feet higher than the floor of Clark Valley. For at least the past 10,000 years the block of land around Fonts Point has been eroding in a spectacular way with most of the eroded sediment flowing to the south, as you will see when you arrive at the point. After taking in the amazing eroding landscape, return to your vehicle by following the dirt road 1.1 miles north from Fonts Point.

At Fonts Point you may be able to discover a rare, tiny parasite called Thurber's pilostyles or

Wendy Esterly

Coyote

The view to the west

Thurber's stemsucker (*Pilostyles thurberi*). It blooms between November and January along the stems of its host plant white dalea (*Psorothamnus emoryi*). White dalea is commonly called dyebush because pinching a leaf dyes your fingers yellowish-orange. Thurber's pilostyles is not visible until its brownish-maroon flower buds burst from the stem and the 2 mm flowers bloom. Look for small dark bumps, then get out a hand lens if you have one!

An interesting plant on the road to Fonts Point is a desert lily (*Hesperocallis undulata*) that acts like an annual but is really a perennial, growing from an underground bulb. If there has been sufficient water, it sends up a stalk and very distinct leaves with wavy margins that are responsible for its species name. Another surprising fact is that it is in the same family as the desert agave and the Mojave yucca. This monocot flower, like almost all monocot flowers, has three petals and three sepals. The sepals are the same color as the petals, and the flower appears to have six petals. The lily is very fragrant, so be sure to stop and experience the scent. Native Americans would dig up the bulb and eat it. It was called an *ajo* lily (garlic lily) by the Spaniards, referring to the garlic-like flavor of the bulb.

Fonts Point Wash is a good place to look for various tracks in the sand or along dry mudflats. Look for dog-like tracks especially on the dried mudflats where full impressions are best for identifying species. They may be made by coyotes (*Canis latrans*) prowling in the area for something to eat. Look for the claw indentations typical of canids and Canidae. If both the front and hind foot prints are about 2 inches long, they probably belong to the coyote, but if they are only about 1 inch in length, they likely belong to a kit fox (*Vulpes macrotis*). The kit fox is the region's smallest species of this family. The kit fox has very large ears that help to moderate body temperature in desert heat, much like the ears of a jackrabbit. It also has exceptional hearing to alert it to potential danger or prey.

Coyote scat with seeds

Distance:	3 miles, out-and-back
Difficulty:	👫👫
Elevation gain/loss:	Up to 200 feet
Hiking time:	2 hours
Agency:	CSP-CDD (ABDSP)
Notes:	Bring plenty of water
Trailhead GPS:	N33.30275, W116.19801
Optional map:	USGS 7.5-min *Fonts Point*
Atlas square:	E27
Directions:	(Borrego Springs) From S-22 park in turnouts on either side of the road, 12.7 miles east from Christmas Circle in Borrego Springs, just west of milepost 32. The turnout to the south is signed Thimble Trail. The turnout on the north is unsigned. The trail begins on the north side of S-22.

Habitat(s):

Lute Ridge is a dramatic feature in the San Jacinto Fault Zone that is quite accessible. Situated at the southeastern end of Clark Valley, it is a strike-slip pressure-ridge fault scarp that is 2 miles in length along the Clark Fault with a high point of 1172 feet. Lute Ridge is a classic fault scarp and the largest known of its kind on the North American continent, developed in recent unconsolidated sediments.

This is a place where you can see the results of earth movement along a fault scarp. Visible is about 2100 feet of recent displacement along a right-lateral, left-stepping fault. This ridge is moving to the northwest in respect to the rest of the alluvial fan and mountains, which are moving to the southeast. This resulting pressure ridge is continuing to be uplifted.

Begin the hike by heading north about 0.6 mile toward the east foot of Lute Ridge. Before ascending the ridge, hike around to the north side of the ridge to view the fault trace along the alluvial fan created from debris from the Rattlesnake Canyon area. This is where the earth has been uplifted and tipped away from the slope. The trail you are on heads northwest toward Rattlesnake Canyon and Villager/Rabbit peaks. After exploring the fault trace, backtrack to the ridge and begin climbing. It is about 0.7 mile to the top of the ridge. Continue for another 0.1 mile and look for a cairn that marks a survey point called Lute on this ridge.

From the top of the ridge there is a clear view up Clark Valley on the Clark Valley Fault. This fault extends on into Rockhouse Canyon to the northwest and to Arroyo Salado to the

Looking into Clark Valley from the ridge

southeast. There is also a clear view of the approach leading to Villager Peak.

From here, retrace your route to return to your vehicle, or work your way down from the ridge heading southwest to meet the old dirt Truckhaven Trail route and follow this road to the east back to your parked vehicle.

Plants encountered on this hike are typical of the area and include creosote bush, cholla, and brittlebush. Along the trace of the fault scarp there is milkweed, desert-lavender, desert trumpet, barrel cacti, white rhatany or krameria, and catclaw acacia (*Senegalia greggii*). Catclaw acacia has curved claw-like prickles that grow out of the epidermis of the stem. The prickles are not thorns, which arise from branch tissue, or spines, which arise from leaf tissue. The prickles, however, are danger-ous and can easily catch on anything. Catclaw acacia earned the name baby-tear-blanket from the early pioneers. A member of the pea family, catclaw acacia pea pods were eaten by local Indians, but only as a famine food, since they much preferred the tastier honey and screw-bean mesquite.

As you hike through the desert, take a closer look at the spines of the various cacti. You might see the remains of a speared insect, rodent, small bird, or lizard—the work of a masked bandit called the loggerhead shrike (*Lanius ludovicianus*). This stocky songbird acts like a raptor but does not have talons. Instead, it skewers its prey on spines or thorns. It has a gray head and back, whitish undersides, white patches on its black wings, and a black mask across its eyes. The shrike's bill has a small hook.

Catclaw acacia

Loggerhead shrike

Distance:	7.6 miles, out-and-back
Difficulty:	🏃🏃🏃🏃🏃
Elevation gain/loss:	Up to 1700 feet
Hiking time:	5 hours
Agency:	CSP-CDD (ABDSP)
Notes:	Bring plenty of water; a few non-technical dry waterfalls to climb not requiring special equipment
Trailhead GPS:	N33.30279, W116.19793
Optional map:	USGS 7.5-min *Fonts Point*
Atlas square:	E27
Directions:	(Borrego Springs) From S-22 park in turnouts on either side of the road, 12.7 miles east from Christmas Circle in Borrego Springs, just west of milepost 32. The turnout to the south is signed Thimble Trail. The turnout on the north is unsigned. The trail begins on the north side of S-22.

Habitat(s):

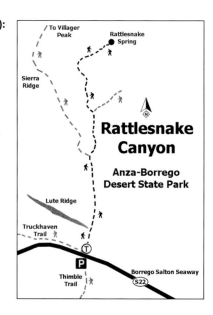

Rattlesnake Canyon is a large, deep canyon at the southern end of the Santa Rosa Mountains and one of the few canyons that flow north to south. It is a major conduit for alluvial material eroded from the Santa Rosas flowing into the Anza-Borrego Desert. Here one gets a firsthand look at water's power to erode stone and rearrange the landscape.

Begin hiking north across a sandy alluvial plane dotted with large ocotillo, creosote bush, and clumps of galleta grass. Initially the trail is not well marked except by footprints of those who have hiked this way before. Further ahead the trail will be well marked with frequent cairns. The Santa Rosa Mountains and Rattlesnake Canyon are directly ahead, but they look closer than they are. The trail crosses the eastern-most end of Lute Ridge after 0.65 mile. Lute Ridge is a 2-mile long fault scarp composed of unconsolidated alluvial sand, gravel, and boulders that are being pushed up by movement along the Clark Fault in the San Jacinto Fault Zone. The Clark Fault is one of many highly active faults in the Anza-Borrego area.

In another 0.4 mile, the trail drops into Rattlesnake Canyon Wash, now headed west, carrying alluvial debris toward Clark Valley. Rattlesnake Canyon itself is entered at about 1.25 miles from the highway. The high walls of unconsolidated alluvial material rising high above you testify to the violence of the flash floods that have carved this canyon.

Approaching the canyon

Most of the trail up the canyon is through soft sand or skirts around large granite and metamorphic boulders.

The Santa Rosa Mountains are composed mainly of the igneous granite-type rocks of the Peninsular Ranges Batholith, but these igneous rocks intruded into much older layers of metamorphic rocks initially formed as layers of sediment under an ancient ocean. Heat and pressure from thousands of feet of overlying material transformed the underlying sand, mud, and carbonate layers into metamorphic rocks, such as schist, marble, quartzite, and gneiss, which have been contorted and exposed by geological events.

Although the vegetation is rather sparse, it includes some large smoke trees, palo verde trees, catclaw acacia, and desert-lavender, as well as many ocotillo and creosote bushes. Smaller common shrubs include brittlebush and white bur-sage (**Ambrosia dumosa**). White bur-sage is the second most common plant in the Anza-Borrego Desert after creosote bush and often appears in association with creosote bush. However, this low gray-green plant that grows up to 3 feet in height is usually not noticed except when in bloom, and even then, it is often overlooked. The fruit is a bur, giving rise to its name along with the fact that it was browsed upon by burros.

Scattered cacti are more common on the canyon hillsides than in the flash flood prone canyon bottom. Look for a shrub with needle-like leaves that look as though they belong on a conifer. This is the pygmy-cedar (**Peucephyllum schottii**), a member of the sunflower family, common elsewhere in the Sonoran Desert, but not frequently found in Anza-Borrego Desert State Park.

At about 3.5 miles from the highway, the canyon makes a sharp turn to the east. Continuing up the canyon a little farther is a high dry fall, about 40 feet high. This is a good place to turn around and retrace your steps back to your vehicle. On the way back, note the distinct line along the fault scarp and enjoy the view to the south.

White bur-sage

Distance:	4.5 miles, out-and-back
Difficulty:	🏃🏃🏃
Elevation gain/loss:	Up to 700 feet
Hiking time:	3 hours
Agency:	CSP-CDD (ABDSP)
Notes:	Bring plenty of water
Trailhead GPS:	N33.29580, W116.18183
Optional map:	USGS 7.5-min *Fonts Point*
Atlas square:	F28
Directions:	(Borrego Springs) From S-22 park in turnouts on either side of the road, 13.8 miles east from Christmas Circle in Borrego Springs, at milepost 33. The trail begins on the north side of S-22.

Habitat(s):

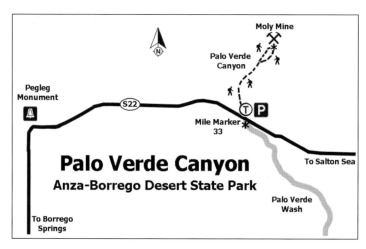

Palo Verde Canyon is aptly named for the many lime green-stemmed blue palo verde trees (*Parkinsonia florida*) in this desert canyon. A hike up this canyon leads to an old abandoned mine long thought to have been a molybdenum prospect. The return hike has a small loop that follows a portion of an ancient Indian trail between Palo Verde Canyon and Smoke Tree Canyon to the east.

Although the most opportune time to hike this canyon is in early April when the bright golden-yellow blooms of the palo verdes are at their peak, it is always a delight in any season because of the variety in both the canyon's plants and geologic features. *Palo verde* is Spanish for green stick, and is a direct reference to the chlorophyll that gives this tree the ability to photosynthesize in its stem as well as its leaves. This allows the tree to cut water loss by dropping its leaves when it's drought stressed and still be able to create food for itself. This is an unusual feature also seen in the wand-like oco-

tillo (*Fouquieria splendens*). The green-barked ocotillo, like the palo verde, is leafless much of the year, thereby saving moisture normally lost through the leaves. The tradeoff for photosynthesizing in the bark versus the leaves is slower plant growth. The ocotillo differs from the palo verde in that it can regrow leaves several times a year. If it has rained recently, each branch will be a wand of green, covered with freshly-grown new leaves within 48 hours of the rain. With a broad and shallow root system, the ocotillo is positioned to catch any rainwater or runoff that comes its way. Once adequate water is no longer available, the ocotillo will drop its leaves and resume the appearance of a leafless dead plant, but it is far from that. Because its bark contains chlorophyll, it can continue to photosynthesize in its bark until the next time water comes along and it can grow new leaves, allowing it to produce more food and grow faster. The ocotillo blooms in April, providing even more canyon color with its flame-tipped

Blue palo verde bloom

that faces west, taking care to watch out for cholla balls that will easily attach to your hiking boots. As with all mines, it is best not to enter not only for your own safety but also because it might disturb possible bat roosts. Carefully work your way down from the mine entrance and up the ridge to the other side where the Indian trail crosses. Follow the Indian trail down 0.3 miles to rejoin the canyon floor to begin the trek back to the trailhead on S-22.

Ocotillo leaves and blooms

tubular flowers that provide nectar for migrating and local hummingbirds. Ranchers used to place the spiny ocotillo staves into the ground to create a living fence.

The hike begins at S-22 across from the entrance to Palo Verde Wash. Follow the gradually ascending canyon, being careful of the very rocky, braided outwash that is strong evidence of what the force of water can move and churn as it spills from a canyon mouth. Generally head north, not straying off course into a smaller canyon to the east of Palo Verde.

The canyon narrows at about 1.5 miles. Begin looking for a steep rocky trail up the granitic canyon wall on the right or east side of the canyon, where a large palo verde tree is found in a small alcove. This is where the return trail will rejoin the canyon. This ancient Cahuilla trail ascends the ridge separating Palo Verde from Smoke Tree Canyon and continues toward Wonderstone Wash, where rocks were quarried by local Indians. The Moly Mine is visible to the north from the trail.

Plants found in the lower part of the canyon wash besides palo verde and ocotillo include creosote bush, white rhatany or krameria, and various cacti. Desert-lavender and smoke trees become visible at higher elevations.

Follow the canyon around to the northeast where it opens into a bowl at 2 miles. Look for a trail up the ridge on the east side of this bowl that will lead to the entrance of the Moly Mine at 2.28 miles into the hike. If you have a flashlight, you can carefully peak into the mine entrance

Ocotillo new leaves and green stem

Distance:	1 to 3 miles, out-and-back
Difficulty:	🚶
Elevation gain/loss:	Up to 200 feet
Hiking time:	1 to 2 hours
Agency:	CSP-CDD (ABDSP)
Notes:	Bring plenty of water
Trailhead GPS:	N33.28207, W116.14112
Optional map:	USGS 7.5-min *Fonts Point*
Atlas square:	F28
Directions:	(Borrego Springs) From S-22 park in turnout on north side of the road, 16.4 miles east from Christmas Circle in Borrego Springs, at milepost 35.5. The trail begins on the north side of S-22. The rocks are visible from the road at the foot of the Santa Rosa Mountains.

Habitat(s):

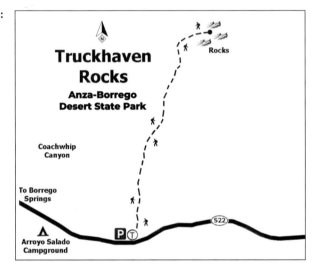

Truckhaven rocks are blocks of reddish-brown sandstone made from sedimentary deposits that were tilted to a 45-degree angle by geological forces eons ago. They rise up 100 feet or more from the alluvial plain and are named for the first road east out of the Borrego Valley—the old Truckhaven Trail. The sandstone has been eroded by wind and rain to create a miniature mountain range, complete with canyons, peaks, and ridges. Located in the eastern part of the Anza-Borrego Desert, it is an area that receives even less rainfall than Borrego Springs, giving the area surrounding the rocks a barren appearance. Keep your eyes open as you hike across the alluvial plain to reach the rocks, as there is a diverse array of life, including wildflowers in the spring. The rocks themselves provide a fascinating place to explore and are highly photogenic. Bring a camera!

Although Truckhaven Rocks can be reached by hiking up Arroyo Salado Wash, it would be a more strenuous hike than the one recommended here. Instead, simply start walking north across the gently tilted alluvial plain from milepost 35.5 toward the rocks, which remain visible throughout the hike. There is no official trail but rather numerous parallel routes across the plain, some of which have been marked with ducks.

The desert floor here is composed of sand and an assortment of granitic and metamorphic boulders that have been carried down from the rapidly eroding Santa Rosa Mountains by intense but infrequent rainstorms. The storms have created a series of interconnected channels of varying age. In the oldest channels are paths of desert pavement lined with random piles of deeply bronzed, desert-varnished boulders. The

Rocks rising from the alluvial plain

more recently carved channels have a sandy floor and the boulders have lost their varnish, if they ever had it.

In this sparsely vegetated area are many of the shrubs found throughout the Anza-Borrego area, including creosote bush, white bur-sage, ocotillo, catclaw acacia, Gander's cholla, California barrel cactus, and beavertail cactus. You can also find some of the less common shrubs, particularly indigo bush.

Take a look around the creosote bushes and in their branches. You might see a desert iguana (***Dipsosaurus dorsalis***). This vegetarian is particularly attracted to yellow flowers such as those on creosote bushes. The creosote bush provides food, shade, and shelter. The desert iguana will take advantage of kangaroo rat holes often found beneath the creosote bush. The holes are handy shelters from predators and are places to escape desert heat, which the desert iguana can tolerate better than any other desert lizard. The desert iguana's tail is one-and-a-half times longer than its cream-colored body, which has a reticulated pattern on its back that becomes banded as it moves down its tail. It also has a slightly enlarged ridge of dorsal scales down its back.

In late winter and early spring, many wild-flowers are scattered over the alluvial fan. Gold poppies are abundant, forming a carpet in patches. Pinnate-leaf or brown-eyed evening-primrose, desert phacelia, Mojave lupine, desert lily, and Mojave desert star can easily be found. The beautiful Mojave desert star (***Monoptilon bellioides***) has white showy flowers with yellow centers that huddle low, barely raising their daisy-like heads above the ground. It is smaller than a nickel with only a few leaves on the plant. Its strategy for life in this dry desert is to live fast and die young.

Desert iguana

Mojave desert star

Distance:	4 miles, out-and-back
Difficulty:	🚶🚶
Elevation gain/loss:	Up to 800 feet
Hiking time:	2 hours
Agency:	CSP-CDD (ABDSP)
Notes:	Bring plenty of water
Trailhead GPS:	N33.28097, W116.09623
Optional map:	USGS 7.5-min *Seventeen Palms*
Atlas square:	F29
Directions:	(Borrego Springs) From S-22 park in turnout on north side of the road, 19.1 miles east of Christmas Circle in Borrego Springs, east of milepost 37.

Habitat(s):

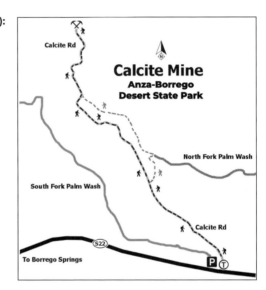

Calcite was an essential component of the Norden bombsight used during World War II and was one of America's most closely guarded secrets during the war. The bombsight was used to calculate the trajectory of a bomb, and enabled American airplanes to hit ground targets in daylight raids from an altitude of six miles.

Calcite has the property of birefringence, which is responsible for the phenomenon of double refraction when a ray of light is split by polarization into two rays with each taking a slightly different course. The calcite crystals needed for bombsights had to be colorless and transparent, which is the type of calcite found and mined in this area for several years until the Polaroid Company discovered a synthetic crystal that did not need to be mined.

Calcite is a very common mineral, a form of calcium carbonate, similar in basic chemi-cal composition to chalk and gypsum and the basic material for cement. There are at least 800 different forms of crystalline calcite. These differ in color and in light transmission from completely opaque to translucent.

To maximize viewing of the area, leave your car at the parking area at the top of the canyon so as not to miss the amazing slot canyon that leads to an abandoned site where calcite crystals were mined during WWII. Vehicles driving to the site will miss the slot canyon. The 4WD-only road is also treacherous and is not recommended. Hiking will also give you the opportunity to note the panoramic views of the Salton Sea to the east and the Borrego Badlands to the south that are visible during this hike.

The hike begins from the parking area on the north side of S-22 at Mile Marker 34, where a truck trail descends sharply into the

Sidewinder eating a common side-blotched lizard

South Fork of Palm Wash. Cross the Wash and proceed northwest up the hill. Approximately 0.75 mile from S-22 will be a signed junction. The road to the left continues on up the hill to the mine while the one on the right goes down to the Palm Wash 4WD trail and provides another way to get to the mine site while hiking through an amazing slot canyon that reveals the sedimentary history of these mountains. When you reach the sandy wash, go left up the wash. After about 0.25 mile, the truck trail ends at a point where the main wash is choked with some huge boulders. The slot canyon leads off to the left at this point. The hike through this canyon leads back to the Calcite Mine 4WD trail at a point about 1.5 miles from the start of the hike. The slot canyon continues north on the other side of the road, should you have time and want to explore some more. For those with more limited time, once you reach the road, turn right and follow the road uphill for another 0.5 mile to the mine site.

Calcite was mined by digging trenches along calcite-containing seams. The trenches can be recognized by their unnatural regularity. Look around and note small calcite crystals everywhere glittering in the sunlight. However, remember that it is illegal to remove any plant, animal, or mineral you might find in the park. Look, experiment with the crystals, but leave them here when you are ready to leave. If you find a transparent crystal, look at some printed matter through it to observe the birefringence or double refraction of the crystal. After exploring the area, return to your vehicle, but pay attention to the tracks that you might find in the sandy open areas of the wash. Chances are that you will see tracks of lizards, possibly dog-like tracks (with claws) of the coyote or kit fox, or cat-like tracks (no claws) of a bobcat, or even sweeping parallel J-shaped tracks of the sidewinder (**Crotalus cerastes**).

Like other pit vipers, the sidewinder is an ambush hunter waiting for prey to pass so that it can strike. The sidewinder is totally adapted to open, sandy terrain. The snake travels by raising its body and throwing raised loops to the side, thereby pushing itself forward. On its triangular-shaped head, it has a raised scale over each eye that look like little horns. The scale folds down over the eye to protect the snake's eye when crawling in burrows or burrowing in sand. Typically the snake will lie covered with sand, except for his head, near kangaroo rat burrows or along lizard or rodent trails waiting for prey. It can control the amount of venom injected, and if the fangs are broken, new ones will grow to replace the old ones. Adults are 12-18 inches long and have a heavy body but a thin neck. The sidewinder's color tends to match the surrounding soil. There is a dark stripe across the eyes and a darker segment next to the rattle. It also has dark blotches on its back.

Desert lily

Distance:	0.3 mile, loop; 0.7 mile, one-way, or 1.4 miles, out-and-back
Difficulty:	🚶
Elevation gain/loss:	Up to 300 feet
Hiking time:	1 hour
Agency:	CSP-CDD (ABDSP
Trail use:	Wheel-chair accessible
Notes:	Concrete-paved and compact dirt trails
Trailhead GPS:	N33.25794, W116.40655
Optional map:	USGS 7.5-min *Borrego Palm Canyon*
Atlas square:	F23
Directions:	(Borrego Springs) From S-22 go west on Palm Canyon Drive for 0.4 mile to the Anza-Borrego Desert State Park Visitor Center parking area.

Habitat(s):

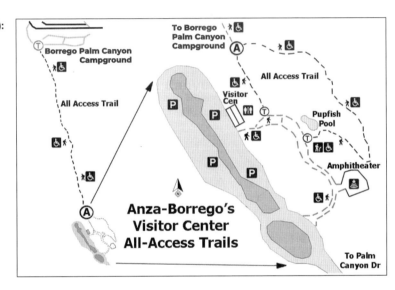

Anza-Borrego Desert State Park offers something for everyone at the park's visitor center, including two trails that are Americans with Disabilities Act (ADA) approved. Both trails start at the visitor center and are clearly marked. The longer 0.7-mile trail leads north from the visitor center to the campground area, ending just west of campsite No. 71, where a drinking fountain is found. The trail is completely paved, has sitting areas, and offers 10 interpretive signs with illustrations that have been set at an angle to make it convenient for people at different heights to read the information. Beneath the interpretive illustrations and descriptions on the panel are similar descriptions written in Braille. Visitors are encouraged to use all their senses to experience the desert surroundings, though care should be taken not to touch the cactus!

This all-accessible trail makes a good introductory trail for first-time visitors. A cautionary sign advises visitors to: carry water; wear light clothing, a hat, and sunglasses; use sunscreen and a lip balm; carry a map; let someone know what trails you will be on and when you intend to return; and call your contact to let them known you have safely returned to avoid unnecessarily starting a search. Another recommendation is to carry a comb and tweezers to remove any spines that might attach to your clothing or skin if you brush against a cactus. Cholla have papery sheaths covering their spines that may also need to be removed.

The interpretive signs describe common desert shrubs, reptiles, insects and spiders, and large and small birds and mammals. Shrubs that surround the trail are typical of desert scrub and include the creosote bush, white

A bench with an interpretive sign

bur-sage, ocotillo, various cholla, brittlebush, and indigo bush. There is even a sign that interprets the relative distances of planets in our solar system. Borrego Springs is one of the few dark sky communities in the United States and one of the best places for night sky viewing.

You are likely to see a desert cottontail (*Sylvilagus audubonii*) or a black-tailed jackrabbit (*Lepus californicus*) scurrying around the many plants. The two differ in many ways.

Cottontails are rabbits and are born blind and naked in a burrow and are totally dependent on their mother for several weeks. Jackrabbits are hares and are born fully furred, eyes open, and ready to run. Jackrabbits do not dig burrows. They separate their young and hide them under shrubs. A jackrabbit is larger, as are its ears, which are half the length of its body. It is called a jackrabbit because its long ears are similar to those of a donkey. The large ears

Black-tailed jackrabbit

Desert cottontail

Diana Lindsay

The All-Access Trail

help the jackrabbit regulate its body temperature while also helping it to hear predators. The long legs give it speed and the ability to jump over shrubs. Jackrabbits have been observed running directly toward a cactus while being pursued, then clearing it at the last moment, leaving the pursuing prey headed for an unwelcomed target.

The shorter 0.25-mile trail begins in front of the visitor center entrance. This loop trail is on compact dirt and is wheelchair accessible and joins a portion of the longer trail before it returns to the main path, leading back to the entrance of the visitor center. The trail has interpretive signs and offers a great variety of desert plants, many of which were planted around the visitor center for the enjoyment and education of visitors. One of the interpretive signs along this trail describes the life of the desert pupfish (*Cyprinodon macularius*) that is able to withstand extreme temperatures. The desert pupfish can also tolerate extreme salinity—over three times that of saltwater—and low oxygen content. It is listed as federally endangered. Although no more than 3 inches in length, the bluish-colored males are very territorial. Females are silvery or tan in color and slightly smaller than the males. The desert pupfish is a very old fish, sometimes referred to as a living fossil. About 10,000 years ago, there were prehistoric Pleistocene lakes in the desert that were interconnected. As the lakes

evaporated and the pupfish genus became isolated, they evolved into the 13 living species known today. The desert pupfish is listed as endangered by the US Fish and Wildlife Service. The pupfish pond is next to the tall native California fan palms.

Keep alert for birds that you might see scurrying around bushes. They might be one of the two species of quail that are known to inhabit the Borrego Valley. Both have the teardrop-shaped plume on their forehead, and males have a black throat. There are subtle distinctions between the two. Gambel's quail (*Callipepla gambelii*) is the typical desert species with a redder head than the bluer-headed California quail (*Callipepla californica*), which has spread east into desert areas. The California quail has a much more distinct scale pattern on its chest compared to Gambel's. Unlike the California quail, Gambel's quail has a cream-colored belly, with the male having a black patch on its belly. The call of the Gambel's quail is a loud waaah, whereas the California quail sounds like chi-ca-go, chi-ca-go (cha-cua-ca, cha-cua-ca south of the border). Typical of quail, both prefer to walk rather than fly. If you do see a small flock or covey of quail, look for a lone male standing on a high point keeping a lookout for danger.

A perfect way to end the hike is to visit the interior of the visitor center, where there are more interpretive signs, films, and volunteer staff who are ready to answer questions about this desert area.

Wendy Esterly

California quail

Distance:	3 miles, out-and-back or a return loop on the alternate trail
Difficulty:	🚶🚶
Elevation gain/loss:	Up to 600 feet
Hiking time:	2 hours
Agency:	CSP-CDD (ABDSP)
Notes:	Parking fee; bring plenty of water
Trailhead GPS:	N33.27016, W116.41843
Optional map:	USGS 7.5-min *Borrego Palm Canyon*
Atlas square:	F23
Directions:	(Borrego Springs) From S-22 go west on Palm Canyon Drive for 0.2 mile. Turn right into the entrance to the Borrego Palm Canyon Campground (if you reach the Anza-Borrego Desert State Park Visitor Center, you have gone too far). Drive to the west end of the campground and park in the day-use parking lot.

Habitat(s):

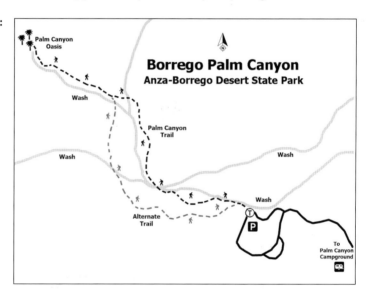

Borrego Palm Canyon is the most popular hike in Anza-Borrego Desert State Park, and it is easy to understand why so many people are drawn to it. Dramatic desert-varnished walls begin to close in as one hikes up a large alluvial fan into the heart of the canyon where a clear bubbling stream flows through a cool, shady oasis of native California fan palms. This palm grove was initially recommended to be part of the proposed California State Park System in March 1928 and officially became Borego (with one r) Palms Desert State Park in November 1932—the first desert park in California. An added bonus on this hike may be a sighting of desert bighorn sheep—the *borrego*s of the canyon—which are common in the canyon but are not always easy to see.

During the wildflower season there may be a profusion of colorful blooms from both annuals and perennials that might include six species of phacelia, chuparosa, indigo bush, apricot mallow, desert-willow, Palmer's loco-weed, ocotillo, pygmy gold-poppy, California fuchsia, and Bigelow's monkey flower. Two annuals that can be found in the sandy wash and any dune areas are desert sand-verbena (*Abronia villosa* var. *villosa*) and dune evening-primrose (*Oenothera deltoides*). The desert sand-verbena is found throughout the park and Borrego Valley and is recognized by its purplish golf-ball-size cluster of multiple blooms that trail in the sand. They have a nice scent, but you will have to get your nose to the ground to smell them. The dune evening-primrose also spreads itself along

Don Endicott

California fan palms at the first grove

the sand growing stalks that emerge from a basal rosette. The large four-petaled white blooms grow at the end of the stalk and turn pink once they have matured. After the plant has gone to seed, the stems curl upward as they dry out, taking the shape of a birdcage, hence one of its common names is birdcage evening-primrose. This is another plant with a sweet smell that attracts pollinators.

There are two trails leading up to the palm grove: the main Palm Canyon Trail and an alternate one. Both begin at the western-most end of the campground near a desert pupfish pond. Most hikers take the main trail that goes up the canyon's floodplain, which occasionally is disturbed by flash floods, the most recent having occurred in the summer of 2013. The 2013 flood was minor compared to that of September 2004, which not only destroyed parts of the main trail, but also devastated many of the palms at the first oasis and caused damage to the campground. Both the palms and the campground were little affected by the latest flash flood and have largely recovered from the devastation of the 2004 flood. However, there are still visible signs along the trail that attest to the awesome power of water during a flash flood.

Diana Lindsay

Desert sand verbena and dune evening-primrose

Evidence of flash flooding

face. Palm trees are an indicator of water at either the surface or just below the surface as they have a shallow root system. If no water is readily available, coyotes will dig for it near palm trees, and they also eat palm fruit. Western yellow bats (*Lasiurus xanthinus*) roost exclusively in the skirts of dead fronds encircling fan palms, which limited their distribution until palms became popular in landscaping. The western yellow bat is a medium-sized bat with yellowish coloration and short ears.

The tourist turnaround is at the main palm grove where there is plenty of water and shade. However, don't drink the water unless you have treated it. Exploration above the main grove leads to other groves but the trail becomes very steep with plenty of boulders.

The canyon has an alternate trail to the grove that is higher on the bajada, largely out of the floodplain, and was not affected by the summer 2013 flood. It joins the main trail about 1 mile up the canyon. Hikers often go up to the first oasis on the main trail and return on the alternate trail.

Borrego Palm Canyon was home to a band of Indians for a good reason. It offered shade, water, and plenty of resources for food including mesquite beans, desert agave, and cactus fruit. Shelter and bow-making resources included desert-willows, palm trees, and ironwood. Creosote bush and sages were of medicinal use, and plenty of granitic rocks made it easy to grind seeds near the source of food. Look for grinding areas on rocks during the hike. Also pick up an interpretive brochure at the trailhead that gives more information about the canyon and the Indians' use of plants.

The canyon was named for the native California fan palms (*Washingtonia filifera*), which are a remnant from a cooler, wetter climate before the desert evolved in this area. With a large leaf surface exposed to the sun and a short root system, the native California fan palm is an unlikely desert plant with its rapid rate of water evaporation and its dependence on water. However, an underground water source close to the surface allows the roots to sit in water while the thick palm frond shag coat provides insulation to keep the tree cool in the hot sun. Palm trees are predominately found in the western canyons of the park where water is close to the sur-

Desert sand verbena

Distance:	7 or 8.8 miles, out-and-back
Difficulty:	🚶🚶🚶🚶🚶
Elevation gain/loss:	Up to 1000 or 3200 feet
Hiking time:	6 or 8 hours
Agency:	CSP-CDD (ABDSP)
Notes:	Parking fee; bring plenty of water; steep, rocky, and cross-country travel
Trailhead GPS:	N33.27010, W116.41854
Optional map:	USGS 7.5-min *Borrego Palm Canyon*
Atlas square:	F23
Directions:	(Borrego Springs) From S-22 go west on Palm Canyon Drive for 0.2 mile. Turn right into the entrance to the Borrego Palm Canyon Campground (if you reach the Anza-Borrego State Desert Park Visitor Center you have gone too far). Drive to the west end of the campground and park in the day-use parking lot.

Habitat(s):

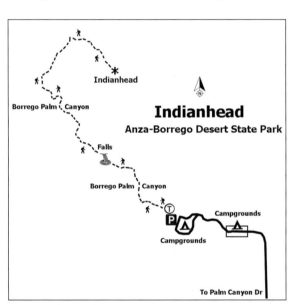

Indianhead is a rugged desert peak in the San Ysidro Mountains that defines the northern side of lower Borrego Palm Canyon. Its close proximity to Borrego Springs and Borrego Palm Canyon invites exploration for those prepared for a challenging, all-day cross-country hike and climb to the 3960-foot summit. Indianhead's steep, rocky slopes provide refuge for bands of threatened desert bighorn sheep. The summit rewards hardy hikers with incredible views of the Borrego Valley, the Santa Rosa Mountains, and the Salton Sea.

This route ascends Borrego Palm Canyon, a rare desert riparian zone and another signature feature of Anza-Borrego Desert State Park. At its base flows a year-round creek, nurturing native California fan palms. This riparian zone begins in earnest at First Grove, which is also called Palm Oasis in state park handouts, 1.5 miles from the trailhead. A small waterfall is usually flowing here in the midst of a remnant palm grove, the largest stand of these trees in the canyon that survived an extremely damaging summer thunderstorm flash flood in 2004.

Although it is not guaranteed, you are likely to encounter the namesake borregos, the desert bighorn sheep of the Peninsular Ranges. These impressive animals may be sighted at any time of the year. The canyon is also home to a wide variety of resident and migratory birds, including the cactus wren, canyon wren, loggerhead shrike, Scott's and Bullock's oriole, and Costa's

Southern maidenhair fern at the waterfall

hummingbird, as well as common raven and prairie falcon. Gray foxes, coyotes, bobcats, and signs of mountain lions may be spotted.

This is an out-and-back route over the same terrain in both directions, although it is possible to include the alternate palm canyon trail on either the descent or the ascent, providing a loop option for the lower section of the hike. Begin from the Borrego Palm Canyon Trailhead, where there is a small man-made pond that hosts California treefrogs and desert pupfish.

There is a well-defined trail to First Grove with numbered sign posts corresponding to a variety of natural features described in a free pamphlet available from the visitor center. The trail crosses and follows the main creek bottom at various points but is likely to be dry until nearing the grove, which is approached on the right or north side of the canyon floor. Between the trailhead and First Grove, there are hundreds of broken off palm trunks and stumps, evidence of the severity of the big flash flood of 2004.

Proceeding beyond First Grove, the trail climbs up and around the waterfall area on the north side, starting a hundred yards or so east of the waterfall. Beyond the grove, there

are only remnants of the former trail. Drop down into the main canyon and cross over to the south side to follow the original trail, a somewhat obscure use-trail since the 2004 flood. It is also possible to hike directly up the canyon, but large boulders and drop-offs can make this a tiring option. Eventually the canyon makes a sharp bend to the right, turning

Climbing around the waterfall

The climb to the south summit

directly toward the steep lower south slopes of Indianhead.

Continue to follow faintly marked trail segments on either side of the canyon. These climb over or around numerous large boulders. Perhaps the most distinctive obstacle before climbing out of the canyon at Third Grove is a small waterfall at the base of a large, dark red gneiss formation unofficially called Anvil of the Sun by some hikers. If the water is low, a short scramble leads up the right side of the waterfall chute. Otherwise, walk up and traverse this large reddish slab and descend to a ledge on its upstream side.

A standard climb out point is near lower Third Grove. Here the route starts up the south-facing slope to reach a ridge that eventually leads to a saddle just west of Indianhead. Since the flood of 2004, only a few palms define Third Grove, but mesquite, catclaw acacia, reeds, and other vegetation abounds. There is usually at least a small flow in the creek here.

For the rest of the hike to the summit, the climb is primarily on or near a ridge leading upward to the north. A good reference landmark on the ridge is to aim for a prominent white boulder outcrop visible from the canyon floor. Once on the ridge you will find traces of use-trail and an occasional trail duck. From here, continue upward to a broad saddle that divides Borrego Palm Canyon and Henderson Canyon. After taking in your first look down the sheer north side of Indianhead, turn

eastward and ascend the western ridge of the mountain, staying primarily on the ridge's south side, taking care to watch your footing and look for lose rock.

The upper section of this route is more easily negotiated than in the past due to a large wildfire on the Los Coyotes Indian Reservation in 2011 that burned into upper Borrego Palm Canyon and here on Indianhead. There are a few large boulders to scramble around but route options should be obvious. The last 0.25 mile to the summit rocks is quite open and nearly level. A summit register is located near the highest point. Reverse the route to return.

If camping in the canyon or on the summit, no ground fires are allowed at any time. Treat or filter any water from the creek you plan on drinking.

The summit

Distance:	3.2 miles, loop
Difficulty:	🚶🚶
Elevation gain/loss:	Up to 500 feet
Hiking time:	2 hours
Agency:	CSP-CDD (ABDSP)
Trail use:	No dogs or bicycles allowed within 0.7 mile of the trailhead.
Notes:	Bring plenty of water
Trailhead GPS:	N33.24853, W116.40534
Optional map:	USGS 7.5-min *Borrego Palm Canyon, Tubb Canyon*
Atlas square:	G23
Directions:	(Borrego Springs) From S-22 turn west into the Hellhole Canyon parking area, 0.8 miles north of Palm Canyon Drive and 16.5 miles east of S-2, at the bottom of the grade. The trailhead is on the east side of the highway directly across from the entrance to the Hellhole Canyon parking area.

Habitat(s):

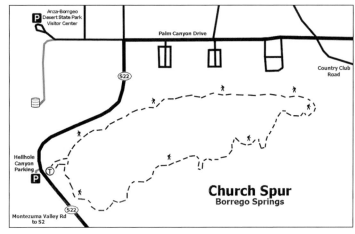

This hike on Church Spur is popular with locals in Borrego Springs. The beginning of the hike is within Anza-Borrego Desert State Park for only a little over 0.5 mile; the remainder of the hike is outside the park. At the eastern end of this spur are several churches and a street named Church Lane, which might account for the spur's name. There is also an annual Easter Sunrise Service held outside along a lower ridge of the spur that has nice views of Borrego Valley. This hike, however, does not extend that far east.

Perhaps it was the view from the spur that caused the original planners of the town to consider routing the Montezuma Highway down to its eastern end. In fact, the front of the Borrego Springs mall was to face the road entering Borrego Springs. The mall was constructed based on the original road plans. When the road plans were modified to its present location, motorists were forced to approach the mall on Palm Canyon Drive from what was supposed to have been the back side.

Geologically, Church Spur is very complex with forces from the late Tertiary Period to the present responsible for detachment faulting in the San Ysidro Mountain block found along Church Spur. This locale may have begun slipping from the main mountain block when compression and detachment faulting began along the San Jacinto Fault Zone and along the Salton Trough. Church Spur is a product of fault slip and motion due to the force of gravity into the Salton Trough. Tremendous pressure within this area has caused some igneous rocks to be metamorphosed into schists and other rocks. Today the spur extends into the valley.

The hike begins across from the Hellhole Canyon parking area and heads east to the mountain block 0.1 mile ahead, passing ocoti-

Fonts Point in the distance

llos, various cacti, brittlebush, and desert-lavender (***Condea emoryi***). Stop and look at the tall, slender, and much branched desert-lavender with soft hairy, blue-gray, ovate leaves. When in bloom it sports inconspicuous, blue-violet flowers. Get a whiff of the wonderful lavender scent of this mint. When it's blooming, you may notice quite a few bees buzzing around the plant, which is one of the reasons it is sometimes called bee sage. You may even hear the bees before you see the shrub. Desert-lavender is a common plant found in desert canyons, in sandy washes, and on alluvial fans. Cahuilla Indians made an infusion from its boiled leaves and blossoms to stop hemorrhages and to stanch heavy menstruation.

Look for the traces of an old jeep road and follow the rutted trail to the right up to the high point of this loop hike at 0.73 mile from the start. This high point is a good place to contemplate how this spur moved down from its mountain block. It is also a good place to peer into Hellhole Canyon, a popular hiking area with palm groves and a waterfall during wet years. Look around this high point and note some of the cleared areas; it's possible that Native Americans used these areas for shelters or hunting blinds.

Follow the winding trail up and down along the ridge, enjoying the view of Borrego Valley. At mile 1.12, look to the south toward Sunset Mountain and down to view the new University of California, Irvine, field station where students and researchers are learning more about this desert. This area of the ridge has some cross trails. Follow trails that tend north and east. At mile 1.5, the trail begins a rapid descent to the valley floor at mile 1.86. From here turn west and follow an old jeep trail around the ridge to complete the loop.

Desert-lavender

Distance:	6 miles, out-and-back
Difficulty:	🚶🚶🚶🚶
Elevation gain/loss:	Up to 1000 feet
Hiking time:	4 hours
Agency:	CSP-CDD (ABDSP)
Notes:	Bring plenty of water; mountain lion sightings in this canyon
Trailhead GPS:	N33.24755, W116.40619
Optional map:	USGS 7.5-min *Tubb Canyon*
Atlas square:	G23
Directions:	(Borrego Springs) From S-22 turn west into the Hellhole Canyon parking area, 0.8 miles north of Palm Canyon Drive and 16.5 miles east of S-2, at the bottom of the grade.

Habitat(s):

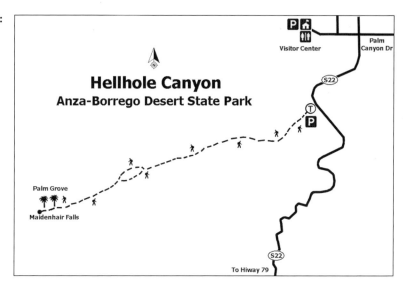

Despite the formidable name, Hellhole Canyon is one of the most delightful canyons in Anza-Borrego Desert State Park with western sycamores, western cottonwoods, and native palm trees fed by intermittent streams. The destination of this hike is the 18-foot waterfall cascade called Maidenhair Falls and the pool below the falls. The face of the fall and the surrounding grotto is surrounded by lacy southern maidenhair fern (*Adiantum capillus-veneris*) and mosses—a rare site in a desert canyon. Just before you reach the falls, look to the left in the dense growth and you may see stream orchids.

Begin the hike from the parking area and follow the wide, well-worn path up the alluvial fan to the narrowing mouth of the canyon where the ribboned pattern of Julian schist becomes visible on the canyon walls. A cautionary sign reminds you that you are in mountain

lion country. Vegetation typical of alluvial fans, such as creosote bush, white bur-sage, chuparosa, cheesebush or burrobrush, silver cholla, desert agave, and desert-lavender give way to desert-willow, brittlebush, jojoba, ocotillo, teddy-bear cholla, and white sage. As the canyon narrows and steepens, the first palm trees and sycamores become visible. Hairy yerba santa is near the first palm grove where flowing water is found. Cottonwoods also lap up the flowing water and provide some shade. At higher elevations, the deep green leaves of sugar bush come into view.

Use caution ascending the narrow canyon that is filled with boulders and spiny mesquite and prickly catclaw acacia (wait-a-minute bush). It is best to hike with long sleeves to avoid scratches. The spiny underbrush led to the name Hellhole Canyon. In earlier days cattle would roam down into the canyon from

Diana Lindsay

Maidenhair Falls

Culp Valley. Cattleman Wid Helm reportedly said that the canyon was "one hell of a hole to get cattle out of."

Keep generally to the south side of the creek. Note the occasional mortero grinding holes in the granitic rocks left by the early-day Indians who frequented this canyon. They harvested the canyon's mesquite beans and palm fruit. Women would pound seeds they collected with a handheld pestle to break them up before placing the crushed material onto a smooth surface, similar to a metate. They would then convert the mass into flour with a rolling-pin action using a smaller rock called a mano. The ground flour would then be cooked into a mush or made into tortilla-like cakes. Clay pots were used for storage only and not for cooking, so mush was made in a basket by adding water and dropping in hot rocks, stirring quickly so as not to burn the basket. The water swelled the basket fibers making it waterproof. Rocks were replaced as they cooled until the contents were cooked. The tortilla-like cakes would be baked by the sun or in a fire.

About 200 yards above a large palm grove of about 20 trees, begin listening for falling water. The falls are hidden in shrubbery behind a large boulder and are easy to miss. The shady grotto makes a great lunch stop before retracing your steps back to the parking area. If you are there in springtime, look into some of the palm fronds as you head down the trail to see if you can spot a hooded oriole (*Icterus cucullatus*) nest. The hooded oriole attaches its nest, a tightly woven pouch, to the underside of leaves by sewing nest fibers into the leaf. They especially like palm leaves for their nests. Look for the orioles flying among the palms. It is easy to identify the male because of his orange head, black face and throat, orange underparts, and black back. The females are a drab green above and yellowish on their underparts. This oriole is a nectar thief because it pierces the flower to get the nectar in such a way as to not pollinate the flower.

Wendy Esterly

Male Hooded oriole

Distance:	5 or 8 miles, one-way
Difficulty:	🚶🚶🚶
Elevation gain/loss:	up to 500/3700 feet
Hiking time:	3 or 6 hours
Agency:	CSP-CDD (ABDSP)
Trail use:	Horses allowed on CRHT
Notes:	Bring plenty of water; optional trips to Pena Spring, Culp Valley Lookout, and Lookout Point
Trailhead GPS:	N33.21064, W116.49106
Optional map:	USGS 7.5-min *Tubb Canyon*
Atlas square:	G22
Directions:	(Ranchita) From S-22 turn south onto the Jasper Trail, 6.8 miles east of S-2, and park off road. The upper trailhead is on the north side of S-22 across from the Jasper Trail sign. The Culp Valley trailhead departs from Culp Valley Primitive Camp, which is on the north side of S-22, 9.2 miles east of S-2. The lower trailhead at the entrance to Hellhole Canyon parking area is on the west side of S-22, 16.5 miles east of S-2.

Habitat(s):

The California Riding and Hiking Trail (CRHT) was created in 1945 as a state-wide recreational trail stretching from San Diego County to the Oregon border, with 100 miles of it passing through San Diego County. The CRHT has been largely abandoned or subsumed by newer trails, modern roads, or re-alignments due in part to funding cuts in the 1960s and private property access issues. Fortunately, a few stretches remain in nearly their original form, one of which is the 8-mile spur described here that provides exceptional views of the San Ysidro Mountains, Borrego Valley, Santa Rosa Mountains, and Salton Sea. It follows a prehistoric Native American pathway and a 20th century cattle drive route. The

route is marked with signature brown fence posts capped with yellow paint, indicating the CRHT. The trailhead is across from the turnoff to the Jasper Trail.

For a one-way thru-hike, arrange a car shuttle from the Hellhole Canyon trailhead near Borrego Springs. The hike can be done from either direction or it can be a challenging 16 miles out-and-back trip. A shorter one-way (5 miles) or out-and-back (10 miles) hike can begin from Culp Valley. Bicycles are allowed on the CRHT only between Culp Valley and the Hellhole Canyon trailhead. Horses are not restricted on the CRHT.

The trail begins at elevation 4100 feet in chaparral mixed with desert species that in-

Borrego Valley view from Lookout Point

clude yucca, desert agave, beavertail cactus, and catclaw acacia. Although infrequent, there can be snow at this elevation as winter storms pass through the area. Mule deer, coyotes, and bobcats may be seen in the upper sections along with occasional tracks or scat left by the elusive mountain lion. Drought and recent fires in the area have thinned the vegetation and Mesozoic Era granite boulders are now more prominent. These exposed remnants of the batholith that rose up to form the Peninsular Range and current Sierra Nevada are testaments to the dynamic geology of our region.

The trail dips and climbs in short stretches as it meanders over and around ravines and outcrops without losing significant elevation

until a descent to Pena Spring. Approximately 0.7 mile from the start, the trail passes a small open galvanized watering tank on the left in vicinity of By Jim Spring. This tank and its associated pipes are in disrepair and typically dry. A nice view of the Salton Sea in the distance is encountered 1 mile from the trailhead, and the first sighting of the Santa Rosa Mountains to the northeast is at 1.3 miles.

At 2.5 miles, the trail descends steeply for 0.33 mile to the Pena Spring Trailhead, the first good access to Hellhole Canyon. A small parking area is located to the right and several use-trails lead to the spring on the left. This is an alternate starting point for a shorter hike or for exploring Pena Spring. Parking here is lim-

Lower trail with Gander's and teddy-bear cholla, California barrel cactus, ocotillo, and desert agave

Southern mule deer doe on the trail

ited to four or possibly five vehicles. Pena Spring provides the only reliable water along this hike and is reached by following one of several short use-trails branching off from the CRHT. Surrounded by riparian vegetation, it is easier to hear the spring than to see where the water gurgles slowly out of a vertical pipe obscured by reeds. This is a good spot for birding and wildlife observation early in the morning or during evening twilight.

From the Pena Spring junction, the trail climbs again then levels off as you approach a junction with the Culp Valley Trail at 3.5 miles. This accessible gravel path arcs 0.5 mile southward to Culp Valley Primitive Camp. Pit toilets are available but there are neither water nor other improvements. Situated 500 feet from the junction on the north side of the CRHT is a viewpoint called Scenic Overlook. From here you can look down Hellhole Canyon and across Borrego Valley to the Santa Rosa Mountains. The Culp Valley Primitive Camp trailhead is an alternate starting point for a 5-mile CRHT hike to the Hellhole Trailhead and the one most commonly used. Mountain bikes are allowed on this section of the trail.

From the Culp Valley Trail junction, the main trail starts a gentle climb before again leveling off and starting a long descent along the ridge between Hellhole Canyon and Dry Canyon. An optional side trip is a short ascent on an unmarked use-trail departing on the right at 0.3 mile from Scenic Overlook. This path leads to another viewpoint called Culp Valley Lookout, the high point of a loop that returns to the CRHT. Another possible side trip is an easy cross-country scramble to Lookout Point, departing the CRHT at 1 mile beyond the Culp Valley Trail junction. Follow the terrain to a ridge overlooking Hellhole Canyon just above Maidenhair Falls. You won't be able to see the falls but you can look down on native California fan palms that thrive in this part of Hellhole Canyon. Consider pausing here for lunch, where at an elevation of 3000 feet, it will be cooler than any point lower on the trail.

Now starts the primary downhill section dropping 2100 feet in the last 3 miles as the CRHT passes through the last of the junipers and transitions to the upper reaches of the Colorado Desert. Plants encountered here include desert agave, ocotillo, prickly-pear cactus, barrel cactus, teddy-bear cholla, springtime belly flowers, and the ubiquitous brittlebush. One last side trail branches from the CRHT 1 mile short of the end of the hike where remnants of the original cattle trail can be followed to the right, eventually coming out at S-22 about 0.75 mile above the Hellhole Canyon parking area. A brown and yellow CRHT post marks this point. Looking out over the Borrego Valley, the Anza-Borrego Desert State Park Visitor Center and the Colorado Desert District Headquarters are the closest structures seen from here. As the trail emerges into the flats of lower Hellhole Canyon, it meets the trail heading up to Maidenhair Falls, a trip best saved for another visit. Head east 0.3 mile to the parking area.

Distance:	12 miles, one-way
Difficulty:	🚶🚶🚶🚶🚶
Elevation gain/loss:	Up to 500/2500 feet
Hiking time:	7 hours
Agency:	CSP-CDD (ABDSP)
Trail use:	Bicycles and dogs on jeep route only; horses on CRHT
Notes:	Bring plenty of water
Trailhead GPS:	N33.21052, W116.49152
Optional map:	USGS 7.5-min *Tubb Canyon*
Atlas square:	G22
Directions:	(Ranchita) From S-22 turn south onto the Jasper Trail, 6.8 miles east of S-2, and park off road.

Habitat(s):

The name of this hike hints at the history of this area. The Jasper Trail is named after Ranchita cattleman Ralph Jasper who, at one time, owned over 5500 acres in portions of Montezuma Valley, Grapevine Canyon, and Yaqui Well, much of which is part of Anza-Borrego Desert State Park today. Jasper developed both Stuart and Angelina springs to make watering holes for his cattle. His father James Jasper, a San Diego County supervisor, had initially homesteaded in Grapevine Canyon, where he had found wild grapes near springs and in the canyon.

This hike begins in the San Ysidro Mountains near the small community of Ranchita and descends 12 miles down the scenic Jasper Trail into Grapevine Canyon, ending at the junction of Grapevine Canyon Road and CA-78 at Yaqui Flat where Sentenac Canyon opens up to the desert. Ralph Jasper used this trail when moving cattle from his ranch in Ranchita down to the warmer climes of Anza-Borrego for the winter.

It is recommended that this hike be done with a shuttle by leaving a car at the terminus on CA-78 at the Plum Canyon trailhead, and then driving 23 miles back to the start of the hike on Jasper Trail off of S-22. This direction makes for a mostly downhill trek, but there will still be sections requiring some gain in altitude before dropping down. The length of the hike can be modified by how far one drives down Jasper Trail before parking and heading out on foot. All distances listed here are assuming that the hike begins at the top of Jasper Trail. A 4WD vehicle is recommended if driving any portion of the Jasper Trail.

The first part of the trail is in a relatively flat open area that burned in the 2013 Ranchita Fire. Expect showy displays of wildflowers for

Trail winds down Grapevine Canyon

the next several years as the transition zone vegetation recovers. There will also be noticeable perennials like tall yellow mounds of 1-inch sunflower-like blooms of interior goldenbush (***Ericameria linearifolia***). Even when the plant is not in bloom, be sure to take time to smell the strongly lemon-scented leaves. The species scientific name is a direct reference to this daisy-like plant's narrow, linear leaves. It is commonly found in pinyon-juniper woodlands.

Approximately 1 mile from S-22, the California Riding and Hiking Trail (CRHT) cuts south off of Jasper Trail and provides escape from motorized activity. You may follow this single track path through stands of desert scrub oak and California juniper. While on the CRHT, you will cross Old Culp Valley Road and rejoin Jasper Trail for a short distance before returning to the CRHT. At 3.5 miles, you will once again rejoin the Jasper Trail and meander up and down the rugged dirt road until finally coming to Grapevine Canyon at 5 miles. The canyon is named after the southern California wild grapes that were found on the canyon floor. The sandy trail that runs through it stretches between the San Felipe Hills and Grapevine Hills. Native Americans either ate the grapes or dried them as raisins and stored them for later use.

Heading east you quickly come to Stuart Spring, the only reliable source of water for many miles, frequented by local animals and insects. With a little hunting it is possible to locate a small water-filled trough constructed by Ralph Jasper. However, be sure to filter the water if you take it from the spring.

Angelina Spring is next at 6.8 miles where the water is subsurface much of the year, identified by lush stands of desert-willow and pink-flowered arrow weed (***Pluchea sericea***), so named for its long straight stems used by the native people in fashioning the shafts of arrows. This area was inhabited by native peoples for thousands of years, first by an older Indian group and later by the more modern Kumeyaay Indians. It is now one of seven cultural reserves in the state park. Native people

Interior goldenbush

Mojave yucca

use the cultural preserve today for gatherings and educational visits.

Follow Grapevine Canyon Road through ocotillo, desert agave, California barrel cactus, teddy-bear cholla, Mojave yucca, and displays of desert wildflowers during spring. Mojave yucca (*Yucca schidigera*) may be recognized by its noticeable trunk and stiff leaf blades with fibrous-shedding margins. The Greek word schidigera refers to its fibrous shredding. This plant was important to Native Americans and was known as *shah'aa* in the Kumeyaay language. It was used like agave as a food and fiber source. A chemical called saponin found in the root was used as soap by mashing the root and adding water. Mojave yucca has an obvious stem with few branches. Leaves have stiff blades with conspicuous fibrous-shedding margins. The flower cluster is compact, the flowers are white and purple-edged, and they bloom at night. Yuccas are exclusively pollinated at night by a species of moth—some host specific—that lays its eggs in the flower's ovary. The Mojave yucca has a specific yucca moth (*Tegeticula yuccasella*) that pollinates it. The co-dependency between the yucca and moth for pollination and larval food and shelter is termed obligate mutualism and has been recognized since 1872. Charles Darwin commented about the coevolution between yuccas and yucca moths.

This yucca is found in chaparral as well as in creosote bush scrub.

At mile 9.9 there is a signed fork in the road. Left goes to the north side of Yaqui Flat and towards Yaqui Well. Keep right for CA-78 and a return to your shuttle car parked at Plum Canyon. This route is a popular 4WD route on weekends, but mid-week there may be little or no traffic. No matter the day, you will discover great views, incredible solitude, and a rewarding trip through some of Anza-Borrego's less-visited landscapes.

Yucca or pronuba moth

Distance:	8.5 miles, out-and-back
Difficulty:	🚶🚶🚶🚶🚶
Elevation gain/loss:	Up to 1400 feet
Hiking time:	6 hours
Agency:	CSP-CDD (ABDSP)
Notes:	4WD recommended; call ABDSP Visitor Center regarding road conditions; bring plenty of water
Trailhead GPS:	N33.19396, W116.48391
Optional map:	USGS 7.5-min *Tubb Canyon*
Atlas square:	H22
Directions:	(Ranchita) From S-22 go south on the Jasper Trail, 6.8 miles east of S-2, for 1.4 miles. Turn left on Old Culp Valley Road, and go 1.5 miles to the signed Wilson trailhead on the right. The trailhead is also accessible from Culp Valley.

Habitat(s):

Wilson Trail and Peak were named for the rancher Alfred Wilson, who ran cattle in this area in the first half of the 20th century. The Wilson Trail goes southeast along Pinyon Ridge for several miles to just beyond Wilson Peak (4573'), which is the ridge high point. The trail goes through an interesting mix of chaparral and desert species. There are scattered pinyon pines and junipers, as well as abundant cholla, sugar bush, mountain-mahogany, and chamise. The area is in the middle of a designated wilderness area and is open only to hikers. Years ago it was open to 4WD vehicles, as well as horses and cattle, but it has been closed to them for many years.

The trail goes over a series of ridges and through intervening valleys on an easily followed decomposed granite path, maintained only by the feet of hikers who have gone before on this trek, just north of Wilson Peak. To reach the peak, look for one of the many improvised trails up to the peak, and don't miss it, as it provides spectacular views in all directions. To the east are the Salton Sea and the Chocolate Mountains in Imperial County. To the southeast are Whale Peak and the Pinyon Mountains. To the southwest are the Laguna and Cuyamaca mountains. To the northeast is Palomar Observatory, while to the north is the sweep of the Santa Rosa Mountains with Borrego Valley below.

The trail is entirely within the transition zone found in the drier and hotter high elevation mountains of San Diego County. There are conifers—junipers and pinyon pines—but not those requiring more rainfall and cooler temperatures. Many typical desert plants are

View toward Borrego Valley

abundant here, especially cholla and other cacti. There also are numerous chaparral species, including sugar bush, desert scrub oaks, Mojave yucca, chamise, big-berry manzanita, and cup-leaf-lilac, which is a desert *Ceanothus*.

The 2013 Ranchita fire left blackened skeletons of many of these plants. Some may not be recognizable as most of their distinguishing characteristics were burned. However, others are now sprouting new growth from their bases or were only minimally damaged by the fire.

The Wilson Trail is best visited in spring when there are spectacular wildflowers. There are large patches of white layia, tidy tips, cream cups, southern goldfields, baby blue eyes, desert bluebell, yellow pincushion, and many others. The many seeds produced by the various plants

attract birds to the area. One of the most common birds that may be seen is the mourning dove (***Zenaida macroura***), small-headed and long-tailed. It feeds on the ground, swallowing seeds rapidly and storing them in its crop, an enlarged part of its esophagus. When the crop is full, the bird flies to a safe place where it can digest the seeds. The crop can hold hundreds to thousands of seeds. The mourning dove may eat up to 20% of its weight per day. One reason it survives in the desert is its ability to drink brackish spring water with a salinity content up to half that of ocean water.

Even if you can't make it during the wildflower season, the trail provides spectacular views in all directions and an abundance of huge granite boulders eroded into fantastic shapes.

Mourning dove

Boulder near the summit

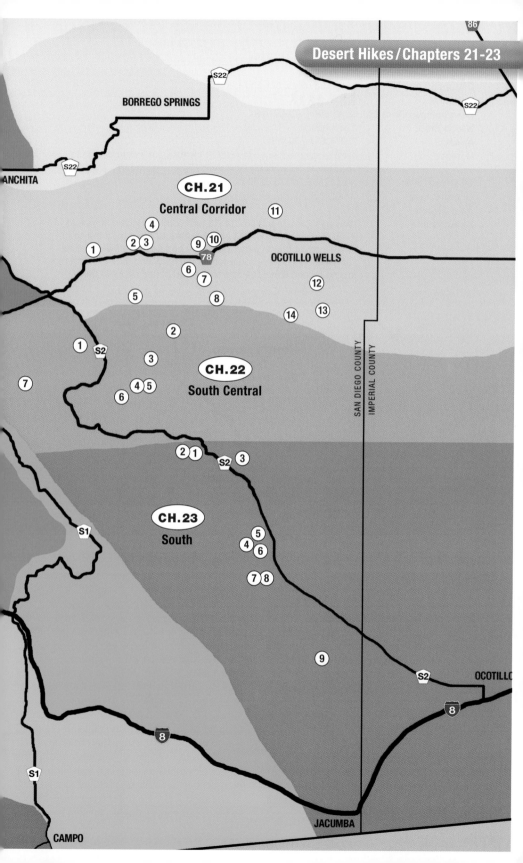

Distance:	2.8 or 6.3 miles, out-and-back
Difficulty:	
Elevation gain/loss:	Up to 600 or 1000 feet
Hiking time:	2 or 4 hours
Agency:	CSP-CDD (ABDSP)
Notes:	4WD recommended; call ABDSP Visitor Center regarding road conditions; bring plenty of water
Trailhead GPS:	N33.12865, W116.42526
Optional map:	USGS 7.5-min *Tubb Canyon*
Atlas square:	I23
Directions:	(Scissors Crossing) From CA-78 turn south into the entrance to Plum Canyon, 4 miles east of S-2, after a sharp turn to the east. There is an option to either park here and begin the hike or drive 1.4 miles on a dirt road to a fork in the road, and take the right fork, driving an additional 0.4 mile to the end of the road and park.

Habitat(s):

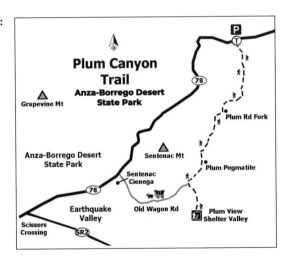

There are no plum trees in Plum Canyon. It is possibly a misnomer caused by incorrectly identifying a desert apricot tree (*Prunus fremontii*) as a desert plum. In fact, there are no desert plums in the Anza-Borrego area. A plant that is similar to a desert apricot that is also found in this region is the desert almond, but not in Plum Canyon. Another possibility for the name of the canyon is attributed to cattleman John McCain who, with his brother, constructed a wagon road through to Plum Canyon to travel between Shelter or Earthquake Valley and Yaqui Well, sometime before 1913, many years before CA-78 was constructed. McCain grew plums on his ranch in Julian in the 1890s, so perhaps there is a connection there. An earlier name for this canyon was Wagon Wash, named for the wagon road that the McCains constructed.

Today it is difficult to fathom that a wagon road was cut from Shelter/Earthquake Valley to Plum Canyon as rockslides have made it impassable. However, as a hiking route it is well worth exploring. The California Riding and Hiking Trail (CRHT) follows upper Plum Canyon and continues on to the Pinyon Mountain Road in Shelter Valley and then on into Blair Valley. The canyon has a wide diversity of plants—with 191 taxa identified—because of its location in the Desert Transition Zone. Begin the hike at the entrance to Plum Canyon for a longer but more interesting hike. It is a good way to experience the transition from lower elevation desert vegetation to that found in the higher elevations, making it a favored hike for members of the California Native Plant Society.

The road forks 1.4 miles from the entrance to Plum Canyon. Go right. The dirt road ends

CRHT sign post

on the trail. At 2.4 miles look for a large and interesting pegmatite dike with quartz and black tourmaline and wind caves on the right. About 0.25 mile further is a side canyon where the old Plum Canyon Road came into the wash from Shelter/Earthquake Valley. If exploring this side canyon, look for traces of the old wagon road. Continuing up the main wash, there is another CRHT sign before a steep climb that leads to the overview of Shelter/Earthquake Valley at elevation 2720 feet at mile 3.17. Enjoy the view of Granite Mountain to the west. The start of the old wagon road is not visible from this point as the view is blocked. Retrace steps back to your vehicle.

Desert apricot

at mile 1.8. The shorter hike begins here. Plants seen in this lower elevation area include desert agave, desert-lavender, creosote bush, chuparosa, brittlebush, ocotillo, and a variety of cacti. Many smoke trees are found in the wash. Soon after leaving the upper parking area is the first encounter with desert apricot trees, California juniper, Mojave yucca, desert-willow, and California barrel cactus. This mixed transition area also has catclaw acacia and ephedra (*Ephedra* spp.).

Ephedra is a broom-like shrub with joint stems and scale-like leaves that is a gymnosperm or cone-bearing plant, like those in the cypress family and the pine family. Common names associated with it include joint fir, Mormon tea, and Indian tea. Ephedra stems, branches, and roots contain ephedrine, which stimulates the central nervous system, much like an amphetamine. The Mormons drank a tea made from ephedra because their religious practices discouraged using coffee as a stimulant. The Morman Battalion drank it when they marched almost 2000 miles from Council Bluffs, Iowa, to San Diego, California, in 1846. Local Indians used ephedra as a general tonic.

At 2.11 miles the trail goes to the right and over a dry waterfall. A sign indicates that it is part of the CRHT and that horses are allowed

Ephedra

Distance:	1.6 miles, out-and-back
Difficulty:	🚶
Elevation gain/loss:	Up to 100 feet
Hiking time:	1 hour
Agency:	CSP-CDD (ABDSP)
Notes:	Bring plenty of water
Trailhead GPS:	N33.13836, W116.37652
Optional map:	USGS 7.5-min *Tubb Canyon*
Atlas square:	I24
Directions:	(Tamarisk Grove Campground) From CA-78 go north on S-3 (Yaqui Pass Road) for 0.3 mile to the entrance of the Tamarisk Grove Campground and park off the road. The trailhead is across the street from the entrance to the campground on the west side of the ranger residence.

Habitat(s):

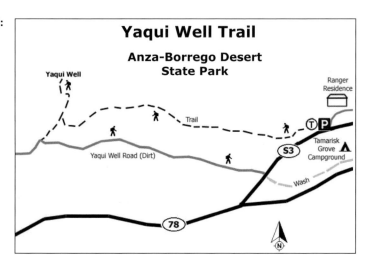

Yaqui Well is a small seep situated on the San Felipe Fault in San Felipe Wash that has been used for hundreds of years by Native Americans, cattlemen, prospectors, and travelers alike. Many lost-gold stories and legends of ghostly apparitions are associated with the area. The name of the well is said to have derived from a Yaqui Indian of Sonora, Mexico, who lived with a local Kumeyaay woman near the well. It was first developed as a cattle camp sometime after 1909 by Paul Sentenac, for whom Sentenac Canyon is named.

Large magnificent desert ironwoods and mesquite trees grow here, some heavily festooned with desert mistletoe (***Phoradendron californicum***). Listen for the characteristic questioning call of the phainopepla (***Phainopepla nitens***) that has a rising intonation that sounds like *hỏi*, the Vietnamese word for ask. This black silky, crested flycatcher-like bird,

with a long tail, and white wing patches visible in flight, is commonly seen and heard in the area as it feasts on the red berries of the desert mistletoe. This is the male of the phainopepla; the female is gray. The name phainopepla comes from the Greek meaning shining robe and refers to its black shiny feathers. The phainopepla is a bird primarily found in washes and riparian areas. An individual bird can eat up to 1100 berries a day. The phainopepla is responsible for helping spread the hemi-parasitic mistletoe by defecating seeds, which it does not digest, onto branches. The seeds then take root onto the host plant. The leafless desert mistletoe takes water and minerals from its host plant but does its own photosynthesizing. This bird rarely drinks water. It gets the moisture it needs from the desert mistletoe berries. The phainopepla will mimic the calls of other birds when pursued by predators.

Desert mistletoe

Yaqui Well is considered a birding hotspot. Over 80 species of birds have been observed in the area including the California quail, Costa's hummingbird, least Bell's vireo, cactus wren, verdin, loggerhead shrike, house finch, black-throated sparrow, black-tailed gnatcatcher, common raven, and the greater roadrunner (*Geococcyx californianus*). There is a reason this bird is called a roadrunner—it can run up to 20 miles per hour. Native Americans revered its speed, endurance, and courage. The roadrunner has a distinctive X-shaped footprint with two toes in front and two toes in back. It can eat venomous prey with no ill

effect. It is about 2 feet long, including its tails which is nearly half its body length. It is often seen in open areas, running to catch its preferred food—lizards and snakes. It is one of the few birds that will attack and kill rattlesnakes. It often does this cooperatively with one bird distracting the snake while the other pounces on it for the kill.

The Yaqui Well trail begins just west of the ranger residence across from Tamarisk Grove Campground. The trail follows a rocky ridge with typical creosote desert scrub. Plants found here include desert-lavender, desert agave, jojoba, white rhatany or krameria, alkalai goldenbush, trixis, brittlebush, chuparosa, creosote bush, and various cacti. Also found is many-fruit saltbush (*Atriplex polycarpa*) that is indicative of an area with alkali soil. The habitat changes to a wash woodland as the trail drops into San Felipe Wash where large ironwoods and honey mesquite are found along with catclaw acacia, palo verde, and smoke tree. The creosote bush is larger here.

The water in the Yaqui Well seep can vary from year to year. In times past the seep has been surrounded with cattails. In recent times there has been very little surface water. From the seep, hikers have a choice of retracing their steps back the same way or completing the loop by following the trail south to the Yaqui Well primitive camping area and road. Camp toilets are visible before reaching the dirt road. While walking east along the dirt road, you will see several large desert-willow trees. From the junction with the pavement, it is only 0.2 mile back to the trailhead.

Phainopepla

Greater roadrunner

Distance:	0.6 mile, out-and-back
Difficulty:	🚶
Elevation gain/loss:	Up to 200 feet
Hiking time:	1 hour
Agency:	CSP-CDD (ABDSP)
Trailhead GPS:	N33.13874, W116.37497
Optional map:	USGS 7.5-min *Tubb Canyon*
Atlas square:	I24
Directions:	(Tamarisk Grove Campground) From CA-78 go north on S-3 (Yaqui Pass Road) for 0.3 mile to the entrance of the Tamarisk Grove Campground and park off the road. The trailhead is across the street from the campground entrance on the east side of the ranger residence.

Habitat(s):

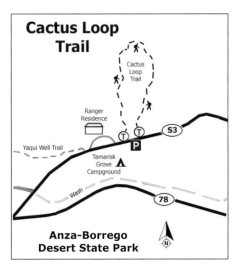

One of the easiest ways to compare the differences between the various types of cacti and to learn how plants survive on steep, rocky slopes is to visit the Cactus Loop Trail. A nature trail guide, available at the trailhead, provides interpretive information at 14 numbered stops along the loop.

Cacti found on this trail include Engelmann's hedgehog, fish-hook, Gander's cholla, beavertail, teddy-bear or jumping cholla, diamond or pencil cholla, and barrel cactus. The most notable is the teddy-bear cholla (**Cylindropuntia bigelovii**), which is a forest of shrubs on this trail; some specimens are almost 6 feet tall.

If you are unlucky enough to have a cactus spine attach itself to you, use caution when attempting to remove it, as cactus spines can easily pierce the skin. It's a good idea to carry a comb and/or tweezers as part of your desert hiking gear; they are excellent aids for re-

moving most spines or thorns. The beavertail cactus (**Opuntia basilaris**) is deceptive in its appearance with its flat, rounded pads. There are no visible long spines. Instead, it has very tiny, almost microscopic barbed bristles called glochids that can easily penetrate the skin. The best way to remove these barbed hairs is with a piece of duct tape. One desert animal that is seemingly unaffected by cactus spines is Bryant's woodrat or pack rat (**Neotoma bryanti**). It will gather cholla balls and mound them up and spread them around its nest as a defense against predators. Look for these nests on this hike.

The Cactus Loop Trail gradually climbs up and over a ridge. From the top of this ridge there are views to the southeast of Mescal Bajada with its overlapping alluvial fans covered with desert agave (mescal). There is also a close-up view of the San Felipe fault trace. One

Teddy-bear cholla

of the numbered stops overlooks a desert wash that clearly shows the work of water during flash floods that can move massive amounts of material to help form the landscape.

This trail is also a study on how perennial plants are able to survive the extremes of desert temperatures. Some plants have tiny leaves or even a shiny, oily coating on their leaves to reflect sunlight, like the creosote bush (*Larrea tridentata*), while another will have a hairy leaf surface that provides shade when it is hot, like the brittlebush or incienso (*Encelia farinosa*). Other plants will quickly drop their leaves if dry and grow leaves anew if they receive moisture, like the ocotillo (*Fouquieria splendens*). The California barrel cactus (*Ferocactus cylindraceus*) expands to store water during dry times, and the desert agave (*Agave deserti*) has thick leaves that also store water. The spines of cacti help protect the plant from browsing animals while also providing some shade. These are a few examples of the many techniques plants have evolved to survive desert heat and aridity.

Another thing to note on this hike is the rust-colored stains found on the rocks. Known as desert varnish, it is not clear how it has formed over thousands of years, but it is conjectured that bacteria that live on the rocks absorb manganese and iron oxide, imparting the reddish hue. It is further believed that the bacteria cements tiny particles of clay to themselves to prevent drying out, contributing a brownish hue.

Ocotillo bloom

California barrel cactus

Distance:	1.2 miles, loop
Difficulty:	🏃
Elevation gain/loss:	Minimal
Hiking time:	1 hour
Agency:	CSP-CDD (ABDSP)
Notes:	Bring plenty of water
Trailhead GPS:	N33.14662, W116.35212
Optional map:	USGS 7.5-min *Borrego Sink*
Atlas square:	I24
Directions:	(Tamarisk Grove Campground) From CA-78 go north on S-3 (Yaqui Pass Road) for 1.9 miles and park at the pullout about 60 yards from milepost 2 and next to the San Diego County call box S-3-18. Parking also available on the north side of the milepost in the primitive camp area.

Habitat(s):

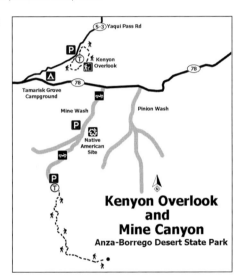

**Kenyon Overlook
and
Mine Canyon**
Anza-Borrego Desert State Park

The view at the top of the overlook of the Bill Kenyon Trail is best during morning hours or later afternoon when shadows are most prominent on the Pinyon Mountains and the overlapping skirts of the alluvial fans flowing down from the mountainsides. The overlook offers a vast view of the surrounding area through which San Felipe Wash passes between Sentenac Canyon and Borrego Mountain. This is an easy loop hike with a variety of plants and interesting granitic outcrops. The trail is well marked with only one very short unmarked turnoff that leads to the viewpoint.

The viewpoint is named for William L. Kenyon, a former Anza-Borrego Desert State Park supervisor who set up ranger patrol districts that continue to this day. A monument to Kenyon is at the overlook as well as an interpretive sign for the view of Mescal Bajada seen to the south on

the opposite side of CA-78. Mescal is another name for the desert agave or century plant that is abundant on the depositional material that flows down from the Pinyon Mountains. *Bajar* is Spanish for to go down or descend.

Because this is a loop hike, cars can be parked either at the pull out or at the Yaqui Pass Primitive Camp area. A trail sign is at both locations. The elevation of the pass is 1750 feet with only a small variance in elevation throughout the gentle undulating trail that goes over rocky slopes and down small gullies. The granitic outcrops are dark with a desert varnish or patina covering. The reddish brown to black coating common in arid areas is thought to be caused by manganese-oxidizing microbes. Desert varnish forms on stabilized rock surfaces.

Plants seen on this hike, typical of desert scrub found on rocky slopes, include creo-

The trail

a large, densely branched, spiny shrub that can reach a height of 10 feet. It has small needle-like linear blue-gray or green leaves dotted with glands. The leaves grow in bunches. The name indigo refers to the color of the flower, which is between a deep blue and violet. In early spring it can be a striking plant when covered with indigo-colored pea flowers that emit a fragrant odor to attract pollinators such as bees and insects. After the flowers disappear, there is an egg-shaped fruit with raised dark red spots.

Brittlebush or incienso is easy to identify when in bloom with its yellow daisy flowers on long wand stems above the low-rounded shrub, generally less than 4 feet tall. It is known as brittlebush because the stems become very brittle when dry. It is also known as incienso because its yellow sap was once collected from various species of *Encelia* and burned as incense in the California missions. Brittlebush is a drought tolerant plant that constantly adapts to available moisture. In spring, when it is cool and moist, leaves are green and shiny and grow rapidly. As it becomes warmer, leaves will turn gray and develop a hairy surface that will provide shade and reflect sunlight. As it becomes hot, leaves produced will have more hairs to slow down water loss. If necessary, portions of the plant will die back to conserve water. In the spring, hillsides are dotted with the bright yellow blooms of brittlebush.

sote bush, white bur-sage, Gander's and teddy-bear cholla, beavertail, California barrel cactus, desert agave, desert-lavender, white rhatany or krameria, indigo bush (*Psorothamnus schottii*) and brittlebush (*Encelia farinosa*). The indigo bush is in the pea family, as is the smoke tree, which it resembles. It is

Indigo bush

Brittlebush

Distance:	5 miles, out-and-back
Difficulty:	🏃🏃🏃
Elevation gain/loss:	Up to 500 feet
Hiking time:	3 hours
Agency:	CSP-CDD (ABDSP)
Trail use:	Dogs and horses on jeep trail only
Notes:	4WD recommended; call ABDSP Visitor Center regarding road conditions; bring plenty of water
Trailhead GPS:	N33.07918, W116.36907
Optional map:	USGS 7.5-min *Whale Peak*
Atlas square:	K24
Directions:	(Tamarisk Grove Campground) From CA-78 go south on Mine Wash, 2.8 miles east of S-3 (Yaqui Pass Road). Continue off road for 1.6 miles to the Kumeyaay Village, then 3.1 miles past the village to Mine Canyon.

Habitat(s):

A major archeological site, a treasure trove of fascinating plants and animals, and beautiful scenery ranging from wide-open desert views to narrow winding mountain canyons all await anyone who takes a drive to and hike up Mine Wash and Canyon.

The first stop is the Kumeyaay village site peppered with morteros and metate-like slicks on the granitic rock surrounded by areas of darkened earth indicating sites of old agave roasting pits. The Kumeyaay traveled seasonally to harvest plants from the coast, mountains, and desert areas. They used large rock pestles for pounding various nuts and seeds in morteros and manos or smaller smooth rocks for grinding seeds and grains on portable metates or slicks on granitic rock. Also note the scat-

tered pottery shards in the village area. Observe only. All cultural features are protected by the state park and by the federal Antiquities Act. Collecting artifacts is subject to prosecution.

Return to your vehicle and drive another 3 miles up-canyon, stopping at the end of the road where there is a barrier preventing vehicles from going farther. The remains of an abandoned gold mine, for which the wash and canyon are named, are located on the northwest bank of the wash. From here begin exploration of the canyon by following the road up-canyon beyond the barrier. Eventually you come to another barrier that blocks vehicles from entering the canyon when approaching it from Earthquake Valley. The old road, now a trail, continues beyond this second barrier,

Kumeyaay village site

val stage. Look for miniature caves in the rock walls or in sandy soils at ground level that collect wind-blown sand and house immature antlions identified by their funnel-shaped pits in the sand. The larval antlions wait at the bottom of the pit under cover of soft sand with only their mandibles exposed. Ants and other small insects slide to the bottom of the pit where antlions suck out their body fluids then fling the carcasses out and wait for the next meal. In this larval stage, it has an incomplete digestive track. Waste materials accumulate in the midgut and then are expelled near the end of the pupal stage after the anus is finally connected. As an adult, after it emerges from its cocoon, it resembles a damselfly that has clubbed antenna, delicate when compared to the immature larval stage with its large hairy body and piercing mandibles. The antlion life cycle is two to three years with the last remaining days spent as an adult that cannot eat.

eventually connecting with the Pinyon Mountain Road. However, before reaching Pinyon Mountain Road, there is a viewpoint overlooking Earthquake/Shelter Valley with views beyond to Granite Mountain. This is good place to turn around.

Near low-growing shrubs or cacti, look for the black-throated sparrow (*Amphispiza bilineata*), a year-round resident, and the white-crowned sparrow (*Zonotrichia leucophrys*), a winter visitor. The two are easy to differentiate by the pattern of black and white on their heads. The black-throated sparrow is sometimes referred to as the desert sparrow because of its preference for desert scrub and arid hillsides. It has a gray body, a black throat, and white face stripes. It is a ground forager looking for insects to eat. The white-crowned sparrow is found in several habitats and patronizes backyard feeders. Adults are easily recognized by their black-and-white-striped head, a pale pink to yellow bill, gray underparts, and gray-and-rusty striped back. It is a large sparrow with a small bill and a long tail. White-crowned sparrows forage mainly on the ground, looking primarily for seeds, insects, and berries. Also look for phainopeplas near catclaw acacias that have large growths of mistletoe.

Another interesting animal found here is the antlion (**family Myrmeleontidae**); it is not an ant but a winged insect with an interesting lar-

White-crowned sparrow

Antlion

Distance:	8 miles, loop
Difficulty:	🏃🏃🏃🏃
Elevation gain/loss:	Up to 1300 feet
Hiking time:	5 hours
Agency:	CSP-CDD (ABDSP)
Notes:	4WD recommended; call ABDSP Visitor Center regarding road conditions; bring plenty of water; trekking poles recommended
Trailhead GPS:	N33.11334, W116.31787
Optional map:	USGS 7.5-min *Whale Peak*
Atlas square:	J25
Directions:	(Tamarisk Grove Campground) From CA-78 turn south on Pinyon Wash, 4.1 miles east of S-3 (Yaqui Pass Road). Go south 1.6 miles on the Pinyon Wash dirt road to the junction with Nolina Wash and park safely off the road.

Habitat(s):

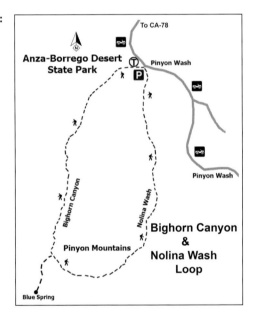

This Anza-Borrego desert hike is an adventure through infrequently visited canyons where one may encounter a bighorn sheep, view fascinating rock formations, and find some interesting native plants. It is also interesting to compare these two canyons and their washes. While similar, they also have their differences. Ironwood trees are relatively rare in Bighorn Canyon and common in Nolina Wash, and the yucca relative, Parry's bear-grass or nolina, appears to be confined to Nolina Wash.

Although the route is obvious, for most of the distance there is no maintained trail, and some boulder hopping is necessary. From your parked vehicle at the junction of the Pinyon Wash jeep trail and the Nolina jeep trail, start

hiking west across the flat, sandy Mescal Bajada. About 0.3 mile from your vehicle, begin tending southwest and continue until Bighorn Canyon is visible ahead, which you will enter after covering about 1 mile. The canyon gradually narrows as you hike south through scattered catclaw acacia, black-banded rabbitbrush, desert agave, California barrel and fishhook cactus, two kinds of cholla, ephedra or Mormon tea, and occasional juniper trees.

Blue Spring, on the north-facing slope of Pinyon Mountain, is 3.75 miles from your vehicle, if you choose to take an optional side trip. It was developed as a guzzler for desert bighorn sheep (***Ovis canadensis nelsoni***) in the Pinyon Mountains and is not a source of water

Rock formation near the saddle

Ironwood trees (*Olneya tesota*) are scattered in this canyon wash. These are the tall desert trees that can grow to 30 feet and live well over 1000 years. The species name refers to the hardness of the wood. It is the only species in its genus. The cream to lavender-colored pea flowers bloom from April to May. Indians gathered the seed pods, roasted them, and ground them into flour. They were used for cakes, porridge, and stored dried for later use. The taste is similar to peanuts. The wood was used to make things that required extreme hardness, such as throwing sticks and clubs and was also used for firewood. After contemplating the majesty of the ironwood, continue following the jeep trail through soft sand back to your vehicle.

A collared ewe

for humans. The best chance for seeing the elusive sheep is just to remain quiet and carefully scan the steep rocky slopes above the spring or near some of their favorites forage plants found here that include catclaw acacia, brittlebush or incienso, rush sweetbush, and white rhatany or krameria. Their efficient digestive system allows them to maximize removal of nutrients from what can be well-armed dry and abrasive plants. Males may weigh over 200 pounds and have huge horns to match. The local population has rebounded from a low of around 200 individuals in the early 1990s. They are listed as endangered by the US Fish and Wildlife Service.

If you do go to Blue Spring, reverse your steps until the low pass to the east that separates Bighorn Canyon and Nolina Wash is visible. Then go toward it, following the ducks that lead over the pass and down into Nolina Wash. Take care making your way down-canyon, where you must carefully negotiate some short dry falls. The Nolina Wash jeep trail is 1.75 miles from the pass summit. Scrambling over rocks ends here and hiking becomes easy again.

Cheesebush

Distance:	6 miles, out-and-back
Difficulty:	🏃🏃🏃🏃
Elevation gain/loss:	Up to 2000 feet
Hiking time:	5 hours
Agency:	CSP-CDD (ABDSP)
Notes:	4WD recommended; call ABDSP Visitor Center regarding road conditions; bring plenty of water; trekking poles recommended; trail is not obvious—bring GPS or map and compass for route finding
Trailhead GPS:	N33.10509, W116.30082
Optional map:	USGS 7.5-min *Whale Peak*
Atlas square:	J25
Directions:	(Tamarisk Grove Campground) From CA-78 turn south on Pinyon Wash, 4.1 miles east of S-3 (Yaqui Pass Road). Go south 1.6 miles on the Pinyon Wash dirt road to the junction with Nolina Wash. Keep left, staying in Pinyon Wash. Go 1 mile farther and park. (If concerned about driving in the wash, park at the junction and begin the hike there.)

Habitat(s):

Sunset Mountain (3657') takes its name from the last rays of the setting sun that enshroud the peak. The peak is located south of CA-78 between Pinyon Wash and Harper Canyon. From the top, there are views to the Salton Sea beyond the Borrego Badlands, which make the hike well worth the effort. Borrego Valley lies to the north, and the Pinyon Mountains and Whale Peak are to the southwest. The bulk of the Vallecito Mountains stretch out toward Fish Creek.

If hiking in the early part of the year, plan accordingly for short days of sunlight. Carry a light and a jacket if starting the climb any time after 12 noon. Take extra care hiking down,

which can be more difficult than hiking up because of the steepness and loose rocks. Sunset Mountain can be climbed from various sides, but the route from Pinyon Wash is the easiest.

From the parked vehicle, begin hiking to the east and climb up toward the low point of the broad ridge that lies to the west of the peak. There is no real trail, but one should not be concerned about getting lost. By heading for the saddle and then walking the ridge, you will avoid the many big boulders that would be encountered if you just went straight up. Keep the summit in view and look back at the trail often for landmarks for the return trip. The main

Germar Bernard

Sunset Mountain at sunset

challenge will be finding a way around large rocks, desert agave, and cacti. After you've ascended the ridge, follow it to the summit where there is a US Geological Survey benchmark and a climber's log to record your name. Retrace your path for the return hike.

Take care passing boulders and working your way down-canyon to the wash as you will be in rattlesnake country. Both the red diamond rattlesnake (*Crotalus ruber*) and the speckled rattlesnake (*Crotalus mitchellii*) prefer areas with rocks, boulders, and rocky outcrops surrounded by typical desert vegetation. Both species hunt at dusk, night, and dawn during the heat of summer and then during days when the temperature cools. Small mammals, birds, and lizards are on the menu. They may wait near an-

imal trails for unsuspecting prey, striking it and then following it until the prey collapses and they can eat it whole.

When alarmed they will shake their tail, rattling segments that are added every time the snake sheds its skin, which is at least once each year. Newborn snakes do not have a rattle. Adult red diamonds are larger (2-4.5 feet) than speckled rattlesnakes (2-3.5 feet), and both have a heavy body and the typical triangular-shaped head of pit vipers. Red diamonds vary in color from pink to reddish brown with diamond-shaped blotches on the back and black and white rings around the tail. Speckled rattlesnakes have a great variance in color to allow them to blend into their background. Colors vary from off white to yellow, pinkish,

Alan King

Red diamond rattlesnake

Alan King

Speckled rattlesnake

Heading down the mountain

gray, tan, to brown, but they all have speckled, banded marking. There are alternating dark and light rings on the tail with the tail color in contrast to the body color.

These snakes are not aggressive, but they will defend themselves. They will provide a warning with a rattle. Your first line of defense is to remain motionless. They will bite only if provoked and if not given an escape route. One in five bites to humans is a dry bite with no release of venom, as the snake needs to save his venom for hunting. Nevertheless, a bite from a rattlesnake needs immediate medical treatment.

A variety of plants can be found on this hike in the wash area as well as higher elevations. Cheesebush or burrobrush (*Ambrosia salsola* var. *salsola*) is a small shrub standing 2-3 feet in height with needle-like leaves on a thin stem. The plant emits an odor that is said to resemble Limburger cheese. In summer and fall it has a straw-like appearance. In spring this member of the sunflower family has both small male and female flowers on the same plant, making this a monoecious plant. It grows in washes and sandy soils and is often found in association with other wash plants such as smoke trees, chuparosa, and desert-lavender. At higher elevations look for jojoba and ephedra. A variety of cacti and desert agave are found at all elevations. Be particularly cautious of the agave staves and the catclaw acacia. Long pants and a long-sleeve shirt offer some protection.

This area has an abundance of cholla cactus. The spines do not bother the cactus wren (*Campylorhynchus brunneicapillus*), which sleeps safely at night protected by cholla spines. It builds its football-shaped nest with its entrance on the side in a cactus or thorny tree. The cactus wren has a brown cap, a white eye streak, and brown upperparts streaked and mottled white. The underparts are boldly spotted with black on a background that shades from whitish to tawny. It is the largest of California's wrens and is a true desert bird that can survive without drinking water. It forages for insects and spiders.

Cactus wren

Distance:	3 miles, out-and-back
Difficulty:	🚶🚶
Elevation gain/loss:	Up to 500 feet
Hiking time:	2 hours
Agency:	CSP-CDD (ABDSP)
Notes:	4WD recommended; call ABDSP Visitor Center regarding road conditions; bring plenty of water
Trailhead GPS:	N33.07802, W116.28805
Optional map:	USGS 7.5-min *Whale Peak*
Atlas square:	K26
Directions:	(Tamarisk Grove Campground) From CA-78 turn south on Pinyon Wash, 4.1 miles east of S-3 (Yaqui Pass Road). Go south 1.6 miles on the Pinyon Wash dirt road to the junction with Nolina Wash. Keep left, staying in Pinyon Wash. Go 3.3 miles to the end of the road and park.

Habitat(s):

This hike takes you into one of the more remote areas of Anza-Borrego Desert State Park that was used by Native Americans. A well-marked trail begins at the end of the Pinyon Wash road and continues through the canyon and past a stand of imposing boulders. After some rugged ups and downs over the rocks, the route will level off in a mostly smooth, sandy streambed, gradually angling up-hill.

If it's spring and the rains have come, you're in for a colorful treat. Clumps of brilliant yellow brittlebush and rivers of golden poppies will spill down the boulder-strewn hillsides, as spiny teddy-bear chollas raise their furry arms. Gander's chollas make their stand in the pale blue-lavender seas of color formed by wild-heliotrope

or common phacelia (*Phacelia distans*), if the rains have cooperated.

Unlike its name, teddy-bear cholla (*Cylindropuntia bigelovii*) is not a cactus that one would cuddle. It is fiercely armed with joints that easily detach, hence its other name of jumping cholla. Mature specimens are surrounded with cholla balls that can easily and quickly catch a ride on hiking boots, clothing, and passing wildlife. The fallen balls are able to root and grow into a new plant. Look for small teddy-bear plants surrounding mature larger plants. Wild-heliotrope's bell-shaped flowers are arranged in a coil, resembling a scorpion's tail and providing another common name by which it is known—scorpionweed. It has five petals and green, fine-

Fish-hook cactus in bloom

ders. Native peoples used these grinding holes in the preparation of food. As you wander and search along the edge of the hillside, also keep an eye out for broken shards of pottery and obsidian flakings left from the making of arrow points or other tools. Look and photograph, but do not collect or pick up anything as the exact position of artifacts is important to archaeologists who record these sites. All antiquities are protected by state and federal law and may not be removed. Possession of artifacts is subject to prosecution.

In addition to native artifacts, watch for the magenta blooms of beavertail cactus (*Opuntia basilaris*) and the creamy blossoms of the small fish-hook cactus (*Mammillaria dioica*) hiding under bushes. Note the hooked barbs that give this plant its name. If you're lucky, you may spot a banded rock lizard (*Petrosaurus mearnsi*) with a black collar on its neck and a banded tail. These agile lizards live on large boulders where they escape predators by running up vertical rock faces or skittering around to the opposite side of the rock to hide.

After about 0.5 mile, you will reach two large rocks, maybe 15 feet high. The sheltered space between them is a fine place to relax and have a snack among the Native American grinding holes before retracing your steps back to your vehicle. Keep your eyes open for treasures and pleasures you missed on the way in.

ly-haired, fern-like leaves. It usually grows up through other surrounding plants to a height of 1-3 feet. This hardy annual grows in many habitats including desert, chaparral, and grasslands.

The elevation is high enough that jojoba or goatnut (*Simmondsia chinensis*) is found along the trail. Look for a small rounded shrub with thick leathery leaves. The nutty fruit of this dioecious (separate male and female plants) evergreen shrub contains an oil that is really a liquid wax. It has been harvested commercially as a substitute for sperm whale oil, which it chemically resembles. It is used in shampoos and to lubricate machinery. In the 1970s and 1980s jojoba was planted in southern California as a commercial crop. This was a financial gamble with poor results because only female plants produce seed. It can take over five years to discover if the young plants are male or female! The nuts are the ripened ovary of the female flower. Jojoba nuts are a favorite of desert bighorn sheep. Native Americans ate the flowers but ate the fruit (the nuts) only as a supplemental food because it is bitter and hard to digest. A tea made from the leaves was used to treat a variety of problems including rheumatism, asthma, emphysema, and hemorrhoids. The fruit was ground and applied to the hair as a shampoo.

After about 1 mile, the wash opens up into a large flat area. Scanning Harper Flat, you will see the conspicuous ocotillo and creosote bush. Turn left along the hillside and start looking for multiple bedrock mortars worn into the boul-

Beavertail cactus

Distance:	2 miles, loop and out-and-back
Difficulty:	
Elevation gain/loss:	Up to 200 feet
Hiking time:	1 hour
Agency:	CSP-CDD (ABDSP)
Notes:	Bring plenty of water
Trailhead GPS:	N33.13065, W116.30143
Optional map:	USGS 7.5-min *Borrego Sink*
Atlas square:	I25
Directions:	(Tamarisk Grove Campground) From CA-78 turn south into the Narrows Earth Trail parking area along the highway, 4.7 miles east of S-3 (Yaqui Pass Road), where the road turns abruptly to the left.

Habitat(s):

The Narrows Earth Trail is located at The Narrows where San Felipe Creek turns abruptly northeast, just east of the junction with Pinyon Wash. It is the perfect place to observe geology and earth movement in action. The short 0.5 mile trail is located in a small side canyon called Powder Dump Canyon that was once used to store explosives in a bunker at the mouth of the canyon when CA-78 was under construction.

Quartz Vein Wash is the next canyon to the east where you can look for some of the same features found on the Narrows Earth Trail. In addition, Quartz Vein Wash has great examples of pegmatite dikes and black tourmaline or schorl in quartz. Large ironwood trees are scattered throughout the wash, making it a veritable forest. Wind caves show the force of wind as it has weathered and eroded canyon walls.

Begin the hike at the Narrows Earth Trail by picking up an interpretive guide at the first station. The contact zone for the Aguanga-San Felipe Fault is visible. This is a very complex area displaying region-wide detachment faulting. Along the walk are displays of prominent fault gouging. The earth movement in this area has exposed pre-Cretaceous metasedimentary rocks that were originally laid down some 500 million years ago as alternating layers of sand and mud from an ancient seabed. These are some of the oldest exposed rocks of this desert

Many geologic features on the hike

area. They can be noted as bands of light and dark material in outcrops along the trail and in Quartz Vein Wash.

After this introduction to local geology, head east to the mouth and entrance to Quartz Vein Wash. This out-and-back hike is 1.5 miles in length and, unlike the Narrows Earth Trail, climbs about 200 feet. Begin walking on the dirt road up-canyon.

Almost immediately after starting the hike note a small cove on the right with ironwood trees—a perfect campsite with shade. Soon after passing this cove will be a turnoff to the right with a sign that says "no vehicles." Follow this wash up-canyon, passing the forest of ironwood trees. Common plants that are found here in addition to the many ironwood trees include desert-lavender, creosote bush, chuparosa, ocotillo, brittlebush, catclaw acacias, and Gander's cholla. But the most noticeable are the ironwood trees

At about 0.5 mile, begin looking for black tourmaline or schorl found in the pegmatite quartz along the canyon walls. Schorl is the most common form of tourmaline. Also note that the walls are pocked with interesting wind caves. Look for dark patches of rock within larger granitic boulders as you are hiking. These are called xenoliths—literally strangers in the rock. They are older chunks of surface rock that were broken up when molten rock intruded and captured the chunks as the rock solidified.

As the canyon begins to fork, stay to the right and work around the many boulders that appear as the canyon narrows. Note desert agave and California barrel cactus in this area. The steep ridge on the right separates this canyon from Powder Dump Canyon. Climb as far as comfortable, and then turn around and return to your vehicle.

Free trail guide describes features

Distance:	1.5 miles, loop
Difficulty:	
Elevation gain/loss:	Up to 100 feet
Hiking time:	1 hour
Agency:	CSP-CDD (ABDSP)
Notes:	Bring plenty of water
Trailhead GPS:	N33.13948, W116.28976
Optional map:	USGS 7.5-min *Borrego Sink*
Atlas square:	I26
Directions:	(Tamarisk Grove Campground) From CA-78 turn south into the entrance to Nude Wash entrance, 5.7 miles east of S-3 (Yaqui Pass Road), just beyond the electrical substation. A short dirt road extends into the wash. Park here.

Habitat(s):

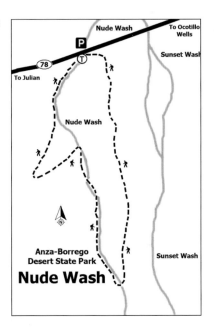

An often overlooked small wash and canyon in the Anza-Borrego area with interesting geology and vegetation is Nude Wash. The unusual name for this wash is attributed to California State Park Ranger Merle Beckman who was checking the canyon in the late 1950s and found a man in the nude sun bathing. He thought it an appropriate name for the wash. The wash is to the east of The Narrows and north of Sunset Mountain where San Felipe Creek turns northeast toward Borrego Mountain.

Park in the wide sandy area near CA-78, and then start hiking south, down the dirt road, and past scattered ironwood trees. The road forks in about 0.1 mile with the left fork leading further down the wash while the right fork leads to a small tributary canyon that is worthy of a detour. About 100 yards into the tributary there is a dry fall with exposed, highly eroded, colorful metasedimentary rocks. Although the falls could easily be climbed, go back out to the main Nude Wash road and continue hiking south. Note the variety of spiny plants found in this wash that includes ocotillo, several kinds of cholla, barrel and beavertail cacti, catclaw acacia, and mesquite.

The dirt road ends 0.4 mile from the highway, but continue hiking into The narrow canyon where you will have to scale three small waterfalls. The vegetation includes not only the various spiny plants and ironwood trees found in the sandy wash, but also desert-lavender,

Desert wishbone plant

nal, it is fairly easily seen and recognized by its white stripe found along its side, extending from its shoulder to its hip, and its general reddish appearance. It resembles a chipmunk, except its white lateral stripe does not extend to its head.

The hike offers an opportunity to see many interesting geological phenomena as well. The Vallecito Mountains were formed when igneous plumes of granite pushed up through the ancient metamorphic layers that had lain here since the Paleozoic era, about 500 million years ago. That is about 420 million years before the Vallecito Mountains even began to be uplifted. The structures found here include evidence of faulting and anticlines that were formed as The metamorphic layers were bent and broken by the intruding igneous plume.

creosote bush, brittlebush, and desert wishbone plant (*Mirabilis laevis* var. *retrorsa*). The unusual common name for this perennial herb refers to the forked stems that are reminiscent of a wishbone. At the base of the fork are opposite dark green ovate leaves. Because of the wishbone forked stems and opposite leaves, the plant can easily be identified even when not in bloom. This plant is in the four o'clock family. Flowers are mostly white. The varietal name refers to short retrorse (bending forward or upward) hairs on the plant.

One small mammal that you might see searching for seeds is the white-tailed antelope ground squirrel (*Ammospermophilus leucurus*). Since this ground squirrel is diur-

A mudstone dry waterfall

At 0.6 mile from the highway, look for traces of a trail going up the hillside on the left. Take this trail to the saddle for an overlook into the much larger Sunset Wash, a major channel carrying debris from rapidly eroding Sunset Mountain into the San Felipe Wash. Once on the ridge, follow it north, but don't try to cut down into either Sunset or Nude Wash. Instead, hike up the middle of the ridge. It will gradually descend into Nude Wash near where you parked your vehicle.

White-tailed antelope ground squirrel

Distance:	3.5 miles, out-and-back, two different routes
Difficulty:	𝀭𝀭
Elevation gain/loss:	Up to 400 feet
Hiking time:	2 hours
Agency:	CSP-CDD (ABDSP)
Notes:	4WD recommended; call ABDSP Visitor Center regarding road conditions; bring plenty of water; trail identified by ducks and frequent use patterns
Trailhead GPS:	N33.18205, W116.21415
Optional map:	USGS 7.5-min *Borrego Mountain*
Atlas square:	H27
Directions:	(Ocotillo Wells) From CA-78 go north on the unpaved Buttes Pass Road, 1.5 miles east of Borrego Springs Road. The small sign for Buttes Pass can easily be missed. Go 1 mile to a fork in the road. Go left at the fork and continue another 0.8 mile to The Slot and the West Butte trailhead and park. Watch for some areas of soft sand and a few potholes.

Habitat(s):

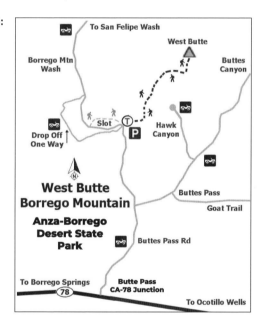

This is one of the most popular hikes in the Anza-Borrego Desert. From the top of the West Butte of Borrego Mountain there is an almost 360-degree view that includes a major part of the state park and the state vehicular recreation area and views of Borrego Springs, the Borrego Badlands, and the Santa Rosa, Vallecito, and San Ysidro mountains.

An added bonus is The Slot on Borrego Mountain, which is the only slot marked on a map. There are many slot canyons—narrow passages carved by water flowing through easily eroded soft formations such as sandstone or siltstone—in Anza-Borrego, but this one is the most frequently visited. It is such a narrow passage through towering sandstone canyon walls that you may have to take your daypack off and edge through sideways.

Start the trip to the slot from the parking area. Find the heavily traveled trail leading a short distance down into the canyon below. After reaching the bottom, go left. The canyon quickly narrows as you descend. In places the path is convoluted, in others it is straight and very narrow, occasionally less than shoulder width. You may have to squeeze through sideways. At one

Don Fosket

Hikers near the top of the butte

point the trail passes under a precarious rock that bridges the walls of the canyon. It looks as though it could fall at any minute, but it has been there for many years. The narrowest section is fairly short. In less than 0.5 mile, it widens to a broad sandy bottom and joins a jeep road. Head back to your car by either following this road or returning the way you came to experience The Slot for a second time.

Once you reach your car, start your journey up the West Butte by hiking up the abandoned dirt road leading east and signed "NO Motorized Vehicles." The road ends in a small box canyon within 0.25 mile. Look for ducks and a well-traveled footpath leading up a ridge at the road's end. At the top of the ridge, the trail continues to climb up the west-facing slope of the mountain. The lower reaches of West Butte are heavily eroded sandstone and cobble with very sparse vegetation, mainly with creosote bush and brittlebush. Nearing the top, the trail scrambles around decomposing desert-varnished granite boulders. The view from the top is impressive at any time. Especially dramatic is the vista of the Borrego Badlands to the northeast when seen in the late afternoon. After taking in the view, go back the way you came, paying attention to any movement that you might see under shrubs, on rocks, or in sandy areas. Chances are you might spot some interesting insects or reptiles, such as the flat-tailed horned lizard (**Phrynosoma mcallii**), which is a species of conservation concern because of its shrinking range in the Lower Colorado Desert,

often impacted by off-roaders, the development of golf courses, agriculture, and wind and solar energy projects.

The flat-tailed horned lizard is a master of camouflage with its ability to blend in with the color of surrounding soil and to minimize its shadow by lying flat against the ground. It has a wide oval-shaped body about 2-3 inches long from snout to vent at the base of its tail with a dark stripe running down the length of its back. It has pointed scales on its body with eight horns at the back of its head—the two central horns are long and sharp. It can quickly burrow in sand to hide or to keep cool. Although it can run quickly, its major defense is to remain motionless and blend into its surrounding area. It is not known to shoot blood out of its eyes for defense as many other horned lizards can do. It eats ants, especially harvester ants.

Alan Marshall

Flat-tailed horned lizard

Distance:	1.1 miles, loop
Difficulty:	
Elevation gain/loss:	Up to 100 feet
Hiking time:	1 hour
Agency:	CSP-CDD (ABDSP)
Notes:	Usually okay for 2WD; call ABDSP Visitor Center regarding road conditions; bring plenty of water
Trailhead GPS:	N33.06828, W116.11665
Optional map:	USGS 7.5-min *Borrego Mountain NE*
Atlas square:	K29
Directions:	(Ocotillo Wells) From CA-78 go south on Split Mountain Road for 5.8 miles. Turn right onto the signed dirt road leading to the trailhead. Go 1 mile, and park.

Habitat(s):

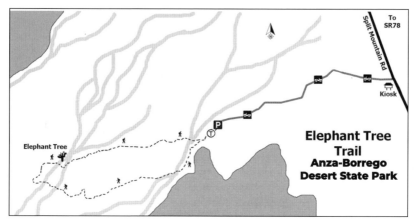

The small-leaf elephant tree (**Bursera microphylla**) is rare in the United States. It is found in the Gila Range of Arizona and, more commonly, in Baja California and Sonora, Mexico. For many years it was thought not to exist in the United States. The first sighting in the Colorado Desert was made in 1911, but its exact location remained a mystery until an elephant tree hunt was organized in 1937 by representatives from the San Diego Natural History Museum and the state park, and the site was officially recorded. Since that time, other stands have been found in the Santa Rosa Mountains near Clark Dry Lake, Indian and Bow Willow canyon areas, Bisnaga Alta Wash, Fish Creek Mountains, and In-Ko-Pah Gorge.

The tree is usually found in rocky areas and on slopes. The common name derives from its swollen trunk which stores water and has the resemblance of an elephant's thick, massive leg. It stands usually 6-10 feet tall, rarely as high as 30 feet. The tree has low spreading branches, a yellowish paper-like shredding bark, copper-colored upper branches, small green leaves, white flowers, purple fruit, and exudes a pinkish-red resin. It has a strong pungent smell reminiscent of turpentine, pine needles, and tangerines and is in the same family as myrrh and frankincense of the Middle East. It had the same sacred and special medicinal value to Native Americans as myrrh and frankincense had to the early Arabic and Judaic cultures, which also found it economically important as a source of incense and perfume.

The Elephant Tree Trail is well marked and has 13 numbered posts that relate to a free interpretive nature trail guide available at the turnoff to Elephant Tree Trail from Split Mountain Road or from the park's visitor center. The guide is a good way to learn about common desert plants and strategies they have to survive in the desert. For those interested in annual wildflowers, this is the

Small-leaf elephant tree

first place to check each season as annuals will flower at the lower and hotter elevations first.

The trail has changed from previous years due to flash flooding in the wash. There is now only one tree on this trail, and it is a shorter hike than it was previously. Large piled rocks and boulders on the sides and in the wash testify to the force of running water and its ability to reshape trails that are in washes. At about 0.5 mile, note the many downed ocotillos that were toppled in a flash flood. Also look to the northwest for a tall tree that stands out on the side of the wash. That is the lone elephant tree found on this hike, a little further at mile 0.65. The tree is large, standing almost 15 feet in height. The trail continues to loop around the wash rejoining almost at the trailhead at signpost No. 2.

More elephant trees persist farther up the bajada and in a canyon emerging from the Vallecito Mountains to the west, making this area one of the largest concentrated herds in the Anza-Borrego area.

Small-leaf elephant tree

Distance:	2 miles, out-and-back
Difficulty:	
Elevation gain/loss:	Up to 300 feet
Hiking time:	1 hour
Agency:	CSP-CDD (ABDSP)
Trail use:	Dogs and horses on designated roads only
Notes:	4WD recommended; call ABDSP Visitor Center regarding road conditions; bring plenty of water
Trailhead GPS:	N32.99313, W116.11842
Optional map:	USGS 7.5-min *Carrizo Mtn NE*
Atlas square:	L29
Directions:	(Ocotillo Wells) From CA-78 go south on Split Mountain Road for 8.1miles. Turn right on Fish Creek Wash. Go 4.2 miles on the unpaved road to the signed trailhead for the Wind Caves on the left and park.

Habitat(s):

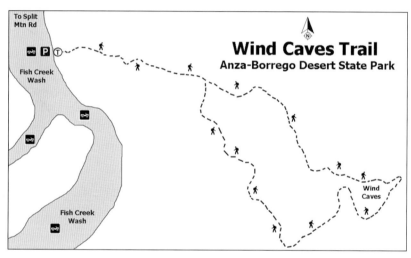

On the eastern edge of Anza-Borrego Desert State Park lie Split Mountain, the Carrizo Badlands, and a feature known as the Wind Caves. Here the exposed sandstone of the marine beds from the 5 million-year-old Imperial Formation have been slowly eroded by wind into fantastic shapes that evoke whimsical images of boats with portholes, spaceships, and even the fictional town of Bedrock, hometown of the prehistoric Flintstone family.

The journey to the Wind Caves starts by driving off-road up Fish Creek Wash towards Split Mountain Gorge. The Fish Creek Primitive Campground is to the left or east at mile 1.4 from the pavement. If unsure of clearance or driving in loose sand further into the wash, this is a good place to park your vehicle and continue on foot. This adds another 5.5 miles (round trip) to the hike.

Continuing on, you will soon enter the realm of Split Mountain Gorge with its sheer vertical walls towering hundreds of feet. The road winds through the gorge that is the dividing line between the Vallecito Mountains on the west and the Fish Creek Mountains on the east. Split Mountain Gorge was cut by an ancient stream that ran through a fault between the two ranges a million years ago. As the mountains continued to rise, the stream held its course and slowly eroded the gorge that we see today.

At 2.5 miles there is an arch-like formation on the west wall (right side) of the gorge known as the anticline. It was formed about 5 million years ago when an earthquake caused a massive landslide that deposited hundreds of millions of cubic yards of rock into the shallow sea that once covered this area. The force and speed of the slide warped the sand of the seafloor into

Don Fosket

Arizona lupine

the semi-circular layers seen here, much like carpeting being pushed against a wall.

Be on the lookout for the green leaves and purple flowers of Orcutt's woody aster clinging to the rock walls of the gorge. Amongst other desert bloomers, the yellow tassel-topped flowers of California trixis (*Trixis californica*) and the purple flower stalk of Arizona lupine (*Lupinus arizonicus*) may be found in the shade along the sides of the wash. The lupine is phototropic— the leaves track the movement of the sun from morning to dusk in order to maximize photosynthesis and fast growth to produce seeds before it dies. It is a race against desert heat and drought.

The gorge suddenly opens at about 4 miles, and in another 0.2 mile, there is a sign for the Wind Caves Trail on the left. Be sure to park in hard-packed sand, otherwise your vehicle may need to be towed or pushed upon return.

The hike begins with a climb up the east side of Split Mountain Wash on a series of rocky steps. As the trail ascends, there are outstanding views of the Carrizo Badlands, looking like huge frozen waves on a rough ocean. The Elephant Knees Formation is the prominent feature to the south. The fluted hills, while resembling the knees of giant elephants, are the remnants of a fossil reef formed 20 million years ago when the Gulf of California covered the region. If you have time after this hike, you may want to drive over to the Elephant Knees area to get a closer look.

After walking 0.2 mile, go straight and continue to climb at the first fork in the trail. The trail to the right will be the return route. In a few hundred feet go to the right and onto the Wind Caves—the left fork continues for 1 mile to the 1700-foot summit of Split Mountain East. After turning right at the fork and continuing about 0.7 mile, the Wind Caves will come into view. Spend time exploring the various rooms, alcoves, and tunnels found here. See if you can identify the formations known as The Phantom and The Ghost. Also contemplate the role that wind plays in the formation of desert lands along with earth movement and water. Surprisingly of the three, water plays the greater role in this dry land. When it does appear in the form of flash floods, it has the ability to move mountains.

There is evidence that Native Americans used some of these wind caves for shelter. As you enjoy a snack or lunch, try to imagine these past inhabitants doing the same. Remember there is no collecting of any kind allowed in the park, so do not move anything found so others may enjoy it also. All Indian artifacts are protected by the American Antiquities Act of 1906.

When finished exploring, find a route down to the trail immediately below the caves. Take this less-used single track west as it descends to another small collection of sandstone caves. This track rejoins the main trail not far above the wash and makes for a nice loop hike. Descend to the wash and your vehicle to retrace your drive through Split Mountain Gorge and to the paved road.

Jim Varnell

California trixis

Distance:	7 miles, out-and-back
Difficulty:	
Elevation gain/loss:	Up to 1000 feet
Hiking time:	5 hours
Agency:	CSP-CDD (ABDSP)
Notes:	4WD recommended; call ABDSP Visitor Center regarding road conditions; bring plenty of water
Trailhead GPS:	N32.97919, W116.21470
Optional map:	USGS 7.5-min *Arroyo Tapiado*
Atlas square:	M27
Directions:	(Ocotillo Wells) From CA-78 go south on Split Mountain Road for 8.1 miles. Turn right on Fish Creek Wash. Go 12.5 miles on the unpaved road to the signed entrance for Sandstone Canyon on left, and park.

Habitat(s):

Sandstone Canyon is one of several long canyons that stretch down the flanks of the rapidly eroding Vallecito Mountains. Frequent visitors to this part of the Anza-Borrego Desert consider Sandstone Canyon to be the most dramatic of these because of the high sheer sandstone cliffs found in this narrow canyon. It is also home to desert bighorn sheep and two uncommon sensitive plants, Orcutt's woody aster (*Xylorhiza orcuttii*) and the rush milkweed or ajamete (*Asclepias subulata*), making a visit here interesting for its biology as well as its dramatic geology.

Orcutt's woody aster is native to southern California and northern Baja California, Mexico. It prefers the dry canyons of the Sonora Desert and clay, rocky, and sandy substrates

and alkaline soils. While fairly common in the Fish Creek canyons, it is rare in most other areas of the state park. It is easily recognized in bloom with its lavender-to-pale-blue daisy flowers.

Rush milkweed is a native of southwestern deserts and northern Mexico that grows in sandy washes or arroyos. It is an erect perennial herb, usually 2-4 feet tall, with blue-green, mostly leafless, wand-like stems and creamy-white flowers when in bloom. It also has a milky sap. Milkweed contains poisonous toxins that do not bother the flashy monarch butterfly or the brightly-colored red and black milkweed bug (**family Lygaeidae**) that both exhibit warning coloration to potential predators. Birds learn quickly to avoid eating

Entrance to Sandstone Canyon

them. Milkweed bugs, like ladybugs, do not go through a complete metamorphosis in developing from egg to adult. The nymphs resemble the adults except they don't have wings or reproductive organs and lack the black spots of the adults. Nymphs grow to adults through a series of molts (shedding of skin) in stages called instars. Each instar lasts about a week. With each molt, they become larger until they reach adulthood.

Orcutt's woody aster

Begin hiking from your parked car at the mouth of the Sandstone Canyon even though a jeep road continues up Sandstone Canyon for another 2 miles or so. Watch for vehicles in the canyon, as it is a popular destination for off-roaders. The walls of the canyon close in rapidly as you progress west-northwest up the sandy wash. In places, sheer cliffs of layered sedimentary rock tower above the canyon floor. The layers are rocks known as fanglomerate (alluvial fan and conglomerate), mudstone and sandstone that accumulated over the course of the past 5 million years. Each layer represents mud, sand, gravel, and rocks eroded from the Vallecito Mountains. Some of the layers contain fossils that tell us about the animals that lived here in the past 1.5 million years, including the ancestor of the modern camel.

This hike follows the canyon 2.4 miles up the wash where there is a narrow slot canyon tributary on the left leading to June Wash Overlook. Take care as the slot canyon is easily missed. The slot canyon is so narrow that it does not appear to be an important tributary. It can be followed for more than 1 mile. The slot canyon widens and turns toward the southwest as you continue. It also becomes steeper with more vegetation, chiefly teddy-bear cholla, silver cholla, California barrel cactus, ocotillo, catclaw acacia, and brittlebush. Keep to the left

Don Fosket

Badlands view from June Wash saddle

at each fork to reach the June Wash Overlook. Enjoy the view, and then return to the same way to your vehicle.

If time allows, there are two tributary canyons to the east to explore during the trip to the June Wash Overlook and back. The first is a small tributary located 1.2 miles into Sandstone Canyon that leads to a usually dry fall, but after a storm, water may continue to flow over it and into a small pool at its base. The second tributary is at 2.1 miles and leads to an overlook of Olla Wash. Explore these tributaries before returning again to Sandstone Canyon.

Don Fosket

Bill Howell

Milkweed bug

Sandstone Canyon's narrow walls

Distance:	3 miles, out-and-back
Difficulty:	🏃🏃
Elevation gain/loss:	Up to100 feet
Hiking time:	2 hours
Agency:	CSP-CDD (ABDSP)
Notes:	Bring plenty of water
Trailhead GPS:	N33.04760, W116.43503
Optional map:	USGS 7.5-min *Earthquake Valley*
Atlas square:	K23
Directions:	(Scissors Crossing) From S-2 go west on an unsigned dirt road, 4.4 miles south of CA-78 and 0.4 mile south of Stagecoach Trails RV Park. Go 1.3 miles to the end of the road and park. The Cool Canyon access road is narrow and unimproved, mostly sandy road with a few rocks, but passenger cars should have no difficulty.

Habitat(s):

Cool Canyon is unlikely to be cool most of the year as far as the daytime temperature is concerned, but it is definitely cool in the colloquial sense. Hike up this east-west oriented canyon and observe the change from the Sonoran desert scrub vegetation of Earthquake Valley to the foothill chaparral transition zone where you will find junipers and manzanita in an otherwise arid desert setting. The geology is fascinating with large exposed expanses of colorful metamorphic Julian schist with numerous intrusions of igneous granite, schorl or black tourmaline, and quartz. The Julian schist rock formation held the gold that attracted miners to the Julian area in the 19th century.

There is no official trail. From the end of the road, simply start walking up the sandy wash. The vegetation near the start of the hike includes typical common subshrubs of the

low desert such as white bur-sage, cheesebush or burrobrush, creosote bush, ocotillo, and catclaw acacia. Sunflower-like plants commonly in flower here include brittlebush and Parish's golden-eyes (***Bahiopsis parishii***). Parish's golden-eyes is recognized by the bright yellow, 2-inch flowers and shiny green triangular-shaped leaves, mostly opposite, with grayish-white hairs. Stems have a whitish hoary cast to them. Cactus found here includes Gander's cholla (***Cylindropuntia ganderi***), one of the most common chollas in the Anza-Borrego area. It is often confused with silver cholla (***Cylindropuntia echinocarpa***) that is very similar in appearance but with distinct differences and not found in Cool Canyon. Both have greenish blooms, but the tips of the perianth (the part of the flower surrounding the sexual organs—petals and se-

Metamorphic rock with cacti

An old gnarled California juniper

pals) of Gander's cholla is reddish-brown. The most distinguishing feature is the position of the branches. Gander's cholla branches angle upward and reach for the sky while those of the silver cholla are spreading with many at right angles to the main stem.

The first mile is easy walking in soft sand with occasional small dry falls. Then a series of somewhat larger dry falls are encountered. If concerned, this might be a good place to turn back. The dry waterfalls can be surmounted without climbing skills, but a little bit of care is necessary. The canyon branches beyond these obstacles. Take the canyon to the right that heads in a westerly direction. Here the sandy walk continues with only a

modest amount of boulder hopping. On your left is a beautiful old California juniper with a gnarled trunk and a big-berry manzanita growing next to it. Junipers are common here, as is desert agave, but manzanita is relatively rare here.

At a little over 1.5 miles from the start of the hike, there is thick brush in the canyon bottom. One option is to navigate up onto the ridge on the right and continue to the point where Earthquake Valley can be viewed. A more adventurous alternative would be to hike to the top of Granite Mountain from here, but that is beyond the scope of this trip. This also may be the best place to turn around and head back.

Gander's cholla

Gander's cholla bloom

Distance:	4 miles, out-and-back
Difficulty:	🚶🚶🚶
Elevation gain/loss:	up to 1500 feet
Hiking time:	3 hours
Agency:	CSP-CDD (ABDSP)
Notes:	4WD recommended; call ABDSP Visitor Center regarding road conditions; bring plenty of water; trekking poles recommended; bring GPS or map and compass for route finding; best in October to May
Trailhead GPS:	N33.05046, W116.33309
Optional map:	USGS 7.5-min *Whale Peak*
Atlas square:	K25
Directions:	(Scissors Crossing) From S-2 go east on the signed Pinyon Mountain Area Road, 4.3 miles south of CA-78 and 0.3 mile south of Stagecoach Trails RV Park. Almost immediately the dirt road splits. Bear right and go 5.7 miles over areas of deep soft sand, bumps, deep ruts, and rocks, and park where there is a short spur road going off to the south toward Whale Peak. Be sure to note your mileage after turning off S-2 as there are similar spur roads going toward Whale Peak at 4.1 and 6.3 miles. All three have been used as starting points but the route starting at mile 5.7 is the most frequently used to Whale Peak, and the one described here.

Habitat(s):

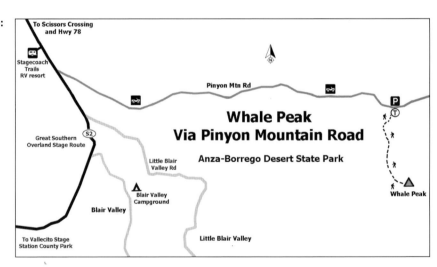

Whale Peak (5349'), though not the highest peak in the Anza-Borrego Desert State Park, is high enough to offer spectacular views of much of the park and beyond to mountain ranges in Mexico and Arizona. It is also high enough to support an extensive beautiful forest of miniature trees that includes the single-leaf pinyon (*Pinus monophylla*). Pinyons are usually found in association with California juniper, which is a cypress. The biome they create is called a pinyon-juniper woodland. The single-leaf pinyon is found in pinyon-juniper

woodlands or chaparral above 3000 feet on desert and mountain slopes.

The single-leaf pinyon is unusual because it has a single leaf or needle. Other pines have three, four, or five leaves or needles. Common pines in San Diego County with three leaves or needles in a bundle include the Jeffrey or yellow (*Pinus Jeffreyi*), Coulter (*Pinus coulteri*), and Pacific ponderosa (*Pinus ponderosa*). They are best identified by their cones rather than their needles. A Parry pinyon (*Pinus quadrifolia*) generally has four leaves. Pines

Don Fosket

Summit panorama

with five leaves or needles include the Torrey pine (**Pinus torreyana**) and the sugar pine (**Pinus lambertiana**).

Pinyon pines were a major staple for desert Indians. Because of fierce competition with animals and birds for the cones, the Kumeyaay Indians picked the cones in early summer before they were fully ripened. They roasted the cones in a pit which would cause them to open. The Kumeyaay were careful to collect the cones before the heaviest drop occurred, so as to beat the animals and birds. The Kumeyaay collected the cones by knocking them down from the trees. They ate the nuts whole, ground, or made into a mush. They would also store them for later use or as a trade food. Pine nuts were among the four most important foods that desert Indians gathered, which also included desert agave, mesquite, and acorns. Pinyon needles were used in basketry and pine pitch was used as an adhesive for mending pottery and baskets.

At mile 5.7, start hiking up the steep, boulder-choked canyon straight ahead. Consistently look back for landmarks while climbing around and over boulders to help guide you on the return trip. Occasionally stacked rocks or ducks mark the path. After climbing about 0.25 mile, there is a sandy flat. Starting at this point, there will be an obvious path created by hundreds of other hikers who have ventured up this mountain. Although marked with frequent ducks, don't rely too much on them as there are numerous other routes going in various directions, also marked with ducks. This hike offers an excellent opportunity to practice route finding skills.

There are three more ridges to climb before reaching a point where the final ascent to the top of the broad, relatively flat, Whale Peak begins. Explore the peak area to find the best vantage points to view the Salton Sea to the east, Agua Caliente County Park to the west some 4000 feet below, and Borrego Valley, the Santa Rosa Mountains, and beyond to Mount San Jacinto to the northeast. Be sure and sign the register at the summit.

Although the views are inspiring, be sure to take some time to observe the variety of plant life in this juniper-pinyon woodland. In addition to the single-leaf pinyon and the California juniper, you will also find desert scrub oak, huge Mojave yuccas, an abundance of Gander's cholla as well as the occasional beavertail cactus, and desert apricot.

Once you have thoroughly explored the peak area, return to your car the way you came. Be careful when selecting a route based on ducks or you could end up many miles from your vehicle. If you paid attention for landmarks on the way up, it will be easier to find your way down.

Don Fosket

Single-leaf pinyon

Distance:	8.75 miles, out-and-back
Difficulty:	🚶🚶🚶🚶🚶
Elevation gain/loss:	Up to 2600 feet
Hiking time:	7 hours
Agency:	CSP-CDD (ABDSP)
Notes:	Usually okay for 2WD; call ABDSP Visitor Center regarding road conditions; bring plenty of water; overnight option; if camping—no open fires; boulder scrambling; route finding
Trailhead GPS:	N33.01963, W116.35958
Optional map:	USGS 7.5-min *Whale Peak*
Atlas square:	L25
Directions:	(Scissors Crossing) From S-2 go east at the Blair Valley turnoff, 5.9 miles south of CA-78. Follow the dirt road into and around Blair Valley for 2.7 miles. Turn left at the signed fork with the Ghost Mountain turnoff. Go 2.4 miles following the sign to Morteros and Pictographs that leads to the Pictograph trailhead in Little Blair Valley. The road can be muddy and/or sandy depending on recent weather conditions.

Habitat(s):

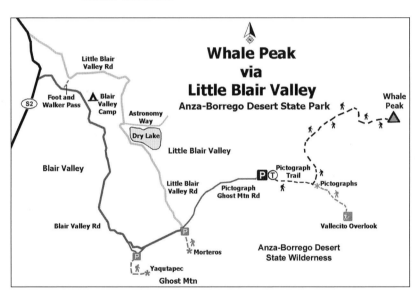

Whale Peak stands thousands of feet above the surrounding desert floor and features an abundance of single-leaf pinyon pine, California juniper (*Juniperus californica*), and Parry's bear-grass (*Nolina parryi*). The summit is an island oasis for native plants and animals more comfortable with cooler temperatures and more moisture. This was also a seasonal home for Kumeyaay families for millennia who gathered pinyon pine nuts, juniper berries, and fruit from the nolina. Look for these plants on the hike.

California juniper is a dioecious shrub or small multi-trunked tree found on dry desert slopes and flats of pinyon-juniper woodlands. It has either pollen cones or bluish seed cones. Native Americans gathered and consumed berries between June and August each year, although individual trees only produced berries every other year. They ate the berries fresh, or dried them for later use. During times of famine, they ate the inner bark. The bark can be used in a tea to treat colds, fevers, and constipation. The Kumeyaay used an infusion of leaves and bark as a relief from hangovers and for high blood pressure as well as using it to treat hiccups. They also used the bark in making clothing and mattresses.

California juniper with berries or female seed cones

Parry's bear-grass is not a grass but a no-lina, which is a yucca-like species that grows exceptionally tall on Whale Peak. Nolinas differ from yuccas in having huge clusters of long, thin, and pliant fibrous leaves that are not spiny tipped and do not shed. Nolinas and yuccas are in separate families. The common name bear-grass probably refers to the grass-like appearance of the leaves. Flowering stalks may reach 10 feet and may be 1-2 feet across. Nolinas are generally dioecious, having unisexual flowers that distinguish male and female plants. Native Americans baked nolina, much like desert agave and yucca, but it has a bitter taste. Like the yucca, its flowers also attract moths who feed on the plant in the larval stage. Parry's bear-grass is the host plant for a nolina moth (*Mesepiola specca*), a cousin of the yucca moth. The flowers also attract bees and various insects.

The open cross-country terrain of Whale Peak invites exploration in every direction. For backpackers prepared to spend the night, Whale Peak provides solitude and exceptional sunrise and sunset views. Its triangular evening shadow thrusts out miles to east and is a sight to remember. Following winter storms, the upper elevations may even be snow covered for a few days.

Begin the hike on the well-defined Picto-graph Trail that starts in the far southeast quadrant of Little Blair Valley. A short, gradual ascent up a ravine leads to upper Smuggler Canyon, an open wash trending north-south

California juniper with male pollen cones

Good campsites on the summit

that defines the western base of Whale Peak. The namesake pictographs, a form of Kumeyaay rock art painted on the east face of a large boulder, are located less than 1 mile from the parking area and are well worth a visit on the way to Whale Peak or on your return.

The most direct route departs from Pictograph Trail and heads east approximately 0.7 mile from the start. There is no defined turnoff, but you may see informal use-trails leading easterly. Once in the wash, follow it north-northeast as it arcs around to a large cove and an unnamed canyon leading upward. Here, at 3600 feet elevation, the ascent starts in earnest as you scramble over and around boulders and pass short, twisting sandy benches on the canyon floor. If you encounter an obstacle, it is easy to find a path by climbing out onto the adjoining slope, typically on the north side. Watch out for cholla, yucca, and desert agave; avoid their sharp spines.

Eventually the canyon opens up and intersects an unmarked trail at 4600 feet, approximately 3 miles from the trailhead. Turn right and follow a meandering ducked trail for another mile as it climbs gradually to a saddle at 5000 feet. From here scramble up the boulder strewn slope to the east for the final 400 feet to reach the summit plateau. The true high point is 0.2 mile of level walking to the east, identified by a steel sign placed by a Boy Scout troop. A register is here at the summit. Numerous level and wind-protected campsites are available here.

Once on top, drop your pack, have a snack, wander around a bit to take in this patch of high desert Eden. To the southwest is the steep eastern escarpment of the Laguna Mountains and Monument Peak (6271'), while Granite Mountain (5633') stands solitary and prominent to the west, less than 300 feet higher than Whale Peak (5349'). To the east are Vallecito and Fish Creek mountains. To the south, far below, are Vallecito Valley and Carrizo Valley. If this is a dayhike, reverse your route. Be sure to visit the pictographs if you missed them on the way up. If you came with provisions for an overnight stay, set up camp, enjoy sunset and your dinner, and take in the incomparable night sky. Note that no ground fires are allowed.

Weathered summit sign

Distance:	1.6 miles, out-and-back
Difficulty:	🚶
Elevation gain/loss:	Minimal
Hiking time:	1 hour
Agency:	CSP-CDD (ABDSP)
Notes:	Usually okay for 2WD; call ABDSP Visitor Center regarding road conditions; bring plenty of water
Trailhead GPS:	N33.01965, W116.35983
Optional map:	USGS 7.5-min *Whale Peak*
Atlas square:	L25
Directions:	(Scissors Crossing) From S-2 go east at the Blair Valley turnoff, 5.9 miles south of CA-78. Follow the dirt road into and around Blair Valley for 2.7 miles. Turn left at the signed fork with the Ghost Mountain turnoff. Go 2.4 miles following the sign to Morteros and Pictographs that leads to the Pictograph trailhead in Little Blair Valley.

Habitat(s):

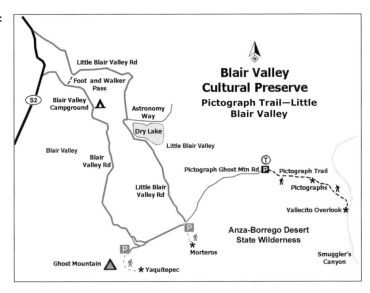

The Kumeyaay of the area painted the Little Blair Valley Pictographs hundreds of years ago. The pictographs are unusual for their well-executed yellow and red symbolic designs that include diamond chains and chevrons, typical of Luiseño rock art. The designs reflect the influence of this Indian group on the neighboring Kumeyaay who chose to use this style of rock art within their territory. Anthropologists are still conjecturing whether they served a specific purpose, such as part of a puberty ceremony, or whether they simply reflect the inclinations of the artist. The pictographs are included in the 4757-acre Little Blair Valley Cultural Preserve that was created in December 2010. This pictograph site is the only one in Anza-Borrego Desert State Park that is advertised to the public.

The hiking trail begins next to an interpretive sign. This is the steepest part of the trail, which goes over a low divide into Smuggler Canyon. Because of the higher elevation of the Blair Valley area, both California juniper and Mojave yucca grow here. The typical desert plants along the trail include creosote bush, brittlebush, ocotillo, desert agave, desert-lavender, catclaw acacia, and various species of cholla. A nice selection of annuals bloom here in spring.

Annual wildflower seeds can lie dormant in the soil for years until there is sufficient rain to allow them to quickly grow, sprout,

Diana Lindsay

Pictographs

bloom, and reproduce, leaving seeds for the next opportune time, before they die. They go through their whole cycle before the summer heats up. Desert chicory (***Rafinesquia neomexicana***) is one of the annuals that is easy to identify with its small daisy-like flower in the sunflower family that has white petals that appear as if they have been trimmed with pinking shears. The ray flowers become longer as they near the outer edge. Desert chicory prefers creosote bush scrub and gravelly or sandy soils.

A small mammal that will be looking for annual seeds to eat is the nocturnal kangaroo rat. Highly adapted to desert living, it is easy to identify by its long tail with a tuft at the end, and large hind feet that allows it to jump like a kangaroo. This large-headed and large-eyed herbivore can survive without drinking any water. It draws all the water it needs from the seeds it eats. The kangaroo rat fills its cheek pouches with seeds and carries them back to its burrow. Often their burrows, as well as those of other rodents, can be found at the base of shrubs, such as a creosote bush, where the root system provides structure to their burrows. The shrubs also give them cover from predators when outside the burrows. The deep burrows help them to avoid the extremes of temperatures at the surface. Four species occur in San Diego County, two in the Anza-Borrego Desert—the small Mer-

riam's kangaroo rat (***Dipodomys merriami***) and the large desert kangaroo rat (***Dipodomys deserti***). The former has an additional competitive advantage, even over other kangaroo rats, in its use of spatial memory. It can remember the location of all of its buried food caches in the absence of any odor.

Look for a prominent boulder on the west side of the streambed less than 1 mile from the trailhead. Grinding areas may be seen next to the rock art. The large boulder may have served as part of a shelter. Most visitors turn around here and head back to their vehicles, missing an extra bonus found by continuing another 0.5 mile where an ancient Kumeyaay seasonal camp was located. To the right are many flat boulder ledges where bedrock mortars are scattered. Where the canyon narrows, there is a low point that may have pooled water supplying the local Kumeyaay hundreds of years ago when this desert was less dry. Pass through the narrow area with boulders to the top edge of a dry waterfall. From this perch a stunning view into the Carrizo Valley dramatically opens up, making this a favorite hidden surprise for many park visitors. The Vallecito Stage Station is also visible from this overlook. Do not attempt to climb down the dry waterfall. It has a sharp drop-off and is slippery. After taking in the view, follow the trail back to your vehicles.

Don Fosket

Desert chicory

Distance:	1 mile, out-and-back
Difficulty:	🚶
Elevation gain/loss:	Minimal
Hiking time:	1 hour
Agency:	CSP-CDD (ABDSP)
Notes:	Usually okay for 2WD; call ABDSP Visitor Center regarding road conditions; bring plenty of water
Trailhead GPS:	N33.00890, W116.37833
Optional map:	USGS 7.5-min *Whale Peak*
Atlas square:	L24
Directions:	(Scissors Crossing) From S-2 go east at the Blair Valley turnoff, 5.9 miles south of CA-78. Follow the dirt road into and around Blair Valley for 2.7 miles. Turn left at the signed fork with the Ghost Mountain turnoff. Go 0.8 mile to the trailhead and parking area for the Morteros Trail.

Habitat(s):

The Morteros Trail is part of the 4757-acre Little Blair Valley Cultural Preserve that was created in December 2010. The area was a seasonal home for the Kumeyaay who harvested and processed the desert agave and juniper berries found in this area. At the trailhead there is both an interpretive sign and a trail guide entitled "The 'Ehmuu—Morteros Trail." There are nine signed sites along this walk to help one understand the significance of this Kumeyaay site. The wealth of cultural materials in this small area is significant and is well interpreted. It is also protected by law, and no collection is allowed.

From the parking area the trail heads to an area peppered with boulders where there are several grinding areas. The kitchen areas among the boulders display both bedrock mortar holes (morteros) and smooth grinding areas (slicks) where women processed collected food resources using either a large stone (pestle) or a smaller hand-held stone (mano).

There are several sites with smaller pounded holes (cupules) that resemble mini-mortero holes that were probably made in association with various ceremonies, such as puberty or coming of age. There is a rock shelter that may have been used to store foods, provide shelter from the elements, or was enclosed as part of a ceremonial sweathouse. The highlight of the trail is 0.5 mile out where a stunning Kumeyaay rock art is found. The sweeping lines of the black pictograph resemble stick figures. The exact meaning of this art is unknown.

Split rock formation

Morteros

The area is rich with plant life. The hillsides are covered with the gray-green rosettes and tall flower stalks of the desert agave (**Agave deserti**), known as 'emally by the Kumeyaay, who harvested this plant. Along the trail are darkened areas in the sand indicating where the agave had been roasted. Desert agave was a major staple for the Indians who used every part of this plant for some purpose, whether it was for food, fiber to make rope, medicine, firewood, or using the sharp spike at the tip of the leaf blade as an awl for basket making, as a needle with attached fiber thread, or as a tool for tattooing. The juice of the root was sometimes applied to fresh wounds as it has antibiotic and anti-inflammatory properties. Only men harvested the agave because of the difficulty of extracting it from the ground. Each spring Native Americans used to come from all around to harvest the newly sprouting flower stalks of agaves. The agaves cooked for several days in heated, rock-lined pits before they were dug up and consumed or dried and stored for later consumption. Baked agave has the flavor of baked yams or pineapple. The Greek name *agave* means noble and refers to the size of the plant and its flower stalks. Look for darkened ground that indicates where agaves had been roasted.

Other common plants in this area include the higher elevation California juniper, jojoba, Mojave yucca, and ephedra or Mormon tea.

Desert agave

Desert agave bloom

Distance:	2 miles, out-and-back
Difficulty:	🏃🏃
Elevation gain/loss:	Up to 500 feet
Hiking time:	Up to 2 hours
Agency:	CSP-CDD (ABDSP)
Notes:	Usually okay for 2WD; call ABDSP Visitor Center regarding road conditions; bring plenty of water; trekking poles recommended
Trailhead GPS:	N33.00349, W116.38987
Optional map:	USGS 7.5-min *Earthquake Valley*
Atlas square:	L24
Directions:	(Scissors Crossing) From S-2 go east at the Blair Valley turnoff, 5.9 miles south of CA-78. Follow the dirt road into and around Blair Valley for 2.7 miles to the Marshal South trailhead. The road can be muddy and/or sandy depending on recent weather conditions.

Habitat(s):

A rugged 1-mile trail up the Ghost Mountain ridge leads to Yaquitepec (3215'), the ruins of an adobe home named and built by poet/author/artist Marshal South and his wife Tanya, about 200 feet below the summit of waterless Ghost Mountain (3412'). The Souths began their 17-year homestead adventure soon after the start of the Great Depression. They wanted solitude and the freedom to live their chosen lifestyle, unencumbered by clothing or civilization. They raised and homeschooled three children on the isolated desert mountaintop. The great experiment ended in 1947. Tanya and the children moved to San Diego. A year later, South died in Julian.

South wrote his popular monthly columns about their experiment in primitive living for *Desert Magazine* for nine years, which have been reprinted in book form as *Marshal South*

and the Ghost Mountain Chronicles. He chronicled how his family survived and thrived under the most primitive conditions. Water had to be hauled up to the adobe to supplement what was caught in catch basins when it occasionally rained. The catch basins are still there next to the adobe ruins. The old homestead is now part of Anza-Borrego Desert State Park.

South introduced a whole generation to the desert through his many timeless articles about the desert's natural features. Among the many plants he described and harvested on Ghost Mountain is chia (***Salvia columbariae***). Chia was one of the most important seed plants for desert Indians. It is known as *awol* to the Kumeyaay and *pasal* to the Cahuilla. The two groups had different techniques for gathering the seeds of this small and nutritious plant in the mint family. The Kumeyaay collected the stalks,

Yaquitepec ruins

which they dried and stored and later beat against a basketry tray to shake lose the seeds. The Cahuilla beat the plants with a seed beater so that the seeds would fall into a collection basket. After being hulled and winnowed, the seeds could then be roasted and parched and ground into flour for mush or cakes or stored in ollas for later use. Chia seeds were eaten before a long journey to sustain extra exertion. The seeds are 20% protein and 34% oil.

South also wrote several popular novels, all published in London. Two of the novels incorporate sites and legends of the Anza-Borrego area, especially stories involved with the Butterfield Overland Stage, which greatly interested him. His two western novels have been reprinted as *Marshal South Rides Again*.

The steep schistose trail up Ghost Mountain is much the same as when used by the Souths to haul up water and supplies. It is well marked,

Yaquitepec in 1943

Marshal South and desert agave

the granitic rocks near the ruins. Some pottery shards may be visible. Also note the one Mojave yucca in front of the house that was originally carried up the trail by the Souths and transplanted on the mountaintop.

A visit to the old South homestead is best during the cooler desert season from November through April. Ghost Mountain's uplift is created by the Elsinore Fault Zone. Highway S-2 basically follows the trace of the fault through this area.

Chia

beginning at an interpretive sign found at the trailhead. Mojave yucca, creosote bush, ocotillo, California juniper, jojoba or goatnut, cholla, beavertail cactus, desert agave, and brittlebush line the many switchbacks heading in a general southwest direction. As elevation increases with a widening view of Blair Valley and its playa, the yuccas gradually disappear as the trail wraps completely around the ridge turning to the northeast. A short climb over a boulder trail leads to the ruins and a spectacular view of the valley below and the Laguna Mountains to the west. A short walk southeast past the ruins of an adobe kiln, used by the Souths in pottery making, reveals the undulating Vallecito Badlands to the east. South described the view of the "old Vanished Sea" from his mountaintop as "rolling blue in its old bed" when the light is right at morning and night. Just below the ridge are Vallecito County Park and the old adobe Butterfield Vallecito stage station.

All cultural and natural features on Ghost Mountain are protected by the state park and can't be collected. Old agave roasting pits, used by both the Souths and the earlier Indians who once called this area home, are visible along the trail and near the adobe ruins. Look for old Indian grinding morteros and slicks on

Chia bloom

Distance:	9 miles, out-and-back
Difficulty:	🚶🚶🚶🚶🚶
Elevation gain/loss:	Up to 2500 feet
Hiking time:	6 hours
Agency:	CSP-CDD (ABDSP)
Trail use:	Bicycles can only use part of this trail
Notes:	4WD recommended; call ABDSP Visitor Center regarding road conditions; bring plenty of water
Trailhead GPS:	N33.01486, W116.49502
Optional map:	USGS 7.5-min *Earthquake Valley*
Atlas square:	L22
Directions:	(Scissors Crossing) From S-2 go west on the signed dirt road for Oriflamme Canyon (the start of the Mason Valley Truck Trail), 9.8 miles south of CA-78. Go 1.9 miles. At the branch for the Rodriguez Truck Trail stay left. Go 0.9 mile to where a road descends a short distance to trees lining Oriflamme Creek and park. Watch out for soft sand, boulders and, after storms, mud or even running water. Part of the road is in the usually dry Vallecito Creek bed.

Habitat(s):

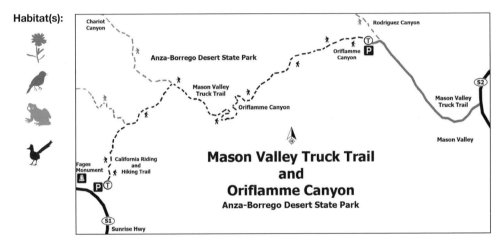

Oriflamme was the name of a side-wheel steamship that brought the first miners to the coast in 1870 during the Julian gold rush. The steamship regularly stopped at San Diego Harbor as part of its route between San Francisco and the Atlantic Ocean. Oriflamme was also the name first given to a mine worked in the area, and the canyon and mountain soon followed.

The name, however, has little to do with the historic and scenic attributes of the canyon, which are considerable. It was the main route between Kumeyaay villages in the desert and summer encampments in the Laguna Mountains. It was the route Col. Pedro Fages took in 1772 while searching for army deserters, making him the first European to set foot in the Anza-Borrego Desert who lived to write about it. In the 1850s Oriflamme Canyon was a leg on a transcontinental mail route called The San Antonio and San Diego Mail Line. It came to be known as the Jackass Mail because mules were used to pull wagons up the steep road through the canyon. Later, cattle ranchers who had settled near Vallecito built a rough road through Oriflamme Canyon to move their cattle to summer pasture in the Laguna Mountains. Much of that road still exists as the Mason Valley Truck Trail and is part of the route of this hike.

If time and energy are available before beginning the hike, explore Oriflamme Canyon's stream course, a riparian habitat containing a lush growth of western sycamores,

Descending into the canyon

willows, western cottonwoods, and mule fat. Indian grinding areas are found among the boulders as well as evidence of an old road camp. In wet years a bubbling stream flows over granite boulders and there is a small waterfall about 1 mile up the canyon.

Begin the actual hike from the parked vehicle, following the truck trail west-southwest as it rises rather steeply up the north side of the canyon, gaining about 1500 feet of elevation in 1.6 miles. The reward is the view down to the Oriflamme stream course, a lively green most of the year but developing yellow and orange colors in the fall. The vegetation initially is typical high desert including California juniper, cholla, prickly-pear cactus, Mojave yucca, and desert agave. Once above the canyon, the vegetation changes into montane chaparral dominated by scrub oaks, birch-leaf mountain-mahogany, chamise, Parish's goldenbush, California buckwheat, Eastwood's manzanita, and many others. When seen at a distance the higher hills appear to be covered with an olive green velvet blanket.

Continue up the road as it enters a side canyon, leaving Oriflamme Canyon in about 0.5 mile. As it leaves the canyon, there is a broad saddle that marks the divide between Oriflamme and Chariot canyons. The road becomes nearly flat and the hiking is easy. Look for a sign for the California Riding and Hiking Trail (CRHT) off to the left and take

it. The next 0.7 mile is also nearly flat, but just ahead is another ascent, this time rising up 500 feet in 0.5 mile to the divide between Oriflamme and Cuyamaca drainages. After 3.85 miles from the start of the hike, the dirt road is left behind as the Pacific Crest Trail is briefly joined, also signed as the CRHT. Continue following the CRHT west-southwest through a series of deer grass meadows to the Fages Monument on the Sunrise Highway (S-1), 4.56 miles from the start of the hike. Reverse direction to return to your vehicle, unless arrangements were made to pick you up at the monument.

If attempting this hike from the Sunrise Highway (S-1), just follow the reverse of the above directions. The Sunrise Highway option is recommended for those without a 4WD. Drive a short distance east from Julian to the junction of CA-78 and CA-79. Go right (south) on CA-79 and continue 6 miles to the Sunrise Highway junction on the left. Continue 1.6 miles on S-1 to the Fages Monument and a roadside parking area on the left. This may also be done as a 4.5-mile one-way trek with a shuttle arrangement.

The trail in Oriflamme Canyon

Distance:	1.5 miles, loop
Difficulty:	🚶🚶
Elevation gain/loss:	Up to 400 feet
Hiking time:	1 hour
Agency:	San Diego County
Notes:	Day-use fee; bring plenty of water; some boulder scrambling
Trailhead GPS:	N32.94849, W116.30326
Optional map:	USGS 7.5-min *Agua Caliente Springs*
Atlas square:	M26
Directions:	(Agua Caliente County Park) From S-2 go south to the entrance of Agua Caliente County Park, 26.5 miles north of I-8 and 21.8 miles south of CA-78. The trailhead is next to campsite 140, across from the shuffleboard court where day-use parking is available.

Habitat(s):

Agua Caliente County Park is one of the special places in the Anza-Borrego Desert area that has wide appeal, offering not only a very popular hiking trail but also full camping facilities and both outdoor and indoor pools with geothermally-heated mineral water to soak in after a vigorous hike through a beautiful canyon. This small county park is tucked into the much larger Anza-Borrego Desert State Park. It is located on a spur of the very active Elsinore fault that causes heated water to percolate to the surface in springs that dot this portion of the Tierra Blanca Mountains.

The hike described here reverses the normal designated Moonlight Canyon Trail loop that begins across from the shuffleboard courts and next to campsite No. 140. This reverse loop allows everyone to experience Moonlight Canyon while giving the option of turning

back at the more challenging section, which is at the end of this hike or at the beginning of the normal designated hike. Challenges include traversing boulders and short dry waterfalls.

From the signed Moonlight Canyon Trail End near the caravan area and campsite No. 63, head in a southeasterly direction across the flat, sandy desert through tall ocotillo, white bur-sage, desert agave, creosote bush, cholla, and possibly masses of wildflowers if the timing of your visit is right. The trail turns south as it enters Moonlight Canyon. The canyon becomes progressively narrower as you proceed. After you have hiked about 0.5 mile, you come to The Narrows where the canyon walls are only a few feet apart. As you go through The Narrows, note the white granite rocks for which the Tierra Blanca Mountains and Moonlight Canyon were named. This is also a

Chuparosa

Male Costa's hummingbird

wet area where year-round water permits lush vegetation to grow. Plants here include mesquite, catclaw acacia, desert-willow, apricot mallow, chuparosa, and desert-lavender. While some of these are rather prickly, you can enjoy the scent of the desert-lavender and the colorful red chuparosa (***Justicia californica***) almost year-round.

The chuparosa takes its name from the Spanish *chupa* and *rosa*, literally to suck red, referring to its red tubular flower that is a favorite of hummingbirds and also earning it another common name—hummingbird plant. Costa's hummingbird (***Calypte costae***) is one of the hummingbirds that you might see. It is the most desert-adapted hummingbird of North America. Costa's primarily feed on nectar from brightly-colored flowers including chuparosa, ocotillo, red penstemon, and desert agave. They will also eat small insects. Males have an iridescent violet head and throat, while females are plain green above and whitish below.

In less than 0.2 mile the canyon widens somewhat and you resume hiking over soft sand. Turn back here if you want to avoid the more challenging section of the trail. The trail leaves Moonlight Canyon 0.85 mile from the start and proceeds up a smaller tributary canyon. If you are still in Moonlight Canyon beyond this point you will come to a large red sign saying "DO NOT ENTER" indicating a dangerous route that is best not taken. If you find yourself there, you missed the turn. Back up a bit and look for the trail nearer the west side of the canyon. The trail rises more steeply

in the next 0.25 mile until it reaches the top of a saddle. As you are climbing, note the numerous large California barrel cacti and abundant desert agave. It is downhill from this point to the campground, but take care getting down the dry falls.

Moonlight Trail

Distance:	5 miles, out-and-back
Difficulty:	
Elevation gain/loss:	Up to 800 feet
Hiking time:	4 hours
Agency:	BLM-CDD; San Diego County
Notes:	Day-use fee; bring plenty of water; trekking poles recommended
Trailhead GPS:	N32.94843, W116.30324
Optional map:	USGS 7.5-min *Agua Caliente Springs*
Atlas square:	M26
Directions:	(Agua Caliente County Park) From S-2 go south to the entrance of Agua Caliente County Park, 26.5 miles north of I-8 and 21.8 miles south of CA-78. The trailhead is next to campsite 140, across from the shuffleboard court where day-use parking is available. This is also the trailhead for the Moonlight Canyon Loop Trail.
Habitat(s):	

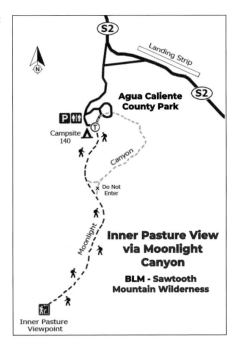

The Inner Pasture is a remarkable geographic feature of the Anza-Borrego Desert. It is a large, isolated, almost flat plain that appears to be completely surrounded by mountains. The jagged Sawtooth Mountains rise steeply on its southern and western boundary while the Tierra Blanca Mountains rise up sharply on its northern and eastern flanks. In the recent past, cattle ranchers used it as a secure place to graze their cattle, but before that era it was home, perhaps for a thousand years, to a band of Kumeyaay. During your visit to this remote location you can enjoy a silence and solitude you are unlikely to find in San Diego.

Keep in mind that generations of people once lived here. Evidence of their presence is easily found in the sands and rocks of the Inner Pasture. All artifacts are protected by law—enjoy and leave them where they are found. There is also a chance to see desert bighorn sheep and abundant wildflowers in a wet year.

Moonlight Canyon is in the Tierra Blanca Mountains near Agua Caliente County Park. The canyon runs roughly east and west. The hike begins at the northern end of the Moonlight Canyon Loop Trail, next to campsite No. 140. The well-marked and heavily-traveled loop trail takes you up an unnamed can-

View of Inner Pasture

yon to a saddle and then down a Moonlight Canyon tributary before it enters the named canyon. The loop trail continues to the east down the canyon, eventually returning to the campground.

To get to the Inner Pasture you need to go right at the saddle of the loop trail, in a westerly direction to follow Moonlight Canyon toward Inner Pasture. However, at the turnoff to Moonlight Canyon, there is a large sign posted stating "DO NOT ENTER." The sign warns of a 30-foot dry fall a short distance up the canyon that is not climbable and very dangerous for the average boulder hopper. Don't try it! Instead, you will have to work your way around this dry waterfall. If you have gotten this far, go back the way you came to a small narrow canyon on your left—the one you should have taken originally. Here you will see a small red flag and a stack of stones or ducks marking a little-used trail that leads up and over the ridge dividing this canyon from Moonlight Canyon, reaching Moonlight Canyon at a point above the dry falls that are not climbable.

Now that you have been warned, you can avoid this problem by taking the somewhat easier, improvised trail that leads off to the right as you start to descend from the saddle, 0.8 mile into the hike. Again follow the ducks and keep a close eye on the faint trail, and it will lead you to Moonlight Canyon further up from the dry falls barrier. From here the trail is easily followed, though it involves periodic boulder hopping and a few dry falls to climb, but also with long stretches of easy walking through sand. At about 2.5 miles into the hike

you suddenly come to a saddle overlooking the Inner Pasture and the end of Moonlight Canyon. This is a good place for lunch and perhaps a rest while enjoying the view. Return the way you came, or if you want to explore further and extend your hike by several miles, follow the canyon down into Inner Pasture for a quick exploration before returning. If you head west in Inner Pasture, and don't mind hiking about 4 miles farther, you can explore the remains of a cattleman's rock house built against a rock base southwest of Moonlight Canyon.

As you climb over rocks on this hike, look for reptiles that might be hiding in the rock crevices or sunning themselves. If you are lucky, you might see a common chuckwalla (*Sauromalus ater*), considered a delicacy by the Native Americans who hunted for them. When threatened, the common chuckwalla will seek a rock crevice and lodge its body into the space. If a predator attempts to pull it out, it will gulp air to inflate its body, making it difficult to pull out. The Indians would find a sharp stick or use a tool with a hook to puncture the chuckwalla, deflating it and forcing it to release pressure, so that it could be pull out. It was then cooked and eaten or smoked and dried for later use. The common chuckwalla is the largest lizard of the Anza-Borrego area at 5-9 inches from snout to vent. It is the third largest reptile of North America—the largest is the gila monster. The common chuckwalla is a flat lizard with a large round belly. Males usually have a darker head and body with a lighter cream-colored tail. Females are lighter with a banded tail. The tail will regenerate if detached. They like to eat creosote flowers and various plants.

Common chuckwalla

Distance:	10 miles, out-and-back
Difficulty:	🏃🏃🏃🏃🏃
Elevation gain/loss:	up to 1300 feet
Hiking time:	7 hours
Agency:	CSP-CDD (ABDSP)
Notes:	4WD recommended; call ABDSP Visitor Center regarding road conditions; bring plenty of water; soft sand at beginning of hike
Trailhead GPS:	N32.93839, W116.26247
Optional map:	USGS 7.5-min *Agua Caliente Springs*
Atlas square:	N27
Directions:	(Ocotillo) From S-2 go east on June Wash, 22.8 miles north of I-8 and 24.5 miles south of CA-78. Go 0.5 mile up June Wash and park where the road takes a 90-degree turn to the right. This dirt road has some soft sand. If concerned about the sand, park at the entrance to June Wash and walk the 0.5 mile to this point to begin the hike.

Habitat(s):

Ironwood Wash and Canyon are not on any map printed before March 11, 2010. That was the date that the US Board on Geographic Names unanimously approved the official naming of this wash and canyon, including its East Fork, as originally proposed by Canebrake Community resident Frank Colver in the fall of 2008. Colver counted over 100 ironwood trees in the wash and canyon. He followed the correct protocol to properly assign a geographic name to an area, including an endorsement and approval for the name by state park officials.

In the application, Colver also listed other features, including multiple palisades and side canyons in its serpentine reach toward Whale Peak. The higher reaches of the canyon have views toward June Wash and the Mud Palisades. The wash flows south to its confluence with Vallecito Creek. Ironwood Wash and Canyon are within the protected state wilderness area. No vehicles, bicycles, or dogs are allowed in this area and nothing may be removed. Leave only footprints.

The desert ironwood (***Olneya tesota***) is an evergreen tree that is a member of the pea family. It only grows in the Sonora Desert of southwestern Arizona, southern California, and northwestern Mexico in washes and low valleys along seeps under 2500 feet in elevation. It is considered somewhat of an indicator

Hiking in Ironwood Wash

species of the greater Sonora Desert, although it appears less frequently in our Colorado Desert area west of the Colorado River. The flower resembles a sweet pea. Flowers vary in color from cream to lavender and bloom from April to May. Leaves are bluish-green and are pinnately compound. Pinnate leaves are like feathers with leaflets on each side of a common axis. A compound leaf has a number of leaflets on a common stalk. At the base of each pinnate leaf petiole that attaches the leaf blade to the stem are two spines. The abundance of ironwoods in this canyon is noteworthy. Ironwoods create a microhabitat around them, providing food and shade for animals, including various insects, birds, reptiles, and rodents, which in turn attract various predators such as hawks, rattlesnakes, bobcats, and coyotes. Nitrogen-fixing nodules in their root system combine with leaf litter to make a rich soil and fertilizer for surrounding plants. Desert ironwoods are pollinated by native bees.

The key to finding the wash and canyon from the parking area is to scan the area looking toward Whale Peak and to look for a line of ironwood trees in the distance that are in a wash. Hike toward the ironwood trees and keep in the same wash. After about 3 miles, there will be a fork. Stay in the main canyon, and do not take the East Fork, which does not have any ironwood trees. From this point, the canyon walls begin to emerge and the force of flashfloods that have carved deeply into the banks becomes evident. Some of the ironwood roots along the banks are exposed.

As one walks deeper and higher into the canyon, the walls constrict and large palisades begin to form. The canyon curves and bends with side canyons becoming evident. At about mile 4 within the main canyon, there is a small opening to a side canyon to the left that can be explored for about 0.5 mile where there is a hole in the sandstone wall through which the sky is visible. Beyond this side exploration, the main canyon continues to narrow as it approaches the base of Whale Peak. When it becomes too difficult to hike because of tumbled boulders, it is a good place to turn around and head back down the canyon.

In addition to the many ironwood trees, there are mini-forests of teddy-bear cholla. The hillsides have many fine large specimens of California barrel cactus. Chuparosa, brittlebush, cheesebush or burrobrush, ocotillo, desert agave, and catclaw acacia are found in the canyon floor.

Frank Colver in Ironwood Wash

Ironwood tree leaves and thorns

Distance:	8.7 or 6.7 miles, out-and-back or loop depending on parking area
Difficulty:	🚶🚶🚶🚶 or 🚶🚶🚶🚶🚶
Elevation gain/loss:	Up to 1000 feet
Hiking time:	5 hours
Agency:	CSP-CDD (ABDSP)
Notes:	4WD recommended; call ABDSP Visitor Center regarding road conditions; bring plenty of water; trekking poles recommended on loop hike
Trailhead GPS:	N32.87057, W116.23475
Optional map:	USGS 7.5-min *Sweeney Pass*
Atlas square:	O27
Directions:	(Ocotillo) From S-2 go west on the dirt to Indian Gorge, 18.2 miles north of I-8 and 29.2 miles south of CA-78, midway between mileposts 46 and 47. Go 0.7 mile and park or continue 1.7 miles with a 4WD to the well-marked Torote Canyon trailhead on your right.

Habitat(s):

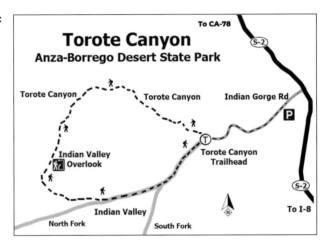

Torote is the Spanish name for the small-leaf elephant tree found in this canyon. Although there are many specimens in the canyon, the individual trees are quite scattered and are commonly found higher up on the canyon slopes. A pair of binoculars would come in handy here.

There is no official or maintained trail into the canyon. Begin by following the footsteps of numerous hikers who have preceded you into this well-trod canyon. After covering about 0.25 mile, there will be a pile of boulders and small dry falls that appear to block this narrow canyon. However, these are easily surmounted and the canyon begins to widen as the boulders give way to a broad sandy wash.

The west-facing canyon wall is cloaked with a forest of teddy-bear cholla, with scattered ocotillo and torote. In spring the air will be scented with desert-lavender. You will also find California copperleaf, desert wishbone plant, white-stem or giant milkweed, chuparosa, and broom matchweed (*Gutierrezia sarothrae*) in bloom, as well as annual wildflowers. Later in the spring expect blooming catclaw acacia and many cacti, but by April, most of the annuals are gone.

Broom matchweed or snakeweed is a perennial herb or shrub in the sunflower family that may be familiar to those who hike from coast to cactus, as it is found in a variety of habitats. It stands 1-2 feet high and is diffusely branched with daisy-like yellow flower heads at the end of long stems arising from a woody base. It has 5 to15 ray flowers and 4 to13 disk flowers per head. Leaves are linear, alternate, and about 2 inches long. The plant is toxic to livestock.

The canyon forks about 1.20 miles from the trailhead with Torote Canyon going north-

Small-leaf elephant tree

west, off to the right. The first significant dry falls are encountered at mile 1.54. It is about 20 feet high, but it can be relatively easy and safely overcome. Thereafter, there are a few smaller dry falls, followed by a long stretch of easy walking up the sandy canyon bottom. After 2.22 miles the canyon widens significantly as tributaries join the main canyon. Torote Canyon continues as the middle branch, which takes you in a southwesterly direction.

The easy stroll along the sandy canyon floor ends with a pile of boulders that must be climbed, 2.65 miles from your vehicle. Af-

ter this hurdle, the easy walking resumes after hiking 3.35 miles when you arrive at the Indian Valley Overlook. This is a major decision point. You can return to your vehicle the way you came, or you can make this a loop hike. The total distance is the same either way, but for the loop hike, there is a steep descent of 0.4 mile through a boulder- and cholla-choked canyon leading down to the North Fork of Indian Valley. Once you reach the dry creek bed on the canyon floor, follow it east until it joins the North Fork 4WD road, which you will follow back to your vehicle.

Torote Canyon entrance

Broom matchweed

Distance:	5 miles, out-and-back
Difficulty:	🚶🚶🚶
Elevation gain/loss:	Up to 300 feet
Hiking time:	3 hours
Agency:	CSP-CDD (ABDSP)
Notes:	4WD recommended; call ABDSP Visitor Center regarding road conditions; bring plenty of water; trekking poles recommended; one-way hike possible with second vehicle
Trailhead GPS:	N32.87532, W116.21800
Optional map:	USGS 7.5-min *Arroyo Tapiado, Sweeney Pass*
Atlas square:	O27
Directions:	(Ocotillo) From S-2 go west on the dirt to Indian Gorge, 18.2 miles north of I-8 and 29.2 miles south of CA-78, midway between mileposts 46 and 47. Go 0.7 mile and park.

Habitat(s):

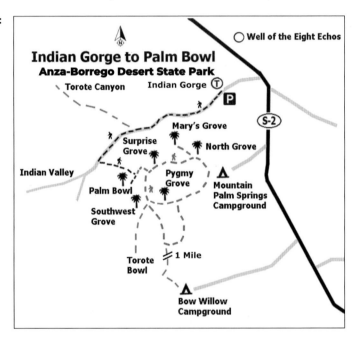

Palm Bowl is the most remote of the six palm groves of Mountain Palm Springs. A direct route to this hidden grove is through Anza-Borrego's Indian Gorge. A ridge route drops into a small mesquite-filled valley leading to this large grove where Kumeyaay Indians once camped and harvested mesquite pods and palm fruit. The shady grove makes a nice rest stop. An added treat of going into Indian Gorge is visiting a side canyon called Torote where elephant trees grow (see previous hike).

Begin at the signed entrance to Indian Gorge, walking through typical desert plants that include chuparosa, cholla, ocotillo, desert-lavender, catclaw acacia, brittlebush, and smoke

tree (*Psorothamnus spinosus*), a large shrub or small tree with many rigid branches and a crooked trunk. The slender twigs are blue-gray and thorn-tipped. The leaves are blue-gray with a smoky hue. Smoke trees are a common plant found in low desert washes, needing running water to tumble, abrade, and carry its seeds a measured distance away from the parent tree before they can germinate, assuring that the offspring do not compete for water. Carried too far and overly abraded, they will not germinate. A member of the pea family, the smoke tree can grow up to 25 feet and appears leafless and ashen most of the year, but lovely purple blooms appear briefly around June.

Smoke trees at canyon entrance

As you pass the smoke trees, look for possible verdin (*Auriparus flaviceps*) nests. The verdin is a small songbird with a gray body and a yellow face. It builds an enclosed nest with the entrance a small hole. The male builds the exterior and the female lines the interior. The nest is often placed in the outer branches of a thorny tree such as the smoke tree, deterring predators not by concealment but by the sharp thorns of the tree and of the twigs covering the exterior of the nest. Smoke trees become thin as the gorge opens up into Indian Canyon where desert agave and California barrel cactus are visible on the hillsides.

Hike up the canyon toward a large desert-willow tree, about 0.2 mile past the entrance to Torote Canyon. A state park boundary sign marks the beginning of state wilderness lands. Just beyond this sign to the south is the beginning of the trail that leads over the ridge to Palm Bowl. Follow this trail into the next canyon where Palm Bowl will be clearly visible to the west. A short walk through the mesquite grove will lead to the palm trees.

Look for grinding areas once used by the local Indians. The palm trees are California fan palms (*Washingtonia filifera*), the only native palm tree in the western United States. The name fan refers to the shape of the leaves as opposed to the spear-like leaves that are characteristic of the Mediterranean date palms. Local Indians harvested the palm fruit and used the leaf fibers to make sandals, baskets, and

thatch roofs and walls for their houses. Palm oases were favorite living areas for the local Kumeyaay bands of this area and also for the Cahuilla bands that lived further north. They provided shade, water, and resource materials needed for survival, including animals to hunt and trap that visit palm oases.

From the palm grove, it is about 2 miles to return to the entrance of Indian Gorge. An option is to follow the canyon to the next grove, which is Surprise Grove, and then to either continue following the canyon down to the Mountain Palm Springs trailhead or to take another trail over the ridge at Surprise Grove and follow it to Southwest Grove and then out to the Mountain Palm Springs trailhead via Pygmy Grove (see next hike description). If no car is positioned at this trailhead, it will be a long hike back. Mountain Palm Springs has a vault toilet but no water.

Fan palm leaf

539 SOUTH

Distance:	2.5 miles, loop
Difficulty:	🚶🚶
Elevation gain/loss:	Up to 500 feet
Hiking time:	2 hours
Agency:	CSP-CDD (ABDSP)
Notes:	Usually okay for 2WD; call ABDSP Visitor Center regarding road conditions; bring plenty of water; optional side trips available
Trailhead GPS:	N32.86255, W116.21879
Optional map:	USGS 7.5-min *Sweeney Pass*
Atlas square:	O27
Directions:	(Ocotillo) From S-2 go west on the dirt to Mountain Palm Springs Camp, 17.2 miles north of I-8 and 30.2 miles south of CA-78. Go 0.6 mile to trailhead parking.

Habitat(s):

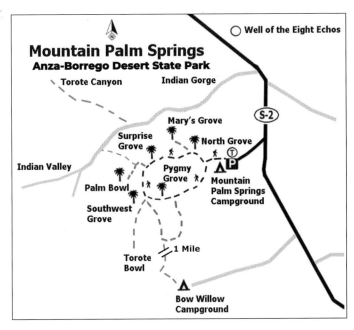

The best place to visit accessible desert palm groves in the southern Anza-Borrego Desert State Park is Mountain Palm Springs found at the foot of the Tierra Blanca Mountains. Six oases with well-established trees provide shade for hikers and a nice respite for wildlife with intermittent streams of water. The palms are remnants from a time before there was a desert when the climate could accommodate more tropical plants. A large owl that may be seen near the palm groves is the great horned owl. The groves provided a sheltered home for the early Kumeyaay Indians who collected palm fruit and used palm leaves for construction material and fiber to make baskets. Several grinding areas are near the groves.

The approach to the trailhead from S-2 is up a well-drained alluvial fan with a rich desert scrub community consisting of several varieties of cactus, ocotillo, creosote bush, white bur-sage, and desert-holly (***Atriplex hymenelytra***), a silvery-gray to white shrub that is the most drought-tolerant saltbush in the desert. The name refers to its resemblance to Christmas holly because of its toothed leaves and red fruit.

Honey mesquite (***Prosopis glandulosa*** var. *torreyana*) is in the canyon drainage and was a major source of food for the local Kumeyaay. Mesquite and desert agave were the two major plants harvested in the desert by all desert Indians. The best seasonal camps and village sites

Diana Lindsay

Honey mesquite beans

were located near these two resources along with a water source and granitic rocks that could be used to process these plants. The two major higher elevation plants needed for survival were oak trees for their acorns and pine trees for their pine nuts. The commonality for these four food resources is the abundance that could be harvested in some years and the ability to store them for use during years of famine or to use them as trade items.

There are two species of spiny mesquite that were harvested. The honey mesquite is the most common and was preferred because of its long nutritious pods. The other is screw-bean mesquite (***Prosopis pubescens***), which is uncommon and has tightly coiled beans. Both plants have long tap roots that secure a permanent source of water. Both also had a variety of ways in which they were used by local Indians besides being a food source. Limbs were used in construction of homes and granaries. Wood was used to make such things as bowls, cooking and pottery tools, digging tools, and agave cutters. Leaves, twigs, and other parts of the plant had medicinal uses also.

The most popular hike in this area is a loop of almost 2.5 miles that visits four groves starting from an interpretive panel at the trailhead. Shortly after starting the hike is Pygmy Grove on the north side of the trail with almost 40 trees, many with burned skirts and trunks from a fire but very much alive with new seedlings in the grove. The surrounding hillsides are covered with tall California barrel cactus and occasional milkweed. Brittlebush or encelia and white rhatany or krameria are found along the trail.

The trail curves to the left and then back to the right following a ridge west that leads to Southwest Grove with well over 100 trees. This grove is about 0.5 mile from the beginning trailhead. If hikers want to extend this loop hike by 1 mile, they can follow the well-marked trail up the steep ridge to the south another 0.5 mile to Torote Bowl where several elephant trees are found.

Across from the Torote Bowl trail sign is a narrow and rather obscure trail that climbs a ridge on the north side. This is the trail to Surprise Grove that drops into the next canyon after a little more than a 0.5 mile. Surprise Grove has over 30 trees. Up-canyon less than 0.5 mile from Surprise Grove is Palm Bowl tucked into a large mesquite-filled bowl with well over 50 trees. Retrace your way back to Surprise Grove and follow the canyon down another 0.5 mile to the junction with a canyon leading north to North Grove and Mary's Grove. The 2.5-mile loop hike turns right and heads back to the parking area and trailhead that is clearly visible.

By turning to the left or north at the junction of Surprise Canyon another mile is added to the hike. North Grove is visible from the junction and from the trailhead. The wind can knock down many of the palm fronds that can be slick to walk on, so use caution. There are about 20 trees strewn in this narrow canyon. The climb becomes steep and rocky as one continues on to Mary's Grove where there are over 30 trees in scattered groupings. Hike back down-canyon to return to your vehicle.

Jim Zuell

Screw-bean mesquite

Distance:	4 miles, loop
Difficulty:	🚶🚶
Elevation gain/loss:	Up to 400 feet
Hiking time:	2 hours
Agency:	CSP-CDD (ABDSP)
Notes:	Usually okay for 2WD; call ABDSP Visitor Center regarding road conditions; bring plenty of water; trekking poles recommended
Trailhead GPS:	N32.84319, W116.22667
Optional map:	USGS 7.5-min *Sweeney Pass*
Atlas square:	P27
Directions:	(Ocotillo) From S-2 go west on the dirt road to Bow Willow Campground, 15.9 miles north of I-8 and 31.5 miles south of CA-78. Go 1.5 miles to trailhead parking.

Habitat(s):

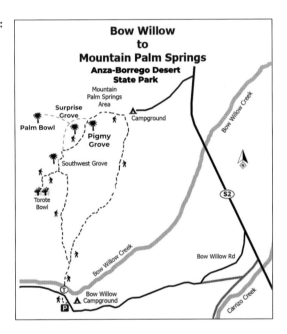

The present Bow Willow Campground was the site of a large seasonal Kumeyaay village. Many trails radiate out from the campground area making it a choice staging area for adventure. One trail heads into the Laguna Mountains while another leads to an historic rock house, a remnant of a different era when cattlemen roamed these hills. Still another trail, the one described here, leads to the beautiful palm oases at Mountain Palm Springs. En route, there is an opportunity to visit the elephant tree forest at Torote Bowl with its dramatic views east to the Carrizo Badlands and marsh.

Start walking northwest from the campground trailhead, crossing the wide sandy Bow Willow Creek wash. Look for weathered 4x4

posts with yellow tops that mark the trail. An unpainted sign identifies this as the Mountain Palm Springs Trail, and a sign about 0.3 mile from the trailhead marks the direction for the Southwest Grove and Torote Bowl.

The ubiquitous creosote bush (***Larrea tridentata***) is found along the trail. It is a mounded plant that is waist to head high and is characterized by tiny deep green leaves, open branching structure, and small yellow flowers in spring. The creosote bush is one of the oldest and most widespread plants of the California deserts. It has the ability to clone itself out from the original seedling by sending out fresh new outer branches as the center of the plant dies. This results in a circle of plants that are genetically

View east of Torote Bowl

the same as the original seed that may have sprouted thousands of years ago. The oldest and largest known ring of creosotes is in the Coachella Valley. Scientists estimate that these plants are over 11,000 years old, older than the ancient bristlecone pine. Creosote is an indicator plant for the Colorado Desert and is the desert's most drought-tolerant plant capable of surviving up to 70% loss of water, despite the fact that it is an evergreen. It does this by using many strategies to protect its leaf moisture from the hot desert sun. The leaves are leathery, shiny, tiny, ta-co-shaped, and at an angle to the sun. This maximizes its ability to conserve water. Thick leaves protect the plant; shininess reflects the sun; tiny means less leaf surface from which to lose water; and folded leaves at an angle to the sun reduces the surface area exposed to the direct intensity of the sun. The creosote bush is the most commonly used plant for medicinal purposes by southwestern Indian groups. It is sometimes referred to as the cure-all or drug store of the desert because of its antioxidant and antiseptic properties used to cure a variety of ailments.

Creosote

Diana Lindsay

Creosote flower

While you are looking at the creosote bush, look for the creosote bush walking stick (*Diapheromera covilleae*) that might be on the plant. This insect does not have wings but walks along branches. It is a hard-to-find insect as it is even more skillful at disguise than a chameleon. It sways from side-to-side with a breeze, and times each leg movement to an almost imperceptible crawl. Its graceful, stick-like body matches the greens and browns of the creosote bark and leaves that it feeds upon. Its tiny head is topped by long, sensitive antennae. The desert hosts several species of walking sticks including some that feed on mesquite. The insects produce flask-shaped eggs that look like tiny seeds. Sometimes ants mistake the eggs for food and bring them into their warm, dark nest. Once inside, the ants are fooled, and the walking stick's larvae are free to develop in a protected environment that is much safer for them than above ground.

Also near the creosote may be the black and white Sackeni's velvet ant (*Dasymutilla sackenii*), which is actually a wasp and not an ant. Females are wingless and resemble the fruit of the creosote and may look like a creosote bush fruit blowing across the desert floor.

The trail continues up the hillside on the north side of the wash, opening up some grand vistas as you gain elevation. At a fork in the trail, take the left branch to proceed to Torote Bowl, about 0.5 mile ahead.

The Torote Bowl is the upper end of an unnamed canyon and is home to at least 15 large small-leaf elephant trees (*Bursera microphylla*) or *torote*, as it is known in Spanish.

The Spanish name means twisted, and indeed the short, stubby branches of this hardy tree are contorted. This large concentration of elephant trees is well worth the hike to view this unusual plant. Also, the view from Torote Bowl out to the Carrizo Badlands and marsh is not to be missed and is another reason to take this short side trip. After examining the elephant trees and taking in the view, return to the trail junction and take the signed trail to the Southwest Grove of palms in Mountain Palm Springs, 1.9 miles from Bow Willow. This large well-watered palm grove offers shade and a cool respite from the hot desert sun.

At this point there are two return options. Either head back the same way for a slightly less than 4 miles out-and-back hike, or take the well-worn trail east from the Southwest Grove toward the Mountain Palm Springs primitive campground for an alternate return hike. There is an assumption that the exploration of the six major palm groves in the Mountain Palm Springs area will be left for another day's exploration. The route described here takes the alternate route back.

Find a well-used but unsigned trail leading south up a small gully shortly before arriving at the Mountain Palm Springs trailhead parking area. Following this trail requires close attention, but it is marked with frequent ducks, and it is easy walking through the Sonoran scrub. If the trail is lost, just keep walking west-south-west until Bow Willow Campground comes into view.

Bill Howell

Sackeni's velvet ant and creosote seeds

Distance:	7.5 miles, loop
Difficulty:	🚶🚶🚶🚶
Elevation gain/loss:	Up to 700 feet
Hiking time:	5 hours
Agency:	CSP-CDD (ABDSP); BLM-CDD
Notes:	Usually okay for 2WD; call ABDSP Visitor Center regarding road conditions; bring plenty of water; trekking poles recommended; boulder scrabbling
Trailhead GPS:	N32.84325, W116.22709
Optional map:	USGS 7.5-min *Sweeney Pass*
Atlas square:	P27
Directions:	((Ocotillo) From S-2 go west on the dirt road to Bow Willow Campground, 15.9 miles north of I-8 and 31.5 miles south of CA-78. Go 1.5 miles to trailhead parking.

Habitat(s):

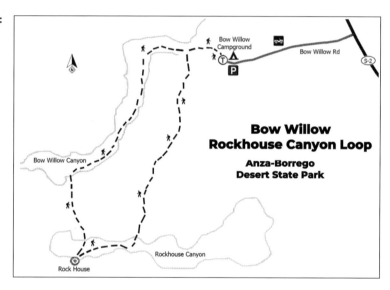

Many of the Anza-Borrego area's first settlers were cattlemen who needed the wide open spaces for winter grazing. Cow camps were established in several areas beginning around the 1890s. Cattleman Darrel McCain built the rock house located in the Bureau of Land Management's Carrizo Gorge Wilderness south of Bow Willow in 1933. The small 10x12-foot shelter was built to get out of the wind. McCain used two large boulders for the back and side and used rock and mortar for the other sides. It also had a fireplace and a window. This hike follows Bow Willow Canyon Wash to an arroyo that leads to the rock house and returns via Rockhouse Canyon, named for this historic line shack.

From Bow Willow Campground, walk west up the sandy, wide Bow Willow Can-yon Wash, past the scattered desert-willows (*Chilopsis linearis*) that are abundant here. The Kumeyaay Indians used these trees to make their hunting bows, giving the canyon its name. However, this tree or large shrub, which can grow up to 21 feet, is not a willow, but a member of the bignonia family, related to the purple-flowering jacaranda, an ornamental commonly seen in urban San Diego. The desert-willow is a phreatophyte—a water indicating plant found where there is a water source along washes or where there is standing water by a stream or spring. It is deciduous, has narrow leaves, and blooms from April to August with a pink to light lavender two-lipped flower. The Indians made a tea from the dried flowers and seed pods. The bark was used to make shirts, breechcloths, and cordage for nets. The

The rock shelter

After exploring the area, head across the valley to the low point in the hills to the north, almost directly across from Rockhouse Canyon. An old Indian trail leads over this pass to Bow Willow Canyon. At one time the park maintained this trail, but it no longer does, and it may be hard to follow in places. Still, you can't get lost. Once you reach the saddle, you will see the sandy Bow Willow Canyon Wash spread out below you. Continue hiking north for about 1 mile, then bear eastward, following the canyon back to the campground.

Desert willow

wood was also used to make house frames and granaries.

At 0.5 mile from the trailhead parking area, start hiking up the side canyon to your left. Unofficially it is called Lone Palm Canyon for reasons you will soon discover. Huge desert-varnished granite boulders cover the walls of the canyon, and the canyon bottom is choked with boulders that have fallen from above. There is no maintained trail up Lone Palm Canyon and it requires a fair amount of boulder hopping, but the route is marked with ducks and is not difficult. The boulder field is only 0.5 mile long and is followed by easy hiking in a relatively flat, sandy canyon that continues for another 2 miles. The canyon bottom may be sprinkled with dwarf poppy, desert dandelion, Spanish-needles, purple mat, and other colorful annuals in early spring following a good rainfall, as well as flowering shrubs, including desert-lavender, chuparosa, desert apricot, and creosote bush. At about 3 miles from the Bow Willow Campground is Rockhouse Canyon. Go west, up the canyon for another 0.6 mile to the famous rock house ruins. The house was a surprisingly small, cramped shack that once had a tin roof over its rock and concrete walls, forming a single room that served as kitchen, living room, and bedroom. It is the only such structure for miles around, and it is interesting to imagine what life might have been like for the cowboys who spent months here looking after their cattle.

Desert willow

Distance:	5 miles, loop
Difficulty:	🏃🏃
Elevation gain/loss:	Up to 900 feet
Hiking time:	4 hours
Agency:	CSP-CDD (ABDSP)
Notes:	4WD recommended; call ABDSP Visitor Center regarding road conditions; bring plenty of water; bring GPS or map and compass to find railroad camp
Trailhead GPS:	N32.75775, W116.15885
Optional map:	USGS 7.5-min *Sweeney Pass*
Atlas square:	R28
Directions:	(Ocotillo) From S-2 go south on Mortero Wash, 8.5 miles north of I-8 and 38.9 miles south of CA-78. Go 4 miles to its intersection with Dos Cabezas Road, which is not signed. There are several roads in this area. The topo map is not a reliable guide here as the road that needs to be taken is not on the map. It is roughly 0.1 miles east of the railroad tracks and looks down on the tracks and the rusty water tower beside them. Go right on this road and proceed north/ northwest for approximately 1.5 miles paralleling the tracks. Look for a low railroad undercrossing and park on the east side of the tracks.

Habitat(s):

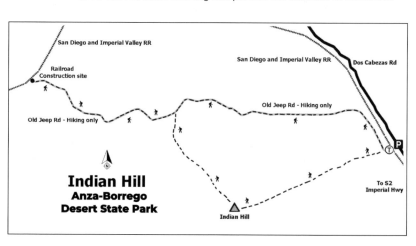

Visiting Indian Hill gives us a renewed appreciation for this desert area. Humans have used the area perhaps for several thousand years. The last Indian cultural group to occupy this area was the Kumeyaay. It was later used by local cattlemen and much later, beginning in 1912, by construction crews of the San Diego & Arizona Eastern Railway (SD&AE)—the Impossible Railroad—who dug tunnels, laid track, and built a large wooden trestle through Carrizo Gorge to connect with San Diego. Their construction camp was located near what is marked as Indian Hill on the USGS topographic map. The real Indian Hill, however, is another rocky hill to the southeast with a large shelter and morteros on its north side.

In looking at the area now, it is hard to see how it could have supported human life, let alone cattle. However, it is likely that the climate was more favorable in the past than it is currently. Also the Indian groups living here had the ingenuity and culture necessary to make a living in this harsh climate, using the available resources at hand.

When beginning the hike, avoid the illegal jeep road that crosses the railroad track and continues up the wash and an intermittent stream, ending within 100 yards of Indian Hill. This illegal road is a laborious trudge through soft sand churned up by the many vehicles that have used this route, scarring the fragile desert. There is a better way to get there.

Approaching Indian Hill

Rock enhancements found at Indian Hill

From your parked vehicle, go under the railroad tracks at the crossing and proceed west, across a broad sandy plain with abundant cholla. Stay on the south side of the roughly 400-foot high hill, about 0.5 mile from the crossing. The slopes of this hill are covered with a magnificent cactus garden, including California barrel cactus (***Ferocactus cylindraceus***). Some of the specimens are as tall as an average human—they can grow up to 9 feet and have 20-30 ribs. They also lean toward the south or southwest. They are phototropic, bending toward the most intense light. Sometimes it is called a compass cactus.

The California barrel cactus—especially larger ones with lower surface to volume ratio—is highly drought and temperature tolerant because its shape exposes a smaller surface area to evaporation. It has a greater capacity to store water, like a barrel. This characteristic has led to the lore that the barrel cactus can provide water for thirsty desert travelers. This is far from the truth, however, in that the work involved in extracting the water would outweigh the gain. In addition, the mucilaginous slime induces headaches and diarrhea.

At this point in the hike, look west-southwest for a pile of highly eroded, large granite boulders about 0.4 mile straight ahead. That is the real Indian Hill. The boulders have been weathered in a way that has created numerous caves, narrow passages, and rocky overhangs. One large cave in particular on the north side had been inhabited by Indian groups for thousands of years, as early as when the desert was still evolving and much cooler and wetter than it is today. The roof of this cave still retains soot from past cooking fires. Morteros are found next to the large cave and scattered around the hill area, attesting to the heavy Indian use of this area. You may find pottery

Rock wall in old railroad camp

shards scattered about. Do not move these as the exact location of artifacts is important to archaeologists who record cultural sites. The area is culturally important and protected and continues to be studied by archaeologists. Damage to or removal of cultural artifacts is subject to prosecution. It is important to treat this site with respect. Look and photograph if desired, but do not touch. Care must be taken when photographing any pictographs that may be found in this area as any contact with the pigment will damage or destroy them.

After exploring Indian Hill, head up the ridge leading northwest to an old construction site for the SD&AE Railway. In about 0.25 mile, there will be a 4WD road. Go left on the road, and it will lead to the old construction site.

About 100 years ago, over 400 workers building the segment of the railroad through Carrizo Canyon lived and worked at this site, then known as China Camp. Little remains of the camp other than an old stone wall, a cement slab, and some rusting artifacts. The name suggests that Chinese labor helped to build this railroad, but it is a mistake to think so. There is no evidence to prove this. While exploring this area, think about the heroic effort that was required to build a railroad through the rugged Jacumba Mountains.

An optional extension to this trip is to hike down to Carrizo Palms, following an old road to the west that overlooks the railroad tracks. However, the route is very rugged and steep. The railroad workers pumped water from Carrizo Palms to the railroad camp.

Return the same way or follow the dirt road between the camp and the railroad tracks back to your vehicle. Although motorized vehicles are not allowed to use this road either, you will find abundant evidence of frequent illegal vehicle use. The soft sand created by this activity makes for unpleasant walking.

California barrel cactus

Species and Habitats by Common Name

Type	Common/Scientific name	Beach/Salt Marsh/Lagoon	Coastal Sage Scrub	Grassland	Chaparral	Oak Woodland	Riparian	Freshwater Marsh/Montane Meadow/Vernal Pool	Mixed Conifer Forest	Desert
Algae, Bacteria & Fungi	Frankia (*Frankia* sp.)		x		x	x	x			x
Algae, Bacteria & Fungi	Freshwater Green Algae (*Spirogyra* spp.)							x		
Algae, Bacteria & Fungi	Giant Kelp (*Macrocystis pyrifera*)	x								
Algae, Bacteria & Fungi	Green Algae (*Trebouxia* spp.)		x	x	x	x	x	x	x	x
Algae, Bacteria & Fungi	Lichen (phylum Ascomycota)		x	x	x	x	x	x	x	x
Algae, Bacteria & Fungi	Pond scums, Pond-mosses (*Spirogyra* spp.)							x		
Birds	Acorn Woodpecker (*Melanerpes formicivorus*)					x			x	
Birds	Allen's Hummingbird (*Selasphorus sasin*)		x							
Birds	American Avocet (*Recurvirostra americana*)	x								
Birds	American Coot (*Fulica americana*)							x		
Birds	American Crow (*Corvus brachyrhynchos*)						x			
Birds	American Goldfinch (*Spinus tristis*)						x			
Birds	American Kestrel (*Falco sparverius*)				x					
Birds	American Pipit (*Anthus rubescens*)				x					
Birds	American White Pelican (*Pelecanus erythrorhynchos*)	x						x		
Birds	Anna's Hummingbird (*Calypte anna*)		x		x	x	x			
Birds	Bald Eagle (*Haliaeetus leucocephalus*)	x		x			x	x		
Birds	Band-tailed Pigeon (*Patagioenas fasciata*)					x			x	
Birds	Barn Owl (*Tyto alba*)				x		x	x		
Birds	Belding's Savannah Sparrow (*Passerculus sandwichensis beldingi*)	x								
Birds	Belted Kingfisher (*Megaceryle alcyon*)	x						x		
Birds	Bewick's Wren (*Thryomanes bewickii*)		x		x					
Birds	Black Phoebe (*Sayornis nigricans*)						x	x		
Birds	Black-crowned Night Heron (*Nycticorax nycticorax*)	x						x		
Birds	Black-headed Grosbeak (*Pheucticus melanocephalus*)				x	x	x		x	
Birds	Black-necked Stilt (*Himantopus mexicanus*)	x								
Birds	Black-throated Magpie-jay (*Calocitta colliei*)						x			
Birds	Black-throated Sparrow (*Amphispiza bilineata*)									x
Birds	Brandt's Cormorant (*Phalacrocorax penicillatus*)	x								
Birds	Brown-headed Cowbird (*Molothrus ater*)				x		x			
Birds	Bufflehead (*Bucephala albeola*)	x								
Birds	Bullock's Oriole (*Icterus bullockii*)						x			
Birds	Bushtit (*Psaltriparus minimus*)		x		x	x	x			
Birds	Cactus Wren (*Campylorhynchus brunneicapillus*)		x							x
Birds	California Brown Pelican (*Pelecanus occidentalis californicus*)	x								
Birds	California Gnatcatcher (*Polioptila californica californica*)		x							
Birds	California Quail (*Callipepla californica*)		x		x	x	x			
Birds	California Thrasher (*Toxostoma redivivum*)		x		x					
Birds	California Towhee (*Melozone crissalis*)		x							
Birds	Calliope Hummingbird (*Selasphorus calliope*)								x	
Birds	Cinnamon Teal (*Anas cyanoptera*)							x		
Birds	Cliff Swallow (*Petrochelidon pyrrhonota*)							x		
Birds	Common Raven (*Corvus corax*)		x	x						x
Birds	Costa's Hummingbird (*Calypte costae*)		x		x					x
Birds	Gambel's Quail (*Callipepla gambelii*)									x
Birds	Golden Eagle (*Aquila chrysaetos*)				x	x	x			x
Birds	Gray Vireo (*Vireo vicinior*)				x					

Legend for Habitats

 Beach/Salt Marsh/Lagoon

 Coastal Sage Scrub

 Grassland

 Chaparral

 Oak Woodland

 Riparian

 Freshwater Marsh Montane Meadow/Vernal Pool

 Mixed Conifer Forest

 Desert

Type	Common/Scientific name									
Birds	Great Blue Heron (*Ardea herodias*)	X								
Birds	Great Egret (*Ardea alba*)	X								
Birds	Great Horned Owl (*Bubo virginianus*)					X				
Birds	Greater Roadrunner (*Geococcyx californianus*)		X							X
Birds	Green Heron (*Butorides virescens*)							X		
Birds	Gulls (family Laridae, subfamily Larinae)	X								
Birds	Hooded Oriole (*Icterus cucullatus*)						X			X
Birds	Horned Lark (*Eremophila alpestris*)			X						
Birds	House Finch (*Haemorhous mexicanus*)		X	X	X		X			X
Birds	Killdeer (*Charadrius vociferus*)	X		X				X		
Birds	Lark Sparrow (*Chondestes grammacus*)			X						
Birds	Lazuli Bunting (*Passerina amoena*)				X	X	X		X	
Birds	Least Bell's Vireo (*Vireo bellii pusillus*)						X			
Birds	Least Tern (*Sternula antillarum*)	X								
Birds	Lesser Goldfinch (*Spinus psaltria*)				X		X			
Birds	Lesser Scaup (*Aythya affinis*)	X						X		
Birds	Light-footed Ridgway's Rail (*Rallus obsoletus levipes*)	X						X		
Birds	Loggerhead Shrike (*Lanius ludovicianus*)			X	X					X
Birds	Mallard (*Anas platyrhynchos*)						X			
Birds	Mountain Bluebird (*Sialia currucoides*)			X						X
Birds	Mountain Chickadee (*Poecile gambeli*)								X	
Birds	Mourning Dove (*Zenaida macroura*)			X	X					X
Birds	Northern Harrier (*Circus cyaneus*)	X					X			
Birds	Northern Mockingbird (*Mimus polyglottos*)			X						X
Birds	Osprey (*Pandion haliaetus*)	X					X			
Birds	Peregrine Falcon (*Falco peregrinus*)	X		X			X			
Birds	Phainopepla (*Phainopepla nitens*)					X	X			X
Birds	Pied-billed Grebe (*Podilymbus podiceps*)	X					X			
Birds	Prairie Falcon (*Falco mexicanus*)			X						X
Birds	Red-shouldered Hawk (*Buteo lineatus*)					X				
Birds	Red-tailed Hawk (*Buteo jamaicensis*)			X	X					
Birds	Red-winged Blackbird (*Agelaius phoeniceus*)						X			
Birds	Reddish Egret (*Egretta rufescens*)	X								
Birds	Ruby-crowned Kinglet (*Regulus calendula*)				X	X	X		X	
Birds	Ruddy Duck (*Oxyura jamaicensis*)	X					X			
Birds	Sanderling (*Calidris alba*)	X								
Birds	Say's Phoebe (*Sayornis saya*)			X						X
Birds	Snowy Egret (*Egretta thula*)	X								
Birds	Southwestern Willow Flycatcher (*Empidonax traillii extimus*)					X				
Birds	Spotted Owl (*Strix occidentalis*)					X			X	
Birds	Spotted Towhee (*Pipilo maculatus*)				X	X	X			
Birds	Steller's Jay (*Cyanocitta stelleri*)								X	
Birds	Swallows (family Hirundinidae)	X		X			X	X	X	
Birds	Swifts (family Apodidae)	X		X	X		X			X
Birds	Terns (family Laridae, subfamily Sterninae)	X					X			
Birds	Turkey Vulture (*Cathartes aura*)			X	X					
Birds	Verdin (*Auriparus flaviceps*)									X
Birds	Western Bluebird (*Sialia mexicana*)					X			X	
Birds	Western Flycatcher (*Empidonax difficilis*)					X				
Birds	Western Grebe (*Aechmophorus occidentalis*)	X					X			
Birds	Western Gull (*Larus occidentalis*)	X								
Birds	Western Meadowlark (*Sturnella neglecta*)			X						
Birds	Western Sandpiper (*Calidris mauri*)	X								
Birds	Western Scrub-jay (*Aphelocoma californica*)				X	X				
Birds	Western Snowy Plover (*Charadrius nivosus*)	X								
Birds	Western Tanager (*Piranga ludoviciana*)								X	
Birds	Western Wood-pewee (*Contopus sordidulus*)					X			X	
Birds	White-breasted Nuthatch (*Sitta carolinensis*)					X			X	
Birds	White-crowned Sparrow (*Zonotrichia leucophrys*)		X	X	X					X
Birds	White-tailed Kite (*Elanus leucurus*)			X						
Birds	Wild Turkey (*Meleagris gallopavo*)					X			X	
Birds	Willet (*Tringa semipalmata*)	X								
Birds	Wrentit (*Chamaea fasciata*)		X		X					

Type	Common/*Scientific* name	1	2	3	4	5	6	7	8	9
Birds	Yellow-rumped Warbler (*Setophaga coronata*)		X	X		X				
Invertebrates	Antlions (family *Myrmeleontidae*)		X		X	X			X	X
Invertebrates	Argentine Ant (*Linepithema humile*)		X	X	X		X			
Invertebrates	Argiope spider (*Argiope aurantia*)		X	X	X					
Invertebrates	Big-headed Ants (*Pheidole hyatti*)				X					X
Invertebrates	Black Widow (*Latrodectus hesperus*)	X	X	X	X		X		X	X
Invertebrates	Brown Widow (*Latrodectus geometricus*)		X	X	X	X	X			
Invertebrates	Cabbage White Butterfly (*Pieris rapae*)		X	X	X	X	X			
Invertebrates	California Aglaja (*Navanax inermis*)	X								
Invertebrates	California Harvester Ant (*Pogonomyrmex californicus*)		X		X	X				X
Invertebrates	California Trapdoor Spider (*Bothriocyrtum californicum*)		X	X	X	X			X	
Invertebrates	California Velvety Tree Ant (*Liometopum occidentale*)					X	X		X	
Invertebrates	Ceanothus Silk Moth (*Hyalophora euryalus*)		X		X					
Invertebrates	Chitons (phylum Mollusca)	X								
Invertebrates	Cochineal Scale (*Dactylopius coccus*)		X		X					
Invertebrates	Common Water Strider (*Aquarius remigis*)						X	X		
Invertebrates	Creosote Bush Walking Stick (*Diapheromera covilleae*)									X
Invertebrates	Dainty Sulphur Butterfly (*Nathalis iole*)		X	X	X	X			X	X
Invertebrates	Damselflies (order Odonata)						X	X		
Invertebrates	Dragonflies (order Odonata)		X	X	X	X	X	X	X	X
Invertebrates	Earthworms (family Lumbricidae)						X	X	X	
Invertebrates	European Earthworm (*Lumbricus rubellus*)						X	X	X	
Invertebrates	European Honey Bee (*Apis mellifera*)		X	X	X	X	X	X	X	X
Invertebrates	Fairy Shrimps (*Branchinecta* spp.)		X							
Invertebrates	Fiddler Crab (*Uca pugilator*)	X								
Invertebrates	Five-spined Engraver Beetle (*Ips paraconfusus*)								X	
Invertebrates	Funnel Weaver Spiders (family Agelenidae)		X	X	X					
Invertebrates	Goldspotted Oak Borer (*Agrilus auroguttatus*)					X				
Invertebrates	Grasshoppers (family Acrididae)		X	X	X	X	X	X	X	X
Invertebrates	Gray Bird Grasshopper (*Schistocerca nitens*)		X	X	X	X	X	X	X	X
Invertebrates	Harbison's Dun Skipper (*Euphyes vestris harbisoni*)					X	X			
Invertebrates	Harlequin Bug (*Murgantia histrionica*)		X							X
Invertebrates	Hermes Copper Butterfly (*Lycaena hermes*)		X		X					
Invertebrates	Horsehair worms (phylum Nematomorpha)		X	X	X	X				
Invertebrates	House Ants (*Tapimona sessile*)		X	X	X	X	X		X	X
Invertebrates	Jerusalem Crickets (*Stenopelmatus* spp.)		X	X	X	X			X	X
Invertebrates	Kelp Flies (*Coelopa* spp.)	X								
Invertebrates	Ladybug, Ladybird Beetles (family Coccinellidae)		X	X	X	X	X	X	X	X
Invertebrates	Limpets (phylum Mollusca)	X								
Invertebrates	Milkweed bugs (family Lygaeidae)		X	X	X	X			X	X
Invertebrates	Monarch Butterfly (*Danaus plexippus*)		X	X	X	X	X		X	X
Invertebrates	Native Bees (superfamily Apoidea)		X	X	X	X	X		X	X
Invertebrates	Nolina Moth (*Mesepiola specca*)				X					X
Invertebrates	Northern White Skipper (*Heliopetes ericetorum*)				X	X				X
Invertebrates	Nudibranchs (class Gastropoda)	X								
Invertebrates	Oak Gall Wasps (family Cynipidae)					X				
Invertebrates	Pacific Banana Slug (*Ariolimax columbianus*)					X				
Invertebrates	Pacific Velvet Ant (*Dasymutilla aureola*)		X	X	X					
Invertebrates	Painted Lady (*Vanessa cardui*)		X	X	X	X	X		X	X
Invertebrates	Pink Abalone (*Haliotis corrugata*)	X								
Invertebrates	Queen Butterfly (*Danaus gilippus*)									X
Invertebrates	Quino Checkerspot Butterfly (*Euphydryas editha quino*)		X	X						
Invertebrates	Red Turpentine Beetle (*Dendroctonus valens*)								X	
Invertebrates	Sackeni's Velvet Ant (*Dasymutilla sackenii*)		X	X	X					
Invertebrates	San Diego Fairy Shrimp (*Branchinecta sandiegonensis*)		X							
Invertebrates	Sand Crabs (*Emerita analoga*)	X								
Invertebrates	Sand Tubeworms (phylum Annelida)	X								
Invertebrates	Sara Orangetip Butterfly (*Anthocharis sara*)		X	X	X	X	X		X	X
Invertebrates	Satyr Angelwing (*Polygonia satyrus*)						X			
Invertebrates	Sea Anemones (*Anthopleura* spp.)	X								
Invertebrates	Spanish Shawl (*Flabellina iodinea*)	X								
Invertebrates	Spittle Bugs (*Aphorphora* spp.)		X	X	X	X	X	X		X
Invertebrates	Squash Bee (*Peponapis pruinosa*)		X		X	X				X

Type	Common/*Scientific* name	🐦	🌼	🌾	🐦	🍇	🦊	🦋	🌲	🦤
Invertebrates	Squash Bees (*Peponapis* spp.)				x		x	x		x
Invertebrates	Squash Bees (*Xenoglossa* spp.)				x		x	x		x
Invertebrates	Stigmella Moth (*Stigmella* sp.)				x		x	x		
Invertebrates	Stink Beetle (*Eleodes* sp.)				x	x	x	x	x		x	x
Invertebrates	Tarantula (*Aphonopelma* sp.)				x	x	x			x
Invertebrates	Tarantula Hawk Wasp (*Pepsis* sp.)				x	x	x	x		x	x
Invertebrates	Tick (*Dermacentor* sp.)				x	x	x	x	x		x
Invertebrates	Tiny Blue Butterflies (family Lycaenidae)				x		x	x		x	x
Invertebrates	True Bugs (order Hemiptera)	x		x	x	x	x	x	x	x	x
Invertebrates	Water Penny Beetles (family Psephenidae)						x			
Invertebrates	Western Blue Pygmy Butterfly (*Brephidium exilis*)	x								x
Invertebrates	Western Tiger Swallowtail Butterfly (*Papilio rutulus*)				x	x	x	x	x		x	x
Invertebrates	Willow Gall Sawfly (*Pontania* sp.)						x			
Invertebrates	Yucca Moth (*Tegeticula yuccasella*)				x		x			x
Invertebrates	Yucca or Pronuba Moth (*Tegeticula maculata*)				x		x	x		
Mammals	Badger (*Taxidea taxus*)				x		x	x	x	x	x
Mammals	Bats (order Chiroptera)				x	x	x	x	x	x	x
Mammals	Big-eared Woodrat (*Neotoma macrotis*)				x		x	x	x	x	x
Mammals	Black-tailed Jackrabbit (*Lepus californicus*)	x	x		x	x	x	x	x		x
Mammals	Bobcat (*Lynx rufus*)	x	x		x	x	x	x	x	x	x
Mammals	Botta's Pocket Gopher (*Thomomys bottae*)	x	x		x	x	x	x	x	x	x
Mammals	Brush Rabbit (*Sylvilagus bachmani*)	x	x		x		x	x	x		x
Mammals	Bryant's Woodrat (*Neotoma bryanti*)				x		x	x		x	x
Mammals	California Black Bear (*Ursus americanus californiensis*)				x	x	x	x	x	x	x
Mammals	California Ground Squirrel (*Otospermophilus beecheyi*)	x	x		x	x	x	x	x	x	x
Mammals	California Sea Lion (*Zalophus californianus*)	x								
Mammals	California Vole (*Microtus californicus*)	x	x		x	x	x	x		
Mammals	California Weasel (*Mustela frenata*)	x	x				x	x	x	x	x
Mammals	Coyote (*Canis latrans*)	x	x		x	x	x	x	x	x	x
Mammals	Desert Bighorn Sheep (*Ovis canadensis nelsoni*)									x
Mammals	Desert Cottontail (*Sylvilagus audubonii*)	x	x		x	x	x	x	x	x	x
Mammals	Desert Kangaroo Rat (*Dipodomys deserti*)				x		x	x		
Mammals	Feral Pig (*Sus scrofa*)				x	x	x		x	x	
Mammals	Gray Fox (*Urocyon cinereoargenteus*)	x	x		x	x	x	x	x	x	x
Mammals	Harbor Seal (*Phoca vitulina*)	x								
Mammals	Kit Fox (*Vulpes macrotis*)									x
Mammals	Merriam's Kangaroo Rat (*Dipodomys merriami*)				x	x		x	x		x
Mammals	Mexican Free-tailed Bat (*Tadarida brasiliensis*)				x	x	x	x	x	x	x
Mammals	Mountain Lion (*Puma concolor*)	x	x		x	x	x	x	x	x	x
Mammals	Northern Raccoon (*Procyon lotor*)	x					x	x	x	
Mammals	Ringtail (*Bassariscus astutus*)					x	x	x	x	x	x
Mammals	Roof Rat (*Rattus rattus*)				x	x	x	x	x	x	x
Mammals	San Diego Pocket Mouse (*Chaetodipus fallax*)				x	x	x			
Mammals	Southern Mule Deer (*Odocoileus hemionus*)	x	x		x	x	x	x	x	x	x
Mammals	Striped Skunk (*Mephitis mephitis*)	x	x		x	x	x	x	x	x	x
Mammals	Virginia Opossum (*Didelphis virginiana*)				x	x	x	x	x	x	x
Mammals	Western Gray Squirrel (*Sciurus griseus*)						x			
Mammals	Western Yellow Bat (*Lasiurus xanthinus*)				x	x	x	x	x	x	x
Mammals	White-tailed Antelope Ground Squirrel (*Ammospermophilus leucurus*)									x
Plants	Alkali-heath (*Frankenia salina*)	x								
Plants	Aquatic Hairy Clover Fern (*Marsilea vestita*)						x			
Plants	Arizona Lupine (*Lupinus arizonicus*)									x
Plants	Arrow Weed (*Pluchea sericea*)						x	x		
Plants	Arroyo Willow (*Salix lasiolepis*)						x	x		
Plants	Artichoke Thistle (*Cynara cardunculus*)				x	x	x			
Plants	Beach Sun Cup (*Camissoniopsis cheiranthifolia* subsp. *suffruticosa*)	x								
Plants	Beavertail Cactus (*Opuntia basilaris*)									x
Plants	Bedstraws (*Galium* spp.)				x		x	x		x
Plants	Big Saltbush (*Atriplex lentiformis*)	x								
Plants	Big-berry Manzanita (*Arctostaphylos glauca*)						x	x		
Plants	Big-cone Douglas Fir (*Pseudotsuga macrocarpa*)								x	
Plants	Birch-leaf Mountain-mahogany (*Cercocarpus betuloides*)						x		x	
Plants	Black Mustard (*Brassica nigra*)				x	x				

554 COAST TO CACTUS

Type	Common/*Scientific* name									
Plants	Black Sage (*Salvia mellifera*)				x	x				
Plants	Blue Dicks (*Dichelostemma capitatum* subsp. *capitatum*)				x	x	x			
Plants	Blue Elderberry (*Sambucus nigra*)				x	x		x	x	
Plants	Blue Palo Verde (*Parkinsonia florida*)									x
Plants	Blue-eyed-grass (*Sisyrinchium bellum*)					x				
Plants	Brittlebush (*Encelia farinosa*)									x
Plants	Broad-leaf Peppergrass (*Lepidium latifolium*)				x	x	x			
Plants	Bromes (*Bromus* spp.)				x		x			
Plants	Broom Baccharis (*Baccharis sarothroides*)	x					x			
Plants	Broom Matchweed (*Gutierrezia sarothrae*)					x	x	x		
Plants	Bulrushes (*Schoenoplectus* spp.)							x		
Plants	Burrobrush (*Ambrosia salsola* var. *salsola*)									x
Plants	Bush Monkey Flower (*Diplacus longiflorus*)				x		x			
Plants	California Barrel Cactus (*Ferocactus cylindraceus*)									x
Plants	California Black Oak (*Quercus kelloggii*)								x	
Plants	California Buckwheat (*Eriogonum fasciculatum*)				x		x			
Plants	California Buttercup (*Ranunculus californicus*)				x	x	x		x	
Plants	California Cord Grass (*Spartina foliosa*)	x								
Plants	California Desert Thorn (*Lycium californicum*)	x	x							
Plants	California Encelia (*Encelia californica*)	x	x		x					
Plants	California Fan Palm (*Washingtonia filifera*)									x
Plants	California Incense Cedar (*Calocedrus decurrens*)								x	
Plants	California Juniper (*Juniperus californica*)									x
Plants	California Large-leaf Filaree (*California macrophylla*)				x					
Plants	California Peony (*Paeonia californica*)						x			
Plants	California Poppy (*Eschscholzia californica*)				x	x	x			
Plants	California Rock-cress (*Boechera californica*)					x	x			
Plants	California Rose (*Rosa californica*)							x	x	x
Plants	California Thistle (*Cirsium occidentale* var. *californicum*)						x		x	
Plants	California Trixis (*Trixis californica*)									x
Plants	California/Round-hood Milkweed (*Asclepias californica*)					x	x	x	x	
Plants	Canchalagua (*Zeltnera venusta*)				x	x	x			
Plants	Canyon Live Oak (*Quercus chrysolepis*)						x		x	
Plants	Cardinal/Scarlet Larkspur (*Delphinium cardinale*)					x				
Plants	Catclaw Acacia (*Senegalia greggii*)									x
Plants	Cattails (*Typha* spp.)	x						x	x	
Plants	Ceanothus species (*Ceanothus* spp.)						x	x	x	
Plants	Chalk Dudleya (*Dudleya pulverulenta*)				x		x			
Plants	Chamise (*Adenostoma fasciculatum*)						x	x		
Plants	Chaparral Broom or Coyote Brush (*Baccharis pilularis*)				x					
Plants	Chaparral Bushmallow (*Malacothamnus fasciculatus*)				x					
Plants	Chaparral Candle (*Hesperoyucca whipplei*)				x	x	x	x		
Plants	Chaparral Whitethorn (*Ceanothus leucodermis*)						x	x	x	
Plants	Cheat Grass (*Bromus tectorum*)					x	x	x	x	
Plants	Cheesebush (*Ambrosia salsola* var. *salsola*)									x
Plants	Chia (*Salvia columbariae*)				x		x			
Plants	Chocolate Lily (*Fritillaria biflora*)				x	x				
Plants	Christmas Berry (*Heteromeles arbutifolia*)				x	x	x	x		
Plants	Chuparosa (*Justicia californica*)									x
Plants	Coast Barrel Cactus (*Ferocactus viridescens*)				x					
Plants	Coast Bladderpod (*Peritoma arborea* var. *arborea*)				x	x				
Plants	Coast Cholla (*Cylindropuntia prolifera*)				x					
Plants	Coast Live Oak (*Quercus agrifolia* var. *agrifolia*)						x	x		
Plants	Coast Monkey Flower (*Diplacus puniceus*)				x		x			
Plants	Coast Prickly-pear (*Opuntia littoralis*)				x		x			
Plants	Coast Spice Bush or Bush-rue (*Cneoridium dumosum*)				x		x			
Plants	Coastal Goldenbush (*Isocoma menziesii* var. *vernonioides*)	x						x	x	
Plants	Coastal Sagebrush (*Artemisia californica*)	x			x	x	x			
Plants	Coffeeberry (*Frangula californica*)						x		x	
Plants	Common Eel-grass (*Zostera marina*)	x								
Plants	Common Poison Hemlock (*Conium maculatum*)							x	x	
Plants	Common Snowberry (*Symphoricarpos albus*)								x	
Plants	Compact Brome (*Bromus madritensis*)				x	x	x	x	x	

Type	Common/Scientific name										
Plants	Coues's Cassia (*Senna Covesii*)			X	X						
Plants	Coulter Pine (*Pinus coulteri*)									X	
Plants	Coyote Melon (*Cucurbita foetidissima*)		X	X							
Plants	Cream Cups (*Platystemon californicus*)		X			X					
Plants	Creosote Bush (*Larrea tridentata*)										X
Plants	Crystalline Iceplant (*Mesembryanthemum crystallinum*)	X									
Plants	Cuyamaca Lake Downingia (*Downingia concolor*)							X	X		
Plants	Deergrass (*Muhlenbergia rigens*)						X	X	X		
Plants	Deerweed (*Acmispon glaber*)		X	X	X	X				X	X
Plants	Dehesa Nolina (*Nolina interrata*)					X					
Plants	Del Mar Manzanita (*Arctostaphylos glandulosa* subsp. *crassifolia*)					X					
Plants	Desert Agave (*Agave deserti*)										X
Plants	Desert Apricot (*Prunus fremontii*)										X
Plants	Desert Baccharis (*Baccharis sergiloides*)					X				X	X
Plants	Desert Chicory (*Rafinesquia neomexicana*)										X
Plants	Desert Lily (*Hesperocallis undulata*)										X
Plants	Desert Mistletoe (*Phoradendron californicum*)										X
Plants	Desert Sand-verbena (*Abronia villosa* var. *villosa*)										X
Plants	Desert Thornapple (*Datura discolor*)										X
Plants	Desert Wishbone Plant (*Mirabilis laevis* var. *retrorsa*)										X
Plants	Desert-holly (*Atriplex hymenelytra*)										X
Plants	Desert-lavender (*Condea emoryi*)										X
Plants	Desert-willow (*Chilopsis linearis*)										X
Plants	Dodders (*Cuscuta* spp.)	X	X		X						
Plants	Dot-seed Plantain (*Plantago erecta*)		X	X	X						
Plants	Dune Evening primrose (*Oenothera deltoides*)								X	X	
Plants	Eastwood's Manzanita (*Arctostaphylos glandulosa* subsp. *glandulosa*)					X					
Plants	Engelmann Oak/Mesa Blue Oak (*Quercus engelmannii*)					X	X				
Plants	Ephedras (*Ephedra* spp.)					X					X
Plants	Eucalypti (*Eucalyptus* spp.)					X	X	X			
Plants	Felt-leaf Yerba Santa (*Eriodictyon crassifolium* var. *crassifolium*)				X	X					
Plants	Filarees (*Erodium* spp.)		X	X	X	X				X	X
Plants	Fire Poppy (*Papaver californicum*)				X	X					
Plants	Fish-hook Cactus (*Mammillaria dioica*)										X
Plants	Flatsedges (*Cyperus* spp.)							X	X		
Plants	Fleshy Jaumea (*Jaumea carnosa*)	X									
Plants	Four-spot Clarkia (*Clarkia purpurea* subsp. *quadrivulnera*)				X	X	X	X		X	
Plants	Fragrant Sage (*Salvia clevelandii*)					X					
Plants	Fuchsia-flower Gooseberry (*Ribes speciosum*)				X			X			
Plants	Gander's Cholla (*Cylindropuntia ganderi*)										X
Plants	Garland Daisy (*Glebionis coronaria*)	X	X								
Plants	Giant Reed (*Arundo donax*)							X			
Plants	Goatnut (*Simmondsia chinensis*)										X
Plants	Goodding's Black Willow (*Salix gooddingii*)							X	X		
Plants	Grape Soda Lupine (*Lupinus excubitus* var. *austromontanus*)									X	
Plants	Grass (family Poaceae)		X	X	X	X	X	X	X	X	X
Plants	Greene's Ground-cherry (*Physalis crassifolia*)				X	X					X
Plants	Hairy Matilija Poppy (*Romneya trichocalyx*)				X	X					
Plants	Hoary Nettle (*Urtica dioica*)							X	X		
Plants	Holly-leaf Cherry (*Prunus ilicifolia* subsp. *ilicifolia*)					X	X				
Plants	Holly-leaf Redberry (*Rhamnus ilicifolia*)					X				X	
Plants	Honey Mesquite (*Prosopis glandulosa* var. *torreyana*)										X
Plants	Honeysuckles (*Lonicera* spp.)					X	X			X	
Plants	Hooked Skunkweed (*Navarretia hamata*)				X	X					
Plants	Horehound (*Marrubium vulgare*)		X	X	X						
Plants	Hottentot-fig (*Carpobrotus edulis*)	X	X								
Plants	Incienso (*Encelia farinosa*)										X
Plants	Indian Milkweed (*Asclepias eriocarpa*)									X	
Plants	Indigo Bush (*Psorothamnus schottii*)										X
Plants	Interior Coast Live Oak (*Quercus agrifolia* var. *oxyadenia*)						X			X	
Plants	Interior Goldenbush (*Ericameria linearifolia*)				X	X					
Plants	Interior Live Oak (*Quercus wislizeni*)						X			X	
Plants	Ironwood (*Olneya tesota*)										X

Type	Common/Scientific name									
Plants	Islay (*Prunus ilicifolia* subsp. *ilicifolia*)				x	x				
Plants	Jeffrey/Yellow Pine (*Pinus jeffreyi*)								x	
Plants	Jojoba (*Simmondsia chinensis*)									x
Plants	Joshua Tree (*Yucca brevifolia*)									x
Plants	Laguna Mountain Aster (*Dieteria asteroides* var. *lagunensis*)					x			x	
Plants	Laguna/Orcutt's Linanthus (*Linanthus orcuttii*)				x				x	
Plants	Lakeside-lilac (*Ceanothus cyaneus*)				x					
Plants	Laurel Sumac (*Malosma laurina*)		x	x	x		x			
Plants	Lemonadeberry (*Rhus integrifolia*)		x	x	x					
Plants	Lupines (*Lupinus* spp.)		x	x	x	x	x		x	x
Plants	Many-fruit Saltbush (*Atriplex polycarpa*)									x
Plants	Manzanitas (*Arctostaphylos* spp.)					x				
Plants	Mariposa Lilies (*Calochortus* spp.)		x	x	x	x				
Plants	Mexican Fan Palm (*Washingtonia robusta*)						x			
Plants	Milkweeds (*Asclepias* spp.)		x	x	x	x			x	x
Plants	Mission Manzanita (*Xylococcus bicolor*)		x			x				
Plants	Mission Prickly-pear or Indian-fig (*Opuntia ficus-indica*)		x			x				
Plants	Mohave Desert Star (*Monoptilon bellioides*)									x
Plants	Mojave Yucca (*Yucca schidigera*)		x			x				
Plants	Mosses (phylum Bryophyta)		x	x	x	x			x	x
Plants	Mountain-mahoganies (*Cercocarpus* spp.)					x	x		x	
Plants	Mule-fat (*Baccharis salicifolia*)	x						x		
Plants	Narrow-leaf Willow (*Salix exigua*)		x	x	x	x	x			
Plants	Nightshades (family *Solanaceae*)		x	x	x	x	x		x	x
Plants	Nuttall's Scrub Oak (*Quercus dumosa*)		x							
Plants	Nuttall's Snapdragon (*Antirrhinum nuttallianum*)		x			x				
Plants	Oaks (*Quercus* spp.)			x	x	x			x	
Plants	Oats (*Avena* spp.)			x	x	x			x	
Plants	Ocellated Lily (*Lilium humboldtii*)			x	x					
Plants	Ocotillo (*Fouquieria splendens*)									x
Plants	Oleander (*Nerium oleander*)						x			
Plants	Orcutt's Bird's Beak (*Dicranostegia orcuttiana*)		x							
Plants	Orcutt's Brodiaea (*Brodiaea orcuttii*)		x	x			x	x	x	
Plants	Orcutt's Goldenbush (*Hazardia orcuttii*)		x							
Plants	Orcutt's Woody Aster (*Xylorhiza orcuttii*)									x
Plants	Pacific Mosquito Fern (*Azolla filiculoides*)						x	x		
Plants	Pacific Pickleweed (*Salicornia pacifica*)	x								
Plants	Pacific Ponderosa Pine (*Pinus ponderosa*)								x	
Plants	Paintbrushes (*Castilleja* spp.)		x		x	x			x	
Plants	Palmer's-lilac (*Ceanothus palmeri*)								x	
Plants	Parish's Golden-eyes (*Bahiopsis parishii*)									x
Plants	Parish's Stream Lupine (*Lupinus latifolius*)						x			
Plants	Parry Pinyon (*Pinus quadrifolia*)								x	
Plants	Parry's Bear-grass (*Nolina parryi*)									x
Plants	Parry's Tetracoccus (*Tetracoccus dioicus*)		x			x				
Plants	Perez's Marsh-rosemary (*Limonium perezii*)	x	x							
Plants	Pickleweeds (*Salicornia* spp.)	x								
Plants	Pima Rhatany (*Krameria erecta*)									x
Plants	Pipestem Virgin's Bower (*Clematis lasiantha*)		x			x		x	x	
Plants	Poodle-dog Bush (*Eriodictyon parryi*)					x	x			
Plants	Prickly Poppy (*Argemone munita*)		x			x	x		x	
Plants	Prickly-pears (*Opuntia* spp.)		x							
Plants	Prostrate/Nuttall's Lotus (*Acmispon prostratus*)		x							
Plants	Purple Needle Grass (*Stipa pulchra*)		x	x						
Plants	Purple Owl's-clover (*Castilleja exserta* subsp. *exserta*)				x	x				
Plants	Purple-heather (*Krameria erecta*)									x
Plants	Purple-spot Gilia (*Gilia clivorum*)				x					
Plants	Pygmy-cedar (*Peucephyllum schottii*)									x
Plants	Rainbow Manzanita (*Arctostaphylos rainbowensis*)				x					
Plants	Ramona-lilac (*Ceanothus tomentosus*)				x					
Plants	Red Shank (*Adenostoma sparsifolium*)				x					
Plants	Red-stem Filaree (*Erodium cicutarium*)		x	x					x	x
Plants	Ripgut Grass (*Bromus diandrus*)		x	x	x	x			x	

Type	Common/Scientific name	🦅	🌼	🌾	🪶	🍇	🐟	🦋	🌲	🐦
Plants	Rushes (*Juncus* spp.)	X					X	X			X
Plants	Rush Milkweed (*Asclepias subulata*)										X
Plants	Sacapellote (*Acourtia microcephala*)			X		X				
Plants	Salt Heliotrope (*Heliotropium curassavicum*)			X						
Plants	Salt Marsh Bird's Beak (*Chloropyron maritimum*)	X								
Plants	Saltcedar (*Tamarix ramosissima*)	X					X			
Plants	San Diego Ambrosia (*Ambrosia pumila*)					X	X			
Plants	San Diego Hulsea (*Hulsea californica*)					X	X		X	
Plants	San Diego Mountain-mahogany (*Cercocarpus minutiflorus*)			X		X	X			
Plants	San Diego Sedge (*Carex spissa*)						X			
Plants	San Diego Sunflower (*Bahiopsis laciniata*)			X	X					
Plants	San Diego Wreath-plant (*Stephanomeria diegensis*)			X	X					
Plants	San Miguel Savory (*Clinopodium chandleri*)			X		X				
Plants	Santa Rosa Basalt Brodiaea (*Brodiaea santarosae*)					X				
Plants	Scarlet Bugler (*Penstemon centranthifolius*)						X		X	
Plants	School Bells (*Dichelostemma capitatum* subsp. *capitatum*)			X	X		X			
Plants	Screw-bean Mesquite (*Prosopis pubescens*)										X
Plants	Sea-fig (*Carpobrotus chilensis*)	X								
Plants	Selloa Pampas Grass (*Cortaderia selloana*)						X			
Plants	Short-lobe Phacelia (*Phacelia brachyloba*)				X	X	X		X	
Plants	Short-pod Mustard (*Hirschfeldia incana*)	X		X	X					
Plants	Showy Penstemon (*Penstemon spectabilis* var. *spectabilis*)						X			
Plants	Sierra Gooseberry (*Ribes roezlii*)								X	
Plants	Silver Cholla (*Cylindropuntia echinocarpa*)										X
Plants	Single-leaf Pinyon (*Pinus monophylla*)								X	
Plants	Skunkbush or Basket Bush (*Rhus aromatica*)					X	X	X		
Plants	Slender Wild Oat (*Avena barbata*)			X	X					
Plants	Small-leaf Elephant Tree (*Bursera microphylla*)										X
Plants	Smoke Tree (*Psorothamnus spinosus*)										X
Plants	Snake Cholla (*Cylindropuntia californica*)			X						
Plants	Southern California Wild Grape (*Vitis girdiana*)					X	X			
Plants	Southern Jewelflower (*Streptanthus campestris*)					X	X		X	
Plants	Southern Maidenhair Fern (*Adiantum capillus-veneris*)					X	X	X		X
Plants	Southern Pink (*Silene laciniata*)			X		X				
Plants	Spineshrub (*Adolphia californica*)			X	X					
Plants	Spiny Redberry (*Rhamnus crocea*)			X	X					
Plants	Splendid Mariposa Lily (*Calochortus splendens*)			X	X		X			
Plants	Sticky Nama (*Eriodictyon parryi*)					X	X			
Plants	Storksbill (*Erodium cicutarium*)			X	X				X	X
Plants	Storksbills (*Erodium* spp.)			X	X	X			X	X
Plants	Stream Orchid (*Epipactis gigantea*)						X	X		
Plants	Sugar Bush (*Rhus ovata*)					X	X			
Plants	Sugar Pine (*Pinus lambertiana*)								X	
Plants	Summer Snow (*Leptosiphon floribundus*)					X	X		X	
Plants	Sunflowers (family *Asteraceae*)	X	X	X	X	X	X	X	X	X
Plants	Sweet Fennel (*Foeniculum vulgare*)			X	X					
Plants	Tarplants (*Deinandra* spp.)			X	X		X			
Plants	Tecate Cypress (*Hesperocyparis forbesii*)					X				
Plants	Teddy-bear Cholla (*Cylindropuntia bigelovii*)										X
Plants	Telegraph Weed (*Heterotheca grandiflora*)			X						
Plants	Thimbleberry (*Rubus parviflorus*)								X	
Plants	Thornmint (*Acanthomintha ilicifolia*)			X		X				
Plants	Three-awn Grass (*Aristida purpurea*)	X		X	X	X					X
Plants	Thurber's Pilostyles (*Pilostyles thurberi*)										X
Plants	Tidy Tips (*Layia platyglossa*)			X		X			X	
Plants	Torrey Pine (*Pinus torreyana*)					X				
Plants	Torrey's Scrub Oak (*Quercus Xacutidens*)					X				
Plants	Toyon (*Heteromeles arbutifolia*)			X		X	X	X		
Plants	Tree Tobacco (*Nicotiana glauca*)										X
Plants	Wallace's Woolly Daisy (*Eriophyllum wallacei*)			X	X	X	X				X
Plants	Weed's Mariposa Lily (*Calochortus weedii* var. *weedii*)			X	X					
Plants	Western Azalea (*Rhododendron occidentale*)							X		X
Plants	Western Blue Flag (*Iris missouriensis*)							X	X	X

Type	Common/*Scientific* name									
Plants	Western Choke Cherry (*Prunus virginiana* var. *demissa*)								x	
Plants	Western Cottonwood (*Populus fremontii*)							x		
Plants	Western Jimson Weed (*Datura wrightii*)		x	x		x				
Plants	Western Poison-oak (*Toxicodendron diversilobum*)						x	x		
Plants	Western Redbud (*Cercis occidentalis*)				x	x	x		x	
Plants	Western Sycamore (*Platanus racemosa*)							x	x	
Plants	White Alder (*Alnus rhombifolia*)							x		
Plants	White Bur-sage (*Ambrosia dumosa*)									x
Plants	White Dalea (*Psorothamnus emoryi*)									x
Plants	White Globe Lily (*Calochortus albus*)							x		
Plants	White Rhatany (*Krameria bicolor*)									x
Plants	White Sage (*Salvia apiana*)		x	x	x	x				
Plants	Wild-cucumber or Manroot (*Marah macrocarpa*)		x							
Plants	Wild-heliotrope (*Phacelia distans*)	x	x			x				
Plants	Willows (*Salix* spp.)						x			
Plants	Yerba de Chiva (*Clematis ligusticifolia*)			x	x		x		x	
Plants	Yerba Mansa (*Anemopsis californica*)						x	x		
Reptiles, Amphibians & Fish	Arroyo Toad (*Anaxyrus californicus*)						x			
Reptiles, Amphibians & Fish	Banded Rock Lizard (*Petrosaurus mearnsi*)									x
Reptiles, Amphibians & Fish	Blainville's Horned Lizard (*Phrynosoma blainvillii*)		x	x	x	x			x	
Reptiles, Amphibians & Fish	California Grunion (*Leuresthes tenuis*)	x								
Reptiles, Amphibians & Fish	California Treefrog (*Pseudacris cadaverina*)						x	x		x
Reptiles, Amphibians & Fish	Coachwhip (*Coluber flagellum*)		x	x	x					x
Reptiles, Amphibians & Fish	Common Chuckwalla (*Sauromalus ater*)									x
Reptiles, Amphibians & Fish	Common Side-blotched Lizard (*Uta stansburiana*)		x	x	x	x	x		x	x
Reptiles, Amphibians & Fish	Desert Iguana (*Dipsosaurus dorsalis*)									x
Reptiles, Amphibians & Fish	Desert Pupfish (*Cyprinodon macularius*)									x
Reptiles, Amphibians & Fish	Flat-tailed Horned Lizard (*Phrynosoma mcallii*)									x
Reptiles, Amphibians & Fish	Garibaldi (*Hypsypops rubicundus*)	x								
Reptiles, Amphibians & Fish	Gilbert's Skink (*Plestiodon gilberti*)		x	x	x	x	x		x	
Reptiles, Amphibians & Fish	Gophersnake (*Pituophis catenifer*)		x	x	x	x				x
Reptiles, Amphibians & Fish	Horned Lizard (*Phrynosoma* sp.)		x	x	x	x			x	x
Reptiles, Amphibians & Fish	Orange-throated Whiptail (*Aspidoscelis hyperythra*)		x	x	x					
Reptiles, Amphibians & Fish	Pacific Treefrog (*Pseudacris regilla*)							x		
Reptiles, Amphibians & Fish	Rattlesnakes (*Crotalus* spp.)		x	x	x	x	x	x	x	x
Reptiles, Amphibians & Fish	Red Diamond Rattlesnake (*Crotalus ruber*)		x	x	x	x				x
Reptiles, Amphibians & Fish	Rosy Boa (*Lichanura trivirgata*)		x	x	x	x				x
Reptiles, Amphibians & Fish	Sidewinder (*Crotalus cerastes*)									x
Reptiles, Amphibians & Fish	Southern Alligator Lizard (*Elgaria multicarinata*)		x	x	x	x	x		x	
Reptiles, Amphibians & Fish	Speckled Rattlesnake (*Crotalus mitchellii*)		x		x	x				x
Reptiles, Amphibians & Fish	Two-striped Gartersnake (*Thamnophis hammondii*)						x	x		
Reptiles, Amphibians & Fish	Western Fence Lizard (*Sceloporus occidentalis*)		x	x	x	x	x		x	
Reptiles, Amphibians & Fish	Western Rattlesnake (*Crotalus oreganus*)		x	x	x	x	x			
Reptiles, Amphibians & Fish	Western Skink (*Plestiodon skiltonianus*)		x	x	x	x	x		x	
Reptiles, Amphibians & Fish	Western Toad (*Anaxyrus boreas*)						x	x	x	

Species and Habitats by Scientific Name

Type	Scientific/Common name	Beach/Salt Marsh/Lagoon	Coastal Sage Scrub	Grassland	Chaparral	Oak Woodland	Freshwater Marsh/Montane Meadow/Vernal Pool	Mixed Conifer Forest	Desert
Algae, Bacteria & Fungi	Ascomycota (Phylum of Lichens)	x	x	x	x	x	x	x	x
Algae, Bacteria & Fungi	Frankia sp. (Frankia)	x			x	x	x		x
Algae, Bacteria & Fungi	Macrocystis pyrifera (Giant Kelp)	x							
Algae, Bacteria & Fungi	Spirogyra spp. (Freshwater Green Algae, Pond Scums, Pond-mosses)							x	
Algae, Bacteria & Fungi	Trebouxia spp. (Green Algae)	x		x	x	x	x	x	x
Birds	Aechmophorus occidentalis (Western Grebe)	x					x		
Birds	Agelaius phoeniceus (Red-winged Blackbird)						x		
Birds	Amphispiza bilineata (Black-throated Sparrow)								x
Birds	Apodidae (Family of Swifts)	x			x	x		x	x
Birds	Anas cyanoptera (Cinnamon Teal)						x		
Birds	Anas platyrhynchos (Mallard)						x		
Birds	Anthus rubescens (American Pipit)			x					
Birds	Aphelocoma californica (Western Scrub-jay)				x	x			
Birds	Aquila chrysaetos (Golden Eagle)			x	x	x			
Birds	Ardea alba (Great Egret)	x							
Birds	Ardea herodias (Great Blue Heron)	x							
Birds	Auriparus flaviceps (Verdin)								x
Birds	Aythya affinis (Lesser Scaup)	x					x		
Birds	Bubo virginianus (Great Horned Owl)					x			
Birds	Bucephala albeola (Bufflehead)	x							
Birds	Buteo jamaicensis (Red-tailed Hawk)			x	x				
Birds	Buteo lineatus (Red-shouldered Hawk)					x			
Birds	Butorides virescens (Green Heron)						x		
Birds	Calidris alba (Sanderling)	x							
Birds	Calidris mauri (Western Sandpiper)	x							
Birds	Callipepla californica (California Quail)		x		x	x	x		
Birds	Callipepla gambelii (Gambel's Quail)								x
Birds	Calocitta colliei (Black-throated Magpie-jay)					x			
Birds	Calypte anna (Anna's Hummingbird)		x		x	x	x		
Birds	Calypte costae (Costa's Hummingbird)		x		x				x
Birds	Campylorhynchus brunneicapillus (Cactus Wren)		x						x
Birds	Cathartes aura (Turkey Vulture)			x	x				
Birds	Chamaea fasciata (Wrentit)		x		x				
Birds	Charadrius nivosus (Western Snowy Plover)	x							
Birds	Charadrius vociferus (Killdeer)	x		x			x		
Birds	Chondestes grammacus (Lark Sparrow)			x					
Birds	Circus cyaneus (Northern Harrier)	x					x		
Birds	Contopus sordidulus (Western Wood-pewee)					x		x	
Birds	Corvus brachyrhynchos (American Crow)					x			
Birds	Corvus corax (Common Raven)			x	x				x
Birds	Cyanocitta stelleri (Steller's Jay)							x	
Birds	Egretta rufescens (Reddish Egret)	x							
Birds	Egretta thula (Snowy Egret)	x							
Birds	Elanus leucurus (White-tailed Kite)					x			
Birds	Empidonax difficilis (Western Flycatcher)						x		
Birds	Empidonax traillii extimus (Southwestern Willow Flycatcher)						x		
Birds	Eremophila alpestris (Horned Lark)			x					

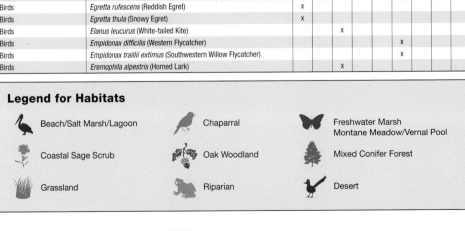

Legend for Habitats

- Beach/Salt Marsh/Lagoon
- Coastal Sage Scrub
- Grassland
- Chaparral
- Oak Woodland
- Riparian
- Freshwater Marsh Montane Meadow/Vernal Pool
- Mixed Conifer Forest
- Desert

Type	Scientific/Common name								
Birds	*Falco mexicanus* (Prairie Falcon)		x						x
Birds	*Falco peregrinus* (Peregrine Falcon)	x	x				x		
Birds	*Falco sparverius* (American Kestrel)		x						
Birds	*Fulica americana* (American Coot)						x		
Birds	*Geococcyx californianus* (Greater Roadrunner)		x						x
Birds	*Haemorhous mexicanus* (House Finch)		x	x	x		x		x
Birds	*Haliaeetus leucocephalus* (Bald Eagle)	x	x				x	x	
Birds	*Himantopus mexicanus* (Black-necked Stilt)	x							
Birds	Hirundinidae (Family of Swallows)	x	x				x	x	x
Birds	*Icterus bullockii* (Bullock's Oriole)						x		
Birds	*Icterus cucullatus* (Hooded Oriole)						x		x
Birds	*Lanius ludovicianus* (Loggerhead Shrike)		x	x					x
Birds	Laridae (Family of Gulls and Terns)	x							
Birds	Larinae (Subfamily of Gulls)	x					x		
Birds	*Larus occidentalis* (Western Gull)	x							
Birds	*Megaceryle alcyon* (Belted Kingfisher)	x					x		
Birds	*Melanerpes formicivorus* (Acorn Woodpecker)				x			x	
Birds	*Meleagris gallopavo* (Wild Turkey)				x			x	
Birds	*Melozone crissalis* (California Towhee)		x						
Birds	*Mimus polyglottos* (Northern Mockingbird)		x						x
Birds	*Molothrus ater* (Brown-headed Cowbird)			x		x			
Birds	*Nycticorax nycticorax* (Black-crowned Night Heron)	x					x		
Birds	*Oxyura jamaicensis* (Ruddy Duck)	x					x		
Birds	*Pandion haliaetus* (Osprey)	x					x		
Birds	*Passerculus sandwichensis beldingi* (Belding's Savannah Sparrow)	x							
Birds	*Passerina amoena* (Lazuli Bunting)				x	x	x		x
Birds	*Patagioenas fasciata* (Band-tailed Pigeon)				x			x	
Birds	*Pelecanus erythrorhynchos* (American White Pelican)	x					x		
Birds	*Pelecanus occidentalis californicus* (California Brown Pelican)	x							
Birds	*Petrochelidon pyrrhonota* (Cliff Swallow)						x		
Birds	*Phainopepla nitens* (Phainopepla)				x	x			x
Birds	*Phalacrocorax penicillatus* (Brandt's Cormorant)	x							
Birds	*Pheucticus melanocephalus* (Black-headed Grosbeak)				x	x		x	
Birds	*Pipilo maculatus* (Spotted Towhee)				x	x	x		
Birds	*Piranga ludoviciana* (Western Tanager)							x	
Birds	*Podilymbus podiceps* (Pied-billed Grebe)	x					x		
Birds	*Poecile gambeli* (Mountain Chickadee)							x	
Birds	*Polioptila californica californica* (California Gnatcatcher)		x						
Birds	*Psaltriparus minimus* (Bushtit)		x		x	x	x		
Birds	*Rallus obsoletus levipes* (Light-footed Ridgway's Rail)	x					x		
Birds	*Recurvirostra americana* (American Avocet)	x							
Birds	*Regulus calendula* (Ruby-crowned Kinglet)				x	x	x		x
Birds	*Sayornis nigricans* (Black Phoebe)						x	x	
Birds	*Sayornis saya* (Say's Phoebe)			x					x
Birds	*Selasphorus calliope* (Calliope Hummingbird)							x	
Birds	*Selasphorus sasin* (Allen's Hummingbird)		x						
Birds	*Setophaga coronata* (Yellow-rumped Warbler)		x	x		x			
Birds	*Sialia currucoides* (Mountain Bluebird)			x					x
Birds	*Sialia mexicana* (Western Bluebird)					x		x	
Birds	*Sitta carolinensis* (White-breasted Nuthatch)					x		x	
Birds	*Spinus psaltria* (Lesser Goldfinch)				x	x			
Birds	*Spinus tristis* (American Goldfinch)					x			
Birds	*Sternula antillarum* (Least Tern)	x							
Birds	*Strix occidentalis* (Spotted Owl)					x		x	
Birds	*Sturnella neglecta* (Western Meadowlark)		x						
Birds	Sterninae (Subfamily of Terns)	x					x		
Birds	*Thryomanes bewickii* (Bewick's Wren)		x		x				
Birds	*Toxostoma redivivum* (California Thrasher)		x		x				
Birds	*Tringa semipalmata* (Willet)	x							
Birds	*Tyto alba* (Barn Owl)			x		x	x		
Birds	*Vireo bellii pusillus* (Least Bell's Vireo)						x		
Birds	*Vireo vicinior* (Gray Vireo)				x				
Birds	*Zenaida macroura* (Mourning Dove)		x	x					x

Type	Scientific/Common name									
Birds	Zonotrichia leucophrys (White-crowned Sparrow)	x	x	x						x
Invertebrates	Acrididae (Family of Grasshoppers)	x	x	x	x	x	x	x	x
Invertebrates	Agelenidae (Family of Funnel Weaver Spiders)	x	x	x						
Invertebrates	Agrilus auroguttatus (Goldspotted Oak Borer)						x			
Invertebrates	Annelida (Phylum Sand Tubeworms)	x								
Invertebrates	Anthocharis sara (Sara Orangetip Butterfly)	x	x	x	x	x	x		x	x
Invertebrates	Anthopleura spp. (Sea Anemones)	x								
Invertebrates	Aphonopelma sp. (Tarantula)	x	x	x						x
Invertebrates	Aphorphora spp. (Spittle Bugs)	x	x	x	x	x	x	x	x
Invertebrates	Apis mellifera (European Honey Bee)	x	x	x	x	x	x	x	x
Invertebrates	Apoidea (Superfamily of Native Bees)	x	x	x	x	x	x	x	x
Invertebrates	Aquarius remijis (Common Water Strider)							x	x	
Invertebrates	Argiope aurantia (Argiope spider)	x	x	x						
Invertebrates	Ariolimax columbianus (Pacific Banana Slug)						x			
Invertebrates	Bothriocyrtum californicum (California Trapdoor Spider)	x	x	x	x				x	
Invertebrates	Branchinecta sandiegonensis (San Diego Fairy Shrimp)	x								
Invertebrates	Branchinecta spp. (Fairy Shrimps)	x								
Invertebrates	Brephidium exilis (Western Blue Pygmy Butterfly)	x								x
Invertebrates	Coccinellidae (Family of Ladybugs, Ladybird Beetles)	x	x	x	x	x	x	x	x
Invertebrates	Coelopa spp. (Kelp Flies)	x								
Invertebrates	Cynipidae (Family of Oak Gall Wasps)						x			
Invertebrates	Dactylopius coccus (Cochineal Scale)	x		x						
Invertebrates	Danaus gilippus (Queen Butterfly)									x
Invertebrates	Danaus plexippus (Monarch Butterfly)	x	x	x	x				x	x
Invertebrates	Dasymutilla aureola (Pacific Velvet Ant)	x	x	x						
Invertebrates	Dasymutilla sackenii (Sackeni's Velvet Ant)	x	x	x	x					x
Invertebrates	Dendroctonus valens (Red Turpentine Beetle)								x	
Invertebrates	Dermacentor sp. (Tick)	x	x	x	x	x			x	x
Invertebrates	Diapheromera covilleae (Creosote Bush Walking Stick)									x
Invertebrates	Eleodes sp. (Stink Beetle)	x	x	x	x	x			x	x
Invertebrates	Emerita analoga (Sand Crabs)	x								
Invertebrates	Euphydryas editha quino (Quino Checkerspot Butterfly)	x	x							
Invertebrates	Euphyes vestris harbisoni (Harbison's Dun Skipper)				x	x				
Invertebrates	Flabellina iodinea (Spanish Shawl)	x								
Invertebrates	Gastropoda (Class of Nudibranchs)	x								
Invertebrates	Haliotis corrugata (Pink Abalone)	x								
Invertebrates	Heliopetes ericetorum (Northern White Skipper)				x	x				x
Invertebrates	Hemiptera (Order of True Bugs)	x	x	x	x	x	x	x	x
Invertebrates	Hyalophora euryalus (Ceanothus Silk Moth)	x		x						
Invertebrates	Ips paraconfusus (Five-spined Engraver Beetle)								x	
Invertebrates	Latrodectus geometricus (Brown Widow)	x	x	x	x	x				
Invertebrates	Latrodectus hesperus (Black Widow)	x	x	x	x	x	x		x	x
Invertebrates	Linepithema humile (Argentine Ant)	x	x	x		x				
Invertebrates	Liometopum occidentale (California Velvety Tree Ant)						x	x	x	
Invertebrates	Lumbricidae (Family of Earthworms)						x	x	x	
Invertebrates	Lumbricus rubellus (European Earthworm)						x	x	x	
Invertebrates	Lycaena hermes (Hermes Copper Butterfly)	x		x						
Invertebrates	Lycaenidae (Family of Tiny Blue Butterflies)	x			x	x			x	x
Invertebrates	Lygaeidae (Family of Milkweed bugs)	x	x	x	x				x	x
Invertebrates	Mesepiola specca (Nolina Moth)			x						x
Invertebrates	Mollusca (Phylum of Chitons and Limpets)	x								
Invertebrates	Murgantia histrionica (Harlequin Bug)	x								x
Invertebrates	Myrmeleontidae (Family of Antlions)	x		x	x				x	x
Invertebrates	Nathalis iole (Dainty Sulphur Butterfly)	x	x	x	x				x	x
Invertebrates	Navanax inermis (California Aglaja)	x								
Invertebrates	Nematomorpha (Phylum of Horsehair worms)	x	x	x	x	x	x	x	x
Invertebrates	Odonata (Order of Damselflies and Dragonflies)	x	x	x	x	x	x	x	x
Invertebrates	Papilio rutulus (Western Tiger Swallowtail Butterfly)	x	x	x	x	x			x	x
Invertebrates	Peponapis pruinosa (Squash Bee)	x		x	x					x
Invertebrates	Peponapis spp. (Squash Bees)	x		x	x					x
Invertebrates	Pepsis sp. (Tarantula Hawk Wasp)	x	x	x	x				x	x
Invertebrates	Pheidole hyatti (Big-headed Ants)	x								x
Invertebrates	Pieris rapae (Cabbage White Butterfly)	x	x	x	x	x				

Type	Scientific/Common name									
Invertebrates	*Pogonomyrmex californicus* (California Harvester Ant)		x		x	x				x
Invertebrates	*Polygonia satyrus* (Satyr Angelwing)							x		
Invertebrates	*Pontania* sp. (Willow Gall Sawfly)							x		
Invertebrates	*Psephenidae* (Family of Water Penny Beetles)							x		
Invertebrates	*Schistocerca nitens* (Gray Bird Grasshopper)		x	x	x	x	x	x	x	x
Invertebrates	*Stenopelmatus* spp. (Jerusalem Cricket)		x	x	x	x			x	x
Invertebrates	*Stigmella* sp. (Stigmella Moth)		x		x	x				
Invertebrates	*Tapimona sessile* (House Ants)		x	x	x	x	x		x	x
Invertebrates	*Tegeticula maculata* (Yucca or Pronuba Moth)		x		x	x				
Invertebrates	*Tegeticula yuccasella* (Yucca Moth)		x		x					x
Invertebrates	*Uca pugilator* (Fiddler Crab)	x								
Invertebrates	*Vanessa cardui* (Painted Lady)		x		x	x	x			x
Invertebrates	*Xenoglossa* spp. (Squash Bees)		x		x	x				x
Mammals	*Ammospermophilus leucurus* (White-tailed Antelope Ground Squirrel)									x
Mammals	*Bassariscus astutus* (Ringtail)				x	x	x	x	x	x
Mammals	*Canis latrans* (Coyote)	x	x	x	x	x	x	x	x	x
Mammals	*Chaetodipus fallax* (San Diego Pocket Mouse)				x	x	x			
Mammals	*Chiroptera* (Order of Bats)		x		x	x	x	x	x	x
Mammals	*Didelphis virginiana* (Virginia Opossum)		x		x	x	x	x	x	x
Mammals	*Dipodomys deserti* (Desert Kangaroo Rat)		x		x	x				
Mammals	*Dipodomys merriami* (Merriam's Kangaroo Rat)		x	x		x	x			x
Mammals	*Lasiurus xanthinus* (Western Yellow Bat)		x		x	x	x	x	x	x
Mammals	*Lepus californicus* (Black-tailed Jackrabbit)	x	x		x	x	x	x	x	x
Mammals	*Lynx rufus* (Bobcat)	x	x		x	x	x	x	x	x
Mammals	*Mephitis mephitis* (Striped Skunk)	x	x		x	x	x	x	x	x
Mammals	*Microtus californicus* (California Vole)	x	x	x	x	x	x	x		
Mammals	*Mustela frenata* (California Weasel)	x	x			x	x	x		
Mammals	*Neotoma bryanti* (Bryant's Woodrat)		x		x	x	x		x	x
Mammals	*Neotoma macrotis* (Big-eared Woodrat)		x			x	x	x	x	x
Mammals	*Odocoileus hemionus* (Southern Mule Deer)	x	x	x	x	x	x	x	x	x
Mammals	*Otospermophilus beecheyi* (California Ground Squirrel)	x	x	x	x	x	x	x	x	x
Mammals	*Ovis canadensis nelsoni* (Desert Bighorn Sheep)									x
Mammals	*Phoca vitulina* (Harbor Seal)	x								
Mammals	*Procyon lotor* (Northern Raccoon)	x				x	x	x		
Mammals	*Puma concolor* (Mountain Lion)	x	x	x	x	x	x	x	x	x
Mammals	*Rattus rattus* (Roof Rat)		x	x	x	x	x	x	x	x
Mammals	*Sciurus griseus* (Western Gray Squirrel)					x				
Mammals	*Sus scrofa* (Feral Pig)		x	x	x	x			x	x
Mammals	*Sylvilagus audubonii* (Desert Cottontail)	x	x	x	x	x	x	x	x	x
Mammals	*Sylvilagus bachmani* (Brush Rabbit)	x	x		x	x	x	x	x	x
Mammals	*Tadarida brasiliensis* (Mexican Free-tailed Bat)		x	x	x	x	x	x	x	x
Mammals	*Taxidea taxus* (Badger)		x			x	x	x	x	x
Mammals	*Thomomys bottae* (Botta's Pocket Gopher)	x	x	x	x	x	x	x	x	x
Mammals	*Urocyon cinereoargenteus* (Gray Fox)	x	x	x	x	x	x	x	x	x
Mammals	*Ursus americanus californiensis* (California Black Bear)		x	x	x	x	x	x	x	x
Mammals	*Vulpes macrotis* (Kit Fox)									x
Mammals	*Zalophus californianus* (California Sea Lion)	x								
Plants	*Abronia villosa* var. *villosa* (Desert Sand-verbena)									x
Plants	*Acanthomintha ilicifolia* (Thornmint)		x		x					
Plants	*Acmispon glaber* (Deerweed)		x	x	x	x			x	x
Plants	*Acmispon prostratus* (Prostrate/Nuttall's Lotus)		x							
Plants	*Acourtia microcephala* (Sacapellote)		x		x					
Plants	*Adenostoma fasciculatum* (Chamise)					x	x			
Plants	*Adenostoma sparsifolium* (Red Shank)					x				
Plants	*Adiantum capillus-veneris* (Southern Maidenhair Fern)					x	x		x	x
Plants	*Adolphia californica* (Spineshrub)		x	x						
Plants	*Agave deserti* (Desert Agave)									x
Plants	*Alnus rhombifolia* (White Alder)					x				
Plants	*Ambrosia dumosa* (White Bur-sage)									x
Plants	*Ambrosia pumila* (San Diego Ambrosia)				x		x			
Plants	*Ambrosia salsola* var. *salsola* (Cheesebush, Burrobrush)									x
Plants	*Anemopsis californica* (Yerba Mansa)					x	x			
Plants	*Antirrhinum nuttallianum* (Nuttall's Snapdragon)		x		x					

Type	Scientific/Common name									
Plants	*Arctostaphylos glandulosa* subsp. *crassifolia* (Del Mar Manzanita)				X					
Plants	*Arctostaphylos glandulosa* subsp. *glandulosa* (Eastwood's Manzanita)				X					
Plants	*Arctostaphylos glauca* (Big-berry Manzanita)				X	X				
Plants	*Arctostaphylos rainbowensis* (Rainbow Manzanita)				X					
Plants	*Arctostaphylos* spp. (Manzanitas)				X					
Plants	*Argemone munita* (Prickly Poppy)		X		X	X			X	
Plants	*Aristida purpurea* (Three-awn Grass)	X	X	X	X	X				X
Plants	*Artemisia californica* (Coastal Sagebrush)	X	X	X	X					
Plants	*Arundo donax* (Giant Reed)						X			
Plants	*Asclepias californica* (California/Round-hood Milkweed)			X	X	X			X	
Plants	*Asclepias eriocarpa* (Indian Milkweed)								X	
Plants	*Asclepias* spp. (Milkweeds)			X	X				X	X
Plants	*Asclepias subulata* (Rush Milkweed)									X
Plants	Asteraceae (Family of Sunflowers)	X	X	X	X	X	X	X	X	X
Plants	*Atriplex hymenelytra* (Desert-holly)									X
Plants	*Atriplex lentiformis* (Big Saltbush)	X								
Plants	*Atriplex polycarpa* (Many-fruit Saltbush)									X
Plants	*Avena barbata* (Slender Wild Oat)		X	X						
Plants	*Avena* spp. (Oats)			X	X	X			X	
Plants	*Azolla filiculoides* (Pacific Mosquito Fern)						X	X		
Plants	*Baccharis pilularis* (Chaparral Broom or Coyote Brush)			X						
Plants	*Baccharis salicifolia* (Mule-fat)	X						X		
Plants	*Baccharis sarothroides* (Broom Baccharis)	X					X			
Plants	*Baccharis sergiloides* (Desert Baccharis)				X				X	X
Plants	*Bahiopsis laciniata* (San Diego Sunflower)			X	X					
Plants	*Bahiopsis parishii* (Parish's Golden-eyes)									X
Plants	*Boechera californica* (California Rock-cress)				X	X				
Plants	*Brassica nigra* (Black Mustard)		X	X						
Plants	*Brodiaea orcuttii* (Orcutt's Brodiaea)			X	X		X		X	X
Plants	*Brodiaea santarosae* (Santa Rosa Basalt Brodiaea)				X					
Plants	*Bromus diandrus* (Ripgut Grass)			X	X	X	X		X	
Plants	*Bromus madritensis* (Compact Brome)			X	X	X	X	X	X	
Plants	*Bromus* spp. (Bromes)			X			X			
Plants	*Bromus tectorum* (Cheat Grass)				X	X	X		X	
Plants	Bryophyta (Phylum of Mosses)			X	X	X	X	X	X	X
Plants	*Bursera microphylla* (Small-leaf Elephant Tree)									X
Plants	*California macrophylla* (California Large-leaf Filaree)				X					
Plants	*Calocedrus decurrens* (California Incense Cedar)								X	
Plants	*Calochortus albus* (White Globe Lily)								X	
Plants	*Calochortus splendens* (Splendid Mariposa Lily)			X	X		X			
Plants	*Calochortus* spp. (Mariposa Lilies)			X	X	X	X			
Plants	*Calochortus weedii* var. *weedii* (Weed's Mariposa Lily)			X	X					
Plants	*Camissoniopsis cheiranthifolia* subsp. *suffruticosa* (Beach Sun Cup)	X								
Plants	*Carex spissa* (San Diego Sedge)							X		
Plants	*Carpobrotus chilensis* (Sea-fig)	X								
Plants	*Carpobrotus edulis* (Hottentot-fig)	X	X							
Plants	*Castilleja exserta* subsp. *exserta* (Purple Owl's-clover)				X		X			
Plants	*Castilleja* spp. (Paintbrushes)		X		X	X			X	
Plants	*Ceanothus cyaneus* (Lakeside-lilac)				X					
Plants	*Ceanothus leucodermis* (Chaparral Whitethorn)				X	X			X	
Plants	*Ceanothus palmeri* (Palmer's-lilac)				X				X	
Plants	*Ceanothus* spp. (Ceanothus species)				X	X			X	
Plants	*Ceanothus tomentosus* (Ramona-lilac)				X					
Plants	*Cercis occidentalis* (Western Redbud)				X	X	X		X	
Plants	*Cercocarpus betuloides* (Birch-leaf Mountain-mahogany)				X		X		X	
Plants	*Cercocarpus minutiflorus* (San Diego Mountain-mahogany)		X		X		X			
Plants	*Cercocarpus* spp. (Mountain-mahoganies)				X	X			X	
Plants	*Chilopsis linearis* (Desert-willow)									X
Plants	*Chloropyron maritimum* (Salt Marsh Bird's Beak)	X								
Plants	*Cirsium occidentale* var. *californicum* (California Thistle)						X		X	
Plants	*Clarkia purpurea* subsp. *quadrivulnera* (Four-spot Clarkia)			X	X	X	X		X	
Plants	*Clematis lasiantha* (Pipestem Virgin's Bower)		X		X		X		X	
Plants	*Clematis ligusticifolia* (Yerba de Chiva)			X	X		X		X	

Type	Scientific/Common name									
Plants	*Clinopodium chandleri* (San Miguel Savory)		X		X					
Plants	*Cneoridium dumosum* (Coast Spice Bush or Bush-rue)		X		X					
Plants	*Condea emoryi* (Desert-lavender)									X
Plants	*Conium maculatum* (Common Poison Hemlock)						X	X		
Plants	*Cortaderia selloana* (Selloa Pampas Grass)						X			
Plants	*Cucurbita foetidissima* (Coyote Melon)		X	X						
Plants	*Cuscuta* spp. (Dodders)	X	X		X					X
Plants	*Cylindropuntia bigelovii* (Teddy-bear Cholla)									X
Plants	*Cylindropuntia californica* (Snake Cholla)		X							
Plants	*Cylindropuntia echinocarpa* (Silver Cholla)									X
Plants	*Cylindropuntia ganderi* (Gander's Cholla)									X
Plants	*Cylindropuntia prolifera* (Coast Cholla)		X							
Plants	*Cynara cardunculus* (Artichoke Thistle)		X	X	X					
Plants	*Cyperus* spp. (Flatsedges)						X	X		
Plants	*Datura discolor* (Desert Thornapple)									X
Plants	*Datura wrightii* (Western Jimson Weed)		X	X		X				
Plants	*Deinandra* spp. (Tarplants)		X	X	X	X				
Plants	*Delphinium cardinale* (Cardinal/Scarlet Larkspur)					X				
Plants	*Dichelostemma capitatum* subsp. *capitatum* (Blue Dicks, School Bells)		X	X		X				
Plants	*Dicranostegia orcuttiana* (Orcutt's Bird's Beak)		X							
Plants	*Dieteria asteroides* var. *lagunensis* (Laguna Mountain Aster)					X		X		
Plants	*Diplacus longiflorus* (Bush Monkey Flower)		X		X	X				
Plants	*Diplacus puniceus* (Coast Monkey Flower)		X		X					
Plants	*Downingia concolor* (Cuyamaca Lake Downingia)						X	X		
Plants	*Dudleya pulverulenta* (Chalk Dudleya)		X		X					
Plants	*Encelia californica* (California Encelia)	X	X	X						
Plants	*Encelia farinosa* (Brittlebush, Incienso)									X
Plants	*Ephedra* spp. (Ephedras)					X				X
Plants	*Epipactis gigantea* (Stream Orchid)						X	X		
Plants	*Ericameria linearifolia* (Interior Goldenbush)		X	X						
Plants	*Eriodictyon crassifolium* var. *crassifolium* (Felt-leaf Yerba Santa)		X		X					
Plants	*Eriodictyon parryi* (Poodle-dog Bush, Sticky Nama)		X	X						
Plants	*Eriogonum fasciculatum* (California Buckwheat)		X		X					
Plants	*Eriophyllum wallacei* (Wallace's Woolly Daisy)		X	X	X	X				X
Plants	*Erodium cicutarium* (Red-stem Filaree, Storksbill)		X	X					X	X
Plants	*Erodium* spp. (Filarees, Storksbills)		X	X	X	X			X	X
Plants	*Eschscholzia californica* (California Poppy)		X	X		X				
Plants	*Eucalyptus* spp. (Eucalypti)					X	X	X		
Plants	*Ferocactus cylindraceus* (California Barrel Cactus)									X
Plants	*Ferocactus viridescens* (Coast Barrel Cactus)		X							
Plants	*Foeniculum vulgare* (Sweet Fennel)		X	X						
Plants	*Fouquieria splendens* (Ocotillo)									X
Plants	*Frangula californica* (Coffeeberry)					X			X	
Plants	*Frankenia salina* (Alkali-heath)	X								
Plants	*Fritillaria biflora* (Chocolate Lily)		X	X						
Plants	*Galium* spp. (Bedstraws)		X		X	X			X	
Plants	*Gilia clivorum* (Purple-spot Gilia)		X							
Plants	*Glebionis coronaria* (Garland Daisy)	X	X							
Plants	*Gutierrezia sarothrae* (Broom Matchweed)			X	X	X				
Plants	*Hazardia orcuttii* (Orcutt's Goldenbush)		X							
Plants	*Heliotropium curassavicum* (Salt Heliotrope)		X							
Plants	*Hesperocallis undulata* (Desert Lily)									X
Plants	*Hesperocyparis forbesii* (Tecate Cypress)					X				
Plants	*Hesperoyucca whipplei* (Chaparral Candle)		X	X	X	X				
Plants	*Heteromeles arbutifolia* (Toyon, Christmas Berry)		X		X	X	X			
Plants	*Heterotheca grandiflora* (Telegraph Weed)		X							
Plants	*Hirschfeldia incana* (Short-pod Mustard)	X	X	X						
Plants	*Hulsea californica* (San Diego Hulsea)					X	X		X	
Plants	*Iris missouriensis* (Western Blue Flag)						X	X	X	
Plants	*Isocoma menziesii* var. *vernonioides* (Coastal Goldenbush)	X					X	X		
Plants	*Jaumea carnosa* (Fleshy Jaumea)	X								
Plants	*Juncus* spp. (Rushes)	X					X	X		X
Plants	*Juniperus californica* (California Juniper)									X

Type	Scientific/Common name										
Plants	*Justicia californica* (Chuparosa)										x
Plants	*Krameria bicolor* (White Rhatany)										x
Plants	*Krameria erecta* (Pima Rhatany, Purple-heather)										x
Plants	*Larrea tridentata* (Creosote Bush)										x
Plants	*Layia platyglossa* (Tidy Tips)		x			x			x		
Plants	*Lepidium latifolium* (Broad-leaf Peppergrass)		x	x		x					
Plants	*Leptosiphon floribundus* (Summer Snow)					x	x		x		
Plants	*Lilium humboldtii* (Ocellated Lily)					x	x				
Plants	*Limonium perezii* (Perez's Marsh-rosemary)	x	x								
Plants	*Linanthus orcuttii* (Laguna/Orcutt's Linanthus)					x			x		
Plants	*Lonicera* spp. (Honeysuckles)					x	x		x		
Plants	*Lupinus arizonicus* (Arizona Lupine)										x
Plants	*Lupinus excubitus* var. *austromontanus* (Grape Soda Lupine)								x		
Plants	*Lupinus latifolius* (Parish's Stream Lupine)							x			
Plants	*Lupinus* spp. (Lupines)		x	x	x	x	x	x		x	x
Plants	*Lycium californicum* (California Desert Thorn)	x	x								
Plants	*Malacothamnus fasciculatus* (Chaparral Bushmallow)		x								
Plants	*Malosma laurina* (Laurel Sumac)		x	x		x		x			
Plants	*Mammillaria dioica* (Fish-hook Cactus)										x
Plants	*Marah macrocarpa* (Wild-cucumber or Manroot)		x								
Plants	*Marrubium vulgare* (Horehound)		x	x		x					
Plants	*Marsilea vestita* (Aquatic Hairy Clover Fern)							x			
Plants	*Mesembryanthemum crystallinum* (Crystalline Iceplant)	x									
Plants	*Mirabilis laevis* var. *retrorsa* (Desert Wishbone Plant)										x
Plants	*Monoptilon bellioides* (Mohave Desert Star)										x
Plants	*Muhlenbergia rigens* (Deergrass)						x	x	x		
Plants	*Navarretia hamata* (Hooked Skunkweed)		x			x					
Plants	*Nerium oleander* (Oleander)							x			
Plants	*Nicotiana glauca* (Tree Tobacco)										x
Plants	*Nolina interrata* (Dehesa Nolina)					x					
Plants	*Nolina parryi* (Parry's Bear-grass)										x
Plants	*Oenothera deltoides* (Dune Evening-primrose)							x	x		
Plants	*Olneya tesota* (ironwood)										x
Plants	*Opuntia basilaris* (Beavertail Cactus)										x
Plants	*Opuntia ficus-indica* (Mission Prickly-pear or Indian-fig)		x			x					
Plants	*Opuntia littoralis* (Coast Prickly-pear)		x			x					
Plants	*Opuntia* spp. (Prickly-pears)		x								
Plants	*Paeonia californica* (California Peony)						x				
Plants	*Papaver californicum* (Fire Poppy)		x			x					
Plants	*Parkinsonia florida* (Blue Palo Verde)										x
Plants	*Penstemon centranthifolius* (Scarlet Bugler)						x		x		
Plants	*Penstemon spectabilis* var. *spectabilis* (Showy Penstemon)						x				
Plants	*Peritoma arborea* var. *arborea* (Coast Bladderpod)		x	x							
Plants	*Peucephyllum schottii* (Pygmy-cedar)										x
Plants	*Phacelia brachyloba* (Short-lobe Phacelia)				x	x	x		x		
Plants	*Phacelia distans* (Wild-heliotrope)	x	x			x					
Plants	*Phoradendron californicum* (Desert Mistletoe)										x
Plants	*Physalis crassifolia* (Greene's Ground-cherry)		x			x					x
Plants	*Pilostyles thurberi* (Thurber's Pilostyles)										x
Plants	*Pinus coulteri* (Coulter Pine)									x	
Plants	*Pinus jeffreyi* (Jeffrey/Yellow Pine)									x	
Plants	*Pinus lambertiana* (Sugar Pine)									x	
Plants	*Pinus monophylla* (Single-leaf Pinyon)									x	
Plants	*Pinus ponderosa* (Pacific Ponderosa Pine)									x	
Plants	*Pinus quadrifolia* (Parry Pinyon)									x	
Plants	*Pinus torreyana* (Torrey Pine)					x					
Plants	*Plantago erecta* (Dot-seed Plantain)		x	x		x					
Plants	*Platanus racemosa* (Western Sycamore)							x	x		
Plants	*Platystemon californicus* (Cream Cups)				x		x				
Plants	*Pluchea sericea* (Arrow Weed)							x	x		
Plants	Poaceae (Family of Grasses)	x	x	x	x	x	x	x	x		
Plants	*Populus fremontii* (Western Cottonwood)							x			
Plants	*Prosopis glandulosa* var. *torreyana* (Honey Mesquite)										x

Type	Scientific/Common name	🦤	🌼	🌾	🐦	🦎	🦦	🦋	🌲	🦃
Plants	*Prosopis pubescens* (Screw-bean Mesquite)									x
Plants	*Prunus fremontii* (Desert Apricot)									x
Plants	*Prunus ilicifolia* subsp. *ilicifolia* (Islay, Holly-leaf Cherry)				x	x				
Plants	*Prunus virginiana* var. *demissa* (Western Choke Cherry)								x	
Plants	*Pseudotsuga macrocarpa* (Big-cone Douglas Fir)								x	
Plants	*Psorothamnus emoryi* (White Dalea)									x
Plants	*Psorothamnus schottii* (Indigo Bush)									x
Plants	*Psorothamnus spinosus* (Smoke Tree)									x
Plants	*Quercus agrifolia* var. *agrifolia* (Coast Live Oak)					x	x			
Plants	*Quercus agrifolia* var. *oxyadenia* (Interior Coast Live Oak)					x			x	
Plants	*Quercus chrysolepis* (Canyon Live Oak)					x			x	
Plants	*Quercus dumosa* (Nuttall's Scrub Oak)		x							
Plants	*Quercus engelmannii* (Engelmann Oak/Mesa Blue Oak)				x	x				
Plants	*Quercus kelloggii* (California Black Oak)								x	
Plants	*Quercus* spp. (Oaks)			x	x	x			x	
Plants	*Quercus wislizeni* (Interior Live Oak)					x			x	
Plants	*Quercus* X*acutidens* (Torrey's Scrub Oak)				x					
Plants	*Rafinesquia neomexicana* (Desert Chicory)									x
Plants	*Ranunculus californicus* (California Buttercup)				x	x	x			
Plants	*Rhamnus crocea* (Spiny Redberry)		x	x						
Plants	*Rhamnus ilicifolia* (Holly-Leaf Redberry)					x			x	
Plants	*Rhododendron occidentale* (Western Azalea)							x		
Plants	*Rhus aromatica* (Skunkbush or Basket Bush)				x	x			x	
Plants	*Rhus integrifolia* (Lemonadeberry)		x	x	x					
Plants	*Rhus ovata* (Sugar Bush)				x	x				
Plants	*Ribes roezlii* (Sierra Gooseberry)								x	
Plants	*Ribes speciosum* (Fuchsia-flower Gooseberry)		x				x			
Plants	*Romneya trichocalyx* (Hairy Matilija Poppy)		x		x					
Plants	*Rosa californica* (California Rose)						x	x	x	
Plants	*Rubus parviflorus* (Thimbleberry)								x	
Plants	*Salicornia pacifica* (Pacific Pickleweed)	x								
Plants	*Salicornia* spp. (Pickleweeds)	x								
Plants	*Salix exigua* (Narrow-leaf Willow)		x	x	x	x	x			
Plants	*Salix gooddingii* (Goodding's Black Willow)						x	x		
Plants	*Salix lasiolepis* (Arroyo Willow)						x	x		
Plants	*Salix* spp. (Willows)						x			
Plants	*Salvia apiana* (White Sage)		x	x	x	x				
Plants	*Salvia clevelandii* (Fragrant Sage)				x					
Plants	*Salvia columbariae* (Chia)		x		x					
Plants	*Salvia mellifera* (Black Sage)		x	x						
Plants	*Sambucus nigra* (Blue Elderberry)		x	x			x		x	
Plants	*Schoenoplectus* spp. (Bulrushes)							x		
Plants	*Senegalia greggii* (Catclaw Acacia)									x
Plants	*Senna Covesii* (Coues's Cassia)			x	x					
Plants	*Silene laciniata* (Southern Pink)		x		x					
Plants	*Simmondsia chinensis* (Jojoba, Goatnut)									x
Plants	*Sisyrinchium bellum* (Blue-eyed-grass)				x					
Plants	Solanaceae (Family of Nightshades)			x	x	x		x	x	x
Plants	*Spartina foliosa* (California Cord Grass)	x								
Plants	*Stephanomeria diegensis* (San Diego Wreath-plant)		x	x						
Plants	*Stipa pulchra* (Purple Needle Grass)		x	x						
Plants	*Streptanthus campestris* (Southern Jewelflower)				x	x			x	
Plants	*Symphoricarpos albus* (Common Snowberry)								x	
Plants	*Tamarix ramosissima* (Saltcedar)	x					x			
Plants	*Tetracoccus dioicus* (Parry's Tetracoccus)			x		x				
Plants	*Toxicodendron diversilobum* (Western Poison-oak)					x	x			
Plants	*Trixis californica* (California Trixis)									x
Plants	*Typha* spp. (Cattails)	x					x	x		
Plants	*Urtica dioica* (Hoary Nettle)						x	x		
Plants	*Vitis girdiana* (Southern California Wild Grape)					x	x			
Plants	*Washingtonia filifera* (California Fan Palm)									x
Plants	*Washingtonia robusta* (Mexican Fan Palm)									
Plants	*Xylococcus bicolor* (Mission Manzanita)		x			x				

Type	Scientific/Common name									
Plants	*Xylorhiza orcuttii* (Orcutt's Woody Aster)									x
Plants	*Yucca brevifolia* (Joshua Tree)									x
Plants	*Yucca schidigera* (Mojave Yucca)		x		x					
Plants	*Zeltnera venusta* (Canchalagua)		x	x		x				
Plants	*Zostera marina* (Common Eel-grass)	x								
Reptiles, amphibians and fish	*Anaxyrus boreas* (Western Toad)						x	x	x	
Reptiles, amphibians and fish	*Anaxyrus californicus* (Arroyo Toad)						x			
Reptiles, amphibians and fish	*Aspidoscelis hyperythra* (Orange-throated Whiptail)		x	x	x					
Reptiles, amphibians and fish	*Coluber flagellum* (Coachwhip)		x	x	x					x
Reptiles, amphibians and fish	*Crotalus cerastes* (Sidewinder)									x
Reptiles, amphibians and fish	*Crotalus mitchellii* (Speckled Rattlesnake)		x		x	x				x
Reptiles, amphibians and fish	*Crotalus oreganus* (Western Rattlesnake)		x	x	x	x	x			
Reptiles, amphibians and fish	*Crotalus ruber* (Red Diamond Rattlesnake)		x	x	x	x				x
Reptiles, amphibians and fish	*Crotalus* spp. (Rattlesnakes)		x	x	x	x	x	x	x	x
Reptiles, amphibians and fish	*Cyprinodon macularius* (Desert Pupfish)									x
Reptiles, amphibians and fish	*Dipsosaurus dorsalis* (Desert Iguana)									x
Reptiles, amphibians and fish	*Elgaria multicarinata* (Southern Alligator Lizard)		x	x	x	x	x		x	
Reptiles, amphibians and fish	*Hypsypops rubicundus* (Garibaldi)	x								
Reptiles, amphibians and fish	*Leuresthes tenuis* (California Grunion)	x								
Reptiles, amphibians and fish	*Lichanura trivirgata* (Rosy Boa)		x	x	x	x				x
Reptiles, amphibians and fish	*Petrosaurus mearnsi* (Banded Rock Lizard)									x
Reptiles, amphibians and fish	*Phrynosoma blainvillii* (Blainville's Horned Lizard)		x	x	x	x			x	
Reptiles, amphibians and fish	*Phrynosoma mcallii* (Flat-tailed Horned Lizard)									x
Reptiles, amphibians and fish	*Phrynosoma* sp. (Horned Lizard)		x	x	x	x			x	x
Reptiles, amphibians and fish	*Pituophis catenifer* (Gophersnake)		x	x	x	x				x
Reptiles, amphibians and fish	*Plestiodon gilberti* (Gilbert's Skink)		x	x	x	x	x		x	
Reptiles, amphibians and fish	*Plestiodon skiltonianus* (Western Skink)		x	x	x	x	x		x	
Reptiles, amphibians and fish	*Pseudacris cadaverina* (California Treefrog)						x	x		x
Reptiles, amphibians and fish	*Pseudacris regilla* (Pacific Treefrog)						x			
Reptiles, amphibians and fish	*Sauromalus ater* (Common Chuckwalla)									x
Reptiles, amphibians and fish	*Sceloporus occidentalis* (Western Fence Lizard)		x	x	x	x	x		x	
Reptiles, amphibians and fish	*Thamnophis hammondii* (Two-striped Gartersnake)						x	x		
Reptiles, amphibians and fish	*Uta stansburiana* (Common Side-blotched Lizard)		x	x	x	x	x		x	x

Managing Agencies

"At a Glance" abbreviation	Agency	phone	WEB
ABDSP	Anza-Borrego Desert State Park	(760) 767-5311	www.parks.ca.gov
BLM-CDD	Bureau of Land Management-California Desert District	(951) 697-5200	www.blm.gov/ca
CDFW	California Department of Fish & Wildlife-South Coast Region	(858) 467-4201	www.wildlife.ca.gov
City of Carlsbad	City of Carlsbad	(760) 434-2826	www.carlsbadca.gov
City of Chula Vista	City of Chula Vista	(619) 409-5900	www.chulavistaca.gov
City of Encinitas	City of Encinitas	(760) 633-2740	www.encinitasca.gov
City of Escondido	City of Escondido	(760) 839-4691	www.escondido.org
City of Oceanside	City of Oceanside	(760) 435-4500	www.ci.oceanside.ca.us
City of Poway	City of Poway	(858) 668-4400	www.poway.org
City of San Diego	City of San Diego	(619) 525-8213	www.sandiego.gov
City of San Marcos	City of San Marcos	(760) 744-9000	www.ci.san-marcos.ca.us
City of Santee	City of Santee	(619) 258-4100 ext. 222	www.ci.santee.ca.us
City of Vista	City of Vista	(760) 639-6151	www.cityofvista.com
CNLM	Center for Natural Lands Management	(760) 731-7790	www.cnlm.org
CSP-CDD	California State Parks-Colorado Desert District	(760) 767-4037	www.parks.ca.gov
CSP-SDCD	California State Park-San Diego Coastal District	(619) 688-3260	www.parks.ca.gov
FLC	Fallbrook Land Conservancy	(760) 728-0889	www.fallbrooklandconservancy.org
FTC	Fallbrook Trails Council	(760) 723-8780.	www.fallbrooktrailscouncil.com
HWD	Helix Water District	(619) 443-2510	www.lakejennings.org
LCDC	Living Coast Discovery Center	(619) 409-5900	www.thelivingcoast.org
LCR&PD	Lake Cuyamaca Recreation & Park District	(877) 581-9904	www.lakecuyamaca.org
LRPC	Lakeside's River Park Conservancy	(619) 443-4770	www.lakesideriverpark.org
NPS	National Park Service	(619) 557-5450	www.nps.gov
NRS-UCSD	Natural Reserve System-University of California, San Diego	(858) 534-2077	www.nrs.ucsd.edu
NWR	National Wildlife Refuge	(619) 468-9245	www.fws.gov
OMWD	Olivenhain Municipal Water District	(760) 632-4212	www.olivenhain.com
RCP	RCP Riverside County Regional Parks and Open Space District	(951) 677-6951	www.rivcoparks.org
RMWD	Ramona Municipal Water District	(760) 789-1330	www.rmwd.org/lake-ramona
San Diego County	San Diego County	(858) 694-3030	www.sandiegocounty.gov/parks
SD Audubon	San Diego Audubon	(858) 273-7800	www.sandiegoaudubon.org
SDRP	San Dieguito River Park JPA	(858) 674-2275	www.sdrp.org
SDRPF	San Diego River Park Foundation	(619) 297-7380	www.sandiegoriver.org
SLRP	Santee Lakes Recreation Preserve	(619) 596-3141	www.santeelakes.com
SR&SJMNM	Santa Rosa and San Jacinto Mountains National Monument	(760) 862-9984	www.blm.gov
Sweetwater Authority	Sweetwater Authority	(619) 420-1413	www.sweetwater.org
TNC	The Nature Conservancy - CA Field Office	(415) 777-0487	www.nature.org
USFS/CNF-DRD	U.S. Forest Service/Cleveland National Forest-Descanso Ranger District	(619) 445-6235	www.fs.usda.gov
USFS/CNF-PRD	U.S. Forest Service/Cleveland National Forest-Palomar Ranger District	(760) 788-0250	www.fs.usda.gov
USFW	US Fish & Wildlife Service	(619(476-9150	www.fws.gov

Local Supporting Organizations

Local Supporting Organizations	Web
Anza-Borrego Desert Natural History Association	www.abdnha.org
Anza-Borrego Foundation	www.theabf.org
Batiquitos Lagoon Foundation	www.batiquitosfoundation.org
Blue Sky Ecological Reserve	www.blueskyreserve.org
Buena Vista Lagoon Foundation	www.buenavistalagoon.org
California Native Plant Society San Diego Chapter	www.cnpssd.org
Canyoneers of the San Diego Natural History Museum	www.sdnat.org/canyoneers
Cleveland National Forest Foundation	www.cnff.org
Cuyamaca Rancho State Park Interpretive Association	www.crspia.org
Desert Protective Council	www.dpcinc.org
Earth Discovery Institute	www.earthdiscovery.org
Friends of Palomar Mountain State Park	www.friendsofpalomarsp.org
Hiking Meetups	www.hiking.meetup.com
Kumeyaay Diegueño Land Conservancy	www.kdlc.org
Kumeyaay Information	www.kumeyaay.info
La Jolla Indian Reservation	www.lajollaindians.com
Laguna Mountain Volunteer Association	www.lmva.net
Otay Valley Regional Park (OVRP)	www.ovrp.org
San Diego Audubon Society	www.sandiegoaudubon.org
San Diego Canyonlands, Inc.	www.sdcanyonlands.org
San Diego Hiking Club	www.sandiegohikingclub.org
San Dieguito River Valley Conservancy	www.sandieguitorivervalleyconservancy.org
San Elijo Lagoon Conservancy	www.sanelijo.org
Sierra Club, San Diego Chapter	www.sandiegosierraclub.org
Tijuana River National Estuarine Research Reserve	www.trnerr.org
Torrey Pines Association	www.torreypines.org
US Fish & Wildlfe - National Wildlife Refuge, San Diego	www.fws.gov/refuge/San_Diego
US Fish & Wildlfe - National Wildlife Refuge, San Diego Bay	www.fws.gov/refuge/San_Diego_Bay
Volcan Mountain Foundation	www.volcanmt.org
Walkabout International	www.walkabout-int.org

Acknowledgments

You, our reader, can be the judge of whether this village of contributors has succeeded in creating a product that is much more than a trail guide. We hope it will be a source for constant discovery of something new and surprising about this incredible county that is home to a myriad of plant and animal species within a very diverse geographical setting. Below is the team that has worked to create our virtual Canyoneer.

The editing team of Paula Knoll, Terri Varnell, and Diana Lindsay prepared the articles for the weekly submission to the San Diego Reader. When work began on the book, it was their task to bring all these articles together in a cohesive whole. This involved a two-part process. First was checking the accuracy of species descriptions and their locations. San Diego Natural History Museum scientists—Jim Berrian, Bradford Hollingsworth, Jon Rebman, Scott Tremor, Phil Unitt, Michael Wall—and other scientists including botanists Tom Oberbauer and Kate Harper—were instrumental in this most critical step. Second was text editing for readability and understanding, which was provided by Mary Duffy, Ellen Esch, Don Fosket, Richard Halsey, Joanne Ingwall, Daniel Keddy, Lowell Lindsay, and Enrique Medina, and followed by overall editing and proofing by Maggie Thompson.

Patric Knoll created all of the trail maps with the assistance of Paula Knoll who checked for accuracy. Patric's good humor through several revisions of the maps was greatly appreciated. Jim Varnell checked the GPS for all trailheads and wrote the driving instructions to the trailhead for each hike. Jim also plotted the position of trailheads for each hike on a map that was used by designer Barry Age, who created the master geographical maps used in this book. Marcus Lubich, Park Project Manager, San Diego County Parks and Recreation, gave us permission to use the Regional Trails Map and the base map for county watersheds. Kathleen Wise recreated the watershed map for our use.

Terri Varnell managed the "At a Glance" information for each trail, and with input from the Museum curators, ensured the accuracy of the species lists by habitats. Ellen Esch wrote the introduction to San Diego County's ecosystems and habitats and provided initial input for species information. Ellen also suggested the cover format of a coastal setting with cactus for this book, using her Scripps Reserve research station as the location for the photo cover. Bill Edwards provided the draft for the introductory material related to equipment, hazards, and trail etiquette.

Those who submitted articles for the Reader also submitted accompanying photographs that were used in this book. Canyoneers Alan King, Wendy Esterly, and Don Fosket also provided numerous photographs from their collections to fill in areas where photos were needed. Others who provided specific photos included Mary Duffy, Don Endicott, Richard Halsey, John Hopper, Bill Howell, Pauline Jimenez, Walter Konopka, Jon Lindsay, Keir Morse, Jim Varnell, and Jim Zuehl. Great appreciation goes to our models for the front cover, Diane Murbach, and back cover, Ken Busby.

Museum President and CEO Michael W. Hager supported this project from the very beginning. Other Museum staff members who collaborated in the project include Rebecca Handelsman, Senior Director of Communications, who led the charge on marketing the book to the public and forging a partnership with Subaru of America for the Canyoneer program and this publication, and Mary Lou Morreal, Art Director, who offered valuable suggestions for the book's design elements.

This book would not have been possible without the full support of the Canyoneers and associated friends who faithfully contribute weekly to the "Roam-O-Rama" column. Particular recognition goes to Don Fosket who contributed 89 articles, did initial groundwork for the listing of habitats found on each hike, and was always quick to assist where and when needed. Many Canyoneers contributed trail descriptions, photographs, and species information that were eventually incorporated into this book.

The 63 contributors to this work include, in alphabetical order: Judy Alvarez, Germar Bernhard, Ellen Bevier, Richard Campbell, Karen Cassimatis, Sami Collins, Russ Colton, Cynthia Cordle, Andrew Currie, Joan Dowd, Mary Duffy, Glenn Dunham, Bill Edwards, Don Endicott, Ellen Esch, Wendy Esterly, Joe Fader, Frederick Fitch, Don Fosket, Sam Gabriel, Rochelle Gaudette, Henry Geffroy, Richard Halsey, Maggie Holloway, Annie Hoppe, John Hopper, Bill Howell, Pauline Jimenez, Walter Konopka, Janine Kardokus, Daniel Keddy, Alan King, Victor Knarreborg, Paula Knoll, Diana Lindsay, Jon Lindsay, Mary Lueking, Alan Marshall, Anne McCammon, Eva McCatty, Enrique Medina, Susan Nelson, Doug Nolff, Janet Peyton, Sandi Rosenthal, Sue Stiver, Jennifer Stone, Marcia Stoner, Brian Swanson, Tim Sweet, Thuy Ta, Ellen Taylor, Maggie Thompson, Duane Trombly, Liz Tymkiw, George Varga, Jim Varnell, Terri Varnell, Stacey Vielma, Jessie Vinje, Pam Weinisch, Nic Wiseman, and Donna Zoll.

Many individuals in various agencies checked the text and maps for accuracy and provided editorial corrections for their areas of concern. Great appreciation for time spent on reviewing the text, offering suggestions for improvement, and general support of this project goes to: Kevin Best, Kathy Dice, Don Falat, and Norb Ruhmke from the Colorado Desert District, California State Parks; Garratt Aitchison, Robin Greene, Dylan Hardenbrook, and Lisa Urbach from the San Diego Coast District, California State Parks; Lindsey Steinwachs from Descanso Ranger District, Cleveland National Forest; Rangers Heidi Gutknecht and Andy Quinn with Mission Trails Regional Park; Maggie Holloway and Jay Wilson with Mission Trails Regional Park Foundation; Rob Hutsel with the San Diego River Park Foundation; and Shawna Anderson, Leana Bulay, and Kevin McKernan with the San Dieguito River Park, Joint Powers Authority.

Several individuals, organizations, media and business representatives reviewed the final text and gave us their impressions of our work. We are most appreciative of the kind words of endorsement coming from these individual listed in alphabetical order: Janet Anderson, President, Desert Protective Council; Robert Buehler, President, Walkabout International; Cathy Chadwick, President/Director, Earth Discovery Institute; Roy Coffman, Store Manager, Patagonia Cardiff-by-the-Sea; Karen Eagleton, President/Chairman of the Board, The Wilderness Association of San Diego and San Diego Hiking Club; Jim Holman, Editor and Publisher, San Diego Reader; Mark Jorgensen, Retired Superintendent, Anza-Borrego Desert State Park; David Kimball, President, San Diego Audubon Society; Duncan McFetridge, Director, Cleveland National Forest Foundation; Annette McGivney, Southwest Editor, Backpacker Magazine; John D. Mead, President, Adventure 16; Eric Park, Zone Retail Marketing Manager, Subaru of America; Carrie Schneider, President, San Diego Canyonlands; Bobbie Stephenson, President, San Diego Chapter, California Native Plant Society; Davin Widgerow, Chair, Steering Committee, Sierra Club San Diego; and Ed Zieralski, Outdoor Writer.

Once everything was checked and reviewed, the manuscript was ready for the creative magic that turns words on paper and assorted photographs into a stunning product. Special thanks go to Barry Age who did superb work under very tight deadlines. He was assisted by typographer Simone Matern. Once the pages were set, it was up to Dianna Haught to create the index needed for the book—so very important for directing readers to the pages containing detailed information for the more than 500 species featured in this book. Debi Young, Publications Manager for Sunbelt Publications, Inc., orchestrated the entire production.

Sincere appreciation also goes to the following who made it possible to fully fund this publication, which provides financial support to the San Diego Natural History Museum through sales of the book. At the time of this printing, names include: Patrick L. Abbott; Lyle and Helen Arnold; Wayne and Lauralee Bennett; By The Sea Realty; Richard and Anne Bogardt; Anita Busquets and William Ladd; Ingrid and Bob Coffin; Decco Castings, Inc., El Cajon; Glenn Dunham; David and Peg Engel; Dowd Family; Don Fosket; Debbie Fritsch and Pat Boyce; J. David Garmon, MD, and Frank D. Gilman, MD; Jon and Linda Gilbert; Charlene Glacy; Bob Gordon, MD; Tory, Rick, and Luke Gulley; Mick and Denise Hager; Jeriah and Josha Hildwine; John and Maggie Holloway; John Hopper; Timothy E. Horning, CPA; Frank and Diane Hydoski; Pauline Jimenez; Becky Keller; in honor of Paul Knoll; Walter F. Konopka, Jr.; Bill and Suzanne Lawrence; Sally Marshall; Anne and Andy McCammon; Enrique Medina; Monte and Diane Murbach; Eric and Amee Mustonen; in honor of Nancy Nenow; Linda Pardy; Janet M. Peyton; Michael Pinto; Joan and Marty Rosen; Sandi Rosenthal; George Sardina, MD; Carrie Schneider; Sue Stiver; Brian Swanson; Thuy Ta and Lance Walsh; John and Elena Thompson; Maggie Thompson with friends and family; Jim and Terri Varnell; Pam Weinisch; Richard J. Corky Wharton; and others who wish to remain anonymous.

Additional Acknowledgments

Third Printing 2018. A special thanks to the following: Nico Goossens read the entire book, making note of discrepancies or typos that have been corrected in this new printing. Jim Varnell updated over 100 maps. Barry Age provided more information on the cover and interior area maps to make them easier to use. John Hopper took replacement photos requested by MTRP. Jon Rebman provided replacement photos for four plants that had been misidentified. Michele Hernandez and Fran Wade provided replacement photos of Cuyamaca Lake downingia and common chuckwall, respectively. The editorial team took advantage of the reprint opportunity to add chapter numbers to trip numbers in the headers to make the book easier to use. We hope you enjoy the improvements added to this 3rd printing.

Fourth Printing 2021. Appreciate additional corrections for this printing from Dave and Betsy Chamberlin, Bill Howell, and Kay Stewart.

Index

Page numbers in **bold** indicate that detailed information about a species is on that page. All hike titles in the Table of Contents are listed with inclusive page numbers <u>underlined</u>. (P) indicates pages with photos.

Index (continued)

Index (continued)

Index (continued)

Index (continued)

frankia (*Frankia* sp.), **93**
Frankia sp. (frankia), **93**
Fred Canyon, 413
French Creek, 312
French Valley, 322
French Valley Trail, 312
freshwater green algae (*Spirogyra* spp.), **231** (P)
Freshwater marsh/Montane Meadow/Vernal Pool (habitat), xxviii
Fries, Alice, 72
Fritillaria biflora (chocolate lily), **59**
frogs and toads. *See* arroyo toad, California treefrog, Pacific treefrog, western toad
Fry Creek Trail, 307–308
Fry-Koegel Trail, 158, 161 (map)
fuchsia-flower gooseberry (*Ribes speciosum*), 170, 171 (P), 173, 175, 229
Fulica americana (American coot), **136–137** (P)
funnel weaver spider (family Agelenidae), **177** (P)

G

Gadwall duck, 200
Galium spp. (bedstraw), 9, **138**, 139 (P)
Gambel's quail (*Callipepla gambelii*), **464**
Gander's cholla (*Cylindropuntia ganderi*), 499, **514–515** (P)
garibaldi (*Hypsypops rubicundus*), **33**
garland daisy (*Glebionis coronaria*), **178–179**
Garnet Peak, 299, 394-395, 405
Garra Revolt, 433
Gaskill Peak, 424
Gastropoda class (Nudibranchs), **30**
Geococcyx californianus (greater roadrunner), 105, 292, **487** (P)
Ghost Mountain—Blair Valley, 391, 525–527
giant kelp (*Macrocystis pyrifera*), **4–5**, 37, **44**, 45 (P)
giant reed (*Arundo donax*), 7, **113–114** (P), 233
Gilbert's skink (*Plestiodon gilberti*), **297**
gilia clivorum (purple-spot gilia), 361
Gill, Irving, 197
Glebionis coronaria (garland daisy), 178–179
Glen's View, 340, 341
Glider Point Marker, 138
goatnut. *See* jojoba (*Simmondsia chinensis*)
golden eagle (*Aquila chrysaetos*), 68, 155–156, 390, **425**
goldspotted oak borer (*Agrilus auroguttatus*), **xxvi**, **341**
Gonzales Canyon, 140
Goodan Ranch Sycamore Canyon Preserve, 202–203, 220–221
Goodding's black willow (*Salix gooddingii*), 60, 74, **161–162** (P)
gophersnake (*Pituophis catenifer*), 65, **85–86** (P)
GPS use, xxxiii–xxxv, xxxix
Gradwohl, Judith, xvi
Granite Mountain, 339, 343, 485, 493, 515, 520
Granite Spring, 379
grape soda lupine (*Lupinus excubitus* var. *austromontanus*), 366, 370, **407** (P)
Grapevine Canyon, xxxi, 478–480
Grapevine Hills, 479
grasses (family Poaceae), **372–373**
grasshoppers (family Acrididae), **261**, 263
Grassland (habitat), xxiii–xxiv
gray bird grasshopper (*Schistocerca nitens*), **261**
gray fox (*Urocyon cinereoargenteus*), **316**

gray vireo (*Vireo vicinior*), **413**
great blue heron (*Ardea herodias*), 9, **211**, 212 (P)
great egret (*Ardea alba*), 41 (P), 208, 223, 278, 349
great horned owl (*Bubo virginianus*), 129, **184**, 188 (P), 223
greater roadrunner (*Geococcyx californianus*), 105, 292, 487 (P)
green algae (*Trebouxia* spp.), **251**
green heron (*Butorides virescens*), 135 (P)
Green Valley Campground, 381–382
Green Valley Falls Loop, 383–384
Green Valley Truck Trail, 164
Greene's ground-cherry (*Physalis crassifolia*), **447**, 448 (P)
grinding holes. *See* morteros
grizzly bear, 413
Guajome Regional Park, 67–69
Guatay Mountain, 350–351
gulls (family Laridae, subfamily Larinae), 3, **6**, 68, 189
Gunpowder Point, 44
Gutierrezia sarothrae (broom matchweed), **536**, 537 (P)
Guy Fleming Trail—Torrey Pines State Natural Reserve, 16–17

H

Habitats, xxxv
  Beach/Salt Marsh/Lagoon, xxii
  Chaparral, xxiv–xxv
  Coastal Sage Scrub, xxiii
  Desert, xxix
  Freshwater Marsh/Montane Meadow/Vernal Pool, xxviii
  Grassland, xxiii–xxiv
  Mixed Conifer Forest, xxviii–xxix
  Oak Woodland, xxv–xxvi
  Riparian, xxvi–xxviii
Haemorhous mexicanus (house finch), **154** (P), 487
Hager, Michael W., xvi, xvii
Hairy matilija poppy (*Romneya trichocalyx*), **192**
Hale Telescope, 357
Haliaeetus leucocephalus (bald eagle), 81, **321**, 355, 361
Haliotis corrugata (pink abalone), **43**
Harbison's dun skipper (*Euphyes vestris harbisoni*), **296–297** (P)
harbor seal (*Phoca vitulina*), **32**
harlequin bug (*Murgantia histrionica*), **28** (P), 192, 316 (P)
Harper Canyon, 496
Harper Creek, 375–376, 280
Harper family, 390
Harper Flat, 500
Harvey Moore Trail, 380
Hauser Canyon, 428
Hatfield, Charles, 428
Hazardia orcuttii (Orcutt's goldenbush), 115, **121**, 122 (P)
Heart Pond, 281
Heise Park, 343
Heliopetes ericetorum (northern white skipper butterfly), **259** (P)
Heliotropium curassavicum (salt heliotrope), 48, **152** (P)
Hell Creek/Trail, 76–77
Hellhole Canyon and Maidenhair Falls, 473–474 Trailhead, 477
Hellhole Canyon Preserve, 76–77
Helm, Wid, 474
Hemiptera order (true bugs), 12, 316
Henshaw Dam, 322
Hermes copper butterfly (*Lycaena hermes*), **273**, 274 (P)

Index (continued)

Recommended Reading List

Baja California Plant Field Guide, 3rd edition
Jon Rebman and Norman Roberts
This manual to native and naturalized plants is a valuable guide for the entire Sonoran Desert and for southern California, as 50% of the species covered also occur in these regions. Over 715 different plants in 111 plant families are identified with both scientific and common names, detailed descriptions, and photographs.

Coast to Crest and Beyond: Across San Diego County by Car along the San Dieguito River
Wolf Berger
This book introduces the reader to the biodiversity of San Diego County via a drive along the San Dieguito River, following the general course of the Coast to Crest Trail beginning at the beach in Del Mar and ending at the source of the San Dieguito River on Volcan Mountain.

Coloring Plants Used by Desert Indians
Diana Lindsay
This book has 40 key plants that desert Indians primarily living in the Sonora Desert of southern California, Baja California (Mexico), and Arizona have used for centuries. Detailed information about how the plants were used make this a real "Color and Learn" experience.

Cycling the Trails of San Diego:
A Mountain Biker's Guide to the County
Nelson Copp
Explore the excellent mountain bike trails found throughout San Diego County, from the International Border up to Palomar Mountain, and from the coast out to Anza-Borrego Desert, with state-of-the-art route maps and detailed trip descriptions for 50 great rides, many of which are equally suitable for hiking.

Fire, Chaparral, and Survival in Southern California
Richard W. Halsey
This book covers what southern Californians need to know about fire, fire-fighting, and the chaparral ecosystem. Weaved together are the crucial elements of fire behavior and knowledge of the natural environment. Full-color photos and descriptions of common chaparral plants are included.

Kumeyaay Ethnobotany: Shared Heritage of the Californias
Michael Wilken-Robertson
Kumeyaay people of northern Baja California and southern California made their homes in the diverse landscapes of the region, interacting with native plants and learning skills to transform native plants into food, medicine, arts, tools, regalia, construction materials, and ceremonial items. This beautiful full-color book has in-depth descriptions and uses of 47 plants.

Nature Adventures! A Guidebook of Nature Facts, Songs, and Hikes in San Diego County
Linda Gallo Hawley
This resource guide for parents, teachers, and children is focused on studying the animal and plant species found in San Diego County. It teaches the reader to develop observation skills, to notice signs of wildlife, and to enjoy and connect with the natural world.

Pacific Peaks & Picnics:
Day Journeys in San Diego County
Linda McMillin Pyle
A guide to the hiking and biking trails and natural history of both popular and off-the-beaten-track areas of the county. Included are routes for easy, moderate, or strenuous day hikes: some colorful trailside lore; and the author's "trail-tested" recipes.

Rise and Fall of San Diego: 150 Million Years Recorded in Sedimentary Rocks
Patrick Abbott
The story of San Diego's prehistoric landscape is captured in the region's sedimentary rocks. Line drawings, illustrations, photographs, and maps help explain the concepts and make the text easy to understand. Numerous field trips guide the reader to key locations and features discussed in the book.

San Diego: An Introduction to the Region,
5th edition
Philip Pryde
This is the essential one-volume reference to the history, economics, demographics, natural features, earth science, and environmental issues of the San Diego region provides a great overview of the area.

San Diego County Mammal Atlas
Scott Tremor
This 432-page, full-color book is the definitive guide to the mammals of San Diego County, the biodiversity of which is one of the greatest in the United States. Covered is the biology of all 91 terrestrial species and 31 inshore marine visitors known to have occurred in the county during recorded history (since 1769).